PROBATION, PAROLE, AND COMMUNITY-BASED CORRECTIONS:

Supervision, Treatment, and Evidence-Based Practices

PROBATION, PAROLE, AND COMMUNITY-BASED CORRECTIONS:

Supervision, Treatment, and Evidence-Based Practices

Gerald Bayens
Washburn University

John Ortiz Smykla
University of West Florida

The McGraw·Hill Companies

PROBATION, PAROLE, AND COMMUNITY-BASED CORRECTIONS: SUPERVISION, TREATMENT, AND EVIDENCE-BASED PRACTICES

Published by McGraw-Hill, a business unit of The McGraw-Hill Companies, Inc., 1221 Avenue of the Americas, New York, NY 10020.

This book is printed on acid-free paper.

1 2 3 4 5 6 7 8 9 0 RJE/RJE 1 0 9 8 7 6 5 4 3 2

ISBN 978-0-07-811150-1
MHID 0-07-811150-1

Vice President & Editor-in-Chief: *Michael Ryan*
Vice President of Specialized Publishing: *Janice M. Roerig-Blong*
Editorial Director: *William Glass*
Sponsoring Editor: *Jessica Cannavo*
Marketing Coordinator: *Angela R. FitzPatrick*
Developmental Editor: *Robin A. Reed*
Lead Project Manager: *Jane Mohr*
Design Coordinator: *Brenda A. Rolwes*
Cover Designer: *Studio Montage, St. Louis, Missouri*
Photo Research Coordinator: *LouAnn Wilson*
Cover Image: © *Digital Vision/PunchStock RF*
Buyer: *Susan K. Culbertson*
Media Project Manager: *Sridevi Palani*
Compositor: *Lachina Publishing Services*
Typeface: *10/12 Times LT Std*
Printer: *R.R. Donnelley*

Library of Congress Cataloging-in-Publication Data

Bayens, Gerald J.
Probation, parole, and community-based corrections : supervision, treatment, and evidence-based practices / Gerald Bayens, John Ortiz Smykla.
p. cm. — (Connect, learn, succeed).
Includes index.
ISBN-13: 978-0-07-811150-1 (alk. paper)
1. Community-based corrections—United States. 2. Probation—United States. 3. Parole—United States. I. Smykla, John Ortiz. II. Title.
HV9304.B377 2012
364.60973—dc23 2011036300

www.mhhe.com

Carol Bayens and Mary Scarlett

Great Women—Greater Moms!

—Gerald Bayens

For my granddaughter, Harper Grace

—John Ortiz Smykla

about the authors

Gerald Bayens, Ph.D., is professor and chair of the Department of Criminal Justice and Legal Studies at Washburn University. He also provides direct services and technical assistance to criminal justice agencies, focusing on strategic planning and policy development.

Dr. Bayens teaches courses primarily in law enforcement and correctional management, criminal justice policy, and research methods. He earned a Ph.D. in criminal justice from the Union Institute, a master's in criminal justice from The University of Alabama, and bachelor's in criminal justice from Washburn University.

Dr. Bayens worked in the criminal justice field for 22 years in both law enforcement and corrections. He is a former Special Agent of the Kansas Bureau of Investigations and Director of Juvenile Corrections and Intensive Supervised Probation. Dr. Bayens served as a military police officer in the U.S. Marine Corps from 1974 through 1978.

Dr. Bayens is the author of numerous research articles, government reports, and books, including the second edition of *Criminal Justice Research Methods: Theory & Practice* (co-authored with Cliff Roberson). As a former corrections practitioner, his research interests continue to be focused on intensive supervised probation, alternatives to jail incarceration, and juvenile diversion programs.

Dr. Bayens is a member of the Academy of Criminal Justice Sciences currently serving as chair of the Academic Review and Certification Committee. He is also a member of the American Correctional Association and from 1992–1993 served as president and past president of the state affiliate Kansas Correctional Association. Dr. Bayens is the recipient of the 1993 Washburn Fellow Award.

John Ortiz Smykla, Ph.D., is Distinguished University Professor at the University of West Florida, Pensacola, Florida. He holds a doctorate from the School of Criminal Justice at Michigan State University.

From 1977 to 2002, Dr. Smykla taught criminal justice, international studies and women's studies at the University of Alabama. He served as criminal justice department chair from 1986–1996. From 2002 to 2005, he served as chair of the department of political science and criminal justice at the University of South Alabama, Mobile, Alabama. In 2005, he accepted the position of chair of criminal justice and legal studies at the University of West Florida. He returned to full-time faculty status in 2009.

In 1986, Dr. Smykla was a Senior Fulbright Scholar to Argentina and Uruguay. In 1987, his paper on Uruguayan corrections won third place in the Academy of Criminal Justice Sciences (ACJS) International Paper Competition. In 2011, Drs. Smykla and Bayens traveled with 20 students to the University of the West of Scotland to study Scottish criminal justice.

Dr. Smykla is the author of numerous articles and books, including the sixth edition of *Corrections in the 21st Century* (co-authored with Frank Schmalleger). His dataset, *Executions in the United States, 1608–2008: The Espy File*, is one of the most frequently requested data files from the University of Michigan's ICPSR.

At present, Dr. Smykla and a colleague are evaluating federal reentry court. For many years he served on the Mobile County Jail Planning Committee working with other professionals to develop and maintain strategies to reduce jail crowding. In 2008, he raised a quarter of a million dollars to convert a classroom into a high tech mock trial courtroom on the campus of UWF, the first mock trial courtroom of its kind outside a law school in the state of Florida.

Dr. Smykla is a member of ACJS and the Southern Criminal Justice Association (SCJA). In 1996, SCJA named him Educator of the Year for his contributions to criminal justice education. In 1997, he served as program chair for the annual program committee and in 2000 he served as president of SCJA. In 2011, the University of West Florida named him Distinguished University Professor.

brief contents

contents

preface

Community-based corrections is the most exciting and important field in criminal justice for one simple fact: almost all offenders end up under some type of community supervision after adjudication.

Whether sentenced to jail, prison, or community-based correctional programs (e.g., probation, halfway house, drug court), all offenders receive some kind of community supervision. The numbers tell the story and suggest the importance of this text:

108,700	Number of juveniles in detention, correctional, or shelter facilities
562,600	Number of juveniles on probation
767,000	Number of adults in jail
819,000	Number of adults on parole
1,600,000	Number of adults in prison
4,200,000	Number of adults on probation

Yet for all its importance, community-based corrections has lagged behind its counterpart—institutional corrections (jails and prisons)—in academic coverage and criminal justice policy.

However, community-based corrections predates institutional corrections by centuries. The criminal codes of Hammurabi (nineteenth century B.C.) and the Persian Empire (sixteenth century B.C.), the Hebrew Law of Moses (fifteenth through ninth centuries B.C.), and the Twelve Tables (the first written laws of Rome issued in 451 B.C.) required various forms of public (and oftentimes brutal) punishment, but not incarceration. These same codes also ordered offenders to make compensation and restitution and to enter servitude. Only with the advent of nation-states in the Middle Ages did the state become the victim and did incarceration replace victim restitution as punishment. Incarceration as we know it today did not emerge until the late eighteenth century.

In the 1960s in the United States, community-based corrections flourished as new ideas, philosophy, and politics of offender punishment and treatment surfaced. However, its promise to reduce crime was vastly oversold. Lacking results, it soon fell out of favor with legislators and corrections policymakers. For the next few decades incarceration took center stage in policy and the classroom.

In the 1990s, liberals and conservatives returned to the concept of community-based corrections for two reasons: community-based corrections was cheaper than institutional corrections, and new strategies in community-based corrections (e.g., electronic monitoring, boot camps, intensive supervision) offered more control and higher-quality treatment of offenders in the community than did their predecessors of the 1960s.

Today's budget crisis has moved community-based corrections back to center stage as governors, legislatures, and departments of corrections work to reduce spending on expensive institutional corrections. Just a decade ago it would have been unthinkable and political suicide for politicians to advocate publicly for closing prisons, increasing parole and early release, and creating a class of ex-prisoners whose parole would not be revoked. But today, such activity is advanced as being "smart on crime," cost-effective, and in many cases evidence-based. Many of those ideas are discussed in this book.

Most colleges and universities offer a course on institutional corrections and another on community-based corrections. Sometimes the institutional corrections course is a lower-level undergraduate course, and the community-based corrections course is an upper-level undergraduate one. Some programs have them on equal footing. For the most part, however, it is safe to say that *Probation, Parole, and Community-Based Corrections* will fit any level undergraduate course in community-based corrections.

The Approach of This Text

The two of us have been teaching community-based corrections for 50 years combined. Both of us have also worked in juvenile community-based corrections. The problem we've seen with most community-based corrections textbooks is they are overly prescriptive or a compilation of disjointed chapters. They appear to be more helpful as "tool kits" for agency professionals than developing critical thinking skills in the next generation of professionals.

When we had the opportunity to write this book, we wanted an approach that would introduce students to the key issues and programmatic developments that are current in the field today that are helpful in getting started as a community-based corrections professional, but we wanted more. We wanted students to achieve critical thinking skills. Knowledge and understanding are critical to successful employment today, but higher-order learning objectives are key to career development.

Our approach has four themes: Explain and demonstrate the importance that evidence-based corrections (EBC) plays in the field. Embrace professionalism and theory as key components in EBC. And demonstrate that the acquisition of higher-order learning objectives can produce more EBC, and thereby control crime and increase public safety. These four themes serve as this textbook's organizing principles.

1. **Evidence-Based Corrections.** Today a new elephant has entered the room, so to speak—evidence-based corrections—by which we mean the application of social scientific techniques to the study of everyday corrections practices in order to increase effectiveness and enhance the efficient use of available resources. In evidence-based corrections, evaluation research is used to construct guidelines for correctional practices that will reduce crime.

   The Center for Evidence-Based Corrections at the University of California, Irvine, describes the discipline this way:

   > Evidence-based policy . . . helps people make well-informed decisions about policies and programs by putting the best available evidence from research at the heart of policy development and implementation. This approach stands in contrast to opinion-based policy, which relies heavily on either the selective use of evidence (e.g., on single studies irrespective of quality) or on the untested views of individuals or groups, often inspired by ideological views and speculative conjecture.

   Our text is the first to make evidence-based practices in community-based corrections a dominant theme. We introduce and define the concept in Chapter 1.

In later chapters we discuss the evidence-based literature that applies to a range of intermediate sanctions: pretrial release, diversion, probation, parole, therapeutic courts, residential and non-residential programs, and so on. Where additional research is still needed, we note that—for example, with regard to faith-based programs, day fines, and work release programs.

2. **Professionalism.** Evidence-based corrections is grounded in the assumption that corrections personnel embrace research results as fundamental to effective practice. In our book, we define corrections professionalism as an attitude that develops among all program staff regardless of level of education, training, or credentialing and that demonstrates respect for evidence-based approaches, acknowledges the problem-solving potential of social science research methods, and accepts program evaluation as an integral means of improving treatment effectiveness.
3. **Theory.** A major task of evidence-based corrections is to build theories related to correctional interventions that work and to unmask those that don't. Some community-based texts pay lip service to theory, and others don't mention it at all, believing perhaps that students have learned all they need to learn in a stand-alone course on criminological and criminal justice theory. We do not believe that approach is sufficient in the context of evidence-based corrections. Thus, in Chapter 3, we cover theories of crime causation and the pivotal role theory plays in the development of evidence-based community corrections.

   One of the most promising theoretical approaches we discuss is the evolving "principles of effective correctional intervention." This approach is rooted in the empirical literature of criminology, behavioral psychology, and correctional evaluation.

   Our approach to theory will work for instructors who teach community-based corrections at comprehensive research universities as well as at regional and two-year schools.
4. **Critical Thinking.** We may not always want to think critically in our day-to-day existence, but we need those skills when dealing with the difficult subject of crime and criminals.

   The new world of evidence-based corrections requires us to rely on reason rather than emotion. It requires us to follow evidence where it leads and to be more concerned with finding the best explanation than with being right.

   Critical thinkers are by nature skeptical, they ask questions and analyze, and they are open to new ideas and perspectives. By contrast, noncritical thinkers see things in either/or terms. They take their facts as the only relevant facts, their own perspective as the only sensible one, and their goals as the only valid ones. The history of risk assessment discussed in Chapter 4 is a case in point.

   For the first half of the twentieth century, the belief in risk assessment was that as community corrections officers gained knowledge and experience, they developed an intuitive sense, or a "gut" feeling, of an offender's risks and needs and of the probability that he/she might reoffend. Their intuitive sense guided the case plans they developed and the interventions they believed would protect the public. However, as many scholars have since pointed out, clinical assessment was oftentimes biased and subjective. Too often community corrections officers missed important information while overemphasizing trivial information. Unfortunately, too many probation and parole agencies nationwide still believe that "professional opinion is adequate."

To counterbalance such beliefs, our book engages students in developing higher order thinking skills. Thus, we have not written a "how-to" book. While we believe that students must be familiar with the types of community-based programs in operation today, we know those programs will be short-lived. Instead, by creating a book that encourages students to be critical thinkers, to analyze and evaluate evidence, we are preparing them for tomorrow.

Organization

Probation, Parole, and Community-Based Corrections is presented in 12 chapters and is easily adapted to most academic calendars. Every chapter begins with a high-profile case taken from today's headlines that provide timely corrections coverage and the background needed to understand the role of community-based corrections in today's world.

Chapter 1 introduces the case of U.S. District Senior Judge Jack Camp, who received the same community-based sentence that he had been handing down for 25 years after he was convicted of paying a stripper for sex, using and attempting to purchase illegal drugs, and giving the stripper his government-issued laptop. We present the student with an understanding of community-based corrections by explaining what community-based corrections is and isn't. We explain the importance of evidence-based corrections, outline the major strategies of community-based corrections and intermediate sanctions, and compare the goals of retributive and restorative justice in the context of community-based corrections.

Chapter 2 asks the reader to critically evaluate whether Leandro Andrade should have been sentenced to life in prison with no possibility of parole because his third felony was petty theft with a prior conviction—he stole $150 worth of videotapes from two Kmart stores in California. Would a community-based sentence have been more appropriate? We explain how the four filters affecting community-based corrections (the legislative filter, the apprehension filter, the adjudication filter, and the corrections filter) impact community-based sentencing. We also explain what community corrections acts are and why states use them. The chapter discusses the relationship between arrest rates and corrections, the influence that drug offenders have on the criminal justice system, the relationship between sentencing laws and community-based corrections, and provides examples of the policy changes that are occurring as a result of the current economic crisis.

Chapter 3 begins with the question "Why did Sean Penn break the camera of a photographer filming a story about paparazzi?" Our focus is on theories of offender treatment. No one theory explains crime or offers a magic bullet for crime control. Therefore students are given a brief introduction to the major theoretical approaches of the classical and positivist schools of criminology, and a discussion of what community-based corrections policies would flow from each theoretical perspective.

Chapter 4 uses the story of California sex offender Phillip Garrido, who kidnapped and sexually assaulted Jaycee Lee Dugard for 18 years, to explain the importance of classification in assessing offender risk and the guidance provided by the risk-need-responsivity principle. We sketch the history of risk and needs assessment from clinical judgment to a scientific approach that not only identifies an offender's potential risk of reoffending and his/her criminogenic needs, but also the services, in what duration, and with what level of intensity, that will produce the best outcomes based on the assessed risks and needs. We explain where risk and needs assessment are conducted, who special-needs offenders are and what corrections is doing to assess their risks and needs, project what classification might be like in the future, and identify sound principles for classification and risk/needs assessment.

Chapter 5 uses the case of Rush Limbaugh, who entered an 18-month substance abuse treatment program for addiction to painkillers and for "doctor shopping" to explain pretrial diversion as an alternative to prosecution. We explain how pretrial release developed in the United States, how it operates, how risk assessment is used to facilitate its use, what the benefits and challenges are, and the policy issues that increase the potential for pretrial defendants to appear in court.

Chapter 6 brings up the simple battery case of Kid Rock and asks if tariff (fixed) fines are a slap on the wrist for the rich who don't feel the sting of punishment and who could afford to pay more. The student is then introduced to the different types of economic sanctions that are used in the United States, the differences between tariff and day fines and restitution and compensation, and the benefits and challenges of community service.

Chapter 7 asks the student to evaluate whether Chris Brown's five years' probation sentence for felony assault by means likely to cause great bodily injury against Robin "Rihanna" Fenty was fair. We explain the difference between probation and intensive supervised probation (ISP) and discuss how remote location monitoring and home confinement/house arrest are often applied as special conditions of ISP. We trace the historical roots of probation, discuss the characteristics of those who are on probation today, explain the differences between the casework and brokerage models of probation, contrast the investigative and supervision roles of probation officers, differentiate between general and special conditions of probation, and explain revocation, the reasons why probation is revoked and what some jurisdictions are doing to scale back revocations noting the economic impact when probation is revoked and more expensive sanctions are applied especially for technical violations. And finally, we sketch how probation is organized in the United States and why some states are turning to probation privatization for supervision of low-risk offenders.

Chapter 8 relates the story of Mike Danton, former National Hockey League player with the St. Louis Blues, to parole. Danton was sentenced to seven-and-a-half years in prison followed by three years of parole for masterminding a murder-for-hire plot. After serving five years in federal prison Danton, a Canadian citizen, was transferred to Canada and later granted parole. Students are asked what conditions should apply to Danton's parole. The chapter also introduces the reader to a brief history of American parole development, the role and function of a paroling authority, the reasons for parole revocation and the impact the U.S. Supreme Court has had on the parole revocation hearing, the changing role of parole officers, how today's budget cuts are affecting a parolee's successful reentry, promising innovations to inmate reentry, the importance of gender-based reentry, and we conclude with a discussion of why evidence-based practices in parole are important.

Chapter 9 begins with a quote by Lieutenant Colonel Bruce Conover, Chief of Corrections with the U.S. Army. Conover's quote compares military and correctional boot camps and hints at the importance of aftercare for both. The reader is then introduced to the major features of correctional boot camps and what the evidence-based literature tells us about boot camps. The second half of Chapter 9 introduces the student to jail-based issues of work release, community service, reentry, substance abuse treatment, and therapeutic communities.

Chapter 10 explains the transition of Grammy-winning rap artist "T.I." from federal prison to a residential community center after conviction on federal weapons charges. The student is asked to evaluate if residential community centers provide public safety and offender rehabilitation. We then trace the development of residential community centers in the United States, describe their characteristics and the role that cognitive-behavioral therapy plays in treatment. The second half of Chapter 10 introduces two other community-based programs: day reporting centers and drug courts. Their characteristics are discussed as well as what we know about their effectiveness from the evidence-based literature.

Chapter 11 introduces the issue of special population offenders by relating the problem of "sexting" and sex offenders. Shortly after turning 18, Phillip Alpert sent nude pictures of his 16-year old girlfriend to her family and friends. Alpert was found guilty of distributing child pornography and required to register as a sex offender. Special needs offenders—persons who suffer from mental illness, sex offenders, and some women offenders—present unique treatment needs and public safety concerns. This chapter discusses theoretical explanations for their behavior, the problems they face in the criminal justice system, and how communities can assist in their successful reintegration.

Chapter 12 asks how a 14-year old boy can be tried as an adult. The case of Lionel Tate is both complex and disturbing yet it highlights the importance of community-based programming for youth under the age of 18. The chapter also traces the history of juvenile community-based corrections in the United States, the major U.S. Supreme Court decisions that have shaped juvenile justice, how and why juveniles are transferred to adult court, the services juvenile probation agencies provide these young offenders, the groundswell of innovative and evidence-based practices we find in juvenile community-based corrections, and we conclude with a discussion of the importance of gender-specific programming for juvenile female offenders.

Special Features

The special features we developed to support our four themes are:

1. **Chapter Outline and Learning Objectives**. To provide students with an overview of the chapter structure and a clear idea of their learning goals, each chapter opens with these reading and learning aids.
2. **Chapter-Opening Stories**. These high-profile community-based corrections cases are taken from recent headlines and focus on the chapter topic as well as the application of theory.
3. **Career Profiles**. In this feature, we introduce individuals who are working in the field of community-based corrections while acquainting students with the types of jobs available, the training and credentials required for such jobs, and the real-life experience of those who hold such positions.
4. **Policy Implications**. Every chapter concludes with a discussion of the policy implications for community-based corrections. From theory to practice, every chapter suggests how evidence-based community corrections practices can shape criminal justice policy.
5. **CBC Online**. Every chapter includes at least three online exercises that direct students to an Internet Web site. Questions related to what they've read or viewed at the Web site ask them to employ critical thinking. Each chapter also includes at

least three Web-based exercises of this kind on the text's Online Learning Center, located at www.mhhe.com/bayens1e.

6. **Chapter Summaries**. Each chapter ends with a summary of the important concepts keyed to the chapter's learning objectives.
7. **Key Terms**. Each chapter also ends with a list of terms that have been defined in the chapter, and tagged with page references so students can use them for review.
8. **Questions for Review**. These objective study questions are keyed to chapter objectives and summary points, thus allowing students to test their knowledge of the chapter's essential elements and prepare for exams.
9. **Question of Policy**. These real-life scenarios, which also appear at the end of each chapter, provide insight into the dilemmas facing corrections professionals and ask students to offer opinions or analysis.
10. **What Would You Do?** These real-life scenarios, which appear at the end of each chapter, prompt students to focus on professional values and integrity and consider how they would act in specific situations.
11. **End-of-Book Glossary**. This comprehensive tool includes all key terms with definitions.
12. **International Perspectives in Community-Based Corrections**. These narratives, available at the book's Web site, www.mhhe.com/bayens1e, present examples of community-based corrections programs and practices around the world, especially evidence-based practices where available. Including this feature reinforces our themes of evidence-based community corrections, professionalism and theory.

Supplements

An extensive package of supplemental aids accompanies this edition of *Probation, Parole, and Community-Based Corrections*. Visit our Online Learning Center at www.mhhe.com/bayens1e for robust student and instructor resources.

For Students

Student resources include three Internet exercises per chapter, CBC Online exercises, International Perspectives in Community-Based Corrections, and multiple-choice quizzes.

For Instructors

The password-protected instructor portion of the Web site includes the instructor's manual, a comprehensive computerized test bank using the EZ Test® test generator, and PowerPoint lecture slides.

Additional instructor resources include:

This text is available as an eBook at www.CourseSmart.com. At CourseSmart, your students can take advantage of significant savings off the cost of a print textbook, reduce their impact on the environment, and gain access to powerful Web tools for learning. CourseSmart eBooks can be viewed online or downloaded to a computer. The eBooks allow students to do full text searches, add highlighting and notes, and share notes with classmates. CourseSmart has the largest selection of eBooks available anywhere. Visit www.CourseSmart.com to learn more and to try a sample chapter.

Craft your teaching resources to match the way you teach! With McGraw-Hill Create™, www.mcgrawhillcreate.com, you can easily rearrange chapters, combine material from other content sources, and quickly upload content you have written such as your course syllabus or teaching notes. Find the content you need in Create by searching through thousands of leading McGraw-Hill textbooks. Arrange your book to fit your teaching style. Create even allows you to personalize your book's appearance by selecting the cover and adding your name, school, and course information. Order a Create book and you'll receive a complimentary print review copy in 3–5 business days or a complimentary electronic review copy (eComp) via email in minutes. Go to www.mcgrawhillcreate.com today and register to experience how McGraw-Hill Create™ empowers you to teach *your* students *your* way.

In Appreciation

In writing *Probation, Parole, and Community-Based Corrections*, we were greatly assisted by people who merit special recognition. Special thanks to Anthony Lopez for his ideas on chapter opening stories; to Phyllis Berry for her contribution to our chapter on special offenders; and Don Hummer at Penn State Harrisburg for his early involvement with the project.

We greatly appreciate the help and support of the dedicated community-based corrections professionals who provided their career profiles that make this book come alive. They are:

Chapter 1: Jesse Montgomery, Chief of Parole, Illinois Department of Corrections

Chapter 2: Beverly Morgan, Supervising U.S. Probation Officer, Western District of North Carolina

Chapter 3: Matthew Crow, Associate Professor of Criminal Justice, University of West Florida

Chapter 4: Beth Robinson, Corrections Counselor, Clark County District Court, Vancouver, Washington

Chapter 5: Kimberly Rieger, Supervising U.S. Probation and Pretrial Officer, Western District of Oklahoma

Chapter 6: Dan Petersen, Senior Faculty, National Victim Assistance Academy

Chapter 7: Kelli Matthews, U.S. Probation Officer Assistant, Southern District of Alabama

Chapter 8: Rick Robinson, Community Corrections Officer, Washington State Department of Corrections

Chapter 9: Joseph Schuetz, Reentry Officer, Shawnee County, Kansas Department of Corrections

Chapter 10: Lora Hawkins Cole, Deputy Commissioner of Community Corrections, State of Mississippi

Chapter 11: Angela Goering, Senior Vice President of Clinical Operations, Armor Correctional Health Services, Inc., Miami, Florida

Chapter 12: Randy McWilliams, Juvenile Probation Officer, 46th Judicial Juvenile District, Vernon, Texas

Reviewers pointed out the book's strengths and weaknesses. We took their comments seriously and hope they find their educational needs met more fully. They are:

Pierrette Ayotte, Thomas College
Elmer Bailey, Houston Community College
John Stuart Batchelder, North Georgia College and State University
Robert Bing, University of Texas–Arlington
Curtis Blakely, Truman State University
Brenda Brady, Rowan-Cabarrus Community College
Barbara Carson, Minnesota State University–Mankato
Gary Cornelius, George Mason University
David Johnson, University of Baltimore
Robert Keeton, Gulf Coast Community College
Kathryn Morgan, University of Alabama–Birmingham
Amy Nemmetz, University of Wisconsin–Platteville
Don Peavy, Sr., Canyon College
Diane Kay Sjuts, Metropolitan Community College
Steve Unterreiner, Southeast Missouri State University

We also want to acknowledge the special debt that we owe to the McGraw-Hill team, including Jessica Cannavo, Sponsoring Editor; Robin Reed, Developmental Editor; Angela FitzPatrick, Marketing Coordinator; Jane Mohr, Project Manager; Brenda Rolwes, Design Coordinator; Sue Culbertson, Buyer; and finally to Katie Stevens for encouraging us to write this book even though it took us several years to answer her call. A special thank you also goes out to Susan Messer, who obtained some very valuable reviewer feedback and helped us develop the chapters.

Ultimately, however, the full responsibility for the book is ours alone.

Gerald Bayens
Professor and Chair
Department of Criminal Justice and Legal Studies
Washburn University
gerald.bayens@washburn.edu

John Ortiz Smykla
Distinguished University Professor
University of West Florida
jsmykla@uwf.edu

PROBATION, PAROLE, AND COMMUNITY-BASED CORRECTIONS:

Supervision, Treatment, and Evidence-Based Practices

CHAPTER 1

Why Study Community-Based Corrections?:

Using Evidence-Based Practices, Risk Assessment, and Intermediate Sanctions to Reduce Crime and Protect the Community

OBJECTIVES

1. Explain what community-based corrections is and isn't.
2. Show how evidence-based corrections is the opposite of "correctional quackery."
3. Outline the major strategies of community-based corrections and intermediate sanctions.
4. Describe the Community Corrections Acts.
5. Compare the correctional goals of retributive justice and restorative justice.
6. Defend the six key components of the Pew Center on the States' publication *Policy Framework to Strengthen Community Corrections.*

OUTLINE

Drugs, guns, and strippers rocked the federal judiciary in 2011, when former U.S. District Senior Judge Jack Camp broke the very law that he had sworn to uphold.[1] *Camp pleaded guilty to a felony drug charge and two misdemeanors. He was sentenced to 30 days in federal prison plus a year of probation, a $1,000 fine, and 400 hours of community service. He was also ordered to reimburse the government for the cost of its prosecution.*

Since his appointment to the federal bench in 1987 by President Ronald Reagan, Camp had sentenced hundreds of offenders in the community. In spite of his lifetime appointment to the federal bench, his marriage and two adult children, and his honorable military service in the Vietnam War, in May 2010, 67-year-old Camp went astray. He began frequenting the Goldrush Show Bar (a nude strip club) in Atlanta, Georgia. One evening he invited a dancer to give him a lap dance. Soon afterward, Camp was paying her for sex, and they began smoking marijuana and snorting cocaine.

What Camp did not know was that the dancer was cooperating with the FBI. In October 2010, in an undercover drug sting, Camp was arrested in a parking lot by federal agents after he gave the stripper $160 for a drug deal. The agents also recovered two guns from the front seat of his car and discovered that he had given the stripper his $850 government-issued laptop computer. Camp resigned from the federal bench in November 2010.

Camp's probation, fine, and community service highlight the growing role of community corrections and alternatives to incarceration in criminal justice today. To introduce you to these important subjects, this chapter (1) defines the field of community-based corrections; (2) explains what evidence-based practices are and how they are reshaping community corrections today; (3) defines the concept of intermediate sanctions and lists the major types in use today; (4) outlines what Community Corrections Acts are and how they promote community-based practices at the local level; and (5) examines the goals and policies of community-based corrections today and for the future.

What Is Community-Based Corrections?

From Washington, D.C., to the smallest community in America, an effort is underway to identify more strategic, more effective, and more sustainable approaches to addressing crime. This means supporting community-based corrections programs that are backed by evidence of effectiveness, not simply feel-good policies or ideology.

In this book, we define **community corrections** as a philosophy of correctional treatment that embraces (1) decentralization of authority from state to local levels; (2) citizen participation in program planning, design, implementation, and evaluation; (3) redefinition of the population of offenders for whom incarceration is most appropriate; and (4) emphasis on rehabilitation through community programs. Community

HEARING TO ASSESS ALTERNATIVES TO INCARCERATION FOR DRUG INVOLVED OFFENDERS

In this hearing before the House of Representatives' Subcommittee on Domestic Policy, several experts discuss alternatives to incarceration in state, local, and tribal criminal justice systems. They also address the Department of Justice's commitment to reducing crime by focusing on evidence-based practices. If you were a member of this subcommittee, what questions would you ask these experts after you heard their testimony?

Visit CBC Online 1.1 at www.mhhe.com/bayens1e

corrections is an exciting field of criminal justice employing highly educated professionals who create innovative and evidence-based strategies to reduce **recidivism**—the repetition of criminal behavior, generally defined as rearrest.

Community corrections employs a continuum of sanctions other than prison. In such programs, offenders can be supervised in court-mandated community settings and complete their sentences while working, receiving treatment, and engaging with family. Community corrections programs are neighborhood-based, and they span a continuum from nonresidential programs such as probation, day-reporting centers, and home confinement to residential reentry centers such as halfway houses, boot camps, and work release centers as highlighted in CBC Online 1.1.

The philosophy behind community-based corrections recognizes the importance of the community in responding to crime. In short, the idea is that our communities not only have a right to safe streets and homes but also bear responsibility for making them safe. Today, all major components of the criminal justice system have alliances with the community. These include the following:

- Community policing—a law enforcement strategy to get residents involved in making their neighborhoods safer by focusing on crime prevention, nonemergency services, public accountability, and decentralized decision making.
- Community-based prosecution—a strategy founded on the idea that prosecutors have a responsibility not only to prosecute cases but to solve public safety problems, prevent crime, and improve public confidence in the justice system; prosecutors work out of neighborhood offices and collaborate with others in the development of problem-solving initiatives, setting the crime-fighting agenda, and participating in the solutions.
- Community-based defender services—a strategy that provides continuity in representation of indigent defendants and helps them with personal and family problems that can lead to legal troubles.
- Community courts—a strategy of harnessing the power of the justice system to hearing criminal cases in the community that are most affected by the case and including that community in case disposition to address local problems.

These alliances have been born out of necessity, or, to quote Plato, the Greek author and philosopher, "Necessity is the mother of invention," meaning that inventiveness and ingenuity are stimulated by difficulty. The current economic crisis is causing many states to face difficult budget choices. Legislators and corrections policymakers across the country are realizing that spending over *$52 billion* per year to incarcerate over 1.5 million adults in prison and another 800,000 in jail is reducing resources available for social structures such as education and healthcare and for improvements in physical structures such as roads, bridges, and national parks. As a result, many states are moving away from what Missouri Chief Justice William Ray Price calls "anger-based sentencing that ignores cost and effectiveness." Instead, he says, they are moving toward "evidence-based sentencing that focuses on results—sentencing that assesses each offender's risk and then fits that offender with the cheapest and most effective rehabilitation that he or she needs . . . because they cannot afford such a great waste of resources."[2]

For example, Mississippi legislators recently changed the law so nonviolent offenders are eligible for parole after they serve 25 percent of their sentences.[3] Missouri started informing judges how much their sentences will affect the public budget, and Colorado may soon be doing the same thing.[4] Missouri judges now know that three years in prison will cost $37,000, while three years on probation costs $6,770. More examples of how states are using community-based alternatives to reduce prison populations are shown in Exhibit 1.1. The common thread running across these examples is this: States are relying on professionalism in corrections and the use of social science data and theory to generate evidence-based practices, the major themes of this textbook. We turn now to a discussion of what that means for criminal justice professionals today and in the future.

Evidence-Based Corrections

As offender populations continue to grow, corrections officials are looking to community corrections and evidence-based practices to alleviate overcrowding in prisons and jails and to reduce new crimes and new victimization. The term **evidence-based corrections** (also called evidence-based practices) refers to the application of social scientific techniques to the study of everyday corrections procedures for the purpose of increasing effectiveness and enhancing the efficient use of available resources.

Used originally in the health and social science fields, evidence-based practice focuses on approaches that have been demonstrated to be effective through empirical research rather than through anecdote or professional experience alone. To say that a practice is evidence-based implies that (1) it has a definable outcome; (2) the outcome is measurable; and (3) the outcome is defined according to practical realities such as recidivism, victim satisfaction, employment rates of offenders, level of offenders' participation in substance abuse treatment, or level of offenders' participation in educational or vocational programming. An evidence-based approach not only meets the public's expectations for quality, efficiency, and effectiveness; it also reflects fairness, justice, and accountability.

Evidence-based practice draws on the highest form of empirical evidence, meaning that it is objective, balanced, and based on the best available data. Moreover, it is used to guide policy such that outcomes for consumers are improved. In the case of corrections, consumers include offenders, victims, communities, and other key stakeholders. As we will demonstrate in the chapters that follow, currently available evidence has already produced validated principles and demonstrated remarkable outcomes with correctional populations. Evidence-based research indicates that certain programs

Evidence-based research indicates that certain programs and intervention strategies, when applied to a variety of offender populations, reliably produce significant reductions in recidivism. When an offender's risk factors are identified through objective assessment processes, the probability of recidivism declines, leading to ex-offender autonomy and self-sufficiency. How can probation and parole officers respond to an offender's needs with job placement, family issues, vocational and educational training, anger management, and substance abuse treatment?

and intervention strategies, when applied to a variety of offender populations, reliably produce significant reductions in recidivism. Documented reductions in recidivism in some populations have exceeded 30 percent.

The traditional approach to offender supervision in the United States has emphasized individual accountability from offenders, and probation and parole officers were expected to rely on their personal experience and instincts to determine the most effective interventions for their clients. (We critique this method of offender classification in Chapter 4.) Though probation and parole officers made their best efforts, they were not provided with the full range of information needed to implement risk-reduction strategies. Even today, probation and parole officers continue to be trained with standards that stress quantity rather than quality of interactions with clients. And officers are not so much clearly directed what *to* do, as what *not* to do.

Academic researchers in the United States and Canada refer to this approach as "correctional quackery," an approach that is dismissive of scientific knowledge, training, and expertise. Its posture is strikingly overconfident, if not arrogant. It embraces the notion that interventions are best rooted in "common sense," in personal experiences (or clinical knowledge), in tradition, and in superstition. "What works" is thus felt to be "obvious," derived only from years of an individual's experience, and is legitimized by an appeal to custom.

Correctional quackery, therefore, is the use of treatment interventions that are based on neither (1) existing knowledge of the causes of crime nor (2) existing knowledge of which programs have been shown to change offender behavior.

Evidence-based practice is the opposite of "correctional quackery." It is the body of research that describes contemporary correctional assessment, programming, and supervision strategies that lead to improved correctional outcomes such as the rehabilitation of offenders and increased public safety.[5]

Within the field of community corrections, evidence-based practices can be research-tested principles that guide intervention, or they can refer to intervention

1.2

CBC Online

RESEARCH FOR THE REAL WORLD SEMINAR SERIES: SOLUTIONS IN CORRECTIONS USING EVIDENCE-BASED KNOWLEDGE

This National Institute of Justice seminar features Dr. Ed Latessa, professor of criminal justice at the University of Cincinnati, discussing evidence-based programs, practices, and policies that are both practical and useful in the field. Dr. Latessa describes how he and his team assessed more than 550 programs and saw the best and the worst. He shares five lessons and offers examples of states that are using evidence-based knowledge to improve correctional programs.

After you've reviewed the seminar materials, answer these questions:

1. In Lesson 1, did any of the correctional programs that did not work surprise you? Why or why not?
2. Why is Lesson 2 important?
3. Are you an example of Lesson 3?
4. Lesson 4 is about the importance of program integrity. Explain what that is and why it is important.
5. How can we achieve Lesson 5?

Visit CBC Online 1.2 at www.mhhe.com/bayens1e

models proven to lead to desirable outcomes. Ultimately, the goal of evidence-based approaches is to have professionals use the professional literature to find good evidence, and then implement it effectively to support policy and practice. Of course, not all research findings pertaining to a specific intervention or strategy reach the same conclusion for all samples and across all settings, and additional findings may one day provide refuting evidence. In other words, once evidence-based is not always evidence-based.

Nevertheless, adopting evidence-based practices is not an indication that community corrections is "soft" on crime or criminals. In fact, it is quite the opposite. Evidence-based practice provides more assurance that professionals are using the "right" theories, strategies, and approaches, which will result in reduced misconduct and enhanced safety for all. The profession of community-based corrections is evolving into a complex array of knowledge and skills related to the application of evidence-based best practices, as highlighted in CBC Online 1.2.

Recently the Justice Policy Institute, a Washington, D.C., think tank that is committed to reducing society's reliance on incarceration, reported on the innovative community-based corrections strategies that Georgia, Kansas, Michigan, Nevada, New Jersey, and Texas are using to reduce their prison populations. These states and others are relying on evidence-based practices to release nonviolent offenders early from prison to community supervision and to place them on the intermediate sanctions discussed later in this chapter. These states and others are also improving their offender risk-needs assessment procedures (discussed in Chapter 4) to reduce the chances that offenders will recidivate. A summary of what these states are doing is shown in Exhibit 1.1.

We do not mean to oversell what can be achieved with any specific evidence-based intervention. Nor do we mean to suggest that any strategy is guaranteed, failsafe, or a "magic bullet." Reducing recidivism is a complex process that depends on a number of theoretical variables. In addition, evidence-based practices must be implemented as closely as possible to the original approach in order to replicate their results. This means hiring community corrections professionals who are versed in theory and

EXHIBIT 1.1 Using Community-Based Corrections and Evidence-Based Practice to Reduce Prison Populations and Save Money

GEORGIA—As part of the National Institute of Correction's Transition from Prison to the Community Initiative (TPCI), Georgia began implementing a data-driven, outcome-based approach to parole, with the goal of improving completion rates for people on parole. As part of the initiative, parole officers serve as advocates, providing access to treatment, training, and other services. The TPCI also includes improved risk assessment instruments designed to more accurately predict whether a person is at high risk of being reconvicted of a new crime.

KANSAS—Under 2007 legislation, Kansas granted people in prison a 60-day credit for participating in certain programs designed to facilitate reintegration into the community. The state projects savings of approximately $80 million in the next five years. Prior to the legislation, Kansas had already changed the philosophy of parole by hiring social workers to be parole officers. Moreover, rather than simply monitoring offenders to catch them if they violate the terms of probation, parole officers are asked to ensure that people on parole stay out of prison.

MICHIGAN—Evidence-based practices in Michigan increased the rate of parole to its highest level in 16 years and decreased the state prison population from 51,500 in 2007 to 45,000 in 2009. Governor Jennifer M. Granholm has approved 133 commutations, expanded the state's parole board, and recently proposed a budget that presumes 7,500 fewer prisoners next year for savings of more than $130 million. The state has also expanded programs for people returning to their communities, directing millions of dollars toward helping them stay out of prison.

NEVADA—In 2007, Nevada passed a bill allowing people on probation to earn credits toward the reduction of their sentences. The legislation also established a series of graduated sanctions for violation of the terms of parole to prevent the immediate return to prison.

NEW JERSEY—The Halfway Back Program in New Jersey works with people on parole who are at risk of returning to prison on technical violations by assisting them with job placement, family, vocational and educational training, anger management, and substance abuse treatment. Investments in this program, in combination with the addition of risk assessment centers, were estimated to save $14 million in FY2010.

TEXAS—In May 2007, Texas enacted various community-based corrections policies that saved the state $210.5 million over the 2008–2009 fiscal year. Those policies included creating 3,800 beds for residential and outpatient drug treatment for people on probation, establishing maximum-sentence lengths for people on probation, establishing maximum case limits for parole officers, and developing incentives for counties that establish progressive sanctioning models for parole and probation systems. If new treatment and diversion programs are successful and no additional prisons are constructed, the state will save an additional $233 million.

Source: Justice Policy Institute, *How to Safely Reduce Prison Populations and Support People Returning to Their Communities* (Washington, D.C.: Justice Policy Institute, June 2010), pp. 8–9.

research methods. For insight into the career of one such professional, read the profile of Jesse Montgomery. A commitment to professionalism and continuous quality improvement is needed both to ensure that interventions are replicated closely and that new evidence is incorporated as it becomes available. The "best available evidence" evolves as the body of community corrections research grows.

JESSE MONTGOMERY, CHIEF OF PAROLE

Jesse Montgomery was named Chief of Parole for the Illinois Department of Corrections (IDOC) in 2007. His primary responsibilities include oversight and command authority for the state's parole division, which includes 31,000 adult and 2,000 juvenile parolees, 400 agents, 40 supervisors, and 50 support staff. Montgomery also oversees seven adult transition centers serving 2,000 inmates with 400 staff. He is also responsible for the Victim Services Unit; the Interstate Compact, which is the agreement between states to supervise offenders who are sentenced in one state but have requested to move (usually for family or work reasons) to another state; and the Apprehension and Extradition Units.

Montgomery joined IDOC as a correctional officer at Joliet Correctional Center in 1990 and was promoted to correctional sergeant in 1996. He became an administrative assistant at Joliet in 1997 and was named acting unit superintendent in 1999. That same year, he was named assistant warden for programs at Pontiac Correctional Center; the next year, he became assistant warden of operations at Stateville Correctional Center, and soon thereafter became superintendent of Illinois Youth Center–Joliet. He was appointed deputy director of District 2 in May 2003, with primary operational and budgetary oversight for seven correctional facilities ranging from maximum security to work release, as well as four adult transition centers. In November 2004, he was named deputy director of the Parole Division and remained in that position until his appointment as chief of parole in 2007. Montgomery is a U.S. Marine Corps veteran. He earned his associate's degree in applied science from Prairie State College in 1999, and in 2008 he earned his bachelor's degree in liberal arts with a minor in criminal justice from Governors State University.

Transitioning from employment with IDOC institutional corrections to community corrections was a learning experience for Montgomery. "I started my career with the IDOC as a correctional officer working in a maximum-security prison. When you're a CO in a max-security prison, your thought process is locked in on surviving as opposed to rehabilitating offenders. I was part of that thought process: Lock them up and make it to another day. However, I saw that this kind of thinking, along with a lack of reentry resources, only reinforced the recidivism rollercoaster. As I gained responsibility for inmate transition services, I learned that if you don't want the inmates to come back, you cannot incarcerate without a plan on the back-end.

"I worked on completing my degree. I advocated that it was cheaper and more prudent for parole agents with a caseload of no more than 90 to supervise offenders in the community with wraparound services. I called for reduced recidivism through targeted program policies, automated case management systems, enhanced staff training initiatives including unique training programs for special populations, cost-savings programs including paperless reports and early discharge policies, and community-based collaborations. I also strengthened reentry systems and wraparound services, and worked on legislative proposals to enhance public safety. Working with the IDOC has been very rewarding for me."

Montgomery's advice for persons interested in a career in corrections is this: "There was no magic bullet to my career path other than being my own person. One should always learn to think without prompting, leave peer pressure alone, question practice if it does not meet policy and vice versa, and make sure you finish your degree. If something does not seem correct, be brave enough to question and have a solution to present. If I sum up anything in my career it is treating **ALL** with respect—offenders, staff, families in the community, and more than anyone—yourself."

Intermediate Sanctions

The basic premise underlying community corrections is that sanctions are imposed on individuals according to the nature and severity of the offense, moving from limited interventions to more restrictive actions if the offender continues criminal activities. We refer to the punishments along this continuum as **intermediate sanctions**. Intermediate sanctions are criminal sentences that fall between standard probation and incarceration.

Intermediate sanctions serve a dual purpose in the criminal justice system. First, they reduce prison overcrowding and ease the burden on our nation's prison system. Second, they reduce recidivism by targeting the behaviors of the offender that led to the crime. For example, a batterer who can attend an anger management treatment program rather than go to prison, and who succeeds in the program, is less likely to commit future crimes. Intermediate sanctions can be effective if used appropriately.

Let us briefly introduce the intermediate sanctions that you will read about in later chapters.

Intensive supervision probation or **parole (ISP)**. This is a form of community supervision with frequent contact between offenders and their supervision officers. ISP is a restrictive form of community supervision for higher-risk offenders, and it usually includes strict enforcement of conditions, random drug and alcohol testing, and other intermediate sanctions.

Day reporting centers (DRC). These are nonresidential community correctional centers to which an offender reports either every day or several times a week depending on the level of supervision and treatment required. DRCs typically offer numerous services, such as counseling and job training, to address an offender's problems, and they typically supervise offenders in a setting that is more restrictive than probation but less inhibiting than prison. DRCs combine high levels of control with intensive delivery of services.

Home confinement/house arrest. This arrangement restricts an offender to his/her residence in one of three ways: under curfew, home detention, or home incarceration. Curfew requires offenders to stay in their residence during specified hours. Depending on the situation, an offender's behavior outside the curfew hours may or may not be regulated. Home detention requires an offender to stay home except for pre-approved activities such as work and education or for medical or religious purposes. The offender's movements are structured and monitored throughout the day to verify compliance. The most restrictive house arrest program is home incarceration. It requires offenders to stay home at *all* times with limited exceptions such as medical or religious purposes. The offender is subject to random contacts, and his or her behavior is tightly monitored to verify compliance.

Remote location monitoring (also referred to as electronic monitoring). Remote location monitoring is a technological tool that probation and parole officers use to monitor offenders remotely. Remote location monitoring involves either periodic or continuous surveillance of an offender through electronic means such as an ankle bracelet, voice verification, or GPS. It is a way to monitor the offender's presence in a proscribed location and is used with other intermediate sanctions, such as ISP, curfew, home detention, or home incarceration.

Fines. These financial sanctions require an offender to pay a specified amount of money to the court. Fines are usually based on the seriousness of the crime committed but can also be based on the offender's income. A fine is one of the oldest forms of punishment and is often given to first-time offenders for a variety of less serious offenses such as shoplifting, minor drug possession, violation of fish and game regulations, and even first-time drunk driving cases. In more serious cases, judges combine fines with other punishments such as probation and even incarceration. Recall this chapter's opening story about federal judge Jack Camp, who was sentenced to 30 days in federal prison plus a year of probation, a $1,000 fine, and 400 hours of community service.

Restitution. Whereas fines paid by offenders go to the court, restitution goes to victims for damages. Restitution refers to compensation for financial, physical, or emotional loss suffered by a crime victim. Offenders may be ordered to replace stolen or damaged property, cover medical treatment for physical injuries, or pay funeral and other costs. Offenders usually make payments to the victim through the court.

Community service. An offender under a community service order performs labor for a certain length of time for the community, such as cleaning a park of debris, or for charitable nonprofit organizations, such as domestic violence shelters, or for governmental offices, such as courthouses. Because the work takes away an offender's time, it is sometimes called a "fine of time."

Boot camps. Typically used for young offenders, boot camps provide structured and military-like activities focusing on discipline, physical labor, and education. Boot camps are designed to develop self-discipline, respect for authority, responsibility, and a sense of accomplishment. Once a popular type of intermediate sanction, boot camps are now on the decline, as you will learn.

Residential community centers (RCC). These minimum-security residential facilities provide convicted offenders with housing, treatment services, and access to community resources for employment and education. In RCCs, a resident's movements, behavior, and attitude are continuously monitored. Some RCCs are halfway houses, or transitional residences for offenders leaving prison or being sent there as a sentence instead of going to prison. Other examples of RCCs include work release centers and drug treatment facilities. Offenders in RCCs work at jobs in the community and pay rent, restitution, and family support. They only leave the RCC for work and other approved community activity such as religious worship or treatment. They return to the RCC promptly after the approved activity.

Drug court. This specialized court handles cases involving drug-addicted offenders. Drug courts use the power of the court to treat, sanction, and reward drug offenders with punishment more restrictive than regular probation but less severe than incarceration. Drug courts are more healing and restorative than regular courts. They integrate substance abuse treatment, sanctions, incentives, and frequent court appearances with case processing to place drug-involved offenders in judicially supervised rehabilitation programs. Successful completion of the treatment program results in dismissal of the charges, reduced or set-aside sentences, lesser penalties, or a combination of these.

Each of these intermediate sanctions can be used on its own as a penalty or interconnected with other correctional options, usually probation and parole. For example, Mindy McCready, a country music singer known for her number one hit "Guys Do It All the Time" and top 10 hit "A Girl's Gotta Do (What A Girl's Gotta Do)," was fined $4,000, sentenced to three years' probation, and ordered to perform 200 hours of community service for using a fake prescription to buy the painkiller OxyContin.

Typically, offenders given intermediate sanctions are under some form of probation supervision, whether it is regular probation or intensive. For instance, an offender on ISP may also be required to pay restitution and perform community service when he or she is financially and logistically able.

Intermediate sanctions are designed for offenders who require more punitive and restrictive monitoring than routine probation offers but who do not need to be imprisoned. However, intermediate sanctions are also used for persons accused of crimes and released into the community during court proceedings; for persons convicted of misdemeanors or felonies and then directly sentenced to an intermediate sanction; and for persons on probation, in jail, in prison, or on parole.

Information is readily available regarding the number of persons in a community who are on probation and parole. However, citing the number of offenders involved in intermediate sanctions, or even the number of intermediate sanction programs that exist across the nation, is difficult because intermediate sanctions have sprung up independently in many jurisdictions. Local public or private agencies rather than federal or state agencies often introduce them, and we do not yet have a complete inventory of all of them or of the numbers they are serving. Suffice it to say, thousands of offenders are involved in intermediate sanctions on any given day. For example, at midyear 2009, 8.3 percent of the 837,833 adults who were sentenced to jail were supervised outside a jail facility in the following intermediate sanctions:[6]

17,738 in community service
12,439 in pretrial supervision
11,834 in remote location monitoring
11,212 in weekend programs
6,492 in day reporting centers
5,912 in other work programs
2,082 in treatment programs
1,766 in other forms of sanction
738 in home detention

The American Corrections Association, the oldest and largest international corrections association in the world, has embraced community corrections and intermediate sanctions. Their statement of support is shown in Exhibit 1.2.

Community-Based Corrections Acts

This spirit of correctional collaboration and community partnership has led 35 states and the District of Columbia to pass **community corrections acts** (CCAs) (see Exhibit 1.3). CCAs are state laws that give economic grants to local communities to establish community corrections goals and policies and to develop and operate community corrections programs. Most CCAs transfer some state functions to local communities, decentralizing services and engaging communities in the process of reintegrating offenders. The goal of CCAs in most states is to divert certain prison-bound offenders into local-, city-, or county-level programs where they can receive treatment and community support instead of incarceration. A recent example is found in Kansas, where the state offered $4 million in grants to local community corrections programs that agreed to reduce their probation revocations by 20 percent (probation revocations are discussed in Chapter 7). In California, community corrections legislation is being updated. The new plan is called "realignment." In order to preserve expensive prison cells for more serious offenses, the new plan is to reduce the number of people going to state prison for select low-level, nonviolent drug or property offenses by providing

EXHIBIT 1.2 American Correctional Association Public Correctional Policy on Community Corrections

Introduction

Community corrections programs are an integral component of a graduated system of sanctions and services. They enable offenders to work and pay taxes, make restitution, meet court obligations, maintain family ties, and develop or maintain critical support systems with the community. To be successful, community corrections programs must promote public safety and a continuum of care that responds to the needs of victims, offenders, and the community. These programs should include a collaborative comprehensive planning process for the development of effective policies and services.

Policy Statement

Community corrections programs include residential and nonresidential programs. Most community corrections programs require offenders to participate in certain activities or special programs that are specifically directed toward reducing their risk to the community. Those responsible for community corrections programs, services, and supervision should:

- seek statutory authority and adequate funding, both public and private, for community programs and services as part of a comprehensive corrections strategy
- develop and ensure access to a wide array of residential and nonresidential services that address the identifiable needs of victims, offenders, and the community
- inform the public about the benefits of community programs and services, the criteria used to select individuals for these programs, and the requirements for successful completion
- recognize that public acceptance of community corrections is enhanced by the provision of victim services, community service, and conciliation programs
- mobilize the participation of a well-informed constituency, including citizen advisory boards and broad-based coalitions, to address community corrections issues
- participate in collaborative, comprehensive planning efforts which provide a framework to assess community needs and develop a system-wide plan for services
- ensure the integrity and accountability of community programs by establishing a reliable system for monitoring and measuring performance in accordance with accepted standards of professional practices and sound evaluation methodology.

This Public Correctional Policy was unanimously ratified by the American Correctional Association Delegate Assembly at the Winter Conference in Orlando, Florida, on January 20, 1985. It was reviewed and amended on January 29, 1997, at the Winter Conference in Indianapolis, Indiana. It was reviewed and amended again on January 14, 2002, at the Winter Conference in San Antonio, Texas.

counties with either $11,000 per offender (the Republican proposal) or $24,000 per offender (the Democratic proposal) kept at the local level who would otherwise have been sent to state prison, which costs $50,000 per offender per year.[7] Counties can use the money to create new offender services and improve existing ones. Research shows that locally designed sanctions have a better chance of succeeding because they are based in the community where offenders' families, friends, and other social supports are, and they are cheaper.[8]

EXHIBIT 1.3 States with Community Corrections

Source: Data from Mary Shilton, "Community Corrections Acts by States, 2007," Center for Community Corrections, www.centerforcommunitycorrections.org (accessed August 11, 2010).

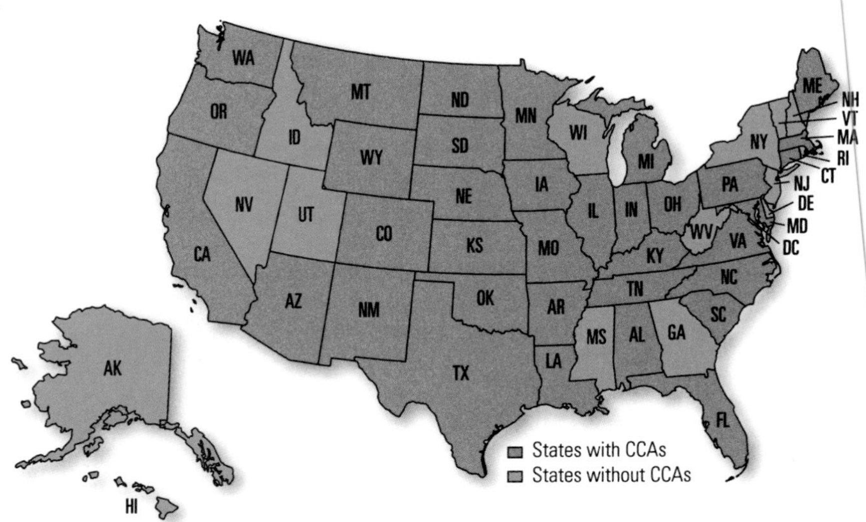

In 1973, Minnesota became the first state to adopt a CCA. Minnesota officials wanted to reduce fragmentation in criminal justice service delivery, to control costs, and to redefine the population of offenders for whom state incarceration was most appropriate. Communities throughout Minnesota were willing to assume greater correctional responsibility for less serious offenders, as long as the communities were also given state subsidies and significant control over planning and service delivery. The huge success of Minnesota's CCA can be seen in Minnesota's incarceration rate, one of the lowest in the United States today. While the crime rate is not much different from those of other states,[9] the incarceration rate is only 189 persons for every 100,000 residents. (The U.S. average on January 1, 2009, was 502 per 100,000 residents.[10]) The majority of Minnesota's offenders are handled under the CCA. CCAs in Minnesota and other states are discussed in Chapter 2.

Simply having a correctional program in a community does not mean that it will succeed. A set of consistent goals and approaches to achieving those goals is the backbone of successful community corrections. Adopting community corrections legislation can help accomplish that consistency.

Goals of Community-Based Corrections

High-profile faces and cases taken from today's headlines introduce each chapter in this textbook and demonstrate the two broad purposes of contemporary sentencing: retributive justice and restorative justice.

Retributive justice is a theory of justice that states that everyone should get what they deserve. Retributive justice focuses on the law and the need for the community to exact punishment.

Restorative justice is a theory of justice that emphasizes repairing the harm caused by criminal behavior. It focuses on the needs of victims and offenders instead of the need to satisfy the abstract principles of law or the need for the community to exact punishment. Both restorative justice and retributive justice are goals in community corrections sentencing today.

Retributive justice goals include revenge, retribution, just desserts, deterrence, incapacitation, and rehabilitation. Restoration is the goal of restorative justice. Each is described below.

Revenge (also known as vengeance) is a harmful act taken in response to criminal victimization. The goal of revenge usually consists of forcing the offender to suffer the same or greater pain than that which was originally inflicted on the victim.

Retribution implies the infliction of punishment on those who deserve to be punished and scaled relative to the severity of the offending behavior. A retributive system punishes severe crime more harshly than minor crime, but this does not mean that the punishment has to be equivalent to the crime. Historically, retribution has been explained as "an eye for an eye and a tooth for a tooth."

Just deserts is similar to revenge and retribution, but it deemphasizes the emotional component. It is based solely on the severity of the crime and not on individual characteristics. Just deserts claims that criminal acts are deserving of punishment, that offenders are morally blameworthy and must be punished. Defendants convicted of the same crime should receive the same punishment.

Deterrence is another form of retributive justice. Unlike revenge, retribution, and just deserts, which focus on the past, deterrence is centered on the future. Advocates of deterrence argue that punishment serves a useful purpose because it restrains the individual offender (**specific deterrence**) or the population as a whole (**general deterrence**). Deterrence is synonymous with what has been called the "pleasure–pain principle"—that is, if the pain of punishment is greater than the pleasure of crime, an offender will stop committing crime.

Incapacitation restrains offenders from committing additional crimes by isolating them, generally in jail or in prison. Advocates of community-based corrections argue that home confinement/house arrest is a less expensive way to isolate offenders.

And finally, **rehabilitation** is a structured effort to alter the attitudes and behaviors of offenders and change criminal lifestyles into law-abiding ones by using medical and psychological treatments and social-skills training. Elsewhere in this textbook we discuss the use of motivational interviewing and cognitive behavioral therapy in community-based corrections as evidence-based practices that correct problems that lead individuals to crime.

Whereas retributive justice goals define crime as a violation of law and give primacy to punishing offenders, restorative justice focuses on allowing offenders to make amends to their victims. Instead of viewing crime as a violation against the state, restorative justice views crime as a violation of one person by another. An excellent discussion of restorative justice is presented in CBC Online 1.3.

Advocates of restorative justice believe that retributive justice may be counterproductive, resulting in stigmatization, humiliation, isolation of offenders, and exclusion of victims. Moreover, retributive justice lacks the message that the offender should repair damages to the victim. In contrast, intermediate sanctions such as community service and restitution offer new ways to respond to crime and criminal behavior while at the same time involving victims, offenders, and the community. Programs typically identified with restorative justice include victim–offender mediation, meaning a meeting between the victim and offender facilitated by a trained mediator in which the victim and offender begin to resolve the conflict and construct their own approach to achieving justice in the face of their particular crime. Second, such programs include

AN INTERVIEW WITH DR. HOWARD ZEHR, FOUNDER OF THE RESTORATIVE JUSTICE MOVEMENT

In two videos, Dr. Howard Zehr, founder of the restorative justice movement and professor of sociology and restorative justice at Eastern Mennonite University, Harrisonburg, Virginia, discusses the meaning, uses, and issues surrounding restorative justice with Ann Helmke, director of the Peace Center in San Antonio, Texas.

Watch the videos and then answer this question: If you had the opportunity to interview Dr. Zehr, what three questions would you ask him?

Visit CBC Online 1.3 at www.mhhe.com/bayens1e

conferencing, which is similar to victim–offender mediation but also includes the participation of families, community support groups, police, social welfare officials, and attorneys. A third component can be circle sentencing, a common approach in Native American communities. In circle sentencing, participants—who can be anyone in the community concerned about the crime—form a circle for a session chaired by a respected member of the community. Discussion goes beyond the offense and the offender to include discussion of

- similar crimes in the community
- causes of crimes
- life in the community before the crime
- impact on victims
- what can be done to prevent the behavior in the future
- what must be done to help heal the offender, the victim, and the community
- what the sentence will be
- who will carry out the sentence
- who will support the victim and offender to ensure the sentence is successfully implemented.

A key aspect of such circles is the recognition that the offender has deep roots and commitment in the community.

A fourth common component of restorative justice is victim assistance—meaning programs that provide services to victims as they recover from the crime and proceed through the criminal justice process.

In short, restorative approaches are characterized by four key values: (1) to provide opportunities for victims, offenders, and community members who want to meet to discuss the crime and its consequences; (2) to provide opportunities for offenders to take steps to repair the harm they have caused; (3) to provide opportunities for victims and offenders to once again become whole, contributing members of society; and (4) to provide opportunities for parties with a stake in specific crimes to participate in their resolution.

The groundswell in evidence-based practice, a continuum of intermediate sanctions, development of community corrections acts, and emergence of new sentencing goals are contributing to a stronger and more effective system of community-based corrections and have the potential to redirect a portion of the money spent on incarceration. We turn now to a discussion of future policy in community-based corrections.

Dr. Howard Zehr is founder of the restorative justice (RJ) movement and professor of sociology and restorative justice at Eastern Mennonite University, Harrisonburg, Virginia. RJ focuses on allowing offenders to make amends to their victims. Instead of viewing crime as a violation against the state, restorative justice views crime as a violation of one person by another. How is RJ different from retributive justice?

Policy Implications

The current budget crisis in the United States has prompted many states to retool their sentencing and corrections options to better manage the 7.3 million Americans under correctional control. In the view of the Pew Center on the States, "If we had stronger community corrections, we wouldn't need to lock up so many people at such a great cost. By redirecting a portion of the dollars currently spent on imprisoning the lowest-risk inmates, we could significantly increase the intensity and quality of supervision and services directed at the same type of offender in the community."[11]

To help create a national agenda for stronger and more effective community-based corrections, the Pew Center brought together leading policymakers, correctional practitioners, and researchers from states (including Arizona, Kansas, and Texas) that were already considering which offenders should be locked up and which might be managed effectively in the community. An additional purpose of the meeting was to identify ways to help correctional agencies adopt the most effective evidence-based practices. The result was publication of the document *Policy Framework to Strengthen Community Corrections.* The policy framework includes incentives for offenders to stay crime- and drug-free, fiscal incentives for agencies to improve their success rates, and ways to focus treatment and punishment toward one goal—preventing crime—which is more effective than either punishment or treatment alone. Here we briefly detail the six key components of that framework.

1. Sort Offenders by Risk to Public Safety. Accurately separate those who are more likely to cause great harm from those who may cause relatively little harm. The risk-assessment tools discussed in Chapter 4 can help corrections officials more accurately predict not only how likely a person is to commit a new crime, but also whether that offense will be a violent one. The risk score can then be used to guide decisions about whether an offender should go to prison or remain under community control, and which cognitive treatment interventions will change the offender's thinking and reasoning that drive criminal activity. The Pew Center report points out, however, that risk assessment is not risk elimination. Risk assessment is an estimate of what a given person might do. The science continues to evolve.
2. Base Intervention Programs on Science. Similar to the Pew Center report, this book promotes the application of evidence-based practices. In later chapters you will learn that evidence-based practices are associated with an average decrease in crime of between 10 and 20 percent, whereas data on non-evidence-based programs tend show no decrease and in some cases even reveal slight increases in crime. Interventions that follow all evidence-based practices have been associated with reductions in criminal activity of as much as 30 percent.

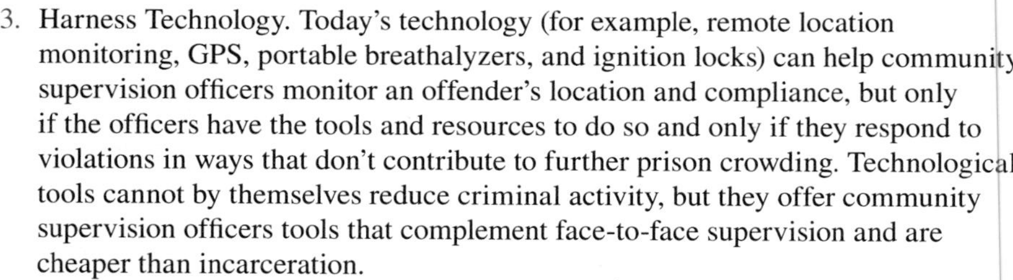

3. Harness Technology. Today's technology (for example, remote location monitoring, GPS, portable breathalyzers, and ignition locks) can help community supervision officers monitor an offender's location and compliance, but only if the officers have the tools and resources to do so and only if they respond to violations in ways that don't contribute to further prison crowding. Technological tools cannot by themselves reduce criminal activity, but they offer community supervision officers tools that complement face-to-face supervision and are cheaper than incarceration.

To help create a national agenda for stronger and more effective community-based corrections, the Pew Center brought together the nation's leading policymakers, correctional practitioners, and researchers to develop a framework to help correctional agencies adopt the most effective evidence-based practices. What are the six key components of that framework?

4. Impose Swift and Certain Sanctions for Violation. Today, too many probation and parole agencies are underfunded and understaffed. They struggle with high caseloads and lack legal authority to impose graduated sanctions for violations. Many community supervision officers delay pursuing violations until an offender has committed a new crime or a significant number of technical violations, at which point return to prison is likely. The framework suggested by the Pew Center gives probation and parole officers authority to impose graduated sanctions on violators without first requiring a time-consuming trip back to court. The framework documents the success of a program in Georgia called Probation Options Management, which allows chief probation officers (POs) to impose sanctions on violators in certain circumstances. The program reduced the number of days offenders spent in jail awaiting court disposition by 70 percent, saved local jails $1.1 million, and reduced the amount of time POs spent waiting in courthouses for violation cases to be heard.

5. Create Incentives for Success. This applies to both offenders and community supervision agencies. Arizona is a case in point. In 2008, Arizona adopted the Safe Communities Act. For every month an offender complies with the terms of supervision, the act authorizes the courts to reduce the offender's length of probation by 20 days. In addition, counties that reduce recidivism are awarded 40 percent of the money the state saves by not having to incarcerate rule violators in state prison.
6. Measure Progress. Policymakers, practitioners, and researchers agree that accurate and timely statistics, deployment of resources where they are most needed, effective human service strategies, and ongoing follow-up and assessment are critical to knowing what impact corrections has on reducing criminal activity. Yes, the goal is to reduce recidivism, but as we will report in Chapter 7, the American Probation and Parole Association urges its members to also collect data on other key performance measures such as amount of restitution collected, number

1.4

COMMUNITY CORRECTIONS, MONROE COUNTY, INDIANA

This informational video and PowerPoint presentation introduces you to community corrections in Monroe County, Indiana. It reviews a number of topics covered in this chapter, such as the goals and mission of community corrections, as well as types of intermediate sanctions. It follows a defendant from his sentencing through 180 days of house arrest and successful program completion.

After viewing this presentation, consider this question: How could the use of community corrections expand to include more serious crimes while still protecting the community?

Visit CBC Online 1.4 at www.mhhe.com/bayens1e.

CBC Online

of offenders employed, amount of fines and fees collected, hours of community service performed, number of treatment sessions attended, percentage of financial obligations collected, educational attainment, and number of days drug-free.

This set of sentencing and correctional principles is offered as a way to better balance public safety, offender accountability, and the realities of today's economic crisis. We agree with the Pew Center and its experts that better performance in community corrections can reduce criminal activity and the expensive use of imprisonment for low-risk offenders.

Will the American public support using community-based corrections to respond to non-serious crime? The answer is that a majority will. One month after the Pew Center published its framework, the National Council on Crime and Delinquency (NCCD) commissioned Zogby International to conduct a national public opinion poll about American voter attitudes toward intermediate sanctions for non-serious, nonsexual crimes. This poll showed that striking majorities favor methods other than incarceration for responding to these offenders. Almost eight in 10 believe non-serious, nonsexual offenders should receive the kind of intermediate sanctions discussed in this chapter; almost eight in 10 do not believe that intermediate sanctions decrease public safety; half believe that intermediate sanctions save money; and almost half believe that intermediate sanctions are more effective at reducing recidivism than prison or jail time. NCCD estimates that over $7 billion can be saved if 80 percent of nonviolent, non-serious, and nonsexual offenders are sentenced to alternatives instead of incarceration. A savings of this magnitude in the current economic crisis would reduce the economic burden on institutional corrections while also providing funding for community-based corrections and for the intermediate sanctions that are more appropriate for non-serious, nonviolent, and nonsexual offenders. CBC Online 1.4, which focuses on community corrections in Monroe County, Indiana, demonstrates the safety and savings of community corrections.

We conclude this chapter with Exhibit 1.4, an interview that Dr. Joan Petersilia, one of the nation's most respected experts on community-based corrections, gave in 2007. In that interview, she spoke with Pew's Public Safety Performance Project about what works in community corrections.

EXHIBIT 1.4 What Works in Community Corrections: An Interview with Dr. Joan Petersilia[12]

Q: To start us off, what are community corrections and what are their goals?

A: Simply defined, "community corrections" are non-prison sanctions that are imposed on convicted adults or adjudicated juveniles either by a court instead of a prison sentence or by a parole board following release from prison. Community corrections programs are usually operated by probation and parole agencies, and the programs can include general community supervision as well as day reporting centers, halfway houses and other residential facilities, work release, and other community programs.

All community corrections programs have the multiple goals of providing offender accountability, delivering rehabilitation services and surveillance, and achieving fiscal efficiency.

Q: Would you describe a few of the most effective community corrections programs and the results they deliver?

A: First, it is important to note that probably 99 percent of all community corrections programs in the U.S. today have not been scientifically evaluated. So identifying which ones are most effective is impossible. I suspect there are many excellent programs operating today (such as faith-based mentoring, etc.) that, if subject to evaluation, might be effective. But the corrections literature includes evaluations mostly of large federally funded programs, and most of those are services for drug-addicted felons. From that literature, we know that intensive community supervision combined with rehabilitation services can reduce recidivism between 10 and 20 percent. Some drug courts have also had similarly encouraging results.

Q: And what does the research say about ineffective programs?

A: We know more about what doesn't work than what does. Research has shown that boot camps, house arrest, and routine probation and parole supervision do not reduce recidivism. But again, the majority of community corrections programs have never been scientifically tested so you have to view these results cautiously as well.

Q: In your view, what are the principles or themes that run through effective community corrections programs?

A: At the core of any good community corrections program is the use of an objective risk and needs assessment. Assessments allow correctional agencies to assign offenders to the programs that will most likely benefit them. The "risk" part of the assessment instrument assesses risk to reoffend, and that information is critical to assigning probationers or parolees to levels of surveillance and supervision, such as specialized caseloads, frequent drug testing, or electronic monitoring. The "need" portion of the assessment instrument identifies the subset of the offender population that research has shown will benefit from being in rehabilitation treatment programs. Research has shown that for high- and moderate-risk offenders, participation in treatment programs and services has high payoff, but for those with a low risk to reoffend, life skills programs are more appropriate. This is the most efficient use of scarce correctional resources as well as the best way to increase public safety.

Of course, the next core principle is to make certain that the rehabilitation programs are of sufficient quality to make a difference. There are now several scoring methods that rate the quality of rehabilitation programs along such dimensions as staff qualifications and training, use of a tested curriculum or program model, and use of cognitive-behavioral or social learning methods. These and other program characteristics have been shown to increase success. In short, effective corrections programs must get the right offender in the right program. And then of course, we must continually evaluate costs and program outcomes and revise accordingly.

Research over the last several decades also reinforces the importance of the community and familial supports as sources of informal social control. Effective programs involve family and community members in a very real and proactive way. Effective programs recognize that government programs ultimately end, and the handoff between the formal and informal systems is ultimately what determines success. In my opinion, community corrections agencies that collaborate closely with nonprofits and other community organizations, who in turn work to integrate the offender's family and social support system, will have the most success.

Q: How have community corrections programs changed, and what does the future hold?

A: There are two major trends that I see in community corrections today. The first has to do with technology to monitor compliance with court-ordered conditions, such as drug testing, global positioning systems, alcohol breathalyzers, and so on. The second has to do with "wraparound services." Every agency, including probation and parole, recognizes that reducing criminal behavior is incredibly difficult, and no one agency can do it alone. More and more, I see wraparound services, where mental health, alcohol and drug abuse, housing, and medical services agencies are creating an offender's case management plan together. This is very promising. And then, of course, there is reentry, which is now the new correctional buzzword. If inmate reentry were our focus, then the divide between incarceration and community corrections would begin to blur, and that would be a good thing, in my view.

Q: Saving the best for last, what are the key questions policymakers should be asking when they confront decisions about correctional strategy and spending? How should they think about striking the right balance between building more prisons and expanding community corrections?

A: To me, policymakers need to understand that it is not one or the other: build prisons or support community corrections. We need strong systems of each. We need to create enough prison space to house the truly violent and those with no desire to change their criminal behavior, and at the same time, we need to invest heavily in helping offenders who are not yet steeped in criminal behavior and wish to chart a different path. Sending someone to prison should be our last resort; it is expensive, it is stigmatizing, and it can increase risk for future criminal behavior. Moreover, it impacts not only the person incarcerated but also his or her family and children. Investing in quality community corrections programs is, in my view, just good public policy.

chapter 1 review

Summary

Community-based corrections is a philosophy of correctional treatment that embraces (1) decentralization of authority from state to local levels; (2) citizen participation in program planning, design, implementation, and evaluation; (3) redefinition of the population of offenders for whom incarceration is most appropriate; and (4) emphasis on rehabilitation through community programs.

Evidence-based practice is based in research. In the context of community corrections, it focuses on contemporary correctional assessment, programming, and supervision strategies that can lead to improved correctional outcomes such as the rehabilitation of offenders and increased public safety. Correctional quackery is dismissive of scientific knowledge, training, and expertise. It embraces the notion that interventions are best rooted in common sense, personal experiences (or clinical knowledge), tradition, and superstition.

The major strategies of community-based corrections are the intermediate sanctions, including intensive supervised probation, day reporting centers, home confinement and house arrest, remote location monitoring, fines, restitution, community service, boot camp, residential community centers, and drug courts.

Community Corrections Acts (CCAs) are state laws that give economic grants to local communities to establish community corrections goals and policies and to develop and operate community corrections programs. CCAs transfer some state functions to local communities, decentralizing services and engaging communities in the process of reintegrating offenders. The goal of CCAs in most states is to divert certain prison-bound offenders into local, city, or county programs where they can receive treatment and community support instead of incarceration.

Retributive justice is a theory of justice that emphasizes the principle that everyone should get what they deserve. Retributive justice focuses on the law and the need of the community to exact punishment. Restorative justice is a theory of justice that emphasizes repairing the harm caused by criminal behavior. It focuses on the needs of victims and offenders, instead of the need to satisfy the abstract principles of law or the need of the community to exact punishment.

To build a stronger and more effective system of community-based corrections and to redirect a portion of the money spent on imprisoning the lowest-risk offenders, criminal justice professionals should sort offenders by risk to public safety, base intervention programs on evidence-based practices, use technological tools that complement face-to-face supervision and are cheaper than incarceration, give probation and parole officers authority to impose graduated sanctions on violators without first requiring a time-consuming trip back to court, create incentives for offenders and programs to succeed, and measure progress so communities can know what impact corrections has on reducing criminal activity.

Key Terms

boot camp, p.11
community corrections, p.3
community corrections acts (CCA), p.12
community service, p.11
day reporting centers (DRC), p.10
deterrence, p.15
drug court, p.11
evidence-based corrections, p.5
fines, p.10
general deterrence, p.15
home confinement/house arrest, p.10
incapacitation, p.15
intensive supervision probation (ISP), p.10
intermediate sanctions, p.10
just deserts, p.15
recidivism, p.4
rehabilitation, p.15
remote location monitoring, p.10
residential community centers (RCC), p.11
restitution, p.11
restorative justice, p.14
revenge, p.15
retribution, p.15
retributive justice, p.14
specific deterrence, p.15

Questions for Review

1. What is/isn't community-based corrections?
2. How is evidence-based corrections the opposite of "correctional quackery"?
3. What are the major strategies of community-based corrections?
4. How would you explain Community Corrections Acts?
5. How would you contrast the correctional goals of retributive justice and restorative justice?

6. How would you implement the six key components of the Pew Center on the States' publication, *Policy Framework to Strengthen Community Corrections*?

Question of Policy

Community Corrections Improvement Act of 2010

The 2010 legislative agenda of the International Community Corrections Association (ICCA) is to pursue new Congressional legislation entitled *Community Corrections Improvement Act of 2010.* The 2010 Legislative Agenda and the Act can be found at the ICCA Web site (www.iccaweb.org under the link "Public Policy") or by using any Internet search engine with the key terms "international community corrections association community corrections improvement act of 2010."

After reading through the Web site, answer this question: How do the five sections of the act relate to ideas discussed in this chapter?

What Would You Do?

In CBC Online 1.2, on using evidence-based knowledge, Professor Ed Latessa tells us that if we want to reduce recidivism, we should focus on offenders most likely to recidivate and use evidence-based practices. Sounds easy enough in the abstract, but which offenders are most likely to recidivate? If you want to evaluate whether your state is focusing on offenders who are most likely to recidivate, what would you do? (Hint: Contact your state department of corrections. Most have a research division.) What evidence-based practices are they using to reduce recidivism? Is your state really focusing on the offenders most likely to recidivate, or are they taking the simpler route of focusing on less severe offenders? If you find the latter, what would you do to bring about change?

Endnotes

1. Bill Rankin, "Ex-judge Caught with Drugs, Stripper Gets 30 Days," *Atlanta Journal and Constitution*, March 11, 2011, www.ajc.com (accessed March 22, 2011), and "Ex-Federal Judge Gets 30 Days in Prison for Crimes With Stripper," www.thecrimereport.org (accessed March 22, 2011).
2. "Chief Justice Delivers 2010 State of the Judiciary Address," February 3, 2010, *www.courts.mo.gov/page.jsp?id=36875* (accessed February 10, 2010).
3. John Buntin, "Mississippi's Corrections Reform," *Governing*, August 2010, www.governing.com (accessed September 2010).
4. Editorial, "Weighing the Cost of Justice," *The Denver Post*, www.denverpost.com, September 24, 2010 (accessed September 27, 2010).
5. Edward Latessa, Frank Cullen, and Paul Gendreau, "Beyond Professional Quackery: Professionalism and the Possibility of Professional Treatment," *Federal Probation*, vol. 66, no. 2 (September 2002), pp. 43–49.
6. Todd D. Minton, *Jail Inmates at Midyear 2009—Statistical Tables* (Washington, DC: U.S. Department of Justice, Bureau of Justice Statistics, June 2010).
7. Jeanne Woodford, "Viewpoints: California's Bloated Prison System Threatens Public Safety," *The Sacramento Bee*, October 4, 2010, www.sacbee.com (accessed October 6, 2010).
8. Mary. K. Shilton, *Community Corrections Acts for State and Local Partnerships* (Laurel, MD: American Correctional Association, 1992), and Woodford, "Viewpoints: California's Bloated Prison System Threatens Public Safety."
9. Federal Bureau of Investigation, *2008 Crime in the United States* (Washington, DC: U.S. Department of Justice, Federal Bureau of Investigation), www.fbi.gov (accessed July 28, 2010).
10. Heather C. West, William J. Sabol, and Sarah J. Greenman, *Prisoners in 2009* (Washington, DC: U.S. Department of Justice, Bureau of Justice Statistics, December 2010).
11. Pew Center on the States, *One in 31: The Long Reach of American Corrections* (New York: Pew Charitable Trusts, March 2009), p. 3.
12. The Pew Charitable Trusts, *What Works in Community Corrections: An Interview with Dr. Joan Petersilia* (Washington, DC: Pew Charitable Trusts, November 2007).

CHAPTER 2

Legislation, Apprehension, Adjudication, and Corrections:

The Four Filters Affecting Community-Based Corrections

OBJECTIVES

1 Explain the importance of community corrections acts in the evolution of community-based correctional programs.

2 Demonstrate an understanding of the connection between arrest rates and corrections.

3 Describe the "war on drugs" and the influence that drug offenders have on the criminal justice system.

4 Describe the relationship between mandatory sentencing laws and community-based corrections.

5 Provide examples of policy changes that have occurred to meet the economic constraints of the times.

OUTLINE

In November 1995, Leandro Andrade was charged with two felony counts of petty theft with a prior conviction after he stole approximately $150 worth of videotapes from Kmarts located in two cities in California. Under California's "three-strikes" law, any felony can constitute the third strike and subject a defendant to a prison term of 25 years to life.

A jury found Andrade guilty and then found that he had prior convictions that qualified as serious felonies under the three-strikes law. Because each of his petty theft convictions triggered a separate application of the three-strikes law, the judge sentenced Andrade to life in prison with no possibility of parole for 50 years. Andrade appealed his sentence, alleging that California's law was grossly disproportionate to the crime and thereby constituted cruel and unusual punishment in violation of the Eighth Amendment. In a 5–4 decision, the U.S. Supreme Court disagreed and upheld the conviction (Lockyer v. *Andrade, 538 U.S. 63, 123 S. Ct. 1166, L. Ed. 2d (2003).*[1] *The essence of the Court's ruling was that a sentence of two consecutive terms of 25 years to life in prison for a "third strike" conviction did not violate the Eighth Amendment prohibition on cruel and unusual punishment.*

In this chapter we will address how legislation and other aspects of the criminal justice system have greatly influenced the delivery of correctional services in the United States. As you read the chapter, consider whether Andrade's punishment fit the crime. That is, should he have been sentenced to 50 years behind bars for petty theft? Also, consider the financial burden society takes on in a case like Andrade's, where incarceration rather than community-based sanctions is imposed by the courts.

Community-Based Corrections and the Criminal Justice System

The corrections profession is the third component of a broader criminal justice system, which also consists of law enforcement and the courts. While all three components enjoy a great deal of autonomy from each other, combined they constitute an interconnected system of justice in the United States. Moreover, the nature of the criminal justice system is such that changes occurring in one component typically affect changes in the other components.

Exhibit 2.1 summarizes the most common events in the criminal and juvenile justice systems, including entry into the criminal justice system, prosecution and pretrial services, adjudication, sentencing and sanctions, and corrections. Although located toward the end of the diagram, the field of corrections plays a key role in promoting public safety at nearly every stage of the justice system. After making an arrest, for example, a police officer transports the accused to the local jail and releases him or her to corrections officials for booking. There the arrestee is searched, photographed, fingerprinted, and provided a copy of the charges. If bail is granted, corrections personnel prepare a bond that specifies the conditions of the release and the court appearance

EXHIBIT 2.1 Sequence of Events in the U.S. Criminal Justice System

Source: Bureau of Justice Statistics, *http://bjs.ojp.usdoj.gov/content/largechart.cfm*

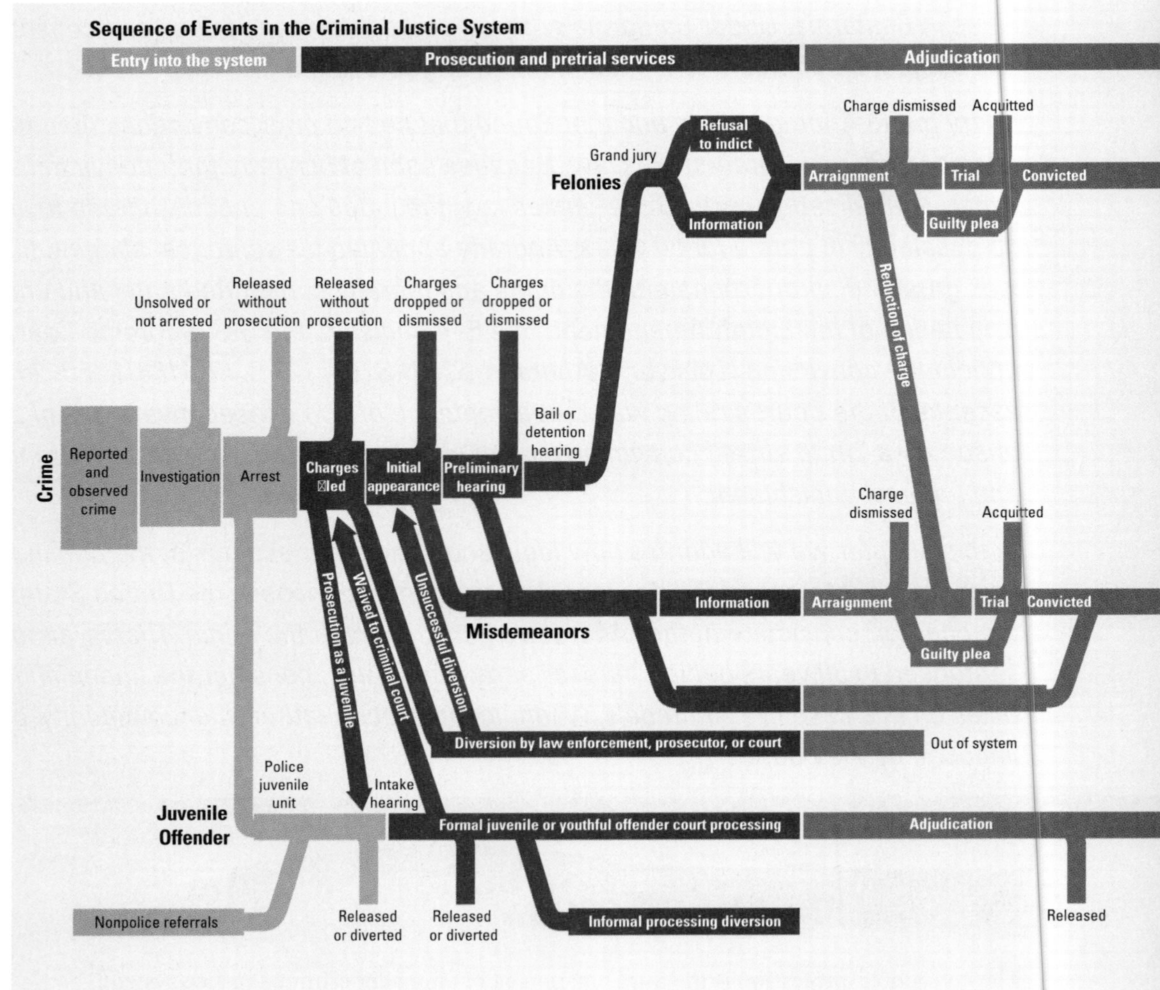

date. In many jurisdictions, local probation agencies supervise pretrial release individuals in the community. Individuals who are not released are remanded to the care and custody of corrections.

As the accused proceeds through the criminal court process of prosecution, sentencing, and sanctions, corrections officials are active each step along the way. During trial or other court proceedings, correctional officials may transport persons to and from the jail to the courtroom. If the defendant is found guilty, courts rely heavily on presentence reports by probation agencies to investigate the circumstances surrounding the convicted person's criminal behavior.

Sentencing may include incarceration, probation, or intermediate sanctions (e.g., boot camps, electronic monitoring). Corrections officials are responsible for the operations of all of these sanctions. Finally, offenders sentenced to incarceration in prison usually become eligible for parole after serving a specific part of the sentence. The decision to grant parole varies widely among jurisdictions but typically is made through

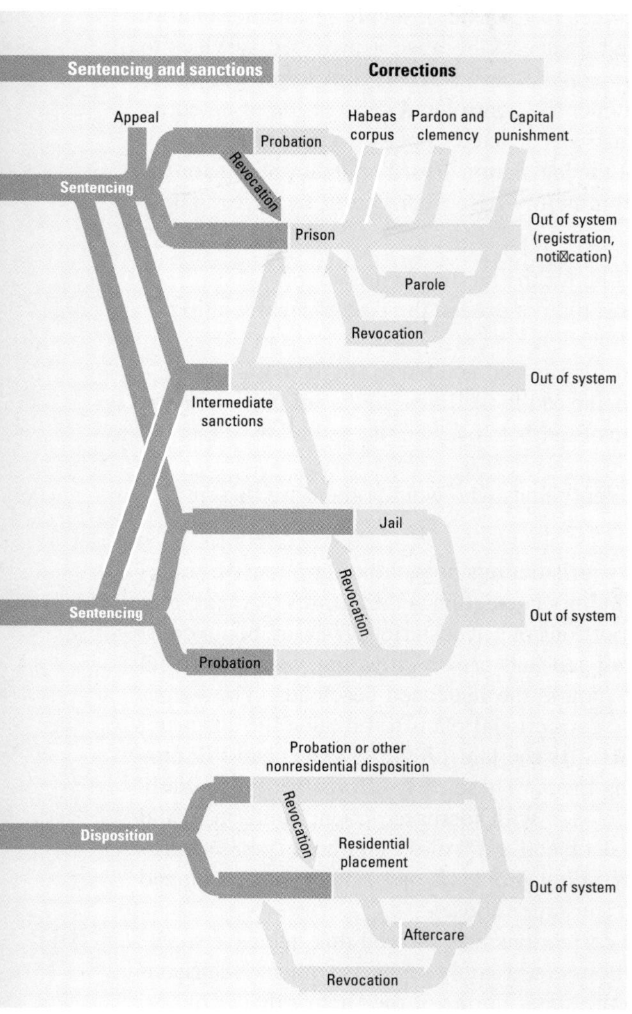

collaborative efforts between corrections officials and an authority such as a parole board. While the offender is on parole, he or she is normally supervised in the community by a parole service administered by the state department of corrections.

Within corrections we generally distinguish between institutional corrections (i.e., prisons and jails) and community-based corrections (i.e., probation, parole, and other non-institutional services). In Chapters 7 and 8, we will discuss the evolution of probation and parole, and the efforts of such pioneers as John Augustus and Alexander Maconochie. However, for the purposes of addressing matters relating to the four filters of community-based corrections (i.e., legislation, apprehension, adjudication, and corrections), we begin our overview of the development of community-based correctional programs from the perspective of more recent expansions of state laws that were passed in the 1970s and 1980s under the general title of "community corrections."

To start, community corrections began with Minnesota's Community Corrections Act (CCA), which became law in 1973. The act was based on the assumption that local communities are in the best position to define community correction needs and programs, and that most offenders can remain in the community without loss of public protection. An important feature of the Minnesota CCA was the formation of local community corrections advisory boards. Membership composition of these boards was specified by statute and consisted of county sheriffs, chiefs of police, court officials, judicial officers, educators, and citizens within the community. Working together with community corrections officials, the advisory board was charged with creating an annual comprehensive correctional plan to improve the administration of justice at the local level. This plan details the punishment options available in the community to judges when sentencing offenders.

Widespread development of Community Correction Acts in the United States continued in the 1970s as local and state partnerships emerged in Oregon, Colorado, Kansas, and Ohio. A common theme of each state's act was to offer residential correctional services such as halfway houses and work release centers to divert nonviolent offenders from jails and state prisons. One example is a community-based correctional facility called "MonDay," which was established in 1979 as part of the Ohio Community Corrections Act as a response to prison overcrowding.[2] The MonDay facility offered work release, education, and other training services to felons at a secure residential facility in Dayton, Ohio. MonDay was considered a success because it provided services to low-level, nonviolent felony offenders who would otherwise have gone to prison. Moreover, this community-based facility was under the control and supervision of an entity other than the state or local jail. Legislation was enacted to permit the construction of similar facilities around the state of Ohio; the legislation also set out conditions for the relationship between the state and the community-based correction facilities. These conditions included the following:

1st: The state would provide the funding for the facilities without local contribution, provided that the cost did not exceed the cost of incarcerating an offender in prison.

2nd: Local control of the facilities was guaranteed and placed in the common pleas courts that would be sentencing to the facilities. Judges of participating courts formed Judicial Corrections Boards to oversee the operation of the facilities.

3rd: The target population was nonviolent felons who would otherwise be sent to prison.[3]

In addition to residential services, many jurisdictions began to offer intensive supervised probation (ISP) as part of their community correction act programs. A major reason for the movement was that higher proportions of serious offenders were being court ordered to traditional probation because of jail and prison crowding, and most local probation programs were ill-equipped to handle the increased caseloads. The intent, then, was to build ISP into comprehensive correctional plans to broaden the spectrum of criminal sanctions available to the courts. By the late 1980s, 45 states had ISP programs or were in the process of developing them.[4] These early efforts were essentially predicated on the notion that smaller caseloads with increased client contacts would lead to favorable outcomes. The principal objective of these community-based programs was to assist probationers in overcoming problems associated with continued criminal activity (e.g., unemployment and substance abuse).[5]

Evaluation studies of state community corrections acts showed that intensive supervised probation and other alternative sanctions could safely supervise otherwise prison-bound offenders and at a reduced cost to the state. In one of the first of these studies, the Kansas Department of Corrections commissioned Temple University to conduct a study of the Kansas Community Act of 1978. The evaluation addressed three primary areas of policy interest, as well as a number of subsidiary issues. First, the evaluation explored the extent to which community corrections projects had reduced commitments to state prisons by diverting first- or second-felony, nonviolent offenders (e.g., theft, burglary, drugs) into alternative programs. The second major research question concerned the effects of the community corrections act on public safety. Three years of rearrests and reconvictions data was collected on offenders assigned to community corrections, probation, and prison, then compared to see if offenders were more likely to reoffend while on community corrections. The third major area of inquiry focused on costs (i.e., expense of community corrections programs versus imprisonment).[6]

In all three major areas, positive results were found. First, community corrections programs did draw the majority of clients from a prison-bound population. The findings suggested that prison crowding problems faced by Kansas would have been far worse without the community corrections act. Second, with regard to public safety concerns, data indicated that the same proportion of target-category offenders reoffended whether they were placed in prison or community-based programs. Last, the evaluation showed that in nearly every way in which costs were analyzed, community-based programs saved the state of Kansas money. Overall, the decision to send a community-corrections-eligible offender to prison for 18 months easily represented as much as a six- or sevenfold difference in cost (i.e., $18,000 for prison custody; $2,700 for community-based supervision).[7]

Currently, community-based alternatives to prison are either state-administered programs or county-operated programs that are subsidized by the state. In some states, nonprofit organizations run programs such as halfway houses, which are also subsidized by the state. More and more states and communities are experimenting with less and less restrictive forms of supervision and treatment, and are seeing treatment programs as part of a vital system that rehabilitates offenders. This approach emerged from changes in correctional philosophies that developed in the 1980s, which placed greater emphasis on risk control and risk reduction. Electronic monitoring, surveillance, intensive supervised probation, and other intermediate sanctions have become popular because they control risk by promoting the legitimate power of local and state criminal justice systems to impose greater leverage on offenders in the community. At the same time and of equal importance, they reduce risk by giving offenders greater access to community treatment services and more opportunities to be rehabilitated. Treatment programs, employment training, educational opportunities, and other needs-based services are acknowledged to be an important counterbalance to risk control mechanisms and necessary to the overall success of community-based corrections.

While this attempt to strike a balance between risk control and risk reduction is the prevailing ideological force behind today's community-based corrections, in practice this approach is often difficult to achieve and even harder to maintain. External forces, both within and outside the criminal justice system, regularly apply pressures that interfere with the operations and often the effectiveness of community-based corrections. Perhaps the most influential force is that of the crime control policies that were legislated in the 1980s and 1990s. During this **get-tough era** of criminal justice, new laws were passed on the federal and state levels that increased the number of offenders entering the criminal justice system. The resulting domino effect is that more people than ever before are now under some type of correctional authority. In the next section we take a closer look at the extent to which the criminal justice population has increased in the United States during the past 20 years and the resulting economic impact of this growth.

Crime Trends Affecting Community-Based Corrections

The number of reported crimes in the United States has decreased in the past 10 years. Data from the **Uniform Crime Report (UCR)** show a decrease of 3.1 percent in violent crimes between 1999 and 2008. Property crime dropped 5.3 percent nationwide between 2004 and 2008. A similar story of the national trends in crime over time emerges when one examines the findings of the **National Crime Victimization Survey (NCVS)**. Unlike the UCR data, which reflect crimes reported to the police, the NCVS violent crime estimates are based on periodic surveys of a random sample of households in the United States. Accordingly, estimates show the violent crime rate declined by 41 percent, and the property crime rate fell by 32 percent over the 10-year period from 1999 through 2008.[8]

Notwithstanding the declines, crime is still arguably the number one social and political issue facing the United States. The FBI estimated that more than 14 million arrests

EXHIBIT 2.2 Number of Persons under Correctional Supervision, 2000–2009

Year	Total Estimated Correctional Population	Community Supervision		Incarceration	
		Probation	Parole	Jail	Prison
2000	6,445,100	3,826,209	723,898	621,149	1,316,333
2001	6,581,700	3,931,731	732,333	631,240	1,330,007
2002	6,758,800	4,024,067	750,934	665,475	1,367,547
2003	6,924,500	4,120,012	769,925	691,301	1,390,279
2004	6,995,000	4,143,792	771,852	713,990	1,421,345
2005	7,051,900	4,166,757	780,616	747,529	1,448,344
2006	7,182,100	4,215,361	799,875	65,819	1,492,973
2007	7,274,300	4,234,471	821,177	80,174	1,517,867
2008	7,308,200	4,270,917	828,169	785,556	1,518,559
2009	7,225,800	4,203,967	819,308	760,400	1,524,513

Source: Bureau of Justice Statistics Bulletin, NCJ 231681 (December, 2010).

occurred in 2008 for all offenses (except traffic violations). Of these arrests, 594,911 were for violent crimes, and 1,687,345 were for property crimes. The most frequent arrests made in 2008 were for drug abuse violations (estimated at 1,702,537 arrests).[9] Because the number of arrests directly influences the number of persons entering correctional custody, it is not surprising that the United States incarcerates more people than any country in the world. At year-end 2009, over 7.2 million men and women were under some form of correctional supervision, including offenders supervised in the community (5,018,900) on probation or parole, and those incarcerated (2,284,900) in state or federal prisons and local jails.[10] Moreover, the upward trend in correctional populations has remained relatively constant for nearly a decade (see Exhibit 2.2).

The number of persons under community supervision displayed in Exhibit 2.2 includes sentenced persons on probation and persons under postrelease supervision while on parole. While this number is high, the data do not account for all persons under jurisdiction of community-based corrections. As a sanction ordered by the courts, community-based services can also be imposed at other stages of the criminal justice process, including pretrial and presentence. In the pretrial stage, conditional supervised release can be granted as an alternative to incarceration, and this allows arrested defendants to be released from jail while they await disposition of their criminal charges. Many jurisdictions rely heavily on pretrial release to reduce the stigma of confinement and as a mechanism to lower jail populations and associated costs. For example, a law passed in 2009 allows any interested jurisdiction in New York to establish a local conditional release commission to determine whether certain eligible residents may be released early from local jails and be placed under the supervision of its local probation department. If granted release, the person is under one year of conditional release supervision performed by the supervising probation department.[11]

Supervised conditional release may also be imposed once a defendant is found guilty of a crime. While release from confinement prior to sentencing occurs less frequently than in the pretrial stage, most jurisdictions maintain policies that require the least restrictive alternatives to incarceration while the court determines an appropriate punishment. The judge typically requires the court services or probation program to prepare a presentence investigation report. Interviews are conducted with the victim of the crime, the defendant, and the defendant's family, and a written report is prepared for the judge. The presentence report is made available to the defendant, defense counsel, and the prosecutor's office. In Chapters 5 and 7, we will take an in-depth review of the presentence investigation report, as well as bail and other mechanisms of pretrial services.

As we have noted, the number of persons being supervised in the community in each of the four stages of the criminal justice process (pretrial, presentence, sentenced, and postrelease) depends to a great extent on the number of arrests and convictions. That is, the greater the number of persons entering the criminal justice system, the greater the demand for community-based corrections. To complicate matters, the cost of incarceration has skyrocketed in the past 20 years, to the point that many local and state policy makers are shifting their support for get-tough philosophies that require incarceration to "alternative" community-based corrections as a means to alleviate overcrowded jails and prisons and budget pressures. For example, as in many other states, Ohio legislators enacted a law specifying nonresidential prison alternatives to allow lower-level felons to be diverted from expensive state penal institutions into cheaper community-based programs. In fiscal year 2009, 10,114 prison offenders and 20,859 jail offenders were diverted into community-based programs. In addition to averting the average daily cost of confinement, the following characteristics describe supplementary cost savings:

- Jail diversion offenders earned $41,152,732; paid $394,709 in restitution; paid $2,490,974 in court costs and fines; paid $798,183 in child support; and completed 207,346 hours of community work service.
- Prison diversion offenders earned $24,571,297; paid $873,270 in restitution; paid $2,073,590 in court costs and fines; paid $907,978 in child support; and completed 140,766 hours of community work service.[12]

The Cost of Community Corrections

With more than five million offenders under community supervision (the equivalent of about one in every 45 adults) and two million in lockup (the equivalent of one in every 100 adults), state spending for corrections totaled $52 billion in fiscal year 2008 and is estimated to increase 1.8% ($53 billion) in 2009.[13] To get a better understanding of how states invest their corrections dollars, the Pew Center on the States, along with the American Probation and Parole Association, the Crime and Justice Institute, and other partners, completed a survey of corrections spending in 34 states across the country. The results of the study showed that in FY 2008, these 34 states spent $18.65 billion on prisons but just $2.52 billion on probation and parole, a ratio of more than seven to one.[14] Clearly this represents a huge discrepancy in state spending.

Although more than double the offender population is under supervision in the community, only 10 percent of the state funding goes to community-based corrections. Another way to illustrate the cost difference is by comparing average daily costs. Among the 34 states participating in the Pew Research Center study, prisons cost an average of about $79 per inmate per day—or almost $29,000 per year. In contrast, the average daily cost for managing an offender in the community ranged from $3.42 per day for probationers to $7.47 per day for parolees, or about $1,250 to $2,750 a year, respectively.[15]

2.1

CBC Online

REALLOCATING PRISON EXPENSES TO FUND STRONGER PROBATION AND PAROLE PROGRAMS

Produced by the National Institute of Justice in 2009, this three-minute video interview of Adam Gelb, Director of the Public Safety Performance Project, Pew Center on the States, Washington, D.C., addresses costs associated with imprisonment compared to probation.

After viewing the video, describe three factors mentioned by Mr. Gelb that have contributed to increased costs of corrections.

Visit CBC Online 2.1 at www.mhhe.com/bayens1e

The nexus between increased number of offenders entering the criminal justice system and the lopsidedness of state budget allocations for imprisonment has stretched community-based corrections programs throughout the country (see CBC Online 2.1). Parole and probation officer caseloads are typically high, translating to minimal personal contact and supervision. In North Carolina for example, the Division of Community Corrections is responsible for supervising 128,000 adult offenders on probation, parole or postrelease supervision in the state. Probation Officers (PO1s) supervise cases adjudicated as community punishment, which may include fines, restitution, community service, and/or substance abuse treatment. The nature of the supervision requires limited field contacts with offenders and represents more traditional probation strategies, primarily in an office setting. In addition to such supervision, PO1s are responsible for performing administrative work for the courts, such as presentence investigations and processing of new cases. In January 2009, the average caseload for PO1s in North Carolina was 110 offenders.[16]

The Legislative Filter

Shifting demographics, the strength of the economy, and many other factors influence the crime rate and subsequent size and cost of the criminal justice system in the United States. For corrections, the adoption of new crime control legislation in the 1980s and 1990s, such as harsher drug laws and mandatory minimum sentences, began to fill newly built prisons beyond their capacities with **front-end offenders**. As overcrowding occurred and budgets became deficient, policymakers shifted their focus to boot camps, intensive supervised probation, work release, and other community-based corrections as viable alternatives to imprisonment. In addition, many states focused on more effective and efficient methods of managing **back-end offenders** who were on postrelease supervision in the community. Let's look at a couple examples of federal legislation that increased the number of arrests, which in turn increased prison commitments and ultimately led to the development of community-based corrections.

Violent Crime Control and Law Enforcement Act of 1994

Between 1984 and 1994, Congress passed three omnibus federal crime bills. Of these bills, the Violent Crime Control and Law Enforcement Act of 1994[17] was arguably the most far-reaching and comprehensive, authorizing funding for law enforcement and prevention measures that included increasing the number of crimes punishable by death and establishing a three-strikes provision for violent offenders. As we illustrated in our opening story, tough sentencing policies like three strikes in California and throughout the United States were thought to be the most effective option to incapacitate serious offenders and deter future criminal behavior.

In the 1994 crime bill, Congress authorized nearly $10 billion to states for prison construction and other alternative correctional facilities such as boot camps. The primary goal of these grants was to free prison space for the confinement of violent offenders. In the area of community-based corrections, the act funded state initiatives that integrated correctional facilities with job skills programs, educational programs, pre-release prisoner assessment, and postrelease assistance for offenders on parole.[18]

In the area of juvenile justice, the act took primarily a community-based corrections approach. Congress made grants to states so they could develop alternative methods of punishment for young offenders. These alternative punishments were to promote reduced recidivism, particularly for young offenders who could be punished more effectively in an environment other than a traditional correctional facility. Funding was allocated for

1. Alternative sanctions that create accountability and certain kinds of punishment for young offenders
2. Restitution programs for young offenders
3. Innovative projects consisting of education and job training activities for incarcerated young offenders
4. Correctional options such as community-based incarceration, weekend incarceration, and electronic monitoring
5. Community service programs that provide work service placement for young offenders at nonprofit, private organizations and community organizations
6. Innovative methods that address the problems of young offenders convicted of serious substance abuse (including alcohol abuse) and gang-related offenses
7. Appropriate postrelease programs for young offenders, such as substance abuse treatment, education programs, vocational training, job placement counseling, family counseling, and other support programs.[19]

The War on Drugs

During the same period, as public fears of drug abuse increased, Congress enacted the Anti-Drug Abuse Act of 1986.[20] This act created mandatory minimum sentences for drug trafficking and distribution, using the quantity of the drug involved to determine the minimum terms of imprisonment. Drug "kingpins," or high-level dealers who possessed large quantities of powder cocaine or heroin, faced a minimum 10-year prison sentence. Offenders possessing smaller amounts—considered mid-level dealers—faced a minimum five-year sentence.

Two years later, Congress broadened the mandatory minimums to cover conspiracy in certain drug offenses.[21] The 1988 act also established a minimum sentence for simple possession of crack cocaine—which became the focus of the war on drugs. The reasoning behind this concentration was that although crack and powder cocaine are the same chemical substance, crack can be smoked and sells more cheaply on the

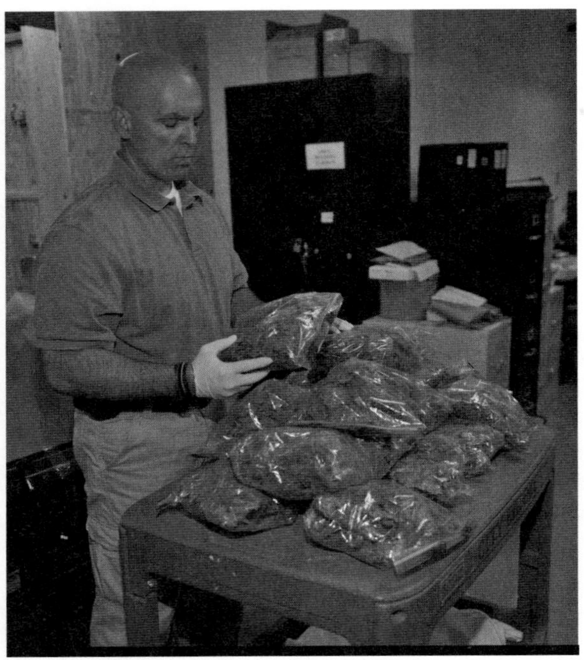

In the 1980s and 1990s, state and federal governments passed three-strikes and mandatory minimum sentences for drug trafficking and distribution. How have these laws affected the apprehension, adjudication, and corrections stages of criminal justice processing?

streets. As it came into widespread use in the mid-1980s, crack cocaine was associated with violent street crime, so much so that in the summer and fall of 1986, press reports sparked growing popular and congressional concern about a crack "epidemic."[22] If arrested, a first-time offender caught with five grams of crack cocaine was sentenced to no less than five years in prison. In contrast, a person had to possess at least five hundred grams of powder cocaine to receive a five-year sentence.[23]

To gather useful information for local officials on the course of illicit drug use, including crack cocaine, the National Institute of Justice launched the Drug Use Forecasting (DUF) program in 1987. The DUF program collects data from adult and juvenile arrestees booked into jails at major metropolitan areas across the United States. Data collected by the DUF showed that cocaine usage was in decline by 1994, as the public came to recognize the devastating effects of crack addiction. In 1997, the National Institute of Justice expanded and reengineered the DUF study and renamed it the **Arrestee Drug Abuse Monitoring (ADAM)** program—a network of research sites in select U.S. cities. Studies by ADAM show that cocaine usage is still very much a problem in the United States. Consider the following characteristics provided by the White House Office of the National Drug Control Policy.

- In 1998, approximately 138,000 convicted jail inmates were under the influence of drugs at the time of the offense that resulted in their incarceration. About 43 percent (59,000) had used cocaine or crack, and most reported that they had committed their offense to get money for drugs.
- In 2000, Americans spent an estimated $36 billion on cocaine.
- In 2000, although research suggested that perhaps the worst of the crack epidemic was over, data indicate use among arrestees continued at high levels. On average, 30 percent of arrestees tested positive for cocaine. Moreover, in the ADAM sites studied, the overwhelming majority of cocaine-positive arrestees (88 percent) were using crack, not powder.
- In 2001, 1.7 million persons over the age of 12 used cocaine. It was the drug most commonly used by female arrestees.
- In 2007, an estimated 626 metric tons of cocaine entered the United States from South America.
- In 2008, cocaine was the second most commonly detected substance among arrestees, except in Atlanta, where it was the most commonly detected drug.[24]

Ever since crime control became focused as a national issue in the get-tough era, there has been greater emphasis on increased law enforcement resources that would net higher apprehension rates and thereby increase public safety. However, as we will see in the next section, increasing police resources doesn't necessarily equate to secure custody for those serious offenders who present a danger to the physical safety of citizens.

The Apprehension Filter

The impact of the war on drugs and the federal crime bills of the 1980s and 1990s was that arrests increased immediately, followed by increases in the correctional population. In Exhibit 2.3, we provide 1980, 1990, and 2000 arrest data for the purposes of comparing drug crimes, violent crimes, and property crimes during the "get-tough-on-crime" era. We also provide the most current arrest data provided by the FBI (2008) for a contemporary comparison.

After the passage of get-tough legislation, the total number of arrests for drug-related crimes nearly doubled—from 580,900 in 1980 to 1,089,500 in 1990. In 2000, nearly 1 million more persons were arrested for drugs than in 1980. Note, though, that the number of arrests for marijuana, especially possession arrests, has consumed much of the law enforcement effort in the war on drugs. In 2008, 49.8 percent (half) of the 1,702,537 total arrests for drug abuse violations were for marijuana—a total of 847,863 arrests. Of those, 754,224 people were arrested for marijuana possession alone.

A major contributor to drug usage in the United States is that the cost of drugs has decreased in the past 30 years. According to the U.S. Office of National Drug Control Policy, the cost of cocaine at the retail level declined from an average estimated $544.59 per gram in 1981 to $106.54 per gram in 2003. At the wholesale level, the drop went from $201.18 per gram in 1981 to $37.96 per gram in 2003. The purity of cocaine also went up during that time. At the retail level, it averaged 40% purity in 1981 and 70% purity in 2003, while at the wholesale level, cocaine averaged 56% purity in 1981 and 63% purity in 2003.[26]

The evolution of the illegal drug market has been linked to the rising crimes rates of the late 1980s and early 1990s. Note in Exhibit 2.3 that in 1980 and 1990, as drug arrests increased, so too did the number of arrests for violent crimes and property offenses. However, the relationship between drug enforcement and crimes against persons and property has been controversial. Consider again Exhibit 2.3; the data for 2000 and 2008 show that while drug arrests continued to increase, violent crime decreased and property crime remained fairly constant. Some studies have suggested that drug offenders are far more likely to recidivate for a drug offense than for a violent or property offense. Furthermore, violent offenders who are rearrested tend to recidivate most often for a new violent crime, and property offenders are most likely to recidivate for another property crime.[27]

EXHIBIT 2.3 Comparison of Arrests Data for 1980, 1990, 2000, and 2008

Year	Total Arrests	Total Drug Arrests	Total Marijuana Arrests	Marijuana Trafficking/ Sale Arrests	Marijuana Possession Arrests	Total Violent Crime Arrests	Total Property Crime Arrests
2008	14,005,615	1,702,537	847,863	93,640	754,224	594,911	1,687,345
2000	13,980,297	1,579,566	734,497	88,455	646,042	625,132	1,620,928
1990	14,195,100	1,089,500	326,850	66,460	260,390	705,500	2,217,800
1980	10,441,000	580,900	401,982	63,318	338,664	475,160	1,863,300

Source: FBI Uniform Crime Reports for 1980, 1990, 2000, and 2008. Bureau of Justice Statistics 1970–2003.[25]

2.2

CBC Online

U.S. SUPPORT FOR LEGALIZING MARIJUANA REACHES NEW HIGH

This October 2009 Gallup poll finds 44% of Americans in favor of making marijuana legal and taxed as a way of raising revenue for state governments. Read the brief article and consider how the war on drugs would be affected should marijuana be decriminalized.

Visit CBC Online 2.2 at www.mhhe.com/bayens1e

Between 1990 and 2000, the number of drug offenders incarcerated in state prisons across the country increased from approximately 149,700 to 251,100—accounting for 20% of total growth in the state prison population. Moreover, surveys of prisoners conducted during this same period showed a high level of drug usage, many just prior to committing crimes. For example, in 1991, a survey of prisoners showed that 32% of prisoners reported using cocaine or crack regularly, and 15% used heroin or opiates regularly.[28]

Lastly, a snapshot of offenders sentenced to probation and parole on December 31, 2001, showed a total of 3,932,751 adult men and women were on probation in the United States. Approximately 25% of these probationers had committed a drug law violation, and nearly 33% of parole releases from state prison were drug offenders.[29] This trend continues throughout the 21st century (see CBC Online 2.2). In 2008, for example, the most common type of offense for which probationers were under supervision was a drug offense. About three in 10 probationers were under supervision for a drug offense in 2008, up from about a quarter (24%) of all probationers in 2000. In 2008, parolees were more likely to have served a sentence for a drug offense.[30]

The Adjudication/Sentencing Filter

While the war on drugs and federal crime bills of the get-tough era have greatly influenced the modern criminal justice system, another key factor, especially with regard to the growth of the correctional population, is mandatory sentencing. For the purposes of our discussion here, we address stricter sentencing and release laws by emphasizing two policy changes that took place in the criminal justice system during the 1980s and 1990s. They are three strikes and **determinate sentencing**.

Three Strikes

In the mid-1990s, 24 states and the federal government enacted sentencing policy reforms that aimed to protect the public by incapacitating dangerous offenders. These "three-strikes-and-you're-out" laws, which provide longer prison terms for some criminals with repeat felony convictions, are presently still among the most controversial, because the majority call for life sentences without the possibility of release for at least

25 years. Critics of three strikes argue that these laws are too harsh or unnecessary because habitual-offender laws are already in place. Supporters claim that such laws are needed to prevent the escalation of serious or violent crimes, but they often accentuate the "violent" aspects of the law and deemphasize the fact that some of the serious crimes also include property offenses such as theft, burglary, and arson.

As we noted in our opening story, the Supreme Court case *Lockyer* v. *Andrade,* 538 U.S. 63 (2003), caused California's version of the three-strikes law to be at the center of attention. Referred to as the "the largest penal experiment in American history,"[31] legal challenges to California's three-strikes law have occurred in part because the state applies its law with a great deal of regularity. Between April 1994 and December 1996, well over 90 percent of the strike sentences handed down in jurisdictions with these laws were in California.[32] It is worth noting, though, that while California is universally connected with pioneering the three-strikes law, other states (i.e., Washington and Texas) were actually the first to pass sentencing reforms requiring a term of life imprisonment without the possibility of parole for persons convicted for a third time of certain specified violent or serious felonies. In 1980, for example, the Supreme Court upheld Texas statutes when William Rummel challenged a life sentence after being convicted of three nonviolent felonies that occurred over a 15-year period.[33]

Three-strikes laws and other mandatory sentencing laws allow enhanced length of imprisonment for frequency but not necessarily seriousness of crimes committed. Justification for such laws is grounded in the punitive ideologies of deterrence, incapacitation, and/or just deserts. General deterrence is achieved by delivering lengthy prison terms to punish offenders who habitually commit crime. The goal is to suppress the criminal tendencies of potential offenders. Incapacitation effects may be achieved by accurately targeting recidivists and sentencing them to lengthy prison terms. By physically removing them from society, future offenses are prevented rather than merely deterred. The idea of just deserts, which argues that criminal sanctions should be commensurate with the seriousness of the offense, is achieved by ensuring that repeat offenders receive harsh punishment for their continued disregard for laws. As we mentioned in Chapter 1, one facet of this form of retributive justice is that repeat offenders deserve punishment in direct proportion to the harm inflicted to society over time. The more crimes offenders commit, the more punishment they deserve.

When considering mandatory sentencing versus community-based corrections, one must weigh the need to incarcerate criminals who commit serious crime against the ability of corrections to supervise them in the community. At the center of this debate and an ever-present force behind the justification of three strikes is the media's attention to **predatory crimes**. News accounts of criminal cases, especially violent murders involving convicted felons on postrelease supervision, have greatly influenced public opinion and given rise to support for mandatory sentencing laws.

Consider, for example, the tragic death of Diane Ballasiotes, in Washington, who was murdered by a convicted rapist who had been released from prison. In October 1988, Gene Kane Jr., an escapee from a Seattle work-release facility, brutally stabbed Ballasiotes to death in the course of an attempted rape, robbery, and kidnapping. A few years later, 12-year-old Polly Klaas was abducted from her home in Petaluma, California, by another repeat felon, Richard Allen Davis. That same evening, Davis strangled Polly to death and was charged with murder, kidnapping, and attempted sexual molestation. In each of these highly publicized cases, citizens were dismayed at the inability of parole and other community-based correctional programs to adequately supervise these offenders. As a result, the parole system in the United States underwent legislative

2.3

CBC Online

TWO TORN FAMILIES SHOW FLIP SIDE OF THREE-STRIKES LAW

This seven-minute broadcast, aired in October 2009 by National Public Radio, is the first of a three-part series providing an overview of the three-strikes law and its impact on the state of California. Hyperlinks are provided to parts two and three of the series, which are titled "Crime Locale Is Key In California's 3 Strikes Law" and "Cases Show Disparity of California's 3 Strikes Law."

After listening to these audio presentations, what conclusions can you draw about the support for three-strikes laws in California?

Visit CBC Online 2.3 at www.mhhe.com/bayens1e

scrutiny, and in several jurisdictions, significant changes were made to abolish parole boards, increase the enforcement of parole conditions, and adopt zero-tolerance policies that send more parolees back to prison (see CBC Online 2.3).

Determinate Sentencing

Between 1930 and 1970, the dominant sentencing model in the United States maintained the fundamental philosophy that each court case should be handled individually, with the goal of rehabilitation. This approach of **indeterminate sentencing** featured broad judicial discretion and heavy reliance on probation services and parole boards to determine an offender's readiness to be released into the community. With indeterminate sentencing, judges could consider the defendant's character and background as well as the type of crime that had been committed. Sentences were scaled to reflect punishments that best fit the offender's needs rather than his or her crime.

The **Model Penal Code (MPC)**, developed in the 1950s, was the high point in the conceptualization of indeterminate sentencing. Developed by the American Law Institute, the purpose of the MPC was to assist state legislatures in standardizing penal law in the United States. Since its promulgation, the code has played an important part in the widespread revision and codification of U.S. criminal law. Moreover, thousands of court opinions have cited the Model Penal Code as a persuasive authority for the interpretation of existing statutes or the exercise of a court's occasional power to formulate a criminal law doctrine.[34]

At the same time that the war on drugs and application of three strikes were occurring, support for indeterminate sentencing declined due to questions regarding rehabilitation and fairness. A movement toward determinate sentencing emerged to address concerns that judges and parole boards possessed too much discretion and that rehabilitation was not reducing crime. Proponents of the deterrence model of punishment contended that people would be deterred from committing crimes if the consequences were sufficiently severe, and thus they called for the enactment of **sentencing guidelines**.

By the 1990s, some states had replaced indeterminate sentencing with structured sentencing guidelines aimed at increasing uniformity. During this period, approximately 20 percent of states moved to presumptive sentencing guidelines, 18 percent passed voluntary guidelines, and one state enacted mandatory guidelines.[35] The major objectives of sentencing reform were to (1) reduce sentencing disparities by sex or race, (2) reduce disparity in judicial decisions regarding incarceration and sentence length, and (3) institutionalize principles of just deserts and deterrence.[36] By 2004, 24 states had active sentencing commissions and some form of sentencing guidelines.[37]

Sentencing Guidelines

To explain sentencing guidelines, we first reiterate the principal elements of indeterminate sentencing that were viewed as unfair: unbridled judicial discretion and unruliness in the parole system. Before states passed sentencing guidelines, the personality of a judge mattered in a criminal case. Judges possessed nearly unlimited authority to hand down sentences and impose a wide range of punishment options that "decided the various goals of sentencing, the relevant aggravating and mitigating circumstances, and the way in which these factors would be combined in determining a specific sentence."[38] Sentences were limited only by statutorily prescribed minimums and maximums. For example, a person convicted of residential burglary might be sentenced to prison for a term of no less than one year and no more than 10 years. Once an offender was in the state correctional system, however, the parole board had the authority to reduce the sentence. Consequently, while a judge might sentence an offender to 10 years, the state's parole authority might release the offender after five.

Under sentencing guidelines, a judge is no longer allowed a broad range of sentencing discretion. Instead, the court's discretion is limited to a grid of sentencing ranges specified by the guidelines, absent a valid ground for departure. The purpose of the restriction is to provide equity in sentencing whereby offenders are sentenced based principally on the severity of the crime and criminal history. That is, criminal offenders who are similar with respect to relevant sentencing criteria ought to receive similar sanctions. To illustrate the rationale behind sentencing guidelines, we note the Minnesota Sentencing Guidelines Commission's statement of purpose:

1. Sentencing should be neutral with respect to the race, gender, social, or economic status of convicted felons.
2. While commitment to the Commissioner of Corrections is the most severe sanction that can follow conviction of a felony, it is not the only significant sanction available to the sentencing judge. Development of a rational and consistent sentencing policy requires that the severity of sanctions increase in direct proportion to increases in the severity of criminal offenses and the severity of criminal histories of convicted felons.
3. Because the capacities of state and local correctional facilities are finite, use of incarcerative sanctions should be limited to those convicted of more serious offenses or those who have longer criminal histories. To ensure such usage of finite resources, sanctions used in sentencing convicted felons should be the least restrictive necessary to achieve the purposes of the sentence.
4. While the sentencing guidelines are advisory to the sentencing judge, departures from the presumptive sentences established in the guidelines should be made only when substantial and compelling circumstances exist.[39]

Under sentencing guidelines, a probation officer, such as Beverly Morgan, featured in the Career Profile, provides a presentence investigation report to the court for consideration. The importance of the report cannot be overstated. In it, the probation

Career Profile

BEVERLY MORGAN, SUPERVISING UNITED STATES PROBATION OFFICER, WESTERN DISTRICT OF NORTH CAROLINA

Beverly L. Morgan earned a Bachelor of Science Degree in Criminal Justice from the University of North Carolina in Charlotte and a Master of Arts degree in Organizational Communication from Queens University. She worked as an NC State Probation and Parole Officer for 14 years before obtaining the position of United States Probation Officer. She has worked for the federal system for 18 years, primarily in the Presentence division. According to Beverly, "One of the most important decisions to be made in the criminal justice system is the determination of a defendant's sentence. The presentence report is the means by which the federal court determines the appropriate sentence for a defendant. The Federal Rules of Criminal Procedure delegate the critical responsibility of preparing the presentence report to the probation officer. As the court's independent and impartial investigator, the probation officer must meet this assignment by investigating the circumstances of the defendant and providing accurate information. The statute (18 U.S.C. § 3661) dictates that 'no limitation shall be placed on the information concerning the background, character, and conduct of a person convicted of an offense which a court of the United States may receive and consider for the purpose of imposing an appropriate sentence.'

"To prepare a presentence report of the highest quality, the officer applies the United States Sentencing Guidelines and determines a total offense level and a criminal-history point category. She or he considers all factors, using a preponderance of evidence standard. Before the court receives a copy of the presentence report, the prosecution and defénse attorneys have an opportunity to object to its content. The probation officer is charged with addressing objections before the final presentence report is disclosed. The presentence report is highly confidential. The court uses it to select the appropriate sentence, the probation officers use it in the supervision of defendants, and the Bureau of Prisons use it to determine inmate classification, program assignment, and release planning."

officer recommends fact findings, guideline calculations, and potential grounds for departure; in many districts, the officer may also recommend factors to be considered in sentencing outside the guideline range.

The last characteristic of sentencing guidelines that we want to briefly discuss is the sentencing grid (Exhibit 2.4). The grid block where the severity level of the crime and the offender's total criminal history (expressed in number of prior convictions) intersect is the presumed sentence, stated in months. Using this grid, a first-time felony offender who is convicted of a severity-level V residential burglary would receive an 18-month non-prison (e.g., probation) sentence. As the number of prior convictions increases, so too does the severity of the punishment. An offender with three prior felony convictions would typically receive a sentence of 33 months in prison, with adjustments between 29 and 39 months available for mitigating or aggravating circumstances.

In most states, such grids serve only as recommendations based on typical circumstances. However, in some states (e.g., Kansas, Washington, and Oregon), sentencing guidelines carry a degree of enforceable legal authority. Trial courts are instructed that they must use the presumptive sentences in the guideline grid in "ordinary"

EXHIBIT 2.4 A Sentencing Grid

Severity Level of Conviction Offense		Criminal History (number of convictions) 0	1	2	3	4	5	6 or more
Murder—2nd Degree	I	306* *261–367*	326 *278–391*	346 *295–415*	366 *312–439*	386 *329–463*	406 *346–480*	426 *363–480*
Aggravated Assault	II	86 *74–103*	98 *84–117*	110 *94–132*	122 *104–146*	134 *114–160*	146 *125–175*	158 *135–189*
Aggravated Robbery	III	48 *41–57*	58 *50–69*	68 *58–81*	78 *67–93*	88 *75–105*	98 *84–117*	108 *92–129*
Controlled Substance Crime	IV	21	27	33	39 *34–46*	45 *39–54*	51 *44–61*	57 *49–68*
Residential Burglary	V	18	23	28	33 *29–39*	38 *33–45*	43 *37–51*	48 *41–57*
Theft Crimes (Over $5,000)	VI	12	13	15	17	19 *17–22*	21 *18–25*	23 *20–27*

* Average number of months of sentence.

Imprisonment—Presumptive commitment to state prison system by number of months.

Non-Imprisonment—Presumptive stayed sentence by number of months; a year in jail and/or other non-jail, community-based sanctions can be imposed as conditions of probation.

cases—which include the majority of all sentencing decisions. However, the trial judge retains discretion to "depart" upward from the guidelines when elements of the criminal act are viewed as egregious. Conversely, a downward departure would signal that a judge has determined that circumstances of the crime were less than ordinary. If the court does depart, the judge must justify the extent of the departure in addition to articulating substantial and compelling reasons for the departure. Any departure from the sentencing grid is subject to appeal.

It's worth mentioning here that research on evidence-based practices (EBP) demonstrates that for a punitive sanction to be effective, both the content of the sentencing decision and the manner in which the court interacts with the offender matter. This is especially true of the relationship between community-based sentences and the goal of reducing recidivism. Among the conclusions reached when applying EBP principles to state felony-sentencing practices are the following:

- The sentencing process matters as much as the specifics of the sentencing decision.
- All communications with the offender in connection with sentencing, especially by the judge, should be conducted in a manner to achieve a mutual goal of the court and the offender.
- The judge should act as a change agent to reinforce the importance of the offender's voluntary compliance, not merely to enforce compliance.
- Judges have the opportunity to maximize the positive effect and minimize any negative effect of court processes by the way they interact with people coming before them.[40]

Truth in Sentencing

In addition to reducing sentencing disparity, determinate sentencing better aligns sentences with the amount of time served in prison by restricting or eliminating parole eligibility and good time. This policy stance, referred to as **truth in sentencing (TIS)**, basically requires that a convicted offender serve 85 percent of the sentence before eligibility for release. In 1984, Washington became the first state to pass truth-in-sentencing legislation, and the U.S. Congress soon thereafter began to authorize additional funding for state prison systems where truth-in-sentencing laws were in place. By 1999, a total of 42 states and the District of Columbia had adopted laws or policies to regulate the percentage of imposed sentences that offenders will serve in prison.[41]

Proponents argue that TIS policies restore public confidence in the sentencing process and further such concepts as deterrence, victim rights, proportionality, and better reliability for correctional population forecasts and management. Opponents claim that TIS is simply another get-tough reform that states have pursued to receive monetary rewards through incentive grants from the government. They argue that some discretion should be retained by the parole authority and that, in the long term, incarcerating offenders for longer periods simply wastes resources and will have little positive effect on public safety.[42] The National Council on Crime and Delinquency (NCCD) suggests that a return to a well-implemented system of parole would revive a motivation for improved standards of behavior in prisons and jails.[43]

The overall impact of truth-in-sentencing policies on incarceration rates and sentence lengths remains unclear. One reason for the uncertainty is that the types of truth-in-sentencing legislation that states have passed differ with respect to the targeted offenders, use of postrelease supervision and parole, and use of good time credits. For example, in an evaluation of the implementation of TIS in Massachusetts, researchers found very little change in sentences imposed in the pre- versus post-TIS sentences, but a measurable increase in the projected length of time to serve.[44] In examining TIS in Mississippi, researchers concluded that the response to TIS by court practitioners, including judges, prosecutors and defense attorneys, has been to adjust sentences to maintain the historic "proportionality in punishment," or same average number of years served in prison. Moreover, they found considerable variation in the enforcement of TIS geographically across the state.[45]

Some evidence suggests that while the amount of serious crime does impact incarceration rates, the availability of resources to increase prison beds has a similar impact. New research suggests that about 30 percent of the change in incarceration rates over the past 30 years is attributable to increases in state resources to increase prison capacity, with crime rates accounting for 32 to 44 percent of the increase.[46] As the average annual grant award to states from federal TIS funding was $7.9 million, it would seem plausible that decreased funding to support TIS would have a correlative effect on prison populations.

The Corrections Filter

Thus far we have noted that since the 1980s, policymakers across the country have turned increasingly to prison as the most effective crime prevention strategy. They have adopted get-tough policies such as mandatory minimum sentences, three-strikes laws, and truth-in-sentencing laws that call for specific and lengthy prison stays (see Exhibit 2.5). As a result, one in every 100 adults in the United States is in jail or prison,

EXHIBIT 2.5 Three Decades of Sentencing Reform—1970s through 1990s[48]

Mandatory Minimum Sentences:	States added statutes requiring offenders to be sentenced to a specified amount of prison time.
Indeterminate Sentencing:	Common in the 1970s, state parole boards maintain the authority to release offenders from prison.
Determinate Sentencing:	States introduced fixed prison terms that could be reduced by good-time or earned-time credits.
Sentencing Guidelines:	States established sentencing commissions and created ranges of sentences based on the severity of offense and offender criminal history.
Truth in Sentencing:	Enacted in 1984, laws requiring offenders to serve a substantial portion of their prison sentence. Parole eligibility and good-time credits are restricted or eliminated.

and spending on corrections has jumped to more than $50 billion, breaking the bank in many states. In both Florida and California, for instance, spending for prisons now exceeds spending for public higher education. In California, the three-strikes law could cost $5.5 billion over a 20-year period. The cost of implementation is expected to rise at least until 2019, when the first wave of third-strike inmates is eligible for release. At that time, other costs, such as parole supervisions, will be incurred. The additional cost of parole supervision for California inmates is estimated at about $20 million per year.[47]

The overwhelming costs associated with prison have forced policymakers to look closer at the profile of the prison inmate. What they have found is that many are first-time, nonviolent criminals, often low-level drug offenders. A snapshot of the Missouri prison population in December 2008 revealed that only 52% (15,833) of the 30,415 inmates were incarcerated for serious crimes against persons. The other 48% were serving prison sentences for property, drugs, DWI, and other offenses. Prison operating costs in Missouri during this time period exceeded $260 million.[49]

In addition to understanding that nonviolent offenders are taking up expensive bed space in our nation's prisons, policymakers have been put on alert that many prison inmates are postrelease parolees who have been sent back to prison for committing "technical" violations, such as missing a meeting with a parole officer. Consider, for example, that in California, only 21 percent of parolees successfully complete parole; two-thirds are returned within the three-year average parole period, and of those, roughly one-fifth are returned because of non-criminal violations of parole.[50] It costs an estimated $46,000 annually to incarcerate someone in California's prisons.[51]

The current budget crisis in the United States is also bearing down on states, forcing them to examine the use of incarceration and the prospects for reducing prison populations by retooling their sentencing and corrections systems. Some states have taken drastic measures to rein in spending, include closing prisons and other correctional facilities and releasing prisoners early. In other states, policymakers are reallocating correctional dollars to provide community-based corrections agencies with more resources and authority. In this final section, we explore the relationship between revenue shortfall and corrections reform. We also highlight some of the programs that are evolving in reaction to a renewed interest in evidence- and community-based practices that are less expensive than prison but provide public safety.

2.4

CBC Online

REDUCING U.S. INCARCERATION RATES

This-one hour video presentation, produced by the Center for American Progress, features Paul Butler, law professor at George Washington University in Washington, D.C., and Glenn Ivey, the state attorney for Prince George's County, Maryland. These panelists discuss current criminal justice system problems, including the number of people imprisoned in the United States and the drug laws that put the majority of inmates behind bars.

After watching the presentation, answer this question: What new solutions do the panelists suggest for reducing the U.S. prison population? What are the strengths and weaknesses of their suggestions?

Visit CBC Online 2.4 at www.mhhe.com/bayens1e

State and local governments are swimming in red ink. The Center on Budget and Policy Priorities offers the bleak forecast that state budget shortfalls are likely to reach a whopping $180 billion for the 2011 fiscal year. Strategies adopted by states to bridge budget shortfalls include reducing spending, raising taxes, and cutting funds to local governments. In New Jersey, for example, taxes have been raised and budget cuts of 25 percent have been made in state agencies to offset a deficit of $9 billion.[52]

As budgets have tightened, state and local criminal justice agencies are getting creative in reducing costs within their operations. Several states are taking action that includes court cutbacks and fee increases. Oregon will try to save $3.1 million by closing its courthouses every Friday for four months and cutting the pay of 1,800 court workers by 20 percent. New Hampshire suspended civil and criminal jury trials in eight counties for a month and postponed filling seven of the state's 59 vacant judgeships.[53]

Law enforcement agencies throughout the country have cut spending in a variety of areas. A survey conducted by the Police Executive Research Forum found that of the 233 larger police departments across the country, 63 percent are preparing to cut their total funding for the next fiscal year. Most of the agencies (53%) said they already have implemented a hiring freeze for non-sworn personnel, and 27 percent said they have implemented a freeze for sworn positions.[54] Likewise, state highway patrol agencies in Alabama, Pennsylvania, and Tennessee are scrambling to continue the same level of services without replacing vacant trooper positions. In Virginia the governor's budget for 2010–2012 proposes $270 million in cuts to sheriff's departments and commonwealth's attorney's offices, in addition to roughly $73 million in cuts to local police departments.

In the area of institutional corrections, New Hampshire, Tennessee, and Kansas are among states that have closed prisons. In Exhibit 2.6 we highlight budget proposals of the Governor's Office in North Carolina for FY 2010–2011 in the area of justice and public safety. While most of the proposals are to reduce or eliminate personnel, equipment, and programs, items 6, 7, and 8 pertain to increasing revenues for community-based programs in the state.

Revisiting Sentencing Options

Reacting to the economic constraints felt in recent years, many states are shifting their criminal justice strategies by looking at non-mandatory minimum sentencing

EXHIBIT 2.6 FY 2010 North Carolina Budget Proposals in Criminal Justice[55]

	ITEM	*Reduction*	*Increase*
1.	Reduce spending in the department of corrections	$54.5 million	
2.	Reduce spending in the state courts system	$7.3 million	
3.	Reduce salaries for the courts' administrative office	$14.4 million	
4.	Close a correctional hospital	$15.4 million	
5.	Close three (3) correctional centers	$3.2 million	
6.	Eliminate 114 positions in the department of corrections	$5.1 million	
7.	Hire 29 chief probation/parole officers		$2.2 million
8.	Hire 117 more probation and parole officers		$7.9 million
9.	Purchase communication devices for community corrections		$1.2 million

approaches such as drug courts and other types of sanctions, which provide a range of sentencing options outside prison. In Illinois, for example, a study estimated costs of alternative sentencing programs, such as substance abuse treatment programs for non-violent offenders, and then compared them with the costs associated with incarceration. A few key findings follow:

1. Nonviolent drug offenders constitute 25% of the Illinois adult inmate population. It costs Illinois taxpayers an estimated $246 million per year to incarcerate these inmates for nonviolent drug offenses.
2. The recidivism rate in Illinois for inmates released is nearly 55%; over one-half of inmates were returned to prison within three years of their release.
3. Effective programs for inmates can increase access to substance abuse treatment for a large number of drug-involved offenders. Drug treatment programs can reduce recidivism by as much as 31%.
4. A national study estimated the average benefit of treatment per person to be three times the cost of treatment. The benefit of treatment to society includes reduced costs related to crime, healthcare, and increased earnings. Using this model, the potential economic benefit of the treatment of 10% of inmates with nonviolent drug offenses to Illinois would be nearly $10 million, compared to an estimated cost of $3.2 million for treatment services.
5. Recent studies of public opinion find that the majority of respondents consider prison sentences for nonviolent drug offenders the wrong approach to the problem of addiction and crime. A public opinion poll in Illinois found that 95% of respondents regarded addiction to be a pervasive illness that affects people across the social spectrum, and 74% thought that mandatory drug treatment is a better response to the problem of nonviolent crime committed by drug users compared to 9% supporting conventional prison sentencing for these offenders.[56]

In New York, policymakers agreed to divert the cases of thousands of lower-level, nonviolent drug offenders to an expanded treatment initiative that would rely on the discretion of state judges. The sentencing reform referred to as the Rockefeller Drug Law Reform Act of 2009 eliminated mandatory minimum sentences and maximums of up to life in prison for offenders caught with relatively small amounts of drugs. A main

Cuts in corrections budgets have forced many states, including Michigan, Ohio, and Texas, to close prison guard towers because they are obsolete and expensive to operate. Corrections officials tell us that advances in technology can secure public safety at lower cost. How have other advances in technology shaped corrections today?

goal of the new legislation was to give judges back the discretion to send first-time nonviolent offenders into treatment over the objections of prosecutors. Offenders who commit other crimes, such as burglary linked to their drug use, also would be eligible for diversion into treatment programs under the agreement. As noted earlier, it costs about $45,000 a year to incarcerate an inmate in state prison but only about $15,000 a year to provide addicts with substance abuse treatment at a residential facility.

As a result of such policies in New York, admission of people sentenced to prison for drug violations fell from 8,227 in 2000 to 5,190 in 2008.[57] In 2000, more than 22,000 prison beds were occupied by people convicted of drug violations, comprising 31 percent of the population behind bars. By 2008, with some 8,800 fewer drug prisoners, that proportion had dropped to just 21 percent. Estimates are that eventual cost savings to the state will be $250 million a year.[58] In a follow-up study of the effectiveness of the drug law reform statute, researchers found that early release from prison not only led to considerable cost savings, but also resulted in a very low rate of return to prison. The data support the legislative judgment that the old drug law sentences were excessive and longer than necessary to protect the community.[59]

In some jurisdictions, policymakers are also revisiting truth-in-sentencing laws. For example, the governor of Michigan proposed to end the state's truth-in-sentencing policy, which requires that every prisoner serve at least the minimum sentence. Michigan is attempting to resolve a $1.6 billion budget shortfall without increasing taxes, and currently, the state's annual corrections budget is close to $2 billion, exceeding the amount the state spends each year on its 15 public universities. The recommendation is projected to save $120 million in the 2011 budget by using electronic tether monitors and community residential programs to drop the number of prisoners behind bars to 35,500 from 45,200 by October 2011 and by closing five prisons. The governor also proposes hiring 40 more probation and parole officers to supervise the additional parolees.[60] In New York, inmates convicted of serious offenses may now earn a six-month, merit-time credit by achieving a "significant programmatic accomplishment," which is statutorily defined as participating in at least two years of college programming; obtaining a master's or professional studies degree; successfully participating as an inmate program associate for no less than two years; receiving certification from the State Department of Labor for successful participation in an apprenticeship program; or successfully working as an inmate hospice aide for a period of no less than two years.[61] Lastly, the states of Louisiana, Texas, and Mississippi have revised laws to restore good-time credit that reduces the time served in prison for persons who complete approved educational programs, treatment programs, and other programs.[62]

Alternative Sanctions for Prison-Bound Offenders

In addition to revising mandatory minimum sentences and truth-in-sentencing requirements, many states are adopting laws designed to expand alternatives to incarceration. The prevailing thought is that a wider range of alternatives may enable states to reach multiple correctional goals and do so in an economical way. Four state initiatives that expand community-based correction services are the Illinois Crime Reduction Act, the California Community Corrections Performance Incentive Act, the Arizona Safe Communities Act, and the Kansas Reduction Initiative. All of these new laws place a great deal of emphasis on evidence-based practices. We provide a brief description of each.

The Illinois Crime Reduction Act of 2009 was drafted by Chicago Metropolis 2020, a business-based civic organization working for, among other things, better outcomes in the legal and corrections systems. The primary product of the legislation was to create the Adult Redeploy Illinois program, which offers state funds to local jurisdictions to assess offenders and provide a continuum of sanctions and treatment alternatives for offenders who would be incarcerated if those local services and sanctions did not exist. The act also calls for an automated, integrated system to link courts, probation, prison, and parole in order to formulate an offender's reentry plan and reduce recidivism. A collaborative goal is to identify resources and services needed, such as substance abuse programming and job placement, as well as characteristics of offenders, including education level, skills, attitude, and relationships that can affect the reentry process. Finally, the act requires the Parole Division of the Department of Corrections and the Prisoner Review Board to adopt a statewide standardized risk assessment tool to assure that at least 75% of individuals are being supervised in accordance with evidence-based practices.[63]

The California Community Corrections Performance Incentive Act was enacted in 2009 in an attempt to reduce the number of probation revocations. In California, 40 percent of new admissions to state prison are offenders who have failed on felony probation. These offenders are currently under community supervision, but little is being done to stop their cycle of offending. The act calls for enhanced funding to counties that succeed in reducing the rate of adult probationers sent to prison. Grants are allocated for use in evidence-based probation programs that include risk and needs assessments and intermediate sanctions. Successful implementation will achieve an estimated reduction of 1,915 inmates. In addition, programs for alternative custody for low-risk offenders will achieve a 4,800 reduction. The law also requires performance measurement and stipulates that counties use at least 5 percent of the monies allocated to them to evaluate recidivism reduction programs.[64]

2.5

CBC Online

PEW CENTER ON THE STATES, PUBLIC SAFETY PERFORMANCE PROJECT ON THE NEED FOR CORRECTIONS REFORMS

The Public Safety Performance Project of the Pew Center on the States asked business leaders in five states to participate in a question-and-answer session on their approach to working with policymakers on public safety issues. Chicago Metropolis 2020 Executive Director Frank Beal was one of the featured leaders discussing innovative approaches. The responses were compiled in a document titled "Right-Sizing Prisons: Business Leaders Make the Case for Corrections Reform."

After reading the document, discuss these business leaders' ideas for protecting public safety and holding offenders accountable in cost-effective ways. Which ideas sound best to you and why?

Visit CBC Online 2.5 at www.mhhe.com/bayens1e

Similar to the new laws in Illinois and California, the Arizona Safe Communities Act provides financial incentives to probation departments to reduce crime and violations committed by people under probation supervision. The conditions that led to the new legislation was that during FY 2008, the average number of people on probation was 82,576, and by the end of year, a total of 7,720 dispositions had resulted in probation being revoked. Counties that reduce recidivism are now awarded 40 percent of the money the state saves by not having to house repeat offenders and probation-rule violators in its prisons. The counties then use the refund to improve victims' services and expand access to drug treatment and other recidivism-reducing programs. Projections show that if counties reduce probation revocations by 10 percent, the state could save nearly $10 million, with 40 percent of that amount returned to the local level. Another section of the Act provides incentives for the offenders to pay court-ordered restitution, complete community service assignments, and comply with their other conditions of supervision. For every month that an offender complies with the terms of supervision, the act authorizes the courts to reduce the length of probation by up to 20 days. Shortening probation terms for successful individuals not only will provide an incentive for probationers to comply with their conditions of supervision, but will also allow probation departments to concentrate existing resources on individuals who are more difficult to supervise and pose a greater risk to public safety (see CBC Online 2.5).[65]

In FY 2008, the Kansas Legislature appropriated $4 million as grant funds to local community corrections agencies through the SB14 Risk Reduction Initiative, a competitive grant process implemented by the Kansas Department of Corrections to enhance risk reduction efforts and reduce revocation rates by at least 20%. The three specific goals of the initiative are to increase public safety, reduce the risks posed by probationers on community corrections supervision, and increase the percentage of probationers successfully completing community corrections supervision. Agencies funded under this initiative have committed to these goals by targeting the criminogenic needs of medium- and high-risk probationers utilizing evidence-based community supervision methods and practices. Statewide, between FY 2006 and FY 2009 there has been a 24.9% decrease in revocations to prison—thus surpassing the goal of reducing community corrections revocation rates by at least 20% (using their FY 2006 revocation rate as a baseline)—and a 28.6% increase in number of probationers successfully completing supervision.[66]

Policy Implications

Throughout this chapter we have explored the influence of get-tough-on-crime policies and their impacts on the criminal justice system. Moreover, we have discussed the economic impact these policies are having on state budgets. Realizing that 13 states now devote more than $1 billion a year in general funds to their corrections systems, the need for investing in sound correctional policies and practices cannot be overstated. A key challenge is to devise strategies to ensure that reform efforts and policy initiatives are sustainable once external financial support has been reduced or terminated.

On the bright side, reforms in several states appear to be yielding positive results. A renewed emphasis on evidence-based practices is assisting practitioners and policymakers in developing sentencing and correctional principles that meet both current economic challenges and needs for public safety. Some states are developing new supervision strategies and technologies to hold drug offenders and other nonviolent offenders accountable in the community, at lower cost and with better results than incarceration achieves. Still other states are beginning to reallocate correctional budgets to better support new approaches in community corrections that are aimed at reducing parole and probation revocations for offenders violating the terms of their supervision agreements.

Evidence-based policies will have their greatest influence on correctional programs and services if the public better understands the criminal justice system and the impact of such policies. For example, opinion polls consistently report that Americans believe crime is on the rise both across the United States and in their local areas. A 2009 Gallup Poll found that 74% of Americans believed there is more crime in the United States than there was a year ago, the highest measured since the early 1990s.[67] Citizens are also critical of perceived judicial leniency in sentencing.[68] However, many citizens lack knowledge of the criminal justice system and the wide range of sentencing options available for offenders. For example, much of the general public equates sentencing with imprisonment. When focus group participants are asked to sentence hypothetical offenders, they overwhelmingly choose incarceration.[69] However, when given information about alternative sanctions, the respondents chose incarceration for only a small percentage of the offenders. These findings suggest that if the public knew more about community alternatives to imprisonment, they might be more supportive of such alternatives.

Countering false beliefs about crime rates, sentencing, and the criminal justice system in general is a primary concern for community-based corrections. What is known is that most crimes are neither as serious as the public perceives them to be nor as heinous as the media portrays them. Yet many arrests result in prison terms. The result is that the cost to the community for drug, property, and other low-level crimes is only a fraction of the costs of incarcerating those who are arrested and convicted for these types of crimes. Moreover, states that have experienced the greatest increases in incarceration rates are not necessarily seeing a corresponding drop in crime rates.[70] Such results do not support continued overreliance on incarceration, particularly in a time of fiscal crisis.

Summary

Community Corrections Acts were passed in the United States in the 1970s and 1980s to offer residential correctional services such as halfway houses and work release centers that would divert nonviolent offenders from jails and state prisons into local alternative punishment programs. Evaluation studies of state community corrections acts showed that intensive supervised probation (ISP) and other alternative sanctions could safely supervise otherwise prison-bound offenders at a reduced cost to the state.

During the get-tough era of criminal justice, the war on drugs and other federal crime bills caused arrests to increase, immediately followed by increases in the correctional population.

Under sentencing guidelines, the court's discretion is limited to a grid of sentencing ranges absent a valid ground for departure. The purpose of the restriction is to provide equity in sentencing whereby offenders are sentenced based principally on the severity of the crime and criminal history.

To better align sentences with the amount of time served in prison by restricting or eliminating parole eligibility and good time, truth-in-sentencing laws have been passed, requiring that a convicted offender serve 85 percent of a sentence before becoming eligible for release.

Reacting to the economic constraints felt in recent years, many states are shifting their criminal justice strategies by looking at non-mandatory minimum sentencing approaches, such as drug courts and other types of sanctions, which provide a range of sentencing options outside prison.

Key Terms

Arrestee Drug Abuse Monitoring (ADAM), p. 34
back-end offenders, p. 32
determinate sentencing, p. 36
front-end offenders, p. 32
get-tough era, p. 29
indeterminate sentencing, p. 38
Model Penal Code (MPC), p. 38
National Crime Victimization Survey (NCVS), p. 29
predatory crime, p. 37
sentencing guidelines, p. 38
truth in sentencing (TIS), p.42
Uniform Crime Report (UCR), p. 29

Questions for Review

1. What role have community corrections acts played in the establishment of community-based correctional programs?
2. What are the current trends between crime rates and corrections?
3. How has the "war on drugs" influenced the criminal justice system?
4. What are determinate sentencing and truth in sentencing?
5. What actions are states taking to meet the economic constraints of the times?

Question of Policy

Fairness in Sentencing

Central to the philosophy of determinate sentencing is the declaration that sentencing should be fair. The idea is that legislative mandates will eliminate the impact of socioeconomic differences among offenders by ensuring that punishment is proportionate to the offense and that it still allows the court to consider the criminal history of offenders. The first part of this equation—that punishment be based on the seriousness of the crime—does address concern for public safety and is consistent with public-supported ideas that serious crimes can be avoided in the future with harsher sentences. However, the secondary mandate—requiring a judge to add on time for an individual's second or third conviction—is often viewed as unjust. Referring back to our opening story, three-strike laws can result in life imprisonment for individuals who commit theft or other low-level offenses. Additionally, from a pragmatic point of view, the more offenders who enter the prison system, the more economic resources are needed to support increased prison populations.

Discuss your views on the requirement to provide consistency in sentencing versus financial concerns that stem from prison crowding during less prosperous times.

What Would You Do?

As a probation officer in the Intensive Supervised Probation Department, you have a caseload of 40 offenders, most of whom are drug offenders on intermediate supervision. Your agency operates under mandatory sentencing statutes that require one year in prison without parole for persons convicted of drug offenses committed in "drug-free zones." Under state law, such zones include any place within 1,000 feet of a school or 500 feet of a park, library, museum, or public housing project. The law also imposes a mandatory 90-day prison term on anyone possessing drug paraphernalia.

One of your female offenders is a single mother with a six-year-old daughter who attends elementary school near your office. Knowing that she has lunch with her daughter every Wednesday, you schedule this offender's next probation appointment to meet with you immediately after her visit at the school. When the offender arrives at your office, you search her coat and find a small glass pipe and two off-white nuggets that resemble crack cocaine. When questioned, the offender readily admits that she had visited her daughter's school prior to the probation appointment. However, she tells you that the coat was borrowed from a friend because of the cold weather.

1. What dilemmas are presented in this situation?
2. Setting aside any required action, how would you react to this situation?

Endnotes

1. See Cal. Penal Code §§ 667(d)(1), 1170.12(b)(1) and In re Cervera, 16 P.3d 176, 177 (Cal. 2001).
2. Ohio Department of Rehabilitation and Correction, *Best Practices Tool-Kit: Community Corrections and Evidence-Based Practices*, accessed March 22, 2010, www.drc.state.oh.us/WEB/iej_files/EvidenceBasedPracticesInCommunityCorrections.pdf.
3. Susan Boyer, *A Short History of Community Based Corrections Facilities in Ohio: Welcome to a New Chapter in an Ongoing Success Story*, accessed March 22, 2010, www.ohiojudges.org/_cms/tools/act_Download.cfm?FileID=1387&/CBCF%20Trans%20History.pdf.
4. Emily Herrick, "Intensive Probation Supervision," *Corrections Compendium*, vol. 12, no. 12, 1988, pp. 4–14.
5. Christopher Baird, *Report on Intensive Probation Supervision Programs in Probation and Parole* (Washington, DC: National Institute of Corrections, 1984).
6. M. Kay Harris and Peter Jones, *The Kansas Community Corrections Act: An Assessment of a Public Policy Initiative* (Philadelphia, PA: Final Report of the Temple University, September, 1990).
7. Ibid.
8. "Crime Victimization, 2008" (Washington, DC: Bureau of Justice Statistics, September, 2009).
9. "Crime in the United States, 2008" (Washington, DC: Federal Bureau of Investigations, September, 2009).
10. Lauren Glaze, *Correctional Populations in the United States, 2009* (Washington, DC: Bureau of Justice Statistics, December, 2010).
11. State of New York Article 12: Correction Law §§ 271 and 272: Local Conditional Release Commission (April 7, 2009).
12. Ohio Department of Rehabilitation and Corrections, *Data Source Reports—CCA Programs Annual Reports* (August, 2009).
13. National Association of State Budget Officers, *State Expenditure Report 2008*, accessed April 10, 2010, www.nasbo.org.
14. Pew Center on the States, *One in 31: The Long Reach of American Corrections* (Washington, DC: The Pew Charitable Trusts, March, 2009).
15. Ibid.
16. State of North Carolina, Division of Community Corrections, *Legislative Report on Probation and Parole Caseloads* (Raleigh, NC: Department of Corrections, March, 2009).
17. Comprehensive Crime Control Act of 1984. Pub. L. No. 98–473, Title II, October 12, 1984, 98 Stat. 1976 to 2193.
18. Ibid. See Subtitle A. Violent Offender Incarceration and Truth in Sentencing Incentive Grants. Section 20101: Grants for Correctional Facilities.
19. Ibid. See Part R. Certain Punishment for Young Offenders. Section 1801: Grant Authorization.
20. Anti-Drug Abuse Act of 1986, Pub. L. No. 99–570, 100 Stat. 3207 (1986).

21. Anti-Drug Abuse Act of 1988. Pub. L. No. 100–690, § 6470(a), 102 Stat. 4377 (21 U.S.C.A. §§ 846, 963).

22. Brian Landsberg, ed., *Anti-Drug Abuse Act (1986): Major Acts of Congress* (Farmington Hills, MI: Macmillan-Thomson Gale Publishing, 2004).

23. Ibid. See 21 U.S.C.A. §§ 841(b)(1)(B) (ii)-(iii) [[1982 & Supp. V 1987]].

24. See *White House Office of National Drug Control Policy (ONDCP) Drug Policy Information Clearinghouse. Fact Sheets: Drug Data Summary* (March 2003); *ADAM Preliminary 2000 Findings on Drug Use & Drug Markets—Adult Male Arrestees* (December, 2001); and *ADAM II Annual Report, 2008* (April, 2009).

25. See Crime in America: *FBI Uniform Crime Reports 2008, Table 29* (Washington, DC: U.S. Dept. of Justice, 2008)*; Uniform Crime Reports for the United States 2000, Tables 29 and 4.1* (Washington DC: U.S. Government Printing Office, 2001)*; FBI, UCR for the US 1990* (Washington, DC: U.S. Government Printing Office, 1991); *FBI, UCR for the U.S. 1980* Washington, DC: US Government Printing Office, 1981); and *Bureau of Justice Statistics, Chart of arrests by age group, number and rates for total offenses, violent offenses, and property offenses, 1970–2003* (December 2004).

26. Office of National Drug Control Policy. *The Price and Purity of Illicit Drugs: 1981 Through the Second Quarter of 2003, Tables 1 and 2,* Pub. L. No. NCJ 207768 (Washington DC: Executive Office of the President, November 2004), pp. 58–59.

27. Bruce Benson and David Rasmussen, *Independent Policy Report: Illicit Drugs and Crime* (Oakland, CA: The Independent Institute, 1996).

28. Survey of State Prison Inmates, *Bureau of Justice Statistics Report No. NCJ-136949* (Washington, DC: Bureau of Justice Statistics, 1991).

29. Lauren Glaze, *Probation and Parole in the United States, 2001* (Washington, DC: Bureau of Justice Statistics, August, 2002).

30. Supra (see 5).

31. Franklin Zimring, Gordon Hawkins, and Sam Kamin, *Punishment and Democracy: Three Strikes and You're Out in California* (Oxford: Oxford University Press, 2001).

32. Joanna Shepherd, "Fear of the First Strike: The Full Deterrent Effect of California's Two- and Three-Strikes Legislation," *The Journal of Legal Studies,* vol. 31, no. 1 (January 2002), pp. 159–201.

33. *Rummel* v. *Estelle* 445 U.S. 263 (1980).

34. Paul Robinson and Markus Dubber, "An Introduction to the Model Penal Code," *New Criminal Law Review*, vol. 10, no. 3 (Summer, 2007), pp 319–341.

35. Michael Tonry, "The Fragmentation of Sentencing and Corrections in America," *Sentencing & Corrections, Issues for the 21st Century, 1,* Bureau of Justice Statistics Publication: NCJ 175721 (Washington, DC: National Institute of Justice, 1999).

36. Rodney Engen and Sara Steen, "The Power to Punish: Discretion and Sentencing Reform in the War on Drugs," *American Journal of Sociology*, vol. 105, no. 5 (March 2000), pp. 1357–1395.

37. David Rottman and Shauna Strickland, *State Court Organization, 2004* (Washington, DC: U.S. Department of Justice, Bureau of Justice Statistics, 2006).

38. II U.S. Sentencing Commission, *The Federal Sentencing Guidelines: A Report on the Operation of the Guidelines System and Short-Term Impacts on Disparity in Sentencing, Use of Incarceration, and Prosecutorial Discretion and Plea Bargaining* (December 1991).

39. Minnesota Sentencing Guidelines Commission, *Minnesota Sentencing Guidelines and Commentary*, accessed April 20, 2010, www.msgc.state.mn.us/guidelines/guide09.pdf.

40. Roger Warren, *Evidence-Based Practice to Reduce Recidivism: Implications for State Judiciaries* (Washington, DC: U.S. Department of Justice, National Institute of Corrections, August 2007).

41. William J. Sabol, Katherine Rosich, Kamala Mallik Kane, David P. Kirk, and Glenn Dubin, *The Influences of Truth-in-Sentencing Reforms on Changes in States' Sentencing Practices and*

Prison Populations (Chicago: IL: The Urban Institute, April 2002).

42. Brian Ostrom, Fred Cheesman, Ann Jones, Meredith Peterson, and Neal Kauder, *Truth-in-Sentencing in Virginia* (Williamsburg, VA: National Center for State Courts, April 2001).

43. National Council on Crime and Delinquency, *Criminal Justice Sentencing Policy Statement 2005*, accessed April 22, 2010, http://nccd-crc.issuelab.org/research.

44. Massachusetts Sentencing Commission, *Survey of Sentencing Practices: Truth-in-Sentencing Reform in Massachusetts* (Boston, MA: Massachusetts Sentencing Commission, 2000).

45. Peter Wood and Roy Dunaway, "Consequences of Truth-in-Sentencing: The Mississippi Case," *Punishment and Society*, vol. 5, no. 2 (2003), pp. 139–154.

46. William Spelman, "Crime, Cash, and Limited Options: Explaining the Prison Boom," *Criminology and Public Policy,* vol. 8, no. 1 (February, 2009), pp. 29–77.

47. Albert Dichiara, "Costs Exceed Benefits Of Three-Strikes Law," *Hartford Business Journal Online*, February 2008, accessed April 22, 2010, www.hartfordinfo.org/issues/documents/prisonerre-entry /hbj_020408.asp.

48. Adapted from Paula Ditton and Doris Wilson, *Truth in Sentencing in State Prisons* (Washington, DC: U.S. Department of Justice, Bureau of Justice Statistics, January 1999).

49. *Missouri Department of Corrections Annual Report 2008,* accessed April 22, 2010, http://doc .mo.gov/documents/ publications/AR2008.pdf.

50. Joan Petersilia, *Understanding California Corrections* (Berkeley, CA: California Policy Research Center, May 2006).

51. Skaidra Smith-Heisters, *The Nonviolent Offender Rehabilitation Act: Prison Overcrowding, Parole and Sentencing Reform (Proposition 5).* (Los Angeles, CA: The Reason Foundation, October 2008).

52. Shannon McCaffrey, "State Budget Shortfalls May Reach $180 Billion this Year," *The Boston Globe*, January 4, 2010.

53. Lauren Altdoerffer, *Cutting Costs in the Criminal Justice System* (Sacramento, CA: Criminal Justice Legal Foundation, April 2009).

54. The Police Executive Research Forum, *63 Percent of Local Police Departments are Facing Cuts in Their Total Funding, Survey Shows*, accessed April 24, 2010, www.policeforum.org.

55. "The North Carolina State Budget Recommended Operating Budget 2009–2011 with Performance Management Information," *Justice and Public Safety Section*, vol. 4 (Raleigh, NC: Office of State Budget and Management Office of the Governor, March 2009).

56. Lise McKean and Susan Shapiro, *Sentencing Reform for Nonviolent Offenses: Benefits and Estimated Savings for Illinois* (Chicago, IL: Center for Impact Research, December 2004).

57. "New York State Department of Correctional Services, 2000–2008 Annual Reports," *Statistical Overview of Court Commitments.*

58. New York State Assembly (February 2009) Bill Number A06085.

59. William Gibney and Terence Davidson, *Drug Laws Resentencing: Saving Tax Dollars with Minimal Community Risk* (New York, NY: The Legal Aid Society, January 2010).

60. Editorial, "Shorter Sentences Ease Budget Strain," *The Detroit News*, February 22, 2010, http://detnews.com/article /20100222/OPINION01/2220308/Editorial-Shorter-sentences-ease-budget-strain (accessed April 24, 2010).

61. N.Y. CORRECTION LAW § 803–b: Article 24: Provisions Applicable to Sentences Imposed Under the Revised Penal Plan. NY Code—Section 803–B: *Limited Credit Time Allowances for Inmates Serving Indeterminate or Determinate Sentences Imposed for Specified Offenses.*

62. Nicole Porter, *The State of Sentencing 2009 Developments in Policy and Practice* (Washington, DC: The Sentencing Project, 2010).

63. Illinois General Assembly Public Act 096-0761: Illinois Crime Reduction Act of 2009.

64. California Senate Bill 678: Chapter 608, Statutes of 2009 (an act to add and repeal Chapter 3 [Commencing with Section 1228] of Title 8 of

Part 2 of the Penal Code, relating to probation) (October 2009).

65. Section 13–901, Arizona Revised Statutes. Also see *Safe Communities Act* (Phoenix, AZ: Arizona Supreme Court Adult Probation Services Division, November 2009). Probation data available at www.supreme.state.az.us/apsd/azprobpop.htm.

66. The Kansas Department of Corrections, *2010 Risk Reduction Initiative Report*, accessed April 25, 2010, www.doc.ks.gov/publications/the-senate-bill-14-risk-reduction-initiative.

67. Gallup, *Americans Perceive Increased Crime in U.S.,* accessed April 25, 2010, www.gallup.com/poll/123644/Americans-Perceive-Increased-Crime.aspx.

68. David Rottman, "Public Perceptions of the State Courts: A Primer," *The Court Manager*, vol. 15 no. 3 (2000), pp. 1–14. Also see Ronald Fagan, "Public Support for the Courts: An Examination of Alternative Explanations," *Journal of Criminal Justice*, vol. 9 no. 6 (1981), pp. 403–417.

69. Julian Roberts, "Public Opinion, Crime and Criminal Justice," *Crime and Justice: A Review of Research*, vol. 16 (1992), pp. 99–180.

70. Justice Policy Institute, *Pruning Prisons: How Cutting Corrections Can Save Money and Protect Public Safety*, accessed April 25, 2010, www.justicepolicy.org/images/upload/09_05_REP_PruningPrisons_AC_PS.pdf.

CHAPTER 3

Theories of Offender Treatment:

Reasons to Have a Theoretical Roadmap

OBJECTIVES

1. Explain the classical school of criminology and the crime control policies that stem from it.
2. Contrast the classical branch of criminology with the two positivist branches—the psychological and the sociological schools.
3. Explain the biological school of criminology and the crime control policies that stem from it.
4. Outline the psychological school of criminology and the crime control policies that stem from it.
5. Outline the sociological approaches of anomie and social disorganization theory and the crime control policies that stem from it.
6. Describe the sociological approach of social learning theory and the crime control policies that stem from it.
7. Outline the sociological approach of social control and self-control theories and the crime control policies that stem from it.
8. Explain the sociological approach of social reaction theory and the crime control policies that stem from it.
9. Outline the sociological approach of conflict theory and the crime control policies that stem from critical, Marxist, and feminist theories.

OUTLINE

Vandalism refers to the willful damaging or defacing of the property of others. Over five million acts of vandalism are committed annually in the United States.[1]

One of those acts drew national attention on October 4, 2009, when Oscar-winning actor and political activist Sean Penn broke the camera of photographer Jordan Dawes, who was at the Brentwood Country Mart, a shopping and dining complex in western Los Angeles, filming a story about paparazzi.[2]

On May 13, 2010, Penn pleaded no contest to the charge of misdemeanor vandalism.[3] *When pleading no contest, the defendant neither admits to nor disputes a charge. While not technically a guilty plea, a no contest plea has the same immediate effect as a guilty plea, and the defendant is sentenced.*

Penn was sentenced to three years' probation and ordered to attend 36 hours of anger management classes, perform 300 hours of community service, and stay at least 100 yards away from Dawes in the future.

Why did Penn behave in this way, and why was he sentenced to community-based correction? Criminologists seek to understand the complexity of human behavior and the appropriate criminal-justice response to it, so they have offered numerous responses to such questions. Which of the following explanations do you agree with?

1. He did it because he thought he could get away with it.
2. He did it because of psychological or physical forces over which he had no control.
3. He did it because of the environment in which he was raised.
4. He did it because his social environment includes friends or family who find vandalism acceptable.
5. He did it because he felt this was the only way he could get the paparazzi to leave him alone.
6. He did it because he has a poor self-image and weak ties to family.
7. In previous encounters with the criminal justice system, Penn was treated as deviant, which shaped his identity as a deviant and prompted further deviant behavior. In 1987 and 2006 he was sentenced for fighting with photographers.
8. Defining Penn's behavior as criminal is a means for those in power to promote conformity.
9. The criminal justice system prosecuted him because it is prejudiced against Hollywood actors.

Each one of these explanations represents a criminological theory discussed in this chapter. Criminological theory is an attempt to answer the question "Why do individuals commit crime?" The first explanation—he did it because he thought he could get away with it—represents the ***classical school of criminology****, the belief that crime is a matter of individual choice. Individuals are free to do as they wish and as their intelligence directs. According to this theory, then, the individual rationally calculates the benefits of committing crime against its potential costs.*

The other explanations represent theories of the ***positivist school of criminology****, which assert that criminal behavior is explained by factors beyond the individual's control. The original positivist criminologists looked mainly at biological factors, but later criminologists shifted their focus to psychological and then to social factors in their attempts to locate the causes of crime.*

Understanding criminological theory is important because effective community-based corrections is rooted not only in the evidence-based practices discussed across these chapters, but also in the professional attitudes of the corrections staff. These attitudes are in turn shaped by particular theoretical views of human behavior that guide society's response to crime and to designing systems of punishment that reduce crime. In the sections that follow, we will explore the dominant theoretical perspectives and their policy implications.

Classical School of Criminology

The classical school of criminology is a broad label for a group of thinkers of crime and punishment in the 18th and early 19th centuries who rebelled against the spiritual explanations of crime that formed the criminal justice policies in most of Europe. Its most prominent writer is Cesare Beccaria, who believed that human beings were hedonistic, acting in their own self-interest, but rational and capable of considering which course of action served them best. Classical theorists believed that a well-ordered state would construct laws and punishments in such a way that people would understand peaceful and noncriminal actions to be in their self-interest through strategies of punishment based on deterrence.

Cesare Beccaria and the Classical School

Cesare Beccaria (1738–1794), considered the founder of the classical school of criminology, is one of the most famous criminal justice theorists of all time. He lived during a time when a spiritual explanation of crime had dominated Europe for over a thousand years—that is, crime was seen as the work of the devil. Because crime was identified with sin, the state used horrible and gruesome torture on criminals to set them up as examples and instill terror in other sinners.

Even though the writings of more enlightened citizens such as Thomas Hobbes (1588–1678), John Locke (1632–1704), Baron de Montesquieu (1689–1755), Francois Marie Arouet (1694–1778), better known by his pen name of Voltaire, and Jean-Jacques Rousseau (1712–1778) were well known and widely accepted by the middle of the 1700s, they did not represent the thinking of the powerful elite. This more enlightened way of thinking, called **social contract philosophy**, was at odds with the spiritual explanation of crime because it substituted naturalistic explanations for spiritual ones. Social contract theorists argued that people naturally pursue their own interests without caring whether they hurt anyone. But because human beings are rational, they realize this situation is not in their best interest and agree to forgo their selfish behavior, thus forming a social contract with an enforcement mechanism (giving the state the right to use force to maintain the contract).

Beccaria's *On Crimes and Punishments* was published in 1764, and it embodied this social contract philosophy. In it he opposed the arbitrary and capricious nature of the criminal justice system of the time. He proposed that law and the administration of justice should be based on rationality and human rights, neither of which was then commonly applied. He argued for a system of criminal justice based on legal definitions of crime rather than on a concern with criminal behavior.

Beccaria's treatise is the first succinct and systematic statement of principles governing criminal punishment. The argument of the book is based on the utilitarian principle that governmental policy should seek the greatest good for the greatest number. The objective of the penal system, he argued, should be to devise penalties only severe enough to achieve the proper purposes of security and order; anything in excess is tyranny. He also argued that the effectiveness of criminal justice depends largely on the certainty of punishment rather than on its severity. Penalties should be scaled to the importance of the offense. Beccaria also advocated the abolition of capital punishment.

Beccaria feared a political backlash from the powerful elite, so at first he published the book anonymously. In fact, the Roman Catholic Church did condemn the book because its rationalistic ideas abandoned the spiritual approach, placing *On Crimes and Punishment* on its *Index of Forbidden Books,* where it remained for over 200 years. Nevertheless, the book was widely accepted by Beccaria's contemporaries. The treatise was publicly praised by Catherine the Great and Maria Theresa of Austria–Hungry, and it was quoted by Voltaire, Thomas Jefferson, and John Adams. It was published in many languages all over the world and was influential in the creation and reform of penal systems across the globe.

Around the time that Beccaria was writing *On Crimes and Punishments,* the American colonies were coming together as a nation. Thus, the U.S. Constitution and Bill of Rights were greatly influenced by Beccaria's work, specifically its void-for-vagueness rules, right to public trial, right to be judged by peers, right to dismiss certain jurors, right against unusual punishments, right to speedy trial, right to examine witnesses, rules invalidating coerced or tortured confessions, right to be informed of accused acts, and right to bear arms.

The greatest practical difficulty with the Classical school that grew out of Beccaria's work was that everyone was treated exactly alike, since the determinant of punishment was the act and not the offender. Thus, juveniles were treated the same as adults, first offenders were treated the same as repeaters, and those who were mentally challenged were treated the same as those who were not. Critics complained about this and championed the need for revisions so judges could exercise discretion in considering age, criminal history, mental condition, and external forces. These practical revisions led to what is called the **neoclassical school of criminology**.

Although crime statistics were not regularly collected during the 18th and 19th centuries, the dominant belief was that changes in punishment policies alone would not reduce crime. This concern gave rise to a new way of thinking about crime called the Positivist school, whose goal was to study the causes of crime whether in the individual or in the society at large. After considering the policy implications of the classical school approach to criminology, we will explore Positivist thinking.

Policy Implications

Two of the major concepts of the Classical school, deterrence and rationality, continue to shape modern theory and criminal justice polices. Two relevant theories are rational choice theory and routine activities theory. Ronald Clarke and Derek Cornish, researchers with the British government's research crime unit, proposed the first. Their **rational choice theory** asserts that an individual makes a rational choice to commit a crime by weighing the risks and benefits of doing so. If the risks of apprehension and punishment outweigh the benefits, then the person will not commit the act. The opposite is also true. Rational choice theory became popular in the 1970s when practitioners and scholars began questioning whether crime-producing traits and factors could be isolated, and whether treatment could be administered to eliminate or control the trait or factor. Once again the focus was on the offense committed, not on the offender. Policies such as mandatory sentencing and "three strikes and you're out" are based on choice theory and the principle that since humans are hedonistic, efforts should be placed on making the risks higher than any benefit derived from committing offenses.

Routine activities theory is also based on the tenets of deterrence and rationality. It was developed by University of Illinois sociologists Lawrence Cohen and Marcus Felson. It argues that crime occurs when there are motivated offenders, suitable targets (for example, something worth stealing), and an absence of capable guardians—meaning nobody or nothing is present to prevent the crime (such as high walls, security officers, guard dogs, or closed circuit television cameras). If all of these components are present, the probability of crime increases. If one of these components is missing, crime becomes less likely. How might one of these Classical theorists explain why

Routine activities theory argues that crime occurs when there are motivated offenders, suitable targets, and an absence of capable guardians. What crime control policies would a routine activities theorist propose to reduce home burglaries?

EXHIBIT 3.1 Classical Theory, Theorists, Principles, and Policy Implications

Theory	Classical—crime is a product of the individual's free choice. Contemporary versions are rational choice and routine activities.
Theorists	Cesare Beccaria (founder), Ronald Clarke and Derek Cornish (rational choice), and Lawrence Cohen and Marcus Felson (routine activities)
Principles	Nine principles summarize Classical theory: (1) The role of the legislature should be to define crimes and specific punishments for each crime. (2) The role of judges is to determine guilt and follow the strict letter of the law in determining punishment. (3) The seriousness of crime should be determined only by the harm it inflicts on society. (4) Punishment should be proportionate to the seriousness of the crime, and the purpose of punishment should be to deter crime. (5) The only justification for punishment is deterrence. Punishment is unjust when it exceeds what is necessary to achieve deterrence. (6) Excessive severity increases crime. (7) Punishment should be prompt and closely follow the commission of crime for it to have a lasting impact. (8) Punishment should be certain. (9) Preventing crime is better than punishing crime. Rational choice tells us that an individual commits crime because she or he makes a rational choice to do so by weighing the risks and benefits of committing the act. Routine activities argues that crime occurs when there are motivated offenders, suitable targets, and an absence of capable guardians.
Policy Implications	Classical theory proposes creating a system of criminal justice based on the legal definitions of crime rather than on a concern with criminal behavior. Rational choice theory has given rise to mandatory sentencing and "three-strikes-and-you're-out" policies. Routine activities proposes making targets less vulnerable (e.g., via better locks, anti-theft plastic devices found on clothing, development of community watches, and more policing).

Sean Penn committed the crime of vandalism? Exhibit 3.1 summarizes Classical theory along with its representative theorists, principles, and policy implications.

Positivist School of Criminology

The positivist school dates back to the early- to mid-19th century and continues through today. What all the positivist approaches have in common is the use of science to study the causes of criminal behavior. Some approaches focus on biological causes, others psychological, and still others social. It is impossible to account for every positivist approach that developed over the past 200 years in this brief introduction. However, we will point out that the positivist approaches were developed to explain crime, not to promote community-based punishments. Research on the positivist approaches has yielded mixed results, and a great deal more investigation is needed. The discussion presented here by necessity only provides sketches of the many positivist approaches that have emerged over the past 200 years, with examples of how a particular approach might be compatible with a community-based punishment. As you read the positivist explanations for crime, consider how each might explain Sean Penn's behavior.

3.1

CBC Online

BIOLOGICAL DISPOSITIONS TO CRIME

Modern biological theories have integrated biological, psychological, and social concepts into general theories of crime. Read the essay "Genetic and Environmental Influences on Criminal Behavior" and the peer commentaries that follow the essay.

After reading the debate, explain what biological factors offer criminology theory today.

Visit CBC Online 3.1 at www.mhhe.com/bayens1e

Cesare Lombroso and the Biological School

The **biological school of criminology** is associated with the name of Cesare Lombroso (1835–1909), a physician and professor of legal medicine in Italy. In 1876 he published *The Criminal Man*. In it he proposed that criminals were biological throwbacks to an earlier evolutionary stage, people who were more primitive and less highly evolved than their noncriminal counterparts. Lombroso used the term **atavistic** (meaning "derived from ancestor") to describe such people. As his thinking matured, Lombroso looked more toward environmental factors than strictly biological ones to explain crime and eventually conceded that socio-environmental factors such as religion, gender, marriage, criminal law, climate, rainfall, and taxation influence crime.

Lombroso maintained that there are three classes of criminals: (1) born criminals, or atavistic reversions to a lower or more primitive evolutionary form of development; (2) insane criminals, meaning those he termed idiots, imbeciles, sufferers from melancholia, and those afflicted with alcoholism, epilepsy, or hysteria; and (3) criminaloids, which included a large class without special physical characteristics or recognizable mental disorders but whose mental and emotional makeup are such that under certain circumstances they indulge in criminal behavior. Lombroso's research with prisoners concluded that well over one-half of all criminals were criminaloids.

By the time of his death in 1909, Lombroso's theories were perceived as too simple and naïve. Psychiatry and psychology were producing evidence to show that the relationship between crime and alcoholism or crime and insanity was much more complex and involved than Lombroso assumed. Still, Lombroso's theory of the atavistic criminal received enormous public attention. As a result he continues to be described as the first criminologist to search for the causes of crime and therefore has been given the mantel "founder of the Positivist school of criminology."

Today we continue to discuss biological factors and criminal behavior; however, theorists no longer argue for biological determinism as did Lombroso. Instead they argue that certain biological characteristics increase the chances that individuals will engage in criminal behavior (see CBC Online 3.1). No one is willing to make an absolute prediction—for example, that everyone with these characteristics will commit crime—only to assert an increased probability. Many of today's biological theories also point to a high degree of interaction with the social and physical environment.

Some of the more interesting biological theories relating to criminal behavior researched in the 20th century involve physical appearance (body type), family studies, twin and adoption studies, neurotransmitters, hormones, the central nervous system, the autonomic nervous system, and environmentally induced biological components of behavior. Some of these theoretical explanations have serious methodological problems, such as failure to adequately define crime, dependence on official crime statistics that record only known offenses, errors that result from the use of small samples, and failure to control for environmental influences. As Professors Mark Lanier and Stuart Henry say, "the relationship between biology and crime is not simple, and probably not linear but more likely reciprocal, with both biological and environmental factors feeding into and enhancing each other. . . . Not only might biological factors result from behavioral and environmental ones, but the biological factors are not immutable and can be altered by changes in behavior and environment."[4] In short, only in conjunction with certain environmental or social factors do biological factors limit choices that result in criminality. Although the research of the following criminologists does not sufficiently explore this complex interaction, we present brief summaries of their perspectives so you will be familiar with the range of people working in this field.

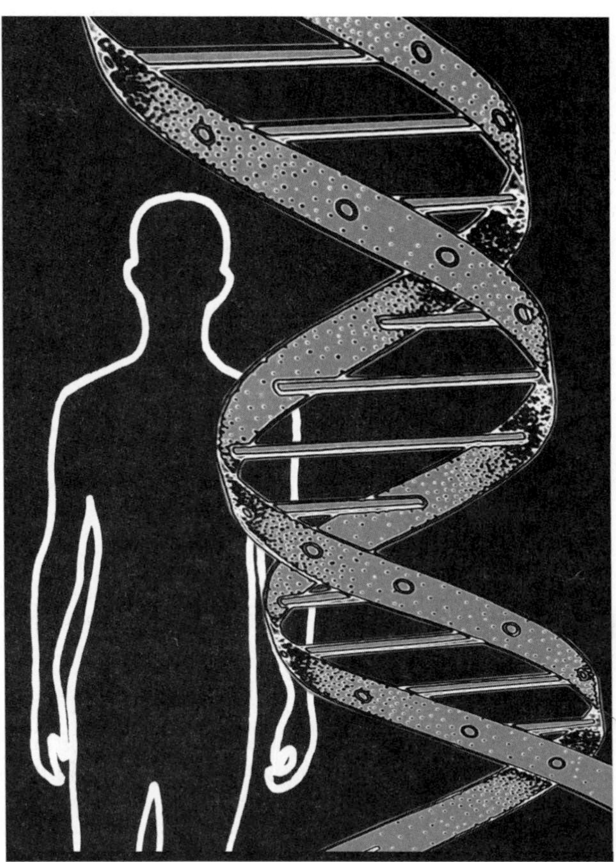

The biological school of criminology argues that certain biological characteristics increase the chances that individuals will engage in criminal behavior. What are some of the contemporary biological explanations for criminal behavior? What methodological problems do these explanations have, and what are the policy implications?

To begin our survey, physical-appearance theorists William Sheldon and Eleanor Glueck argue that persons with muscular skeletons are more likely to commit acts of aggression.[5] Family-study researcher Charles Goring asserted that criminality is associated with the inherited characteristics of height and weight.[6] He found criminals were on average two inches shorter than noncriminals and weighed three to seven pounds less. Goring believed these differences demonstrated hereditary inferiority.

Twin and adoption researcher Karl Christiansen found stronger patterns of criminal behavior among identical twins than among fraternal twins.[7] Moving into the realm of brain chemistry, Adrian Raine and Angela Scerbo studied the impact of neurotransmitters (chemicals that allow for the transmission of electrical impulses within the brain and that are the basis for the brain's processing of information) on behavior and found three neurotransmitters that may be associated with criminal behavior: serotonin, dopamine, and norepinephrine.[8] In short, they theorized, antisocial people have lower levels of serotonin than the general population, and these lower levels may account for criminal behavior.

In an initial study of the role of hormones and the central nervous system (CNS) in crime, Raine failed to find a strong relationship.[9] In another study, she examined the relationship between crime and the CNS and concluded that we do not yet know enough about the processes by which brain-wave activity affects behavior to come to any firm conclusions.[10]

Biological criminologist Sarnoff Mednick studied the relationship between the autonomic nervous system (ANS) and criminal behavior and found that people who are not easily aroused emotionally are less responsive to conditioning, whether punishment or rewards.[11] They are also more likely to resist socialization and more likely to break the law without fearing legal consequences.

Moving on to other research on crime and biological factors, psychologist Alfred Friedman finds a consistently strong relationship between alcohol and violence, especially for males, but the reason for the relationship, he says, is as yet unclear.[12]

Other researchers, such as Tufts University psychologist Robin Kanarek, have found a relationship between diet—for example, high sugar intake—hyperactivity, and criminal behavior, but again, the methodological limitations of these studies make it difficult to form solid conclusions.[13] Exposure to lead in diet and in one's environment has been shown to negatively affect brain functioning, resulting in learning disabilities and hyperactive attention deficit disorder in children. And although it may increase the risk for criminal behavior, more methodologically solid research is needed before solid conclusions affecting policy can be drawn.

Mednick also examined the impact of head injury on criminal behavior,[14] but whether the relationship is causal—meaning the presence of one affects the other—or whether the two conditions are only associated—meaning where you find one, you tend to find the other—is still unclear.

And finally, biological criminologists Elizabeth Kandel and Sarnoff Mednick have examined the link between pregnancy, delivery complications, and criminal behavior and found that pregnancy complications were not significantly related to offending behavior, but delivery complications were.[15] Others have found that delivery complications followed by the mother rejecting the new baby are strongly associated with criminal offending.[16]

Policy Implications

If research does determine that biological factors increase the likelihood that an individual will engage in criminal behavior, crime control policy will shift to a medical model that involves identification of those with the relevant biological factors in order to treat them and in turn prevent crime. Treatment might include surgery or drugs, incapacitation, eugenics for those who are untreatable, genetic counseling, and/or environmental manipulation. The most extreme policy would be to prevent the proliferation of criminals by stopping their procreation either through the genetic testing of fetuses or parents as carriers of certain traits. A less extreme measure would be to treat the "sickness" (the biological cause of the criminal behavior) with expert science and an indeterminate sentence for each individual offender based on his/her needs. Community-based punishments could be a viable option for offenders whose biological factors do not threaten public safety.

Exhibit 3.2 summarizes the theory, representative theorists, principles and policy implications related to the biological approach to crime research.

Psychological School

It was Sigmund Freud (1856–1939) who first studied the role of the unconscious mind in shaping behavior, and thus began psychology as an academic discipline. Since then, the **psychological school of criminology** has progressed from the study of the unconscious to a focus on intelligence, personality, and impulsivity as the causes of crime.

Although Freud wrote very little on crime, the argument that grew out of his psychoanalytic line of thinking is that crime is an expression of buried internal conflicts that result from traumas and deprivations during childhood, such as a poor early relationship with the mother or father, fixation at a stage of emotional development, and/or repressed sexuality or guilt. Most criminologists have discredited the psycho-

EXHIBIT 3.2 Biological Theory, Theorists, Principles, and Policy Implications

Theory	Biological – based on the proposition that certain biological characteristics increase the probability that individuals will engage in crime.
Theorists	Cesare Lombroso (founder) Sheldon and Gluecks (physical appearance as key to criminality) Goring (family as key factor in criminality) Christiansen (genetics as basis for criminality supported by twin and adoption studies) Raine and Scerbo (research on neurotransmitters) Raine (research on testosterone levels and criminality; also on CNS) Mednick (research on ANS responses and criminality; also research on possible relation between head injuries and criminality) Friedman (influence of alcohol and drugs) Kanarek (influence of diet) Kandel and Mednick (relations between pregnancy, delivery complications, and criminality)
Principles	Criminals are biological throwbacks to an earlier evolutionary stage. There are three classes of criminals: (1) born criminals; (2) insane criminals; and (3) criminaloids. Contemporary biological criminologists argue that certain biological characteristics increase the chances that individuals will engage in criminal behavior, but they have not demonstrated with certainty that everyone with these characteristics will commit crime. Some biological areas being researched today involve physical appearance, family studies, twin and adoption studies, neurotransmitters, hormones, central nervous system, autonomic nervous system, and environmentally induced biological components of behavior.
Policy Implications	Crime control policy follows the medical model: identification, prevention, and treatment (surgery, drugs, incapacitation, or eugenics for those who are untreatable). The most extreme policy is to prevent procreation.

analytic approach because it lacks empirical measurement. Because the id, ego, and superego are located in the individual's unconscious, unknown even to the offender, it is impossible to deny or confirm their existence. Only the interpretation of the therapist determines when and how an internal conflict is present. Still, the ultimate value of Freudian analysis is in helping individuals overcome their problems and highlighting the importance of mental processes in producing behavioral outcomes.

Other psychological approaches to criminal behavior date back to the turn of the 20th century when German and French psychologists developed intelligence testing. Soon researchers in Europe and the United States began studying the relationship between low IQ and criminal behavior. It was Henry H. Goddard, prominent American psychologist, who popularized the theory of a relationship between IQ and crime with his studies at the New Jersey Training School for the Feeble Minded and other public institutions.[17] Goddard administered IQ tests to inmates and found 70 percent had IQ scores below 70. He therefore concluded that most criminals were feebleminded and that the only way to eliminate feeblemindedness was through selective breeding (eugenics).

However, by the mid-20th century, low intelligence as a cause of crime fell out of favor, when researchers showed little to no difference in intelligence between criminals

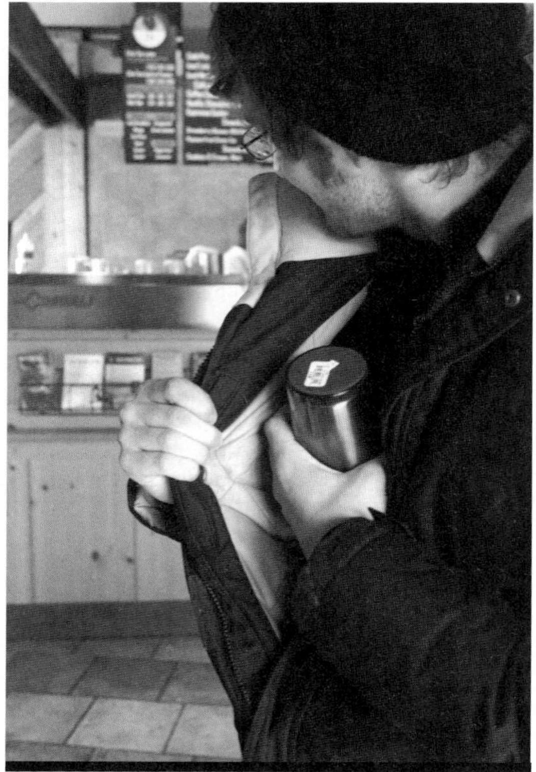

One of the more widely accepted psychological explanations for criminal behavior focuses on impulsivity—acting without thinking. Impulsivity theorists argue that changing thinking patterns will reduce crime. How would cognitive restructuring correct the thinking patterns of persons who steal?

and noncriminals and criticized the methodological limitations of Goddard and his followers. Today researchers argue that intervening factors such as ineffective child-rearing practices, school failure, and failure to learn cognitive skills such as moral reasoning, empathy, or problem-solving, not IQ, result in criminal behavior. Keep in mind also that intelligence cannot be observed directly. It is measured indirectly through reading ability or the motivation to succeed on testing. Any difference in IQ scores between criminals and noncriminals may reflect broader social and environmental influences rather than psychological or genetic ones.

Personality theories have also been advanced as a psychological roadmap to understanding criminal behavior. Theorists in this camp have focused on qualities or traits of individual behavior. The basic proposition is that delinquents and criminals have abnormal, inadequate, or specific criminal personalities or personality traits that differentiate them from law-abiding citizens. Words such as *self-centered, shameless, guiltless, impulsive, no life plan, superficial, disconnected, impersonal, deceptive, lack of empathy, unresponsive to interpersonal relations, unable to sustain enduring relationships,* and *blames others for problems* have been used to describe criminals and their behavior. The personality approach gained center stage with the Gluecks' study of delinquent and non-delinquent boys in 1950. Here is an excerpt:

> [D]elinquents are more extroverted, vivacious, impulsive, and less self-controlled than the non-delinquents. They are more hostile, resentful, defiant, suspicious, and destructive. They are less fearful of failure or defeat than the non-delinquents. . .. They are, as a group, more

socially assertive. To a greater extent than the control group, they express feelings of not being recognized or appreciated.[18]

These are clearly broad generalizations, but today's personality theorists continue to argue in favor of a relationship between personality type and criminal behavior. Along these lines, the American Psychological Association and the American Psychiatric Association have attempted to provide precise definitions of the terms *psychopath, sociopath,* and *antisocial personality disorder.* However, Hervey Cleckley, professor of psychiatry at the Medical College of Georgia, and others point out that sometimes psychologists, psychiatrists, and hospital staff apply these terms so broadly that they might apply to almost any person.[19]

Criticism of the theoretical relationship between personality differences and criminal behavior has followed the same path as theories about IQ. Research using personality tests and comparing mean scores from criminals with those from non-criminals has not been able to consistently support any particular personality traits as major causes of delinquent and criminal behavior. Personality differences may simply reflect differences in situations and circumstances of offenders' lives, rather than any innate personality difference.

One psychological approach that garners support among criminologists and stands up to methodological challenges focuses on the relationship between impulsivity and crime. *Impulsivity* is defined as acting without thinking—a tendency to become impatient, seek immediate gratification and become distracted. After examining youths in Dunedin, New Zealand, and Pittsburgh, Pennsylvania, University of Wisconsin psychologist Avshalom Caspi and colleagues found that a tendency to criminal behavior was associated with impulsivity and negative emotionality (e.g., anger, anxiety, and irritability).[20] Using a Wild West analogy, they described these youth as "quick on the draw."

Policy Implications

Except for the personality characteristic of impulsivity, which recent research consistently links to a large volume of delinquent and criminal behavior, researchers have concluded that most psychological approaches "seem to consist of fancy labels that psychologists and psychiatrists apply to criminals, but they do not add anything to our knowledge about the causes of crime or our ability to reduce it."[21] On the other hand, if certain personality traits can be linked to criminal behavior, then they can be measured and used to predict and prevent future delinquency and criminality. Moreover, these traits could be counteracted with therapeutic interventions. However, moral questions arise about screening young children for personality traits, defining them as "at risk" early in life, and giving them "preventive" treatment.

Even the research on impulsivity has policy limitations. Research has only discovered that impulsivity is *associated* with delinquent and criminal behavior, meaning that where we find one, we find the other. We still have no evidence that impulsivity *causes* crime. Nevertheless, two theorists have advanced ways to reduce impulsivity patterns. Glenn Walters, psychologist with the Federal Bureau of Prisons, for example, connected impulsivity to eight thinking patterns.[22] Change the thinking patterns, he argued, and crime will be reduced. The eight thinking patterns are:

1. Mollification—criminals point out the inequities and unfairness of life and blame others for their own choices

2. Cutoff—a visual image or verbal cue that has the effect of terminating all thought in the moment and allowing the person to act without thinking about the consequences
3. Entitlement—any action is considered justifiable to achieve what one wants
4. Power orientation—those who are strong can do what they want and get away with it
5. Sentimentality—looking back over the good things one has done in life and claiming the good things overshadow the bad
6. Super-optimism—the belief that nothing bad will ever happen to them, including punishment for crime
7. Cognitive indolence—a tendency to overlook details
8. Discontinuity—a tendency not to follow through on commitments or focus on goals over time

Walters advocates for **cognitive restructuring**, a problem-focused intervention that emphasizes changing the way one perceives, reflects, and thinks through modeling, graduated practice, role playing, reinforcement, and concrete verbal suggestions. He also asserts that cognitive restructuring has produced a statistically significant 7 to 8 percent average reduction in recidivism rates for program participants compared with a treatment-as-usual group.[23]

In additional research on impulsivity and crime,[24] Terrie Moffitt, University of Wisconsin psychologist, focuses on factors such as the mother's drug use or poor nutrition while pregnant, complications at birth resulting in brain damage, deprivation of affection, or child abuse and neglect after birth. According to this theory, these problems lead to impulsive behaviors such as acting without thinking, impatience, seeking immediate gratification, and distraction. As the child ages, the early tendencies toward impulsivity interfere with the child's ability to control his/her behavior and consider consequences. Other researchers believe that crime control policies resulting from the impulsivity approach have great potential for reducing delinquency and crime because they provide for (1) early intervention in the lives of young and troubled children, and (2) parenting-skills instruction for parents of high-risk children.[25]

Overall, the policy implications from a psychological perspective are quite clear: Use therapeutic intervention to correct and control personality traits and mental processes that are associated with criminal behavior. Thus, the psychoanalytical approach focuses on childhood root causes and bringing these to consciousness so that the problems they produce can be effectively controlled. In contrast, interventions based on trait-based personality theory focus on intensive individual counseling and treatment designed to teach offenders new rules and guide them toward understanding the punishment they will receive for committing criminal behavior. Finally, impulsivity theory favors interventions that control potentially criminal behavior by correcting problematic thought patterns and responses.

Psychological approaches to understanding and reducing criminal behavior have become a routine part of criminal justice, including community-based corrections. Offenders sentenced to probation, intermediate sanctions, and parole are often required to attend treatment sessions as a condition of their freedom. Moreover, offenders are diagnosed using a variety of risk-assessment instruments (discussed in Chapter 4) to determine what forms of counseling and treatment they need. Exhibit 3.3 summarizes the theory that grows out of the psychological approach, its representative theorists,

EXHIBIT 3.3 Psychological Theory, Theorists, Principles, and Policy Implications

Theory	Psychological—the belief that psychological characteristics of the individual explain crime.
Theorists	Freud (psychoanalytic) Goddard (IQ) Gluecks (personality) Caspi, Walters, and Moffitt (impulsivity)
Principles	Psychoanalytic: Crime is an expression of buried internal conflicts that result from traumas and deprivations during childhood. IQ: Low intelligence produces crime. Personality: Particular personality traits/drives produce behavioral responses that lead to crime. Impulsivity: The tendency to act without thinking is associated with criminal behavior.
Policy Implications	Correct and control through therapeutic intervention. The psychoanalytical approach focuses on childhood root causes and bringing these to consciousness so that problems can be effectively controlled. Policy stemming from intelligence theory deals with school failure. Trait-based personality theory favors individualized treatment for offenders to learn new rules, perceive punishment, or experience pain. Impulsivity theory favors behavior control through reinforcement and correcting faulty learning.

principles, and policy implications. The Career Profile of Dr. Matthew Crow focuses on the importance of theory in the work of criminology.

Sociological School

In contrast to the classical and psychological approaches, which focus on the characteristics of the individual, the **sociological school of criminology** shifts the discussion to external forces affecting individual behavior. The sociological school encompasses the largest number of criminological theories. What follows is a brief overview of the major branches of sociological thought.

To begin, **social disorganization theory** asserts that persons become criminals when they are isolated from mainstream culture and are instead immersed in impoverished and dilapidated neighborhoods that have their own sets of norms and values. These socially disorganized areas often result in **anomie**, a breakdown of social norms, and a condition in which those norms no longer control the activity of society's members. Without clear rules, individuals have difficulty adjusting to changing conditions of life, which leads them to dissatisfaction, frustration, conflict, and ultimately criminal behavior.

The theory of anomie was first developed by 19th century French sociologist Emile Durkheim. Durkheim studied crime and suicide rates in French society during the Industrial Revolution. Rapid industrialization, commercialization, and urbanization bred such extensive changes that existing norms no longer applied, which in turn led to an absence of social regulation. This deregulated condition in which people had inadequate control over their lives produced anomie.

Career Profile

MATTHEW S. CROW, PROFESSOR AND RESEARCHER

Matthew Crow is associate professor in the School of Justice Studies and Social Work at the University of West Florida (UWF) in Pensacola, Florida. He started his career at UWF in 2005 after completing his Ph.D. in Criminology and Criminal Justice from Florida State University. Dr. Crow teaches and conducts research on judicial process, specialized policing, and criminological and criminal justice theory. He incorporates theory into all his undergraduate and graduate classes and all the research he conducts, noting that "students are often intimidated about learning criminology and criminal justice theories. But once they understand its importance and its role in policy and practice, they realize that having this knowledge will help them succeed in their careers."

"Although this is not always explicitly stated," Crow asserts, theory is critical to developing good policy and practice in community-based corrections. "Criminological and criminal justice theories help us understand why people engage in criminal behavior, why judges sentence offenders to community punishments, and how probation, parole, and other community-based practices can reduce recidivism and the costs of incarceration."

Theory guides all of the research Dr. Crow conducts. For example, he has published a number of studies on criminal sentencing. His primary focus is on discovering the factors that affect judges' decisions about whether to sentence offenders to prison or to community supervision. Several theories, including the focal concerns perspective of sentencing, guide his selection of variables and the interpretation of results. By analyzing a large data set of offenders in the state of Florida, this research has provided a better understanding of how policy, race, gender, and community-related factors influence sentencing decisions. "Theory is essential in the process of building scientific knowledge. My research has built on the work of other scholars in contributing to our theoretical explanations of criminal sentencing. These explanations, in turn, can assist policymakers in crafting policies that are more effective and just."

Dr. Crow's advice to persons interested in a career as a professor or researcher in criminal justice is this: "Work to develop knowledge of criminological and criminal justice theories, research methods, and statistics while you are a student. Seek out opportunities to participate in research. I love working with students on research projects. Many of the students with whom I have conducted research end up seeking advanced degrees to continue on a path toward a career as a professor or researcher."

Columbia University sociologist Robert Merton further developed the concept of anomie, which is still among the most influential of all criminological theories today. Merton believed that the "split" between cultural goals and the institutionalized means for achieving those goals was the cause of anomie. The U.S. value system, he asserted, teaches us both what we should strive for (cultural goals, such as success) and how best to achieve those goals (social means, such as a good education). In a pluralistic society, people differ in degree of access to these goals and means. So, for example, the contradiction that Merton defines as anomie can be seen in the emphasis on the goal of accumulated wealth and the assertion that this goal is possible for all persons when, in fact, the social structure limits the possibilities of individuals within certain groups to

EXHIBIT 3.4 Anomie Theory, Theorists, and Principles

Theory	Anomie—the claim that breakdowns in social regulations (Durkheim) or social structure (Merton) explain crime.
Theorists	Emile Durkheim Robert Merton
Principles	Durkheim theorized that anomie is caused by a breakdown of social norms. Without clear rules, individuals have difficulty adjusting to changing conditions of life. That leads to dissatisfaction, frustration, conflict, and ultimately criminal behavior. Merton asserted that the "split" between cultural goals and the institutionalized means for achieving those goals was the cause of anomie.

achieve this goal. To succeed, then, individuals adopt what Merton referred to as "alternative modes of adaptation." Each of these modes—referred to as conformist, innovator, ritualist, retreatist, and rebel—is formed by combinations of accepting, rejecting, or substituting the cultural goals and institutionalized means. Exhibit 3.4 summarizes anomie theory and its representative theorists and principles. Policy implications for all the sociological approaches are presented later in the chapter.

Social disorganization theory was first developed in the studies of urban crime and delinquency by Robert Park, Earnest Burgess, Clifford Shaw, and Henry McKay, sociologists and researchers at the University of Chicago in the 1920s and 1930s. These researchers plotted the residences of youth who had been refereed to juvenile court. The studies showed that the rates of delinquency in lower-class neighborhoods were highest near the inner city and decreased outwardly toward the more affluent areas. In addition to high rates of delinquency, the inner city also had high rates of adult crime, drug addiction, alcoholism, prostitution, and mental illness. Subsequent researchers found that the inner-city neighborhoods maintained the high rates of delinquency and crime over decades regardless of the racial and ethnic makeup of the population in those areas. Thus, they concluded, residents in this area were not biologically or psychologically abnormal. Instead, their crime and delinquency were normal responses to abnormal conditions. Exhibit 3.5 summarizes social disorganization theory and its representative theorists and principles. For more on this subject, read CBC Online 3.2.

EXHIBIT 3.5 Social Disorganization Theory, Theorists, and Principles

Theory	Social Disorganization—the theory that low economic status, a mixture of ethnic groups, a population that moves frequently in and out of the area, and disrupted families and broken homes explain crime.
Theorists	Robert Park Earnest Burgess Clifford Shaw Henry McKay
Principles	Persons become criminal when they are isolated from the mainstream culture and are immersed in impoverished and dilapidated neighborhoods that have their own norms and values. Delinquency and crime are highest near the inner city and decrease outwardly toward the more affluent areas.

3.2

CBC Online

COMPUTER MAPPING AND SOCIAL DISORGANIZATION

As noted, the theory of social disorganization argues that persons become criminal when they are isolated from the mainstream culture and are in impoverished neighborhoods with different norms and values. The theory includes the idea that there are "hot spots" in communities where frequent criminal activity occurs. The Justice Atlas of Sentencing and Corrections is an interactive tool that maps residential patterns of populations who are admitted to prison and of those who return to their communities from prison. The map shows highly concentrated pockets of criminal justice activity in just a few neighborhoods in major cities and certain rural regions. For example, in New York City, neighborhoods that are home to 18 percent of the city's adult population account for more than 50 percent of prison admissions each year. Use the map to investigate major cities in your state or a neighboring state. What, if anything, can you conclude from these patterns about the theory of social disorganization?

Visit CBC Online 3.2 at www.mhhe.com/bayens1e

As the theories of social disorganization and anomie were developing, the tenets of social learning were also taking shape. **Social learning theory** argues that behavior may be reinforced not only with rewards and punishments, but also with expectations that are learned by watching what happens to other people. More specifically, Indiana University sociologist Edwin Sutherland and his colleague Donald Cressey theorized that criminals learn to commit crimes just as they learn any other behavior. They referred to this idea as **differential association theory**. According to this theory, we learn values from important people (parents, family, close friends, business associates) around us. Those values either support or oppose criminal behavior. The core proposition of differential association is this: a person becomes delinquent because of an excess of definitions favorable to violation of the law over definitions unfavorable to violation of law. To the extent that the weight of those values is against criminal behavior, we will be law abiding. However, if the weight of values supports criminal behavior, we will commit crime.

Later scholars such as Robert Burgess, Ronald Akers, and C. Ray Jeffrey refined Sutherland and Cressey's original theory. They argued that learning criminal behavior depends on the feedback people receive from their environment and how they evaluate their own behavior through interaction with significant other people and groups. They termed their approach **differential reinforcement theory**.

A final social learning approach we will cover is referred to as **neutralization theory**. This theory focuses on the words and phrases offenders use to justify or excuse lawbreaking behavior, such as claiming an action was in self-defense. Offenders develop rationalizations that neutralize their potential guilt. Princeton sociologists Gresham Sykes and David Matza developed this theory and proposed five "techniques of neutralization" that offenders use.

1. Denial of responsibility—"It's not my fault. I was drunk at the time."
2. Denial of injury—"Nobody got hurt."
3. Denial of victim—"She had it coming."

EXHIBIT 3.6 Social Learning Theory, Theorists, and Principles

Theory	Social learning—the theory that behavior may be reinforced not only through rewards and punishments, but also through expectations that are learned by watching what happens to other people.
Theorists	Sutherland and Cressey (differential association) Burgess, Akers, and Jeffrey (differential reinforcement) Sykes and Matza (neutralization)
Principles	Differential association argues that criminal behavior is based on interactions and communications we have with others and the values we receive from others during those interactions. The core proposition is that a person becomes delinquent because of an excess of definitions favorable to violation of the law over definitions unfavorable to violation of law. Differential reinforcement: argues that learning criminal behavior depends on the feedback a person receives from his or her environment and how he or she evaluates his or her own behavior through interaction with significant other people and groups. Neutralization focuses on the words and phrases that offenders use to justify or excuse lawbreaking behavior.

4. Condemnation of the condemners—"Prosecutors are just as corrupt because they withhold evidence."
5. Appeal to higher loyalties—"I stole it to feed my family."

As with most social learning theories, the theory of neutralization has been updated since Sykes and Matza introduced it in 1957. Later scholars have added additional types of neutralizations (for example, the claim of normality—"Everybody is doing it"), criticized some of the original techniques for overlapping (for example, denial of injury and denial of victim), and called attention not to the neutralizations themselves but to the wider context of how an individual makes sense of his or her world. Exhibit 3.6 summarizes social learning theory and its representative theorists and principles.

Whereas the previous theories ask why some people commit crime, social- and self-control theories asks why people obey rules instead of breaking them. The quick answer is that we conform because social controls prevent us from committing crime. **Social control theory** stresses the idea that people commit delinquent or criminal acts because the forces restraining them from doing so are weak, not because the forces driving them to do so are strong. Only when controls break down is criminal behavior likely to result.

Yale University sociologist Albert Reiss developed the initial groundwork in social control theory in the 1950s. He attributed the cause of delinquency to the failure of personal and social controls. Personal controls are internalized. Social controls operate externally, through both formal (legal) and informal social channels. But it was Travis Hirschi, University of Arizona Professor Emeritus, who later refined the concept of social control, renaming it social bonding theory. Hirschi is still regarded as the major control theorist.

"Elements of social bonding," Hirschi wrote, "include attachment to families, commitment to social norms and institutions (school, employment), involvement in activities, and the belief that these things are important."[26] The stronger these bonds are with parents, adults, school teachers, coaches and peers, the more the individual's behavior will be controlled in the direction of conformity. The weaker the bonds are, the more likely the individual will be to violate the law. Furthermore, the four elements of bonding are highly correlated; weakening one will probably be accompanied by a weakening in another.

Attachment, the first element, refers to an individual's close ties to others, especially one's parents. The theory suggests that the more we admire and identify those with whom we have close affectional ties, and the more we care about their expectations, the less likely we will be to violate their norms. Next is commitment, the investment one has in conventional society. Commitment implies that "the interests of most persons would be endangered if they were to engage in criminal acts."[27] Involvement is the time and energy spent on participation in conventional activities. The more time spent doing conventional activities, the less time is available for criminal acts. And finally, the social bond is solidified by belief. If a person shares values/norms with others in their subgroup and believes in the authority of those limiting their behavior, then the motivation to deviate will be minimal.

A large number of researchers have tested social bond theory with adults and juveniles. Most have found strong data to support it, especially the elements of attachment and commitment.

More recently, Hirschi and his colleague Michael Gottfredson, vice chancellor and provost and professor of criminology at the University of California at Irvine, presented a new approach that focuses on what they call **self-control theory**, or the lack of it that results in impulsive behavior. In contrast to the four elements in social bond, this is a single-concept theory. Another difference is that self-control is internal to the individual, whereas the four elements of social bond largely reside in the external social environment.

Self-control theory argues that impulsive behavior is a tendency in all humans; all are motivated to break rules, and all make rational choices about whether to do so. In this sense, self-control draws on the rational choice theory of the Classical school discussed earlier in this chapter. As Hirschi and Gottfredson write, "The quality that prevents crime among some people more than it does among others . . . we call 'self-control,'" which is "the tendency to consider the broader or long-term consequences of one's acts"[28] and "the tendency to avoid acts whose long-term costs exceed their immediate or short-term benefits."[29] The source of low self-control is ineffective or incomplete socialization, especially ineffective childrearing practices. Taken together, the theory goes, inadequate monitoring, inappropriate recognition, and ineffective punishment result in dysfunctional child rearing and set the stage for delinquency and adult criminal behavior.

The simplicity of Hirschi and Gottfredson's theory is its biggest strength as well as its biggest limitation. It is appealing to accept the argument that those who "have a high degree of self-control avoid acts potentially damaging to their future prospects . . . . Those with a low degree of self-control are easily swayed by current benefits and tend to forget future costs."[30] But others argue that criminal behavior is far too complex to be explained by a single element, particularly a simple one. Exhibit 3.7 summarizes social- and self-control theories and their representative theorists and principles.

So far, the theories discussed have examined how the social environment influences individuals to engage in crime, but they devote little attention to the official reaction

EXHIBIT 3.7 Social and Self-Control Theories, Theorists, and Principles

Theory	Social control—the theory that people commit delinquent or criminal acts because of the weakness of the external forces restraining them. Self-control theory focuses on forces internal to the individual.
Theorists	Hirschi (social control) Hirschi and Gottfredson (self-control)
Principles	Social control is the bond between an individual and society. It is composed of four elements: attachment, commitment, involvement, and belief. The stronger these elements are, the more the individual's behavior will be controlled in the direction of conformity. Self-control theory argues that impulsive behavior is a tendency in all humans; all are motivated to break rules and all make rational-choice decisions about whether to do so.

to crime—that is, to the reaction of the police, courts, and corrections agencies. **Social reaction theory** (also referred to as **labeling theory**) fills in this gap. It was Edwin Lemert, professor of sociology at UCLA and later at the University of California at Davis, who in 1951 introduced the concepts of primary and secondary deviance as a way to explain the process of labeling. *Primary deviance* refers to the initial law-violating behavior an individual engages in. *Secondary deviance* refers to behaviors that result after a person's primary deviance is reacted to by authorities, particularly by the social control agents (police, courts, and corrections) of the criminal justice system.

When a person is arrested or convicted of a crime, however mild, the corrections system punishes the individual. However, punishment does not necessarily stop crime, so the individual might commit the same primary deviance again, bringing even harsher reactions from the correctional system. At this point, the individual's feelings of resentment toward the criminal justice system build, while the system brings escalated punishments. Eventually, the community stigmatizes the individual as deviant. Unable to shed the label, the individual ultimately accepts his or her role as criminal, and will commit criminal acts that fit the role of a criminal.

Following Lemert, it was Howard Becker, professor of sociology at the University of California at Santa Barbara, who more fully developed social reaction theory and explained the power of the definition process. Becker first described the process of how a person adopts a deviant role in a study of musicians with whom he once worked. He later studied identity formation in marijuana smokers. This study was the basis of his 1963 book *Outsiders*. This work became the manifesto of the labeling-theory movement among sociologists. In his opening, Becker writes this:

> [S]ocial groups create deviance by making rules whose infraction creates deviance, and by applying those rules to particular people and labeling them as outsiders. From this point of view, deviance is not a quality of the act the person commits, but rather a consequence of the application by others of rules and sanctions to an "offender." The deviant is one to whom that label has been successfully applied; deviant behavior is behavior that people so label.[31]

According to labeling theory, official efforts to control crime often increase crime. Individuals who are arrested, prosecuted, and punished are labeled as criminals. When confronted with a label applied by those with power and authority, the individual has little power to resist his or her identification with it. Others then view and treat these people as criminals, and this increases the likelihood of subsequent crime for several reasons. Labeled individuals may have trouble obtaining legitimate employment, which increases their level of strain and reduces their stake in conformity. Labeled individuals may also find that noncriminals are reluctant to associate with them, and they may instead associate with other criminals as a result. This reduces their bond with conventional others and fosters the social learning of crime. Finally, labeled individuals may eventually come to view themselves as criminals and act in accord with this self-concept.

John Braithwaite, professor of criminology at the Australian National University, argues that labeling increases crime in some circumstances and reduces it in others. Labeling increases crime when no effort is made to reintegrate the offender back into conventional society—that is, when offenders are rejected or informally labeled on a long-term basis. But labeling reduces crime when efforts are made to reintegrate punished offenders back into conventional society. In particular, labeling reduces crime when offenders are made to feel shame or guilt for what they have done, but are eventually forgiven and reintegrated into conventional groups such as family and peer groups. Such reintegration may occur "through words or gestures of forgiveness or ceremonies to decertify the offender as deviant."[32] Braithwaite calls this process **reintegrative shaming**. Reintegrative shaming is said to be more likely in certain types of social settings—for example, where individuals are closely attached to their parents, neighbors, and others. Braithwaite's theory has not yet been well tested, but it helps make sense of the mixed results of past research on labeling theory. Exhibit 3.8 summarizes social reaction theory and its representative theorists and principles.

The final theory of the sociological school that we will discuss is critical theory. We use the term **critical theory** as an umbrella term encompassing a number of emerging perspectives that share several features: (1) knowledge is not seen as neutral but is influenced by human interests and reflects the power and social relationships within society; (2) science, while an empirically based tradition, is also seen as being influenced by values of the scientist and the scientific community; (3) the goal of any research should be a more just and democratic society, which can be achieved by linking the results of social inquiry to action for marginalized groups such as women, ethnic/racial minorities, members of the gay and lesbian communities, people with disabilities, offenders, and those who are poor; and (4) crime is seen as a result of the

EXHIBIT 3.8 Social Reaction Theory, Theorists, and Principles

Theory	Social reaction theory (also referred to as labeling) focuses on the official reaction to crime.
Theorists	Lemert (primary and secondary deviance) Becker (power of definitions) Braithwaite (reintegrative shaming)
Principles	Primary deviance is the initial law-violating behavior an individual engages in. Secondary deviance refers to behaviors that result after a person's primary deviance is reacted to by the agents of the criminal justice system. Power of definitions argues that deviance is not a quality of the act the person commits, but rather a consequence of the application by others of rules and sanctions to an offender. Reintegrative shaming brings the offender back into society as a law-abiding citizen through words or gestures of forgiveness or ceremonies to decertify the offender as deviant.

way society is organized—that is, most crime is the result of large forces (for example, economic and government structures). This final section of the chapter briefly examines three of these emerging critical approaches: conflict theory, Marxist theory, and feminist theory. We begin with conflict theory.

Conflict theory views law as a social-control mechanism reflecting the values and interests of the dominant group. Further, the theory goes, crime is inevitable in capitalist societies because certain groups will become marginalized and unequal. In seeking equality, members of these groups often turn to crime to gain the material wealth that brings equality in capitalist economic states. Conflict theory derives its name from the fact that its theorists reject the idea of a consensual social contract between state and citizen. Most if not all of the theories discussed previously assume that a consensus of values exists in every society—that is, that people share a sense of what is good, right, and just. Conflict theorists, on the other hand, believe that conflict, not consensus, is at the center of human society. Values do not represent common interests but rather the interests of those with sufficient power to take control. The more power people have, the less likely they are to be arrested, convicted, and punished. Powerful people are free to pursue self-interests, while less powerful people who pursue self-interests are more likely to be officially defined and processed as criminal.

The civil rights movement and the Vietnam War of the 1960s resulted in enormous social and political turmoil in the United States and saw the rise of several minority power groups (women, prisoners, African Americans, and students). Suddenly conflict theory came to the forefront in criminology, and several theorists added to the conflict approach. Here we comment on two of them.

Austin Turk, professor of sociology at the University of California at Riverside, argued that in the search for an explanation of criminality, "one is led to investigate the tendency of laws to penalize persons whose behavior is more characteristic of the less powerful than of the more powerful and the extent to which some persons and groups can and do use legal processes and agencies to maintain and enhance their power position vis-à-vis other persons and groups."[33] In his 1969 seminal work, *Criminality and Legal Order,* Turk wrote that in any attempt to explain criminality, "it is more useful to view the social order as mainly a pattern of conflict" rather than to offer explanations for crime based on behavioral or psychological approaches. Turk, like most conflict criminologists, views the law as a powerful tool in the service of prominent social groups seeking continued control over others. Crime is the natural consequence of such intergroup struggle because it results from the definitions imposed by the laws of the powerful on the less powerful.

Another prominent conflict theory of the time was advanced by William Chambliss, professor of sociology at George Washington University, and Robert Seidman, professor of law at Boston University. Chambliss and Seidman argue that the probability of a particular group's norms being encompassed within the law is directly related to the group's political and economic power. The ruling class controls the resources of society and uses law as a means of control. Thus, the law reflects the perspectives, values, definitions of reality, and morality of the upper and middle classes while at the same time being in opposition to the values and morality of the poor. To test their theory, they examined appellate court decisions and observed the functioning of the criminal justice agencies. They found that appellate court decisions overwhelmingly reflect the needs and desires of the wealthy and powerful, and because criminal justice agencies depend on political organizations for their resources, they process a disproportionately high number of the politically weak and powerless while ignoring the violations of

3.3

CBC Online

AMERICANS UNDERESTIMATE U.S. WEALTH INEQUALITY

The term "wealth inequality" refers to the unequal distribution of financial assets among a group of people. In the United States, the top 20 percent of people have 85 percent of the wealth. Harvard Business School professor Michael Norton talks with National Public Radio about what Americans think they know about wealth inequality.

When Professor Norton asked respondents how much wealth the top 20 percent of Americans should have, what did they say? Do you think wealth inequality relates to crime? If so, how? If not, why not?

Visit CBC Online 3.3 at www.mhhe.com/bayens1e

those with power.[34] They conclude that both in structure and in function, the law operates in the interests of power groups. "The public interest is represented only to the extent that it coincides with the interests of those power groups."[35]

Marxist theory, named after Karl Marx (1818–1883), the German Jewish philosopher, political economist, historian, theorist and sociologist, links economic development to social, political, and historical change. The principal idea of Marxist theory is the conflict between those who own the material means of production and the wage laborers who produce the goods. Marx wrote very little about crime, but criminologists adapted his general ideas to their explanations of crime. Marx believed conflict in society was due to a scarcity of resources and inequality in the distribution of those resources. The inequality produces conflict between those with power (the bourgeoisie, the owners of production) and those without (the proletariat, the working class). As the working class becomes aware of their true position and realizes that the structure of society is not in their best interest, they join forces and initiate conflict with the ruling class. Just as capitalism replaced feudalism, Marx believed socialism would replace capitalism and lead to a stateless, classless society called communism.

Marxist criminologists assume that the conflict between classes affects crime in three ways. First, they agree with conflict theorists that law is a tool of the dominant class. The definitions of crime reflect the interests of the dominant class and protect the concept of property, which is the foundation of capitalism. Second, they view crime as a product of class struggle. The emphasis on wealth and property and the exclusion of the working class from the means of production leads to conflict—for example, workers' strikes, destruction of property, and violence—between the classes and even within the classes. The third way conflict between the classes affects crime concerns the amount of surplus labor (the unemployed and underemployed) in a capitalist society. As long as there is not a large surplus of labor, there is no immediate threat to the dominant class, and the dominant class expends few resources on control. However if the surplus grows, and people become unproductive and demoralized, the potential for conflict grows, as was the case during the Great Depression when over a third of all Americans (and over 50 percent of minorities) were out of work. Hungry crowds rioted and vandalized food markets and cleared out the shelves. In Wisconsin, dairy farmers stopped milk trucks on the way to market and dumped the milk into ditches. Violence against minorities increased as whites competed for jobs traditionally held by minorities. For more about wealth inequality, see CBC Online 3.3.

Feminist theory, one of the more recent sociological explanations for criminal behavior, focuses on the role of gender relations. What are the major principles of feminist theory that might explain women's incarceration? What crime control policies flow from gender-based explanations?

As our last sociological perspective on crime, we discuss feminist theory. **Feminist theory** poses the question of whether traditional criminological theories, which are created primarily by men and used men as their subjects, can be generalized to explain women's criminality.[36] Feminist theory seeks to rectify this bias by examining the role of gender relations in crime and criminal justice. Feminist criminology is made up of numerous perspectives. Here we discuss three—the liberation hypothesis, the power-control theory, and the pathways to crime theory.

The **liberation hypothesis**, first proposed by Freda Adler, professor of criminal justice at Rutgers University, argues that the women's movement brought about changes in traditional sex roles, greater equality for women, and an increase of women in the labor force. One unintended consequence of the women's movement, Adler asserts, is a greater involvement of women in criminal activity. As she explains, "In the same way that women are demanding equal opportunity in fields of legitimate endeavor, a similar number of determined women are forcing their way into the world of major crimes. . .formerly committed by males only. . .. Like her sisters in legitimate fields, the female criminal is fighting for her niche in the hierarchy of crime."[37] However, except for an increase of women convicted of shoplifting, the liberation hypothesis has not received much empirical support.

The **power-control theory** proposed by John Hagan, professor of sociology at Northwestern University, argues that socialization within the family places tighter controls on girls than on boys. That is, socialization teaches boys to be risk-takers and girls to be risk-averse, especially in patriarchal families where the father's occupation places him in a "command" position, giving orders to others, and where the mother either does not work outside the home or where she works in a position where she takes orders from supervisors. Hagan writes, "[P]ower-control theory predicts that patriarchal families will be characterized by large gender differences in delinquent behavior, while egalitarian families will be characterized by smaller gender differences in delinquency."[38] Here, too, research results are mixed. Hagan's data from Canada support the theory, but other researchers found that class and gender differences, the low involvement of fathers in exercising parental control, and other internal family variables have weak effects on delinquency patterns. That is, they found that gender differences in delinquency are about the same for patriarchal and egalitarian families.[39]

The **pathways to crime theory**—developed by Barbara Bloom, professor of criminology at California State University, Fresno; Barbara Owens, professor of criminal justice at Sonoma State University; and Stephanie Covington, co-director of the Institute for Relational Development in LaJolla, California—seeks to identify the most common pathways for producing and sustaining female criminality.[40] Their key findings are listed here:

1. Female offenders have histories of sexual and/or physical abuse rooted in delinquency, addiction, and criminality. Frequently, women have their first encounters with the justice system as juveniles who have run away from home to escape violence and sexual or physical abuse. Prostitution, property crime, and drug use often become a way of life for these individuals.
2. Mental illness and substance abuse contribute to criminal pathways for women. Many female offenders suffer from some form of mental illness or co-occurring disorder. Nearly eight in 10 female offenders with a mental illness experienced prior physical or sexual abuse. The link between female criminality and drug use is also very strong. Research indicates that women who use drugs are more likely to be involved in crime. Approximately 80 percent of women in state prisons have substance abuse problems, and about 50 percent of female offenders in state prisons had been using alcohol, drugs, or both at the time of their offense.
3. Many women on the social and economic margins struggle to survive outside legitimate enterprises, which brings them into contact with the criminal justice system. Economic marginalization, often shaped by disconnections from conventional institutions, such as school, work, and families, further increases the likelihood of criminal behavior.
4. Homelessness is also a frequent complication in the lives of women involved in the criminal justice system. Homeless women are far more likely than their male counterparts to have young children in their care and to be more dependent on public assistance and crime if necessary.
5. Criminal involvement of female offenders often comes about through relationships with family members and significant others. For example, women are often first introduced to drugs by partners who frequently continue to be their

EXHIBIT 3.9 Critical Reaction Theory, Theorists, and Principles

Theory	The term *critical* refers to several ideas: (1) that knowledge is not neutral; (2) that science is influenced by values of the scientist and the scientific community; (3) that the goal of research should be a more just and democratic society; and (4) that crime is a result of the way society is organized.
Theorists	Turk, Chambliss, and Seidman (conflict) Marx (Marxist) Adler (feminist—liberation) Hagan (feminist—power control) Bloom, Owen and Covington (feminist—pathways)
Principles	Conflict views law as a social-control mechanism that reflects the values and interests of the dominant group. Crime is inevitable when certain groups become marginalized and unequal. Marxism argues that conflict occurs between those who own the material forces of production and the wage laborers who produce the goods when the working class becomes aware of its position in society and realizes that the structure of society is not in its best interest. Liberation hypothesis argues that the unintended consequence of the women's movement is a greater involvement of women in criminal activity. Power-control argues that socialization within the family controls girls more than boys. Socialization teaches boys to be risk-takers and girls to be risk-averse. Pathways to crime argues that women's victimization is a risk factor contributing to their criminal involvement.

suppliers. Women's attempts to get off drugs, and their failure to supply partners with drugs through prostitution, often elicit violence from the partners; however, many women remain attached to partners despite neglect and abuse.

Many view the pathways perspective as a promising way to develop gender-responsive principles, policy, and practice in the criminal justice system. However, the pathways perspective is a newcomer in criminological theory, and as such, its ideas remains relatively untested. Still, supporters argue that we know enough about women's abuse, early family life, children, street life, and marginality that the right thing to do is respond to these problems, even if doing so doesn't reduce their criminality. Exhibit 3.9 summarizes critical theory and its representative theorists and principles.

We now turn our attention to the policy implications of these five sociological explanations of crime.

Policy Implications

"Easier said than done" describes the dilemma we face in suggesting new criminal justice policy and practices that reflect the sociological perspectives just described. Changes in the social structure of the United States, the socialization of children, parenting skills, the stigma of negative labeling, the balance of power and privilege, and the pathways that lead women into crime will neither happen overnight nor everywhere at the same time. However, all social institutions do change. Prison as punishment was unheard of until the Philadelphia Quakers advocated for its development at the end of the 18th century. Probation and parole didn't exist until reformers in the middle of the 19th century struggled for their acceptance. Proposing to detain offenders at home with remote-control monitoring would have ended a politician's career only a decade ago. But as a result of the global economic crisis in the first decade of the 21st century, governors and legislatures across the country are discussing such recommendations and openly advocating for community-based corrections, in part because they are cheaper than prison.

Thus, while some policy implications to reduce crime may not be realistic in the present day—for example, full employment and well-organized local communities that are invested in conventional society—others are more doable, such as teaching parents and child caregivers the requirements of early childhood socialization. What follows is a summary of policy implications that flow from each of the sociological approaches discussed.

To begin, anomie is a macro-level theory. As it relates to criminology, it highlights the idea that structured inequality leads to crime. Because the theory focuses on social structure, social processes, social problems, and their interrelationships, the policy implications for reducing crime are aimed at modifying the social structure. Thus, one focus would be the equitable distribution of means to reach goals and the reduction of strain that comes of over-promoting unrealistic goals or expectations. Other recommendations are to provide increased job opportunities, work programs, and educational opportunities, and to decrease school dropout rates.

In contrast, social disorganization theory suggests focusing on high-crime neighborhoods and creating community organizations that integrate those high-crime neighborhoods with wider social, political, and economic networks and resources. The theory includes targeting "hot spots" in the community that have frequent criminal activity; stopping neighborhood decay by cleaning up trash and graffiti; increasing adult and youth social relationships through organized activities; and creating mixed-use areas of housing, shopping, and entertainment.

Next, social learning theory asserts that people learn to commit crime as a result of exposure to others' criminal behaviors and ideas that are favorable to violating the law. To prevent crime in the first place, then, children must be kept away from bad influences, and communities, media, and schools can show why following the law is important. If such efforts do not succeed and individuals are too dangerous to others, segregation into various levels of incarceration remains an option.

When people "neutralize" their criminal action with excuses and justifications, the policy implication is to help them see how people are harmed so that they can accept responsibility for their actions. Ethics education starting in elementary school, cognitive restructuring, and the practice of restorative justice are strategies to offset techniques of neutralization.

The policy implications of social- and self-control theories are similar to those of social learning theory. Social control proposes placing restraints on behavior grounded in problems of attachment, involvement and commitment. Self-control theory focuses on improving early-childhood parenting practices.

Examples of social control policy at work can be seen in programs where conventional values are taught, such as recreation and sports programs, academic programs, faith-based programs, Big Brothers/Big Sisters, and YMCA and YWCA. Each of these programs stresses the value of the "American way," meaning engagement in legitimate activity, commitment to an economic system, and belief in the law. They also keep children busy, based on the principle that the more activities children are engaged in, and the more they are involved in conventional activities, the less time they have for delinquency activity.

Self-control policies, on the other hand, focus on enhancing that trait in children eight years of age and younger, based on the principle that only policies that take effect early in life and that have a positive impact on families have a chance of reducing crime and delinquency. Relevant programs work to prevent pregnancy among unmarried adolescent girls and to teach skills to reduce conflict through settlement and negotiation, reduce abuse and neglect, and promote positive parent-child interaction, including effective discipline strategies.

Social reaction theory posits that people become delinquent or criminal as a result of negative labeling by society's informal and formal agents of social control such as family, school, and the criminal justice system. Social reaction theorists argue that our identities change as a result of interactions with others and based on how others see us. Thus, the overarching social reaction policy focus is to prevent labeling by encouraging greater tolerance from informal agents of social control, such as the family, and limiting progression through formal systems of social control. Some of the social reaction policies we've seen develop over the past few decades are decriminalization of victimless crimes, such as prostitution, alcoholism, homosexuality, gambling, and the sale, possession and use of marijuana; diversion programs to avoid negative labeling; community-based programming in lieu of incarceration; decarceration of prison populations that are nonviolent; and victim-offender interaction and reintegrative labeling based on the principles of restorative justice.

Policy implications of critical theory conclude this chapter. Conflict theory focuses on group interests—for example, those based on class, race, ethnicity, and gender—and views law as a set of rules enforced by the powerful to maintain their economic, political, and social positions. As such, conflict theory has contributed to a concern with equality in the criminal justice sentencing. Austin Turk identified 11 concrete measures to reduce crime, of which at least five (proposals 5 through 10) relate to community-based corrections:[41]

1. establish a public information resource center on crime and justice to organize research favoring structural transformation
2. establish gun control nationwide
3. abolish capital punishment
4. indefinitely incarcerate heinous violent offenders
5. stop building prisons
6. create part-time community service jobs for all young people
7. decriminalize drug possession and use
8. decriminalize all consensual sexual activities
9. decriminalize all forms of recreational gambling
10. declare a moratorium on all mandatory sentencing
11. establish community policing and community development

Other policy proposals include reforming the bail system to provide equal justice to arrested individuals, abolishing mandatory sentences, prosecuting corporate crimes, reducing prison overcrowding, and developing more informal arbitration and mediation courts to keep people out of the criminal justice system. The latter policy, referred to as diversion, is a major community-based corrections alternative and is discussed extensively in Chapter 5.

Moving now to Marxist theory, the second critical approach we discussed, its policy implications are clear and controversial: if social structure is the cause of class conflict, the only solution is to change the social structure and remove or considerably reduce economic inequality in society. Marxist theory does not focus on criminal justice per se because the criminal justice system cannot alter fundamental economic inequalities and social structure. Marx believed that the working class would eventually recognize their plight and revolt. Whether the vision of a capitalist society such as that in the United States moving toward true economic equality is strictly utopian remains to be seen. What we wish to point out is that Marxist theory focuses on forces external to the individual as causes of crime in the same way that other positivist theorists do.

Still, some contemporary Marxist criminologists take a more limited approach, focusing on how the criminal justice system can respond to the causes of crime and reduce the economic marginality, social alienation, and political oppression of the lower and working classes. As such, they favor decentralized community-based alliances, similar to those discussed in Chapter 1, namely community policing, community-based prosecution, community-based defender services, community courts, and community-based corrections. Other policy recommendations include equal justice in the bail system, more prosecution of corporate offenders, less use of prison, more use of community-based alternatives, regulating (as opposed to criminalizing) victimless crimes, and addressing the major health, housing, and educational needs of inner-city residents as long-term solutions to dealing with drug problems. Other Marxist criminologists, however, believe that these kinds of social action and reform are futile because they do nothing about the underlying problems of a capitalist society.

Finally, we turn to the contribution and policy implication of feminist theory, which focus on gender inequalities and how they should be addressed. Many of the policy changes that flow from gender-based theories are not directly focused on crime. Instead, they build on the principle that eliminating male domination would result in improved conditions for everyone, and that crime would lessen as a byproduct of those improvements. Feminist theory leads to policies that would end gender discrimination with laws that ban sexual harassment, stalking, and date rape. Additional policies would support the reporting of violence against women at home and at work and an increased role for women in all spheres of life, including as criminal justice professionals. Finally, to quote University of Houston researchers Frank Williams and Marilyn McShane, "[P]erhaps as important as any of the programmatic efforts, the victims' rights movement reflects many gender concerns and is the most extensive policy direction in criminal justice."[42] Exhibit 3.10 summarizes the policy implications of the sociological school.

In conclusion, at the beginning of the 20th century, criminological theory was limited to the ideas set forth by Beccaria and Lombroso. As the century progressed and science, technology, and education advanced, the number and diversity of theories proliferated, as this chapter has shown.

What causes crime? We leave that for you to decide. What we hope is that reading about these theories has given you a better understanding of the complexity of

EXHIBIT 3.10 Policy Implications of the Sociological School

Sociological Approach	Policy Implications
Anomie	Modify the social structure. Equitably distribute the institutionalized means to reach cultural goals and reduce strain by not over-promoting goals or raising people's expectations beyond their capabilities. Provide increased job opportunities, work programs, and educational opportunities, and decrease school dropout rates.
Social disorganization	Focus on high-crime neighborhoods rather than the people. Create community organizations and integrate those informal organizations with wider social, political, and economic networks and resources. Target "hot spots" with frequent criminal activity; clean up trash and graffiti; increase adult and youth social relationships through organized activities; and create mixed-use areas of housing, shopping, and entertainment.
Social control and self-control	Social control focuses on policies grounded in increasing attachment, involvement, and commitment via such programs as recreation and sports, academic, faith-based, Big Brothers/Big Sisters, and YMCA and YWCA. Self-control focuses on early childhood parenting practices, pregnancy prevention among unmarried adolescent girls, and early intervention programs that teach skills to reduce conflict through settlement and negotiation, reduce abuse and neglect, promote positive parent-child interaction, and teach effective discipline strategies.
Social reaction	Prevent labeling by encouraging greater tolerance from informal agents of social control (family) and limiting progression through formal systems of social control. Policies for achieving these goals include decriminalization of victimless crimes; diversion programs; community-based programming in lieu of incarceration; decarceration; victim-offender interaction; and reintegrative labeling.
Critical (conflict, Marxist, and feminist)	Conflict recommendations include reforming the bail system to provide equal justice to arrested individuals, abolishing mandatory sentences, prosecuting corporate crimes, reducing prison overcrowding, and developing more diversion programs to keep people out of the criminal justice system. Large-scale Marxist recommendations are to change the social structure and remove or considerably reduce economic inequality in society. Limited Marxist approaches favor community policing, community-based prosecution, community-based defender services, community courts, and community-based corrections. Feminist theory favors eliminating male domination, ending gender discrimination, enhancing systems for reporting violence against women at home and at work, expanding the roles of women in all spheres of life, and furthering the victims' rights movement.

responding to crime. As you can see, we have no quick fixes, no easy answers. If the answers were easy and simple, crime would have been solved a long time ago.

Our goal has been to introduce you to the field of criminological theory and to stimulate your interest in using theory to advance community-based corrections. As criminologists become more sophisticated in their thinking, and as the tools of research develop, crime policies will address causes and solutions heretofore unknown. Think how far we've come in our understanding of crime since the days of Beccaria and Lombroso.

SUMMARY

The classical school of criminology is a broad label for a group of thinkers in the 18th and early 19th centuries who rebelled against the spiritual explanations for crime that formed the criminal justice policies in most of Europe. Its most prominent writer and founder was Cesare Beccaria. Beccaria opposed the arbitrary and capricious nature of the criminal justice system of the time. He proposed that law and the administration of justice be based on rationality and human rights, neither of which was then commonly applied. He argued for a system of criminal justice based on the legal definitions of crime rather than on a concern with criminal behavior. The objective of the penal system, he argued, should be to devise penalties only severe enough to achieve the proper purposes of security and order. He also argued that the effectiveness of criminal justice depends largely on the certainty of punishment rather than on its severity. Penalties should be scaled to the importance of the offense. Contemporary policies grounded in the classical school include "three strikes and you're out" and mandatory sentencing.

In contrast to the classical and psychological approaches that focus on the crime and characteristics of the individual, respectively, the sociological approach shifts the discussion to external forces affecting individual behavior.

The biological school of criminology and its founder, Cesare Lombroso, believed that criminals were born. The biological approach was later refined to examine physical appearance (body type); family patterns, including twin and adoption studies; neurotransmitters; hormones; the central and the autonomic nervous systems; and environmentally induced biological components of behavior. The crime control policy that grows out of the biological school follows the medical model, which involves identification, prevention, and treatment. Treatment might include surgery or drugs, incapacitation, eugenics for those who are untreatable, genetic counseling, and environmental manipulation.

Sigmund Freud first studied the role of the unconscious mind in shaping behavior and thus began psychology as an academic discipline and the technique of psychoanalytic therapy. Intelligence testing and personality traits have also been advanced as psychological roadmaps to understanding criminal behavior. However, research has found little to no difference in intelligence and personality between criminals and noncriminals. Intelligence and personality differences may simply reflect differences in situations and circumstances of offenders' lives, rather than any innate tendency toward crime. One psychological approach that garners support among criminologists is the relationship between impulsivity (acting without thinking) and crime. Overall, the policy implications from a psychological perspective are to correct and control personality traits and mental processes through therapeutic intervention. Offenders sentenced to probation, intermediate sanctions, and parole are often required to attend treatment sessions as a condition of their freedom in the community.

Of the sociological approaches, social disorganization theorists argue that persons become criminal when they are isolated from the mainstream culture and are immersed in their own impoverished and dilapidated neighborhoods, which have their own sets of norms and values. This isolation often results in anomie, a breakdown of social norms and a condition in which those norms no longer control an individual's or group's activities. Because the focus here is on social structure, social processes, social problems, and their interrelationships, the policy recommendation is to modify the social structure beginning with the equitable distribution of institutionalized means to reach cultural goals and the reduction of strain. Other recommendations are to increase job and educational opportunities, to decrease school dropout rates, and to target efforts on "hot spots." The approach also proposes that we create community organizations and integrate those informal organizations with wider social, political, and economic networks and resources.

Two important social-learning theories are (1) differential association and (2) neutralization. Differential association posits that criminal behavior is based on the interactions and communications we have with others and the values we learn from others during those interactions. Neutralization refers to the words and phrases offenders use to justify or excuse their lawbreaking behavior. To prevent crime, policy that grows out of social learning theory focuses on keeping children away from bad influences and publicly and frequently showing them why they need to obey the law. The policy implication of neutralization is to identify how people are harmed and communicate this to offenders so that they will accept responsibility for their actions. Ethics education starting in elementary school, cognitive restructuring, and the practice of restorative justice are strategies to offset offenders' patterns of neutralization.

Social control and self-control theories ask why people obey rules instead of breaking them. External social controls, the theory goes, are formed through attachment, commitment, involvement and belief. Internal self-controls are a product of child-rearing practices and are formed by the age of eight.

Social reaction theory, also referred to as labeling, focuses on the official reaction to crime. The idea here is that people become delinquent or criminal as a result of negative labeling by society's informal and formal agents of social control such as family, school, and the criminal justice system. Individuals come to view themselves as criminal and act in accord with this self-concept. The policy implication is to prevent labeling by encouraging greater tolerance from both informal and formal systems of social control.

Critical theory focuses on conflict, and includes both Marxist and feminist approaches. Conflict criminology theorists view law as a social-control mechanism that reflects the values and interests of the dominant group. Moreover, they view crime as inevitable in capitalist societies because certain groups will become marginalized and unequal. Marxist theory proposes that conflict in society is due to a scarcity of resources and inequality in the distribution of those resources. The inequality produces conflict between those with power and those without; for example, destruction of property and violence during the Great Depression.

Feminist liberation theorists argue that the women's movement brought about changes in traditional sex roles, greater equality for women, and an increase of women in the labor force. Power-control theorists argue that socialization within the family focuses greater control on girls than boys. Pathways theory argues that we know enough about women's abuse, the impact on children of early family life, street life, and the impact of marginality that the right thing to do is respond to these problems. Policy-wise these approaches advocate elimination of male domination and gender discrimination, intervention in the pathways that lead women into crime, and development of the victims' rights movement.

Key Terms

anomie, p. 69
atavistic, p. 62
biological school of criminology, p. 62
classical school of criminology, p. 58
cognitive restructuring, p. 68
conflict theory, p. 77
critical theory, p. 76
differential association theory, p. 72
differential reinforcement theory, p. 72
feminist theory, p. 79
liberation hypothesis, p. 79
Marxist theory, p. 78
neoclassical school of criminology, p. 59
neutralization theory, p. 72
pathways to crime theory, p. 80
positivist school of criminology, p. 58
power-control theory, p. 80
psychological school of criminology, p. 64
rational choice theory, p. 60
reintegrative shaming, p. 76
routine activities theory, p. 60
self-control theory, p. 74
social contract philosophy, p. 59
social control theory, p. 73
social disorganization theory, p. 69
social learning theory, p. 72
social reaction/labeling theory p. 75
sociological school of criminology, p. 69

Questions for Review

1. What is the classical school of criminology, and what crime control policies does it propose?
2. How does the positivist school of criminology differ from the classical school of criminology?
3. What is the biological school of criminology, and what crime control policies does it propose?
4. What is the psychological school of criminology, and what crime control policies does it propose?
5. How do anomie and social disorganization theories explain crime, and what crime control policies do they propose?
6. What does social learning theory say about crime causation, and what crime control policies does it propose?
7. How do social control and self-control theories explain crime, and what crime control policies do they propose?
8. What is the social-reaction explanation of crime, and what crime control policies does it propose?
9. How does critical criminology explain crime, and what crime control policies does it propose?

Question of Policy

Public Policy on Gender Responsive Programs

On January 29, 2006, the International Community Corrections Association (ICCA) Board of Directors adopted its Public Policy on Gender Responsive Programs. The policy can be found at the ICCA Web site (http://iccaweb.org/public.html). How does the policy relate to ideas discussed in this chapter?

What Would You Do?

The mother of one of your students is the chief circuit judge in your state. She sees the criminological theory book her daughter is reading for your class. She contacts you and asks if you would speak to the next meeting of the circuit court judges. She explains that some judges are "old school" and believe that persons commit crime because they choose to do so. Other judges believe that persons commit crime because of influences external to them. The chief circuit judge tells you that she believes in the value of community-based corrections and would like you to address how community-based corrections can satisfy the "old school" judges and those who believe crime causation is external to the individual. What would you do?

Endnotes

1. Patsy Klaus, *Crime and the Nation's Households, 2005* (Washington, DC: U.S. Department of Justice, Bureau of Justice Statistics, April 2007), p. 2.
2. Shelby Grad, "Sean Penn Sentenced to Probation for Incident With Photographer," *Los Angeles Times*, May 12, 2010, http://articles.latimes.com (accessed October 28, 2010).
3. Laura Fishman, "Actor Sean Penn Sentenced for Vandalism, Avoids Battery Conviction," *The Los Angeles Criminal Law Blog*, May 13, 2010, http://losangelescriminallegalblog.com (accessed October 28, 2010).
4. Mark M. Lanier and Stuart Henry, *Essential Criminology,* 3rd ed. (Boulder, CO: Westview Press, 2010), pp. 111–112.
5. William H. Sheldon, Emil H. Hastl, and Eugene McDermott, *Varieties of Delinquent Youth* (New York: Harper, 1949) and Sheldon Glueck and Eleanor Glueck, *Unraveling Juvenile Delinquency* (New York: Commonwealth Fund, 1950).
6. Charles Goring, *The English Convict: A Statistical Study* (Montclair, NJ: Patterson Smith, [[1913]], 1972).
7. Karl O. Christiansen, "A Preliminary Study of Criminality Among Twins," in Sarnoff Mednick and Karl O. Christiansen (eds.), *Biological Basis of Criminal Behavior* (New York: Gardner, 1977), pp. 45–88.
8. Adrian Raine and Angela Scerbo, "Neurotransmitters and Antisocial Behavior: A Meta-Analysis," reported in Adrian Raine, *The Psychopathology of Crime* (San Diego, CA: Academic Press, 1993), p. 87.
9. Adrian Raine, *The Psychopathology of Crime,* pp. 81–102.
10. Adrian Raine, *The Psychopathology of Crime*, pp. 103–127.
11. Sarnoff Mednick, "A Biosocial Theory of the Learning of Law-Abiding Behavior," in Mednick and Christiansen (eds.), *Biological Basis of Criminal Behavior*, pp. 1–8.
12. Alfred S. Friedman, "Substance Use/Abuse as a Predictor to Illegal and Violent Behavior: A Review of the Relevant Literature," *Aggression and Violent Behavior*, vol. 34, no. 4 (1998), pp. 339–355.
13. Robin B. Kanarek, "Nutrition and Violent Behavior," in Albert Reiss, Klaus Miczek and Jeffrey Roth (eds.), *Understanding and Preventing Violence, Volume 2* (Washington, DC: National Academy Press, 1994), pp. 515–539.
14. Mednick and Christiansen (eds.), "Biology and Violence," in *Biological Basis of Criminal Behavior*, pp. 52–58.
15. Elizabeth Kandel and Sarnoff A. Mednick, "Perinatal Complications Predict Violent Offending," *Criminology*, vol. 29, no. 3 (August 1991), pp. 519–529.
16. Adrian Raine, Patricia Brennan, and Sarnoff A. Mednick, "Interaction Between Birth Complications and Early Maternal Rejection

in Predisposing Individuals to Adult Violence: Specificity to Serious, Early-Onset Violence," *American Journal of Psychiatry*, vol. 159, no. 4 (September 1997), pp. 1265–1271.

17. Henry H. Goddard, *Feeblemindedness: Its Causes and Consequences* (New York: Macmillan, [[1914]], reprinted by Arno, 1972).
18. Sheldon Glueck and Eleanor Glueck, *Unraveling Juvenile Delinquency* (New York: Coommonwealth Fund, 1950), p. 275.
19. Hervey Cleckley, *The Mask of Sanity*, (St. Louis, MO: Mosby, 1976), p. 263.
20. Avshalom Caspi, Terrie E. Moffitt, Phil A. Silva, Magda Stouthamer-Loeber, Robert F. Krueger, and Pamela S. Schmutte, "Are Some People Crime-Prone?" *Criminology*, vol. 32, no. 2 (1994), pp. 163–195.
21. George B. Vold, Thomas J. Bernard, and Jeffrey B. Snipes, *Theoretical Criminology*, 5th ed. (New York: Oxford, 2002).
22. Glenn D. Walters, *The Criminal Lifestyle: Patterns of Serious Criminal Conduct* (Newbury Park, CA: Sage, 1990).
23. Glenn D. Walters, "Short-Term Outcomes of Inmates Participating in Lifestyle Change Program," *Criminal Justice and Behavior*, vol. 26, no. 3 (1999), pp. 322–337.
24. Terrie E. Moffitt, "Life-Course-Persistent and Adolescent-Limited Antisocial Behavior," *Psychological Review*, vol. 100 (1993), pp. 674–701.
25. Vold, Bernard, and Snipes, p. 81.
26. Travis Hirschi, *Causes of Delinquency* (Berkeley, CA: University of California Press, 1969), p. 16.
27. Ibid., 21.
28. Travis Hirschi and Michael R. Gottfredson, "Social Control and Self-Control Theory," in Stuart Henry and Mark M. Lanier (eds.), *The Essential Criminology Reader* (Boulder, CO: Westview Press, 2006), p. 114.
29. __________ , "Self-Control Theory" in Raymond Paternoster and Ronet Bachman (eds.), *Explaining Criminals and Crime* (Los Angeles: Roxbury Press, 2001), p. 82.
30. Ibid., 82.
31. Howard Becker, *Outsiders: Studies in the Sociology of Deviance* (New York: Free Press, 1963), p. 8.
32. John Braithwaite, *Crime, Shame and Reintegration* (Cambridge, UK: Cambridge University Press, 1989), pp. 100–101.
33. Austin Turk, *Criminality and Legal Order* (Chicago: Rand McNally, 1969), p. vii.
34. William J. Chambliss and Robert B. Seidman, *Law, Order, and Power* (Reading, MA: Addison-Wesley, 1971).
35. Ibid., 503.
36. Kathleen Daly and Meda Chesney-Lind, "Feminism and Criminology," *Justice Quarterly*, vol. 5, no. 4 (1988), pp. 497–538.
37. Freda Adler, *Sisters in Crime: The Rise of the New Female Criminal* (New York: McGraw-Hill, 1975), pp. 13–14.
38. John Hagan, *Structural Criminology* (New Brunswick, NJ: Rutgers University Press, 1989), p. 158.
39. Merry Morash and Meda Chesney-Lind, "A Reformulation and Partial Test of the Power Control Theory of Delinquency," *Justice Quarterly*, vol. 8, no. 3 (1991), pp. 347–378.
40. Barbara Bloom, Barbara Owen and Stephanie Covington, *Gender Responsive Strategies: Research, Practice and Guiding Principles for Women Offenders* (Washington, DC: U.S. Department of Justice, National Institute of Corrections, June 2003).
41. Austin T. Turk, "Transformation versus Revolutionalism and Reformism: Policy Implications of Conflict Theory," in High Barlow (ed.), *Crime and Public Policy* (Boulder, CO: Westview Press, 1995), pp. 15–27.
42. Frank P. Williams III and Marilyn D. McShane, *Criminological Theory,* 4th ed. (Upper Saddle River, NJ: Pearson, 2004), p. 264.

CHAPTER 4

Assessing the Risk: The Importance of Classification

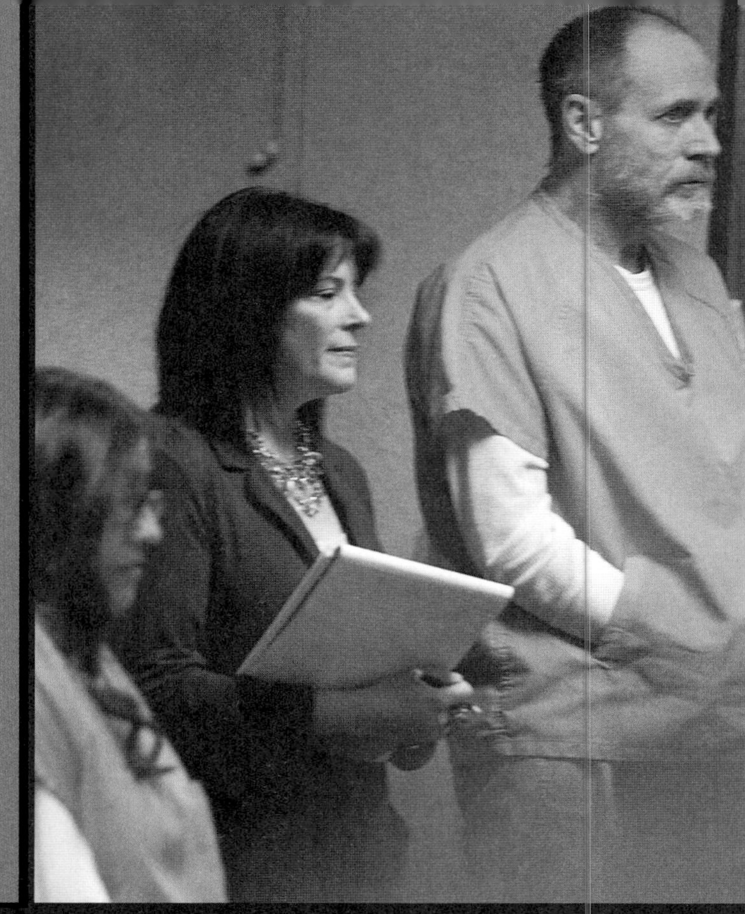

OBJECTIVES

1. Explain classification and the risk-need-responsivity principle.
2. Outline the five eras in the historical development of risk and needs assessment.
3. Name the five stages of criminal justice processing in which risk and needs assessments are conducted.
4. Explain who special-needs offenders are and what corrections agencies are doing to assess their risk and needs.
5. Project what classification and risk/needs assessment might be like in the future.
6. Express sound principles for classification and risk/needs assessment.

OUTLINE

In August 2009, Phillip Craig Garrido and his wife, Nancy, were arrested and charged with the 1991 kidnapping and sexual assault of then 11-year-old Jaycee Lee Dugard. In the 18 years following the kidnapping, Garrido reportedly held Jaycee captive on the grounds of his residence in Antioch, California, sexually assaulting her and fathering her two children. When he was arrested, Garrido had been under parole supervision in California since 1999. According to the investigation of his case, Garrido had at least six parole agents over a decade but was barely supervised.[1]

On November 4, 2009, the California Office of the Inspector General issued a report saying that errors by the California Department of Corrections and Rehabilitation contributed to Dugard's continued captivity.[2] *The report said that Garrido had been incorrectly classified as needing only low-level sex offender supervision and that all other errors were derived from that classification. In his report, the Inspector General described an instance in which a parole agent encountered a 12-year-old girl at Garrido's home, but accepted Garrido's explanation that she was his brother's daughter, so the agent did nothing to verify it.*

The Inspector General said further that the assessment of Garrido as a low-risk sex offender came as a result of (1) sparse information from federal parole officials and (2) state corrections agents' failure to research Garrido's background on their own.

Specifically, during the 10-year period that the California Department of Corrections and Rehabilitation (CDCR) supervised parolee Garrido, the CDCR failed in the following ways:[3]

- It did not adequately classify and supervise Garrido.
- It did not obtain key information from federal parole authorities.
- It did not properly supervise parole agents responsible for Garrido.
- It ignored other opportunities to determine that Garrido was violating the terms of his parole.
- It did not refer Garrido for mental health assessment.
- It did not train parole agents to conduct parolee home visits.
- It missed at least four opportunities to discover the existence of Garrido's three victims by investigating the following:
    - clearly visible utility wires running from Garrido's house toward the concealed compound
    - the presence of a 12-year-old female during a home visit
    - feedback from neighbors or local public safety agencies
    - information clearly demonstrating that Garrido had violated his parole terms

The Inspector General pointed out that if Garrido had been properly classified as a high-risk sex offender from the beginning, he would have been dealing with more seasoned parole agents who would have had half the caseload of agents supervising low-risk offenders. As a result of all these failures and oversights, corrections officials are instituting a field training program to pair veteran parole agents with rookies, and they are restructuring the parole academy to better train agents in classifying sex offenders and spotting deception.

In July 2010, the California legislature approved a payment of $20 million to Jaycee Lee Dugard's family. The settlement will be used to provide therapy for Dugard and her daughters, ages 12 and 15, and go toward their education. Dugard's daughters have never been to school. The settlement will provide an income for the family for the rest of their lives, and Dugard will use part of the settlement to establish a foundation to help others in situations like hers.

What happened to Jaycee Lee Dugard is tragic. It demonstrates what can go horribly wrong if an offender's risk and needs are not properly assessed and if that assessment is not linked with case decisions and management.

This chapter and sections of Chapter 5 introduce you to the role and importance of classification and its connection to risk and needs assessment in community-based corrections. We begin by explaining the concepts, then introduce you to the history of classification as well as the stages of risk and needs development. We follow that with a discussion of where in the criminal justice process risk and needs assessments are conducted. We also investigate the specialized instruments that agencies use to assess the risk and special needs of offenders like Garrido, and conclude the chapter with a question about the future and policy implications of classification and risk assessment.

Classification and Risk Assessment

On a daily basis, community corrections officials make decisions on sentencing recommendations, supervision levels, treatment interventions, violations for non-compliance with orders and conditions of the court, and multiple other areas that affect public safety. Risk assessment methods enhance decision-making by ensuring that factors empirically proven to predict risk are considered in a systematic manner. What these methods are and how they relate to an offender's classification is the subject of this chapter. We begin by explaining the important concepts of classification, risk assessment, and risk and needs.

Classification

The cornerstone of effective community-based corrections is **classification**, a process of separating offenders into discrete groups in such a way that offenders in the same group are similar or close to each other on certain common characteristics in order to effectively supervise and manage them. Classification is important because (1) it enables authorities to make decisions about appropriate offender program placements, (2) it helps to identify an offender's needs and specific treatment interventions, and (3) the accurate placement of offenders into appropriate supervision and treatment strategies is crucial if resources are not to be wasted and unintended harm inflicted on offenders.

Risk Assessment

Risk assessment is the process whereby offenders are assessed on several key variables empirically known to increase the likelihood of committing an offense. The purpose of risk assessment is to predict future crime and manage offender risk throughout the course of the criminal justice process. But how do we distinguish a high-risk offender from a low-risk one and intervene effectively? The approach is called the **risk-need-responsivity model (RNR).**[4] The model is based on the theory of general personality and cognitive learning, which refers to how one learns and processes thoughts.

The risk-need-responsivity model has been used with increasing success to assess and rehabilitate criminals. It is based on these three principles:

1. The **risk principle** focuses on who should be treated. It asserts that criminal behavior can be reliably predicted and that treatment should focus on the higher-risk offenders. This is because higher-risk cases tend to respond better to intensive and extensive service, while low-risk cases respond better to minimal or no intervention.
2. The **need principle** focuses on which behavior patterns should be treated. It highlights the importance of criminogenic needs in the design and delivery of treatment. Criminogenic needs are attributes of offenders that are strongly correlated with risk of recidivism, such as who an offender associates with and whether an offender uses substances.
3. The **responsivity principle** is perhaps the most important of the three. It has been a largely neglected area of study, despite the fact that offender responsivity and other variables related to offender motivation are widely recognized as critical to the success of treatment. The principle states that styles and modes of treatment service must be closely matched to the preferred learning style, motivation, and abilities of the offender. Treatment readiness and offender motivation or responsivity must be assessed and considered in treatment planning if the maximum effectiveness of supervision and treatment programs is to be realized and if we want to ensure the successful reintegration of the offender into the community. Offenders differ significantly, not only in their levels of motivation to participate in treatment, but also in terms of their responsivity to various styles or modes of intervention.

   According to the responsivity principle, these factors impact directly on the effectiveness of correctional treatment and ultimately on recidivism. Individual factors that interfere with or facilitate learning can be considered responsivity factors. Therefore, the assessment of responsivity-related variables is the first step in determining how best to address an offender's criminogenic needs. This, in turn, can ensure that offenders derive the maximum therapeutic benefit from

> treatment. Therefore, prior to targeting criminogenic needs, it is important that responsivity factors be examined to prepare the offender for treatment.
>
> If the responsivity principle is not adhered to, treatment programs can fail, not because they do not have therapeutic integrity or competent therapists, but because other offender-related barriers, such as cognitive/intellectual deficits, were not addressed, preventing the offender from understanding the content of the program. Thus, the three components of responsivity include the following: matching the treatment approach with the learning style of the offender; matching the characteristics of the offender with those of the counselor; and matching the skills of the counselor with the type of program they conduct.

Evidence-based research has shown that if all three principles are considered, recidivism can be reduced by up to 35 percent. If none of the principles is considered, treatment will have little, and often negative, effect on recidivism.[5]

Risk and Needs

In the context of community-based corrections, risk and need refer to an offender's criminogenic needs and the potential they have for prompting her or him to reoffend. Assessing an offender to determine his or her risk and needs is an important tool in promoting public safety. Such assessments can help a community-based corrections agency focus its resources on offenders who most need control and supervision. The goal of allocating staff and other resources effectively is a central reason for assessing offenders' risk/needs.

Risk/needs factors can be classified as either "static" or "dynamic." Static risk factors are unchanging. For example, age at first arrest, history of violent felony convictions,

The cornerstone of effective community-based corrections is classification. Evidence-based research has shown that if the risk-need-responsivity principles are followed, recidivism can be reduced by up to 35 percent. Which principle is perhaps the most important and why?

and severity of the current crime are static risk factors that often appear in risk assessment measures. We might mention here that "crime severity" is not as static as some might believe. We can probably agree that some crimes such as murder and rape are severe. However, corrections officers often evaluate the severity of theft, degrees of robbery, drug violations, and dozens of other crimes more subjectively. Subjective scoring can skew workload imbalances and the distribution of agency resources, as we will point out later.

Dynamic risk/need factors are items associated with future behavior and can change over time. For example, one can lose and find a job, or start or stop abusing drugs. Andrews and Bonta, Canadian psychologists and leading researchers in the field of risk assessment, identified seven major risk/need factors that should be assessed when considering treatment to reduce offending behavior:[6]

1. Antisocial personality pattern
2. Pro-criminal attitudes
3. Social support for crime
4. Substance abuse
5. Family/marital relationships
6. School/work
7. Absence of pro-social recreational activities

Identifying an offender's criminogenic needs makes it possible to provide appropriate treatment, programs, and support to improve his or her chances for success and to reduce the likelihood of reoffending. Exhibit 4.1 lists the seven major risk/needs

EXHIBIT 4.1 Risk/Need Items, Behavioral Indicators, and Treatment Goals

Risk/Need Items	Behavioral Indicators	Treatment Goals
Antisocial personality pattern	Impulsive, adventurous, pleasure seeking, restlessly aggressive and irritable	Build self-management skills, teach anger management
Pro-criminal attitudes	Rationalizations for crime, negative attitudes toward the law	Counter rationalizations with pro-social attitudes; build up a pro-social identity
Social supports for crime	Criminal friends, isolation from pro-social others	Replace pro-criminal friends and associates with pro-social friends and associates
Substance abuse	Abuse of alcohol and/or drugs	Reduce substance abuse, enhance alternatives to substance use
Family/marital relationships	Inappropriate parental monitoring and disciplining, poor family relationships	Teach parenting skills, enhance warmth and caring
School/work	Poor performance, low levels of satisfaction	Enhance work/study skills, nurture interpersonal relationships within the context of work and school
Pro-social recreational activities	Lack of involvement in pro-social recreational/leisure activities	Encourage participation in pro-social recreational activities, teach pro-social hobbies and sports

Source: James Bonta and D.A. Andrews, *Risk-Need-Responsivity Model for Offender Assessment and Rehabilitation, 2006-07* (Canada: Her Majesty the Queen in Right of Canada, 2007).

EVIDENCE-BASED PRACTICES IN COMMUNITY CORRECTIONS

The goal of North Carolina's Division of Community Corrections is to use practices that have been empirically tested and shown to reduce recidivism among offenders. The division's Web site lists eight principles of evidence-based practices that should be followed in order to reach the agency's overall goal of no new crime and no new victims.

After visiting the division's Web site, ask yourself how these eight principles relate to classification and risk/needs assessment.

Visit CBC Online 4.1 at www.mhhe.com/bayens1e

factors, behavioral indicators of each, and suggested treatment goals. CBC Online 4.1 gives insight into one state's approach to classification and risk/needs assessment.

History of Risk and Needs Assessment

The first person to use a scientific approach to predict criminal traits was Cesare Lombroso, a 19th-century Italian physician turned criminologist. Lombroso was famous in the 19th century because he claimed to have discovered the cause of crime. His principal work, *L'Uomodelinquente,* or *The Criminal Man*, was published in 1876. In it he rejected the classical thinking of his day, which held that crime was a trait of human nature and that rational choices were the foundation of behavior. Using detailed anthropometric studies of cadavers (the measurement of physical attributes of deceased human beings, such as head width, length of little finger, and length of torso), Lombroso claimed that the bodies of criminals were physically different from those of normal people. The "born criminal" could be distinguished by physical stigmata (signs) such as abnormal dimensions of the skull and jaw, a sloping forehead, ears of unusual size, asymmetry of the face, prognathism (an extension or bulging out of the lower jaw that occurs when the shape of the face bones cause the teeth to be improperly lined up), excessive length of arms, and asymmetry of the cranium. Lombroso also maintained that criminals had less sensitivity to pain and touch; more acute sight; a lack of moral sense, including an absence of remorse; more vanity, impulsiveness, vindictiveness, and cruelty; and other manifestations, such as a special criminal argot and the excessive use of tattooing.

However, in his measurements of cadavers, Lombroso did not compare criminals with non-criminals. Had he employed adequate control groups he might have altered his general conclusions, as a number of his "physical stigmata" are found equally among criminals and non-criminals.

Even though his ideas are no longer considered valid, he is called the founder of the Positive School of Criminology because he was the first person to use the scientific method to study crime. His theory marks the starting point of the positivist (use of the scientific method) tradition of predicting criminal behavior.

For our purposes we will trace the modern-day history of risk and needs assessment through five stages of development: the professional or clinical assessment era, the actuarial assessment era, the dynamic risk assessment era Phase I, the dynamic risk assessment era Phase II, and the newest era, a user-friendly risk and needs assessment that keeps pace with changes in an offender's life.[7] Our discussion is not technical, nor is it designed to teach you how to use the assessment instruments. Those are responsibilities one learns on the job and outside the scope of this chapter. The discussion here introduces you to the five stages, points out the weaknesses and strengths of each, and raises critical questions about the use of risk and needs assessments.

Note too that as new assessments were introduced, old ways of assessing an offender's risks and needs did not disappear. Rather, new thinking challenged the thinking of previous eras and facilitated the development of new policy, including the shift toward evidence-based community corrections built on theory and professionalism.

Professional or Clinical Assessment Era

For the first half of the 20th century, assessment of risk/needs was a matter of **professional/clinical assessment**. The belief was that as community corrections officers gained knowledge and experience, they developed an intuitive sense, or a "gut" feeling, of what an offender's risks and needs were and what the probability was that he/she might reoffend. Their intuitive sense guided the case plans they developed for offenders and the interventions they believed would protect the public. However, as Harris and others have pointed out, clinical assessment was oftentimes biased and subjective.[8] Too often, community corrections officers missed important information while overemphasizing trivial information. Of all the approaches discussed here, the professional/clinical judgment era is the least accurate risk assessment method. Some have referred to professional/clinical assessment as "no classification system" because it left classification and supervision to the discretion of the supervising officer.[9] Of the 18 percent of U.S. probation and parole agencies nationwide that do not use standardized, objective risk assessment instruments, one-third still believe that "professional opinion is adequate."[10]

Actuarial Assessment Era

The problems of clinical assessment gave rise to the period of **actuarial assessment**, the science of applying mathematical and statistical methods to assess risk. Actuarial assessment first developed in the insurance and finance industries. For example, actuarial risk is used to calculate how much we pay for our vehicle and life insurance policies based on how likely we are to have car accidents and how long we are likely to live.

The first person to use actuarial models in criminal justice on a large scale was University of Chicago sociologist Earnest W. Burgess.[11] Burgess conducted a study of 3,000 Illinois inmates paroled in the four to five years prior to 1924. His goal was to find a statistical relationship between success on parole and some two dozen factors to see which factors were associated with success on parole. Some of Burgess's factors, however, suffered from the same bias and subjectivity of the clinical judgment era. For example, one of Burgess's categories was the parolee's "social type." The inherent flaw of these categories—hobo, ne'er-do-well, mean citizen, drunkard, gangster, recent immigrant, farm boy, and drug addict—is that they were not objectively defined.

Burgess created a 21-factor score sheet to grade each parolee. He assigned points for each factor and then conducted an analysis to determine the percentage of violators who had high scores. Burgess said, "Predictability is feasible. The prediction would not be absolute in any given case, but, according to the law of averages, would apply to any considerable number of cases."[12]

When John Landesco, one of Burgess's research assistants, was appointed to the Illinois Parole Board, he urged the Illinois legislature to pass a bill to hire sociologists and actuaries to "make analyses and predictions in the cases of all men being considered for parole." By 1939, the Illinois parole board was assisted by three sociologists and actuaries. The actuaries compiled the inmate's information and prepared a report that predicted the likelihood of success on parole based on Burgess's probability scale. Even though Burgess's model was primitive insofar as it merely added up the factors to produce a score, it influenced the development of other actuarial models, including the Salient Factor Score (SFS) developed in the 1970s by the United States Parole Commission. The SFS is still used today by the U.S. Parole Commission and by states that have retained the practice of discretionary parole (see Chapter 8). Like Burgess's model, the SFS estimates an inmate's likelihood of recidivating following his or her release from prison.

The SFS focuses on individual offender characteristics (e.g., number of prior convictions as an adult or adjudications as a juvenile) that are known to increase the risk of reoffending. These individual offender characteristics are then assigned numerical values and totaled into one overall score.

Today, the SFS is based on a series of six static factors, each rated on an objective scale. (Recall that static factors are ones that do not change over time and are known to be related to recidivism through empirically validated research.) For example, one SFS item is the number of prior convictions as an adult or the number of adjudications as a juvenile. The offender may receive a score of three if he or she had none, two points if he or she had one, one point if he or she had two or three, and zero points if he or she had four or more. The total score (a range from 0 to 10) is then calculated. The higher the total score, the lower the likelihood of recidivism. The remaining five salient factor items are:

1. Prior commitment of more than 30 days (if none = 2; one or two = 1; three or more = 0)
2. Age at current offense (there are too many subcategories in this factor to list, but the score varies by age and number of prior commitments)
3. Commitment-free period of three years prior to current offense (if none = 1; otherwise = 0)
4. Neither on probation, parole, confinement, or escape status at the time of the current offense nor committed as a probation, parole, confinement, or escape status violator this time (if none = 1; otherwise = 0)
5. If the offender was 41 years of age or more at the commencement of the current offense (and the total score from Items A - E above is 9 or less) = 1; otherwise = 0

Actuarial risk assessment instruments have several advantages. They can reliably distinguish lower-risk from higher-risk offenders, set standards for officer-offender contacts based on an offender's risk level, and distribute workloads appropriately among staff. However, actuarial risk assessment instruments have three major shortcomings. First, they are atheoretical, meaning that the items are not chosen because they are theoretically relevant. Rather, the factors these instruments are based on (e.g., number of prior convictions as an adult) are chosen because they are easily available and show an association with recidivism. Demonstrating an association, however, does not tell us how weak or strong the association is. For example, two offenders with a score of five are not equal in their likelihoods of recidivism. One may have a substance abuse problem that led to his or her crime and have a higher probability of reoffending than the other offender. However, static factors such as the SFS do not account for this. Dynamic factors—those an offender can modify, which are discussed next—give classification specialists more tools for predicting the likelihood of recidivism.

The second shortcoming of actuarial risk assessments is that the items in the instrument are static factors, meaning they focus on past behavior. Once the score is assigned, it cannot record an offender's progress over time even if the offending behavior changes. For example, if an offender scored positive for a history of drug use, that risk factor score is permanent even if the offender has stopped using drugs; hence, once classified, always classified.

And third, actuarial risk assessment instruments are limited in that they do not provide direction for treatment interventions (what we refer to as case planning or case decision-making). Dynamic risk assessments, the next concept we examine, compensate for these three shortcomings, as they better address treatment linkages and case-specific strategies for offender supervision.

Dynamic Risk Assessment Era: Phase I

The **dynamic risk assessment era** is separated into two phases. The phases are similar in that both utilize many of the past factors of static assessment such as criminal history, but they introduce a new ingredient: dynamic criminogenic need items that are linked to general personality theory and the learning of criminal behavior. Recall that dynamic criminogenic needs are factors an offender can modify, such as substance abuse or employment status.

The two phases differ, however, in terms of whether and how much the risk and needs assessment is actually linked to **case planning**, a process of identifying dynamic risk factors requiring intervention, prioritizing placement in programs and treatment, and assembling the supervision team. The early phase did not address the link between assessment and the type, duration, and intensity of intervention. The officer was left guessing about appropriate interventions. The question of case planning is first raised in Phase II but not fully addressed to the satisfaction of users. The result is that case planning continues to be a core issue in the fifth and current era—the user-friendly era discussed later in this chapter.

The first phase of dynamic risk assessment began in the 1970s when Wisconsin introduced its Client Management Classification System (referred to as either "the Wisconsin system" or simply "the CMC"). The CMC was developed by Drs. Gary Arling and Ken Lerner of the Wisconsin Department of Corrections as a method to budget community-based corrections resources.

The CMC identified 10 dynamic and static factors that contribute to an offender's risk:

1. Address changes in past 12 months
2. Employment in past 12 months
3. Alcohol usage
4. Other drug usage
5. Attitude

6. Age at first conviction
7. Number of prior periods of probation/parole supervision
8. Number of prior revocations
9. Number of prior felony convictions
10. Number of convictions for burglary, theft, auto theft, robbery, or worthless checks or forgery

Probationers and parolees complete the CMC instrument. Supervision officers score the factors and determine both the level of supervision the offenders should receive and the types of services they may require. Because it is "dynamic," the CMC system requires offenders to be reevaluated on a regular basis to account for any changes in risk factors that might alter their supervision requirements or needs levels.

CMC users report both positive and negative comments about such instruments.[13] Those who like the CMC refer to its ease of use, low cost (free), and claim that it has withstood scrutiny. Others, however, say that it doesn't meet the needs of the agencies using them, noting its deficiencies in casework planning and concerns that officers can subjectively score needs factors which in turn can skew officers' workloads.

Moreover, although nearly half (48 percent) of all U.S. probation and parole agencies use some variation of the CMC, it has not been widely studied.[14] The CMC is an improvement over the Burgess model in that it at least considers dynamic variables. However, we have limited research on how well the CMC works with diverse geographical populations (e.g., urban, inner city, rural) and how well it performs on populations distinguished by race, ethnicity, or gender, for example. These concerns have given rise to the second phase of dynamic risk assessment.

Dynamic Risk Assessment Era: Phase II

The second phase of the dynamic risk assessment era began in the late 1970s with the introduction of the Level of Service Inventory—Revised (LSI-R). Whereas the CMC was designed to budget an agency's community-based resources, the LSI-R was designed to build on the "what works" literature by measuring and tracking dynamic factors in offender risk and needs, identifying the criminogenic forces at work in an offender's life, and providing correctional staff with information on offender treatment goals. It helps agency staff make decisions about allocation of agency resources, probation and placement, security-level classifications, and treatment progress. Nearly 14 percent of U.S. probation and parole agencies use this assessment tool, with another 6 percent making plans to implement it.

The LSI-R consists of 54 items that are sorted into the following 10 theoretically based substantive areas (called subscales) related to future criminal behavior:

1. Criminal history (10 items)
2. Education and employment (10 items)
3. Finances (2 items)
4. Family and marital relationships (4 items)
5. Housing and accommodations (3 items)
6. Leisure and recreation (2 items)
7. Friends and acquaintances (5 items)
8. Alcohol and drug use (9 items)

9. Emotional and personal (5 items)
10. Attitudes and orientations (4 items)

To complete the assessment, probation and parole officers conduct a semi-structured, one-on-one interview with the offender. Some items require a "yes/no" response, while others use a structured scale ranging in value from 0 to 3. The interviewer scores the offender on each item, totals the item scores, and determines the offender's overall risk level.

The purpose of the interview is to gather information from the offender in a dynamic way, which translates into a real-time picture of his or her criminogenic needs. But the officer also reviews police files, criminal background records, court files, and probation files. This review of information is important because it gives the officer the opportunity to verify information that comes out in the interview as well as to challenge potential inconsistencies.

Because the LSI-R is dynamic, it is capable of identifying a change in risk scores (for example, because an offender moves or becomes unemployed), which in turn can signal changes in an offender's likelihood of committing a new offense. This dynamic quality is important for correctional programs and for the staff charged with managing offender risk and directing interventions.

Few independent studies have yet evaluated the system's reliability and/or predictive value. A recent study in Pennsylvania found a low level of reliability, while another in Ontario showed more positive results.[15] Thus, although this new approach seems more aligned with the values of community-based corrections and the integration of case planning, we still do not have sufficient empirical evidence to make any broad claims about its effectiveness.

User-Friendly Risk and Needs Assessment

To complete the story of offender risk assessment, the past few years have seen users tell us what they want in risk and needs assessment instruments. They want the next generation to be more user-friendly and to translate complex and abstract factors into easy-to-use, simple, and realistic case planning.

Some user-friendly instruments have already been created at the request of federal probation and pretrial services staff, who need to identify not only an offender's potential risk of reoffending and his or her criminogenic needs, but also the services, in what duration, and with what level of intensity, that will produce the best outcomes based on the assessed risks and needs. As one officer said, "This advancement in assessment will require a tremendous amount of research and advanced statistical methodology, but the field of probation must demand statistically valid connections between risk/needs assessment, case planning and outcomes. . . . Some of these recommendations require the development of statistical technologies that are yet to be developed, but advances can and must be made to improve risk/needs assessment and case planning in order to make officers more effective in the recidivism reduction."[16]

Users have other reasons for seeking a new generation of risk and needs assessment instruments. For example, even though an instrument may predict well overall, it does not necessarily predict well with every subpopulation, such as those living in urban, inner city, or rural areas, or those of diverse races, ethnicities, or genders. Thus, new instruments should be tested with subpopulations and should also clearly indicate the populations they work for.

The next generation of risk and needs assessment instruments not only needs to be "user friendly" and translate complex and abstract factors into easy-to-use, simple, and realistic case planning, but must be tested with subpopulations, such as those living within urban, inner city, or rural areas, and those of diverse races, ethnicities, and genders. What other issues should the next generation of risk and needs assessment instruments consider?

As new instruments are developed, another concern of users is that current risk/needs assessment instruments such as the LSI-R do not allow supervision officers to reassess an offender's changing circumstances in real time. For example, if an offender who has been free of substance use for the past five months suddenly tests positive for cocaine and begins verbalizing antisocial thoughts, should not the assessment instrument and case planning reflect those changes? Many of the assessment instruments in use today are not able to accurately adjust the risk score because they are unable to measure the sudden presence and significance of the change.[17]

Moreover, some assessment tools take too long to administer. For example, completing certain dynamic risk assessment instruments can take two hours. One officer put it this way: "As officers struggle to supervise ever increasing caseloads, the thought of adding hours of work for each offender generates *officer resistance* (italics added)."[18]

Other issues to consider in the new generation of instruments relate to high-profile offenders, such as sex offenders and those with mental health issues. The risk factors used to predict future criminal behavior for these types of offenders are the same as for all other offenders. Yet if someone in this group reoffends, the level of damage to the community is far greater, as are the negative consequences for the supervising agency.

Officers' final concern for the next generation of risk and needs assessment instruments is case-planning capacity, meaning the ability to better link assessment findings with case decisions. Without a direct link between the risk and needs assessment and the type, duration, and intensity of intervention, the entire assessment effort is useless, as the officer must guess about appropriate interventions (see CBC Online 4.2 for information on risk assessments and juvenile detention).

As you can see, then, since the days of Cesare Beccaria, criminal justice professionals have made tremendous progress in classifying offenders in terms of risk, assessing their needs, and assisting them to become more law abiding. Professional/clinical judgments and actuarial assessments are still used by a small percentage of probation and parole agencies today in the United States in spite of their limitations. In the meantime, dynamic risk assessments have matured since they were first introduced in the late 1970s, greatly

4.2

CBC Online

RISK ASSESSMENT AS THE KEY TO JUVENILE DETENTION REFORM IN NEW YORK CITY

In 2011, the Vera Institute of Justice's Center on Youth Justice partnered with representatives of the New York City Criminal Justice Coordinator's Office, the Department of Probation, the Administration for Children's Services, the former Department of Juvenile Justice, the Law Department, the Legal Aid Society, the judiciary, and the Annie E. Casey Foundation's Juvenile Detention Alternatives Initiative to develop a risk assessment to help judges determine a young person's risk of rearrest and failure to appear in court pending his or her sentence, and to establish an array of community-based programs for mid-level risk youth in lieu of detention. After reading the report, answer these questions:

1. Which four factors correlate significantly with failure to appear in court and which six factors correlate significantly with rearrest?
2. Which one factor decreased the likelihood of rearrest?
3. Which 11 factors previously thought to correlate with failure to appear and rearrest actually did not?
4. How do probation officers create summary failure to appear and rearrest scores?
5. How does the risk score matrix work?
6. According to the risk score matrix, which youth are deemed most suited for release with no formal supervision? For detention? For alternatives to detention?
7. Explain the community-based alternatives to detention that were developed alongside the risk-based instrument.
8. Explain the preliminary outcomes.
9. How can risk assessment benefit the youth, their families, and improve public safety?

Visit CBC Online 4.2 at www.mhhe.com/bayens1e

influenced by the theoretically based risk-need-responsivity model. The call to make dynamic risk assessments easier to use and to link them with case planning and decision-making will be the foundation of the next generation of risk and needs assessment.

Risk and Needs Assessments in Practice: Results from a National Survey

In 2003, the National Institute of Corrections (NIC) surveyed 73 corrections agencies representing 44 states and asked them when they conduct risk and needs assessments.[19] NIC learned that these assessments occur at one or more stages of criminal justice processing: (1) at the presentence investigation stage (see Chapter 7); (2) when offenders are under consideration for discretionary release from prison (see Chapter 8); (3) at the beginning of probation or parole supervision; and (4) during the period of supervision. We include a fifth stage—pretrial assessment—to begin our discussion. You will learn more about risk assessment in pretrial release in Chapter 5.

Pretrial agencies are required to gather information about offenders at the initial stage of criminal justice processing so they can assess the likelihood that a defendant will appear later in court or be rearrested; provide recommendations to the court regarding whether a defendant should be detained or released and if released, with or without conditional requirements; and encourage a defendant's voluntary participation in treatment programs pending court.

Career Profile

BETH ROBINSON: CORRECTIONS COUNSELOR

Beth Robinson is a corrections counselor II with Clark County District Court Corrections in Vancouver, Washington. She is currently assigned as a probation officer to the Women's Program, supervising a caseload of women on misdemeanor probation. Robinson often tells people she got into probation "by accident," but maybe it would sound better to say she took a non-traditional route.

Robinson earned her bachelor of arts in communications from Purdue University-Calumet Campus. Her career goal was to become a journalist, but life intervened. For a time, she was a stay-at-home mom. When she moved to Vancouver, she was hired as support staff for the sheriff's office in a temporary position. She says, "During my years in college, a career in criminal justice had never crossed my mind. It wasn't something I had looked at and discarded. I literally never considered it! However, after looking around the department, I thought the job of a custody officer seemed more interesting than preparing payroll and purchase orders. I applied for the position, and I think no one was more surprised than I was when I got hired."

Except for the swing-shift hours, Robinson says that she loved the job. But armed with a four-year college degree and corrections experience, she saw new opportunities in correctional case management with the Washington Department of Corrections. She eventually completed some graduate-level coursework in criminal justice and acquired the theoretical background she had been missing.

Female probationers report to Robinson based on their classification scores, and she is responsible for making sure they comply with their court-ordered conditions. She does not have arrest authority. She does not carry a gun, nor does she make field contacts. If one of her probationers violates the conditions of her probation, and intermediate sanctions have no effect, she files a probation violation and returns the case to court.

When asked about her job, Robinson beams. "I love working with female

A national survey of pretrial service programs found that less than 25 percent rely on objective criteria when assessing risk and making bail decisions, and half of those have never validated their risk assessment instruments.[20] Of those agencies that use a risk assessment instrument, 39 percent adopted theirs from another jurisdiction, and 25 percent developed their own. Since no assessment instrument has universal applicability, pre-existing assessment instruments may not be reliable or valid when developed for one offender group and applied to another.

Risk and needs assessments are also conducted at the presentence investigation stage and when prison inmates are being considered for discretionary release. NIC found that about half the corrections agencies providing probation or both probation and parole supervision conduct risk and needs assessments as a component of the presentence investigation. Also, about half the agencies that exercise discretionary parole release from prison conduct risk and needs assessments in connection with their decision to release an inmate to parole or post-prison supervision.

The survey also found that most corrections agencies conduct risk and needs assessments at the onset of probation or parole supervision. For agencies providing both probation and parole supervision, the proportion is over 90 percent. The proportion is slightly lower in agencies providing only probation supervision, and it drops to 60 percent in agencies that provide only parole supervision.

probationers. Knowing that women are relationship-oriented, my agency keeps the female client with a single officer from intake through completion. Our new Service Planning Instrument (SPIn) classification system, used in conjunction with motivational interviewing, gives me a clearer sense of the client than I could ever get from merely reading her file and studying her criminal history. We look at protective factors, not just risk factors. Our case plans are now more collaborative, and they encompass the clients' hopes and dreams—not just their court-ordered conditions. I see the responses of the women as they help map their futures, and I feel like more than just a paper pusher.

"So many women in the criminal justice system have past trauma issues, and we now are able to more fully explore this gateway to criminal behavior through a support group, which I co-facilitate as part of my assigned job duties. I also act as a community liaison, facilitating a staffing group that brings together a variety of local agencies that are all working with the same clientele. I actively search out local resources that will benefit the clients, and I share the information with my coworkers and others in the community via an e-mail distribution group."

Robinson's advice to persons interested in working as a corrections counselor is this: "Serve as a volunteer or intern. You may find the reality of the job different from what you imagined. Bring your life experience and compassion to the job. Remember that your client is an individual, not the sum of her criminal history. Listen more than you talk. Don't be rigid; the best probation officers I know have the ability to slide back and forth on a continuum between law enforcer and social worker. They're not stuck at either end of the continuum, or even firmly planted in the middle. Instead, they can respond based on the needs of the client and the safety of the community. Finally, be open to new experiences and don't be afraid to actively seek change. I never would have expected that a temporary position would lead to a career for me—a career that I was better suited for than the one I had originally chosen for myself."

Many agencies conduct assessments during the period of supervision and reevaluate offenders' risks and needs to measure any changes in the offending behavior that might alter their supervision requirements. Still, compared with agencies that assess at the beginning of supervision, fewer do so during supervision. Of those that do assessments during the period of supervision, some do so every six months, some do so at three-month intervals and when significant supervision events occur, and others do so annually until the offender reaches a low-risk case level.

Survey respondents identified several other points at which offenders are assessed for risk and needs:

- On referral to a treatment program;
- When placed in a specialized diversion program;
- In prison, for re-entry planning or to determine eligibility for a community sentencing program; and
- At major situational changes, such as arrest or when violations occur.

What we know, then, is that corrections agencies conduct risk and needs assessments at various stages of criminal justice processing (see Career Profile of Beth Robinson and CBC Online 4.3). Many of the responding agencies assess offenders at more

4.3

CBC Online

PRETRIAL RISK ASSESSMENT IN THE FEDERAL COURT

In April 2009, the U.S. Department of Justice, Office of Federal Justice Trustee, published a report called "Pretrial Risk Assessment in the Federal Court." A major purpose of the research was to identify predictors of success or failure in avoiding rearrest pending trial. In short, researchers hoped to develop a classification scheme to scale the risk persons arrested for federal criminal offenses posed if released pending trial.

Review the document. Which of the nine predictors of pretrial outcome are static and which are dynamic? Where does the classification scheme fit into the five eras of risk and needs history developed earlier in this chapter?

Visit CBC Online 4.3 at www.mhhe.com/bayens1e

than one stage, but some assess at only one stage, most often the beginning of probation or parole supervision.

Assessment of Special-Needs Offenders

Special-needs offenders exhibit unique physical, mental, social, and programmatic characteristics that distinguish them from other offenders. This group includes sex offenders, substance abusers, and domestic violence abusers, as well as offenders who present particular treatment needs and management issues—for example, because they have a mental illness, low educational level, or low cognitive functioning (the ability to learn and process thoughts).

How do community corrections agencies assess special-needs offenders to manage the risk they pose? Do they administer specialized risk and needs assessment instruments? Or do they use the agency's general population instrument such as the LSI-R or CMC? To answer this important question we refer to a survey conducted by the National Institute of Corrections.

In 2003, NIC surveyed all state departments of corrections and asked a number of questions about the use of assessment instruments, including which instruments they used to assess the risk posed by special-needs offenders. Forty state agencies responded. Exhibit 4.2 shows the number of agencies that assess special-needs offenders using (1) a general risk and needs assessment instrument such as the CMC or LSI-R versus (2) a specialized assessment instrument. (Row totals may not add to 40 if states used both types of instruments or did not respond.)

The data in Exhibit 4.2 show that most corrections agencies do not administer a specialized assessment instrument for special-needs offenders. Unfortunately, the NIC survey did not ask agencies why they did not use a specialized assessment instrument. However, experts' thoughts on currently available assessment instruments (see pp. 106–108) reveal some of the challenges facing agencies. The following questions/issues must be resolved before an agency adopts any assessment instrument, including a specialized one.

1. What is the purpose of the instrument and how does it fit with the agency's mission? Will the instrument be used to measure risk and case planning of all offenders to reoffend, or only specific populations of offenders?

EXHIBIT 4.2 Use of General and Specialized Risk and Needs Assessments

	State agencies that assess special-needs offenders using a general risk and needs assessment instrument	State agencies that assess special-needs offenders using a specialized assessment instrument
Sex offenders	40	28
Substance abusers	35	25
Domestic violence cases	20	8
Literacy/educational needs	17	4
Low cognitive functioning	14	4
Mentally ill offenders	14	3
Violent offenders	14	2
Developmentally disabled offenders	11	3

Source: National Institute of Corrections, *Topics in Community Corrections: Offender Assessment* (Washington, DC: National Institute of Corrections, 2003).

2. Should the agency use an existing instrument or develop its own? Both options have advantages and disadvantages. To begin, existing instruments such as the CMC or LSI-R have resources already in place, such as forms, training curricula, and software. However existing instruments can be expensive to purchase and require significant staff training. In contrast, an agency that develops a new instrument can involve staff in the process and thereby increase their willingness to use the instrument. The disadvantage in developing new instruments is that they are difficult to create, and their reliability and validity have to be statistically tested—a skill that many staff members lack. Thus, agencies that choose to develop their own instruments will likely need to consult an external expert. A third alternative is to use an instrument that is in the public domain and thus free, such as the Wisconsin Client Management Classification System, discussed earlier, or the Virginia Risk Assessment Instrument, which aims to identify good candidates for diversion from incarceration among nonviolent offenders. But again, whether any instrument already in use works well with a particular agency's offender population must be considered.
3. If an agency wants to introduce a new, specialized instrument, will it require new resources or more time? As a respondent in the NIC survey put it, "It takes 1.5 to 2 hours to conduct [the Addiction Severity Index], which stretches already limited personnel resources."
4. At what stage in the criminal justice process will the instrument be administered: at pretrial, at presentencing, or in the post-supervision phase? Depending on when the instrument will be used, it will take on a different form and have different implications for case planning.
5. Will offenders be reassessed, and if so, how often?
6. Will all offenders be assessed or only targeted ones? And if only targeted offenders—for example, special-needs offenders such as Phillip Garrido—how will they be identified?

CBC Online

SPECIALIZED ASSESSMENT INSTRUMENTS FOR SPECIAL-NEEDS OFFENDERS

Review Exhibit 4.3 to identify the most frequently used specialized assessment instruments for special-needs offenders. Then use the Internet to research the assessment instruments for one special-needs offender group and answer the following questions:

1. What is the purpose of the instrument?
2. What does the instrument measure?
3. For whom is the instrument recommended?
4. Does the instrument include static and dynamic factors?
5. Is the instrument free or purchase only?
6. When was the instrument developed?
7. How many items are on the instrument?
8. How long does it take to complete the instrument?
9. What is the format of the instrument (paper and pencil, face-to-face interview, etc.)

7. How will the assessment results be presented? Will staff understand them? Will the results be user-friendly and assist in case planning?
8. How difficult will the instrument be to administer? How much time will it take? Is it interview-based? Paper–pencil? Web-based? Will offenders understand the questions?

These are not easy questions for probation and parole agencies to grapple with, especially as most of them already work with limited resources and tight deadlines. Moreover, many operate under the scrutiny of the court, media, public, and politicians, especially following a high-profile case like the one of Phillip Garrido.

Even if an agency has answers to all these questions, it still could not be certain that a specialized assessment instrument would more accurately classify a special-needs offender than would a general instrument. This is because we do not yet have a body of literature comparing general risk and needs assessment instruments with specialized instruments *on the same population of special-needs offenders* to know which is better. In the end, then, we cannot know whether different parole supervision of Phillip Garrido could have prevented the kidnapping and sexual assault of Jaycee Lee Dugard. We simply do not know whether we would have seen a different outcome if Garrido had been evaluated with a specialized sex assessment instrument such as the Static-99 or the Minnesota Sex Offender Screening Tool (MnSOST), the two most commonly used instruments for assessing sex offenders' risk and needs.

Exhibit 4.3 concludes this section by listing the most frequently used specialized assessment instruments for each special-needs offender group (see CBC Online 4.4 for more on specialized instruments). The number of agencies using each instrument is shown in parentheses.

What Is the Future of Classification?

The progress made in the field of classification and risk and needs assessment over the past decade suggests a future shaped by evidence-based practices. Moreover, we predict that the National Institute of Corrections will continue to conduct research that

EXHIBIT 4.3 Assessment Instruments for Special-Needs Offenders

Substance Abuse	1. Addiction Severity Index (12)
	2. Simple Screening Instrument (5)
	3. Adult Substance Use Survey (4)
Sex Offenders	1. Static-99 (12)
	2. Minnesota Sex Offender Screening Tool (4)
Mental Illness	1. Minnesota Multiphasic Personality Inventory (1)
	2. Millon Clinical Multiaxial Inventory-III (1)
Domestic Violence	1. Spousal Assault Risk Assessment (5)
	2. Domestic Violence Screening Inventory (3)
	3. Lethality Scale/Index (2)
Violence	1. Hare Psychopathy Checklist–Revised (PCL-R) (1)
	2. Violence Risk Appraisal Guide (VRAG) (1)
Cognitive Skills	1. Kaufman Short Neuropsychological Assessment Procedure (unknown)
	2. Comprehensive Adult Student Assessment System (unknown)
	3. Test of Adult Basic Education (unknown)
Developmentally Disabled Offenders	1. Wechsler Adult Intelligence Scale–III (unknown)
	2. Revised Beta IQ
	3. Kaufman Brief Intelligence Test (unknown)
	3. Kaufman Functional Academic Skills Test (unknown)
Literacy/Educational Needs	1. Wisconsin Reading Aptitude Test (unknown)
	2. Comprehensive Adult Student Assessment System (unknown)
	2. Test of Adult Basic Education (unknown)
	3. ATI Assessment (unknown)

Source: National Institute of Corrections, *Topics in Community Corrections: Annual Issue 2003: Offender Assessment* (Washington, DC: U.S. Department of Justice, National Institute of Corrections, 2003).

helps corrections agencies select validated instruments that work with their particular offender populations. We also believe that assessment instruments will become more user friendly and more adept at translating complex and abstract factors into simple and realistic case planning tools, to address the concerns of agencies. In short, we believe that the advances in classification and risk and needs assessment instrument technology we've seen over the past decade will continue and achieve something along the lines of this promising futuristic scenario:

Probation Officer Wendy Holmes teleworks from home on Tuesdays and Thursdays. She pours herself a cup of coffee, turns on her PDA, and synchronizes data with the PC in her office downtown. She skims through the case plans of her probation caseload and finds an inbox item titled "Alert: Risk Increase." She opens the file and finds a notice that probationer Harper Pepperman's supervision risk crossed a threshold that moves her from medium supervision (Level 2) to high supervision (Level 3). The case plan automatically adjusts her risk of rearrest to 60 percent. Officer Holmes reads that Pepperman missed her second group drug counseling session, and her urinalysis was positive for cocaine for the second time in three months, causing the increase in her risk score. The case plan automatically calls for an immediate face-to-face meeting with Pepperman, application of noninvasive drug technology (a patch on the skin that absorbs perspiration, immediately signals the presence of drugs, and sends an electronic notice to her supervision officer), home confinement, and one-on-one drug counseling for one month before resuming group counseling. The risk-assessment instrument that Officer Holmes relies on was recently validated with her agency's offender population, so she feels that the new case plan is warranted, and she sends her assessment to her supervisor for approval. She spends the next several hours sending e-mails to the rest of the women on her caseload, complimenting them on the progress they are making, and then heads off to lunch.

Policy Implications

Risk assessment may sound easy. You find an instrument, rate an offender, add up the score, check the scale, and identify whether the offender is a low, medium, or high risk. Based on that finding, you identify the case management strategy—for example, the kind of supervision plus treatment. But how do you know if the instrument really works? If it is not accurate, or if staff are not trained to use it properly and provide appropriate case management, the consequences can be devastating for victims, as in the case of Jaycee Lee Dugard.

Tomorrow's community-based corrections officers will be shaped by advances reported by the National Institute of Corrections, assessment of special-needs offenders, and user-friendly risk and needs assessment instruments. How will evidence-based practices affect the future of offender classification?

Did Garrido really deserve low-risk supervision because his score put him in the low-supervision range? We don't know whether federal and California probation authorities assessed Garrido with a specialized sex offender instrument. Chances are they didn't, given the inspector general's conclusions about the case. Clearly, to improve the chances that such travesties will not occur again, the policy threshold we should all expect is one of dynamic and ongoing assessment and case management. That's the policy threshold Dugard's family and others in her situation should demand.

To meet this threshold, the policy implications are that classification and risk/needs assessment instruments will need to be (1) validated to insure that their items are theoretically driven and evidence-based; (2) fair to all offender subpopulations such as women and racial and ethnic minorities; (3) designed so that they generate case management strategies and treatment goals that are commensurate with the risk to public safety; (4) practical, efficient, and simple to implement; (5) designed with staff training and retraining in mind; and (6) systematically re-evaluated as the offender population changes (for example, average age and length of sentence), as new laws are passed, as budgets are cut or increased, and as programs and services increase or are reduced. These are serious undertakings, but they are essential principles for sound classification and risk assessment policy.

Summary

Classification is a process of separating offenders into discrete groups in such a way that the offenders in the same group are similar or close enough to each other on certain common characteristics that they can be effectively supervised and managed. The process of separating offenders into groups is know as risk assessment, a measure of the offender's dangerousness to the community and probability of reoffending. The risk principle focuses on *who* should be treated. It asserts that criminal behavior can be reliably predicted and that treatment should focus on the higher-risk offender. The need principle focuses on *what* should be treated. It highlights the importance of criminogenic needs in the design and delivery of treatment. The responsivity principle helps determine how to treat. It describes how the treatment should be provided.

For the first half of the 20th century, assessment of risk was a professional/clinical matter. The belief was that as community corrections officers gained knowledge and experience, they developed an intuitive sense, or a "gut" feeling, of what an offender's risks and needs were and the probability of reoffending. However, clinical assessment is oftentimes biased and subjective and is considered to be the least accurate risk-assessment method. In contrast, actuarial assessment is the science of applying mathematical and statistical methods to assess risk. It surfaced in corrections in the early part of the 20th century. The shortcomings here are that actuarial assessments are atheoretical and static, and they do not provide specific direction for treatment interventions.

Two phases in dynamic risk assessment followed. They incorporated prior static factors into their assessments but also introduced dynamic criminogenic-need items that an offender can modify, such as substance abuse or employment. The first phase began in the 1970s when the state of Wisconsin introduced the CMC to help budget the agency's resources. The second phase was introduced in the late 1970s and incorporated risk/need factors from the emerging "what works" literature to provide staff with treatment goals. We are currently in the fifth era—moving toward user-friendly risk and needs assessment—the goal being to generate tools that translate complex and abstract factors into simple and realistic case planning strategies.

Corrections agencies conduct risk and needs assessments at one or more stages of criminal justice processing: (1) at pretrial; (2) during presentence investigation; (3) when offenders are under consideration for discretionary release from prison; (4) at the beginning of probation or parole supervision; and (5) during supervision.

Special-needs offenders exhibit unique physical, mental, social, and programmatic characteristics that distinguish them from other offenders. This group includes sex offenders, substance abusers, and domestic violence abusers, as well as offenders with special treatment needs and management issues, such as mental illness, low educational level, and low cognitive functioning (the ability to learn and process thoughts). Most corrections agencies do not administer a specialized assessment instrument for these offenders.

History suggests that (1) evidence-based practices will shape the fields of general and specialized offender classification in the future; (2) the National Institute of Corrections will continue to help corrections agencies select validated instruments that work with their offender populations; (3) assessment instruments will become more user friendly and more adept at translating complex and abstract factors into simple and realistic case planning strategies; and (4) advances in classification and risk and needs assessment technology will continue, making the next generation of assessment instruments easier to use.

The principles for sound policy in classification and risk/needs assessment include validating an instrument to insure that (1) its items are theoretically driven and evidence-based; (2) it is fair to all offender subpopulations; (3) the treatment goals it generates are commensurate with the risk to public safety; (4) it is practical, efficient, and simple to implement; (5) staff are trained and retrained on it; and (6) it is systematically re-evaluated as the offender population changes, as new laws are passed, as budgets are cut or increased, and as programs and services increase or are reduced.

Key Terms

actuarial assessment, p. 97
case planning, p. 99
classification, p. 92
dynamic risk assessment, p. 99
need principle, p. 93
professional/clinical assessment, p. 97
responsivity principle, p. 93
risk assessment, p. 93

risk principle, p. 93
risk-need-responsivity model, p. 93
special-needs offenders, p. 106

Questions for Review

1. Define classification, risk assessment, risk principle, need principle, and responsivity principle.
2. What differences exist from era to era in the development of risk and needs assessment?
3. When in criminal justice processing are risk and needs assessments conducted?
4. Who are special-needs offenders, and how are corrections agencies assessing their risks and needs?
5. What underlying themes will shape classification and risk/needs assessment in the future?
6. What are the principles for sound policy in classification and risk/needs assessment?

Question of Policy

Public Correctional Policy on Classification

On April 23, 1984, the American Correctional Association (ACA) unanimously adopted its Public Correctional Policy on Classification. Since then, the association has reviewed and reaffirmed the policy four times, the latest being on January 12, 2005. The policy can be found at the ACA Web site (http://aca.org) or by using any search engine with the key terms "American correctional association public correctional policy on classification." How does the policy relate to ideas discussed in this chapter?

What Would You Do?

Assume for the moment that you are one of five district community supervision officers in your state responsible for the leadership, administration, organization, and management of all probation staff, offenders, and services in your district. Assume, too, that your state does not use specialized assessment instruments for special-needs offenders. Instead, special-needs offenders are assessed with a general risk/needs assessment instrument similar to the Wisconsin CMC. When that assessment is complete, the staff uses its professional and clinical judgment to set treatment goals for special-needs offenders.

After the case of Phillip Garrido made national headlines in 2009, you began to wonder how valid your state's approach was for sex offenders and others with special needs. You surely don't want to be blamed if a Garrido-like situation happens in your district.

Next month you are meeting with the four other district community supervision officers, your state's secretary of corrections, and her management team to discuss classification of special-needs offenders. She asks all of you to bring your thoughts and concerns about the state's method for assessing special-needs offenders. She also asks that if you recommend changes, you consider the state's fiscal crisis and decreasing budget for corrections. However, as the state's chief corrections officer, she reminds you that her goal is to promote public, staff, and offender safety. What would you do?

Endnotes

1. Maria L. LaGanga and Shane Goldmacher, "Jaycee Lee Dugard's Family Will Receive $20 Million from California," *Los Angeles Times,* July 2, 2010, http://articles.latimes.com/2010/jul/02/local/la-me-0702-dugard-settlement-20100702 (accessed July 12, 2010).
2. C. Johnson and George Warren, "Lawmakers Question Prison Official over Supervision of Phillip Garrido," *News 10*, February 16, 2010, http://www.news10.net/news/local/story.aspx?storyid=75438 (accessed July 8, 2010).
3. Office of the Inspector General, State of California, *2009 Annual Report* (Sacramento, CA: Office of the Inspector General, 2009), p. 8.
4. D. A. Andrews, James Bonta, and R. D. Hoge, "Classification for Effective Rehabilitation: Rediscovering Psychology," *Criminal Justice and Behavior*, vol. 17, no. 1 (1990), pp. 19–52.
5. D.A. Andrews and James Bonta, *The Psychology of Criminal Conduct,* 4th ed. (Newark, NJ: LexisNexis, 2006).

6. D. A. Andrews and James Bonta, (2007) *Public Safety Canada Corrections Research: User Report 2007–06,* 2007, www.publicsafety.gc.ca (accessed July 5, 2010).
7. Scott VanBenschoten, "Risk/Needs Assessment: Is This the Best We Can Do?" *Federal Probation*, vol. 72, no 2 (Summer 2008), pp. 38–42.
8. Patricia M. Harris, "What Community Supervision Officers Need to Know About Actuarial Risk Assessment and Clinical Judgment," *Federal Probation*, vol. 70, no. 2 (September, 2006), pp. 8–14.
9. Todd Clear and Kenneth Gallagher, "Probation and Parole Supervision: A Review of Current Classification Practices," *Crime and Delinquency*, vol. 31 (1985), pp. 423–443.
10. Dana A. Jones, Shelley Johnson, Edward Latessa, and Lawrence F. Travis, "Case Classification in Community Corrections: Preliminary Findings From a National Survey," *Topics in Community Corrections: Annual Issue 1999: Classification and Risk Assessment* (Washington, DC: National Institute of Corrections, 1999), p. 7.
11. Bernard E. Harcourt, *Against Prediction: Profiling, Policing, and Punishing in an Actuarial Age* (Chicago, University of Chicago Press, 2007).
12. As cited in Ibid., p. 58.
13. National Institute of Corrections, *Topics in Community Corrections: Offender Assessment* (Washington, DC: National Institute of Corrections, 2003).
14. Jones, Johnson, Latessa, and Travis, "Case Classification in Community Corrections," p. 8; see also Michele M. Connolly, *Critical Examination of Actuarial Offender-Based Prediction Assessments: Guidance for the Next Generation of Assessments*, (Washington, DC: U. S. Department of Justice, 2003).
15. James Austin and Kenneth McGinnis, *Classification of High-Risk and Special Management Prisoners: A National Assessment of Current Practices* (Washington, DC: National Institute of Corrections, 2004), p. 18.
16. Scott VanBenschoten, "Risk/Needs Assessment: Is This the Best We Can Do?"
17. Ibid., p. 40.
18. Ibid., p. 40.
19. National Institute of Corrections, *Topics in Community Corrections: Offender Assessment.*
20. John Clark and D. Alan Henry, *Pretrial Services Programming at the Start of the 21st Century: A Survey of Pretrial Services Programs* (Washington, DC: U.S. Department of Justice, Bureau of Justice Statistics, 2003).

CHAPTER 5

Pretrial Release and Diversion:

Suspending Progression through the Formal Justice Process

OBJECTIVES

1 Trace the historical roots of pretrial release and diversion programs in the United States.

2 Explain pretrial investigation and how risk assessment is used to facilitate its function.

3 Explain the benefits of pretrial diversion and the purposes of assessment and the diversion agreement.

4 Describe the traditional bail system and assess its effectiveness in assuring that defendants appear in court.

5 Describe three prominent issues regarding policy changes that may increase the potential for pretrial defendants to appear in court.

OUTLINE

In 2003, Palm Beach County, Florida, State Attorney Barry Krischer launched an investigation of Rush Limbaugh after Limbaugh's housekeeper Wilma Cline claimed that she and her husband supplied the talk-show host with illegally obtained OxyContin and other painkillers from 1998 to 2002. Limbaugh admitted to listeners on his radio show on October 10, 2003, that he was addicted to prescription painkillers and stated that he would enter inpatient treatment for 30 days, immediately after the broadcast. Limbaugh further explained that his addiction to painkillers resulted from several years of severe back pain heightened by a botched surgery intended to correct those problems.

On April 28, 2006, the 55-year-old radio commentator surrendered himself at the Palm Beach County jail. The warrant for his arrest charged that Limbaugh withheld information so that he might get a prescription from a second practitioner even though he had received medications from a first practitioner within 30 days, in violation of Florida law. The charge is commonly referred to as "doctor shopping" and is a third-degree felony that could carry a sentence of up to five years in prison.

*However, under the terms of a **diversion** agreement, an alternative to prosecution that seeks to divert offenders from traditional criminal justice processing into a program of supervision and services, the State Attorney agreed to drop the charge after Limbaugh completed an 18-month **substance abuse treatment** program, made a $30,000 payment to the State of Florida to defray the public cost of the investigation, and participated in drug testing.*

What are the advantages for both the prosecutor's office and the alleged offender (Limbaugh) when entering an agreement for pretrial diversion? If Limbaugh failed to comply with any of the terms of the pretrial diversion agreement, what would happen? In this chapter, we will begin by discussing pretrial release and diversion programs as an important means of keeping defendants within the community. Later in the chapter we'll turn our attention to bail, conflict resolution, and programming strategies for offenders on pretrial release or diversion.

Overview and History of Pretrial Release and Diversion

The history of structured **pretrial release** and diversion began in the 1960s in what came to be called the Bail Reform Movement. Starting in 1961, the Vera Foundation developed the Manhattan Bail Project in New York City. The fundamental idea behind the project was to assess whether accused persons could be trusted to return to court without being forced to purchase a bail bond. Over the project's three years, 3,505 defendants were released as a requirement of bail, and less than 2 percent failed to arrive for their court appearances.[1] The result was that many pretrial defendants with community ties were safely released without financial bail.[2]

The Manhattan Bail Project attracted enough national attention that the U.S. Department of Justice organized a national conference on bail and criminal justice. In 1966, then-President Lyndon Johnson signed the Bail Reform Act, and many states rewrote their pretrial release statutes to provide clear guidance to judicial officers by listing the factors they should consider at the release hearing. At the signing of the new legislation on June 22, 1966, President Johnson commented, "The principal purpose of bail is to insure that an accused person will return for trial, if he is released after arrest. How is that purpose met under the present system? The defendant with means can afford to pay bail. He can afford to buy his freedom. But the poorer defendant cannot pay the price. He languishes in jail weeks, months, and perhaps even years before trial. He does not stay in jail because he is guilty. He does not stay in jail because any sentence has been passed. He does not stay in jail because he is any more likely to flee before trial. He stays in jail for one reason only—he stays in jail because he is poor."[3]

As pretrial release of defendants gained popularity, so too did diversion. The first pretrial diversion program in the United States was the Citizen's Probation Authority program, established in 1965 in Flint, Michigan. In pretrial diversion programs, defendants charged with nonserious offenses were diverted at the outset of the case, in lieu of prosecution, if they agreed to complete certain requirements (e.g., remain gainfully employed, participate in counseling services) for 90 days to one year. Satisfactory completion of the program resulted in a dismissal of charges; "failure" meant the resumption of criminal proceedings. Diverting cases from traditional prosecution had the added benefit of reducing criminal court caseloads.

In 1967, the President's Commission of Law Enforcement and Administration of Justice, called the Katzenbach Commission, issued a report titled "The Challenge of Crime in a Free Society." It called for the expanded use of pretrial release and diversion programs and recognized the importance of keeping defendants within the community. Reintegration, not retribution, was central to the philosophical overhaul of correctional thinking at the time. As a result of the commission's recommendation, dozens of sites began receiving funding to establish pretrial diversion programs.

In 1968, the American Bar Association published an initial set of criminal justice standards that addressed the pretrial release decision. These standards were virtually identical to the 1966 Federal Bail Reform Act, with two important additions: first, the standards noted that judicial officers should consider potential danger to the community as a factor in making decisions; and second, the standards called for the abolition of surety bail as an option, citing the long history of abuses associated with the practice.[4] Pretrial programs were becoming established in both urban and rural jurisdictions, and were operated by court services and probation offices, local municipal and county jails, and by private, nonprofit, and independent agencies under contract.

The 1970s was the decade of growth for pretrial diversion. The states of Florida, New York, Massachusetts, and Washington enacted statutes authorizing pretrial diversion and established criteria for diverting defendants. These laws were significant in that they were the first non-drug-diversion laws to be passed at the state level. In addition to new state laws enacting pretrial diversion, state and national professional associations and organizations, including the National Association of Pretrial Services Agencies (NAPSA), were established. In 1976, NAPSA received funding from Law Enforcement Assistance Administration (LEAA) to establish national professional standards and goals to govern pretrial diversion programs and to establish a Pretrial Services Resource Center (PSRC). The PSRC served as a clearinghouse for information on pretrial issues and a technical assistance provider for pretrial practitioners. The PSRC also conducted surveys to determine the status of the pretrial field. That first survey of pretrial programs was produced in 1979—just one year after the first edition of Pretrial Diversion Standards was released by PSRC in 1978.[5] Since then, three other surveys have been conducted; the others were completed in 1989, 2001, and 2009.

Research on pretrial diversion during this time period showed promise as an effective means of reducing recidivism. For example, a 1978 study of the Monroe County, NY, Pretrial Diversion Program found that participants had a 35 percent lower rearrest rate over a one-year period than a similarly situated comparison group.[6] Likewise, a study was conducted of the Shelby County, TN, Pretrial Diversion Program—an alternative to prosecution that seeks to divert certain offenders from traditional criminal justice processing into a program of supervision and services. In this study, findings indicated that over a three-year period, only 28 percent of the 275 program participants were rearrested at least once, while a control group of program-eligible persons selected from court records had a rearrest rate of 39 percent. In addition, less than 10 percent of the program participants were rearrested more than once during the three-year period, compared to 18 percent for the comparison group.[7]

As a result of such positive findings, the application of pretrial diversion to a broader category of offenders took center stage in the 1970s. Local and state programs began to look more closely at diversion as a means to offer pretrial services both in-house and through community-based referrals. One program that emerged during this time was Treatment Alternatives to Street Crime (TASC), an offender management model that was implemented in various forms to treat drug-using offenders as part of an overall strategy to control drug use and associated criminal behaviors.

Treatment Alternatives to Street Crime (TASC)

In 1973, the Nixon Administration formed the White House Special Actions Office for Drug Abuse Prevention (SAODAP). The office was charged with implementing a nationwide program for pretrial and post conviction referral to treat addicted defendants. Called TASC (Treatment Alternatives to Street Crime),[8] the initial idea was derived from criminal justice studies indicating that many drug-addicted arrestees were released on bail while awaiting trial and were likely to continue to commit crimes. Although provisions existed for supervising probationers and parolees who were classified as drug-dependent offenders, no such treatment mechanisms were in place to provide supervision of those awaiting trial.

By the late 1970s, about 40 TASC programs were in operation. These programs initially focused on pretrial diversion of first offenders. The original TASC model was structured around three goals: (1) eliminating or reducing the drug use and criminal behavior of drug-using offenders; (2) shifting offenders from a system based on deterrence and punishment to one that, in addition, fostered treatment and rehabilitation; and (3) diverting drug-involved offenders to community-based facilities so as to limit criminal labeling and to avoid the learning of criminal behavior that occurs in prisons.[9]

TASC served as the precursor for the system of **drug courts** currently operating across the United States and is best described as a diversion program and case management that helps link community corrections and the drug-abuse treatment system. TASC provided assessment, referral, case management, and monitoring services for drug- and alcohol-dependent offenders accused or convicted of nonviolent crimes. Overall, TASC's effectiveness has been established in reducing drug abuse and in keeping drug abusers in treatment for a longer period of time.[10] As an alternative to confinement, it is also cheaper. Incarceration of drug-using offenders costs from $25,000 to $50,000 per year. In contrast, the most comprehensive drug courts cost an average of $3,000 annually for each offender. TASC continues to expand in the 21st century, primarily because it has been recognized by the National Institute on Drug Abuse, the Office of National Drug Control Policy, and the Office of Treatment Improvement as an effective program for reducing drug use and related crime.[11] In Chapter 10 we discuss the effectiveness of drug courts to provide community-based treatment and supervision to offenders who are identified as having substance abuse issues.

The Speedy Trial Act of 1974 and the Federal Pretrial Services Act of 1982

In 1974, the U.S. Congress enacted the **Speedy Trial Act**. One part of the Act (Title II) authorized the Director of the Administrative Office of the U.S. courts to establish **demonstration programs** in pretrial services agencies at 10 judicial districts. At these experimental sites, each federal judicial district was allowed to develop its own unique policies and procedures, with two overall goals: reducing crime by persons released to the community pending trial and reducing unnecessary pretrial detention. The agencies were to interview each person charged with anything other than a petty offense, verify background information, and present a report to the judicial officer considering bail. The agencies also were to supervise persons released to their custody pending trial and to help defendants on bail locate and use **community services**. Five of the agencies were administered by the Administrative Office and five by boards of trustees appointed by the chief judges of the district courts.[12]

These demonstration programs formed the basis of the Federal Pretrial Services Act of 1982, which expanded **pretrial services** to all 94 judicial districts and marked a significant milestone for what is now the U.S. Probation and Pretrial Services System. Since its beginning, the scope of pretrial services in the federal system has expanded and the number of offenders placed in federal pretrial programs has increased. Court officers are now involved in the criminal justice process from the time defendants are arrested on federal charges until they complete community supervision. Exhibit 5.1 describes the role of federal pretrial services officers, and the Career Profile of Kimberly Rieger gives insight into what it is like for one woman working in the field. CBC Online 5.1 gives you a look at the development of pretrial services since its inception.

EXHIBIT 5.1 U.S. Pretrial Services Officers: Who They Are and What They Do[13]

- **They are U.S. district court employees.** As such, they provide services that help the federal courts ensure the fair administration of justice.
- **They are federal law enforcement officers.** As such, they hold the responsibility to investigate and supervise persons charged with and convicted of crimes against the United States.

Two important functions include preparing pretrial reports and making recommendations to the court regarding whether to release or detain the defendant before trial. Pretrial Services Officers also work with defendants to ensure that if released to the community before trial, they will commit no crime while awaiting trial and will return to court as required.

KIMBERLY RIEGER, SUPERVISING U.S. PROBATION AND PRETRIAL SERVICES OFFICER, WESTERN DISTRICT OF OKLAHOMA

Kimberly Rieger is the Supervising U.S. Probation and Pretrial Services Officer for the Western District of Oklahoma. She holds a baccalaureate degree from the University of Oklahoma and a Masters of Corrections Administration from Washburn University. The Western District, which is located in Oklahoma City, employs 52 officers who supervise approximately 500 postconviction offenders and 300 pretrial defendants. They also complete 300 presentence investigation reports annually.

As with other federal law enforcement agencies, Federal Probation and Pretrial Services Officers are subject to age restrictions. At the time of hiring, an officer cannot have reached his or her 37th birthday, and must also retire by age 57. Prior to employment, a candidate for the position of Federal Probation and Pretrial Services Officer must pass a background check and receive a medical standards clearance. During the term of employment, officers are subject to periodic reinvestigations of their backgrounds and to drug testing.

Ms. Rieger's advice for students interested in U.S. Probation and Pretrial Services is "to complete an internship at a criminal justice agency while in college. I did, and it not only gave me hands-on experience which helped in getting my first job in the field, but also gave me an opportunity to see firsthand that I enjoyed the work and found it rewarding."

Career Profile

Get-Tough-on-Crime Legislation

In the 1980s, the LEAA block grant program was terminated, and "get tough" laws were enacted that caused the general diversion movement to lose momentum. With the advent of crime control initiatives such as the "war on drugs," the number of persons prosecuted for drug, weapon, and immigration offenses substantially increased. Fueled by federal dollars for drug law enforcement and the passage of mandatory minimum prison sentencing laws for drug trafficking, arrests for drug crimes escalated. In 1989, for example, 406,000 adults were arrested nationwide for drug trafficking. Between 1984 and 1999, the number of defendants charged with a drug offense in the federal courts increased from 11,854 to 29,306.[14] Also, the profile of jail and prison inmate populations reflected the times, as more drug offenders were being incarcerated than ever before. In Kansas, for example, the makeup of the prison population in the late 1970s was generally split between violent and property offenders.[15] In the late 1980s, however, property offenders were routinely sentenced to intensive supervised probation, thereby altering the composition of the prison population to violent and drug offenders. Interestingly though, at the end of the decade, the increases in drug arrests that resulted from get-tough policies helped diversion regain popularity. That is, with the rapid increase in felony drug arrests, the "drug court" initiative gave diversion new legitimacy, as it enabled the court to do something with a class of defendants who were clogging the court system.[16] We will take a more in-depth look at the operation of drug courts in Chapter 10.

The resurgence of pretrial release and diversion persisted throughout the 1990s and continues today. According to a Bureau of Justice Assistance nationwide study, 300 pretrial service programs were operating in the United States during 2001. More than half of these began after 1990.[17] Pretrial release and diversion programs in the 21st century are touted as a cost-effective alternative to confining persons in local jails for

5.1

CBC Online

JUDICIARY NOW: PRETRIAL SERVICES ACT TURNS 25

This five-minute video shows a presentation by U.S. District Court Judge James G. Carr, Director of the Administrative Office of the U.S. Courts, and others addressing pretrial services officers at the 25th anniversary of the Pretrial Service Act in Cleveland, Ohio.

After reviewing the video, answer this question: In what ways have U.S. federal pretrial services evolved in the past 25 years?

Visit CBC Online 5.1 at www.mhhe.com/bayens1e

lengthy periods of time before trial. Other benefits include (1) ensuring that defendants appear in court, (2) helping to alleviate jail crowding, (3) reducing the number of **failure to appear** arrest warrants, (4) eliminating unnecessary court continuances and delays, (5) reducing the size of court dockets and the number of criminal trials, (6) improving judicial procedural efficiencies by dismissing charges against the defendants upon their successful completion of the pretrial program conditions, and (7) substantially lessening the amount of time the court expends per defendant.[18]

The Influence of Program Evaluation

While the search for cost-effective alternatives to confinement helped to advance pretrial release and diversion programs, so did encouraging findings of earlier research. In 1976, for example, the Pretrial Services Institute (PTSI) of Westchester in White Plains, NY, created a program to interview all criminal court clients, including those who were initially unable to post bail, regarding their eligibility for release from jail. The interview process was developed to objectively assess the defendant's qualifications for release through **ROR** (release on own recognizance). Program operations included screening, eligibility determinations, monitoring where appropriate, and court notification of those who fail to satisfy release requirements. A 1979 assessment of this program showed that PTSI increased the rate of defendant releases on recognizance and reduced the number of defendant failures to appear in court.[19] Interestingly, a 1993 evaluation of PTSI's Bail Expediting Program, which screens defendants being detained at the jail on bail of $5,000 or less, reduced the number of people who remained in jail while awaiting trial. It was estimated that the program saved taxpayers $560,593.[20]

Evaluations of pretrial services like that of the White Plains, NY, program add to the bodies of research aimed at answering the practitioner's question, "What works?" Such evaluations are especially helpful in determining what happens to pretrial defendants after their participation in a program. Outcome evaluations are scientifically and professionally necessary to promote and provide evidence-based practice in the discipline of pretrial services.

Evidence-Based Practices for Pretrial Services

In 2004, the Crime and Justice Institute published a study that discusses eight evidence-based principles for effective community-based interventions:

1. Assessing actuarial risk/needs
2. Enhancing intrinsic motivation
3. Targeting interventions
4. Providing skill training with directed practice (in particular, using cognitive behavioral treatment methods)
5. Increasing positive reinforcement
6. Engaging ongoing support in natural communities
7. Measuring relevant processes/practices
8. Providing measurement feedback

Further, the publication presents an integrated model for effective offender interventions based on these eight interdependent principles. Unfortunately, the publication indicates that only a few community supervision agencies (probation, parole, residential community corrections) are using these effective interventions and their concepts and principles.[21]

In a later publication, Crime and Justice Institute researchers note that evidence-based practices for pretrial services programs must sometimes diverge from those identified for community corrections. One fundamental difference is that pretrial programs deal with defendants who are awaiting trial (presumed innocent), while community corrections programs may supervise offenders who have been convicted of a crime. Thus, the rationales of rehabilitation and punishment differ for the two populations.

Second, pretrial and postconviction programs differ fundamentally in their intended outcomes. Evidence-based practices are considered effective for the postconviction (community corrections) discipline when they reduce offender risk and subsequent recidivism. The intended outcome of pretrial services programs is to reduce pretrial failure to appear in court and risk to the community while awaiting trial. In other words, postconviction discipline seeks to impact long-term criminal behavior, while pretrial services focus on the immediate needs of the defendants to ensure their court appearance and reduce criminal behavior during the pretrial stage. These distinctions should be considered when applying evidence-based practices to the pretrial services field.[22]

The use of evidence-based practices (EBP) in pretrial services improves the ability of the criminal justice system to protect the legal rights of those being processed and presumed innocent by the criminal justice system, while ensuring that the public is protected from high-risk, dangerous offenders who have yet to be convicted of a charged crime. Reinforcing the link between EBP, quality assurance, and data-driven decision making should be a goal for all agencies that provide pretrial release services. CBC Online 5.2 considers the operation of pretrial services in New York City.

Purposes and Process of Pretrial Release and Diversion

Each year approximately 14 million arrests occur in the United States. Most of these arrested persons are booked into a county jail and released on bail within a short period of time. Consider, for example, that between 1990 and 2004, 62 percent of felony defendants in state courts in the 75 largest counties were released prior to the disposition of their case.[23] Given the vast numbers of arrested persons entering the criminal justice system, pretrial release and diversion programs help to maximize the release rate of

THE NEW YORK CITY CRIMINAL JUSTICE AGENCY, INC. (CJA)

CBC Online

CJA is a not-for-profit corporation serving New York City's criminal justice system under contract with the Office of the Coordinator for Criminal Justice. CJA was established in 1973 to provide pretrial services as pioneered and tested by the Vera Institute of Justice's Manhattan Bail Project. CJA staff interview defendants arrested in New York City, make recommendations for pretrial release, and notify defendants of upcoming court dates. Within the agency, a research department conducts studies covering a broad array of criminal justice policy concerns.

Review the research briefs series that summarizes the results of some of these studies. How can CJA's research briefs be useful to pretrial service agencies concerned with evidence-based practices? Does one particular research study conducted by CJA stand out as most important to pretrial services in recent years?

Visit CBC Online 5.2 at www.mhhe.com/bayens1e

persons accused of crimes while minimizing the failure to appear and rearrest rates of those released.

While pretrial release and diversion serve many similar purposes, they also differ in several respects. First, pretrial release is defined as a nonmonetary alternative to detention for defendants who are unable to post bail. While most defendants will continue through the criminal justice system (i.e., prosecution and disposition), they are allowed to maintain residency within the community under limited, if any, supervision in lieu of detention. The two types of pretrial release are release on recognizance (ROR) and **conditional-un/supervised release**. Diversion programs, on the other hand, give first-time offenders a second chance at having a clean criminal history by deferring the defendant from prosecution. The original definition published in 1978 by the National Association of Pretrial Services Agencies Board of Directors still has value in setting the parameters for diversion: "It is a strategy designed to offer a nonpunitive case processing to selected individuals charged with a crime."[24] The two basic categories of pretrial diversion include treatment in lieu of prosecution and alternative sanction before judgment. For the purposes of our discussions in this chapter, we will take up only the matter of diversion in lieu of prosecution. Alternative sanction before judgment, which covers a range of alternative programs available to the courts before sentencing (e.g., drug court), are discussed in other chapters of the text. A brief description of the general characteristics of pretrial release and diversion is provided in Exhibit 5.2.

The Role of Pretrial Services Programs

According to a nationwide study by the Bureau of Justice Administration, a total of 337 jurisdictions either have or might have a pretrial services program.[25] Programs have been developed in a variety of rural, suburban, and urban jurisdictions, and operate in public agencies (i.e., probation departments, court offices, and local jails) and under independent contractors. For example, the private sector pretrial program Maine Pretrial Services, Inc. (MPS) was incorporated in 1983 and provides **pre-arraignment** screening and risk assessment, pretrial release and supervision, and other services to

EXHIBIT 5.2 Characteristics of Pretrial Release and Diversion

Pretrial Release	Diversion
1. Released on recognizance (ROR): The court releases a defendant on a signed agreement that he or she will appear in court.	1. Treatment in lieu of prosecution: Arrest charges against the defendant are dropped if the person completes treatment. The decision to order treatment as part of pretrial diversion typically, though not always, rests with the prosecutor's office.
2. Conditional-un/supervised release— *Unsupervised:* Defendants are released on their promise to adhere to court-ordered conditions. Compliance is without supervision. *Supervised release:* Release conditions such as contact requirements exceed those of conditional release without supervision. Compliance is closely monitored; in some cases house arrest or electronic monitoring is required. *Third-party custody:* Defendants are released to the custody of another individual or agency that assumes responsibility for their appearance in court.	2. Alternative sanction before judgment: The defendant is placed in a program (usually supervised) and the charges are pending. If the alternative sanction is completed, then charges may be dismissed. This happens commonly in traffic court but has recently been applied to low-level nonviolent offenses as well.

criminal defendants in all of Maine's 16 counties.[26] Also, a few pretrial programs are operated by private nonprofit organizations.

A survey of pretrial programs conducted by the Pretrial Justice Institute in 2008 indicates that the number of pretrial programs increased 11 percent since a previous survey in 2001. Nearly half the programs participating in the survey began operating after 1990, including 15 percent that have begun since 2000. Survey data shows that 26 percent of the pretrial programs operated with budgets of $200,000 per year or less. Moreover, 21 percent serve multiple localities, typically two or three counties in a particular region. In 2008, the number of staff increased to an average of 22 personnel, and most programs reported starting annual salaries for line staff between $30,000 and $40,000. More than 70 percent of programs have established a mission statement specific to pretrial services.[27] An example from Merrimack County in New Hampshire appears in Exhibit 5.3.

In general, the purposes of the pretrial release decision include providing **due process (of law)** to those accused of crime, maintaining the integrity of the judicial process by securing defendants for trial, and protecting victims, witnesses, and the community

EXHIBIT 5.3 Merrimack County, New Hampshire, Mission Statement

Merrimack County Pretrial Service's mission is to improve bail setting by providing complete, accurate, and neutral information to the court by identifying those for whom alternatives to pretrial incarceration are appropriate. Arrestees released by the court on pretrial supervision are monitored to ensure compliance with court ordered conditions set to reduce the likelihood of failure to appear or pretrial rearrest. Decisions at bail setting require courts to balance potentially conflicting goals. Nearly all bail laws mandate a presumption of non-financial release, or release on the least restrictive means necessary for persons presumed innocent of a crime. However, these statutes also compel courts to ensure the justice system's integrity, and in some instances, the public's safety in setting bail.[28]

from threat, danger, or interference. Pretrial service officers conduct pretrial investigations to assist the judicial officer (judges and magistrates) when deciding whether to release a defendant on personal recognizance or unsecured appearance bond, release a defendant on a condition or combination of conditions, temporarily detain a defendant, or confine a defendant. They also supervise defendants who are released from detention, monitor their compliance with special conditions of release, and report to the court on the defendant's performance while on pretrial release.

The American Bar Association (ABA) defines the goals of the pretrial release decision as "Providing due process to those accused of crime, maintaining the integrity of the judicial process by securing defendants for trial, and protecting victims, witnesses, and the community from threat, danger, or interference."[29] Achieving these goals requires a balance that maximizes pretrial release while minimizing pretrial misconduct (i.e., failure to appear in court and rearrest on new charges).

Federal and state statutes and standards of both the ABA and the National District Attorneys Association (NDAA) provide guidance on striking this balance. Statutes and standards specify the factors the court is to consider in the pretrial release decision. Typically, these include:[30]

- The nature and circumstance of the offense
- The defendant's ties to the community, length of residence, employment status, and physical and mental condition
- The defendant's prior criminal history and record of appearance in court
- The defendant's current probation, parole, or pretrial release status

Judicial Discretion and Equality. The 1961 Vera Foundation Study, mentioned earlier, reports that in addition to the physical, psychological, and financial burdens of pretrial detention, individuals who appear in court while being confined in jail may receive harsher sentences than those persons who were granted pretrial release. Moreover, the report notes that "the defendant at liberty pending trial stands a better chance of not being convicted or, if convicted, of not receiving a prison sentence."[31] Similarly, in a 1980s study of discrimination practices in the criminal courts, researchers found that defendants with families are more likely to be granted pretrial release and are less likely to receive the harsher types of nonjail sentences than those who do not have families; the mitigating effect of being "family-connected" is stronger for women than men.[32]

Why would defendants who are released from jail pending trial be treated differently by the courts than those kept in confinement? One possible answer is the influence of employment. Defendants who are gainfully employed in the community may be less at risk to reoffend than defendants who are not employed, as unemployment is a major contributor to crime causation. Also, defendants who work are positioned to support their families, pay taxes, and disburse monetary restitution. Research on the effect of unemployment on sentencing seems to support this view. For example, a study of sentencing decisions in Kansas City found that unemployed defendants were significantly more likely than employed defendants to be sentenced to prison. In another study of judicial discretion practices in Chicago, researchers found that unemployed offenders faced longer sentences than employed offenders.[33]

Because of such studies, several legal challenges regarding procedural due process rights of persons being considered for bail and pretrial release programs have occurred in the past three decades. Central to these challenges is the concept of equal justice under law, which is deeply embedded in the U.S. Constitution and is a core value of

American society. In the area of pretrial release/detention decisionmaking, it means that all defendants should have the same opportunity for consideration for release without regard to race, sex, economic status, or other extra-legal case factors. Our opening story of the diversion agreement entered into between the Florida State's Attorney General Office and Mr. Rush Limbaugh demonstrates the application of due process in pretrial release.

The legal basis for which defendants enjoy protections during the pretrial stage can be found in the Constitution of the United States, case law, and state and federal statutes. Exhibit 5.4 provides a brief description of six legal principles that are most critical to defendants whose status is that of awaiting trial. Additionally, the ABA's Standards for Pretrial Release provide information relating to what judges are required to consider. For example, when considering the release of a defendant on own recognizance, section 10-5.1 of the Standards[34] notes that:

1. It should be presumed that defendants are entitled to release on personal recognizance on the condition that they attend all required court proceedings and that they do not commit any criminal offense; and
2. In determining whether there is a substantial risk of nonappearance or threat to the community or any person or to the integrity of the judicial process if the defendant is released, the judicial officer should consider the pretrial services assessment of the defendant's risk of willful failure to appear in court or risk of threat to the safety of the community or any person, victim, or witness.

Pretrial Investigation. Before the initial court appearance, pretrial services personnel collect information about the defendant, primarily by means of interviews and record checks. Typically, all persons who are eligible for bail receive this kind of **pretrial assessment** and are interviewed while in custody. The goal of the interview is to obtain background information (e.g., name and aliases, date of birth, address,

Pretrial release allows defendants to maintain residency in the community under limited, if any, supervision in lieu of detention. What are the two types of pretrial release?

EXHIBIT 5.4 Six Legal Protections Important to Pretrial Defendants

1. Presumption of Innocence. This initial principle can be found in case law dating back to 1895. There, in his opinion for the Supreme Court in *Coffin* v. *United States*, Justice White wrote, "The principle that there is a presumption of innocence in favor of the accused is the undoubted law, axiomatic and elementary, and its enforcement lies at the foundation of the administration of our criminal law . . . It is stated as unquestioned in the textbooks, and has been referred to as a matter of course in the decisions of this court and in the courts of the several States."[35] In brief, the mandate is to ensure a fair process for all persons charged with crimes, to reduce the possibility of an error that would convict an innocent person. In criminal law, Blackstone's formulation, also known as Blackstone's ratio, is popularly stated as "better that ten guilty persons escape than that one innocent suffer."[36]
2. Right to Counsel. The right to counsel in criminal proceedings is found in the Sixth Amendment to the U.S. Constitution, which states that "In all criminal prosecutions, the accused shall enjoy the right to a speedy and public trial . . . and to have the assistance of counsel for his defense." The U.S. Supreme Court developed the Sixth Amendment right to counsel in state proceedings gradually in the 20th century. The acknowledged starting point was in 1932, in *Powell* v. *Alabama*. In *Powell*, also referred to as the "Scottsboro Case," the Court held that counsel was required in all state capital proceedings. Then in 1963, the Sixth Amendment right to counsel was extended to the states by the Court in *Gideon* v. *Wainwright*.[37] In this case the Court unanimously held that an indigent person accused of a serious crime was entitled to the appointment of defense counsel at state expense. The Court clarified the scope of that right in 1972 in *Argersinger* v. *Hamlin*,[38] holding that an indigent defendant must be offered counsel in any misdemeanor case "that actually leads to imprisonment." Under *Argersinger*, a pretrial defendant who is charged with an offense under which imprisonment is a possible sanction qualifies initially for appointed counsel.
3. Right Against Self-incrimination. The Fifth Amendment to the U.S. Constitution states that "No person . . . shall be compelled in any criminal case to be a witness against himself." This amendment gives individuals the right to decline to answer questions or make statements. The U.S. Supreme Court clarified this right in 1966 in *Miranda* v. *Arizona* (along with *Vignera* v. *New York, Westover* v. *United States*, and *California* v. *Stewart*), finding that "when an individual is taken into custody or otherwise deprived of his freedom by the authorities in any significant way and is subjected to questioning, the privilege against self-incrimination is jeopardized. Procedural safeguards must be employed to protect the privilege."[39] The procedural safeguards detailed by the Court are well known in the United States as "Miranda Warnings" and hold that before any questioning by police, a suspect must be informed that he or she has the right to remain silent; that anything said can be used against the suspect in a subsequent criminal proceeding; that he or she has the right to the presence of an attorney during the interrogation; and that, if the suspect cannot afford an attorney, one will be appointed at the state's expense.
4. Due Process of Law. The Fifth Amendment to the U.S. Constitution provides that "No person shall be . . . deprived of life, liberty, or property, without *due process of law*" (emphasis added). The Fourteenth

information relating to the charges) and to verify the information in criminal justice database systems. Information gathered during the interview is held confidential and shared only with the judicial officer making the decision about release.

Pretrial officers are responsible for verifying the interview information as rapidly as possible to complete the process before the defendant's first court appearance. Priority items for verification are residency, employment status, family and community ties, criminal record, and court appearance record. What the officer learns from collateral sources (e.g., other persons, documents, and online research) can verify or contradict the information provided by the defendant.

Risk Assessment. Often a risk assessment tool is used to incorporate the information from the pretrial investigation into a numerical score that guides the release decision. The assessment places the defendant in a risk level (i.e., defendant's risks of failing to appear at future court hearings or posing a risk to community safety) and identifies any condition or combination of conditions designed to address the identified risks. As noted previously, a range of release options is available, such as release on recognizance, restrictive nonfinancial conditions, and as the last resort, financial conditions.

Amendment states that "no State shall . . . deprive any person of life, liberty, or property, without *due process of law* . . ." (emphasis added). The Due Process Clause of the Fifth Amendment applies to the federal government and the Fourteenth Amendment applies to the states. Thus, for the purposes of criminal procedure, all persons charged with a federal offense are guaranteed due process under the Fifth Amendment, and all persons charged with a nonfederal (i.e., state or local) offense are guaranteed due process under the Fourteenth Amendment. Both amendments provide that the government shall not take a person's life, liberty, or property without due process of law.

5. Equal Protection of the Laws. The Fourteenth Amendment to the U.S. Constitution provides that "no State shall make or enforce any law which shall abridge the privileges or immunities of citizens of the United States; nor shall any State deprive any person of life, liberty, or property, without due process of law; nor deny to any person within its jurisdiction the equal protection of the laws." Equal protection of the laws does not mean that all persons must be treated equally at all times. Rather, equal protection means that discrimination among groups must have a rational and constitutional basis. As it applies to pretrial defendants, equal justice has been extended to include a person's financial status. The courts have ruled that pretrial release should not be based solely on a person's ability to pay, and that to do so is a violation of equal protection.[40] This protection further applies to criminal trials. Justice Black made this clear in the 1956 U.S. Supreme Court opinion in *Griffin* v. *Illinois,* in which he wrote, "In criminal trials a State can no more discriminate on account of poverty than on account of religion, race, or color. Plainly the ability to pay costs in advance bears no rational relationship to a defendant's guilt or innocence and could not be used as an excuse to deprive a defendant of a fair trial."[41]
6. Right to Bail that Is Not Excessive. The right to reasonable bail was established in the Judiciary Act of 1789 and the Eighth Amendment to the U.S. Constitution, which states: "Excessive bail shall not be required, nor excessive fines imposed, nor cruel and unusual punishments inflicted." Moreover, the presumption for release pending trial was upheld in two U.S. Supreme Court cases. In *Stack* v. *Boyle*, the court held that the purpose of bail is to assure the presence of the defendant in court, and that any bail amount set higher than an amount reasonably calculated to fulfill this purpose is excessive under the Eighth Amendment to the U.S. Constitution. In *U.S.* v. *Salerno*, the Court upheld a presumption for release. In his opinion, Chief Justice William Rehnquist wrote, "In our society, liberty is the norm, and detention prior to trial or without trial is the carefully limited exception." One of the earliest cases relating to burden of proof (presumption of innocence) in pretrial detention hearings was the 1980 California Supreme Court case of *Van Atta* v. *Scott.* In this case, the court shifted the burden of proof away from defendants, who previously had been forced to demonstrate why they should be released, to prosecutors, who had to show why defendants should not be released.[42]

Conditions are recommended on a graduated basis from least (i.e., minimum number of contacts) to most restrictive (i.e., intense supervision). Community-based programs that are evidence-based rely on valid risk assessment instruments, and for that reason we expand on it in Chapter 4.

Both NAPSA and ABA strongly recommend that pretrial services programs use an objective and research-based risk assessment instrument to assist the judicial officer in making release decisions. NAPSA Standard 3.4 states that "assessment and recommendations should be based on an explicit, objective, and consistent policy for evaluating risks and identifying appropriate release options."[43] ABA Standard 10-4.2 also calls for the use of objective criteria in a pretrial program's risk assessment, explaining that "pretrial services investigation should focus on assembling reliable and objective information relevant to determining pretrial release and should be organized according to an explicit, objective and consistent policy for evaluating risk and identifying appropriate release options."[44] Exhibit 5.5 provides an example of a typical risk assessment instrument that collects data related to length of residence, employment status, substance abuse, prior criminal record, and record of failure to appear in court.

EXHIBIT 5.5 Risk Assessment Instrument

Defendant's Name: ______________ Date of Offense: ______________
Court Case/Docket Number: ______________ Bond Amount: ______________
Date of Pretrial Assessment: ______________ Court Date: ______________

Section I. Charge(s) Information & Criminal History **Verified ✔**

1. Based on sentencing guideline definitions: ☐ ☐
   - 1 = Misdemeanor non-person or drug crime
   - 2 = Misdemeanor person crime
   - 3 = Felony non-person or drug crime
   - 4 = Felony person crime
2. Total number of prior misdemeanor and felony convictions: ☐ ☐
3. Prior failure to appear warrants filed: ☐ ☐
   - 1 = Defendant failed to appear in court in prior case(s)
   - 0 = No failure to appear record

Section II. Community Stability

4. Employed at the time of arrest: ☐ ☐
   - 0 = Defendant is employed full time; retired; disabled; or unable to work
   - 1 = Defendant is employed part time
   - 2 = Defendant is unemployed
5. Defendant lived at his/her current residence for 6 months or more: ☐ ☐
   - 0 = Yes
   - 1 = No

Section III. Health Measures

6. Illegal substance use in the last 90 days: ☐ ☐
   - 0 = No
   - 1 = Yes
7. Self-reported alcohol abuse: ☐ ☐
   - 0 = No
   - 1 = Yes
8. Psychiatric treatment in last year: ☐ ☐
   - 0 = No
   - 1 = Yes

Total SCORE ☐

Assessment Cutoff Scores

Score of 0–3 = Low Risk

Score of 4–7 = Medium Risk Pretrial Services Recommendation: Release ☐ Detain ☐

Score of 8–10 = High Risk Court Decision: Release ☐ Detain ☐

Numerical "risk" scores attempt to predict future behavior of pretrial defendants. The more risk factors that are present at the time of the initial interview, the greater the likelihood of future criminal behavior or noncompliance (i.e., the higher the risk score, the higher the risk potential).[45] Moreover, most pretrial services programs collect supplementary information to better help judges make release decisions or to set conditions that are appropriate for the circumstances of the case. While numerically scored risk assessment instruments are objective, such supplemental data tends to be subjective and reported in narrative form. For example, if the defendant used extreme force in the commission of the crime, the information would be relevant to the judge when making a decision whether to release a pretrial defendant. In this case, a pretrial release officer would likely research the defendant's past for indicators of violent behavior and provide relevant information in the supplemental report.

Some pretrial programs have developed special risk assessment procedures for defendants charged with certain types of crimes. For example, researchers conducting a survey of pretrial services found that one-quarter of the 202 programs that participated in their study had developed special risk assessment procedures for defendants charged with domestic violence offenses. Moreover, some procedures for assessing risk are aimed at specific populations. In the study noted above, it was noted that one Ohio program created a gender-specific risk assessment instrument and had developed special programming to supervise women with co-occurring substance abuse and mental health disorders.[46] Last, risk instruments to assess juvenile defendants may place greater emphasis on factors relating to family, school, and mental and physical development. Characteristics of detention that encourage antisocial behavior, for example, may be of greater concern with juveniles than adult defendants. In his remarks at the Vera Institute of Justice's 2009 Annual Justice Address, U.S. Attorney General Eric Holder noted that "Smart risk assessments can identify which offenders can safely remain in their communities and which require continued detention and more intensive supervision. Data analysis can determine which offenders pose a higher recidivism risk based on the type of crime the offender was charged with and the offender's prior record. For example, risk assessments might determine that removing a 16-year-old, nonviolent, first-time offender from his family and school and placing him in a juvenile detention facility is a bad idea because it would actually increase the risk of recidivism, and waste taxpayer dollars besides."[47]

Pretrial Supervision in the Community. The supervision of pretrial defendants includes contact supervision and referral to community services. Monitoring defendants is individualized and typically based on a determined level of supervision. If the court imposes conditions of release, such as testing for substance use and electronic monitoring, pretrial supervision provides an additional focus on the defendants' compliance with such conditions, as well as regular monitoring required to manage the case.

Pretrial services programs have progressively increased the use of technology to aid in the supervision of defendants. Most pretrial programs use drug and alcohol testing as a supervision tool. **Breathalyzers**, devices for estimating blood alcohol content from a defendant's breath, are commonplace in pretrial service programs. Recent technology, referred to as transdermal alcohol monitoring, also allows testing for alcohol by means of remote systems. A device secured to the defendant's ankle tests the alcohol concentration through the skin. The bracelet is water-resistant and tamper-resistant, and testing usually occurs once or twice and hour. If alcohol is detected, the system can be programmed to automatically begin sampling every 30 minutes until alcohol is no longer present. The results are stored in the bracelet and uploaded each day via a modem in the defendant's home. The results are then analyzed and posted on a secure Web site, so officers can access the information when needed. If the defendant attempts to place products (e.g., tape, paper) between the skin and the bracelet to defeat it, the built-in tamper technology will alert monitoring personnel.

In addition to technologies that aid in the pretrial supervision of defendants' alcohol and drug use, most pretrial programs use at least one form of electronic monitoring. Typically, electronic monitoring involves using continuous signaling devices, which sound an alert if the defendant leaves a restricted area. A more recent innovation in monitoring a defendant's location is the global positioning system (GPS) technology, which allows the exact movements of defendants in the community to be tracked from a remote location on a continuous basis. There are two types of GPS devices: active and passive. Active GPS provides real-time data from satellites to monitoring personnel who can access that data via a secure Web site as it occurs. Passive GPS data is collected and stored throughout the day and reported after the defendant arrives home and places the device in a docking station connected to his or her telephone line. The data can then be reviewed by officers via a secure Web site. Both types of devices utilize an ankle bracelet design. Data collected typically includes date, time, and travel direction. Cell phone technology built into the devices is used to communicate the GPS data to the monitoring center. GPS technology also assists with locating and returning defendants who fail to appear in court.

Managing the Risks of Nonappearance and Public Safety

Defendants on pretrial release pose two major types of risks: nonappearance for scheduled court dates and commission of a new criminal offense. In addressing these issues, a number of pretrial programs have engaged in research to evaluate how well risk assessment works in their agencies. Specific attention has been given to assessing the risk of nonappearance. Also, many agencies have used research to help shape policy and practices (e.g., adoption of **Level of Service Inventory-Revised LSI-R**) relating to monitoring and supervising persons on pretrial release. With regard to new crimes, programs have examined rearrest rates among pretrial defendants.

While much of the research into evidence-based practices related to risk assessment has focused on the relationship between assessment instruments and risks of nonappearance, some studies have concentrated on public safety issues. Typically, these research studies have examined factors that help in predicting recidivism (i.e., rearrest) while on pretrial release. Specific inquiry has been made into such factors as offense type, prior record, the effect of type of release, and community ties. In general, study findings seem to agree that criminal history and community ties are influential predictors of pretrial rearrest. That is, defendants with more serious criminal histories are most likely to be rearrested during the pretrial period. Community ties, particularly employment, reduce the likelihood of pretrial rearrest. In the next section, we examine a few of the research studies related to risk assessment.

Study of the Federal Court System. The largest study on pretrial risk assessment analyzed 565,178 cases processed through the federal pretrial services system between fiscal years 2001 and 2007. A major objective of this research was to identify statistically significant and policy relevant predictors of pretrial risk (failure to appear and danger to the community) of federal criminal defendants.[48]

The average age of the defendants in the study was 34, and men made up 85 percent of all defendants processed by pretrial services. At the time of their initial appearance, 43 percent of all defendants had lived in the area for less than one year. The employment status of defendants varied across years and ranged from 49 to 56 percent employed at the time of the initial appearance, with an average of 52 percent of defendants employed between FY2001 and FY2007. On average, 51 percent of all defendants had a substance abuse problem at the time of the initial appearance. Defendants' primary charge was a felony (92 percent of the time), with drug-related offenses (36 percent) as the most common primary charges for defendants. Eighty-four percent of all defendants had never failed to appear in court.[49]

Failure to appear was measured by whether a defendant had ever failed to appear for a scheduled court appearance or absconded from pretrial supervision while pending trial. Danger to the community was measured by the presence of a bail revocation due to a new arrest for a crime that was allegedly committed while the defendant was released pending trial. Defendants who were deemed to have failed to appear or to have been a danger to the community pending trial were classified "failure," and those defendants who experienced neither and remained in the community during the entire time pending trial were classified "successful."[50]

The results of the study revealed that the best predictors of **pretrial failure** include the following:

1. Primary Charge Category—Defendants charged with a felony were 61 percent more likely to fail pending trial when compared to defendants who were charged with a misdemeanor infraction.
2. Primary Charge Type—When compared to defendants charged with a theft- or fraud-related offense, defendants charged with a firearm offense (51 percent), a drug offense (78 percent), or an immigration law violation (78 percent) were more likely to fail pending trial.
3. Pending Charges—Defendants who had one or more misdemeanor or felony charges pending at the time of arrest were 20 percent more likely to fail pending trial when compared to defendants who did not have a pending charge.
4. Prior Misdemeanor Arrests—Defendants with prior misdemeanor arrests were more likely to fail pending trial when compared to defendants who did not have prior misdemeanor arrests: one prior misdemeanor arrest (13 percent more likely); two prior misdemeanor arrests (32 percent more likely); three prior misdemeanor arrests (45 percent more likely); four misdemeanor arrests (59 percent more likely); and five or more prior misdemeanor arrests (69 percent more likely).
5. Prior Felony Arrests—Defendants with prior felony arrests were more likely to fail pending trial when compared to defendants who did not have prior felony arrests: one prior felony arrest (22 percent more likely) and two or more prior felony arrests (38 percent more likely).
6. Prior Failures to Appear—Defendants with prior failures to appear in court were more likely to fail pending trial when compared to defendants who did not have a prior failure to appear in court: one prior failure to appear (22 percent more likely); and two or more prior failures to appear (35 percent more likely).
7. Employment Status—Defendants who were unemployed at the time of their arrest were 21 percent more likely to fail pending trial when compared to defendants who were employed.
8. Residence Status—Defendants who did not own or were not buying their residence were more likely to fail pending trial when compared to defendants who did own or were buying their residence or had a mortgage on their home: renting

(65 percent more likely); making no financial contribution to residence (74 percent more likely); no residence/place to live (2.1 times or 110 percent more likely); and another type of residence (48 percent more likely).

9. Substance Abuse Type—Defendants who abused alcohol (21 percent), cannabis (23 percent), and narcotics (40 percent) were more likely to fail pending trial when compared to defendants who did not abuse any substances.[51]

The Virginia Pretrial Risk Assessment Instrument. In 2002, the Virginia Pretrial Risk Assessment Instrument (VPRAI)[52] was developed to identify the likelihood of failure to appear in court and the danger to the community posed by a defendant pending trial and to assist pretrial officers in making a bail recommendation. Using personal interviews, criminal history data, court records, and adult criminal justice supervision records, data was collected from a sample of 1,971 adult defendants arrested in select Virginia localities between July 1, 1998, and June 30, 1999. Nine risk factors were identified as the best predictors of pretrial failure. The first six factors were measures of criminal history. The remaining factors were measures of residence, employment/primary child caregiver, and substance abuse. These predictors are quite similar to those found in the study of the federal pretrial services system.

The VPRAI was automated in the statewide Pretrial and Community Corrections Case Management System, and by 2005 all pretrial services agencies in Virginia were using the risk instrument. After two years of statewide usage, the Virginia Department of Criminal Justice Services sought to validate the accuracy of the instrument. In the validation study, 4,378 defendants were selected from a population of defendants who were arrested between January 1 and December 30, 2005, who had both a pretrial investigation and completed VPRAI. A secondary dataset consisted of all defendants released to the supervision of a pretrial services agency between January 1 and December 30, 2005. The sample included 7,174 defendants and consisted of persons released with a condition of pretrial supervision to any of the pretrial services agencies.

When the validation study was completed, the VPRAI was revised and presently consists of eight risk factors. Minor revisions to the descriptions of the risk factors were made during the validation study based on the advisory committee's experience with implementation and use of the VPRAI and to improve understanding of the risk factors. The eight risk factors[53] are provided below.

1. Primary Charge Type—Defendants charged with a felony are more likely to fail pending trial than defendants charged with a misdemeanor.
2. Pending Charge(s)—Defendants who have pending charge(s) at the time of their arrest are more likely to fail pending trial.
3. Criminal History—Defendants with at least one prior misdemeanor or felony conviction are more likely to fail pending trial.
4. Two or More Failures to Appear– Defendants with two or more failures to appear are more likely to fail pending trial.
5. Two or More Violent Convictions—Defendants with two or more violent convictions are more likely to fail pending trial.
6. Length at Current Residence—Defendants who live at their current residence for less than one year are more likely to fail pending trial.
7. Employed/Primary Caregiver—Defendants who have not been employed continuously at one or more jobs during the two years prior to their arrest or who are not primary caregivers are more likely to fail pending trial.

8. History of Drug Abuse—Defendants with a history of drug abuse are more likely to fail pending trial.

Measures of Criminal History and Rearrest. The Bureau of Justice Statistics reports that a survey of state court felony defendants in the 75 largest U.S. counties charged with pretrial misconduct from 1990–2004 show that about 16 percent of all defendants released (no matter the type of bail) were rearrested.[54] In the survey of felony cases, rearrest occurred most often when the defendant had been charged with robbery (21 percent), drug trafficking (21 percent), or motor vehicle theft (20 percent). Defendants age 20 or younger (20 percent) had a higher rearrest rate than older defendants, and males were more likely to be rearrested than female defendants. With regard to prior offense, those defendants who possessed a prior arrest record were three times more likely to be rearrested than defendants with no prior arrest record.[55]

In a series of reports summarizing the research of the New York City Criminal Justice Agency (CJA), pretrial rearrest among defendants was examined from a sample of defendants arrested in New York City during the first quarter of 2001. Data was drawn from a three-month cohort of arrests made from January through March, 2001. The majority of the defendants were male, and the median age was 30 years. Slightly fewer than half the defendants were black, one-third were Hispanic, and the remainder were white or of other ethnicity. Criminal history factors had the strongest impact on the likelihood of pretrial rearrest. Among defendants who were initially arrested on a felony charge and were rearrested during pretrial release, the rearrest charge was as likely to be a nonfelony as a felony. About a third of defendants initially arrested on a lesser-severity charge were rearrested for a felony. The most common rearrest offense type was a drug charge. Approximately 60 percent of those initially arrested on a drug charge were rearrested for the same type of offense.[56]

The Impact of Community-Ties Factors. Studies have shown that defendants with strong community ties (e.g., regular contact with family, residency in the community for a length of time, stable employment) have better outcomes on pretrial release than defendants with weaker ties. Consequently, some agencies rely heavily on these factors to predict pretrial failure to appear. Consider for example, another study conducted by the New York Criminal Justice Agency (CJA) that involved validating a three-year-old risk instrument used to make pretrial release on recognizance (ROR) recommendations for defendants arrested in New York City. In practice, CJA submits a recommendation to the arraigning judge, who makes the first release decision based on the following criteria:

- Character, reputation, habits, and mental condition
- Employment and financial resources
- Family ties and length of residence in the community
- Criminal record
- Record of previous adjudications as a juvenile
- Previous court appearance record
- Probability or improbability of conviction
- Sentence to be imposed if convicted

While a defendant's record and other measures of criminal history are taken into account, the release recommendation by CJA is based solely on a defendant's ties to the community. Defendants who have strong community ties that have been verified are considered low risk and receive a "recommended" evaluation for ROR. Those who have modest ties to the community or who have some unverified community ties are considered moderately at risk and receive a "qualified" rating. Defendants with insufficient community ties are given a "no recommendation rating."

Results of the study to validate the ROR recommendation instrument showed that variables relating to community ties had a statistically significant relationship with pretrial failure to appear. While slight changes were observed in the relative weight of some of the variables relating to community ties, it was concluded that no major adjustments were necessary to the items in the instrument.[57]

The Role of Diversion Programs

In general, the purpose of pretrial diversion is to provide a dispositional alternative for a defendant charged with a crime. Defendants voluntarily enter into a diversion program in lieu of prosecution. If they successfully complete an individualized program plan, the result is dismissal of the arresting charge(s). Diversion programs enhance justice and public safety by addressing the root cause of the defendant's arrest and reducing the stigma that often accompanies a record of conviction. The question of whether an offender should be diverted from further prosecution depends in large part on whether the offender is a low risk to reoffend.

The gatekeeper of the diversion process is the prosecutor. Arrest reports are forwarded from law enforcement to the prosecutor's office for review and possible case filing. If a case is not eligible for prosecution (e.g., for lack of evidence), it is typically dismissed. Sending nonmeritorious cases to diversion would undermine the judicial process along with the integrity of the diversion program. Moreover, it is only after the formal filing that a defendant is fully aware of the charge(s) and the potential consequences of prosecution.

The opportunity to enter into a diversion program is presented to the defendant as soon as possible to facilitate careful consideration of this dispositional alternative. Certain types of crimes, however, require that an evaluation be conducted before diversion is offered to the defendant. In Washington state, for example, a program exists that allows a person suffering from an alcohol problem, a drug addiction, or a mental health issue to seek permission of the court to go through an intensive treatment program in lieu of being prosecuted. The law allows a defendant to request the court for deferral or postponement of their case for five years while he or she seeks treatment for their disease. To qualify for deferred prosecution, the defendant must obtain an evaluation from a state-approved treatment agency. The agency conducts an assessment, and if it concludes that the criminal conduct occurred as a result of alcoholism, drug addiction, or mental health problems and that the defendant is amenable to treatment, the person is eligible for deferred prosecution as long as he or she has never been granted a deferred prosecution before.[58]

Some diversion programs are designed to serve specialized populations. For example, the Substance Abuse and Mental Health Services Administration's (SAMHSA) Center for Mental Health Services (CMHS) funded nine jail diversion programs across the country to learn new ways to divert persons with co-occurring substance abuse and mental health disorders. The goal of these programs was to divert low-level offenders at initial contact with police before formal charges are brought (prebooking programs). Also, court-based and jail-based programs were established for persons to be diverted after arrest and booking (postbooking). From September 1998 to May 2000, nearly 2,000 persons with co-occurring mental illness and substance use disorders were screened and assessed. During that time 1,000 persons were diverted in the programs. A comparison of the characteristics of diverted and nondiverted groups showed that diverted persons were more likely to be female; to have a primary diagnosis of schizophrenia or a mood disorder with psychotic features; and to have received Federal Income Supplements. The diverted participants were also less likely to live with a spouse or partner; to have substance use problems; or to have been arrested and spent time in jail. In general, the diverted group incurred higher community-based treatment costs, and the nondiverted group incurred higher jail costs.[59]

The Merrimack County, New Hampshire, County Attorney's Office offers another example of a diversion program that contains a component to serve a specialized population. The First time Alcohol and Substance Treatment (FAST) program targets first-time marijuana and alcohol offenders (age 16 and older). The goal is to provide services that will help prevent these defendants from committing additional drug and alcohol crimes in the future. Between 2003–2008, over 1,500 individuals have been referred to the FAST Program. According to a study conducted by The University of New Hampshire in 2005, the majority of FAST referrals (approximately 77 percent) completed the program. The recidivism rate for graduates of the FAST Program was only 16 percent. For those participants who didn't complete the FAST Program, the recidivism rate was approximately 25 percent.[60]

Assessment and the Diversion Agreement. Screening for diversion involves assessing the individual risk factors and corresponding needs of the defendant rather than developing an intervention plan based only on the alleged crime. Sometimes referred to as an intervention plan, the diversion agreement is a written, signed contract between the participant and the diversion program that has been individualized to address specific risk factors and encompass only those goals that the defendant can realistically achieve within the given time frame of the program. Recent research on criminal justice EBPs has found that intervention programs directed at reducing recidivism are most successful when they address specific needs and match the level of intensity to the level of risk. These risk and needs principles require use of risk-assessment tools that can determine (1) the most appropriate candidates for diversion; (2) the appropriate offender control mechanisms; and (3) the appropriate conditions to be imposed.[61]

One of the best examples of an assessment tool for identifying good candidates for diversion is the Risk Assessment Instrument developed by the Virginia Criminal Sentencing Commission (VCSC). The VCSC designed the risk assessment instrument to identify defendants charged with nonviolent offenses (i.e., larceny, fraud, and drug offenses) who would otherwise be recommended for incarceration by state sentencing guidelines. Eleven specific factors were incorporated into a risk assessment worksheet, and each was given a score based on its relative degree of importance. A recommendation for diversion is based on an offender's risk assessment point total, with all those scoring nine points or less on the instrument recommended for diversion.

The National Center for State Courts conducted an assessment of the VCSC risk instrument. The research tracked the rate of rearrest of a sample group of offenders, drawn from among 5,158 larceny, fraud, and drug cases in six pilot jurisdictions in Virginia between December 1997 and September 1999.[62] During the period of the study, 2,043 offenders met the basic risk assessment eligibility criteria for diversion, and 555 were actually diverted. Consequently, 27 percent were classified as "good" candidates. That is, in the study "good candidates" is defined as "offenders whose profile—based on the risk assessment score—suggests they pose a minimal risk of recidivating."[63] Of the 555 diverted offenders, 159 (28.6 percent) were rearrested for a new felony or misdemeanor offense, while 76 (13.8 percent) were reconvicted on a new felony or misdemeanor.

Several important findings came from this diversion program study. In the next section we provide a rendering of the study's analyses regarding the utility of the risk instrument to identify appropriate candidates for diversion and the factors that influence recidivism among nonviolent offenders.[64]

1. Which factors on the risk assessment instrument were associated with judges' decisions to divert? Of principal importance, the study found that offenders with lower total risk scores were more likely to be diverted than offenders with higher scores. Judges tended to agree that better candidates for diversion also have lower risk scores. When making the decision to divert, the factors that judges used consistently related to aspects of the offender's prior record and the offender's age.
2. Is the total risk score positively correlated with the likelihood of recidivism? The results confirmed that the risk assessment instrument is a useful tool for predicting recidivism. Whether recidivism was measured by new arrest or new arrest resulting in conviction, the likelihood of recidivism increased as the risk total score rose.
3. Do the individual factors on the risk assessment instrument effectively predict recidivism? Analysis for both measures of recidivism produced very consistent results about which factors were "good" predictors of recidivism. The results indicated that only gender and factors related to prior record were useful for predicting recidivism. Demographics (employment status, marital status, and age of offender) and contemporaneous factors (additional offenses) on the instrument worksheet were not significant predictors of risk.

Control Mechanisms. After being chosen for diversion, defendants typically spend six months to a year under the supervision of a diversion agency. However, in many instances, supervision involves minimum contact between the defendant and the program. Instead, defendants receive treatment at referral services (e.g., drug and alcohol counseling, job placement, remedial education) that have been listed as special conditions of the diversion agreement and must be successfully completed. Defendants who violate the conditions of the agreement by incurring new charges or by failing to participate in treatment services are terminated from the pretrial diversion program and returned to the court on their original charge(s). As a general rule, diversion programs do not have the authority to return program participants directly to prosecution but must recommend such action to the prosecutor or the court. However, the monitoring officers' written account is most important, because once it is handed over to the prosecutor or the court, the report becomes the primary information used for decision making.

Defendants who satisfy the conditions of the agreement are recommended for dismissal, and their cases are dropped at the conclusion of the pretrial diversion period. Moreover, some states have provisions for expunging of records. The Kentucky Court of Appeals, for example, advocates for the expunging of records by noting that "it was clear that the legislature intends for a successful pretrial diversion to, in effect, wipe the slate clean as to these charges."[65] Other states provide an option for successful participants to have their record sealed (see CBC Online 5.3).

Bail and Release on Recognizance

Thus far, we have examined pretrial release services that require defendants to be supervised while in the community awaiting trial or dismissal of charges. In this last

5.3

CBC Online

PRETRIAL DIVERSION AND THE LAW: A SAMPLING OF FOUR

This monograph summarizes 80 state and federal appellate court rulings of the past 40 years in 21 states plus the federal system. The document follows the diversion process, beginning with eligibility determination and admission, then moving on to enrollment in the diversion program, the terms of the diversion agreement, dismissal of charges on successful completion of diversion, consequences of noncompliance, and the use of diversion information outside the diversion setting.

After reviewing the court cases presented in this monograph, which appear to support the contention that prosecutors maintain substantial authority over the operations of pretrial diversion?

Visit CBC Online 5.3 at www.mhhe.com/bayens1e

section, we discuss bail as a legitimate mechanism of the judicial process aimed at ensuring that defendants appear in court while reducing the need for pretrial detention. We will also review evidence-based practices that have stemmed from studies connected to bail reform.

The purpose of bail is to guarantee the appearance of criminal defendants at their court hearings and trial. The theory behind this objective is that defendants will appear at court so they do not lose the amount of the money they posted for pretrial release. Thus, bail (especially large cash and property-valued bail) is believed to provide the incentive to prevent defendants from absconding. Ironically, defendants who are financially secure and can easily afford bail are more likely to absorb bail forfeiture and have the financial capabilities to flee the jurisdiction. In contrast, defendants who are indigent are typically detained because they cannot afford bail. And they are less likely to abscond because they don't have the money to leave town. This paradox has been at the center of the bail debate for decades. In his conclusions of a classic study of the Chicago bail system in the 1920s, Arthur Beeley commented that "the present system [of bail], in too many instances, neither guarantees security to society nor safeguards the rights of the accused. The system is lax with those with whom it should be stringent and stringent with those with whom it could safely be less severe."[66] To illustrate this point, let's consider the pretrial detention and bail amounts of two pretrial defendants: Bernard Madoff and Douglas Maupin. After reading about both offenders (see Exhibit 5.6), it should become apparent that the decision regarding bail is unavoidably discretionary.

There are constitutional guarantees that bail should not be excessive and that the type of bail set for a defendant's pretrial release should be based in large part on the severity of the crime. Generally, the more severe the alleged crime committed, the greater the amount of the bail. Other factors can also influence the bail policies of the court. For example, the size of the jail population often creates or limits the range of bail choices available. When the jail is overcrowded, the courts may feel pressure to reduce bail to allow for the release of more pretrial detainees. Some jurisdictions have implemented around-the-clock bail screening to alleviate jail overcrowding caused by pretrial detainees. In Kentucky, for example, pretrial officers are on call 24 hours a day to interview persons arrested, notify judges by phone of the prisoner's qualifications for release, and supervise the release process if nonfinancial bail is authorized. Many pretrial programs respond to jail population pressures by expanding the range of release options (e.g., conditional and supervised release) and by conducting regular

EXHIBIT 5.6 Bernard Madoff and Douglas Maupin

In December 2008, Bernard Madoff was arrested for securities fraud. Federal prosecutors estimated client losses of almost $65 billion. He was allowed to post a $10 million bail and remain in his $7 million New York penthouse during the pretrial process. At this time, Madoff and his wife sent at least $1 million worth of jewelry as gifts to family members and friends. In addition, prosecutors claimed that Madoff had plans to transfer $200 to $300 million of investors' money to family members and friends. When the authorities searched Madoff's office desk, they found $173 million in signed checks ready to be sent off. In March 2009, Bernard Madoff pleaded guilty to 11 federal crimes, including securities fraud, wire fraud, mail fraud, money laundering, perjury, and making false filings with the U.S. Securities and Exchange Commission. On June 29, 2009, he was sentenced to 150 years in prison, the maximum allowed.

Arlington, Texas, police arrested 35-year-old Douglas L. Maupin on February 15, 2009, after he was stopped for speeding. An NCIC check showed that Maupin was wanted in Collin County (Texas) on a 2003 warrant charging him with failure to appear for jury duty. Unable to afford the $1,500 warrant bail, Maupin was confined in jail pending a court appearance. After months in confinement, Maupin wrote a letter to the *Dallas Morning News* bringing attention to his lengthy incarceration. He was released from jail on May 9, 2009. When interviewed by the *Dallas Morning News* about Maupin's 83 days of incarceration, State District Judge Greg Brewer acknowledged that he knew Maupin had been sitting for months in jail. Further, Judge Brewer had decided not to set a court hearing date for Maupin—or review his requests for a court-appointed attorney—until after some traffic citations were settled. At an average cost of $69.70 per day for a Collin County inmate, Maupin's stay in jail cost the county roughly $5,785.

Research Note: In September 2009, the Collin County Observer newspaper reported that Judge Brewer resigned.[67]

bail reviews for those detained for trial. A National Institute of Justice study found that **supervised release** programs in Miami, Florida; Portland, Oregon; and Milwaukee, Wisconsin, significantly reduced the bail-held population without significantly increasing the risk to public safety.[68]

The decision to grant bail is a difficult one because of the element of uncertainty. Court officials try to assess the personal characteristics of pretrial defendants and choose bail options that reduce the likelihood of nonappearance in court. Even with the best information and effort, the opportunity for an error about a bail decision can be high. One kind of uncertainty is the role others play in influencing the bail decision. Perhaps the greatest uncertainty about the bail decision (particularly for defendants charged with felony offenses) is whether bail bondsmen are willing to post **surety bonds** for pretrial defendants. Slow bail bonding activities typically force pretrial services to conduct more bond-reduction reviews. The final source of uncertainty is related to the conflicting goals of pretrial release. Bail is used not only to guarantee the appearance of defendants in court, but also as a safeguard for the protection of the community. Consideration as to how bail might affect witnesses and victims is of high priority in the pretrial release decision-making process. The difficulty arises when court officials are forced to decide which goal should take precedence.

The Process of Bail

The traditional bail system involves the following categories:

- *Release on Recognizance (ROR):* bail in which the defendant signs an agreement that he or she will appear in court as required. This category also includes citation releases in which arrestees are released pending their first court appearance on a written order issued by law enforcement or jail personnel.
- *Conditional-Un/supervised or Third-Party Release*: bail that requires no financial deposit but sets conditions such as regularly reporting to the court or pretrial services agency, continuing employment or educational status, staying away from the victim, and travel or other restrictions.
- *Cash:* bail that requires the posting of the full amount of the bail bond, to be refunded if the defendant appears as required.
- *Property:* bail that requires posting of property or other assets in lieu of full cash bail with the court.
- *Professional Surety Bail:* requires posting a nonrefundable percentage, usually between 10 and 20 percent, of the full bond amount with a licensed, bonded surety agent who agrees to pay the full amount of the bond if the accused fails to appear as required.

After arrest and before an initial court appearance, bail may be set according to a predetermined schedule established by the judicial district (sometimes referred to as the automatic bond schedule, or ABS). Some local courts authorize release at this point without a bond for traffic or misdemeanor charges, but most bail schedules require the posting of some money as surety against the allure of failing to appear in court. Notwithstanding the ABS, persons in custody awaiting extradition, detainer, or hold from other states or federal authorities are typically not eligible for ABS bond. The same applies to those who have violated probation, parole, or bond condition, or who are believed to pose a danger to the community. Such defendants are taken to an initial court appearance to have bond set. Iowa law, for example, provides an ABS bond schedule that is applicable only if the person was arrested for a crime other than forcible felonies and the courts are not in session. The Iowa judicial code[69] revised the state's ABS in 2007 as shown:

INFRACTION	BOND AMOUNT
• Simple misdemeanor:	$300
• Serious misdemeanor:	$1,000
• Aggravated misdemeanor:	$2,000
• Class D felony:	$5,000
• Class C felony:	$10,000
• Class B felony:	$25,000

Defendants who are not eligible for bail or who otherwise cannot post bail are detained in jail. At the first court appearance, a review of the charges and bail takes place. The judge's decision to release on recognizance (ROR) or to set bail at the first court appearance has an immediate effect on a defendant's liberty. In short, there is a direct relationship between the bail amount and the probability of release. According to a BJS report of felony defendants in state courts in the 75 largest counties, when bail is set under $10,000, most defendants secure release, including seven in 10 defendants with bail under $5,000. The proportion of released defendants declines as the bail amount increases, dropping to one in 10 when bail is $100,000 or higher.[70]

Data on the number of pretrial releases for defendants charged with felony offenses is available from State Court Processing Statistics (SCPS). Every even-numbered year since 1988, SCPS collects data on the processing of felony cases in 40 of the 75 most populous counties in the country. Between 14,000 and 16,000 cases are included in the sample, which are drawn from specified days in the month of May. SCPS collects information on some of the factors that courts consider when making pretrial release decisions—for example, offender demographics, charges and prior criminal records, pretrial release and detention outcomes, adjudication outcomes, sentence, pretrial rearrests, and failure to appear in court. Consistent with its mandate to provide national data, BJS reports the SCPS data from the 40 U.S. counties in the aggregate. Exhibit 5.7 reports data that covers the period of 1990 to 2004. The BJS report notes that the failure to appear rate for ROR is highest (26 percent) compared to the lowest rate (14 percent) for property bail.[71]

Effects of Bail on Court Cases

As noted, pretrial detention can have an adverse effect on case outcomes, especially the likelihood of conviction or harsher sentences, or both.[72] Certain groups may be more negatively affected than others. In a study of the pretrial practices in 87,437 felony cases, researchers found that a greater percentage of male defendants compared to female defendants were denied bail and were detained prior to trial. Male defendants also had a higher average bail amount than female defendants. Extralegal variables, such as race, ethnicity, and type of defense attorney, were also significant predictors of pretrial decisions and outcomes.[73] In another study, data on defendants charged with violent felonies in Detroit Recorder's Court was analyzed to determine the effect of race and gender on the amount of bail imposed and on the defendant's pretrial status. The results in that study suggest that judges take gender, but not race, into account in determining the amount of bail for certain types of cases; more specifically, black females faced lower bail than black males in less serious cases. In contrast, both race and gender affected the likelihood of pretrial release. White defendants were more likely than black defendants to be released pending trial, and females were more likely than males to be released prior to trial. In fact, white females, white males, and black females all were more likely than black males to be released.[74]

EXHIBIT 5.7 1990 to 2004 Failure to Appear Rates by Release Type

Release Type	Failure to Appear	Rearrest	Any Misconduct
Release on recognizance	26%	17%	34%
Conditional release	22%	15%	32%
Deposit bail	22%	14%	30%
Full cash bail	20%	15%	30%
Commercial surety bail	18%	16%	29%
Property bail	14%	17%	27%

Policy Implications

Approximately 25 percent of all persons arrested for felony offenses who are released from detention fail to appear at trial. While some of these failures to appear are excusable, most are unjustifiable and unlawful. After one year, 30 percent of the pretrial felony defendants who initially fail to appear remain fugitives from the law.[75] While these numbers could be improved, from a public policy standpoint, one could argue that pretrial release service is successful because the majority of defendants (i.e., three-fourths) abide by the release contract to appear in court and pose no threat to the community. The success of pretrial programs is even more impressive when considering that 67 percent of convicted offenders released from prison are rearrested within three years and that 51.8 percent of convicted offenders are back in prison either because of a new crime for which they received another prison sentence, or because of a technical violation of their parole.[76] Therefore, it appears that pretrial release defendants are more successful in avoiding rearrest for new crimes or technical violations as compared to offenders released from prison.

In this final section of the chapter, we address two important questions about the effectiveness of pretrial release and diversion. These questions pertain to recent trends in pretrial release policy and practices and the need to implement evidence-based strategies to increase the performance of pretrial services.

1. What current trends in pretrial release practice ensure that defendants will make their court appearances and promote the safety of the community?
2. How can evidence-based practices be used to structure a fairer and more cost-effective system that maximizes the number of pretrial releases while reducing failures to appear and threats to public safety?

Before we focus on these questions, let's assess the difficulties associated with making good pretrial service decisions. First, pretrial release exists to maintain the liberty of persons accused of crimes. The implication is that the criminal justice system should not infringe on the liberty of a defendant except under circumstances when the public's safety comes into question. You'll recall that earlier in the chapter we introduced the U.S. Supreme Court case *U.S.* v. *Salerno*. In this case, the Court upheld detention based on the defendant's dangerousness, ruling that it did not violate due process. The practice of pretrial services then is to be based on sound policy that strikes a balance between protecting individuals' inalienable rights and the public's safety. However, at the center of this seemingly straightforward principle are problems associated with release mechanisms.

Perhaps the most frequently occurring difficulty associated with pretrial release is the accuracy of the decision-making process—that is, the decision as to who should be diverted from detention and who should remain confined during pretrial. In practice, when choosing good candidates for release, the process is far less than exact. Take for example, the ABS, which was discussed earlier. The ABS could be branded as a release mechanism that occurs without good justification. To reiterate, an ABS is a list of charges with a corresponding bail amount prearranged by the court. If, for example, an individual is arrested for criminal trespassing and the ABS amount for this crime is \$500 cash or \$1,000 with surety, the person can be released from jail by simply posting the bail amount. The American Bar Association is against such pretrial release practices and notes that "bail schedules are arbitrary and inflexible: they exclude consideration of factors other than the charge that may be far more relevant to the likelihood that the defendant will appear for court dates . . . They enable the unsupervised release of more affluent defendants who may present real risks of flight or dangerousness, who may be able to post the required amount easily and for whom the posting of bail may be simply the cost of doing 'business as usual.'"[77] So the ABS schedule is a convenience tool to assure that a bail is set, while the release decision is not necessarily based on any sound criteria.

Another policy-related issue that presents problems for decision-makers is the pretrial service program's inherent relationship with jail detention. This is especially true when pretrial service is offered as part of the jail's operations. When the detention facility is overcrowded, pretrial release becomes a means for jail population management and control rather than a method for ensuring that appropriate candidates for pretrial release are selected. This predicament is further compounded if we consider that decision-makers typically do not have ample time to make complicated decisions often associated with bail release, nor do they have the necessary time to validate risk information. Moreover, considering that during the 12 months ending June 29, 2009, local jails admitted almost 13 million persons,[78] the economic effect of deciding for confinement versus release to the community cannot be underestimated. With daily per diem rates for each jail bed space reaching $100.00 or more in some jurisdictions, it would be difficult not to factor in costs to the pretrial release decision (see Exhibit 5.8).

A final area of concern is the slow pace of the court process. There is a point when the caseload per judge becomes so large that even effectively managed courts produce slow case-processing times. The problem, of course, is that the longer it takes to process a case, the higher the potential for rearrest (see Exhibit 5.9).

A recent National Institute of Justice publication examines the "efficiency, timeliness, and quality" of criminal trial courts. This report, which focused on nine trial court jurisdictions, included two findings that are pertinent here. First, the study challenges conventional thinking that timeliness and quality of justice are mutually exclusive, arguing instead that courts can exercise considerable control over how quickly cases move from indictment to resolution without sacrificing advocacy or due process. Second, the relative pace of litigation depended largely on the local legal culture—that is, the expectations and attitudes of judges, prosecutors, and defense attorneys.[79] With these thoughts in mind, let's turn to question number one about which pretrial release practices assure that defendants will make their court appearances.

Increased Use of Detention and Financial Bail

How can current policy increase the potential for pretrial defendants to appear in court? Three issues are prominent in answering this question. First, trend data from pretrial

EXHIBIT 5.8 Selected Jurisdictions with Corresponding Costs for Housing, Feeding, and Supervising Persons in Jail

Jail Location	Daily Per Diem Rate
Missoula County, Montana	$ 56.75
Maricopa County, Arizona	$ 73.46
Kent County, Michigan	$ 74.97
Shawnee County, Kansas	$ 81.00
Monmouth County, New Jersey	$134.00

Source: http://www.co.missoula.mt.us, n.p.; http://www.maricopa.gov, n.p.; http://www.accesskent.com, n.p.; http://www.snco.us, n.p.; and http://co.monmouth.nj.us, n.p.

EXHIBIT 5.9 Cumulative Percentage of Pretrial Misconduct Occurrence[1]

	1 week	1 month	3 months	6 months
Any type	9%	32%	67%	88%
• Failure to appear	9%	32%	68%	89%
• Rearrest	8%	29%	62%	85%

Source: Bureau of Justice Statistics, NCJ 214994, November 2007.

release and detention rates indicates that it does so by diverting fewer defendants from detention for felony offenses. Data from the Administrative Office of the U.S. Courts shows that release rates from 1992 to 2006 have gradually decreased, while confinement rates have increased. As noted in Exhibit 5.10, in 1992, defendants released while awaiting trial averaged a high of 62 percent and decreased to a low of 39 percent in 2006.[80] State court data collected from a representative sample of felony cases filed in large urban counties also shows a trend in the increased use of pretrial detention. In 2004, only 57 percent of felony defendants received a pretrial release prior to adjudication compared to 63 percent in 1992.[81] With regard to jail population trends associated with pretrial detention services, at mid-year 2009, 62 percent of inmates had not been convicted or were awaiting trial, up from 56 percent in 2000.[82]

Second, the courts have begun to rely more heavily on financial release than on release on recognizance. From 1990 through 1994, ROR accounted for 41 percent of releases, compared to 24 percent for surety bond. However, in 2002 and 2004, surety bonds were used for 42 percent of releases, compared to 23 percent for ROR.[83] Data provided by the Bureau of Justice Statistics indicates that this increase in the use of financial bail is well justified. Compared to those released on own recognizance, defendants on financial release were far more likely to make all scheduled court appearances. Defendants released on an unsecured bond were most likely to have a bench warrant issued because they failed to appear in court (see Exhibit 5.11).[84]

EXHIBIT 5.10 U.S. District Courts Pretrial Release & Detention Rates FY 1992–2006

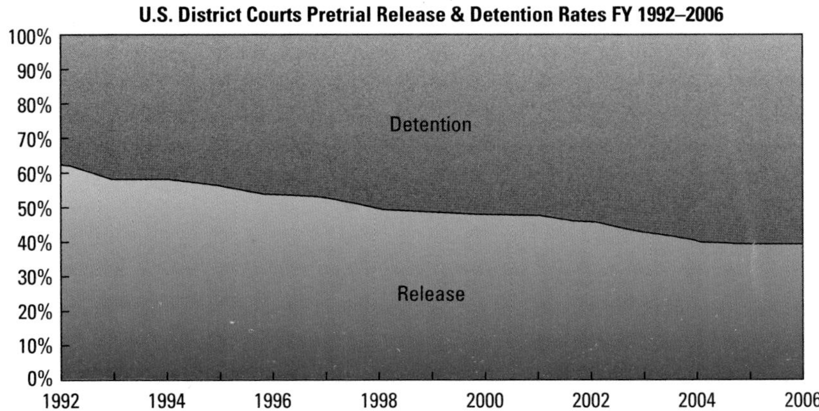

Source: Marie VanNostrand and Gena Keebler, "Our Journey Toward Pretrial Justice," *Federal Probation*, Vol. 71, No. 2 (September 2007), p. 22.

Type of Pretrial Supervision Program

The third policy matter related to improving appearance rates deals with the type and level of supervision provided by pretrial programs. Some pretrial service programs are very proactive, providing case management and pretrial intervention instead of mere release. Intervention usually involves rehabilitative services that address social and economic conditions connected to a defendant's decision to commit crime. Such monitoring and intervention strategies have been touted as significantly affecting whether a defendant will appear in court. Also, enrollment in social services programs appear to affect future criminal involvement by addressing problems that contributed to the defendant's initial criminal activity.

Research studies that explored the relationship between proactive supervision and reduction in rates of failure to appear or pretrial crime have found mixed results. For example, a supervision experiment carried out in the Philadelphia courts found that varying the use of pretrial notification, mode of pretrial notification, and amount of pretrial notifications did not have a significant impact on the likelihood that a defendant would appear in court. Also, minor differences in the forms of supervision (i.e., levels of restrictiveness) did not make a difference in outcomes.[85] However, in another study that combined data from 200 of the nation's pretrial programs, researchers found that a pretrial agency's ability to impose sanctions and report to courts is associated with lower rates of failure to appear. The study also concluded that (1) a pretrial agency's ability to refer a defendant to substance and mental health treatment is associated with lower rates of pretrial rearrest; (2) a pretrial agency's ability to impose urine testing is associated with lower rates of pretrial rearrest; and (3) a pretrial agency's ability to issue warnings to defendants about pretrial behavior is associated with lower rates of pretrial rearrest.[86]

Thus, in addressing our second question—about the use of evidence-based practice to make pretrial services more effective—EBPs clearly can provide guidance for making future policies and implementing practices in the pretrial release and diversion field. Research can help identify practices that work, and, in turn, benchmarks can be established that define optimal pretrial services. At the same time, those who administer pretrial programs must be willing to change practices when research indicates that they do not work. Last, given the ever-present influence of political and economic factors, implementing change based on evidence-based practices will require collaboration among the courts, detention agencies, and pretrial services.

EXHIBIT 5.11 Pretrial Misconduct Rates

Type of Release	Number of Defendants Failing to Appear	Percent Still a Fugitive after 1 Year
All Types	54,485	28%
• Full cash bond	2,179	36%
• Unsecured bond	5,018	33%
• Deposit	4,548	31%
• Property bond	490	30%
• Recognizance	20,883	30%
• Conditional	6,788	27%
• Emergency	1,168	22%
• Surety bond	13,411	19%

Summary

The history of structured pretrial release and diversion began in the 1960s in what came to be called the Bail Reform Movement. In the 1970s, the President's Commission of Law Enforcement and Administration of Justice called for the expanded use of pretrial release and diversion programs. The American Bar Association published criminal justice standards that addressed the pretrial release decision.

Pretrial services conduct pretrial investigations to assist the judicial officers decide whether to release a defendant on personal recognizance or other types of bail. A risk assessment tool is used to incorporate the information from the pretrial investigation into a numerical score that guides the release decision. The assessment places the defendant in a risk level (i.e., defendant's risks of failing to appear at future court hearings or posing a risk to community safety), and identifies any condition or combination of conditions designed to address the identified risks.

Diversion programs give first-time offenders a second chance at having a clean criminal history by deferring the defendant from prosecution. The two basic categories of pretrial diversion include treatment in lieu of prosecution and alternative sanction before judgment. The "gatekeeper" of the diversion process is the prosecutor. Screening for diversion involves assessing the individual risk factors and corresponding needs of the defendant rather than developing an intervention plan based only on alleged crime.

The purpose of bail is to guarantee the appearance of criminal defendants at their court hearings and trial. There are constitutional guarantees that bail should not be excessive, and the type of bail set for a defendant's pretrial release is based in large part on the severity of the crime. From a public policy standpoint, bail is successful because the 75 percent abide by the release contract to appear in court and pose no threat to the community. Also, pretrial release defendants are more successful in avoiding rearrest for new crimes or technical violations when compared to offenders released from prison.

Three prominent issues have the potential to increase pretrial success. The first is the difficulty associated with the accuracy of the decision-making process—that is, the decision as to who should be diverted from detention and who should remain confined during pretrial. The second policy-related issue that presents problems for decision-makers is the pretrial service program's inherent relationship with jail detention. A final area of concern is the slow pace of the court process.

Key Terms

breathalyzers, p. 129
community service, p. 118
conditional-un/supervised release, p. 122
demonstration programs, p. 118
diversion, p. 115
drug court, p. 117
due process (of law) , p. 123
failure to appear, p. 120
level of service inventory-revised (LSI-R), p. 130
pre-arraignment, p.122
pretrial assessment, p. 125
pretrial failure, p. 131
pretrial release, p. 115
pretrial services, p. 118
release on recognizance (ROR), p. 120
speedy trial act, p. 118
substance abuse treatment, p. 115
supervised release, p. 138
surety bond, p. 138

Questions for Review

1. What are the important events that lead to the development of pretrial release and diversion programs in the United States?
2. How does the pretrial investigation and risk assessment function in pretrial services?
3. What is the purpose of assessment when completing a diversion agreement?
4. What does research suggest is the most effective bail in assuring that defendants appear in court? Which form of bail has the least amount of rearrest rates?
5. How has increased use of detention and financial bail and type of pretrial supervision program affected pretrial services?

Question of Policy

The Role of Monitoring and Control in Pretrial Release

Pretrial release officers are primarily responsible for interviewing inmates for pretrial release purposes, validating risk assessments for bondable felony arrestees so the court system can use them to order pretrial conditions, and monitoring defendants released to the community. Consistent with other community corrections programs, pretrial release officers are trained foremost in the importance of monitoring offenders within the community. In the Washington County, Oregon, Circuit Court for example, release assistance officers "monitor compliance with conditions of release. Should violation of any condition on a defendants' pretrial release agreement occur, the release assistance officer will report this information to a judge for immediate action."[87]

This emphasis on monitoring and control is universal within pretrial release services due to concerns about risks that defendants might pose to public safety. However, this control-oriented philosophy may run contrary to the original philosophy promoted by the Katzenbach Commission in 1967. That is, the commission viewed community-correction programs as the *new* alternative, independent from the punitive approaches employed in years past, which relied on incarceration. Moreover, these programs were intended to enhance the reintegration of offenders back into the community.[88]

Do you believe that pretrial service has evolved to function as merely an extension of jail?

Would it be fair to say that many of the Katzenbach Commission's recommendations have become irrelevant to the daily operations of pretrial services and other community corrections programs?

What Would You Do?

In Florida, a woman was charged with exploitation of the elderly, abuse of the elderly, and grand theft. She entered a pretrial diversion program, successfully completed the program, and the charges were dismissed. She then went back to school and became certified as a teacher, only to find that she was rejected for employment by several districts that considered her pretrial diversion program to be an admission of guilt to a crime. She returned to court to move that her dismissal be vacated and the charges reinstated so that she could be exonerated through trial. Unfortunately, the court ruled that there was no legal basis on which a court can vacate a dismissal after completion of a pretrial diversion. The court referred to the pretrial diversion agreement that the defendant had signed years earlier. In it was this condition: "The person who is the subject of a criminal history record that is expunged may lawfully deny or fail to acknowledge the arrests covered by the expunged record, except when the subject of the record is seeking to be employed or licensed by the Office of Teacher Education, Certification, Staff Development, and Professional Practices of the Department of Education, any district school board, or any local governmental entity that licenses child care facilities."[89]

1. Why do you suppose the exception to expungement exists?
2. What policy and procedure might be developed to address this defendant's dilemma?
3. What other actions can be taken to reduce the stigma of a criminal conviction?

Endnotes

1. Joel Fleishman, J. Scott Kohler, & Steven Schindler, *Casebook for the Foundation: A Great American Secret.* NY: Perseus Publishing Group, 2007.
2. Wayne Thomas, *Bail Reform in America.* Berkeley, CA: University of California Press, 1976.
3. John Woolley and Gerhard Peters, *The American Presidency Project* [online], Santa Barbara, CA: University of California (hosted), Gerhard Peters (database), June 22, 1966, www.presidency.ucsb .edu/ws/?pid=27666.
4. John Clark & D. Alan Henry, *The Pretrial Release Decision Making Process: Goals, Current Practices, and Challenges* (Washington, DC: The Pretrial Justice Institute, November 1996).
5. John Bellassai, "Pretrial Diversion: The First Decade in Retrospect," *Pretrial Services Annual Journal* (1978).
6. Donald Pryor, Pluma Kluess, & Jeffrey Smith, "Pretrial Diversion Program in Monroe County,

NY: An Evaluation of Program Impact and Cost Effectiveness," *Pretrial Services Annual Journal* (1978).

7. Richard Thomas, "The Shelby County (Tennessee) Pretrial Diversion Program: An Evaluation," *Pretrial Services Annual Journal* (1980).
8. John Bellassai, *A Short History of the Pretrial Diversion of Adult Defendants from Traditional Criminal Justice Processing Part One: The Early Years.* (Frankfort, KY: National Association of Pretrial Services, 1995).
9. Jerome Jaffe & Faith Jaffe, *Encyclopedia of Drugs, Alcohol, and Addictive Behavior: Treatment Alternatives to Street Crime (TASC)* (Farmington Hills, MI: Gale Group Inc., May 2009).
10. Rosalyn Carson-DeWitt, "Coerced Treatment for Substance Offenders," *Encyclopedia of Drugs, Alcohol, and Addictive Behavior,* 2nd ed. (Farmington Hills, MI: Gale-Cengage, 2001).
11. James Inciardi and Duane McBride, "Reviewing the 'TASC' (Treatment Alternatives to Street Crime) Experience," *Journal of Crime and Justice*, vol. 15, no. 1 (1992), pp. 45–61.
12. James Byrne and Jacob Stowell, "The Impact of the Federal Pretrial Service Act of 1982 on the Release, Supervision, and Detention of Pretrial Defendants," *Federal Probation,* vol. 72, no. 3 (September 2007).
13. Adapted from *U.S. Courts: Probation and Pretrial Services* (August, 2001), www.uscourts.gov/fedprob/officers.html.
14. John Scalia, *Federal Drug Offenders, 1999 with Trends 1984–99* (Washington, DC: Bureau of Justice Statistics NCJ 187285, August 2001).
15. M. Kay Harris and Peter Jones, *The Kansas Community Corrections Act: An Assessment of a Public Policy Initiative.* Technical report presented to the Kansas Department of Corrections, Topeka, KS (September 1990).
16. Joan Mullen, *The Dilemma of Diversion: Resource Materials on Adult Pretrial Intervention Programs* (Washington, DC: U.S. Department of Justice, Law Enforcement Assistance Administration, 1975).
17. John Clark and D. Alan Henry, *Pretrial Services Programming at the Start of the 21st Century: A Survey of Pretrial Services* (Washington, DC: Bureau of Justice Assistance, NCJ 199773, July 2003).
18. John Bellassai, *A Short History of the Pretrial Diversion of Adult Defendants from Traditional Criminal Justice Processing Part One: The Early Years* (Frankfort, KY: National Association of Pretrial Services, 1995).
19. Herman Silverstein, *Pre-Trial Services Institute of Westchester, Inc. Evaluation Report and Impact Assessment* (Washington, DC: National Institute of Justice, NCJ 059326, 1979).
20. Elsa Brenner, "Alternatives to Jail Save $3 Million," *The New York Times*, August 15, 1993, www.nytimes.com/1993/08/15/nyregion/alternatives-to-jail-save-3-million.html.
21. Crime and Justice Institute, *Implementing Evidence-Based Principles in Community Corrections: The Principles of Effective Intervention* (Washington, DC: National Institute of Corrections, 2004).
22. Marie VanNostrand, *Legal and Evidence-Based Practices: Applications of Legal Principles, Laws, and Research to the Field of Pretrial Service* (Boston, MA: Crime and Justice Institute, April 2007).
23. Thomas Cohen and Brian Reaves, *Pretrial Release of Felony Defendants in State Court.* (Washington, DC: Bureau of Justice Statistics, NCJ 214994, November 2007).
24. The National Association of Pretrial Services Agencies, *Informational Report: Pretrial Diversion Abstract* (January 1998), www.napsa.org/publications/diversionabstract.pdf.
25. Supra (See 16).
26. Maine Pretrial Service, Inc. (2008), www.mainepretrial.org/index.htm.
27. Pretrial Justice Institute (2009), www.pretrial.org/PretrialServices/ProgramManagement/Pages/default.aspx.
28. Merrimack County, NH, Pretrial Services, www.merrimackcounty.net/pretrial/about.html.
29. American Bar Association, *ABA Criminal Justice Standards on Pretrial Release,* 3rd ed., Standard 10-1.1 (Washington, DC: American Bar Association, 2007).
30. Ibid.

31. Charles Ares, Ann Rankin, and Herbert Sturz, *The Manhattan Bail Project: An Interim Report on the Use of Pre-Trial Parole*, 38 N.Y.U.L. Rev. 67 (1963), p. 86.
32. Kathleen Daly, "Discrimination in the Criminal Courts: Family, Gender, and the Problem of Equal Treatment," *Social Forces,* vol. 66, no. 1 (September 1987), pp. 152–175.
33. Tracy Nobiling, Cassia Spohn, and Miriam DeLone, "A Tale of Two Counties: Unemployment and Sentence Severity," *Justice Quarterly*, vol. 15, no. 3 (1998), pp. 459–485.
34. American Bar Association, *ABA Criminal Justice Standards, Pretrial Release*, 3rd ed. (Chicago, IL: American Bar Association, 2007), www.abanet.org/crimjust/standards/pretrialrelease_toc.html.
35. *Coffin* v. *United States*, 156 U.S. 432 (1895).
36. Vidar Halvorsen, "Is it Better that Ten Guilty Persons Go Free than that One Innocent Person Be Convicted?" *Criminal Justice Ethics*, vol. 23, no. 2 (Fall 2004), pp. 3–13.
37. *Gideon* v. *Wainwright*, 372 U.S. 335 (1963).
38. *Argersinger* v. *Hamlin*, 407 U.S. 25 (1972).
39. *Miranda* v. *Arizona*, 384 U.S. 436 (1966).
40. *Bandy* v. *United States*, 82 S.Ct. 11 (1961) and *Pugh* v. *Rainwater*, 557 F.2d 1189 (5th Cir. 1977).
41. *Griffin* v. *Illinois*, 351 U.S. 12, (1956).
42. *Van Atta* v. *Scott* (1980) 27 Cal. 3d 424, 450 [166 Cal.Rptr. 149, 613 P.2d 210].
43. National Association of Pretrial Services Agencies, *NAPSA Standards on Pretrial Release*, 3rd ed. (2004). Retrieved from www.napsa.org/publications/2004napsastandards.pdf.
44. Supra (See 23).
45. D. A. (Don) Andrews and James Bonta, *The Level of Supervision Inventory—Revised* (Toronto, ON, Canada: Multi-Health Systems, 1995).
46. Supra (See 16).
47. U.S. Department of Justice, "Remarks as Prepared for Delivery by Attorney General Eric Holder at the Vera Institute of Justice's Third Annual Justice Address" (July 2009), www.usdoj.gov/ag/speeches/2009/ag-speech-090709.html.
48. Marie VanNostrand and Gena Keebler, *Pretrial Risk Assessment in the Federal Court: For the Purpose of Expanding the Use of Alternatives to Detention* (Washington, DC: U.S. Department of Justice, Office of Federal Detention Trustee, April 2009).
49. Ibid.
50. Ibid.
51. Ibid.
52. Marie VanNostrand, *Assessing Risk Among Pretrial Defendants in Virginia: The Virginia Pretrial Risk Assessment Instrument.* (Richmond, VA: Virginia Department of Criminal Justice Services, April 2003).
53. Marie VanNostrand and Kenneth J. Rose, *Pretrial Risk Assessment in Virginia: The Virginia Pretrial Risk Assessment Instrument* (St. Petersburg, FL: Luminosity, Inc., May 2009).
54. Thomas H. Cohen and Brian A. Reaves, *State Court Processing Statistics, 1990–2004 Pretrial Release of Felony Defendants in State Courts* (Washington, DC: Bureau of Justice Statistics, NCJ 214994, November 2007).
55. Ibid.
56. Qudsia Siddiqi, *Pretrial Rearrest Among New York City Defendants* (New York: New York City Criminal Justice Agency, Inc., April 2005).
57. Qudsia Siddiqi, *Prediction of Pretrial Failure to Appear and An Alternative Pretrial Release Risk-Classification Scheme in New York City: A Reassessment Study* (New York: New York City Criminal Justice Agency, Inc., June 2002).
58. *Revised Code of Washington*, Title 10, Chapter 10.05, Section 10.05.020 (2008).
59. Michelle Naples and Henry Steadman, "Can Persons with Co-Occurring Disorders and Violent Charges Be Successfully Diverted?" *International Journal of Forensic Mental Health,* vol. 2, no. 22 (2003), pp. 137–143.
60. Supra (See 28).
61. Roger K. Warren, *Evidence-Based Practice to Reduce Recidivism: Implications for State Judiciaries* (Washington, DC: The Crime and Justice Institute and the National Institute of Corrections, Community Corrections Division, August 2007).
62. Brian Ostrom, et al., *Offender Risk Assessment in Virginia: A Three-Stage Evaluation* (Washington, DC: U.S. Department of Justice Document No.: 196815, September 2002).

63. Ibid.

64. Ibid.

65. *Commonwealth of Kentucky* v. *Shouse*, 183 S.W. 3d 204 (2006).

66. Arthur Beeley, *The Bail System in Chicago* (Chicago, IL: The University of Chicago Press, 1966).

67. Arrest information retrieved from www.co.collin.tx.us/rsp-bin/jlistrv.pgm?IDNO=225115&BOKSEQ=0&caller=JLISTR&Rndpercent20=1326682799524887. Also, see Katie Fairbank, "Judge's Orders Put Collin County Man in Catch-22," *Texas Cable News Report*, May 18, 2009, www.txcn.com/sharedcontent/dws/newslocalnews/stories/051609dnentmaupin.3eaa11d.html.

68. Andy Hall, *Systemwide Strategies to Alleviate Jail Crowding* (Washington, DC: U.S. Department of Justice, National Institute of Justice, January 1987).

69. Iowa Judicial Code § 804.21(5).

70. Supra (See 23).

71. Supra (See 54).

72. Mary Phillips, *Bail, Detention & Felony Case Outcomes*, Research Brief Series, No. 18. (New York: New York City Criminal Justice Agency, 2008).

73. Jeremy Balland and Lisa Growette Bostaph, "He versus She: A Gender-Specific Analysis of Legal and Extralegal Effects on Pretrial Release for Felony Defendants," *Women and Criminal Justice*, vol. 19, no. 2 (April 2009), pp. 95–119.

74. Charles Katz and Cassia Spohn, "The Effect of Race and Gender on Bail Outcomes: A Test of an Interactive Model," *American Journal of Criminal Justice*, vol. 19, no. 2 (April 2008), pp. 161–184.

75. Eric Helland and Alexander Tabarrok, "Public versus Private Law Enforcement: Evidence from Bail Jumping," *The Journal of Law and Economics*, vol. 47, no. 1 (April, 2004), pp. 93–122.

76. Lauren Glaze and Thomas Bonczar, *Probation and Parole in the United States, 2007 Statistical Tables* (Washington, DC: Bureau of Justice Statistics, December 2008).

77. American Bar Association, *ABA Criminal Justice Standards on Pretrial Release*, 3rd ed., Commentary to Standard 10-5.3(e) (2007).

78. Todd Minton, *Jail Inmates at Midyear 2009* (Washington, DC: Bureau of Justice Statistics, June 2010).

79. Brian Ostrom and Roger Hanson, *Efficiency, Timeliness, and Quality: A New Perspective from Nine State Criminal Trial Courts* (Washington, DC: The National Institute of Justice: Research in Brief, June 2000).

80. U.S. District Courts, *Pretrial Release & Detention Rates FY 1992–2006* (Washington, DC: The U.S. Courts: The Federal Judiciary, January, 2007), www.uscourts.gov/fedprob/September_2007/images/journey_figure02.gif.

81. See *Felony Defendants in Large Urban Counties, 2004* (April 2008): NCJ 221152 and *Felony Defendants in Large Urban Counties, 1992* (July, 1995): NCJ 148826. Washington, DC: Bureau of Justice Statistics.

82. Supra (See 78).

83. Supra (See 54).

84. Supra (See 54).

85. John Goldkamp and Michael White, *Restoring Accountability in Pretrial Release: The Philadelphia Pretrial Release Supervision Experiments,* Final Report (Philadelphia, PA: Crime and Justice Research Institute, July 2001).

86. David Levin, *Examining the Efficacy of Pretrial Release Conditions, Sanctions and Screening with the State Court Processing Statistics Data Series.* Paper presentation at the Annual Meeting of the American Society of Criminology (Atlanta, GA, May 2009).

87. Washington County, Oregon Circuit Court, Oregon Judicial Department Webpage, www.ojd.state.or.us/wsh/Criminal/PretrialRelease.htm.

88. Stan Stojkovic, "The President's Crime Commission Recommendations for Corrections: The Twilight of the Idols," in John Conley (ed.), *The 1967 President's Crime Commission Report: Its Impact 25 Years Later* (Highland Heights, KY: Academy of Criminal Justice Sciences/Cincinnati, OH: Anderson Publishing Co., 1994).

89. *State of Florida* v. *Dempsey*, 916 So.2d 856 (2005).

CHAPTER 6

Economic Sanctions:

Fines, Restitution to Victims, and Community Service

OBJECTIVES

1. Summarize the types of economic sanctions that are applied by the criminal justice system.
2. Distinguish between tariff and day fine systems.
3. Explain the functions of restitution and victim compensation programs.
4. Explain the benefits and challenges associated with community service programs.

OUTLINE

In October 2007, Robert J. Ritchie (a.k.a. Kid Rock) was involved in a brawl at a Waffle House in Duluth, Georgia. He was charged with five counts of simple battery. On March 4, 2008, he entered a plea of nolo contendere *to one count, was fined $1,000, required to perform 80 hours of community service, and ordered to complete a six-hour course on anger management. Four other counts of battery were dropped. A week after the court appearance, Rock returned to the Waffle House on Old Peachtree Road in Duluth and raised nearly $20,000 for an Atlanta homeless shelter.*

Rock petitioned Georgia State Court Judge Alvin Wong to allow him to perform his 80 hours of community service in Iraq as a participant in a USO tour, which was scheduled for December 15–21, 2008. But on September 30, 2008, Judge Wong denied the request, writing that Rock had performed for the troops before and "giving him credit for something he would otherwise love to do in front of a camera completely defeats the punitive purpose of performing community service."

On December 2, 2008, the Detroit rocker responded to the denial by posting this message, titled "Getting Something Off My Chest. . ." on www.kidrock.com: "Apparently he (judge) thinks it's more important that I do something else rather than sing, shake hands, take pictures and spend time with the men and women who put themselves in harms [sic] way to protect the very freedom he and all of us live by," the singer wrote in a holiday message on the Web site.

The singer/entertainer ultimately completed the mandatory community service by stuffing envelopes, moving boxes, and shoveling snow at a children's hospital in his native Michigan.

Do you think Kid Rock's community service was a socially productive penalty? Could his energy have been put to better use given his celebrity status and ability to raise money? If Kid Rock violates the conditions of his probation, would you increase his fine? In this chapter we will discuss community service and other restitution programs to give you a range of tools and concepts for considering these questions. First we examine fines, which are described as the most common form of punishment in the United States.

Overview of Economic Sanctions

An economic sanction is a common term to describe a court-ordered requirement for persons to pay money or forfeit property. Multiple applications of economic sanctions can be seen throughout the criminal justice system, ranging from a preset schedule that allows an offender to pay a **fine** directly to the court for a minor offense (e.g., traffic infractions such as speeding or running a stop sign) to the more complex court order that an offender make **restitution** in the form of a large monetary penalty to compensate a victim for damages suffered as a result of a crime (e.g., $3,000 for vandalism to property). Moreover, **community service** is generally included as an economic sanction, whereby the offender completes work for a certain number of hours as reparation to the community.

The use of economic sanctions has increased considerably since the 1980s. As the connection between crime, community, and the economy continues to be a major influence on criminal justice policymaking, a great deal of support now exists to strengthen community punishment. Greater use of fines, restitution, and community service necessarily expands the continuum of correctional sanctions and offers significant opportunities for offenders to be held accountable to victims.

Economic sanctions have several advantages over other types of correctional punishments. First, compared to the costs of confinement, they are substantially cheaper. If we consider that one jail sentence costs taxpayers an average of nearly $60 per day,[1] imposing a fine for a minor offense would save an average of $420 per person per week. The numbers are even more impressive when we consider the confinement of juveniles. The per diem costs of locking up one young person in a juvenile facility ranges from $24 in Wyoming to $726 in Connecticut. The American Correctional Association estimates that, on average, it costs a state $240.99 per day ($1,686.93 a week) for every youth in a juvenile facility.[2]

Second, economic sanctions are flexible in that they can be used alone, with incarceration, with probation, or in a combination of each. In fact, fines for criminal acts in combination with other penalties may produce lower rates of repeat offending. For example, a study of the impact of traditional fines on recidivism in 824 cases in Los Angeles municipal courts found that offenders who received a fine with probation had lower recidivism rates than offenders who received only probation. Similarly, those who received a fine with probation and jail had lower recidivism than offenders who received only probation and jail without the fines.[3] In another study, an examination of the court files of almost 14,000 New York drivers with at least one DUI conviction suggested that economic sanctions were the most effective and consistent factor in reducing recidivism.[4]

A third advantage of economic sanctions is that evaluating their fulfillment is relatively straightforward, as it is usually determined by an offender's level of payment or completion of physical labor assignment.[5] For example, probation officers are routinely responsible for creating restitution payment schedules for probationers under their supervision and also for monitoring the payments made to victims. If victims do not receive scheduled payments, they contact the offender's probation officer through the county probation or court services agencies, and the probation officer can respond appropriately.

A final advantage is that economic sanctions can be tailored to meet rehabilitative and reparative objectives of restorative justice. In short, restorative justice emphasizes repairing the harm caused by crime. Offenders are given an opportunity to make things right with the victim—to the degree possible—through some form of compensation. The relationship between restorative justice and the application of fines, restitution, and community service are addressed throughout the remainder of the chapter, beginning with fines.

Fines: The Most Common Disposition in the United States

Fines are a common punishment for a variety of crimes, especially less serious ones committed by first-time offenders. Offenses that are typically punished by a fine include traffic violations, minor drug possession, and violations of city ordinances.

EXHIBIT 6.1 Fines for Minor Crimes in Selected Cities[7]

Location	Offense	Fine
Southlake, TX	Jaywalking	$ 71
Atlanta, GA	Driving on the sidewalk	$132
Miami, FL	Spray paint–graffiti	$250
Belmar, NJ	Noise violation	$350
Austin, TX	Texting while driving	$500
Bartlesville, OK	Possession of drug paraphernalia	$554

Exhibit 6.1 provides a list of selected offenses and accompanying fines in several U.S. cities. Note that none of these offenses are serious, nor do they involve offenses against persons, but the fines do tend to increase with the seriousness or potential harm involved with the offense. In the United States, over a billion dollars in fines are collected in criminal courts each year. Judges from 126 types of courts around the country report that 36 percent of the time they impose fines alone, while an average of 86 percent of their sentences combine fines with another penalty.[6]

The ability to fine a person gives judges a greater range of remedies at sentencing and may enable them to dispose of a matter without confinement. However, for more serious crimes, judges often combine a fine with another form of punishment, such as jail confinement, an intermediate sanction, or probation. One caveat to this practice is that judges may not convert the fine to imprisonment for those who are unable to pay. In the U.S. Supreme Court case *Tate* v. *Short*, an indigent man from Houston, Texas, was convicted of traffic offenses and fined a total of $425. At the time, state law required that persons unable to pay had to be incarcerated for sufficient time to satisfy their fines, at the rate of $5 per day. In this case, the term of confinement equated to 85 days. The Court held that it was a denial of the equal protection clause of the Fourteenth Amendment to limit punishment to payment of a fine for those who are able to pay it, but to convert the fine to imprisonment for those who could not.[8] On its facts, *Tate* prohibits imprisonment of indigent offenders in cases where a fine is the only punishment prescribed by statute.

Like other forms of punishment, a fine should theoretically impose some deterrent effect on the offender. Holding persons responsible for committing a crime by requiring them to pay may be all that is needed to deter a person from risking criminal liability again. This is especially true of offenders who do not present a serious threat to society and value the chance to make amends for their transgressions without losing their freedom. However, the ability to use fines as an appropriate form of punishment depends to a great extent on the financial resources of the defendant. Therefore, a prime consideration in fixing the dollar amount of a fine is the offender's ability to pay and assuring that the amount is meaningful enough to achieve maximum deterrence. Consider again the offense type and corresponding fine amounts provided in Exhibit 6.1. These **tariff fines** apply to every offender when a particular crime is committed—for example, $132 for any person in Atlanta who drives on the sidewalk, regardless of the offender's income level or ability to pay. For the wealthy, tariff fines can be too small to be a meaningful punishment. For the poor, tariff fines can be too large and

A University of Utah study found that distraction from cell phone use while driving extends a driver's reaction time as much as having a blood alcohol concentration at the legal limit of .08 percent. Many states now fine motorists caught driving while distracted (DWD). Do you support laws restricting any type of cell phone use while driving?

may result in jail time when the offender cannot pay. Consequently, setting a single, fixed amount for all defendants convicted of the same crime could be considered inherently unfair.

Related to the ability of an offender to pay are limitations in the courts' capacity to collect. Collection rates are relatively high for traffic cases, as persons who regularly operate motor vehicles generally are employed or have the chance to become employed, which increases their ability to pay. Typically, methods of payment for court-ordered fines include payment by personal check, credit card, or online payment system. In Michigan, for example, several judicial districts now offer an online payment service for traffic violators. In 2009, 2,100 online ticket payments were made each month in that state. In addition to being a convenience for ticket payers, the online payment system automatically posts transactions without involving court staff, a time savings that frees court employees for other duties.[9]

In contrast to traffic offenders, defendants with criminal charges often have limited financial resources. This is particularly true for defendants who have been or will be confined for an extended period in jail. They generally have difficulty paying because few detainees earn money while in jail. Those who cannot pay their fines upon sentencing may enter into a payment plan or ask the court for some alternative relief. Payment plans allow defendants to meet their financial obligations over time. However, most jurisdictions still struggle with collection. Research suggests that fines are most likely to be paid if the amounts and payment plans are realistic and take into account an offender's ability to pay, if the offender's payments are closely monitored, and if progressively more persuasion is used in response to nonpayment.[10]

An increasing number of jurisdictions throughout the country are forming judicial enforcement or collection units. The collections units may take responsibility for all aspects of fine collection, including processing payments that are made immediately, setting up payment plans, and following up on delinquent accounts. Courts that take this approach typically have enough resources to conduct the entire process. An excellent example of best practices in fine collection comes from the Office of Court Administration's (OCA) Collection Improvement program, which was created in Texas over a decade ago. The OCA program focuses on collecting court costs, fees, and fines assessed against persons who cannot pay at the time of sentencing. This program has two major benefits: It encourages personal responsibility through compliance with court orders, and it increases revenue—leading to an overall increase in Texas collection revenues in 2005 of 86 percent, or $42 million.[11] Between 2006 and 2009, the program generated revenue of more than $270 million. Some key elements that made the program a success are:

- Staff members are committed to collection activities.
- Staff members make it clear to defendants that all court fines are due at the time of sentencing.
- Defendants unable to pay in full on the day of sentencing are required to complete an application for extension of time to pay. This information is verified and evaluated to establish an appropriate payment plan.
- Payment terms are strict (e.g., 50 percent of the total amount due must be paid within 48 hours; 80 percent within 30 days; and 100 percent within 60 days).
- Alternative enforcement options (e.g., community service) are available for those who do not qualify for a payment plan.
- Defendants are closely monitored for compliance, and action is taken promptly for noncompliance, including telephone contact and letter notification when a payment is missed; possible issuance of a warrant for continued noncompliance; and possible application of statutorily permitted collection remedies, such as programs for nonrenewal of driver's license or vehicle registration.
- A county or city may contract with a private attorney or a public or private vendor for the provision of collection services on delinquent cases (61+ days), after in-house collection efforts are exhausted.[12]

In some jurisdictions the probation department rather than the courts manage fine collections. Probation officers are instructed to consider the payment of fines as an important aspect of sentence compliance, and they have the authority to revoke probation for defendants who fail to pay their fines. To monitor compliance, many probation departments rely on Web-based systems to give their staff ready access to offender fine, restitution, and special assessment data. For example, U.S. Probation and Pretrial Services developed the Offender Payment Enhanced Report Access (OPERA) system (see CBC Online 6.1). OPERA is an accounting program of the Probation and Pretrial Services Automated Case Tracking System (PACTS). A probation officer logging into PACTS automatically launches OPERA and can pull up the offender's payment report; the case's financial history, including all dispersals; and the balance owed to each victim.[13]

Some agencies assign staff whose primary task is to collect fines. In Colorado, specialized employees termed "collections investigators" ensure prompt payment of

6.1

CBC Online

OFFENDER PAYMENT ENHANCED REPORT ACCESS (OPERA)

This four-minute video provides an overview of OPERA, a Web-based application that provides U.S. Probation and Pretrial Service Officers with real-time access to offenders' fine and restitution payment records.

After watching the video, describe two major problems that officers hope the application will alleviate.

Visit CBC Online 6.1 at www.mhhe.com/bayens1e

monetary obligations. Collections investigators may work either in probation departments or court clerks' offices. Using Web-based court records, including offender information, probation reports, and past or pending cases, collections investigators ensure that a thorough, consistent collection effort is made in every case.[14] In 1990, the Westchester County, New York, Department of Probation created the Economic Sanctions Unit to benefit crime victims. The goal of the program is to efficiently organize the collection of restitution in one location with computer and direct accountant support. Staff keeps probation officers informed of offenders' progress or any lapses in payments. Since its inception, the Economic Sanctions Unit has collected over $12 million, which has been disbursed directly to victims of crime.[15]

In other jurisdictions, private collection services track offender compliance with court orders. In Arizona, FARE—the Fines/Fees and Restitution Enforcement program—is a partnership between the Arizona Supreme Court and the private Affiliated Computer Services (ACS) company that was created to enhance collection services to Arizona courts. Before the partnership, the amount of unpaid court costs, fines, fees and restitution in Arizona totaled $831 million. Over the four-year period after the partnership with ACS began, the state collected close to $90 million.[16] Under Kansas law, statutes require criminal orders of restitution to be recorded as civil judgments. If a defendant is found noncompliant with a restitution order 60 days after it is issued, the court assigns the case to the attorney general, who contracts with either a private collection agency, a private attorney who specializes in collections, or court trustees to collect the restitution (the attorney general charges a 1 percent administration fee). Collections agencies can impose a surcharge and/or interest (up to 33 percent), calculated on the amount of each payment as opposed to the amount owed. When it receives a case from the attorney general, the collection agency notifies the victim that it has been assigned the case and will try to collect the restitution.[17]

While jurisdictions develop new approaches to fine collection, a fundamental problem with tariff fines will always exist. When a fixed amount is imposed on all defendants convicted of a particular crime, no matter their financial circumstances, the impact of the punishment comes into question. When tariffs are set low, the fines have little punitive or deterrent effect on wealthy offenders. When they are set high, collecting the fine amount from poor defendants is nearly impossible, and indigents may end up in jail. However, as we will see in the next section, a concept known as "day fines" may provide the essential equity for fines to be imposed fairly.

Day Fines: Incorporating an Established European Model in America

In the U.S. criminal justice system, fines are used primarily in courts of limited jurisdiction, especially traffic courts, or as enhancements to other forms of punishment. Earlier we noted that judges impose fines, either alone or in combination with another penalty, in nearly all their sentences. However, fines are generally not used in American courts as an alternative to incarceration or probation. This contrasts sharply with practices in many other countries, where fines are not only used more commonly, but are often the sole penalty, even for repeat offenders and moderately serious offenses.[18]

In the Scandinavian countries and elsewhere in Western Europe, **day fine** systems consider both the severity of the crime and an offender's daily earnings.[19] Thus, day fines differ from tariff fines by making impact of a fine more equitable for wealthy and poor offenders alike.

The success of day fine systems in Europe has been measured in terms of how much they reduce the number of prison sentences. In the mid-1960s, for example, West Germany enacted criminal law reforms calling for fines instead of incarceration for those who would be sentenced to less than six months. Research at the time showed that short sentences did little to rehabilitate offenders, and low-level offenders who were sent to jail for a short period became hardened by the system.[20] Under this policy, between 1968 and 1970, the number of persons incarcerated was reduced from 113,273 to just over 10,000.[21] By 1979, West German courts imposed prison sentences in only 17 percent of cases (for a wide variety of crimes) and fines in 82 percent of cases.[22]

Has the early success of the day fine system in Europe held up over time? A major problem that evolved in Germany and other countries during the 1990s was an increase in the number of fine defaulters. Consequently, persons who did not pay were sent to prison. In 1996, for example, 22 percent of inmates in the German adult prison system had been incarcerated only due to nonpayment of fines. However, a major reason for the high number of defaulters was the high unemployment rate affiliated with bad economic conditions.[23] The unemployment rate in Germany was estimated at 12 percent, and nearly one in eight of Germany's working population was on some form of public support.[24] Elsewhere, the story was about the same, with more persons being incarcerated for nonpayment of fines. In 2005 and 2006 there were 19,477 sentenced receptions to prisons in Scotland. Of these, nearly one-third (6,213) were for fine default.[25]

Besides difficult economic times, increases in European prison populations resulted from attitudes of the judiciary toward tougher sanctions. Consider, for example, that in 2007 Switzerland amended several laws to reduce the number of confined persons. As in other European countries, the Swiss changes included abolishing short-term jail terms and introducing a system of day fines calculated based on a person's income. Although the goal was to reduce the number of persons in confinement, Swiss prison populations grew by 5 percent in 2009. Ironically, the rise occurred despite four years of successive decreases in the number of reported crimes. Martin Killias, a professor of criminology at Zurich University, explained the conflicting trends by noting that "When judges cannot use short sentences they usually impose alternative sanctions, like day fines, but they may also feel such an approach is inappropriate for the crime and impose a heavier custodial sentence of just over six months."[26]

U.S. experimentation with day fines began in the late 1980s with the Staten Island Day-Fine Project in Richmond County, New York. The purpose of the experiment was

EXHIBIT 6.2 Day Fine Unit Scale[27]

Type of Offense	Number of Day Fine Units Discount – PRESUMPTIVE – Premium
• Criminal mischief	
(Damage to property scale)	
$1,000 or more	51 – **60** – 69
$700–$999	42 – **50** – 58
$500–$699	34 – **40** – 46
$300–$499	25 – **30** – 35
$150–$299	17 – **20** – 23
$1–$149	13 – **15** – 17
• Unlawful possession of marijuana	13 – **15** – 17
• Disorderly conduct	13 – **15** – 17
• Trespass	13 – **15** – 17
• Attempted assault	
A. Substantial injury	38 – **45** – 52
Stranger-to-stranger; or where victim is known to assailant, he/she is weaker, vulnerable	
B. Minor injury	30 – **35** – 40
Stranger-to-stranger; or where victim is known to assailant, he/she is weaker, vulnerable; or altercations involving use of a weapon	
C. Substantial injury	17 – **20** – 23
Altercations among acquaintances; brawls	
D. Minor injury	13 – **15** – 17
Altercations among acquaintances; brawls	

to adapt the Western European model to the limited-jurisdiction court on Staten Island and see how judges would use fines when freed from the constraints of the tariff system. To start, a planning group comprised of judges, prosecutors, and defense counsel developed procedures for calculating fine units according to offense severity and income of the offender. They created a scale with presumptive units, including discount and premium options, for particular offenses. Exhibit 6.2 provides an example of selected offense categories in the Staten Island Day Fine Unit Scale. Note that for the offense of trespass, a judge could impose 13, 15, or 17 units depending on extenuating circumstances associated with the offense. Next, the planning group devised a valuation table, specifying the exact dollar amount for each unit based on net daily income

EXHIBIT 6.3 Valuation Table[28]

Net Daily Income	Number of Dependents			
	1	2	3	4
$20	11.22	9.24	5.50	4.50
$30	16.83	13.86	10.89	8.91
$40	22.44	18.48	14.52	11.88
$50	28.05	23.10	18.15	14.85
$60	33.66	27.72	21.78	17.82
$70	39.27	32.34	25.41	20.79
$80	44.88	36.96	29.04	23.76
$90	50.49	41.58	32.67	26.73
$100	56.10	46.20	36.30	29.70

and number of family dependents. Some examples from the full Staten Island day fine scales are provided in Exhibit 6.3.

Using our example of the offender convicted of trespass, a judge would impose the presumptive 15 fine units under normal circumstances. If the offender had two dependents (self and spouse) and earned $80 a day, the offender would pay $36.96 for each fine unit, or a total of $554.40.

The National Institute of Justice evaluated the model to determine the impact of the two-stage procedure on the court's use of day fines. Nearly 5,000 cases were examined over a two-year period. The results were extremely positive and noted the following outcomes:

1. The introduction of the day fines did not affect judges' sentencing decisions.
2. The average fine amounts increased as a result of the new system.
3. The day fine system did not undermine the court's high collection rates.
4. The introduction of the day fine system reduced the number of arrest warrants issued for failure to appear.
5. Low-income offenders were no better or worse at compliance with day fine sentences than with tariff fine sentences.[29]

As the results of the Staten Island evaluation were disseminated, other jurisdictions became interested in the day fine concept. In 1991, the Bureau of Justice Assistance funded a multi-site demonstration project on day fines. Four jurisdictions participated: Maricopa County (Phoenix), Arizona; Polk County (Des Moines), Iowa; Bridgeport, Connecticut; and Marion, Malheur, Coos, and Josephine Counties in Oregon. Although the projects varied considerably in structure and operation, some important lessons can be drawn from them:

- Operationally, structured fines can work effectively. Information about a defendant's financial circumstances can be obtained; calculation of the amount of the structured fine is not difficult; the system is understandable to practitioners who are adequately trained; and the structured fines can be collected in a large number of cases if the system is structured properly and a sound collections system is in place.

- Collection has been a problem in some of the pilot jurisdictions. These problems underline the need for an effective collections system in any structured fine program.
- Practitioners who have used structured fines like the basic concept. Judges, prosecutors, and defense lawyers in the jurisdictions that have instituted pilot programs generally agree that structured fines are fairer than tariff fines.
- The potential effectiveness of structured fines as a sentencing option is significantly impaired by laws establishing mandatory fines, fees, penalty assessments, and other economic sanctions. When the minimum mandatory payment (fine floor) is high, it is difficult to develop a system in which fines can be collected from relatively poor offenders. In contrast, a low maximum fine amount (fine ceiling) in some states results in a system with little meaningful economic impact on relatively affluent offenders.
- To make structured fines work effectively, a great deal of up-front policy formulation and program planning is necessary. Time must be spent on education and training, both before implementation and on a continuing basis. Optimally, a structured fine program will be introduced as an integral part of a jurisdiction's overall development of a rational sentencing policy that includes a full range of intermediate sanctions.[30]

Despite the encouraging results in Staten Island and other U.S. jurisdictions, day fines have failed to gain widespread support in the United States. For example, among persons sentenced for a felony in state courts nationwide in 2006, only 4 percent received a sentence in which a fine, restitution, treatment, or community service was the sole sanction.[31] Yet judges ordered an estimated 38 percent of felony offenders to pay a fine as an additional penalty to probation or confinement. What is it that makes the U.S. courts reluctant to order a fine as the only sentence? Reasons vary, but one issue that bears on the courts' skepticism is the difficulty that occurs when attempting to assess an offender's net income in order to calculate an appropriate day fine. Courts have limited access to an offender's income information, so most of the day fines are assessed based on an offender's self-reported income, which may or may not be reliable. This opens the door for the possibility that courts will be influenced more by the assessment of means than by the seriousness of the crime and imposes small fines for serious matters and large fines for minor offenses.

Another reason for the reluctance is that for the punishment to have achieved its policy goals of **just deserts** and deterrence, offenders must be required to pay their fines. If the offender does not pay, courts must either confine the individual or develop an alternative sanction. If courts resort to confinement on a regular basis for defaulters, it calls into question the soundness of the fining process itself, not just the character of the offenders.

The preservation of the courts' reputation, which is to a great extent influenced by public opinion, is yet another reason that fines will likely never be recognized as a legitimate punishment other than for traffic and low-level offenses. Data from Gallup's most recent annual survey on crime show that a firm majority (65 percent) said that the criminal justice system is too lenient on criminals.[32] Mandatory-minimum sentencing and other get-tough laws are good indicators that U.S. citizens are steadfast in their perceptions that only incarceration can achieve certainty and severity of punishment. Since public opinion creates the boundaries within which the community will support policy, judges will not soon be likely to extend the use of fines as a routine sentence.

Despite the success of the day fine system in Europe and in its pilot programs in the United States and the real possibility of fines being better utilized as an alternative sanction, the criminal justice system in America is not likely to move further in this direction. Too many factors, especially the force of public opinion regarding get-tough punishment, weigh against it.

Restitution and Restorative Justice: Compensating Crime Victims

Restitution requires that offenders partially or fully compensate victims for any financial losses suffered as a result of the crime. Restitution is part of the offender's sentence and can be ordered in both adult and juvenile cases after the defendant is found guilty or pleads guilty. The amount of restitution ordered by the judge depends on the victim's crime-related expenses with consideration of the defendant's financial resources. For certain federal crimes though, restitution is imposed without consideration of the offender's ability to pay.[33] In many jurisdictions, the probation or community corrections department assists the court in determining the amount of restitution. Although normally used to directly compensate a crime victim, courts have ordered restitution payments to family members of deceased victims for funeral costs, expenses related to pain and suffering, and surgery/medical expenses.[34]

Restitution in the United States began in the 1930s with the establishment of penal laws in some states that allowed restitution as part of suspended sentences and probation.[35] Then, in the mid-1970s, the Law Enforcement Assistance Administration offered funding to support states' initiatives to develop restitution programs. At the same time, influential groups like the American Bar Association developed policy statements in support of restitution. However, it wasn't until the victims' rights movement of the 1980s that ordering restitution to crime victims was seen as a legitimate and necessary function of the justice system. One of the most influential actions during the movement was the passage of the Victim and Witness Protection Act (VWPA) of 1982, which required judges to order restitution in criminal cases. Prior to that time, judges could order restitution only as a condition of probation, and such orders were "infrequently used and indifferently enforced."[36] In 1986, the Final Report of the President's Task Force on Victims of Crime reinforced the language of VWPA, calling for legislation that required judges to order restitution or state the reason for not doing so on the record. By July 1985, 29 states had passed laws that mandated restitution to victims as part of the sentencing process.[37]

In 1990, Congress passed the Victims' Rights and Restitution Act, which confirmed that victims had a right to compensation and use of relevant federal services. Five years later, the Victims' Restitution Act of 1995 amended the federal criminal code to require judges to order restitution for victims of the following crimes of violence: property crimes, fraud, consumer product tampering, and drug crimes.[38] By 2000, every state had passed some form of legislation to benefit victims. Florida's state statute is typical, providing that in addition to any punishment, "the court shall order the defendant to make restitution to the victim for damage or loss caused directly or indirectly by the defendant's offense; and damage or loss related to the defendant's criminal episode, unless it finds clear and compelling reasons not to order such restitution. Restitution may be monetary or nonmonetary restitution. If the court does not order restitution, or orders restitution of only a portion of the damages, as provided in this section, it shall state on the record in detail the reasons therefor[e]."[39]

In the federal system, the structure of restitution remained unaltered until Congress passed the Mandatory Victims Restitution Act (the "MVRA" or the "Act") as Title II of the Antiterrorism and Effective Death Penalty Act of 1996. This act expanded the scope of restitution on the federal level, making it mandatory in almost all cases in which the victim suffered an identifiable monetary loss. The MVRA also removed judges' ability to fashion restitution orders based on an offender's ability to pay, by mandating that the court "order restitution to each victim in the full amount of each victim's losses as determined by the court and without consideration of the economic circumstances of the defendant."[40]

Despite the passage of all this legislation, restitution remains one of the most under-enforced rights of crime victims. A fundamental reason is that the criminal justice system is primarily designed to control crime by punishing offenders through harsh sanctions. In order for offenders to receive their just deserts, punishment must be severe

EXHIBIT 6.4 Felons Sentenced to an Additional Penalty in State Courts, by Offense, 2006[43]

	Percentage of Felons with an Additional Penalty of—				
Offense	**Fine**	**Restitution**	**Treatment[a]**	**Community Service**	**Other**
All offenses	38%	18%	11%	11%	2%
Violent offenses	36%	18%	11%	12%	2%
Murder/nonnegligent manslaughter	28	13	8	7	1
Sexual assault	37	18	15	13	2
Rape	38	24	21	19	2
Other sexual assault[b]	36	14	11	9	3
Robbery	26	18	10	9	1
Aggravated assault	40	18	10	12	1
Other violent[c]	36	17	13	15	3
Property offenses	37%	27%	11%	12%	2%
Burglary	34	27	11	12	2
Larceny	35	26	11	13	3
Motor vehicle theft	34	28	20	22	3
Fraud/forgery[d]	42	29	10	11	3
Drug offenses	41%	14%	13%	11%	2%
Possession	36	19	23	20	2
Trafficking	45	11	5	4	2
Weapons offenses	27%	8%	5%	7%	1%
Other Specified Offenses[e]	40%	13%	9%	10%	2%

a Includes any type of counseling, rehabilitation, treatment, or mental hospital confinement

b Includes offenses such as statutory rape and incest with a minor

c Includes offenses such as negligent manslaughter and kidnapping

d Includes embezzlement

e Comprises nonviolent offenses such as vandalism and receiving stolen property

VICTIMINFO.CA: AN ONLINE RESOURCE FOR VICTIMS AND WITNESSES OF CRIME IN BRITISH COLUMBIA, CANADA

6.2

CBC Online

VictimInfo.ca is a Web site created and maintained by the Justice Education Society of British Columbia. The Web site provides resources and information for dealing with the consequences of crime—for example, services for victims, reporting a crime, criminal charges, going to court, and sentencing. Click on "play video" and watch the video guide for victim services. Then click the "Victim Impact Statement" link and watch the video relating to questions and answers about victim impact statements.

Why is it important to complete a victim impact statement shortly after the offense? Can victims update their victim impact statement once it has been submitted to the court?

Visit CBC Online 6.2 at www.mhhe.com/bayens1e

enough to meet the standards of retributive justice. Corresponding to their position on fines, courts are reluctant to sentence a serious offender to restitution unless it's an add-on. The result is an "inherent tension that arises when efforts are made to use the criminal law, with its focus on vindication of society's interests in punishing offenders, to reimburse victims for the harm done them by specific offenders."[41] In the next section, we discuss some of the key issues that obstruct the compensation of victims for losses that result from crime.

Restitution Order and Enforcement

Judges typically order restitution when they can accurately assess the extent of victims' injuries and losses. Thus, they are more likely to order restitution for property crimes when dollar amounts for damages can be objectively determined. For example, an offender found guilty of theft is likely to be ordered to pay restitution commensurate with the value of the stolen property. In contrast, it would be difficult to determine an amount of restitution that could make up for a crime like kidnapping or murder. Exhibit 6.4 provides information from a 2006 Bureau of Justice Statistics survey of state courts on characteristics of felony offenders. Overall, restitution was ordered as an additional penalty in only 18 percent of court cases. About 27 percent of property crime offenders were ordered to pay restitution, while only about 18 percent of violent perpetrators were ordered to do so.[42]

As noted, the difficulty associated with ordering restitution is partly due to problems with assessing victims' injuries and losses. In many jurisdictions, judges rely on the presentence investigation report prepared by the probation department to determine a fair amount of restitution. Although this report focuses primarily on the crime and the defendant's background and criminal history, a **victim impact statement** can be included as part of the presentence report. For this report, victims are asked to describe their physical, psychological, and emotional injuries after an indictment is brought against an offender. Moreover, the report summarizes the economic loss or damage suffered by the victim as a result of the crime. Consequently, a victim impact statement is extremely valuable because it provides the basis for appropriate sentences and suitable restitution. Victim impact statements vary in their format based on the provisions of state statutes. A list of items typically found in an impact statement is provided in Exhibit 6.5. CBC Online 6.2 focuses on resources for victims in Canada.

EXHIBIT 6.5 Victim Impact Statement[44]

1. Please describe how this offense has affected you and your family.
2. What was the *emotional impact* of this crime on you and your family?
3. What was the *financial impact* of this crime on you and your family?
4. What concerns do you have, if any, about your safety and security?
5. What do you want to happen now?
6. Would you like an opportunity to participate in victim/offender programming (such as mediation/dialogue or victim impact panels) that can help hold the offender accountable for his/her actions? (*NOTE: Only utilize this question if such programs are in place, and ensure that the victim has written resources that fully describe such programs*)
7. If community service is recommended as part of the disposition or sentence, do you have a favorite charity or cause you'd like to recommend as a placement?
8. Is there *any other information* you would like to share with the court regarding the offense, and how it affected you and your family?

Documenting Losses for Victim Restitution

To ensure accurate and complete restitution orders, you are required to document your losses in writing for the court or paroling authority. The following considerations can help you document your out-of-pocket expenses and projected future expenses:

- Employer statements (letters or affidavits) that document unpaid time off from work you took as a result of injuries from the crime, or involvement in justice processes.
- Documentation of any workers' compensation claims submitted and/or claims payments received.
- Copies of bills for services directly related to your financial recovery from the crime.
- Any receipts for items or services.
- Documentation that estimates the value of stolen property.
- Photos of valuables that were stolen.
- Copies of any documentation provided by local law enforcement agencies (e.g., records of serial numbers, photos, etc.) that are intended to aid you in the recovery of stolen property.
- Any law enforcement records that indicate the status of your stolen property (e.g., property recovered, recovered but damaged).
- Copies of your applications to and/or copies of checks received from the state victim compensation fund.
- Copies of insurance claims and related correspondence between you and your insurance company, as well as copies of any checks you have received to cover losses.

Immediate Losses

During the presentence investigation, you should be asked to report information about your losses by completing or updating a financial worksheet and providing documentation as described above.

The range of these losses can include the following:

Medical Care

- Emergency transportation to the hospital.
- Rape kit examinations that are not immediately paid by a third party.

- All expenses related to the hospital stay, including the room, laboratory tests, medications, x-rays, and medical supplies.
- HIV testing in cases involving the exchange of bodily fluids, and medical supplies.
- Expenses for care provided by physicians.
- Fees for physical or occupational therapy.
- Replacement of eyeglasses, hearing aids, or other sensory aid items damaged, destroyed, or stolen from the victim.
- Rental and related costs for equipment used for any physical restoration, (e.g., wheelchairs, wheelchair ramps, special beds, crutches).

Mental Health Services

- Fees for counseling or therapy for you and your family members.
- Any costs incurred as a result of your participation in support or therapy groups.
- Expenses for medications that doctors may prescribe to help ease your trauma following the crime.

Funeral Expenses

- Costs associated with burials, i.e., caskets, cemetery plots, memorial services, etc.
- Expenses for travel to plan and/or attend funerals.

Time Off from Work

- To repair damage following property crimes.
- To attend or participate in court or parole proceedings.
- To attend doctors' appointments for injuries or mental health needs directly resulting from the crime.

Other Expenses

- Crime scene cleanup.
- Costs of replacing locks, changing security devices, etc.
- Expenses related to child or elder care when you have to testify in court.
- Relocation expenses.
- Fees incurred in changing banking or credit card accounts.

Projected Expenses

Victimization often results in injuries or losses that are long term. While it is not possible to accurately document such projected expenses, it is possible to document expert opinions as to future financial obligations you might incur as a direct result of the crime.

You should seek documentation (a letter or affidavit) from professionals who are providing you with medical or mental health services that offers an estimate of your future treatment needs, as well as related expenses. Such costs can include:

- Long-term medical treatment.
- Physical or occupational rehabilitation or therapy.
- Mental health counseling or therapy.
- Time that must be taken off from work to receive any of the above services.

In all states, crime victims are allowed to make oral and written statements about the impact of the crime on the victim and the victim's family. Should video productions by the victim's family be allowed to be shown at sentencing?

Problems Associated with Restitution

Although the right to receive restitution is widely recognized, two basic problems limit the effectiveness of the program within the criminal justice system. As we have pointed out, the first is the failure of many courts to even order restitution. Referring again to Exhibit 6.4, judges are two times more likely to order a fine than restitution. Studies regarding adult offenders suggest that judges are more likely to order restitution when the offender is better educated and employed, which make it more likely that the offender will pay the imposed restitution.[45] Moreover, judges order restitution most often when damages are easy to quantify and when the victim was a business.[46] A 1992 Bureau of Justice Statistics report on recidivism of felony offenders on probation revealed that of the 32 counties surveyed, only half required restitution when ordered in felony probation cases.[47]

A second critical problem is that when courts do order restitution, they typically have few efficient procedures for monitoring, enforcement, collection, and disbursement of restitution payments. A Bureau of Justice Statistics study of felony offenders on probation revealed that the average restitution order imposed was $3,368 per probationer. Among those probationers who had completed their sentences, they had paid only 54 percent of the amount of restitution ordered.[48] Similarly, in a study conducted by the American Bar Association, researchers found that only 45 percent of restitution dollars are actually collected.[49] Finally, since the passage of the MVRA, the amount of federal criminal debt has grown from approximately $6 billion in 1996 to over $50 billion in 2007. Eighty percent of the federal criminal debt is the result of uncollected restitution orders owed to third parties. Thus, of the approximately $50 billion in uncollected criminal sanctions, nearly $40 billion is victim restitution.[50]

The Office for Victims of Crime's Joint Center on Violence and Victim Studies has identified a number of barriers that directly influence a jurisdiction's ability to administer successful restitution programs:

- Some justice professionals believe that restitution is simply uncollectible because all offenders are indigent and cannot afford to pay restitution.
- Agencies lack agreements stipulating which of them is responsible for monitoring, enforcing, collecting, and disbursing restitution. Moreover, many probation and parole officers assert that they are not collection agents.
- Even though state laws mandate restitution programs, they fail to provide adequate funding for agencies to fulfill such mandates.
- Restitution orders are often not first in the priority of court-ordered payments, following behind court costs, fines, cost of salaries for justice officials, costs of incarceration, and other financial obligations.
- In jurisdictions where restitution is not mandatory, it is not consistently ordered as a condition of the sentence.
- Agencies lack automation systems to simplify the restitution monitoring and collection processes.
- Many parole boards do not have authority to order restitution as a condition of parole.
- Some crime victims and service providers express cynicism about efforts to collect restitution; their criticism of existing efforts can contribute to lowered employee morale among those responsible for monitoring restitution programs and payments.[51]

Restitution can both positively and negatively affect the psychological recovery of victims from the aftermath of crime. For example, the victims' trauma may be compounded if restitution is not paid and offenders are not held directly accountable for their actions.[52] And victims prefer restitution that comes directly from offenders, as opposed to compensation that is issued by the government. Moreover, some evidence suggests that if victims receive restitution, they are less concerned about further punishment for offenders.[53] Other findings suggest that victims who are involved throughout the restitution process may feel empowered by their experience. Moreover, it allows them an opportunity to make use of a criminal justice process that is often criticized for focusing on offenders rather than victims. In fact, studies have shown that receiving restitution influences most victims' levels of satisfaction with the criminal justice system.[54]

Payment of restitution promotes the active participation of both offenders and victims in the justice process. Because its goals include restoring victims' damages and returning offenders to law-abiding lives, fulfillment of restitution obligations comprises a tenet of restorative justice. As we noted in Chapter 1, the central premise of restorative justice is that victims, offenders, and the affected communities are all key stakeholders in the attempt to repair the harm caused by crime. Participating in the process of paying restitution can serve as an important reminder to offenders about the direct harm they have caused to victims and to their community.

If paying restitution has the potential to benefit all stakeholders in the restorative justice model, shouldn't more be done to monitor offenders' payments and increase

Career Profile

DAN PETERSEN, SENIOR FACULTY WITH THE NATIONAL VICTIM ASSISTANCE ACADEMY

Dr. Petersen is senior faculty with the National Victim Assistance Academy, which is sponsored by the Office for Victims of Crime (OVC), U.S. Department of Justice. His professional career has centered on working with people with disabilities and crime victim services. Dr. Petersen became involved in the crime victim movement in the mid-1980s. At that time he was director of a human services degree program at Montana State University at Billings. According to Dr. Petersen, "In the last twenty-five years the field of victim services has changed dramatically. With the passage of the Victims of Crime Act (VOCA) in 1984 by Congress establishing a Crime Victim Fund, programs serving crime victims sprang up across the country. The Office for Victims of Crime, established a year earlier, became a guiding force and support across the country. Services have greatly expanded in the last few decades, particularly in the areas of domestic violence and sexual assault. While great things have happened, the field of victim services is ever changing and continues to take on new challenges. Areas that still need to be addressed include the balance between victim rights and the defendant's rights in the criminal justice system, continued development and education of victim service providers, the professionalization of the field, the role of victim services in corrections, the development of victim services for persons with disabilities, and many other areas. This is an exciting field to be a part of with huge rewards and challenges."

Last year the Bureau of Justice released the first national report on "findings about nonfatal violent and property crime experienced by persons with disabilities based on the National Crime Victimization Survey (NCVS). This was an exciting event in that for the first time the Office of Justice Program's Bureau of Justice Statistics (BJS) has validated the evidence from smaller studies which indicated that persons with disabilities experienced non-fatal crimes at a rate at least 1.5 times higher than that for persons without disabilities." Dr. Petersen indicated that he has appreciated every moment of his involvement in this field. "This is a field where you encounter passion and purpose and you have a chance to really make a positive difference for people."

their compliance with restitution orders? The answer of course is yes, and many jurisdictions have developed policies and procedures to enhance and streamline restitution collection efforts.

Best Practices to Enhance Restitution Collection

Let's examine a few innovative approaches that make victim compensation a top priority, including victim–offender mediation, restitution court, a program called "project payback," and automated services. For further insight into victim assistance, see the Career Profile of Dan Petersen, who works in this field.

Victim–Offender Mediation. Victim–offender mediation (VOM) is a face-to-face meeting, in the presence of a trained mediator, between the victim of a crime and the person who committed that crime. The practice is also called victim–offender

6.3

CBC Online

RESTORATIVE JUSTICE: VICTIM OFFENDER MEDIATION OVERVIEW

This 10-minute video, facilitated by Dr. Mark Umbreit, founding director of the Center for Restorative Justice and Peacemaking at the University of Minnesota, provides an overview of the core principles of restorative justice and of victim offender mediation and the conferencing process.

After viewing the video, answer the following question: Do you think shame is an important component of the face-to-face meetings between the victim and offenders?

Visit CBC Online 6.3 at www.mhhe.com/bayens1e

reconciliation or restorative justice dialogue. In some practices, the victim and the offender are joined by family and community members. The purpose of the meeting is twofold. First, it allows the victim and the offender to talk about the facts and their feelings related to the crime. Ideally, each will get a glimpse into the other's life and break down any preconceived stereotypes. Mediated sessions address the harm caused by the offender and issues of loss experienced by the victim. The psychological benefit is not just limited to victims. Offenders are also given the opportunity to face the situation, take responsibility for their actions, and correct the harm caused by the crime. Receiving forgiveness for a criminal act is one aspect of victim–offender mediation that is typically not present in traditional criminal proceedings. Often this forgiveness provides offenders with a "clean slate," deterring them from repeating criminal conduct.[55] Second, VOM has the potential for negotiating a mutually agreeable plan for restitution.

Victim–offender mediation first appeared in the United States in the 1970s. A national survey conducted in 2000 revealed that 300 communities nationwide were involved in VOM programs.[56] Further, research indicates that victims and offenders find the mediation process fair and are satisfied with the outcomes.[57] A multi-site study found that 79 percent of victims participating in VOM were satisfied, compared with 57 percent who went through the traditional court system.[58] Victims who participated in VOM reported being less fearful than those in the control group. Research has also shown that victims who participate in mediation sessions receive more restitution than nonparticipants. According to the American Bar Association, 95 percent of mediated cases result in written restitution agreements, and the vast majority of those agreements are completed within one year. In contrast, the rate of payment of court-ordered restitution is typically only 20 to 30 percent.[59]

Recent studies have shown that juvenile offenders who participate in VOM subsequently commit fewer and less serious offenses than their counterparts in the traditional juvenile justice system. A national study of 1,298 juveniles who participated in pretrial VOM found 32 percent less recidivism compared to the control group. Evidence also indicates that among those offenders who recidivate, those who have participated in mediated sessions commit less serious crimes.[60] To learn more about VOM, visit CBC Online 6.3.

Restitution Court In September 2008, the first session of restitution court was held in Maricopa County, Arizona. The purpose of this court—designed for civil proceedings, not probation-revocation hearings—is to determine if a probationer is in contempt of court for nonpayment of restitution. Typically, a judge hears 12–15 cases per month in which probationers are six to 15 months delinquent. At the hearings, judges question probationers about their income, expenses, and financial priorities. Once the questioning is completed, the judge has three options: (1) to direct the person to work with the county's collection unit to develop an acceptable repayment plan; (2) to hold a contempt hearing and find the defendant in contempt, but allow him or her to remain free to develop a repayment plan and make a payment before returning to court the next month; or (3) to hold the contempt hearing, find the individual in contempt, and take him or her into custody, setting a purge amount that is usually equal to the delinquency. The person will stay in custody, with work release, until the purge is paid. As of November 2008, the restitution court has collected nearly $300,000 in delinquent restitution for victims. The program has demonstrated such success in a short time that many counties are considering integrating a similar restitution court in their jurisdictions.[61]

Project Payback Project Payback in Gainesville, Florida, is a restorative justice restitution program administered by the Office of the State Attorney. Its purpose is to monitor and enforce restitution imposed on juvenile offenders. It accomplishes its mission by developing juvenile employment skills, giving juveniles who do not become employed the option of completing community restitution service hours, and improving enforcement procedures used by the various juvenile justice agencies. Juveniles who are employable are required to either be employed or searching for employment, and they must attend three two-hour sessions of job skills training. For juveniles who are not able to become employed, the program requires completion of "community restitution service" hours. For every verified hour the juvenile completes at an approved site, Project Payback forwards minimum wage (currently $7.25/hour) to the victim. If the juvenile does not comply with the program requirements, Project Payback sends the juvenile for a compliance hearing and brings the case to the court's attention. Since the program's inception, $545,000 has been paid back to victims.[62]

California Enhanced Collection Program. In 2007, the California legislature revised the state penal code to require the Judicial Council, a 27-member body responsible for improving the administration of justice in the California courts, to develop performance measures and benchmarks to review the effectiveness of the superior court and county collection programs. Under this program, courts and counties were provided with collections best practices as well as educational tools and resources to assist in establishing or enhancing comprehensive collections programs. Moreover, each superior court and county collections program is required to report to the judicial council regarding its performance and the extent to which it is following best practices.[63] According to revenue figures, this effort is associated with collection of $565,656,730 in delinquent court-ordered debt for FY 2008–2009.[64] In the area of restitution, collections increased from $63.6 million in 2004–2005 to $71.0 million in 2008–2009.[65]

Automated Services. Improvements to restitution collection efforts have been achieved in many jurisdictions through newly designed automated systems. Most of these computer-based systems interface with community-based correctional case-management systems and provide quick access to offender information. These automated systems have also assisted victims, increasing their involvement and knowledge pertaining to the criminal justice process, as well as their sense of personal safety and security. According to the Office for Victims of Crime, automation enhances the restitution process by:

- Reducing the amount of staff time needed to manage and collect restitution
- Automatically generating letters of reminder or bills to offenders related to restitution and other court-ordered fees
- Automatically generating letters to victims informing them about the restitution process, the status of the payments owed to them, and other available services
- Maintaining accurate records of the location of victims and offenders and the status of restitution orders
- Increasing the ability of probation and parole officers, supervisors, and department administrators to access information on the status of an individual offender or of a group of offenders (i.e., all offenders supervised by a particular agent or unit or all offenders ordered to pay restitution throughout the state)
- Enabling agencies to prepare statistical reports quickly and to easily analyze and report progress or results (i.e., collection rates)
- Providing valuable data to evaluate the effectiveness of restitution programs[66]

The Florida Department of Corrections operates its Court-Ordered Payment System (COPS) to track and simplify collections. This automated system is located on the department's mainframe computer and is linked to the offender's criminal history and supervision/inmate record. It provides payment information to 155 probation offices in Florida, 51 major institutions, 32 community correctional centers, and 43 road prisons, work camps, and forestry camps. Offenders make payments to the state, which are then converted to government checks and disbursed to victims and other payees according to the established payment schedules in COPS.[67]

Victim Compensation

Besides restitution, victim compensation programs provide another way to make financial assistance available to crime victims. Unlike restitution programs, in which offenders pay victims for their losses, compensation programs are administered by state governments and funded by both state and federal governments. On the federal level, the Office for Victims of Crime administers the Crime Victims Fund, which was established by the Victims of Crime Act of 1984 (VOCA). It funds victim compensation and assistance programs in every U.S. state and territory, as well as training and demonstration projects designed to enhance the skills of victim service providers. Federal revenues deposited into the fund come from criminal fines, forfeited appearance bonds, special forfeitures of collateral profits from crime, special assessments that range from $25 on individuals convicted of misdemeanors and $400 on corporations convicted of felonies, and gifts, donations, and bequests by private parties. Fiscal year (FY) 2009 was a record-breaking year for deposits, with $1,745,677,602 going into the fund.[68]

Victim compensation programs also received funding through the American Recovery and Reinvestment Act of 2009. The Recovery Act included $4 billion for state, local, and tribal law enforcement as well as other criminal and juvenile justice activities that help prevent crime and improve the criminal justice system in the United States while supporting the creation of jobs and much-needed resources for states and local communities. The Office for Victims of Crime was appropriated $100 million in grant funding, of which $47.5 million was made available for distribution to state crime-victim compensation programs. An additional $47.5 million was allocated to state agencies that administer crime victim assistance programs to support the provision of

EXHIBIT 6.6 FY 09 Recovery Act Victims of Crime Act (VOCA) Victim Compensation Formula Grant Program[70]

Name	Amount
California Victim Compensation & Government Claims Board	$8,110,055
Florida Department of Legal Affairs	$3,050,799
Illinois Court of Claims	$3,029,132
New Jersey Department of Law and Public Safety	$1,410,671
New York Crime Victims Board	$2,829,174
Office of the Ohio Attorney General	$2,000,627
Pennsylvania Commission on Crime and Delinquency	$1,536,233
South Carolina Office of Victim Assistance	$1,153,023
Tennessee Treasury Department Division of Claims Administration	$1,472,799
Texas Office of the Attorney General	$7,771,484

services to victims of crime.[69] Exhibit 6.6 provides a list of the highest monetary grants made to states' victim compensation programs.

Compensation programs make payments to victims, their survivors, or those who have provided services necessitated by the crime. Again, this is distinguished from restitution and civil liability, which hold the offender directly accountable for repairing the harm done to his or her victim (it is of course possible to implement all approaches to helping victims simultaneously). Crime-related expenses include medical costs, funeral and burial costs, mental health counseling, and lost wages or loss of support, to name a few. Typically, property damage and loss are not covered by crime victim funds. Victim assistance includes such services as crisis intervention, emergency shelter, counseling, and criminal justice advocacy. A national evaluation of crime victim compensation programs showed that nearly half (47 percent) of compensation awards, averaging across states, were for medical/dental expenses. Economic support (lost wages and loss of support) accounted for 20 percent of payments, and funeral/burial expenses averaged 13 percent. Mental health expenses averaged 9 percent of payments. One-third of the states use compensation funds to pay for sexual assault forensic exams.[71]

Although each state compensation program is administered independently, most programs have similar eligibility requirements and follow the same basic application procedures. The crime must be reported to law enforcement officials within 72 hours, or there must be good reason why it is not. The victim must submit a timely application to the compensation program, which is generally one year from the date of the crime. The injury sustained by the victim cannot be the result of the victim's own wrongdoing or substantial provocation. Victims must present evidence of their losses, which may include police reports, medical bills, employers' reports of lost wages, and insurance reports.

Compensable expenses are defined by state statute and cover financial assistance that is not reimbursable by insurance or other sources. Decision-making authority varies from state to state, with about a third of the states using part-time boards or commissions to determine eligibility and awards, and the rest authorizing full-time administrative staff (usually program directors) to make determinations. Moreover, the maximum amount of the compensation award is limited in each state. In Idaho, Kansas, and Massachusetts, a crime victim may receive up to $25,000 in compensation. In Michigan and South Carolina, awards from the Crime Victim Compensation Fund are limited to $15,000.

Although there have been a number of substantive reforms in state compensation programs that help honor the rights of victims, the matter of how much a victim's own wrongdoing or provoking behavior contributed to a particular crime is controversial. It is commonly accepted that victims who are involved in the commission of a crime at the time they were victimized should be barred from receiving any compensation. For example, a shoot-out in a liquor store robbery in which the victim is the robber is fairly clear cut. But what about other types of crimes in which participation is not so obvious, such as sexual assault by a spouse? The point to be made here is that decisions about a victim's participation becomes complex at the individual level, and each criminal case is unique and fraught with its own variables. Unfortunately, we have no litmus test to determine the extent of behavior that rises to a level of provocation. Consequently, decisions about whether a victim should be compensated can be subjective and perceived as unfair.

Another matter to consider about victim compensation programs is that compensation boards are routinely under scrutiny because of awards made to victims that do not meet eligibility requirements. Consider, for example, allegations by the New Jersey inspector general regarding personnel from the Victims of Crime Compensation Agency (VCCA). In that matter, the inspector general found that VCCA made payments without obtaining proof that claimants were victims of criminal conduct and without requiring adequate documentation to substantiate claim amounts. In one example, the office paid more than $36,000 in benefits—at least $11,000 above the maximum—to a person who claimed workplace harassment, a crime not even eligible for compensation.[72]

Community Service: Reimbursing Society for Past Harms

Thus far, we have discussed the imposition of fines and restitution as punishment. We have noted that one of the most common reasons judges fail to order these economic sanctions is a defendant's inability to pay. Also, the courts are well aware of the problems associated with collections, which often means that an economic sanction will go unsatisfied. Consequently, indigent defendants face the possibility of incarceration to offset their inability to pay a fine or comply with the restitution order. However, in many cases, the court has another option—to order community service.

Community service is compulsory unpaid public labor performed by an offender as punishment for a crime. The most common type of community service involves neighborhood clean-up and other public improvement projects. Tasks include picking up trash, mowing grass, or painting buildings and other structures. Community service offers a way for the offender to be held accountable and to repair some of the harm caused by his or her criminal conduct. In the United States, community service has not been developed for serious offenders and is typically not a standalone sentence. Rather, it is a court-ordered condition of probation as part of a sentence. If the defendant is indigent, the court can order community service as a substitute for payment of a fine or restitution. In such a situation, hours of work are valued at the minimum wage level, and the work continues until the unpaid fine or restitution has been paid.

Community service emerged in Britain and Wales in 1973 as a desirable alternative to the use of confinement. Within a few short years, thousands of offenders were placed on probation to "work off" community service obligations. By 1987, 8 percent of offenders sentenced for serious crime in England and Wales were sentenced

Some people argue that community service is simply a slap on the wrist. What arguments can you make about the value of this method of punishment as a viable form of justice?

to community service. At the same time in the United States, community service was developed as an alternative to fines or as an additional condition of probation.[73] One of the earliest community service programs in the United States was launched in 1979 as the Community Service Sentencing Project (CSSP) of New York City, an intermediate sanction for repeat misdemeanor offenders. The Vera Institute reports that between 1979 and 1989, CSSP participants logged more than 50,000 hours of unpaid labor each year and saved the city $6.5 million annually in jail operating costs from bed space freed up for more serious offenders.[74]

Today, community service is used in every state and at the federal level. The most recent data from fiscal year 2007 shows that 13.2 percent (26,055) of all postconviction cases in federal courts included community service conditions.[75] Community service is court-ordered for all categories of offenders including adults and juveniles, felons and misdemeanants, probationers and parolees, and those living in residential centers and confinement facilities. Community service offers several benefits with perhaps the most notable being cost-effectiveness. Moreover, the apparent punitiveness of community service enables courts to direct low-risk offenders to such programs without appearing soft on crime. Courts, probation agencies, and correctional programs are eager to show this benefit because of the positive nature of the publicity. Several community service programs from around the country are described in Exhibit 6.7. Note that each agency tracks cost savings to taxpayers and the number of hours offenders are engaged in making reparations to the community.

The benefits of community service extend to the offenders. The interaction between the offender and the community helps restore the offender to the community. Some criminal justice practitioners contend that when offenders work in the community, they find intrinsic value in the work experience, job skills, and socialization opportunities.[81] Others regard community service as a form of creative restitution, a mechanism to fulfill the functions of retribution and deterrence.[82]

EXHIBIT 6.7 Description of Community Service Programs in Selected Jurisdictions

Tarrant County (Fort Worth), Texas—Individuals who are on community supervision can be assigned to one or more of 160 social service, nonprofit, and/or government agencies. These agencies utilize community service restitution volunteers to perform a variety of functions and provide labor such as painting, landscaping, and animal care, which would otherwise not be available due to budget limitations. Community service restitution volunteers provided 414,249 hours of service in FY 2009, which equals $3,003,305 at minimum wage. Approximately 8,893 offenders performed community service hours during FY 2009.[76]

North Carolina Department of Corrections: Division of Community Corrections—The Community Service Work Program (CSWP) receives offenders from the courts or from the Post-Release Supervision and Parole Commission, reviews the offender's history, and places the offender at an agency in the community to perform work. Placements are made to government or nonprofit agencies. Community service hours are ordered as a condition of supervised probation, unsupervised probation or parole; they can be utilized as a supervision tool by the probation officer. In FY 2007–2008, CSWP employees worked with 3,900 agencies across the state to provide meaningful placements for work hours and provided a monetary value to agencies of more than $11.8 million. Taking into account that community service fees amounted to more than $8.6 million, the total value of the program to the state of North Carolina was estimated to exceed $20.4 million.[77]

Paulding County (Paulding), Ohio—Community service is a condition of probation that requires probationers to perform services without compensation for the benefit of the community. This sanction not only provides a service to the community but also enhances accountability and helps instill responsibility. Community service is ordered by the judge and is administered through the probation department. In 2010, probationers served 3,629 community service hours, and the value of work based on minimum wage was $26,492.[78]

Pueblo, Colorado—Adults can also earn credit toward their fines and fees by performing community service for the City of Pueblo. The majority of community service work performed by both juveniles and adults has been in the area of graffiti removal. Throughout 2009, the court's Graffiti Removal/Community Service Program addressed 3,357 separate graffiti sites. Over 12,000 hours of community service was completed at a value of approximately $90,000 based upon minimum wage for juveniles and $10 per hour for adults.[79]

Harris County (Houston), Texas—The Community Service Restitution Program in the juvenile probation department supervises work projects done by probationers and sometimes with their parents at nonprofit agencies or institutions that have been approved as worksites. Worksites are arranged for youth from all divisions of the department including those referred for lesser offenses from intake court services. In 2009, 5,614 probationers and 271 parents worked 63,555 hours at an estimated value of $460,773.[80]

However, administering community service programs has its challenges. First, offenders may not be enthusiastic about completing unpaid work, especially if the number of community service hours is high. You'll remember from our opening chapter story that Kid Rock was sentenced to attend anger management school, pay a large fine, and also complete 80 hours of community service. If his offense had been more serious, the judge would have likely imposed a greater number of community service hours. Consider, for example, that a judge in Rapid City, South Dakota, recently sentenced a 20-year-old man to 10 years probation after he pled guilty to a fourth-degree rape charge for having sex with a girl younger than 16 years old. As a condition of probation, this offender was ordered to complete 1,000 hours of community service and pay restitution of $968, plus court costs.[83]

Exposure to liability for community service programs is also an issue if a probationer is injured while on the job or injures someone else. Generally, judges and court personnel carrying out a judge's order related to participation in community service programs are protected by judicial immunity. If court personnel are acting on their own authority, they may be protected by the doctrine of sovereign immunity for any discretionary decisions they make including work assignments. The doctrine of sovereign, or governmental, immunity extends to certain officers and employees of immune governmental units, provided those officers or employees are acting within the scope of their employment or duties and the conduct does not constitute intentional misconduct or gross negligence. A few states have specific statutes granting immunity to court personnel. North Carolina General Statute 143B–262.4–(d) states:

> [A] person is not liable for damages for any injury or loss sustained by an individual performing community or reparation service under this section unless the injury is caused by the person's gross negligence or intentional wrongdoing. As used in this subsection, "person" includes any governmental unit or agency, nonprofit corporation, or other nonprofit agency that is supervising the individual, or for whom the individual is performing community service work, as well as any person employed by the agency or corporation while acting in the scope and course of the person's employment. This subsection does not affect the immunity from civil liability in tort available to local governmental units or agencies. Notice of the provisions of this subsection shall be furnished to the individual at the time of assignment of community service work by the community service coordinator.[84]

In Louisiana, state statute RS 30:2531.4(c) specifies that:

> A person who participates in a community service litter abatement work program established pursuant to this Section shall have no cause of action for damages against the entity conducting the program or supervising his participation therein, nor against any employee or agent of such entity, for any injury or loss suffered by him during or arising out of his participation in the program, unless the injury or loss was caused by the intentional or grossly negligent act or omission of the entity or its employee or agent. The entity shall not be liable for any injury caused by the individual participating in the program unless the gross negligence or intentional act of the entity or its employee or agent was a substantial factor in causing the injury. No provision hereof shall negate the requirement to provide an offender with necessary medical treatment as statutorily required.[85]

Some jurisdictions charge offenders a program fee to pay a liability insurance premium that covers injuries while participating in community service work. In Olympia, Washington, for example, offenders wishing to participate in the community service program to help pay off court-ordered fines are required to pay a $30 fee, which includes liability insurance and processing by the probation department.[86] In other jurisdictions, community service workers are covered under the workers' compensation insurance policy. Because workers' compensation statutes typically permit remedies only for employee injuries caused by employer negligence, agencies would generally minimize their risk of loss by obtaining coverage under such a statute. Typical statutes do not allow a worker to sue the employer under tort law, thereby averting the risk of enormous damage claims.[87]

Research associated with community service is very limited. The main reason is that community service is primarily used by the courts as an additional sanction for offenders being supervised in the community. Most of the data pertaining to community service comes from self-evaluation studies that assess only program completion rates and cost effectiveness. For example, the state of California collects and reports information on annual program expenditures and juvenile justice outcomes associated with the state's Juvenile Justice Crime Prevention Act. A 2005 annual report indicates that more than 60 percent of the participating counties experienced an increase in the number of youth who completed community service.[88]

A few studies have suggested that courts also use community service as a sentencing option to reduce jail populations. For example, in 1996 the Joint Legislative Audit and Review Commission (JLARC) in Virginia conducted a study of incentives that could be used to reduce the number of prisoners awaiting trial and the number of misdemeanants held in local and regional jails. The study found that community service was one of the primary jail alternative programs that directly resulted in reduced inmate populations.[89] In another study conducted in the 1980s, researchers found that community service sentencing diverted 50 percent of offenders from jail.[90]

Few studies address the matter of whether community service reduces recidivism. However, two studies are noteworthy. The first was conducted in the 1980s by researchers at the Harris County, Texas, Department of Probation. It involved a comparison over 48 months of probationers in standard supervision and those assigned to community service, using randomly selected felony probationers. The study population consisted of 336 felony probationers, 102 of whom were ordered by the court to participate in a Community Service Option Program (CSOP) and 234 of whom were selected from the population of probationers and subject to standard probation supervision. The analysis focused on the effects of community services on both recidivism and fee collections. Data indicated no significant differences in recidivism (measured in law or technical violations) between CSOP and standard supervision cases. However, a higher rate of CSOP probationers successfully completed probation during the study period than those subjected to standard probation supervision (CSOP = 45.3 percent; standard probation = 29.6 percent). Moreover, the results of the study showed that sentencing probationers to community service appears extremely cost effective and consistent with the restorative objective of restitution. CSOP probationers who successfully completed probation supervision paid an average of $565 more in total fees than their standard supervision counterparts.[91]

The second study involves the Department of Rehabilitation and Correction (DRC), which operates Ohio's state correctional system for adult felony offenders. In 1991, DRC embarked on a campaign to involve prison-sentenced inmates in community service work jobs. During the first year of the campaign, prisoners completed 51,000 hours of service work. In 1999, inmates completed a remarkable 4.2 million hours of community service work. A research study was undertaken to examine whether there was any rehabilitative impact on inmates who participated in community service work. A cohort of 4,486 inmates was selected as the study group, comprised of the entire population of inmates who were released from prison during the last three months of 1994. Results indicated that 91.4 percent (4,102) of the study group did not participate in any community service, while 8.6 percent (384) did participate in community service work during their last year of incarceration. The participants in community service comprised the treatment group while the nonparticipants constituted the comparison group. Of the 384 participants in community service, 6.1 percent (273) spent 1–99 hours in community service work and 2.5 percent (111) devoted more than 100 hours of time to community service. The following is a subsequent listing of the research questions and a brief discussion of their findings:

Research Question 1: Did those inmates who participated in community service have lower recidivism rates than those inmates who did not participate in community service?

- For those inmates who did not participate in community service, the recidivism rate was 36.2 percent, while the recidivism rate for those who did participate in community service was 27.9 percent. To express the significance of these findings differently, the success rate of those inmates who participated in community service was 72.1 percent.

Research Question 2: Are inmates who are more involved in community service as measured by the total number of hours of participation in community service less likely to recidivate?

- The results of this research question demonstrated that the more hours of community service participation, the less likely prisoners would be reincarcerated. This research question therefore is answered in the affirmative. Those inmates with no community service had a recidivism rate of 36.2 percent. Inmates with 100 or more hours had a recidivism rate of 26.1 percent.

Research Question 3: For inmates participating in community service, is the length of time between release and reimprisonment longer than the length of time between release and reimprisonment for inmates who did not participate in community service?

- Data were analyzed to examine the length of time between release from prison and return to prison for inmates who participated in community service and inmates who did not. The median survival time for inmates who did not participate in community service was 14.72 months. For those inmates who did participate in community service, the median survival time was 14.25 months. Thus, Research Question 3 cannot be answered affirmatively, as the difference between the two groups is not significant.

Research Question 4: For inmates who are reincarcerated for new crimes, will the ones who participated in community service return for less serious felony violations as measured by sentence length than those who did not participate in community service?

- Data substantiated a clear affirmative answer to this research question. Inmates who had no community service work were recommitted for an average of 8.29 months. Comparatively, offenders who had any community service work experienced an average increase of only 1.51 months. Therefore, there is an almost seven-month difference between the average lengths of reimprisonment time between these two study populations.

Clearly, much more research is required to assess the overall benefits of community service. However, as confinement costs escalate, serious consideration should be given to evidence suggesting that community service may prove successful as an alternative punishment to incarceration. Given that the vast majority of crimes are property, drug, or public disorder offenses, community service, as a diversion program, could potentially reduce jail populations. Moreover, sentencing policies should be re-examined to include consideration of research that suggests positive relationships between community service completion and reductions in recidivism.

Policy Implications

State resources are limited, and there is significant competition for tax dollars between all types of worthwhile public uses, including community-based corrections. Many state policymakers have focused on the fiscal aspects of economic sanctions, seeing them as revenue sources to offset public expenditures in community-based correction programs. For corrections officials, it gives the appearance of being fiscally responsible and partially self-sustaining. Consequently, offenders are required to pay fines, restitution, and complete community service—not to mention fees for services—more than ever before in the history of corrections. The reasoning behind integrating economic sanctions into community-based programs is to hold offenders more accountable and deter future offending. In actuality, though, the increased application of economic sanctions is often less about reducing recidivism and more about generating revenue.

Does increased emphasis on administrative tasks such as the monitoring and collection of economic sanctions infringe upon other important job tasks associated with community-based corrections such as making **collateral contacts**, case planning, and treatment? Given the increased numbers of offenders placed in community-based corrections programs, it seems plausible. As revenue shortages take center stage, it can easily lead to greater emphasis on monitoring and collection, which in turn can undermine the ability of community-based corrections practitioners to effectively manage their caseloads.

An emphasis on collection of economic sanctions also creates unintended consequences for offenders. At the time people are put on probation or another community-based corrections program, there's typically little, if any, inquiry into how much money offenders make. So our tariff system does not take into account what they can afford to pay. But failure to satisfy any portion of a fine, restitution cost, or community service hours typically results in an extension of time in the community-based program—even if the offender has completed all other conditions of the program. The only alternative is to incarcerate the offender, which contradicts the whole rationale behind community-based corrections. So our present policy behind fine collection is such that many offenders are being set up to fail. According to Stephen Bright, professor of law at Yale and Harvard Universities and director of the Southern Center for Human Rights, "It's just a question of, 'You owed this much money and you didn't pay it.' And slam, off you go to jail. The hope a lot of times is that the family will somehow mortgage the house, sell the car, do something to come up with the money so that the person can get back out on the streets again. But we're really running debtor's prisons as a result of this because a lot of families can't come up with the money."[92]

Lastly, what can be said about the underlying assumptions and values of community-based corrections? With the added component of collections quickly creeping into the protocols of many community-based agencies, programs have evolved beyond the original function of providing supervision and treatment of criminal offenders in non-secure settings. For some agencies, the practice of monitoring and collecting fines, restitution, and community service has proliferated to the point that it has become a primary concern of the agency. Consider these excerpts from reports submitted by community-based corrections programs.

- The amount of community service labor provided on an hourly basis for the past fiscal year totaled 10,607 hours. This time, calculated at a rate of $6.55 per hour ($6.55 per hour minimum wage scale for unskilled labor), equated to $67,475.85 worth of labor provided to the county.[93]
- Restitution and other monetary obligations collected from offenders under supervision in FY 2008–2009 totaled $85,151,077.*
- Representatives of the Probation Department's Revenue Recovery Unit can assist victims in submitting claims for restitution to be assigned to those defendants granted probation. In fiscal year 2005–2006, the collections unit collected $2,856,475.84 in restitution, court fines and fees, and probation fines and fees from offenders. A total of $788,176.03 in restitution was returned to victims.[95]

*Community Corrections also collects other costs (crimes compensation, electronic monitoring, drug testing fees, surcharge, subsistence, and additional costs).[94]

Summary

Greater use of fines, restitution, and community service expands the continuum of correctional sanctions and offers significant opportunities for offenders to be held accountable to victims. Economic sanctions are substantially cheaper than incarceration, can be used alone, with incarceration, with probation, or in a combination of each, can be easily evaluated, and can be tailored to meet rehabilitative and reparative objectives of restorative justice.

Tariff fines are set at a single, fixed amount for all defendants convicted of the same crime. The two issues that surface with tariff fines are an offender's ability to pay and limitations in the courts' capacity to collect. Creating special collection units in courts and probation departments, along with contracting with private collection agencies are methods being used to increase fine collection. Day fine systems consider both the severity of the crime and an offender's daily earnings. While successful in Europe, day fines have failed to gain widespread support in the United States.

Restitution requires that offenders compensate victims for any financial losses suffered as a result of the crime. Restitution can both positively and negatively affect the psychological recovery of victims from the aftermath of crime. Victim impact statements are used to assess victims' injuries and losses and many jurisdictions have developed policies and procedures to enhance and streamline restitution collection efforts. Problems related to restitution include the failure of many courts to order restitution and inefficient procedures for monitoring, enforcement, collection, and disbursement of restitution payments. Although legislative support exists to mandate restitution to victims, the U.S. criminal justice system is primarily designed to control crime by punishing offenders through harsh sanctions. State and federal victim compensation programs provide another way that financial assistance is made available to crime victims.

Community service is compulsory unpaid public labor performed by an offender as punishment for a crime. One of the earliest community service programs in New York City was established as an intermediate sanction for repeat misdemeanor offenders. Community service is cost-effective and helps restore the offender to the community. Challenges to community service include the compulsory nature of the sanction and potential exposure to liability. Limited research suggests that several benefits are derived from community service including reduction in cost, jail populations, and recidivism.

Key Terms

collateral contact, p. 179
community service, p. 151
day fine, p. 157
fine(s), p. 151
just deserts, p. 160
restitution, p. 151
tariff fine, p. 153
victim impact statement, p. 163

Questions for Review

1. How does the criminal justice system apply economic sanctions?
2. How do tariff and day fines differ?
3. What are the advantages and disadvantages of restitution and victim compensation programs?
4. What are the benefits and challenges associated with community service programs?

Question of Policy

Proportionality and Equality of Fines

One reported benefit of the day fine is that it achieves proportionality and equality in sentencing offenders with different financial means. It is equitable because it treats the poor and rich offender the same. And it is proportionate because it fines an offender an amount that the offender is capable of paying. However, critics argue that with day fines, the amount of the fine may be influenced more by an offender's financial worth rather than by offense seriousness. In other words, a poor person might be ordered to pay a small fine for a relatively serious matter and a wealthy person could be levied a large fine for a minor offense. Consider, for example, that in 2010, a Swiss millionaire was ordered to pay a fine of $290,000 for a speeding violation. The penalty was calculated based on the motorist's wealth (assessed by the court as $22.7 million) and because he was a repeat traffic offender. "The accused ignored elementary traffic rules with a powerful vehicle out of a pure desire for speed," the court said in its judgment. Swiss media reported that the man owns a villa with five luxury cars, including the Ferrari he was driving when stopped.

1. Do you think the fine amount was fair for the Swiss millionaire?
2. How likely will the fine meet the deterrent goal of punishment?

What Would You Do?

In the agency where you work, probationers who fail to complete a minimum 45 hours of community service usually receive an extension of probation time rather than incarceration. Last year, 35 percent of the offender population was kept on supervision even though they had completed all their probation conditions except community service hours. The typical offender-to-staff supervision ratio is 80 probationers to one probation officer. Because caseloads are high, you have decided to prepare a proposal to allow probation officers to waive the community service requirement. Support for your proposal would require a subtle value shift in your agency, raising the priority of workload matters over community justice and human restoration.

1. Should other conditions besides high caseloads be necessary to justify a waiver?
2. If a change in policy were adopted, what administrative oversight would you propose?
3. Assuming there is an evaluative component to your proposal, what will be evaluated and when?
4. Write the proposal.

Endnotes

1. *The Corrections Yearbook: Adult Corrections 2002* (Middletown, CT: Criminal Justice Institute, Inc., 2003).
2. *The Costs of Confinement: Why Good Juvenile Justice Policies Make Good Fiscal Sense* (Washington, DC: The Justice Policy Institute, May 2009), http://www.justicepolicy.org/images/upload/09_05_REP_CostsOfConfinement_JJ_PS.pdf.
3. M. A. Gordon and D. Glaser, "Use and Effects of Financial Penalties in Municipal Courts," *Criminology*, vol. 29, no. 4 (1991), pp. 651–676.
4. Jiang Yu, "Punishment Celerity and Severity: Testing a Specific Deterrence Model of Drunk Driving Recidivism," *Journal of Criminal Justice,* vol. 22, no. 4 (1994), pp. 355–366.
5. R. Barry Ruback and Mark H. Bergstrom, "Economic Sanctions in Criminal Justice: Purposes, Effects, and Implications," *Criminal Justice and Behavior*, vol. 33, no. 2 (2006), pp. 242–273.
6. Sally T. Hillsman, et al., *Fines as Criminal Sanction*, National Institute of Justice: Research in Brief (Washington, DC: U.S. Department of Justice, September 1987).
7. See www.ci.southlake.tx.us/siteContent/70/documents/Departments/MunicipalCourt/Fines%20by%20Violation.pdf; belmar.com/municipal/municipal-court/schedule-of-fines/; www.atlantaga.gov/client_resources/government/courts/atlanta%20municipal%20court/the%20municipal%20court%20of%20atlanta%20online%20traffic%20fine%20schedule%205-4-09.pdf; www.cityofBartlesville.org/caffeine/uploads/files/Accounting/Excel%20Bond%20Schedule.pdf; and www.iir. com/nygc/Municipal%20Codes/municipal%20codes—graffiti%20tools.htm.
8. *Tate* v. *Short*, 401 U.S. 395 (1971).
9. *Michigan Supreme Court: FY2011 Budget Summary*, http://courts.michigan.gov/supremecourt/AboutCourt/FY11-Budget-Summary-House.pdf.
10. Sally Hillsman, "Fines and Day Fines," in M. Tonry and N. Morris (eds.), *Crime and Justice: A Review of Research 12* (Chicago, IL: University of Chicago Press, 1990), pp. 49–98.
11. Laura Klaversma, *Future Trends in State Courts, 2008* (Williamsburg, VA: National Center for State Courts, 2008), www.ncsconline.org.
12. Collection Improvement Program, Texas Courts Online, www.courts.state.tx.us/oca/collections/collections.asp.
13. "OPERA Brings Information Directly to Probation Officers," *The Third Branch:*

Newsletter of the Federal Courts, vol. 41, no. 12 (December 2009).

14. Paul Litschewski, "Getting a Grip on Court Collections: An Overview of the Colorado Collections Investigator Program," *Court Manager,* vol. 6, no. 3 (1991), p. 13.
15. The Westchester County Department of Probation Economic Sanctions Program, www.westchestergov.com/probation/ Programs%20and%20Services/O'Shea/Economic%20Sanctions.htm.
16. Mark Scolforo, "States Step Up Demands for Restitution," *The Associated Press* (December, 2007).
17. Kan. Stat. Ann. § 75–719, *Collection of Debts Owed to Courts or Restitution; Duties of Attorney General; Contracts for Collection*, www.kslegislature.org/legsrv-statutes/getStatuteFile.do?number=/75-719.html.
18. Sally Hillsman and Judith Greene, "Tailoring Criminal Fines to the Financial Means of the Offender," *Judicature,* vol. 72, no. 1 (1988) pp. 38–45.
19. Sally Hillsman, "Fines and Day Fines," *Crime and Justice, 12* (1990), pp. 49–98.
20. Edwin Zedlewski, *Alternatives to Custodial Supervision: The Day Fine* (Washington, DC: The National Institute of Justice, NCJ 230401, May 2010).
21. Gary Friedman, "The West German Day-Fine System: A Possibility for the United States?" *The University of Chicago Law Review,* vol. 50, no. 1 (Winter 1983), pp. 281–304.
22. Ibid.
23. Frieder Dunkel, "Reducing the Population of Fine Defaulters in Prisons: Experiences with Community Service in Mecklenburg-Western Pomerania (Germany)," in *Crime Policy in Europe: Good Practices and Promising Examples* (Strasbourg, Germany: Council of Europe Publishing, 2005), pp. 127-137.
24. "Economy in Germany," World 66, www.world66.com/europe/germany/economy. Also, see "The Digital Agora 1998" at imej.wfu.edu/articles/1999/1/02/demo/country_profiles/Germany/economy.htm.
25. Scottish Executive Social Research Report: 2006. "Evaluation of the Implementation of the Mandatory Supervised Attendance Order Pilot at Ayr Sheriff and Glasgow District Courts." http://www.scotland.gov.uk/Resource/Doc/169794/0047319.pdf
26. "Experts Reflect on Spike in Prison Population," *Swiss News Worldwide* (January 2010), www.swissinfo.ch/eng/swiss_news/Experts_reflect_on_spike_in_prison_population.html?cid=8167278.
27. Bureau of Justice Assistance, *How To Use Structured Fines (Day Fines) as an Intermediate Sanction* (Washington, DC: NCJ 156242, 1996).
28. Ibid.
29. Laura Winterfield and Sally Hillsman, *The Staten Island Day-Fine Project* (Washington, DC: The National Institute of Justice: Research in Brief, September 1993).
30. Supra (See 26).
31. Sean Rosenmerkel, Matthew Durose, and Donald Farole, *Felony Sentences in State Courts, 2006—Statistical Tables* (Washington, DC: Bureau of Justice Statistics, December 2009).
32. Heather Mason Kiefer, "Gallup Poll: Public on Justice System: Fair, but Still Too Soft," *Gallup* (February 3, 2004), www.gallup.com/poll/10474/public-justice-system-fair-still-too-soft.aspx.
33. 18 U.S.C. § 3663, A Mandatory Restitution to Victims of Certain Crimes (2006).
34. Joan Barrett, *Balancing Charter Interests: Victims' Rights and Third Party Interests* (Ontario, Canada: Carswell Publishing, 2002).
35. Linda Frank, "The Collection of Restitution: An Often Overlooked Service to Crime Victims," *St. John's Journal of Legal Commentary,* vol. 8 (1992), pp. 107–134.
36. Victim and Witness Protection Act of 1982, Pub. L. No. 97-291, § 5, 96 Stat. 1248, 1255 (codified as amended at 18 U.S.C. § 3664 (2006)).
37. *Four Years Later: A Report on the President's Task Force on Victims of Crime* (Washington, DC: U.S. Government Printing Office, May 1986).
38. See 18 U.S.C. § 3663. Victim Restitution Act of 1995.

39. Fla. Stat. ch. 775.089 (2009), www.flsenate.gov/statutes/index.cfm?App_mode=Display_Statute&Search_String=&URL=Ch0775/SEC089.HTM&Title=->2009->Ch0775->Section%20089#0775.089.
40. Supra (See 29).
41. Alan Harland and Catherine Rosen, "Impediments to the Recovery of Restitution by Crime Victims," *Violence and Victims,* vol. 5, no. 2 (1991), pp. 127–1405.
42. Supra (See 30).
43. Ibid.
44. Adapted from pages 22 and 23 of *Promising Practices and Strategies for Victim Services in Corrections* NCJ 166605 (Washington, DC: Office for Victims of Crime, U.S. Department of Justice, July 1999).
45. Arthur Lurigio and Robert Davis, "Does a Threatening Letter Increase Compliance with Restitution Orders? A Field Experiment," *Crime & Delinquency*, vol. 36, no. 4 (1990), pp. 537–548.
46. Maureen Outlaw and R. Barry Ruback, "Predictors and Outcomes of Victim Restitution Orders," *Justice Quarterly*, vol. 16, no. 4 (December 1999), pp. 847–869.
47. Patrick Langan and Mark Cunniff, *Recidivism of Felons on Probation, 1986–89* (Washington, DC: U.S. Department of Justice, Bureau of Justice Statistics, 1992).
48. Robyn Cohen, *Probation and Parole Violation in State Prison, 1991* (Washington, DC: U.S. Department of Justice, Bureau of Justice Statistics, August 1995).
49. Barbara Smith, Robert Davis, and Susan Hillenbrand, "Improving Enforcement of Court-Ordered Restitution," in *Executive Summary: A Study of the American Bar Association, Criminal Justice Section, Victim Witness Project* (Chicago, IL: The American Bar Association, August 1989).
50. Matthew Dickman, "Should Crime Pay?: A Critical Assessment of the Mandatory Victims Restitution Act of 1996," *California Law Review*, vol. 97, no. 6 (December 2009), pp. 1687–1718.
51. Anne Seymour, et al. (eds.), "Financial Assistance for Victims of Crime," *National Victim Assistance Academy Textbook* (Washington, DC: U.S. Department of Justice, Office for Victims of Crime, June 2002). Also, see Anne Seymour, *Victim Restitution: Promising Practices and Strategies for Victim Services in Corrections* (Washington, DC: U.S. Department of Justice, Office for Victims of Crime, 1997).
52. Supra (See 43).
53. Joanna Shapland, "Victims and the Criminal Justice System," in Ezzat Fattah (ed.), *From Crime Policy to Victim Policy: Reorienting the Justice System*. New York: St. Martin's Press, 1986).
54. Office for Victims of Crime, *Ordering Restitution to the Crime Victim. NCJ 189189.* (Washington, DC: U.S. Department of Justice, November, 2002).
55. Mark Umbreit, "Restorative Justice Through Victim Offender Mediation: A Multi-Site Assessment," *Western Criminology Review*, vol. 1, no. 1 (1998), http://wcr.sonoma.edu/v1n1/umbreit.html.
56. Mark S. Umbreit and Jean Greenwood, *National Survey of Victim–Offender Mediation Programs in the United States* (St. Paul, MN: Center for Justice and Peacemaking, April 2000).
57. Mark Umbreit and Robert Coates, "The Impact of Mediating Victim Offender Conflict: An Analysis of Programs in Three States," *Juvenile and Family Court Journal,* vol. 42, no. 1 (1992), pp. 21–29.
58. Mark Umbreit, Robert Coates, and Boris Kalanj, *Victim Meets Offender: The Impact of Restorative Justice and Mediation*, (Monsey, NY: Criminal Justice Press, 1994).
59. Marty Price, "Personalizing Crime: Mediation Produces Restorative Justice for Victims and Offenders," *Dispute Resolution Magazine* (Fall 2001).
60. William Nugent, et al., "Participation in Victim–Offender Mediation Reduces Recidivism," *Connections,* vol. 3, no. 1 (Summer 1999), p. 11.
61. Stephen Hartley, "Court Steps Up Restitution Collection," *Maricopa County, AZ, Superior Court Newsletter, The Judicial Branch News,* vol. 3, no. 11 (November 2008), p. 8. Also, see *2010 Victims' Rights Week Celebration Brochure* at www.azag.gov/victims_rights/VRW/2010-Victims-Rights-Week-Celebration-Program.pdf.

62. The National Center for Victims of Crime, *Webinar Series: Improving the Collection of Crime Victim Restitution* (Washington, DC: Office for Victims of Crime, Office of Justice Programs, U.S. Department of Justice, April 6, 2010), www.ncvc.org/ncvc/AGP.Net/Components/documentViewer/Download.aspxnz?DocumentID=47653.
63. Cal. Penal Code, § 1463.010.
64. "Court and County Collection Programs FY 2008–2009," *Report to the Legislature as Required by Penal Code Section 1463.010* (January 2010), www.courtinfo.ca.gov/reference/documents/collection-courtordered-debt0110.pdf.
65. Supra (See 62).
66. Supra (See 51).
67. Ibid.
68. Crime Victims Fund, *Office of Victims of Crime Fact Sheet* (May 2010), www.ojp.usdoj.gov/ovc/publications/factshts/cvf2010/intro.html.
69 *Recovery Act Funding and OVC* (2009), www.ojp.usdoj.gov/ovc/fund/Recoveryfunds.html.
70. Office of Justice Programs, *Recovery Act Grant Awards: Implementing the American Recovery and Reinvestment Act of 2009 (Recovery Act)*, www.ojp.usdoj.gov/recovery/awards.htm.
71. Lisa Newmark, et al., *National Evaluation of State Victims of Crime Act Assistance and Compensation Programs: Trends and Strategies for the Future* (Washington, DC: U.S. Department of Justice, the Urban Institute, December 2003).
72. Mary Cooper, *Letter to Attorney General Anne Milgram RE: Victims of Crimes Compensation Agency* (July 15, 2008), www.state.nj.us/oig/pdf/lettertoagmilgram_victimsofcrimecompensation.pdf.
73. Norval Morris and Michael Tonry, *Between Prison and Probation: Intermediate Punishments in a Rational Sentencing System* (New York: Oxford University Press, 1990).
74. Vera Institute of Justice, pamphlets about the Community Service Sentencing Project (1979), www.vera.org/content/pamphlets-about-community-service-sentencing-project-cssp.
75. "Offenders Shown Different Way by Community Service," *United States Courts: Inside the Judiciary* (August 25, 2008), www.uscourts.gov/News/News View/08-08-25/Offenders_Shown_Different_Way_By_Community_Service.aspx.
76. Tarrant County, Texas, CSCD Programs and Services, *Community Service Restitution (CSR)* (March 15, 2010), www.tarrantcounty.com/cscd/cwp/view.asp?A=859&Q=475317.
77. North Carolina Department of Corrections, *Community Service Work Program* (February 1, 2009), www.doc.state.nc.us/dcc/Legislative%20Reports/090201%20CSWP%20Legislative%20Report.pdf.
78. Paulding County, Ohio, Probation Department, http://pauldingcountycourt.com/probprog.shtml.
79. Pueblo, Colorado, Municipal Court, *2010 Annual Report* (2010), www.pueblo.us/documents/AnnualReports/2010AnnualReportMunicipalCourt.pdf.
80. Harris County Juvenile Probation Department, *Annual Report* (2010), www.hcjpd.org/probation_service_programs.asp.
81. Douglas McDonald, "Restitution and Community Service," *National Institute of Justice Crime File Study Guide* (Washington, DC: U.S. Government Printing Office, 1988).
82. Barry Nidorf, "Sanction-Oriented Community Corrections: Sales Job? Sellout? Or Response to Reality?" *Perspectives,* vol. 12, no. 3 (1988), pp. 6–11.
83. "Judge Orders 10 Years Probation in Rape Case," *The Rapid City Journal* (June 22, 2010), www.rapidcityjournal.com/news/article_cb244378-7e3b-11df-a4f2-001cc4c002e0.html.
84. N.C. Gen. Stat. § 143B–262.4, *Deferred Prosecution, Community Service Restitution, and Volunteer Program* (2010), www.ncleg.net/gascripts/Statutes/Statutes.asp.
85. La. Rev. Stat. Ann. § RS 30:2531.4, *Community Service Litter Abatement Work Program; Establishment; Limited Liability* (2010), www.legis.state.la.us/lss/tsrssearch.htm.
86. City of Olympia, Washington, *Probation-Community Service* (2010), http://olympiawa.gov/city-government/municipal-court/probation-services/community-service.aspx.
87. Rolando del Carmen, *Liability Issues in Community Service Sanctions* (Washington, DC: National Institute of Corrections, 1986).

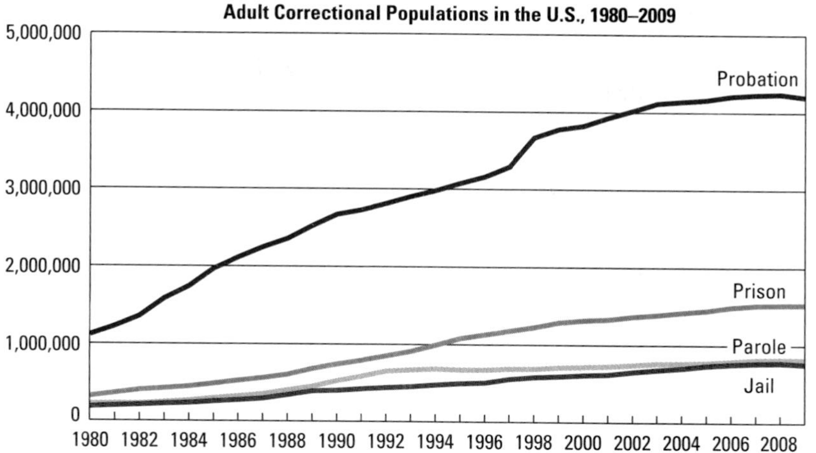

Source: Lauren E. Glaze, Thomas P. Bonczar, and Fan Zhang, *Probation and Parole in the United States, 2009* (Washington, DC: U. S. Department of Justice, Bureau of Justice Statistics, December 2010).

EXHIBIT 7.1 Adult Correctional Populations, 1980–2009

On the other hand, scientific analysis of 10 treatment-oriented ISP programs indicates, on average, a statistically significant 21.9 percent reduction in the recidivism rates of program participants compared with a treatment-as-usual group—what the Washington State Institute for Public Policy calls "extremely successful."[3] It is the treatment—not the intensive monitoring—that results in recidivism reduction. Rearrests are reduced when offenders receive treatment in addition to the increased surveillance and control of ISP programs.

Probation, including ISP, is the most frequently used criminal sanction. At year-end 2009, over 7.3 million people were either on probation or parole or in jail or prison.[4] The vast majority (5,023,275) were under community supervision (see Exhibit 7.1)—the equivalent of about 1 in every 47 adults in the United States, a decrease from about 1 in every 45 adults since 2004. Probationers (4,203,967) represented the majority (84 percent) of this group. Parolees, the subject of the next chapter, accounted for a significantly smaller share (819,308, or 16 percent) of adults under community supervision.

While on probation, offenders are required to fulfill certain conditions. All probationers in Texas, for example, are required to adhere to 15 conditions (refer to Exhibit 7.5 later in this chapter). Among them are (1) Commit no offense against the laws of this or any State or of the United States, (2) Avoid injurious or vicious habits, (3) Avoid the use of all narcotics, habit forming drugs, alcoholic beverages, and controlled substances, (4) Avoid persons or places of disreputable or harmful character, (5) Report to the supervision officer as directed by the judge or the supervision officer, and (6) Obey all orders of the Court and the rules and regulations of the Community Supervision and Corrections Department.

Higher-risk offenders are usually sentenced to ISP and given special conditions that may include wearing an electronic monitor, remaining confined to one's home except for preapproved absences, paying fines and restitution, participating in treatment programs, and adhering to specific rules of conduct while in the community (refer to Special Probation Conditions for Adult Sex Offenders in Indiana in Exhibit 7.6 later in this chapter). Failure to comply with any conditions can result in incarceration. Two special conditions of ISP are discussed here: remote location monitoring and home confinement or house arrest. Fines and restitution are discussed in Chapter 6.

Remote Location Monitoring

In Chapter 1, we defined remote location monitoring (also referred to as electronic monitoring or EM) as a technological tool that probation and parole officers use to monitor offenders remotely. The first recorded use of EM as a court-sanctioned tool can be traced back to 1983, when Jack Love, a district court judge in Albuquerque, New Mexico, persuaded a computer salesperson to develop an electronic tagging system to monitor five offenders.

EM systems were initially home-based and were dependent on a dedicated telephone line to report whether or not the offender being tracked was at home. When the Global Positioning System (GPS) was approved for civilian usage in 1983 and cellular and broadband Internet networks emerged in the mid 1990s, electronic monitoring of offenders emerged as an important surveillance tool that could track an offender's movements anywhere. The number of persons monitored remotely has grown from around 12,000 in 1994 to an estimated 130,000 today.[5] Initially used only for low-risk offenders, such as those convicted of DUI, it has expanded to include offenders awaiting trial or sentencing, offenders on probation and parole, and juvenile offenders.

EM systems can be either "passive" or "active." A passive system generally requires the offender to answer a telephone and speak to an officer or to insert the transmitter into a home monitoring device (HMD) to verify their presence at a location. An active system, by contrast, emits a continuous signal from the transmitter to the HMD. If the offender moves out of range, the HMD alerts the central monitoring center. The central monitoring center also may be alerted if a signal indicates a deviation from the preapproved schedule or a violation of a predetermined set of regulations. A violation requires an immediate response from the appropriate agency. Participants who do not comply with the conditions of their supervision face sanctions ranging from a reprimand to violations for new offenses.

Many active EM systems use GPS technology, voice verification, wrist and ankle bracelets, alcohol and drug testing devices, and other tracking systems to verify a person's physical location, either periodically or continuously, 24 hours a day. Advances in technology now allow probation and parole officers to set up exclusion zones (such as schools, parks, and homes) for offenders who are territory-restricted (e.g., stalkers and child molesters). Approximately half the states now use EM to monitor some sex offenders while they are on parole, and at least eight states (California, Colorado, Florida, Michigan, Missouri, Ohio, Oklahoma, and Wisconsin) have enacted laws permitting lifetime GPS monitoring of some sex offenders.[6]

A major benefit of EM is that it costs less than incarceration. The average cost of incarcerating a prison inmate is between $36 to $123 per day.[7] In contrast, depending on the type of technology used, the daily cost of EM is between $3 and $11 per day.[8] If the offender can afford it, courts order program participants to pay all or part of the costs. Another important benefit is that it allows defendants and offenders to continue to contribute to the support of their families and pay taxes.

EM satisfies three correctional goals. It incapacitates the offender by restricting him or her to a specific location. It is punitive because it forces the offender to stay

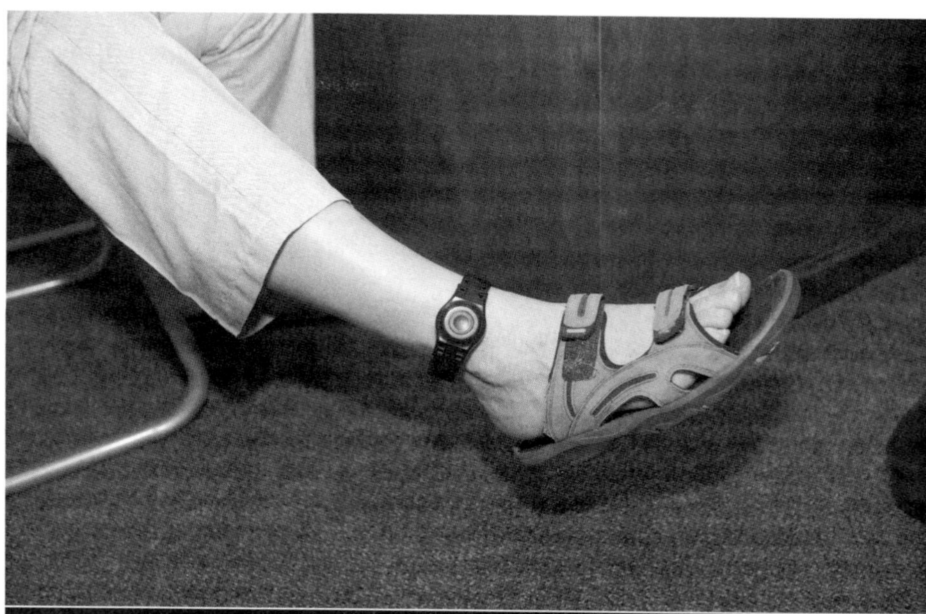

Remote location monitoring is a technological tool that probation and parole officers use to monitor offenders remotely. Why is it difficult to answer the question "Is electronic monitoring effective?"

home when not at work, school, counseling, or community service. And it contributes to rehabilitation by allowing the offender to remain with his or her family and continue employment, education, or vocational training.

It is easy to find evaluations of EM that show positive results. For example, a review of the performance of 17,000 participants in a federal home confinement program found that 89 percent successfully completed the program.[9] And when researchers with the Center for Criminology and Public Policy Research at Florida State University compared the experiences of more than 5,000 medium- and high-risk offenders who were monitored electronically to more than 266,000 offenders not placed on monitoring during a six-year period, they found that electronic monitoring reduced the risk of failure by 31 percent.[10] However, most of the studies do not meet the threshold of scientific rigor. Very few employ the gold standard of research: random assignment of subjects to EM (the experimental group) and others to programs-as-usual (the control group). Without scientific rigor, it is impossible to answer the question "Is EM effective?"

Another problem we see with the literature on EM is that most studies focus only on whether EM suppresses an individual's criminal behavior or changes it. Changes in an offender's cognitive skills of thinking, reasoning, empathy, and problem solving are seldom subject to the same evaluation that control and surveillance are.

Home Confinement or House Arrest

Oftentimes offenders sentenced to ISP with EM are also subject to home confinement or house arrest. In Chapter 1, we defined home confinement or house arrest as a surveillance tool that probation and parole officers use to confine offenders to their place of residence under strict conditions that govern their freedom and actions. Offenders' activities are closely monitored either through the use of EM or manually through frequent staff contacts. Home confinement became a popular intermediate sanction when electronic monitoring devices became inexpensive and easy to use.

There are generally two types of home confinement programs: pretrial and post-adjudication. Pretrial programs, such as those discussed in Chapter 5, use home confinement as an alternative to detention to ensure that individuals appear in court. Post-adjudication programs use home confinement as a sanction that is more severe than regular supervision but less restrictive than incarceration.

Like EM, home confinement satisfies the correctional goals of incapacitation, punishment, and rehabilitation. It confines the person to the home during nonworking hours. It deprives persons of their freedom. And it offers the individual the opportunity to complete a sentence in an environment that allows him or her to work, maintain family relationships and responsibilities, and attend rehabilitation programs that contribute toward addressing the causes of offending.

Home confinement restricts an offender to his or her residence in one of three ways: under curfew, home detention, or home incarceration. Curfew requires offenders to stay in their residence during specified hours. Depending on the situation, an offender's behavior outside the curfew hours may or may not be regulated. Home detention requires an offender to stay home except for preapproved activities such as work, education, or medical or religious purposes. The offender's movements are structured and monitored throughout the day to verify compliance. The most restrictive house arrest program is home incarceration. It requires offenders to stay home at *all* times with limited exceptions such as medical or religious purposes. The offender is subject to random contacts, and his or her behavior is tightly monitored to verify compliance.

There is not a large body of literature assessing the effectiveness of home confinement. As with the literature on electronic monitoring, most of the research suffers from poor research designs and an exclusive use of low-risk adult offenders. Several studies examining both pretrial and post-adjudication home confinement found low recidivism rates using experimental designs, but no significant difference in recidivism between offenders under electronic monitoring and under close manual supervision.[11]

Probation is a key component of the U.S. criminal justice system. How did probation start? What do today's probation officers do? How big are their caseloads? How is probation organized? These are the issues we turn to in this chapter. We begin with a look at the history of probation in the United States.

Probation: Then and Now

In the 19th century, individuals began to question the retributive focus of penal policy and to focus on rehabilitation. Against this backdrop, the origins of probation can be traced back to 1830 and the Boston courtroom of municipal court judge Peter Oxenbridge Thatcher, recognized as the foremost expert on criminal law of his day.[12] It is quite probable, however, that probation in some form was applied earlier.

Searching for a new way to exercise leniency and to humanize the criminal law, Judge Thatcher made the first recorded use of release on recognizance (release on one's personal word) in America when he sentenced Jerusa Chase. Jerusa Chase would have been sentenced for six months and five days in the house of corrections for theft, but she gave her word that she would return to court when the judge requested her presence. Judge Thatcher established the legal concept of probation with the following words:

> The indictment against Jerusa Chase was found at the January term of the court . . . She pleaded guilty to the same and would have been pronounced at that time, but upon the application of her friends, and with the consent of the attorney of the Commonwealth, she was permitted, upon her recognizance for her appearance in this Court whenever she should be called for, to go at large.[13]

We find in Chase's release several characteristics of modern-day probation: suspension of sentence, freedom to stay in the community, conditions on that freedom, and the possibility of revocation of freedom for violation of the conditions.

It was John Augustus, however, who began a campaign to allow discretion in sentencing to help those who were deemed undeserving of harsh sentences and who could be reformed. Augustus advanced the practice of probation in America and is known as its founder.

In 1841, when he was 57 years old, John Augustus, a wealthy Boston shoemaker, became interested in the operation of the courts. Augustus was particularly sensitive to the problems of persons charged with violating Boston's vice or temperance laws. He was a member of the Washington Total Abstinence Society, an organization devoted to the promotion of temperance. By posting bail in selected cases, Augustus had the offenders released to his care and supervision, and so began the work of the nation's first probation officer, an unpaid volunteer.

Augustus carefully screened the offenders he sought to help. Here is an entry from his journal:

> In the month of August, 1841, I was in court one morning . . . in which [a] man was charged with being a common drunkard. The case was clearly made out, but before sentence was passed, I conversed with him for a few moments, and found that he was not yet past all hope of reformation . . . He told me that if he could be saved from the House of Corrections, he never again would taste intoxicating liquors; there was such an earnestness in that one, and a look of firm resolve, that I determined to aid him; I bailed him, by permission of the Court. He was ordered to appear for sentence in three weeks; at the expiration of this period of probation, I accompanied him into the courtroom . . . The Judge expressed himself much pleased with the account we gave of the man, and instead of the usual penalty—imprisonment in the House of Correction—he fined him one cent and costs, amounting in all to $3.76, which was immediately paid. The man continued industrious and sober, and without doubt has been by this treatment, saved from a drunkard's grave.

Augustus had won probation for almost 2,000 adults and several thousand children before he died in 1859. Several aspects of his probation system are still with us. Augustus investigated the age, character, and work habits of each offender. He identified persons he thought redeemable and "whose hearts were not fully depraved, but gave promise of better things." He made probation recommendations to the court; developed conditions of probation; helped offenders with employment, education, and housing; and supervised offenders for periods of, on the average, 30 days. Until 1878, probation continued to be the work of volunteers.

Early Probation Statutes

After Augustus's death in 1859, unpaid volunteers continued his work. In 1878, the Massachusetts legislature passed the first statute authorizing probation and provided for the first paid probation officer. The law applied only to Suffolk County (Boston). It required the mayor of Boston to appoint a probation officer from the police department or citizenry and required the probation officer to report to the chief of police. Three years later, this policy changed, and the probation officer then reported to the state commissioners of prisons.

In 1880, a new law authorized probation as an option in all cities and towns in Massachusetts. But because the law remained voluntary and the probation concept was still new, few cities and towns exercised the power. In 1891, the power to appoint probation officers was transferred from the mayor to the court, in response to criticism that the mayor's appointments were influenced by political considerations. The second state to pass a probation statute was Vermont, in 1898.

As more and more states passed laws authorizing probation, probation became a national institution. By 1925, probation was available for juveniles in every state; by 1956, it was available for adults in every state.

The early laws had little in common. Some allowed probation for adults only. Others allowed it for juveniles only. Some laws restricted the crimes for which probation could be granted. Still others provided for the hiring of probation officers but neglected to provide for paying them. Training for probation officers was brief or nonexistent. Appointments were often based on politics rather than merit, and salaries were typically even lower than those of unskilled laborers.

Data on Probationers Today

As you learned earlier, at the end of 2009, 4,203,967 adults were on probation, up from 3.8 million in 2000. Some facts about the 2009 adult probation population are:[14]

1. 72 percent were on active supervision. Active supervision requires offenders to regularly report to a probation authority in person, by telephone, or by mail.
2. 76 percent were male.
3. Since 2000, the percentage of women sentenced to probation has increased—from 22 percent in 2000 to 24 percent in 2009.
4. 56 percent were white. White probationers also represented a larger share of the probation population in 2009 (56 percent) compared to 2000 (54 percent). During this period the percentage of black probationers declined from 31 percent in 2000 to 30 percent in 2009. The percentage of probationers who are Hispanic or of other races has remained fairly stable.
5. The most common type of offense for which probationers were under supervision was a drug offense (26 percent). Drug offenders represented a larger share of the probation population in 2009 compared to 2000 (24 percent).
6. A quarter (26 percent) of probationers were under supervision for a property offense in 2009, up from 23 percent in 2004.
7. The share of probationers under supervision for a violent offense (19 percent) remained unchanged between 2004 and 2009. (Data on probationers supervised for property and violent offenses were not collected prior to 2002.)
8. Public-order offenders, including those supervised for a DWI or other traffic offense, represented a smaller share of the probation population in 2009 (18 percent) compared to 2000 (24 percent).
9. 50 percent of probationers either completed their full-term probation sentence or received an early discharge.

7.1

PROBATION IN YOUR STATE, 2009

CBC Online

Every year the annual probation and parole surveys collect data on the total number of adults supervised in the community. Review the December 2010 Bureau of Justice Statistics bulletin *Probation and Parole in the United States, 2009*. How does your state compare to the United States as a whole in terms of change in the probation population, the number of adults on probation per 100,000 population, by gender and race, by status of supervision, by type of offense, and by GPS?

Visit CBC Online 7.1 at www.mhhe.com/bayens1e

Probation populations give us a count of the total number of persons on probation (e.g., 4,203,967 offenders on probation at year-end 2009). However if you want to compare the probation population in one state (e.g., California) with another state (e.g., Montana), a total count will not work because the populations are different (California's population is almost 40 million, whereas Montana's population is slightly less than 1 million). Jurisdictions are compared using rates of persons on probation, expressed as the number of probationers per 100,000 residents age 18 and older.

Exhibit 7.2 shows changes in the rate of probation from 2000 through 2009. The rate of probation appears to have remained relatively stable for the United States as a whole (1,836 adults on probation per 100,000 adult residents in 2000 and 1,799 in 2008).

By geographical area we find that the Midwest and the South have consistently higher rates of probation than the Northeast and the West. The rate of probation is highest in Georgia (5,385 per 100,000), and lowest in New Hampshire (434 per 100,000). In terms of sheer number of probationers, Texas has the largest adult probation population (426,331), followed by Georgia (392,688). The smallest adult probation populations are in North Dakota (4,173) and New Hampshire (4,509) (see CBC Online 7.1).

EXHIBIT 7.2 Rate of Probation (per 100,000 adult residents), Total United States and by Region

Year	U.S. Total	Northeast	Midwest	South	West
2000	1,836	1,449	1,884	2,095	1,638
2001	1,849	1,462	1,903	2,117	1,630
2002	1,854	1,469	1,915	2,105	1,658
2003	1,876	1,491	1,926	2,135	1,672
2004	1,884	1,671	1,922	2,196	1,620
2005	1,858	1,658	1,950	2,067	1,546
2006	1,868	1,657	1,981	2,060	1,579
2007	1,873	1,657	2,008	2,033	1,474
2008	1,845	1,690	2,008	2,033	1,474
2009	1,799	1,666	1,964	1,997	1,390

Source: Adapted from Bureau of Justice Statistics publications: *Probation and Parole in the United States* 2000, 2001, 2002, 2003, 2004, 2005, 2006, 2007 Statistical Tables, 2008, and 2009.

EXHIBIT 7.3 Ratio and Percentage of Adult Population under Community Supervision by State, 2007.

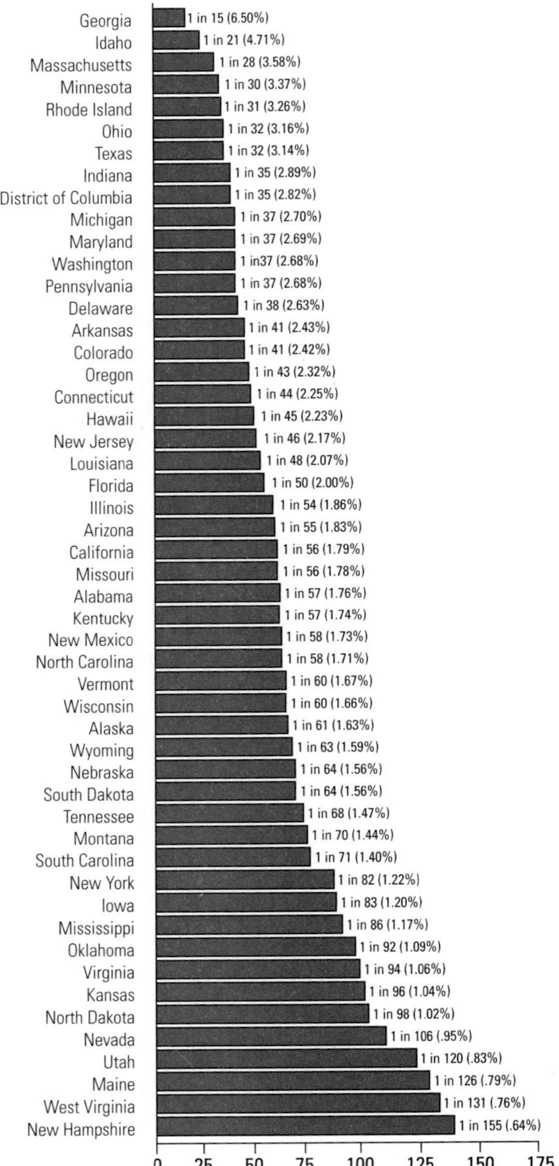

Source: Adapted from Pew Center on the States, "Table 5-A: Adult Community Supervision Rates (Probation and Parole)," *One in 31: The Long Reach of American Corrections* (Washington, DC: The Pew Charitable Trusts, March 2009), p. 44.

Exhibit 7.3 ranks the states in terms of the percentage of their adult population on community supervision (includes both probation and parole) in 2007. It also shows the ratio of adults under community supervision to the adult population in each state. State rankings offer us insight into how states use probation to maintain social order. For example, with one in every 15 adults under community supervision in Georgia, compared to New Hampshire, where only one in every 155 adults is under community supervision, we can begin to ask if what works in New Hampshire might work in Georgia, thereby reducing the scope of control, accepting more diversity, and channeling scarce financial resources into other needed programs such as education, health care, road and bridge maintenance, etc.

Models of Probation Practice

What can probation do to control offending behavior? Over the past 100 years, the probation and parole profession has struggled over its professional orientation. Should probation and parole be seen as law enforcement, social work, or a combination of both? Until about 1970, the supervision process was oriented toward **casework,** or the **medical model**, a philosophy of offender treatment that regarded criminal behavior as a disease to be treated. Probation officers provided the treatment and were viewed as social workers engaged in counseling with their "clients," the probationers.

In the 1950s and 1960s, the casework model slowly gave way to a **community model,** or what some call a **brokerage model**, as researchers, political activists, and others called attention to the influence of the social environment on offending behavior. Crime came to be seen as more than individual choice; forces outside the individual influenced negative behavior. Thus, probation officers turned to community resources for therapeutic, employment, social, educational, and vocational interventions. The probation officer's role was to assess and identify an offender's strengths and needs, develop a therapeutic plan to provide appropriate supports and services, implement the plan using community resources, coordinate and monitor the plan, and evaluate the offender's progress to determine continued need for services. The overall belief was that an offender's needs were the responsibility of other social and government agencies.

When neither the casework nor the community model lowered the crime rate, reduced the prison population, or made the community safer, politicians asserted the belief that society was too soft on crime and ushered in the just deserts model of supervision, which by all accounts is still with us today even though we find a strong mix of evidence-based treatment strategies alongside control strategies. The just deserts model focuses on punishment and supports a philosophy that calls for control, surveillance, and monitoring of probationers using technological tools such as GPS, remote-location monitoring, breathalyzers, and the like. Under the philosophy of just deserts, probationers are punished because they deserve it, and probation officers are viewed as surveillance officers.

Today, evidence-based practices highlight the importance of using scientific research to control offending behavior. We know from sophisticated evaluations in Florida, Maryland, and Washington that surveillance-focused strategies (e.g., intensive probation supervision and remote location monitoring) alone do not reduce criminal activity. However, when those strategies are combined with treatment, probation achieves, on average, a statistically significant 8 to 22 percent reduction in the recidivism rates of program participants compared with a treatment-as-usual group.

Other research has focused on the eight principles of evidence-based practices: (1) assess risk and needs; (2) enhance intrinsic motivation; (3) target interventions; (4) offer skill training with directed practice; (5) increase positive reinforcement; (6) engage ongoing support in natural communities; (7) measure relevant processes and practices; and (8) provide measurable feedback. Research also suggests that if

A DAY IN THE LIFE OF PROBATION AND PAROLE OFFICERS

This 29-minute video provides an overview of a day in the life of probation and parole officers in Washington, D.C., where they are called supervision officers. Host Leonard Sipes talks with Jemell Courtney, supervision officer with the Transitional Interventions for Parole Supervision (TIPS) Unit, and Alexander Portillo, program specialist with the domestic violence prevention unit.

What are the challenges and rewards of being a community supervision officer?

Visit CBC Online 7.2 at www.mhhe.com/bayens1e

probation agencies adhere to these principles, criminal activity can be reduced by as much as 50 percent.[15]

The American Probation and Parole Association (APPA), representing U.S. probation officers nationwide, argues that recidivism rates—generally defined as rearrest—measure just one probation task while ignoring others. The APPA has urged its member agencies to collect data on other outcomes, such as the amount of restitution collected, the number of offenders employed, amount of fines and fees collected, hours of community service performed, number of treatment sessions attended, rate of school enrollment, number of days of employment, educational attainment, and number of days drug-free, thereby focusing attention on what probation officers do.

If you were Chris Brown's probation officer, what benchmarks of success would you want to point to?

What Probation Officers Do

Probation officers are professionals. They are required to hold a college degree; to have specialized knowledge of law, criminal justice, and community resources; to demonstrate strong written and oral communication skills; to adhere to a high standard of professional ethics; and a desire to do a job well (intrinsic motivation) (see CBC Online 7.2).

In 2008, about 103,400 probation officers and correctional treatment specialists (persons who work with probation officers or who may be probation officers themselves and counsel offenders and create treatment plans for them to follow) were employed across the United States.[16] Most jobs are in state or local governments. In some states, probation officers are employed by both state and local governments. At the federal level, probation officers are employed by the U.S. courts, and correctional treatment specialists are employed by the U.S. Department of Justice's Bureau of Prisons (see Career Profile for Kelli Matthews).

Probation work is twofold: case investigation and offender supervision. Depending on resources, size of the jurisdiction, and agency philosophy, probation officers may specialize in either case investigation or offender supervision, or perform both roles. The tendency is to specialize. We now turn to a discussion of those roles.

Career Profile

KELLI MATTHEWS: U.S. PROBATION OFFICER ASSISTANT, SOUTHERN DISTRICT OF ALABAMA

Kelli Matthews is employed as a U.S. Probation Officer Assistant for the Southern District of Alabama. She currently works in the Presentence Unit as a presentence writer/probation officer. Matthews earned her bachelor of arts in history from Stillman College in Tuscaloosa, Alabama, and her masters of science in criminal justice from the University of Alabama.

Matthew's initial interest in probation stemmed from an internship she completed at a juvenile detention center during her senior year in college. There she learned the importance of establishing an effective relationship between offenders and probation officers and especially how important it is for probation officers to display the same level of respect to each offender regardless of the crime committed. In graduate school she concentrated on successful reintegration of ex-offenders, which led her to a career in probation.

As a presentence writer, Matthews attends guilty plea and sentencing hearings; interviews offenders to obtain pertinent background information; investigates leads regarding offenders' education, employment, medical or psychiatric records, and criminal history; conducts home inspections; and prepares detailed presentence reports that follow federal sentencing guidelines and statutes. According to Matthews, "There is never a dull moment in the Presentence Unit. Constant deadlines keep you on your toes. As a presentence writer, you must enjoy reading. My job requires that I read through pages of discovery, federal sentencing guidelines, and federal criminal codes and rule books, which sometimes makes me feel like an attorney."

Her advice to persons interested in working as a federal probation officer is this: "Self-motivation, time management skills, and a sincere respect for others are extremely important in this field. A clear understanding of what the job entails, along with these qualities, should lead to a successful career in probation."

Case Investigation

Case investigation includes preparation of the presentence report (PSR), which provides detailed information on the offense and the defendant's criminal history and characteristics. The judge orders the PSR after finding a defendant guilty. The judge then uses the document to determine whether the offender should be incarcerated or placed on probation.

The PSR also serves other purposes. For example, if the defendant is incarcerated, the federal or state department of corrections will use information to designate the institution where the offender will serve his/her sentence and to determine the offender's eligibility or need for specific correctional programming. Also, depending on the jurisdiction, the PSR can be used to calculate the release date. The probation officer assigned responsibility for the offender's supervision in the community will use the report to make initial and ongoing assessments of case needs and risks during the probation period. Additionally, the report may be used as data by researchers. (Depending on the jurisdiction, the PSR has other names. In some places it is referred to as the PSI/presentence investigation report or the SAR/sentence assessment report.)

CBC Online 7.3 directs you to the PSR used in federal probation. The probation officer completes the 12-page document and provides data on four broad categories. First, the face sheet data lists the case docket number, the name of the judge or magistrate, the defense attorney, and U.S. Attorney, the federal district, the arrest date, the sentencing date, and the demographic data on the offender.

Second is offense data. Here the probation officer details the charge and conviction, the offender's release status, the counts of conviction, whether the offender has any **detainer**s issued against her or him (a detainer is a request from one criminal justice agency to another asking the agency to hold the offender for the requesting agency or to notify the agency when the offender's release is close at hand), whether the crime involved codefendants, the plea agreement, the impact of the crime on the victim, and the defendant's statement of responsibility.

The third section provides detailed information on the defendant's criminal history. The fourth and longest section elaborates on the offender's characteristics. Here the probation officer records every place the offender ever lived; the name, address, and occupation of the defendant's parents and siblings; the defendant's marital status and children, if any; his or her physical, mental, and emotional condition and health; substance use and abuse; vocational skills; scholastic history; military service; employment history; financial condition; and ability to pay restitution, fines, and court costs.

As you can see, the PSR is a detailed background investigation. But how important is all of this information? Does "more" information produce better sentencing and less offender recidivism? Is all the information needed? Is there information missing that should be collected? Not too long ago, the PSR also asked about one's faith and frequency of worship, and some forms even included information about sexual behaviors. The questions appear reasonable on the surface, but are they empirically related to crime control? For example, do less-detailed PSRs produce better or worse sentencing practices and offender recidivism than highly detailed ones? Scholars and practitioners continue the debate with no resolution in sight.

In addition to these questions, several controversies surround the PSR. One is whether the defendant has a constitutional right to see it and challenge the statements it contains. Some judges and probation officers oppose disclosure. They fear that persons having knowledge about the offender will refuse to give information if the defendant could find out that they did. Second, they believe that if the defendant challenges information in the PSR, court proceedings may be delayed. Third, they believe that some kinds of information, such as psychological reports, might be harmful to the defendant. And fourth, they argue that the PSR is a private and confidential court document. A decision by the U.S. Supreme Court has generally supported the position against disclosure. In *Williams* v. *Oklahoma* (1959), the Court held that unless state law or court decisions require disclosure, there is no denial of due process of law when a court considers a PSR without disclosing its contents to the defendant or giving the defendant an opportunity to rebut it.

Still, the trend today is toward limited disclosure of information. The American Bar Association favors disclosure of the factual contents and conclusions of the PSR (not the sources of confidential information) and the defendant's opportunity to rebut them.[17] Federal courts require that the PSR be disclosed to the defendant, his or her counsel, and the attorney for the government, except in three instances: when disclosure might disrupt rehabilitation of the defendant, when information disclosed in the

7.3

CBC Online

FEDERAL PROBATION WORKSHEET FOR PRESENTENCE REPORT

Besides being used to determine an appropriate sentence, the federal PSR has other purposes as discussed in the chapter. Think about the two controversies surrounding the PSR—the defendant's right to see and challenge the contents of the report and the inclusion of hearsay information. If the Federal Bureau of Prisons uses the PSR to designate the prison where the offender will serve his or her time and to determine his or her specific programming, in your opinion should the offender have access to the PSR to challenge hearsay information that might result in more severe punishment? Why or why not?

Visit CBC Online 7.3 at www.mhhe.com/bayens1e

PSR was obtained on the promise of confidentiality, and when disclosure might result in harm to the defendant or any other person. Observers note that jurisdictions that practice limited disclosure have not encountered the problems anticipated by opponents of disclosure.[18]

Another controversy over the PSR is that it contains hearsay information. That is, the probation officer interviews many persons besides the defendant when completing the PSR and shifts from gathering information to analyzing data and, sometimes, applying sentencing guidelines. The final report, however, should only contain accurate, objective information that the court may rely on at sentencing. Probation officers may be skilled in discerning accuracy of information, and senior officers do read their reports before they make a final judgment. However, the PSR does sometimes rely on subjective documents such as police reports or hearsay interviews with victims, employers, neighbors, and so on (see CBC Online 7.3).

Earlier we said that judges use the PSR to determine an appropriate sentence, but how much of the PSR do judges actually read? Researchers asked Utah judges how they use the PSR. Specifically, they asked, "Do you (a) start at the beginning and read the entire report by section, (b) skip over most of the report and focus on the evaluative summary and sentence recommendation, or (c) skim and scan the entire report?" Ninety percent of judges claimed to read the entire report, but only 55 percent of all respondents (judges, prosecutors, public defenders, and probation/parole officers) indicated that they read the entire report section by section. The rest would either skim and scan or ignore most of the report and focus on the sentencing recommendation and evaluative summary.

Offender Supervision

The second major role of probation officers is **offender supervision**. As pointed out at the beginning of this chapter, supervision can be either intensive, with frequent face-to-face meetings between the offender and officer, random drug testing, home confinement, and other special conditions; or it can be regular, with a monthly face-to-face meeting or mail-in report. Probation officers provide offenders with access to services such as job development, substance abuse treatment, counseling, and education. They monitor the probationer's activities through office meetings, alcohol and drug testing, and home and work visits; they also hold offenders accountable by making sure they understand the consequences of violating the criminal law.

Probation officers perform two major roles: case investigation and offender supervision. What does each role entail?

It is in this supervisory role that probation officers experience the job conflict we mentioned earlier—the uneasy combination of enforcing the law and helping the offender. Probation officers have the power to force an offender to do something she or he might not want to do (e.g., complete a substance abuse program) by threatening to revoke the probationer's freedom. However, guiding an offender to do something she or he might not want to do without resorting to the threat of revocation is the source of role conflict.

Although it is difficult to do, probation officers attempt to influence offenders' behavior by gaining their trust and confidence and in turn helping them do what they have to do and want to do in noncriminal ways. The technique is called **motivational interviewing**, a style of offender-centered counseling that facilitates changes in behavior. The core principle of the approach is negotiation rather than conflict. It combines elements of style (e.g., warmth and empathy) with technique (e.g., focused reflective listening). A core tenet of the technique is that the offender's motivation to change is enhanced through negotiation in which the offender, not the probation officer, articulates the benefits and costs involved. A strong principle of this approach is that conflict is unhelpful and that a collaborative relationship between the probation officer and the probationer, in which they tackle the problem together, is essential. The four central principles of motivational interviewing are shown in Exhibit 7.4. As an evidence-based practice, motivational interviewing has been found to be effective for offenders with alcohol and drug problems.[19]

The majority of probationers are male, and almost half are members of minority groups. Slightly more than half the probation officers are female, and three-fourths of all probation officers are white. How can probation officers build rapport across gender, race, and ethnic differences? Without rapport, experts believe, probationers are more likely to miss scheduled appointments, not follow through on referrals, violate

EXHIBIT 7.4 The Four Central Principles of Motivational Interviewing

1. Express empathy by using reflective listening to convey understanding of the offender's point of view and underlying drives.
2. Develop the discrepancy between the offender's most deeply held values and their current behavior (i.e., tease out ways in which current unhealthy behaviors conflict with the wish to "be good").
3. Sidestep resistance by responding with empathy and understanding rather than confrontation.
4. Support self-efficacy by building the offender's confidence that change is possible.

Source: Janet Treasure, "Motivational Interviewing," *Advances in Psychiatric Treatment*, vol. 10 (2004), pp. 331–337.

the conditions of probation, reoffend, and end up back in the system. To lessen the tension and mistrust between probation officers and their probationers, experts suggest five rapport-building strategies:[20]

1. If probation officers are sincere, probationers are more likely to forgive them if they violate a cultural norm such as saying the wrong thing.
2. When probation officers demonstrate high service energy, they send a message that they are in the probationers' corner.
3. Probation officers who demonstrate knowledge of the probationer's culture increase empathy in the cross-cultural counseling relationship.
4. A nonjudgmental attitude increases the officer's credibility.
5. Officers build rapport and credibility when they help probationers with needed resources.

The American Psychological Association (APA) underscores the importance of the officer–offender relationship in the evidence-based literature. In this context, the APA describes a **working alliance**—an effective relationship between a change agent and a client, with negotiated goals and a mutual willingness to compromise to meet the goals or maintain a viable relationship. The APA believes that the establishment of this kind of working alliance contributes far more to the outcomes of treatment and supervision than the type of treatment or intervention delivered.

Another evidence-based strategy for bringing about behavioral change is **cognitive-behavioral treatment (CBT)**, a problem-focused intervention that emphasizes skill training to change the way an individual perceives, reflects, and thinks. CBT is one of the most promising methods of offender rehabilitation. The theory behind it is that offenders' distorted cognition impairs their ability to correctly read social clues, accept blame, and morally reason, thereby creating a sense of entitlement. In addition, their distorted way of thinking leads them to confuse wants with needs, perceive harmless situations as threats, and demand instant gratification.

CBT employs techniques such as modeling, graduated practice, role playing, reinforcement, and concrete verbal suggestions that give offenders a new bank of skills to change offending behavior. The evidence-based literature on CBT shows that it reduces recidivism of program participants by 10 to 35 percent compared with a treatment-as-usual group.[21] The National Institute of Corrections says that, in general, offenders respond far better to CBT than any other program intervention.

7.4

CBC Online

OFFICIAL SITE OF THE NEW YORK DIVISION OF PROBATION AND CORRECTIONAL ALTERNATIVES

The New York Division of Probation and Correctional Alternatives works to advance public safety through a network of public and private agencies. The Division Web site contains a wealth of information on all matters dealing with the Division's functions and initiatives. Click on "FAQs" and then "General FAQs." Read Questions 5 and 15–18. How do they relate to the general and specialized conditions of probations discussed in the chapter?

Visit CBC Online 7.4 at www.mhhe.com/bayens1e

On a daily basis, probation officers try to provide offenders with access to a wide variety of services, such as job development, substance abuse treatment, counseling, and education. They also attempt to monitor the activities of probationers through office meetings, home and work visits, drug and alcohol testing, and contact with family, friends, and employers. And they work to make probationers accountable for their behavior and ensure they understand the consequences of violating the conditions of probation.

Conditions of Probation

Probation is conditional, meaning that the probationer's freedom is subject to compliance with conditions set forth by the court. As noted, it is the probation officer's responsibility to monitor the probationer's compliance with those conditions.

Regardless of their level of supervision, all probationers are subject to **general conditions** of supervision believed to aid in the rehabilitation process. Commonly required general conditions include the following:

1. Refrain from criminal activity.
2. Request permission to travel outside the jurisdiction of the probation agency.
3. Maintain a legal and legitimate residence and employment.
4. Refrain from using or being in possession of alcohol and drugs.
5. Refrain from associating with certain types of people (particularly those with criminal histories) and frequenting certain locales.
6. Refrain from firearms ownership or possession.
7. Pay fines and restitution.

In addition to the general conditions of probation, judges have discretion to assign **special conditions** on certain types of offenders (see CBC Online 7.4). This is especially true with sex offenders or substance abuse offenders, when judges assign extra conditions such as mandatory treatment that they believe have some relation to the crime or the ability of the agency to monitor for potential recidivism. California Superior Court Judge Patricia Schnegg gave Chris Brown a special condition of probation when she signed the protective order that requires Brown to stay at least 50 yards away from Rihanna at all times, except for at industry events, when the distance is shortened to 10 yards.

EXHIBIT 7.5 General Conditions of Community Supervision: State of Texas

1 Commit no offense against the laws of this or any State or of the United States.
2 Avoid injurious or vicious habits.
3 Avoid the use of all narcotics, habit forming drugs, alcoholic beverages, and controlled substances.
4 Avoid persons or places of disreputable or harmful character.
5 Report to the supervision officer as directed by the judge or the supervision officer and obey all orders of the Court and the rules and regulations of the Community Supervision and Corrections Department.
6 Refrain from disorderly conduct, abusive language, or disturbing the peace while present at the office of the Department.
7 Permit the Supervision Officer to visit you at your home or elsewhere.
8 Work faithfully at suitable employment as far as possible.
9 Do not change residence without permission and report changes of employment to Supervision Officer as directed.
10 Remain within ______(County name) or unless given permission to depart by the Supervision Officer.
11 While on community supervision, you must have on your person at all times a current, valid Texas Department of Public Safety photo identification card or a valid Texas Department of Public Safety photo driver's license. You must obtain this photo identification within thirty (30) days of the date of your community supervision.
12 Support your dependents.
13 Submit a urine or breath specimen at the direction of the Supervision Officer and pay all costs if required.
14 All special conditions and court-ordered fees must be paid in full and completed 60 days prior to discharge. If your case is transferred to another state, supervision fees are to be waived beginning on the date of acceptance of the receiving state or return of supervision to Texas.
15 Do not operate a motor vehicle without a valid Texas Driver's License and proof of automobile liability insurance.

Exhibit 7.5 presents the general conditions for all probationers in the State of Texas, and Exhibit 7.6 shows the special conditions for sex offenders in the State of Indiana. If offenders violate the conditions of their probation, they risk having their probation revoked and being removed from the community.

Termination and Revocation of Probation

Probation ends when the probationer either successfully completes his or her probation or when the offender's probationary status is revoked after a **revocation hearing** because he or she has violated the conditions of their probation. A revocation hearing is a due process hearing conducted by the court or probation authority to determine whether the conditions of probation (or parole, as we will see in Chapter 8) have been violated. **Revocation** is the formal termination of an offender's conditional freedom.

The number of persons successfully completing the terms of probation is decreasing. Of the estimated 2.2 million probationers discharged from supervision during 2006, 58 percent had either completed their full-term probation sentence or received an early discharge. By 2009, the rate of completion declined to 50 percent.

EXHIBIT 7.6 Special Probation Conditions for Adult Sex Offenders: State of Indiana

The special conditions checked below apply to you as a result of your sex offense conviction and should be initialed by you after you have read these conditions or after these conditions have been read to you. Violation of any of the special conditions checked below can result in revocation of your probation and incarceration.

Check All Conditions That Apply:

1. ***Applies only to sexually violent predators:*** A sex offender who is a sexually violent predator (as defined in IC 35-38-1-7.5) shall register with local law enforcement authorities within seventy-two (72) hours of being released to probation and shall comply with all other registration requirements.
2. ***Applies only to sex offenders who are NOT sexually violent predators:*** You shall register with local law enforcement authorities as a sex offender within seven (7) days of being released to/placed on probation and shall comply with all other registration requirements.
3. ***Applies only to "offenders against children" as defined in IC 35-42-4-11(a) (1) & (2), including sexually violent predators.*** You shall not reside within one thousand (1,000) feet of school property, a youth program center, or a public park, and you shall not establish a residence within one (1) mile of the victim of your sex offense.
4. You shall not reside within one thousand (1,000) feet of school property as measured from the property line of the sex offender's residence to the property line of the school property, for the period of probation, unless written approval is obtained from the court. *Written approval may not be given to an offender who is a sexually violent predator or an offender against children.*
5. You shall not reside within one (1) mile of the residence of the victim of your sex offense unless granted a waiver from the court. *The court may not grant a waiver for a sexually violent predator or an offender against children.*
6. You shall not establish a new residence within one (1) mile of the residence of the victim of your sex offense (as defined in IC 35-38-2-2.5(b)) unless granted a waiver from the court. *The court may not grant a waiver for a sexually violent predator or an offender against children.*
7. You shall attend, actively participate in, and successfully complete a court-approved sex offender treatment program as directed by the court. Prompt payment of any fees is your responsibility and you must maintain steady progress towards all treatment goals as determined by your treatment provider. Unsuccessful termination from treatment or non-compliance with other required behavioral management requirements will be considered a violation of your probation. You will not be permitted to change treatment providers unless the court gives you prior written approval.
8. You shall not miss any appointments for treatment, psychotherapy, counseling, or self-help groups (any 12 Step Group, Community Support Group, etc.) without the prior approval of your probation officer and the treatment provider involved, or a doctor's excuse. You shall comply with the attendance policy for attending appointments as outlined by the court. You shall continue to take any medication prescribed by your physician.
9. You shall not possess obscene matter as defined by IC 35-49-2-1 or child pornography as defined in 18 U.S.C. § 2256(8), including but not limited to: videos, magazines, books, DVDs, and material downloaded from the Internet. You shall not visit strip clubs, adult bookstores, motels specifically operated for sexual encounters, peep shows, bars where partially nude or exotic dancers perform, or businesses that sell sexual devices or aids.
10. You shall not consume alcohol or use any controlled substance.
11. You shall submit to a substance abuse evaluation and follow all recommendations of your treatment provider at your own expense.
12. You shall be required to inform all persons living at your place of residence about all of your sex-related convictions. You shall notify your probation officer of any changes in home situations or marital status. You shall have only one residence and one mailing address at a time.

The 50 percent completion rate means that one-half do not successfully complete probation. Almost one-fourth had their probationary status revoked because they either committed a **law violation**—that is, they committed a new crime—or they committed a **technical violation**, meaning they did not comply with noncriminal rules such as paying restitution, meeting with the probation officer, or continuing prescribed treatment. Revoking probation for technical reasons is controversial, because if committed

13. You shall not travel alone after 10 P.M. (including but not limited to: driving, walking, bicycling, etc.) unless given permission by your probation officer.
14. You shall not engage in a sexual relationship with any person who has children under the age of 16 years unless given permission by the court and your treatment provider.
15. Your probation officer must first approve any employment and may contact your employer at any time. You will not work in certain occupations that involve being in the private residences of others, such as, but not limited to, door-to-door sales, soliciting, home service visits, or delivery.
16. You shall have no contact with your victim or victim's family unless approved in advance by your probation officer and treatment provider for the benefit of the victim. Contact includes face-to-face, telephonic, written, electronic, or any indirect contact via third parties.
17. You shall have no contact with any person under the age of 16 unless you receive court approval or successfully complete a court-approved sex offender treatment program, pursuant to IC 35-38-2-2.4. Contact includes face-to-face, telephonic, written, electronic, or any indirect contact via third parties.
18. You shall not be present at schools, playgrounds, or day care centers unless given permission by the court.
19. You shall not participate in any activity which involves children under 18 years of age, such as, but not limited to, youth groups, Boy Scouts, Girl Scouts, Cub Scouts, Brownies, 4-H, YMCA, YWCA, or youth sports teams, unless given permission by the Court.
20. You shall sign a waiver of confidentiality, releases of information, or any other document required that permits your probation officer and other behavioral management or treatment providers to examine any and all records relating to you to collaboratively share and discuss your behavioral management conditions, treatment progress, and probation needs as a team. This permission may extend to: (1) sharing your relapse prevention plan and treatment progress with your significant others and/or your victim and victim's therapist as directed by your probation officer or treatment provider(s); and (2) sharing of your modus operandi behaviors with law enforcement personnel.
21. You shall participate in and complete periodic polygraph testing at your own expense at the direction of your probation officer or any other behavioral management professionals who are providing treatment or otherwise assisting your probation officer in monitoring your compliance with your probation conditions.
22. You shall be under intensive supervision and report to your probation officer as directed. You shall complete a travel log and/or journal of daily activities as directed by your probation officer.
23. You shall not access the Internet or any other online service through use of a computer, cell phone, iPod, Xbox, Blackberry, personal digital assistant (PDA), pagers, Palm Pilots, televisions, or any other electronic device at any location (including your place of employment) without prior approval of your probation officer. This includes any Internet service provider, bulletin board system, e-mail system or any other public or private computer network. You shall not possess or use any data encryption technique or program.
24. You shall consent to the search of your personal computer at any time and to the installation on your personal computer or device with Internet capability, at your expense, of one (1) or more hardware or software systems to monitor Internet usage.
25. You are prohibited from accessing or using certain Web sites, chat rooms, or instant messaging programs frequented by children. You are prohibited from deleting, erasing, or tampering with information on your personal computer with intent to conceal an activity prohibited by this condition.
26. ____
____
____.

by someone who is not on probation, these behaviors are not illegal, but if committed by probationers, they can lead to further loss of freedom in the community and even incarceration.

Revocation is a serious matter for several reasons in addition to the offender's loss of freedom. First, processing revocation consumes a significant portion of the court's time, energy, and resources. Also, if revocation results in incarceration the costs are even higher. Finally, imprisoning offenders who otherwise would have been placed on probation may force their families to go on welfare or make greater demands on community resources.

However, revocation is the only way to protect the community from some offenders who refuse to abide by the conditions of probation. Recently a judge in Hawaii took a group of "high-risk" probationers, gave them "warning hearings," and told them that while the rules of probation were not changing, the old rules would now be strictly enforced.[22] Probationers who failed a morning drug test would be arrested immediately, appear in court within hours, and have the terms of their probation modified to include a short jail stay (usually over a weekend in order to promote ongoing employment). The judge also assured those who needed drug treatment, mental health therapy, or other social services that they would get the treatment they needed and were expected to attend and complete the program. Following the judge's action, the overall rate of missed drug tests declined by more than 80 percent, the missed appointment rate fell from 13.3 percent to 2.6 percent, and "dirty" drug tests fell from 49.3 percent to 6.5 percent.

Jurisdictions across the United States now also recognize that revoking even a small percentage of probationers can dramatically affect the prison population. In some states (e.g., California, Oregon, and Texas), over two-thirds of prison admissions are probation or parole violators. While officials must act when they discover violations, prison may not be the best response. State legislatures in Georgia, Mississippi, Oregon, Washington, and elsewhere are trying to reserve prison space for violent offenders by structuring the court's response to technical violations. Georgia and Mississippi use 90-day boot camp programs for probation and parole violators. Oregon and Washington use short jail stays (two to three days). The South Carolina Department

Most probationers are required to pay a monthly supervision fee. What other general conditions of community supervision govern a probationer's behavior?

of Probation, Parole, and Pardon Services was named in the American Correctional Association's Best Practices for its management of probation and parole violations.[23] Its solutions include placing offenders in halfway houses for up to 60 days, in residential or nonresidential treatment facilities, and on home detention, and increasing reporting or drug testing. If an agent cannot resolve a violation case, it goes to an administrative hearing, which is the last step before it goes to the court or parole board. "We're trying to establish consistency in addressing violations," said Joan Meacham, deputy director for field services, South Carolina Department of Probation, Parole and Pardon Services. "We are trying to make it simple for the caseworkers. We make sure we choose the right person to go to court because we don't want to waste anyone's time."

Because revocation is considered so serious, in 1973, in the case of *Gagnon* v. *Scarpelli,* the U.S. Supreme Court extended to probationers the same due process rights it had granted to parolees a year earlier:

1. Written notice of the charge
2. Disclosure to the probationer of the evidence
3. The opportunity to be heard in person and present evidence as well as witnesses
4. The right to confront and cross-examine witnesses
5. The right to judgment by a detached and neutral hearing body
6. A written statement of the reasons for revoking probation
7. The right to counsel under "special circumstances" depending on the offender's competence, case complexity, and mitigating circumstances

Hence we find that probation officers perform two important roles: case investigation and offender supervision. Case investigation includes preparation of the PSR the judge uses to determine an appropriate sentence; if the offender is incarcerated, the PSR is used to determine institutional placement and programming. Offender supervision involves providing offenders services, such as job development, substance abuse treatment, counseling, and education, monitoring the probationer's activities, and holding offenders accountable.

If the offender is placed on probation, her or his freedom is subject to general and sometimes specific conditions. If those conditions are violated, probation may be revoked. We turn next to a brief discussion of caseload size.

Caseload Size

What is the ideal caseload for probation and parole? The issue has been discussed for as long as there have been professionals in the field. The same issue has haunted education for generations. What is the optimal classroom size? Educators, parents, and students believe that generally speaking, smaller classes are better than larger ones because teachers can devote more time to each student.

But small classes alone are not enough. They are a necessary condition for effective instruction, but alone, small classes are not sufficient. What teachers teach, how they teach it, the resources they have to teach it, the support they receive from parents and school administrators are critical factors in the effectiveness of education. Officer caseloads are the equivalent of classroom sizes. Caseloads must be of a size that provides officers with enough time to devote to each offender to achieve supervision, monitoring, and accountability objectives. Just as teachers with overcrowded classes

EXHIBIT 7.7 Adult and Juvenile Caseload Standards

Adult Caseload Standards	
Case Type	Cases-to-Staff Ratio
Intensive	20:1
Moderate to high risk	50:1
Low risk	200:1
Administrative	No limit? 1,000?
Juvenile Standards	
Case Type	Cases-to-Staff Ratio
Intensive	15:1
Moderate to high risk	30:1
Low risk	100:1
Administrative	Not recommended

Source: American Probation and Parole Association, *Caseload Standards for Probation and Parole* (Lexington, KY: APPA, September 2006).

will spend instructional time maintaining order and sending misbehaving students to the principal's office, probation officers with large caseloads can do little more than monitor the offenders and return the noncompliant ones to court. Appropriate class/caseload size is the necessary precondition to effectiveness in these two systems. Without adequate time for supervision (or teaching), effectiveness is just a pipe dream.[24]

Recognizing the need for straightforward caseload standards, in 2006 the APPA consulted experienced practitioners and researchers. It found that using evidence-based practices, it could develop a robust set of effective strategies for correctional treatment, including caseload standards.

To begin, the strategy involved breaking cases down by type based on risk of reoffending, offense type, and criminogenic needs (see Exhibit 7.7). Offenders demonstrating intensive supervision and treatment needs comprise a caseload of no more than 20 and supervised by one probation officer. Administrative caseloads include a variety of offender types who may or may not have any contact with a probation officer, such as those who are only required to submit a monthly progress report, have absconded, or are the subject of an active warrant.

Organization and Privatization of Probation

Probation in the United States is administered by more than 2,000 separate public and private agencies, reflecting local and state customs and the decentralized and fragmented character of contemporary corrections. Adding to the strain on the system, in 2000 the average budget for probation agencies across the United States was $56 million, an increase of only 1 percent ($600,000) from 1992. Meanwhile, the number of persons on probation increased almost 37 percent between 1992 and 2000, from 2.8 to 3.8 million.

To offset declining budgets for probation and parole agencies and provide resources for the increased population, almost all states collect fees from those who can afford to contribute to the cost of their supervision (see Exhibit 7.8).[25]

EXHIBIT 7.8
Supervision Fees for Probationers and Parolees

State	Supervision Fee
Colorado	$50/month
Hawaii	$150/month
Iowa	$250 one-time enrollment fee
Michigan	$135/month (sliding scale)
Missouri	$60/month
New Mexico	$185/month maximum
Rhode Island	$15/month
South Dakota	$15/month

If the probation or parolee is indigent (or a student, as in Pennsylvania) and cannot afford to pay, the fee is waived or reduced in most states.

Exhibit 7.9 shows how probation is administered across the United States. The most common organizational structure, found in 29 states, involves a state executive agency that administers probation services.[26] In three states, probation is administered exclusively through county or multicounty agencies in the executive branch. In eight states, the judicial branch of state government is responsible for probation services. In five states, local agencies in the judicial branch deliver probation services. And in five states, probation services are delivered through some combination of state executive branch, local executive agencies, or local agencies in either the judicial or the executive branch.

Probation agencies in at least 15 states have privatized probation services to supervise low-risk offenders.[27] A listing of these states and short descriptions follow.

EXHIBIT 7.9
Administration of Adult Probation in the States

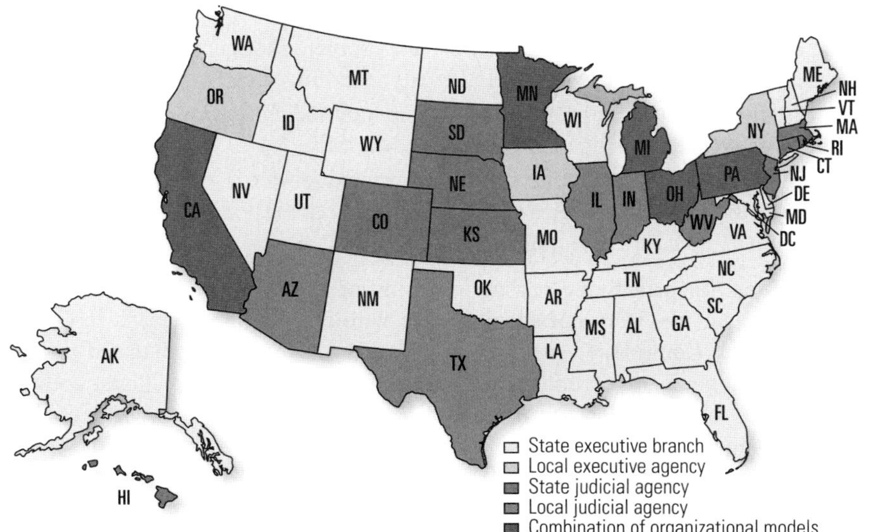

Source: Barbara Krauth and Larry Link, *State Organizational Structures for Delivering Adult Probation Services* (Washington DC: U.S. Department of Justice, National Institute of Corrections, June 1999). Updated by authors.

Colorado: Probation is administered by the judicial branch. In 1996, after an order of the Chief Justice, the state began to use private sector agencies to supervise lower-risk felons and misdemeanants. Further, judicial districts can contract to provide services that offenders pay directly to providers.

Connecticut: The Office of Adult Probation is an agency in the judicial branch. In 1999, the agency was placed under the umbrella of Court Support Services. This office contracts with a single private agency to supervise low-risk cases.

Delaware: There is no specific authorization for privatization, but the Division of Probation and Parole within the Department of Corrections contracts with a private group to supervise offenders under pretrial supervision.

Florida: Probation is located in the Office of Community Corrections within the Florida Department of Corrections. Statutes allow for private agencies to manage misdemeanor cases.

Mississippi: Although there is no statutory authorization, individual courts have made arrangements with private entities to supervise misdemeanor probationers in the community and under house arrest programs.

Missouri: Statutes authorize private services for misdemeanors other than Class A offenses. Approximately 36 private agencies operate within the state.

Montana: Private operators provide misdemeanor supervision.

New Mexico: The Community Corrections Act provides resources to private agencies to deliver intensive services for higher-risk probation and parole cases. Funding is managed by the Probation and Parole Division of the Corrections Department, which arranges contracts through competitive bids.

North Dakota: The Division of Field Services of the Department of Corrections encourages contracts for specific programs such as halfway houses.

Ohio: At least one private provider supervises low-risk offenders.

Oklahoma: At least one private provider supervises low-risk offenders.

Tennessee: Statutes authorize private probation services in misdemeanor cases in some jurisdictions.

Utah: Judges are authorized to order private probation for certain offenses. Private entities operate principally in Salt Lake City, handling mostly misdemeanants.

Wisconsin: A contractor provides electronic monitoring services and administrative supervision of less serious cases only.

Wyoming: Although no statute authorizes private services, some misdemeanants are released to private agencies that provide services to the Field Services Division of the Department of Corrections.

The impetus for privatizing probation is similar across many states. For example, staffing and resources were not keeping pace with increasing caseloads in Connecticut and Georgia. Community supervision officials felt they had exhausted the use of interns and volunteers, and funding for new staff was not possible. Thus, both states partnered with the private sector to monitor low-risk offenders—meaning people who generally have few needs, whose past records reflect little or no violence, and who successfully complete probation about 90 percent of the time. Both the American Probation and Parole Association and the International Community Corrections Association have adopted policy statements supporting privatization, but both also emphasize the need for accountability, standards, performance measurements, and quality.[28]

Growth in the probation population is not expected to slow any time soon. In fact, the Bureau of Labor Statistics predicts that because of growth in the probation population and openings due to large numbers of probation officers who are expected to retire, opportunities for probation officers and correctional treatment specialists are projected to grow faster than the average for all occupations through 2018.[29]

Policy Implications

With over 4.2 million persons on probation, how equipped are states to handle this population of offenders and protect public safety? Consider the resources given to probation. Probation receives only 10 percent of the corrections budget but supervises 80 percent of the corrections population. By contrast, prisons receive 90 percent of the corrections budget while supervising only 20 percent of the corrections population. Probation supporters argue that unless there is adequate funding for community supervision, there will be no reduction in recidivism.

How is probation's success measured? Unfortunately, success with regard to most aspects of corrections, including probation, is measured with a negative standard—recidivism. Whether recidivism is defined as rearrest, reconviction, or reincarceration, it is a negative outcome measure. It's similar to asking students "How well did you do last semester?" and having the student reply, "Great. I only received two Fs and one D."

Probation's success is seldom measured by advancing the kind of positive outcome data urged by the American Probation and Parole Association and reported earlier in this chapter—for example, the amount of restitution collected, number of offenders employed, amount of fines and fees collected, hours of community service performed, number of treatment sessions attended, rate of enrollment in school, number of days employed, level of educational attainment, and number of days drug-free.

The U.S. Bureau of Justice Statistics does report on one positive outcome measure—the number of persons who complete probation. Over the past 20 years, the percentage of persons completing probation has averaged around 64 percent (69 percent in 1990, 60 percent in 2000, and 50 percent in 2009).[30] However, when researchers follow those who complete probation, they report that the vast majority are rearrested within one year, thus making it harder for probation to claim any success and possibly even pointing the finger at probation for failing to produce any lasting impact on those who have been released.

When probation success is measured by examining what happens to offenders while under probation supervision, the revocation rate varies from about 14 percent in some states to 60 percent in others.[31] Because we see such a wide variation in revocation rates, and because we know so little about why that happens, one wonders if these rates tell us more about the politics of decision-making styles and behaviors of legislatures, probation officers and agencies, judges, and police officers than actual differences in a probationer's return to criminal behavior.

Designing policy that might enhance a probationer's success is also hampered by the quality of research design. Many studies lack the gold standard of using experimental and comparison groups.

As we reported earlier, today's economic crisis has forced some states—for example, Georgia, Mississippi, Oregon, South Carolina, and Washington—to rethink their responses to criminal offending, to develop graduated sanctions that are more structured, and to reserve costly incarceration for the most dangerous offenders. Creating policy that reallocates resources to help the most at-risk and least-successful group seems like a reasonable response to crime control, but the road to getting there is long and winding.

Summary

Probation refers to a program in which adult offenders are placed on supervision in the community in lieu of incarceration. When they are on active supervision, probationers must regularly report to a probation authority. When they are on inactive status, probationers are excluded from regularly reporting. Other probation statuses include having only financial conditions remaining, having absconded, or being the subject of an active warrant.

Modern-day probation can be traced back to 1830, when Boston judge Peter Thatcher exercised leniency and ordered that Jerusa Chase be released on recognizance in lieu of incarceration for theft. A decade later, John Augustus began advocating for those he believed did not deserve harsh sentences and petitioned the court for their release into his care and supervision. By 1956, probation was available for adults in every state.

With over 4.2 million adults on probation, the typical probationer is a white male who is on active supervision for a drug offense.

Over the past 100 years, the orientation in probation shifted from (1) the casework or medical model that regarded criminal behavior as a disease to be treated, to (2) a community or brokerage model in which the probation officer turned to community resources for intervention, and recently to (3) the just deserts model, which focuses on punishment, control, surveillance, and monitoring.

A probation officer's job is twofold: case investigation and offender supervision. Case investigation includes preparing the presentence report. Offender supervision means providing offenders with access to community services such as job development, substance abuse treatment, counseling, and education. In this capacity, probation officers monitor the probationer's activities through office meetings, alcohol and drug testing, and home and work visits. By doing so, they hold offenders accountable make sure they understand the consequences of violating the criminal law.

All probationers are subject to general conditions of probation such as refraining from criminal activity and maintaining legal and legitimate employment. They may also be subject to special conditions such as mandatory treatment that judges assign because they believe the conditions have some relation to the crime or the ability of the agency to monitor for potential recidivism.

Revocation is the formal termination of an offender's conditional freedom. A revocation hearing is a due process hearing that must be conducted by the court or probation agency to determine whether the offender violated the law by committing a new crime or by failing to comply with the technical conditions of probation.

More than 2,000 public and private agencies in the United States administer probation. In 29 states, probation is a function of the executive branch of government. In the others, probation is administered through the county or multicounty agencies, by the judicial branch, or through some combination.

Key Terms

case investigation, p. 199
casework/medical model, p. 197
cognitive-behavioral treatment, p. 203
community/brokerage model, p. 197
detainer, p. 200
general condition, p. 204
law violation, p. 206
motivational interviewing, p. 202
offender supervision, p. 201
probation, p. 188
revocation, p. 205
revocation hearing, p. 205
special condition, p. 204
split sentence, p. 186
technical violation, p. 206
working alliance, p. 203

Questions for Review

1. What is probation? What are the supervision statuses of probation?
2. How, where, when, and why did probation develop in the United States?
3. What is the profile of those on probation today?
4. How has the professional orientation of probation changed over the past 100 years?
5. What are the two roles of probation officers?
6. What general and special conditions of probation would you give Chris Brown?
7. How would you defend the reasons for revoking probation in a revocation hearing?

8. In your opinion, which organizational style of probation is better: public or private? And if public, which type? Why?

Question of Policy

Revocation for Technical Violations?

The cost of standard federal probation is about $3,800 a year. Federal incarceration, on the other hand, costs almost $27,251 a year.[32] In 2001, the National Institute of Corrections reported that the most likely reason for prison incarceration of probation violators is technical violations.[33] One analyst in the NIC report wrote, "If our jails and prisons are filled with offenders who are merely noncompliant, there will be no room for the dangerous offender . . . sensible violation policies are essential to the credibility of the system."[34] If you were a corrections professional, what would you do with offenders who violate the technical conditions of their probation? Should there be alternatives to revocation for persons who violate the technical conditions of probation? Explain.

What Would You Do?

After several months of discussion about the success of probation in your agency, your workgroup realizes that they cannot do much if probationers decide to violate the law. After all, you do not shadow your probationers 24 hours a day, and even remote electronic monitoring has its limitations.

You believe that the recidivism statistics reported in the paper and to the state legislature aren't telling the whole story of what your workgroup is doing with the offenders under its supervision, so you decide to act.

Write a list of reasons why recidivism rates don't tell the whole story. Then write a list of other outcome measures you believe your workgroup actually has some control over and could be used in measuring your group's success.

Endnotes

1. Among the sources consulted were George Rush and Nancy Dillon, "Rihanna & Chris Brown Fight Started Over Text Message from Other Woman," *Daily News* (New York), February 11, 2009, www.nydailynews.com (accessed June 1, 2010); George Rush, Laura Schreffler, and Oren Yaniv, "Rihanna Beaten in L.A. & Chris Brown Busted," *Daily News*, February 9, 2009, www.lexisnexis.com (accessed June 1, 2010); Nancy Dillon, "Rihanna Is Torn in Two," *Daily News*, March 7, 2009, www.lexisnexis.com (accessed June 1, 2010); Ryan Christopher DeVault, "Chris Brown Plea Bargain Means No Jail Time for Allegedly Beating Rihanna," *Arts & Entertainment*, June 22, 2009, www.associatedcontent.com (accessed June 28, 2010).

2. U.S. Department of Justice, Bureau of Justice Statistics, *Community Corrections (Probation and Parole), Terms and Definitions*, www.bjs.ojp.usdoj.gov (accessed June 24, 2010).

3. Steve Aos, Marna Miller and Elizabeth Drake, *Evidence-Based Public Policy Options to Reduce Future Prison Construction, Criminal Justice Costs, and Crime Rates* (Olympia, WA: State Institute for Public Policy, 2006); "Washington State Researchers Rate What Works in Treatment," *Criminal Justice Newsletter*, September 1, 2006, p. 2.

4. Lauren E. Glaze, Thomas P. Bonczar and Fan Zhang, *Probation and Parole in the United States, 2009* (Washington, DC: U.S. Department of Justice, Bureau of Justice Statistics, December 2010).

5. Robert S. Gable and Kirkland R. Gable, "The Practical Limitations and Positive Potential of Electronic Monitoring," *Corrections Compendium*, vol. 32, no. 5 (September/October 2007), pp. 4–42.

6. Kathrine Johnson, "States' Use of GPS Offender Tracking Systems," *Journal of Offender Monitoring*, vol. 15, no. 2 (Summer/Fall 2002), pp. 15, 21–22, 26; Katharine Mieszkowski, "Tracking Sex Offenders with GPS," www.salon.com/news/feature/2006/12/19/offenders/index_np.htm (accessed March 19, 2011); Gable and Gable, "The Practical Limitations and Positive Potential of Electronic Monitoring," p. 6.

7. Pew Charitable Trusts, *Public Safety, Public Spending: Forecasting America's Prison Population 2007–2011* (Philadelphia, PA: Pew Charitable Trusts, 2007).

8. Gable and Gable, "The Practical Limitations and Positive Potential of Electronic Monitoring," p. 6.
9. Darren Gowen, "Overview of the Federal Home Confinement Program, 1988–1996," *Federal Probation,* vol. 64, no. 2 (December 2000), pp. 11–18; see also Brian K. Payne and Randy R. Gainey, "The Electronic Monitoring of Offenders Released from Jail or Prison: Safety, Control, and Comparisons to the Incarceration Experience," *The Prison Journal,* vol. 84, no. 4 (December 2004), pp. 413–435.
10. William Bales et al., *A Quantitative and Qualitative Assessment of Electronic Monitoring* (Washington, DC: U.S. Department of Justice, National Institute of Justice, January 2010).
11. Lawrence W. Sherman et al., *Preventing Crime: What Works, What Doesn't, What's Promising* (Washington DC: U.S. Department of Justice, National Institute of Justice, 1998); Joan Petersilia, *Expanding Options for Criminal Sentencing* (Santa Monica, CA: RAND, 1987); Terry L. Baumer and Robert I. Mendelsohn, "Comparing Methods of Monitoring Home Detention: The Results of a Field Experiment." Paper presented at the annual meeting of the American Society of Criminology, San Francisco, CA, November 21–24, 1991; James Bonta, Suzanne Wallace-Capretta, and Jennifer Rooney, "Can Electronic Monitoring Make a Difference? An Evaluation of Three Canadian Programs," *Crime & Delinquency*, vol. 46, no. 1 (2000), pp. 61–75; and James Austin and Patricia Hardyman, *The Use of Early Parole With Electronic Monitoring to Control Prison Crowding: Evaluation of the Oklahoma Department of Corrections Pre-Parole Supervised Release With Electronic Monitoring*. Unpublished report to the U.S. Department of Justice, National Institute of Justice, 1991.
12. Maurice Vanstone, *Supervising Offenders in the Community: A History of Probation Theory and Practice* (Burlington, VT: Ashgate, 2004), p. 17.
13. John Augustus, *A Report on the Labors of John Augustus, for the Last Ten Years, in Aid of the Unfortunate* (Boston: Wright and Hasty, 1852), reprinted as *John Augustus, First Probation Officer* (New York: National Probation Association, 1939), p. 26.
14. Glaze and Bonczar, *Probation and Parole in the United States, 2008.*
15. Mario A. Paparozzi and Matthew DeMichele, "Probation and Parole: Overworked, Misunderstood, and Under-Appreciated: But Why?" *The Howard Journal*, vol. 47, no. 3 (July 2008), pp. 275–296.
16. U.S. Department of Labor, Bureau of Labor Statistics, *Occupational Outlook Handbook, 2010–11 Edition, Probation Officers and Correctional Treatment Specialists*, www.bls.gov/oco/ocos265.htm (accessed June 24, 2010).
17. American Bar Association, *Standards Related to Sentencing Alternatives and Procedures* (Chicago: American Bar Association, n.d.).
18. Paul F. Cromwell, Rolando V. del Carmen, and Leanne F. Alarid, *Community-Based Corrections,* 5th ed. (Belmont, CA: Wadsworth, 2002).
19. Brian L. Burke, Hal Arkowitz, and Marisa Menchola, "The Efficacy of Motivational Interviewing: A Meta-Analysis of Controlled Clinical Trials," *Journal of Consulting and Clinical Psychology*, vol. 71 (2003), pp. 843–861; Chris Dunn, Lisa Deroo, and Frederick Rivara, "The Use of Brief Interventions Adapted from Motivational Interviewing Across Behavioral Domains: A Systematic Review," *Addiction*, vol. 96 (2001), pp. 1725–1742.
20. Mark Sanders, "Building Bridges Instead of Walls: Effective Cross-Cultural Counseling," *Corrections Today*, vol. 65, no. 1 (February 2003), pp. 58–59.
21. Steve Aos, Marna Miller, and Elizabeth Drake, *Evidence-Based Adult Corrections Programs: What Works and What Does Not* (Olympia, WA: Washington State Institute for Public Policy, 2006). See also Frank S. Pearson et al., "The Effects of Behavioral/Cognitive-Behavioral Programs on Recidivism," *Crime & Delinquency*, vol. 48, no. 3 (July 2002), pp. 476–496; Nana A. Landenberger, and Mark W. Lipsey. "The Positive Effects of Cognitive–Behavioral Programs for Offenders: A Meta-Analysis of Factors Associated With Effective Treatment," *Journal of Experimental Criminology* vol. 1 (2005), pp. 451–76; David B. Wilson, Leana Allen Bouffard, and Doris Layton MacKenzie. "A Quantitative Review

of Structured, Group-Oriented, Cognitive–Behavioral Programs for Offenders," *Journal of Criminal Justice and Behavior* vol. 32, no. 2 (2005), pp. 172–204.

22. *HOPE in Hawaii: Swift and Sure Changes in Probation* (Washington, DC: U.S. Department of Justice, National Institute of Justice, June 2008).

23. Meghan Fay, "Effective Ways to Manage Parole and Probation Violations," The Corrections Connection Network News (CCNN), Eye on Corrections, July 24, 2000, www.corrections.com (accessed June 26, 2010)

24. William Burrell, *Caseload Standards for Probation and Parole.* (Lexington, KY: American Probation and Parole Association, 2006).

25. "States Imposing More Fees on Inmates and Probationers," *Corrections Compendium*, January 23, 2006, p. 7.

26. Barbara Karuth and Larry Link, *State Organizational Structures for Delivering Adult Probation Services* (Washington, DC: U.S. Department of Justice, National Institute of Corrections, June 1999), pp. 3–05.

27. Institute for Court Management, *Private Probation in Georgia: A New Direction, Service and Vigilance* (Atlanta: Administrative Office of Courts, May 2001), pp. 24–37.

28. Ibid., p. 25.

29. U.S. Department of Labor, Bureau of Labor Statistics, *Occupational Outlook Handbook, 2010–11 Edition, Probation Officers and Correctional Treatment Specialists.*

30. *National Correctional Population Reaches New High: Grows By 126,400 During 2000 To Total 6.5 Million Adults* (Washington, DC: U.S. Department of Justice, August 28, 2001); Glaze and Bonczar, *Probation and Parole in the United States, 2008.*

31. Michael R. Geerken and Hennessey D. Hayes, "Probation and Parole: Public Risk and the Future of Incarceration Alternatives," *Criminology*, vol. 31, no. 4 (1993), pp. 549–564.

32. "In-Depth: The Federal Probation and Pretrial Services System Reshaping Lives, Protecting Society," May 2010, www.uscourts.gov (accessed June 30, 2010).

33. Peggy Burke, "Probation and Parole Violators: An Overview of Critical Issues," in Madeline M. Carter (ed.), *Responding to Probation and Parole Violators* (Washington, DC: National Institute of Corrections, 2001), p. 6.

34. Ibid., p. 5.

CHAPTER 8

Parole: The Crucial Phase of Reentry

OBJECTIVES

1 Present a brief history of American parole development.

2 Explain the role and function of a paroling authority.

3 Outline reasons for parole revocation and the influence of the U.S. Supreme Court.

4 Discuss the changing role of parole officers.

5 Relate today's budget cuts to the roadblocks that offenders face upon reentry.

6 Contrast promising innovations to inmate reentry.

7 Explain the importance of gender-based programs and theory for women parolees.

8 From a policy perspective, explain why evidence-based practices in parole are important.

OUTLINE

Mike Danton is a Canadian citizen from Brampton, Ontario, and a former National Hockey League player with the St. Louis Blues. At age 23, he was convicted in U.S. District Court in Illinois on charges that he and 19-year-old Katie Wolfmeyer set up a murder-for-hire plot and offered a hit man $10,000 to kill an unidentified male at Danton's St. Louis apartment. The murder was to look like a botched burglary. The U.S. government alleged that the intended victim was Danton's hockey agent, David Frost, and that Danton wanted him killed for giving poor professional advice and threatening to tell the Blues' general manager about Danton's promiscuity and use of alcohol.[1]

However, only recently did Danton reveal to the Canadian National Parole Board that the intended victim was his biological father, Steve Jefferson. Danton claims that as a child he was physically abused by his biological father and suffered an intolerable home environment (cockroaches, no toilet paper, no soap, no food, no clothes, no TV, no telephone). At age 11 Danton left home and moved in with David Frost and his family. Danton met Frost when Danton was a 10-year-old, still going by his family name of Mike Jefferson. Some say that it was then that Frost first began to exert his control over the young hockey player—control that continued throughout Danton's hockey career, from the minor leagues in Toronto and eventually to the National Hockey League.

On November 8, 2004, Danton was sentenced to seven-and-a-half years in prison and three years of supervised probation. After serving five years in U.S. federal prison, Danton was transferred to Canada in March 2009. In September 2009 Danton was granted parole by the Canadian National Parole Board. Soon thereafter he enrolled at St. Mary's University in Halifax, Nova Scotia, majored in psychology and sociology, and played on its hockey team, the Huskies. He said he'd like to work one day as a coach or a hockey psychologist.

Away from hockey for over six years, Danton played his first hockey game with the Huskies on January 27, 2010. He scored a goal in Saint Mary's University's 4–1 loss to Acadia.

If you were a member of the Canadian National Parole Board, what conditions would you set on Danton's parole? In this chapter we examine the process by which offenders are released from prison and the mechanisms in place to determine such conditions and to help them readjust to a life outside prison walls. We begin by looking at the rationale behind parole and learn that early release is not a new idea in corrections.

Parole: Then and Now

Parole is a period of conditional supervised release in the community following a prison term and may be either discretionary or mandatory. **Discretionary parole** applies to persons who entered parole as the result of a parole board decision. **Mandatory parole** applies to persons whose release from prison was not decided by a parole board but instead by determinate sentencing statutes, good-time provisions, or emergency releases. A **parolee** is a criminal offender who has been conditionally released from prison to serve the remaining portion of his/her sentence in the community.

Parole has been one of the more controversial topics in American corrections. Since the recession began in 2007, state leaders have openly discussed what was once politically unthinkable: Close or mothball prisons and increase the number of persons granted parole. Today at least 35 prisons across the United States have closed or been mothballed since state and county government budgets began sliding into red ink; in turn, more states are increasing parole grants for persons who pose lower risks to public safety.

Even before recent budget woes, proponents of parole have vigorously argued that the tenets of parole supervision are crucial to maintaining institutional order and effectively rehabilitating offenders, while opponents charge parole to be little more than a state-sanctioned "get out of jail free" card. In the present climate of scholarly and political debate regarding the merits of parole, it is instructive to examine its historical roots.

The concept of parole in the United States can be traced back to 1655 colonial America, when colonial authorities were charged with supervising convicted felons who had been transported from England. During this period in British–American history, English offenders were typically exiled to America, and then later to Australia, or were transferred to the custody of a contractor who negotiated a system of indentured servitude whereby the offender was technically "free" but had to meet certain conditions to retain that freedom. In 1840, British Navy Captain Alexander Maconochie was appointed superintendent of the most severe British penal colony on Norfolk Island, Australia. He devised a "ticket of leave" system that moved inmates through three stages: imprisonment, conditional release, and complete restoration of liberty. Inmates progressed from one stage to the next by earning "marks" for good behavior and good work habits.

In 1854, Sir Walter Crofton, director of the Irish prisons, implemented a system that was based on Maconochie's "ticket of leave." The "Irish System," as it has been called, required inmates to do the following:

1. Report immediately to the constabulary on arrival and once a week thereafter.
2. Abstain from any violation of the law.
3. Refrain from habitually associating with notoriously bad characters.
4. Refrain from leading an idle and dissolute life.
5. Produce the ticket of leave when asked to do so by a magistrate or police officer.
6. Not change locality without reporting to the constabulary.

In 1876, the Elmira Reformatory in New York was the first U.S. correctional institution to implement an extensive parole program. The institution's superintendent, Zebulon Brockway, implemented a system of upward classification that culminated when inmates made their own living and work arrangements. Brockway's model was predicated on regimens of military discipline that were thought to teach individual discipline, responsibility, and self-control. The goal was to rehabilitate the inmate, and release was predicated not necessarily on the amount of time served but rather on the progress made by the offender, as judged by Brockway and his staff.

Brockway's parole model was viewed as a watershed moment for the "new penology," and correctional facilities across the nation adopted his ideas over the next 50 years. Parole was a fixture in all states and the federal government by 1942. By the middle of the 1950s, indeterminate sentencing and early release were by far the most common means of sentencing and supervising convicted offenders.

From Privilege to Release Valve

Parole has been a fixture of American corrections for nearly 100 years due in part to its utility in the treatment and control of offenders. For several decades, the idea of releasing inmates before their maximum term of incarceration was seen as a useful tool in controlling inmate behavior. The possibility of earning parole might keep inmates from being disruptive during their prison stint so they could earn release more quickly. This in turn made correctional officers' jobs easier.

In the 1970s, however, due to rapid and sharp increases in prison populations nationally, parole became less a reward for model inmate behavior and more a release valve for burgeoning institutional populations. For each inmate entering the facility, another could be identified for parole, thereby stabilizing the population. In other words, parole was something that only the most troublesome inmates *lost* as a result of their behavior or the heinous circumstances of their original crime.

The 1970s also found greater numbers of inmates being released on an annual basis than the parole system could handle, leading to lax supervision in the community and a large number of former inmates who had their parole revoked or were arrested for committing new crimes while on supervised release. Community corrections scholar Joan Petersilia reported that as the 21st century began, the fastest-growing segment of the prison population in America consisted of offenders violating the conditions of their community-based supervision (parole and probation).[2] This trend has led to recent decisions by some states to severely curtail or even abolish early release practices, as we will discuss later in this chapter. As a result, the percentage of inmates released prior to serving their maximum terms reached 30-year lows at the beginning of the 21st century, while the percentage of inmates "maxing out" has grown considerably.

In response to the ever-increasing numbers of offenders violating the conditions of their parole and facing reincarceration, the U.S. Supreme Court made a number of landmark decisions in the 1970s that altered the parole (and probation) revocation process. Three cases in particular are widely cited in the context of parolees and probationers' rights:

1. *Morrissey* v. *Brewer* (1972). This is the seminal parole revocation case. The Court ruled that if parole is to be revoked, the parolee has the right to preliminary and final hearings to determine if indeed a violation occurred that should result in parole or probation being revoked. In addition, the Court declared the minimum due process standards for parole revocation hearings as follows: (1) written notice of the claimed violations of parole; (2) disclosure to the parolee of the evidence to be used against him or her; (3) opportunity to be heard in person and to present witnesses and documentary evidence; (4) the right to confront and cross-examine adverse witnesses (unless the hearing officer specifically finds good cause for not allowing confrontation); (5) a neutral and detached hearing body such as a traditional parole board, members of which need not be judicial officers or lawyers; and (6) a written statement by the fact finders as to evidence relied on and reasons for revoking.

2. *Gagnon* v. *Scarpelli* (1973). The Court ruled that the due process standards applicable to parole revocations established in *Morrissey* v. *Brewer* (1972) apply also to probation revocation hearings. The Court also ruled that offenders do not have an absolute constitutional right to counsel at revocation proceedings; in some circumstances the right to counsel may be required by due process, and in others not required, and that the determination may be made on a case-by-case basis. The Court predicted that "the presence and participation of counsel will probably be both undesirable and unnecessary in most revocation hearings."
3. *Greenholtz* v. *Inmates of the Nebraska Penal and Correctional Complex* (1979). The Court ruled that parole is a privilege, rather than a right, and the full complement of due process rights need not be afforded at parole hearings. The Court also held that when state law requires the state to grant parole whenever a prisoner satisfies certain conditions, due process requires the state to allow the prisoner to present evidence in support of his or her request for parole and to furnish the prisoner a written explanation of the reasons why his or her request has been denied. The Court opined, "The Nebraska procedure affords an opportunity to be heard, and when parole is denied it informs the inmate in what respects he falls short of qualifying for parole; this affords the process that is due under these circumstances. The Constitution does not require more."

Who Is On Parole Today?

Ten years ago, 1,500 inmates were released from prison each day. Today, that number has grown to over 2,000, and most of them are ill-equipped to meet the demands of society. Then as now, three-fourths of all prisoners are released conditionally to probation, parole, supervised mandatory release, or other unspecified conditional releases.[3] Even though the percentage of all persons released from prison conditionally has remained relatively stable, the sheer number of people released from state and federal prison with no community supervision (210,814 in 2009), some say, is cause for alarm and for a rethinking of the role of discretionary release—if not to benefit the individual then to protect public safety.

At year-end 2009, the total parole populations decreased (down 5,526) from 824,834 at year-end 2008 to 819,308.[4] This was the second year in a row that the state parole population declined. The decrease in the state parole population was partially offset by an increase (5,232) in the federal parole population. This was the second consecutive year that the federal system reported the largest increase in the nation.

During 2009, most (33) jurisdictions, including the federal system, reported an increase in their parole populations, amounting to a total of 18,730 parolees (see Exhibit 8.1). The federal system reported the largest absolute increase in the nation, followed by Mississippi and Pennsylvania. The federal system accounted for a third of the total increase in the parole population in 2008, contributing to the large number of federal parolees was the significantly faster growth in entries compared to exits.

Nineteen jurisdictions reported a decline in their parole populations for a total decrease of 29,488 parolees during 2009.[5] In absolute numbers, California and Washington reported the largest declines among the states that reported a decrease, accounting for more than two-thirds of the decrease in the parole population during 2009.

The basic demographics of the parole population in 2009 have not changed considerably since 2000 (see Exhibit 8.2). The parole population is still predominantly male (88 percent), minority (59 percent), and under active supervision, meaning they are

EXHIBIT 8.1 Change in the Parole Population, 2008.*

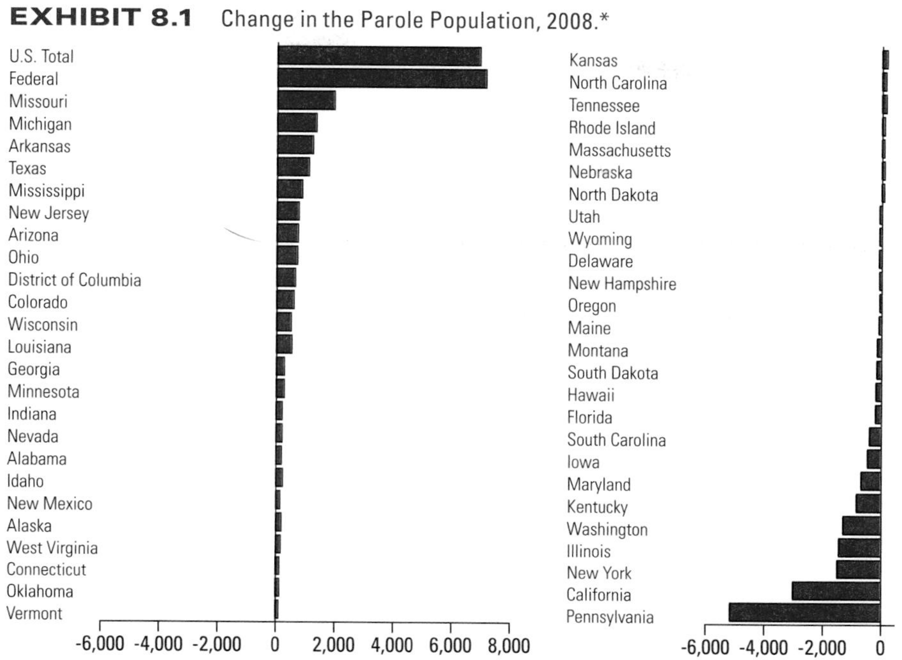

*Virginia was excluded from the graph because the state could not provide data for the January 1, 2008 population.

Source: Lauren E. Glaze and Thomas P. Bonczar, *Probation and Parole in the United States, 2008* (Washington, DC: U.S. Department of Justice Statistics, December 2009), p. 8.

required to regularly report to a parole authority in person, by mail, or by telephone. A small number of parolees (10,494), mostly sex offenders, are tracked by the Global Positioning System (GPS). Most parolees are under supervision for a drug offense. Substance abuse, limited education, and poor job skills continue to define the parole population and contribute to the high rate of recidivism. Almost 30 years ago, the Bureau of Justice Statistics reported that 62.5 percent of parolees are rearrested within three years of release. When the study was replicated in 1993, following a decade of significant growth in prison populations, rearrest rates had not improved. In fact, recidivism had reached 67.5 percent.[6]

What has changed, however, is the balance between the two methods of parole release: discretionary and mandatory. In 1977, 69 percent of parolees received discretionary parole, and 31 percent received mandatory parole. States moved away from discretionary parole in the 1980s in favor of determinate sentences and mandatory parole. Consistent with the adoption of truth in sentencing and other mandatory release statutes, discretionary parole release dropped to 37 percent in 2009, and mandatory parole release increased to 63 percent.[7]

The Move to Abolish Parole

The move to abolish or restrict parole often has political motivations and is not grounded in evidence-based research. More and more offenders are receiving prison

EXHIBIT 8.2
Characteristics of Adults on Parole, 2000, 2008–2009

Characteristics	2000	2008	2009
Total	100%	100%	100%
Sex			
Male	88%	88%	88%
Female	12	12	12
Race and Hispanic or Latino origin			
White	38%	41%	41%
Black	40	38	39
Hispanic or Latino	21	19	18
American Indian/Alaska Native	1	1	1
Asian/Native Hawaiian/other Pacific Islander	...	1	1
Two or more races	...	...	...
Status of supervision			
Active	83%	85%	85%
Inactive	4	4	4
Absconder	7	6	5
Supervised out of state	5	4	4
Financial conditions remaining	...	...	...
Other	1	1	2
Maximum sentence to incarceration			
Less than 1 year	3%	6%	5%
1 year or more	97	94	95
Most serious offense			
Violent	...	26%	27%
Sex offense	...	...	8
Other violent	...	...	19
Property	...	23	23
Drug	...	37	36
Weapon	...	3	3
Other	...	11	10
Adults on parole tracked by GPS	...	...	10,494

Source: Lauren E. Glaze, Thomas P. Bonczar, and Fan Zhang, *Probation and Parole in the United States, 2009* (Washington, DC: U.S. Department of Justice, Bureau of Justice Statistics, December 2010), pp. 36, 43.

time for their crimes under stricter laws enacted during the get-tough era of the 1980s and 1990s. In 2000, approximately 625,000 persons were sent to prison. A decade later, that number has increased 17 percent to more than 730,860, even though crime has decreased by over 11 percent during the same time period.[8] And even though crime is down, prisoners in 2000 and 2009 served the same amount of time (violent offenders, 23.5 months; property and drug offenders, 16 months; and public-order offenders, 14 months).[9]

Having more prisoners behind bars with long sentences also has social and economic consequences. Long-term incarceration leads to **prisonization,** a process whereby the inmate takes on the norms and values of the prison environment and loses the ability to successfully reintegrate into society after prison. Since offenders tend to disproportionately represent communities that are often crime-ridden and lacking in services and support systems, negative elements of prison culture are transmitted more readily in these areas, especially to young males. For example, in Illinois, 51 percent of prisoners released from state correctional institutions in 2001 returned to Chicago, and 34 percent of those prisoners returned to six of Chicago's 77 neighborhoods.[10] Two of those six neighborhoods had no services to help former prisoners reintegrate. Now that we know that returning prisoners concentrate in a handful of neighborhoods in most large cities, we have an opportunity to concentrate our **reentry** efforts in those areas and focus on the transition offenders make from jail or prison to the community.

Why then did some states abolish discretionary parole, which would provide the opportunity for just such targeted reentry efforts? At least four issues were at the heart of the movement. First, opponents of discretionary parole argued that indeterminate sentencing and discretionary parole failed to achieve offender rehabilitation, and too many discretionary parole decisions were influenced by the offender's race, socioeconomic status, and place of conviction. Second, eliminating discretionary parole was touted as a get-tough crime policy during the 1970s and 1980s. Third, discretionary parole board decision-making lacked accountability; parole decisions were made without the benefit of a written set of policies and procedures. And fourth, politicians were able to convince the public that parole was the cause of the rising crime problem in the 1990s and that abolition of parole was the solution.

By the end of 2000, 16 states (Arizona, California, Delaware, Florida, Illinois, Indiana, Kansas, Maine, Minnesota, Mississippi, North Carolina, Ohio, Oregon, Virginia, Washington, and Wisconsin) and the federal government abolished discretionary parole for all offenders. Another four states (Alaska, Louisiana, New York, and Tennessee) had abolished discretionary parole for certain violent offenses or other crimes against a person—primarily first-degree murder and intentional second-degree murder. In these states, postrelease supervision still exists for other kinds of crimes and is referred to as "mandatory supervised release," "controlled release," or "community control." And in these four states, parole boards still have discretion over inmates who were sentenced for crimes committed prior to the effective date of the law that eliminated discretionary parole. They have the responsibility to place such offenders under conditional release, the authority to return an offender to prison for violating the conditions of parole, and the power to grant parole for medical reasons. Exhibit 8.3 shows the amount of discretion that state parole boards have to release inmates as of 2007. Whether or not more states replace discretionary parole with mandatory parole, parole boards will continue to have a role in American corrections. In 1999, the Texas Senate Research Center put it this way: "Parole is not dead, rather it has taken on a new identity."[11]

Also affecting the movement to abolish parole today is the economy. With more inmates serving more time behind bars, state budgets are increasingly dominated by corrections spending. At least five states are now spend more on corrections than they do on higher education (see Exhibit 8.4).

In 2009, with states experiencing significant fiscal crises, legislators and correctional policy makers across the country have enacted policies that could promote public safety by reducing prison populations and increasing the granting of parole, whether the jurisdiction operates discretionary or mandatory parole. Here are some examples:

EXHIBIT 8.3 State Parole Boards, Use of Discretion to Release Inmates

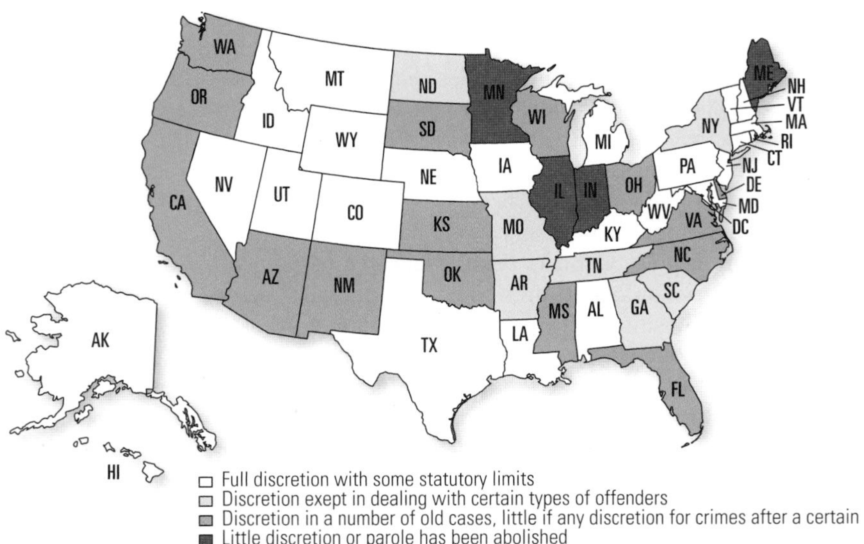

Source: Shamir Ratanski and Stephen M. Cox, *State of Connecticut Assessment and Validation of Connecticut's Salient Factor Score* (New Britain, CT: Connecticut Statistical Analysis Center, Central Connecticut State University, Department of Criminology and Criminal Justice, October 2007). Reprinted with permission.

EXHIBIT 8.4 Ratio of Corrections to Higher Education Spending, 2007

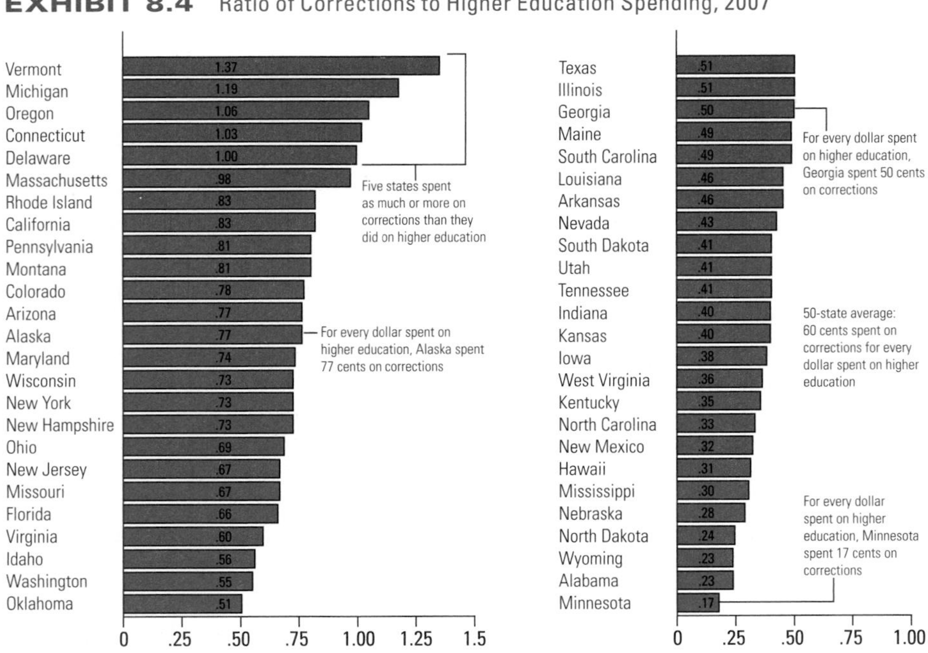

Source: Jennifer Warren, *One in 100: Behind Bars in America, 2008* (Washington, DC: The Pew Charitable Trusts, February 2008). Reprinted with permission.

- **Kentucky—Strengthened Parole Eligibility for Certain Felony Offenses**
  HB 372 provides that persons sentenced to incarceration for nonviolent class D felonies, including certain burglary and first-time drug offenses, are eligible for parole after serving 15 percent or two months of the original sentence—whichever is longer. Additionally, individuals will be released from parole supervision no later than the time when they would have been eligible for discharge had they remained incarcerated.
- **Louisiana—Extended Good-Time Policies to Individuals in State Prisons**
  HB 62 awards up to 180 days of good time to persons who complete approved treatment programs. Those programs include basic education, job skills, and therapeutic programs.
- **Mississippi—Improved Earned Time Programs**
  SB 2039 reduces the time served in prison for persons who complete approved educational programs. Previously, persons were awarded 10 days off of their sentence for 30 days of participation in an educational program. Additionally, the policy capped earned time at 180 days of an individual's sentence. The new policy removes the cap and authorizes the Corrections Commissioner to approve the number of days a person's sentence can be reduced after participation in approved programs and projects.
- **Texas—Restored Good-Time Policy**
  HB 93 granted the Texas Department of Criminal Justice unrestricted administrative authority to restore good conduct time forfeited by an individual as a result of committing an offense or violating a rule of the correctional agency.
- **Washington—Modified Early Release Policies as a Result of Medical Incapacitation**
  HB 2194 authorizes the Department of Corrections to release individuals if they meet certain criteria, including the existence of a medical condition that requires costly treatment or a decision that the individual poses a low risk to the community as a result of physical incapacitation due to age or medical condition and that the early release will result in a cost savings to the state.

Philosophically, Americans must debate whether more and longer prison terms are just punishments for certain types of criminal offenses. The editorial pages of newspapers regularly highlight instances where minor drug offenders end up serving considerable prison time without the possibility of parole, while a violent offender serves less time and is released early. The politicizing of parole has, in the opinion of many, removed the parole process from its core ideals as a rehabilitative instrument and directed the intent toward longer and more intensive supervision of those convicted of crimes. The evidence-based literature has also shown that the term of incarceration loses its deterrent effect after a period of time, so continued incarceration is costly with few tangible benefits.

The changes we've seen in parole over the past 350 years have been enormous. From its roots in colonial America as a form of indentured servitude, to its first indeterminate use at the Elmira Reformatory in 1876 and its spread across the United States, to its shift to mandatory parole and its use as a release valve for reducing prison crowding in the latter part of the 20th century, to what we find today—rethinking the role of discretionary parole to benefit the individual, protect society, reduce prison spending, and rely more on evidence-based literature—echoes the sentiments of the Texas Senate Research Center: Parole is not dead. It has taken on a new identity.

8.1

CBC Online

OFFICIAL SITE OF THE NEW JERSEY STATE PAROLE BOARD

The New Jersey State Parole Board (SPB) is the state's lead reentry agency, working to ensure that ex-prisoners return to society as law-abiding citizens. The SPB Web site contains a wealth of information on all matters dealing with the SPB's functions and initiatives. Click on Parole Eligibility and the list of inmates being considered for parole. Would you grant or deny parole to these individuals and why? What factors would carry the most weight in your decision?

Visit CBC Online 8.1 at www.mhhe.com/bayens1e

Parole Boards, Criteria for Parole, and Parole Revocation

Parole boards lie at the heart of the parole system. In this section you will learn about the roles and responsibilities of parole boards operating in discretionary and mandatory parole systems, the primary factors that guide discretionary parole release, the benefits of using risk assessment instruments such as the Salient Factor Score, the increasing role of technology in the parole hearing, the conditions parole boards set for parolees, and what happens to parolees if they violate those conditions. We begin by discussing what parole boards do.

The Parole Board

Whether it employs discretionary or mandatory parole, every jurisdiction in the United States has a **paroling authority**, often called a parole board or parole commission, that has the authority to grant parole, revoke parole, and discharge from parole. In systems with discretionary parole, the parole board determines when an incarcerated inmate will be released. Further, the board establishes supervision conditions, discharges successful parole and conditional releasees from supervision on the recommendation of the parole officer, and revokes the release of those who have violated the conditions of their supervision. Mike Danton, whose case introduced this chapter, was granted parole by the National Parole Board in Canada. The National Parole Board has discretionary authority to grant, deny, cancel, terminate, or revoke day parole and full parole. Day parole allows offenders to leave the institution for short periods to work or attend school. It is used as preparation for release on full parole.

Under mandatory parole, parole boards establish the conditions of supervision for inmates on postrelease supervision. The board is also responsible for revoking parole for those individuals who have violated their conditions of release. Generally under both systems, the parole board has the responsibility to review executive clemency applications and make recommendations to the governor regarding clemency. Parole boards vary in size from 3 members to 10 or more. Of the 52 jurisdictions—the 50 states, the District of Columbia, and the federal government—only 34 have full-time salaried parole board members. For example, Minnesota's paroling authority is its Commissioner of Corrections. You can learn about New Jersey's Parole Board and what it does to ensure that ex-prisoners return to society as law-abiding citizens by following the link in CBC Online 8.1.

Parole board decision-making relies primarily on two factors: criminal history and institutional behavior. A national survey of parole board members said that the most important factors in the decision to grant or deny parole were the nature of the inmate's offense and the inmate's prior criminal record, attitude toward the victim, institutional adjustment (as measured by the inmate's participation in prison programs), and insight into the causes of past criminal conduct. Least important are the inmate's physical health and age, prison conditions, and the public awareness of the case.

In the 1970s, the U.S. Parole Commission developed the **Salient Factor Score (SFS)**, a risk assessment instrument—first introduced in Chapter 4—to estimate an offender's prison sentence and likelihood of success or failure on parole following his or her release from prison. The SFS has been revised several times since the pilot project in 1972. Today, the SFS is a series of six static factors based on an objective scale through evidence-based research. Static factors are ones that do not change over time and are known to be related to recidivism, such as age at first conviction, prior incarcerations, number and severity of previous arrests or convictions, and supervision failures. The primary benefits of using the SFS are that the items are objective, easily scored, few in number, and unable to be manipulated by offenders.

The salient factor score used by the U.S. Parole Commission today is shown in Exhibit 8.5. Responses to each of the six items are weighted. The total score (a range from 0 to 10) is then calculated. The total score is then placed into one of four risk categories (Poor, 0–3; Fair, 4–5; Good, 6–7; and Very Good, 8–10). Where the SFS intersects with the offense characteristics shown in the first vertical column (category one represents the least serious offenses; category eight represents the most severe) lies the range (in months) of incarceration judges may order at sentencing. Salient factor scores above six predict better chances of success on parole regardless of the offense category.

Every jurisdiction in the United States has a paroling authority that can grant, revoke, or discharge from parole. How do the responsibilities of a paroling authority differ in jurisdictions with discretionary and mandatory parole?

EXHIBIT 8.5 United States Parole Commission Salient Factor Score

Item A. PRIOR CONVICTIONS/ADJUDICATIONS (*ADULT OR JUVENILE*) .... ☐

None = 3; One = 2; Two or three = 1; Four or more = 0

Item B. PRIOR COMMITMENT(S) OF MORE THAN 30 DAYS (*ADULT/JUVENILE*) .... ☐

None = 2; One or two = 1; Three or more = 0

Item C. AGE AT CURRENT OFFENSE/PRIOR COMMITMENTS .... ☐

26 years or more	Three or fewer prior commitments	= 3
	Four prior commitments	= 2
	Five or more commitments	= 1
22-25 years	Three or fewer prior commitments	= 2
	Four prior commitments	= 1
	Five or more commitments	= 0
20-21 years	Three or fewer prior commitments	= 1
	Four prior commitments	= 0
19 years or less	Any number of prior commitments	= 0

Item D. RECENT COMMITMENTS FREE PERIOD (*THREE YEARS*) .... ☐

No prior commitment of more than 30 days (adult or juvenile) or released to the community from last such commitment at least 3 years prior to the commencement of the current offense = 1; Otherwise = 0

Item E. PROBATION/PAROLE/CONFINEMENT/ESCAPE STATUS VIOLATOR THIS TIME .... ☐

Neither on probation, parole, confinement, or escape status at the time of the current offense; nor committed as a probation, parole, confinement, or escape status violator this time = 1; Otherwise = 0

Item F. OLDER OFFENDERS .... ☐

(If the offender was 41 years of age or more at the commencement of the current offense (and the total score from Items A-E above is 9 or less) =1; Otherwise =0

TOTAL SCORE .... ☐

Source: Peter B. Hoffman and James L. Beck, *United States Parole Commission, U.S. Department of Justice* (Washington, DC: United States Parole Commission, March 2004).

Today, the risk assessment instruments discussed in Chapter 4 have become an integral part of the parole process. Parole boards in jurisdictions across the United States use various types of risk assessments, as shown in Exhibit 8.6.

The Parole Hearing

In jurisdictions using discretionary parole, victims, the applicant, the institutional representative, and the hearing examiners or parole board members generally attend the parole hearing. A two-year study of 5,000 parole hearings in Colorado found that the

OFFENSE CHARACTERISTICS:	**OFFENDER CHARACTERISTICS: Parole Prognosis (Salient Factor Score 1998)**			
Severity of Offense Behavior	Very Good (10-8)	Good (7-6)	Fair (5-4)	Poor (3-0)
		Guideline Range		
Category One	≤ 4 months	≤ 8 months	8-12 months	12-16 months
		Guideline Range		
Category Two	≤ 6 months	≤ 10 months	12-16 months	16-22 months
		Guideline Range		
Category Three	≤ 10 months	12-16 months	18-24 months	24-32 months
		Guideline Range		
Category Four	12-18 months	20-26 months	26-34 months	34-44 months
		Guideline Range		
Category Five	24-36 months	36-48 months	48-60 months	60-72 months
		Guideline Range		
Category Six	40-52 months	52-64 months	64-78 months	78-100 months
		Guideline Range		
Category Seven	52-80 months	64-92 months	78-110 months	100-148 months
		Guideline Range		
Category Eight	100+ months	120+ months	150+ months	180+ months

parole board heard too many cases to allow for individualized treatment, hence the important role that risk assessment instruments play in parole decision-making.[12]

In today's high-tech environment, a number of states—West Virginia is one—use video conferencing equipment that links that state's seven regional jails and three prisons. West Virginia's new system saves on travel costs—the five parole board members no longer have to travel around the state to conduct parole hearings at each institution—and permits crime victims to testify without having to be in the same room as the offender.

The final decision to grant or deny parole is based on both eligibility guidelines and the interview. If parole is granted, a contract that defines the release plan is written,

EXHIBIT 8.6 Instruments Used by Other Jurisdictions Across the United States

Jurisdiction	Use a Risk Instrument?	Description of Instrument
Alabama	Yes	A 12-item instrument that consists of 11 static factors and one dynamic factor.
Alaska	No	
Arizona	No	
Arkansas	Yes	A 14-item instrument that examines four categories of predictors; all items are static.
California	No	
Colorado	Yes	An eight-item instrument that consists of one dynamic factor and seven static factors.
Connecticut	Yes	A five-item instrument consisting of static factors.
Delaware	No	
Florida	No Response	
Georgia	Yes	There are 10 risk factors examined, six static factors and four dynamic factors.
Hawaii	No	
Idaho	No Response	
Illinois	No	
Indiana	No Response	
Iowa	No Response	
Kansas	No Response	
Kentucky	Yes	A nine-item instrument that consists of five static items and four dynamic items.
Louisiana	No	
Maine	No Response	
Maryland	Yes	A nine-item risk instrument that has five static risk factors and four dynamic risk factors.
Massachusetts	No	
Michigan	Yes	The instrument consists of 34 items with a combination of static and dynamic factors.
Minnesota	Yes	
Mississippi	No	
Missouri	No Response	
Montana	Yes	A seven-item instrument which consists of six static factors and one dynamic factor.
Nebraska	Yes	A nine-item instrument which consists of eight static factors and one dynamic factor.
Nevada	No	

Source: Shamir Ratanski and Stephen M. Cox, *State of Connecticut Assessment and Validation of Connecticut's Salient Factor Score* (New Britain, CT: Connecticut Statistical Analysis Center, Central Connecticut State University, Department of Criminology and Criminal Justice, October 2007). Reprinted with permission.

New Hampshire	No	
New Jersey	Yes	A 54-item instrument which contains both static and dynamic factors.
New Mexico	No	
New York	Yes	A 17-item instrument that consists of static factors.
North Carolina	No	
North Dakota	No Response	
Ohio	Yes	A six-item instrument that consists of static factors.
Oklahoma	No Response	
Oregon	No	
Pennsylvania	Yes	A 54-item instrument which contains both static and dynamic factors.
Rhode Island	No Response	
South Carolina	Yes	A 10-item instrument which consists of seven static factors and three dynamic factors.
South Dakota	Yes	The instrument contains six items on static factors for risk assessment and three items for the needs assessment.
Tennessee	Yes	A 10-item instrument consisting of static risk factors.
Texas	Yes	An instrument consists of static factors, used for sex offender risk assessment.
Utah	Yes	A seven-item instrument that consists of static risk factors.
Vermont	Yes	A 13-item instrument which consists of seven static risk factors and six dynamic risk factors.
Virginia	No	
Washington	Yes	A 54-item instrument which contains both static and dynamic factors.
West Virginia	Yes	A 10-item instrument which contains five static factors and five dynamic factors.
Wisconsin	No	
Wyoming	No	
U.S. Parole Commission	Yes	A six-item instrument that consists of static factors.
National Parole Board—Canada	Yes	A combination of instruments is used.

SENTENCING THE VICTIM

In 1988, when Joanna Katz was 19 years old, she was raped by four men. Watch the video "Sentencing the Victim" and follow her trauma through every parole hearing. Consider why she and her family feel they are victims in the parole system that is supposed to protect her and them. What changes in South Carolina's parole hearing system would you recommend?

Visit CBC Online 8.2 at www.mhhe.com/bayens1e

and the inmate is given a release date. The inmate who is conditionally released to community supervision is called a parolee.

If parole is denied, the common reasons are "not enough time served," "poor disciplinary record," "need to see movement to lower security and success there," or "lack of satisfactory parole program" (proposed home, work, or treatment in the community). In any of those cases, the inmate remains in prison, and a date is set for the next review. The waiting period between hearings depends on the jurisdiction and the inmate's offense. For example, even though federal offenses committed on or after November 1, 1987, serve determinate terms and are not eligible for parole consideration, federal offenses committed before that date are eligible for parole upon completion of one-third of the prison sentence. Federal postrelease supervision is termed "supervised release."

As one example of parole review, on September 7, 2010, the New York State Parole Board denied parole for the sixth time to Mark David Chapman, the man who shot and killed John Lennon in 1980. The panel of three board members concluded "in written comments that Chapman's discretionary release remains inappropriate at this time and incompatible with the welfare of the community." The New York State Division of Parole received 75 letters arguing against Chapman's release, including one from Lennon's 77-year-old widow, Yoko Ono, who said she believed Chapman posed a risk to her, Lennon's two sons, the public, and even to himself.[13] Chapman was sentenced to 20 years to life in 1980. According to New York law, Chapman is entitled to a parole hearing every two years.

As an example from the victim's point of view, CBC Online 8.2 follows Joanna Katz, a rape victim, through the trauma of driving over 100 miles appearing every year to oppose the parole hearings of the four men who raped her.

Conditions of Parole

Paroling authorities set specific conditions for parole on a case-by-case basis (see Exhibit 8.7). Parolees must comply with these conditions, which apply for an average of three years and may include restitution, substance abuse aftercare, remote-location monitoring, voice and location tracking, and/or house arrest.

Parolees are technically in state or federal custody; they have merely been granted the privilege of living in the community instead of prison. Parole officers, who work closely with the parolee and the paroling authority, are responsible for supervising

EXHIBIT 8.7 New Hampshire Department of Corrections Conditions of Parole

- Report to the Probation/Parole Office at such times and places as directed; comply with PPO instructions and respond truthfully to all inquiries from the PPO.
- Comply with all orders of the Court, Parole Board, or PPO, including any order for payment of money.
- Obtain the PPO's permission before changing residence or employment or traveling out of state.
- Notify the PPO immediately of any arrest, summons, or questioning by a law enforcement officer.
- Diligently seek and maintain lawful employment, notify employer of legal status, and support dependents to the best of ability.
- Not receive, possess, control, or transport any weapon, explosive, or firearm, or simulated weapon, explosive, or firearm.
- Be of good conduct, obey all laws, and remain arrest free.
- Submit to reasonable searches of person, property, and possessions as requested by the PPO and permit the PPO to visit residence at reasonable times for the purpose of examination and inspection in the enforcement of the conditions of probation and parole.
- Not associate with persons having a criminal record or other individuals as directed by the PPO unless specifically authorized to do so by the PPO.
- Not indulge in the illegal use, sale, possession distribution, transportation, or be in the presence of controlled drugs, or use alcoholic beverages to excess.
- Waive extradition to the State of New Hampshire from any state in the United States or any other place and agree to return to New Hampshire if directed by the PPO.
- Participate regularly in Alcoholics Anonymous or other self-help group to the satisfaction of the PPO.
- Secure written permission from PPO prior to purchasing and/or operating a motor vehicle.
- Participate and satisfactorily complete other program(s) as required.
- Enroll and participate in mental health counseling on a regular basis to the satisfaction of the PPO.
- Not be in the unsupervised company of (female/male) minors at any time.
- Not leave the county without permission of the PPO.
- Refrain totally from the use of alcoholic beverages.
- Submit to breath, blood, or urinalysis testing for alcohol or illicit substances at the direction of the PPO.
- Comply with the provisions of house arrest.
- Other (e.g., no contact with victim).

Source: State of New Hampshire Department of Corrections, "Conditions of Probation-Parole." www.nh.gov/nhdoc/index.html, accessed 23 May 2011.

parolees, and they can recommend that parolees be returned to prison if they threaten community safety or otherwise violate the conditions of release. Depending on the severity of the crime and the risk presented by the offender, parole supervision can incorporate several types of contact with and examination of the parolee, including drug testing, setting of a curfew, remote-location monitoring, and employment verification.

Parole Revocation

Parole revocation refers to the formal termination of an offender's freedom in the community. In 2009, slightly more than one-third (34 percent) of the people discharged from parole were reincarcerated, a rate similar to previous years.[14] Nationally,

CBC Online

8.3

IDAHO CORRECTIONS AND PAROLE

On February 24, 2010, the Idaho Joint Legislative Oversight Committee released a report on increasing efficiencies in Idaho's parole process. The report concludes that incarcerating offenders beyond their tentative parole date cost the state nearly $7 million. In this 28-minute video, Idaho Public Broadcasting talks with the Idaho Parole Commissioner, Department of Corrections Director, and two state legislators about the report and what can be done to improve the parole system.

What does the Oversight Committee recommend, and what do the commissioner and director think about those recommendations?

Visit CBC Online 8.3 at www.mhhe.com/bayens1e

two-thirds of all parolees are rearrested within three years, typically within the first six months of release.

Why are they returning? Parole may be revoked if parolees violate a technical condition of parole—for example, they fail to find and/or keep a job, pay restitution and fees, attend drug and alcohol abuse counseling, or commit a new crime.

According to the U.S. Department of Justice, in 2009 one-third of incoming prisoners were admitted for violating parole.[15] Of the parole violators returned to prison, one-fourth were returned for a new conviction and the remainder for technical violations. The Justice Department adds that a significant number of these returns are attributable to incomplete and/or inadequate release planning, imposition of unrealistic rules, and ineffective case management. Other studies tell us that violations are sometimes a function of a client's symptoms or difficulties in following directions. Criminal justice professionals are concerned about such issues, and proposing solutions, as you can see in CBC Online 8.3. The Justice Policy Institute estimates that if states reduced by one-half the number of people sent back to prison for technical violations, together they could save about $1.1 billion in incarceration costs.[16]

When a violation occurs, a revocation hearing is usually the next step. A revocation hearing is a due process hearing that must be conducted to determine whether the conditions of parole have been violated before parole can be revoked and the offender returned to prison. In 1972 the U.S. Supreme Court heard the petition of John Morrissey, who claimed that his parole had been revoked without a hearing and that he was thereby deprived of due process. Listen to the oral arguments and the Justices' questions in CBC Online 8.4. The Court ruled in favor of Morrissey and held the following:

1. Though parole revocation does not call for the full panoply of rights due a defendant in a criminal proceeding, a parolee's liberty involves significant values within the protection of the Due Process Clause of the Fourteenth Amendment, and termination of that liberty requires an informal hearing to give assurance that the finding of a parole violation is based on verified facts to support the revocation.
2. Due process requires a reasonably prompt informal inquiry conducted by an impartial hearing officer near the place of the alleged parole violation or arrest

8.4

CBC Online

MORRISSEY V. BREWER

Listen to the oral arguments presented to the U.S. Supreme Court in *Morrissey* v. *Brewer* on Tuesday, April 11, 1972. If you were in the courtroom, listening to the oral arguments and the Justices' questions, how would you have ruled? What are the facts that would have influenced your decision?

Visit CBC Online 8.4 at www.mhhe.com/bayens1e

to determine if there is reasonable ground to believe that the arrested parolee has violated a parole condition. The parolee should receive prior notice of the inquiry, its purpose, and the alleged violations. The parolee may present relevant information and (absent security considerations) question adverse informants. The hearing officer shall digest the evidence on probable cause and state the reasons for holding the parolee for the parole board's decision.

3. At the revocation hearing, which must be conducted reasonably soon after the parolee's arrest, the minimum due process requirements are: (a) written notice of the claimed violations of parole; (b) disclosure to the parolee of evidence against him or her; (c) the opportunity to be heard in person and to present witnesses and documentary evidence; (d) the right to confront and cross-examine adverse witnesses (unless the hearing officer specifically finds good cause for not allowing confrontation); (e) a "neutral and detached" hearing body, such as a traditional parole board, members of which need not be judicial officers or lawyers; and (f) a written statement.

Revocation is a serious matter for at least five reasons. First, the offender might lose his or her freedom to remain in the community. Second, the process of revoking someone's parole costs parole agencies a lot of time and money. In order to focus its state's limited financial resources on monitoring higher-risk, violent criminals released from prison, California recently launched "nonrevocable parole." Under the new program, low-risk offenders (those convicted of nonviolent and less serious offenses such as misdemeanor spousal abuse, vehicle theft, prostitution or embezzlement) will only be returned to prison if they are arrested for a new offense. They no longer have to report to a parole officer on a regular basis. Third, parole is cheaper than incarceration. For example, the per-person cost of parole supervision in New York is estimated to be one-tenth the cost of incarceration ($3,000 versus $30,000).[17] Fourth, imprisoning offenders who could be kept on parole and therefore remain employed may force their families to go on welfare or make greater demands on community resources. And fifth, a number of jurisdictions now recognize that revoking even a small percentage of the parole population can have a dramatic effect on the prison population. In some states (e.g., California, Oregon, and Texas), over two-thirds of prison admissions are probation or parole violators. While it is important to take action when violations are discovered, prison may not be the best response. Ohio and other states are developing graduated or progressive sanction guidelines to better manage parolees so that persons who repeatedly violate their parole condition can receive increasingly harsher penalties.[18] Ohio's violation grid determines sanctions by assessing the offender's history, risk level and number of previous violations. It thus provides for a structured system that dictates specific responses to offenders' behavior; limits the use of reincarceration; and increases the proportionality of sanction responses. California's nonrevocable parole program offers another way of relieving overcrowded prisons.

What lies at the heart of parole success and failure? We hear and read a lot about the importance of providing parolees with opportunities for work, reunited families, and housing. However, we know from the evidence-based literature that before parolees can take advantage of such opportunities and move toward a different way of life, they must first change their cognitive reasoning—that is, the way they perceive, reflect, think about life, reason, and solve problems. This kind of change is referred to as **cognitive transformation**. Quite possibly the reason that parole has failed to reduce criminal activity and returns to prison is that parole programs have failed to emphasize change on an individual level. Rutgers University professor of criminal justice Dr. Bonita Veysey aptly describes the problem this way: "Telling someone to stop being criminal may work for a period of time, but that person needs a replacement identity, and this identity may be chosen only by the individual who is in the process of change."[19]

For parole to work, two things are needed: a cognitive transformation and a supportive environment in which change is likely to occur. Making these changes will not be easy. If it were, the U.S. Department of Justice statistics reported earlier would not find that two out of every three parolees are rearrested within three years of their release, and that one-half are returned to prison in that same period.

Parole officers are professionals. Once on the job, how can parole officers continue to learn about evidence-based practices and alternatives to incarceration that are consistent with public safety and interests of justice?

EXHIBIT 8.8 American Probation and Parole Association Code of Ethics

1. I will render professional service to the justice system and the community at large in effecting the social adjustment of the offender.
2. I will uphold the law with dignity, displaying an awareness of my responsibility to offenders while recognizing the right of the public to be safeguarded from criminal activity.
3. I will strive to be objective in the performance of my duties, recognizing the inalienable right of all persons, appreciating the inherent worth of the individual, and respecting those confidences which can be reposed in me.
4. I will conduct my personal life with decorum, neither accepting nor granting favors in connection with my office.
5. I will cooperate with my coworkers and related agencies and will continually strive to improve my professional competence through the seeking and sharing of knowledge and understanding.
6. I will distinguish clearly, in public, between my statements and actions as an individual and as a representative of my profession.
7. I will encourage policy, procedures and personnel practices, which will enable others to conduct themselves in accordance with the values, goals, and objectives of the American Probation and Parole Association.
8. I recognize my office as a symbol of public faith and I accept it as a public trust to be held as long as I am true to the ethics of the American Probation and Parole Association.
9. I will constantly strive to achieve these objectives and ideals, dedicating myself to my chosen profession.

Source: American Probation and Parole Association, *Code of Ethics, 2009*, www.appa-net.org/eweb/DynamicPage.aspx?WebCode=IA_CodeEthics#, accessed March 15, 2011. Reprinted with permission.

Parole Officers and Professionalism

Most state parole agencies are located in a department of corrections.[20] In 35 states, an estimated 14,000 full-time parole officers supervise adult offenders on active parole and probation.[21] At mid-year 2006, each full-time parole officer had an average caseload of 38 persons on active parole supervision.[22]

Parole officers enjoy considerable work autonomy, a comfortable salary (annual salaries range from around $34,000 to $63,000[23]), and are commonly engaged in creative and intellectually challenging work. A minimum qualification for most state and federal parole jobs is a bachelor's degree. Because of the personal and confidential nature of parole work, officers are held to strict ethical and moral regulations (see the American Probation and Parole Association Code of Ethics in Exhibit 8.8).

Parole officers' work is to serve crime victims. They monitor offender progress guided by the principles that offenders can achieve more productive, law-abiding lives through counseling, training, education and employment. They supervise and counsel offenders to make sure they complete the requirements ordered as conditions for release. They also encourage and motivate offenders to get the education, job training, and life skills courses that will help them lead successful, productive lives in society.

Career Profile

RICK ROBINSON: COMMUNITY CORRECTIONS OFFICER, WASHINGTON STATE DEPARTMENT OF CORRECTIONS

Rick Robinson is a Community Corrections Officer II with the Washington State Department of Corrections (DOC). He points out that Washington State uses the term "community supervision" instead of "parole" and "probation" for the majority of offenders. He is assigned to the sex offender unit, supervising state and interstate sex offender cases and some kidnappers. Robinson earned an undergraduate degree in social science from Washington State University and then joined the U.S. Air Force and worked for eight years as a law enforcement officer and canine handler for patrol, narcotics detection, and explosive detection. His next career move was to the Washington State DOC, where he served first as a prison correctional officer, then as a prison classification counselor, and later as a correctional unit supervisor.

"Before they are released from prison," Robinson says, "the offenders I supervise are required to have a sponsor and an approved address. One duty I perform is to go to the proposed address and discuss with the sponsor the Department's expectations regarding offenders under supervision. I ask the homeowner if s/he is aware of the offender's crime and of the offender's intent to live there. We discuss home visit requirements, and expectations for the home as a pro-social environment. I also ask whether the homeowner has firearms or alcohol in the home, and what the neighborhood is like in terms of schools, parks, and the presence of minors. I forward my recommendation to my supervisor. Once my supervisor approves the placement, the offender-release plan is complete.

"I am also responsible for conducting the intake interview after the offender is released from prison. This includes reviewing the registration forms with the offender and making sure she or he understands all the conditions of supervision. In certain cases (with the approval of my supervisor), I add special conditions to fit the needs of supervision. For example, if the crime involved alcohol, but a "no alcohol" condition was not listed on the judgment and sentence, I can add that special condition.

"During intake we discuss how often the offender will report to me. Once a month is minimum. I also make home visits. The frequency of home visits depends on the offender's classification. The minimum is twice a month but no less than once every three months. I also make collateral contacts

A parole officer's job is not easy, as each is expected to maintain public safety by actively supervising and enforcing the conditions of early release. At the same time, they must assist the offender in returning to society. As often described, they are "one minute a social worker, and the next minute a cop." This difficult balancing act frequently leads to differing styles of supervision among individual parole officers and/or agencies and a range of results. Moreover, workloads have increased as more offenders enter U.S. prisons, and as budget-strapped states fail to hire sufficient numbers of new parole officers to handle the larger numbers. In turn, offenders have fewer contacts with their parole officers for shorter periods of time than in years past. To manage the large caseloads, parole officers have increasingly tended to recommend revocation of conditional release when technical violations arise.

every month to get input from those involved in the offender's life.

"If the offender violates the conditions of supervision, I have discretion to use intermediate sanctions for minor violations. For example, the first time an offender tests positive for marijuana I can order him or her to enter a chemical dependency treatment program and DOC work crew. For a major violation, I submit a report to the DOC hearing officer and make a sanction recommendation.

"While the offender is under my supervision I am in frequent contact with his or her treatment providers to ensure compliance with the conditions set forth by the court and the DOC. I also ensure that the offender's job is in compliance with the conditions of supervision.

"Another of my duties is drug testing. Once a month I collect approximately 50 urinalyses from male offenders. One to two days a month I am also assigned as the duty officer and required to be available for phone calls and emergency issues.

"I have authority to arrest offenders under my supervision when there is reasonable suspicion that they have violated their conditions, and I request warrants in cases where offenders have not reported in and cannot be found. I also review polygraph reports for indications that violations have occurred and assist in searches and arrests with other officers.

"For safety, I conduct fieldwork with another officer when possible and never conduct home checks with female offenders who are alone. Because of this partnering arrangement, half the time I am conducting fieldwork for another officer's caseload, and half the time he is working on my caseload. When I complete a supervision visit, I notify the court and provide information to them regarding compliance with ordered conditions.

"My advice to persons interested in working in community corrections is this: Make sure you can compartmentalize your work from the rest of your life. Prepare to redefine what you consider success for you and those you supervise. Have some life experiences to draw on when dealing with individuals. Develop empathy, but be prepared to do what is expected of you regardless of the consequences to those you supervise. Be ready to comply with the guidelines of the job. And be prepared to operate in a world that demands flexibility—as you'll need to be part social worker and part enforcement officer on a sliding scale, varying from case to case."

Empirical research has demonstrated that the work of parole officers has shifted from a model predominantly based on individual evaluation and discretion to one bound increasingly by boilerplate regulations and guidelines. Not unlike police officers, who express dissatisfaction with restrictions placed on their discretionary powers, parole officers typically see their duties as less supervisory and more involved with processing offenders through the early release phase of their sentences.

Nevertheless, parole officers play an important professional role. As Tennessee Board of Probation and Parole Chairman Charles Traughber noted, "The justice system depends on the work done by these officers. Their jobs grow more challenging every day. But as professionals, they recognize that their work with offenders is a vital link in keeping communities safe."[24] Robert M. Maccarone, New York State Director of

Parole and Correctional Alternatives, said parole "has a remarkable record as a force for positive change within the justice system." And, he added with regard to parole officers, "through implementing evidence-based practices and program services, embracing victim-sensitive community corrections approaches, and their commitment towards justice and offender accountability, these professionals advance alternatives to incarceration and placement consistent with the public safety and interests of justice."[25] For more on this important role, read the career profile for Rick Robinson.

The Effects of Incarceration, Budget Cuts, and Reentry on the Lives of Parolees

Whether an offender "maxes" out his or her sentence or is conditionally released, a crucial transition point for every offender who has served prison time is leaving the prison subculture and rejoining conventional society. Reentering a traditional community structure after having been subject to the controlled environment of the prison—often for years—is exceedingly difficult and, in the opinion of some observers, a false freedom.

Why is the transition so difficult? Why do so many offenders return to prison? Without question, some inmates leave prison with few, if any, intentions of leading law-abiding lives once outside prison walls; thus their return to custody is simply determined by their ability to elude authorities. However, a majority of offenders do not seek to return to prison, but they face so many impediments to leading a conventional lifestyle that they often feel forced to do whatever they must to get by.

Most of today's prison and jail inmates are high school dropouts.[26] Illiteracy among prison and jail inmates is two and one-half times that of the overall U.S. adult population.[27] Half of all prison and jail inmates have mental health problems, and most

EXHIBIT 8.9 Report Card on How States Deal with the Legal Obstacles Prisoners Face on Reentry

Source: Adapted from Legal Action Center, *After Prison: Roadblocks to Reentry: A Report on State Legal Barriers Facing People With Criminal Records* (New York: Legal Action Center, 2004).

have limited job skills.[28] Over the past 20 years, the annual cost of operating state and federal prisons has skyrocketed from $9 billion to over $52 billion.[29] As states grapple with shrinking budgets, the corrections budget—including parole—is on the chopping block. For example, if the Kansas legislature carries through on its proposal to cut 5 percent from the corrections budget, as many as 125 parole officers might be laid off.[30] Similar cutbacks in community supervision are happening across the United States.

While we all understand that during these economic times budget cuts are inevitable, slashing in-prison and evidence-based community reentry programs is probably the wrong solution to achieving public safety. Shoring up efficiencies in program structures and offerings is a better solution, as many states now realize.

Today's prisons contain only the bare essentials. Programming is one of the first components of prison life to be curtailed or eliminated when budgets are tight, and the result is that correctional facilities do not "correct" so much as warehouse criminal offenders.

The obstacles parolees face when they leave prison include finding suitable housing; getting a Social Security card, driver's license, and birth certificate; arranging transportation; and overcoming the difficult social stigma of having been incarcerated. Taken together, these are significant obstacles to success on the outside. Offenders whose parole is revoked often tell of employers unwilling to hire them, landlords who don't want to rent to them, and family members who are no longer in contact or refuse to help them. The frustration associated with these roadblocks coupled with the shock of reentering society frequently lead former offenders to revert to the behaviors that got them in trouble initially.[31]

Recently, the Legal Action Center (LAC) developed a report card to judge how states deal with major roadblocks that offenders face on reentry: finding employment; obtaining public assistance, food stamps, and housing benefits; voting; gaining access to criminal records; parenting; and driving. States were graded from 1 (being the best) to 10 (the worst). Scores on each roadblock were then totaled for an overall score, which ranged from 6.5 to 46. States with the lowest overall scores have the fewest barriers to reentry. State scores are shown in Exhibit 8.9.

Offender Reentry: A New Era in Offender Treatment and Control

The concept of reentry has received a remarkable surge of federal policy interest over the past two decades. President Clinton's focus on reentry courts, President Bush's passage of the Serious and Violent Offender Reentry Initiative and Second Chance Act, President Obama's $100 million request for reentry programs, and Attorney General Eric Holder's first-ever interagency Cabinet-level "Reentry Council" signal a national movement in reentry to overcome the obstacles of the past.

At the state and local level, hoping to prevent parolees from being shut out of the workforce, some major cities such as Baltimore, Chicago, Los Angeles, Minneapolis, New Haven and Norwich, Connecticut, Oakland, California, and San Francisco have passed "ban the box" laws, which require employers to ask the "Have you ever been convicted?" question at the end, rather than at the beginning, of the application process. Or as an alternative, they require employers to drop the criminal history question altogether from job applications, except for sensitive positions such as with police and schools and positions involving large amounts of money.

Four promising innovations to inmate reentry are offender notification forums; comprehensive, interagency initiatives; reentry courts; and community-based interventions. We discuss each of these below.

Offender notification forums. Since 2000, a Department of Justice-funded program called Project Safe Neighborhoods (PSN) has been implemented in Chicago with the specific charge of reducing the city's high level of homicide and gun violence. In an attempt to address some of the issues returning offenders confront, the PSN taskforce devised a creative reentry program called **offender notification forums (ONF)**.

The basic idea of ONF is twofold: (1) to provide forum attendees with information regarding law enforcement consequences and available service options relevant to crime desistance; and (2) to alter perceptions of law enforcement.

Offenders with a history of gun violence and gang participation who were recently assigned to parole or probation are requested to attend an ONF hosted by the PSN taskforce. The forums are hour-long, round-table style meetings in which approximately 20 offenders sit with federal, state and local law enforcement officials, community representatives, and various service providers. The meetings take place in a location of civic importance (such as a local park, library, or school) and are egalitarian, meaning that offenders sit at the same table as all other participants rather than as passive audience members. The content stresses to offenders the consequences of picking up a gun as well as the choices they have to make to ensure they do not reoffend.

Initial data indicate that the ONF has been remarkably effective in reducing neighborhood crime rates. Homicide rates dropped 37 percent in the target neighborhoods after the program began compared with the previous three years.[32]

Comprehensive, interagency initiatives. The Boston Reentry Initiative (BRI) takes a comprehensive, interagency approach. This unique program targets "high impact offenders" between the ages of 17 and 30 whose prior criminal behavior typically involves gangs, violence, and/or the use of firearms. It is a population considered 100 percent likely to reoffend without intervention.

The BRI represents a partnership between the Boston Police Department, the Suffolk County Sheriff's Department, the Suffolk County District Attorney's Office, Community Resources for Justice, and the U.S. Attorney's Office, as well as probation and parole professionals, social service providers, and faith-based organizations.

Within 45 days of their initial booking into the House of Correction (the local jail), inmates are chosen by the BRI to participate in panels of 12, which are convened monthly. The panel imparts two messages: First, the law enforcement community is aware of the offender's past criminal activity and is prepared to act quickly and decisively if the offender resumes those activities upon release. Second, there are significant resources—employment, housing, educational and other support services—available to aid their transition back into community life. Every inmate is assigned a mentor from a faith-based or community service organization, who assists him or her in implementing the discharge plan they receive upon release.

According to a recently published evaluation, the program is successful. The BRI was associated with significant reductions—on the order of 30 percent—in the overall and violent offender arrest failure rates.[33]

Reentry courts. One of the latest innovations is the **reentry court**. A reentry court manages the return to the community of individuals released from prison, using the authority of the court to apply graduated sanctions and positive reinforcement, and to marshal resources to support the prisoner's reintegration. Reentry courts operate like drug courts or other problem-solving courts (domestic violence court, community court, family court, gun court, and DWI court). Frequent appearances before the court, offers

U.S. District Court Chief Judge Casey Rodgers poses with Michael Robinson, one of the first seven graduates of federal Robert A. Dennis, Jr., Reentry Court. Judge Rodgers started reentry court for the Northern District of Florida in 2010. Reentry court manages the return to the community of individuals released from prison. How do reentry courts operate?

of assistance, and the knowledge of a predetermined range of sanctions for violations of the conditions of release are intended to assist the offender in getting back on track.

Reentry court employs an idea many experts on deterrence call the wave of the future. The idea is to provide constant attention coupled with swift and consistent consequences. In theory this is much more effective than old-school supervision, which involved limited visits and less consistent but far stricter punishment.

Although reentry courts have not yet been rigorously evaluated, some early findings are promising and show reductions in recidivism rates. The largest reentry court in operation today is in Richland County, Ohio. In a 2006 study, Ashland University professor of criminal justice Jeffrey Spelman studied the Richland County reentry court and found that the felony rearrest rate for graduates of the year-long program was 4 percent within one year of their release into the community. The contrast between the 4 percent rearrest rate in Richland County's reentry court and BJS data from a 15-state recidivism study that found a one-year rearrest rate of 44 percent suggests that reentry court is capable of making a difference in the lives of individuals even if they are terminated from the program. However, only time and further research will test the accuracy of these early results.[34]

Community-based interventions. From California to Maryland, communities are creating coalitions of organizations to interact with every person returning home from prison. One such program is the Maryland Re-Entry Partnership (REP), a voluntary ex-offender program that serves men leaving Maryland state prisons and returning to neighborhoods in Baltimore. REP provides intensive community-based case management for one year. It connects ex-offenders with the necessary support services for a positive transition to their communities and provides pre- and post-release programming, housing assistance, substance abuse treatment, mental health counseling, vocational/occupational training, and educational services with the intent of facilitating successful reentry into the community, reductions in recidivism, and enhancement of public safety.

The REP model is to treat each client in a highly individualized manner and to tailor the services to his or her particular assessed needs. REP was evaluated by the Urban Institute and found to be associated with a substantial reduction in homicides. Data showed a decrease from two murders and 11 attempted murders in the comparison group to no murders and no attempted murders in the treatment group.[35]

Considerations for Women Offenders Reentering Communities

For the past decade the proportion of women on parole has held steady at 12 percent. When we look at the parole literature, the inescapable conclusion is that it focuses on male parolees. Perhaps we lack research on female offenders because there are so few women on parole compared to men. What we find instead is criminal justice policy and programs developed and implemented based on findings from the majority—that is, men. To be sure, female and male parolees share critical reentry obstacles: isolation from family and community, poor quality of life conditions, mental illness, and lack of stable and legal employment. An informed perspective on reentry should incorporate neutral principles (what both women and men parolees need) as well as gender-centered approaches. For example, female offenders report more victimization experiences that are violent, sexual, incestuous, and committed by numerous perpetrators over an extended period of time. Those experiences generally contribute to criminalized behaviors such as substance abuse, and they coexist with multiple psychological problems. Unfortunately, we have little gender-based program theory and research pertaining to female offenders overall.

On a positive note, research does indicate that female offenders are more likely than male offenders to successfully complete terms of community supervision. One recent study found that 79 percent of a large sample of women offenders successfully completed their parole or probationary term.[36] The high success rates are likely a combination of the suitability of offenders for community supervision as well as increases in gender-specific programming.

Strategies to address gender-specific concerns are not yet commonplace. However, if gender-specific assessment tools are utilized, and if supervision officers are trained to work with women offenders and their specific needs, then success rates in dealing with female parolees are likely to improve even further. We continue our discussion of the reentry issues facing women offenders in Chapter 11.

What we know about prisoner reentry, then, is that it is difficult for prisoners to transition back to the community. However, the obstacles they face—finding employment, housing, public assistance, a Social Security card, a driver's license, a birth certificate, transportation, voting, and help with parenting, in addition to the importance of gender-specific programming for women—are not insurmountable problems. Evidence-based programming in offender reentry such as the offender notification forums in Chicago; the comprehensive interagency initiatives in Boston; reentry courts in Richland County, Ohio; community-based interventions such as the Maryland Re-Entry Partnership; and federal interest over the past two decades demonstrate that it is possible to overcome the obstacles of the past. Where there is a will, there is a way.

Policy Implications

With over 819,000 offenders on parole, the importance of community supervision and structured release strategies is clear. We've seen in this chapter that programs like offender notification forums, comprehensive interagency initiatives, reentry courts, community-based interventions, and gender-centered approaches have the potential to reverse parole's two-thirds failure rate.

While probation and parole are often discussed interchangeably, there is an important difference between the two concepts. A key component of parole is the re-acculturation of the individual back to a community setting, whereas in probation, community ties are not broken. The culture shock associated with leaving a controlled environment is significant by itself. A large component in easing this culture shock involves helping the released offender establish bonds of normalcy in the community—employment, housing, familial relationships, and so on. These bonds are severed when the inmate enters prison and must effectively be re-established on release. Thus, the weeks immediately after release play a pivotal role in determining whether an offender will succeed or be subsequently incarcerated and continue the cycle of rearrest and imprisonment.

Parole is a key component of American corrections for many reasons. It is a tool for institutional management, has the potential to ease offenders through a difficult transition, and can assist in establishing ties to a law-abiding lifestyle to prevent reoffending, rearrest, and reincarceration. As we move through the 21st century, and as the volume of offenders under supervision continues to grow, progressive national, state and local strategies for working with former inmates in community settings will become increasingly vital. In addition, we will have more empirical research that evaluates existing strategies and points us to those that hold the greatest promise in reducing recidivism. The work of parole boards and officers, while sometimes complicated by policies without empirical backing as well as by politics, will become increasingly vital to the overall efficiency of the criminal justice system.

Put simply, correctional institutions will likely always require a form of meritorious early release as a means of managing inmate behavior and numbers. Public safety, needs of the offending population, and system capacity are competing issues that parole authorities will have to continually balance. Observers of correctional issues generally agree that policies to abolish parole in an attempt to deter or punish offenders further are shortsighted given the impact on prisons and on the communities into which inmates return. In this vein, the Pew Center on the States' report, *Putting Public Safety First,* advocates for "strategies that can reduce recidivism and hold offenders accountable for their actions while also cutting substance abuse and unemployment, and restoring family bonds. Even modest reductions in recidivism will result in fewer crimes, fewer victims, and budget savings for states and localities. Given the sheer numbers of people on probation and parole and the cost to society of new crimes they commit, solid execution of these strategies by community supervision agencies could dramatically improve public safety and free corrections dollars for other pressing public priorities."[37]

Summary

English judges condemned felons as indentured servants and exiled them to colonial America and then to Australia. Captain Alexander Maconochie, superintendent of the British penal colony on Norfolk Island, devised a "ticket of leave" system that moved inmates through stages. Sir Walter Crofton used some of Maconochie's ideas in Ireland. In the United States, Zebulon Brockway implemented a system of upward classification at Elmira Reformatory. By 1970, increases in prison populations led to parole being used less as a reward for model inmate behavior and more as a "release valve" to relieve prison crowding. Today approximately 2,000 inmates are released from prison each day. Two-thirds are rearrested within three years and 25 percent are reincarcerated. In 16 states and the federal government politicians reacted by abolishing discretionary parole.

Paroling authorities play powerful roles in the criminal justice system. They determine the length of incarceration for many offenders and can revoke parole. The paroling authority's policies have a direct impact on an institution's population. Paroling authorities use state laws, information from courts and other criminal justice agencies, and risk assessment instruments to make release decisions.

Revocation refers to the formal termination of an offender's freedom in the community. Parole may be revoked if a parolee commits a new crime or violates a technical condition of his or her parole. The decision to revoke parole was structured by the U.S. Supreme Court ruling in *Morrissey* v. *Brewer.*

Parole officers enjoy considerable work autonomy, a comfortable salary, and creative and intellectually challenging work. Parole officers serve crime victims, monitor offender progress, and supervise and counsel offenders to make sure they complete the requirements ordered as conditions for release. They also encourage and motivate offenders to get the education, job training, and life skills courses that will help them lead successful, productive lives in society.

The work of today's parole officer has shifted from a model based on individual evaluation and discretion to one bound by increasingly boilerplate regulations and guidelines. They typically see their duties as less supervisory and more involved with processing offenders through the early release phase of their sentences and making sure they complete the requirements ordered as conditions of release. As professionals, their work with offenders is a vital link in keeping communities safe.

Chicago's Project Safe Neighborhoods program provides attendees who have a history of gun violence and gang participation with information regarding law enforcement consequences, services that are available to them in the community, and opportunities to alter their negative perceptions of law enforcement. The program reports a 37 percent reduction in homicide rates in the target neighborhoods after the program began compared with the previous three years. The Boston Reentry Initiative (BRI) is a comprehensive, interagency initiative that targets offenders with a history of gang involvement, violence, and/or the use of firearms. Representatives from 10 local agencies meet with small groups of inmates. They explain the services that are available to the offenders to aid their transition back to the community and emphasize that law enforcement is prepared to act quickly and decisively if the offender resumes criminal activities upon release. Every inmate is also assigned a mentor. The BRI reduced the overall and violent arrest failure almost 30 percent. A reentry court manages the return to the community of individuals released from prison. Frequent appearances before the court, offers of assistance, and the knowledge of a predetermined range of sanctions for violations of the conditions of release assist the offender in getting back on track. The reentry court in Richland County, Ohio, found that the felony rearrest rate for graduates of the year-long program was 4 percent within one year of their release into the community. The Maryland Re-Entry Partnership (REP) connects ex-offenders with intensive community-based case management for a positive transition to their communities. The Urban Institute found REP to be associated with a substantial reduction in homicides.

An informed perspective on reentry should incorporate neutral principles of reentry (what women and men parolees both need) and gender-centered approaches. For example, female offenders report more victimization experiences that are violent, sexual, incestuous, and committed by numerous perpetrators over an extended period of time. Those experiences generally contribute to criminalized behaviors such as substance abuse and coexist with multiple psychological problems. If gender-specific assessment tools are utilized, and if supervision officers are trained to work with women offenders and their specific needs, then success rates in dealing with female parolees are likely to improve.

Two-thirds of parolees are rearrested and 25 percent are reincarcerated within three years. Therefore the past few decades have witnessed significant attention paid to evidence-based practices and overcoming the obstacles to reentry by presidents, governors, legislators, and local policymakers. From an economic standpoint, fewer offenders returning to prison means less money spent on prison and more money spent on other important social services. Research and evidence-based practices provide a good understanding of what works and what does not. Far more is known today than a few decades ago about program effectiveness, allowing interventions and services to move toward a policy of evidence-based programming.

Key Terms

cognitive transformation, p. 238
discretionary parole, p. 219
mandatory parole, p. 219
offender notification forums, p. 244
parole, p. 219
parolee, p. 220
paroling authority, p. 228
prisonization, p. 225
reentry, p. 225
reentry court, p. 244
Salient Factor Score, p. 229

Questions for Review

1. Summarize the history of parole development in the United States.
2. How does a paroling authority operate under discretionary parole? Under mandatory parole?
3. How did the U.S. Supreme Court shape parole revocation hearings?
4. How has the role of parole officers changed?
5. What are the roadblocks that offenders face on reentry? How do cuts to correctional budgets affect them?
6. Compare and contrast the initiatives to inmate reentry described in this chapter.
7. Why is gender-based programming and theory for women parolees important?
8. Defend the role of evidence-based practices in the parole system.

Question of Policy

Abolish Parole?

Sixteen states and the federal government abolished discretionary parole release from prison in favor of mandatory parole. Another four states abolished it for certain violent offenses or other crimes against a person. Proponents of discretionary parole release argue that abandonment of discretionary parole has a detrimental effect. They believe that parole serves a beneficial purpose by requiring inmates to focus their efforts on successful reentry from prison to the community or risk revocation and possible reincarceration. They argue that without the prospect of discretionary parole, inmates have fewer incentives for cognitive transformation and, in turn, opportunities for work, reuniting with families, and finding housing.

If you were a corrections professional, what advantages and disadvantages would you see in abolishing discretionary parole in favor of mandatory parole? Explain. If you were a state legislator, what advantages and disadvantages would you see in abolishing discretionary parole in favor of mandatory parole? Explain.

What Would You Do?

After several months of discussion and research, your parole agency decides to create several women-only parole caseloads and asks you to develop the guidelines for gender-based programming that other parole officers will follow. Your boss also tells you to develop a violation grid policy so that women who repeatedly violate the conditions of their parole could receive increasingly harsh punishments in lieu of revocation.

1. What will you do?
2. What will your gender-based programming and the graduated sanctions grid look like?
3. How will you know if gender-based programming and the graduated sanctions grid work?

Endnotes

1. Sources consulted include Geoff Davies, "Danton Just Wants Another Chance," *The Toronto Star*, January 22, 2010, p. A3; James Christie, "Danton Quietly Fitting In," *The Globe and Mail (Canada)*, January 16, p. S4; and "Convicted Danton Awaits OK to Play Hockey at Canadian College," January 12, 2010, CBSSports.com (all accessed March 11, 2010).
2. Joan Petersilia, "Community Corrections," in James Q. Wilson and Joan Petersilia (eds.), *Crime* (Oakland, CA: Institute for Contemporary Studies, 2004), pp. 483–508.
3. William J. Sabol, Heather C. West, and Sarah J. Greenman, *Prisoners in 2009* (Washington, DC: U.S. Department of Justice, Bureau of Justice Statistics, December 2010), p. 26.
4. Lauren E. Glaze, Thomas P. Bonczar, and Fan Zhang, *Probation and Parole in the United States, 2009* (Washington, DC: U.S. Department of Justice, Bureau of Justice Statistics, December 2010), p. 33.
5. Ibid., p. 5.
6. Patrick A. Langan and David J. Levin, *Recidivism of Prisoners Released in 1994* (Washington, DC: U.S. Department of Justice, Bureau of Justice Statistics, June 2002); Glaze, Bonczar, and Zhang, *Probation and Parole in the United States, 2009*, p. 34.
7. Ibid., p. 53.
8. Sabol, West, and Greenman, *Prisoners in 2009*, and Federal Bureau of Investigation, *Crime in the United States 2008* (Washington, DC: U.S. Department of Justice, Federal Bureau of Investigation, 2009); Offense Data, National Data, Table 1 "Crime in the United States, by Volume and Rate per 100,000 Inhabitants, 1989–2008," www.fbi.gov (accessed March 9, 2010).
9. *State Court Sentencing of Convicted Felons, 2004 Statistical Tables*. Electronic format only, www.ojp.usdoj.gov/bjs/abstract/scscfst.htm (accessed March 5, 2010); Sabol, West, and Greenman, *Prisoners in 2009*.
10. Nancy G. La Vigne et al., *Prisoner Reentry and Community Policing Strategies for Enhancing Public Safety* (Washington, DC: Urban Institute, 2006).
11. Senate Research Center, *Parole: Then & Now* (Austin, TX: Senate Research Center, 2009).
12. Mary Wes-Smith, Mark R. Pogrebin, and Eric D. Poole, "Denial of Parole: An Inmate Perspective," *Federal Probation*, vol. 64, no. 2 (December 2000), p. 5.
13. Belinda Goldsmith, "John Lennon's Killer Refused Parole for Sixth Time," *ABC News*, September 8, 2010, www.abcnews.com (accessed September 15, 2010).
14. Glaze, Bonczar, and Zhang, *Probation and Parole in the United States, 2009*, p. 6.
15. Sabol, West, and Greenman, *Prisoners in 2009*, p. 26.
16. Justice Policy Institute, *Pruning Prisons: How Cutting Corrections Can Save Money and Protect Public Safety* (Washington, DC: Justice Policy Institute, May 2009).
17. *Recommendations for Parole Reform in New York State*, www.jjay.cuny.edu/centersinstitutes/pri/pdfs/Recommendations%20NYS%20Parole%20Reform%20With%20Endorsements.pdf (accessed April 15, 2010).
18. Ariel Whitworth, "Strategies for Effective Parole Supervision: Ohio's Graduated Sanction Guidelines," *Corrections Today*, vol. 71, no. 6 (December 2009), pp. 106–107.
19. Bonita M. Veysey, "Rethinking Reentry," *The Criminologist*, vol. 33, no. 3 (May/June 2008), p. 5.
20. Thomas P. Bonczar, *Characteristics of State Parole Supervising Agencies, 2006* (Washington, DC: U.S. Department of Justice, Bureau of Justice Statistics, August 2008), p. 2.
21. Ibid, p. 3.
22. Ibid.
23. Salary data obtained from www.legal-criminal-justice-schools.com/Criminal-Justice-Degrees/Parole-Officer.html (accessed May 18, 2010).
24. *Probation/Parole Officers' Work Honored this Week*, July 14, 2008, http://news.tennesseeanytime.org/node/425 (accessed April 10, 2010).

25. *Governor Patterson Proclaims Probation, Parole, and Community Supervision Week*, Press Release, State of New York, New York State Division of Parole, July 19, 2009.
26. Caroline Wolf Harlow, *Education and Correctional Populations* (Washington, DC: U.S. Department of Justice, Bureau of Justice Statistics, January 2003).
27. Karl O. Haigler, et al., *Executive Summary of Literacy Behind Prison Walls: Profiles of the Prison Population from the National Adult Literacy Survey* (Washington, DC: U.S. Department of Education, National Center for Education Statistics, 1994).
28. Doris J. James and Lauren E. Glaze, *Mental Health Problems of Prison and Jail Inmates* (Washington, DC: U.S. Department of Justice, Bureau of Justice Statistics, September 2006); "Offenders With Health Problems Found to Fare Poorly After Prison," *Criminal Justice Newsletter*, March 17, 2008, pp. 6–7.
29. Jennifer Warren, *One in 100: Behind Bars in America 2008* (Washington, DC: Pew Charitable Trusts, 2009); see also Pew Center on the States, *One in 31: The Long Reach of American Corrections* (New York: Pew Charitable Trusts, March 2009).
30. Tom Potter, "Corrections Budget Cuts Would Spell Disaster, Parole Officers Say," *The Wichita Eagle*, December 23, 2009, www.kansas.com (accessed January 15, 2010).
31. Michael Welch, *Corrections: A Critical Approach* (New York: McGraw-Hill, 2004).
32. Tracey Meares, Andrew V. Papachristos, and Jeffrey Fagan, *Homicide and Gun Violence in Chicago: Evaluation and Summary of Project Safe Neighborhoods Program*, pp. 3–4. Available at www.psnchicago.org/PDFs/2009-PSN-Research-Brief_v2.pdf (accessed March 1, 2010).
33. Anthony A. Braga, Anne M. Piehl, and David Hureau, *Controlling Violent Offenders Released to the Community: An Evaluation of the Boston Reentry Initiative* (Boston, MA: Harvard University, Kennedy School, Program in Criminal Justice Policy and Management, September 2008), pp. 8–9. Available at www.hks.harvard.edu/rappaport/downloads/braga_BRI_final.pdf (Accessed March 5, 2010).
34. Jeffrey Spelman, "An Initial Comparison of Graduates and Terminated Clients in America's Largest Re-Entry Court," *Corrections Today*, vol. 65, no. 2 (August 2003), pp. 74–83; Erik Shilling, "Ohio Court's Re-entry Program Helps Felons Adjust," *USA TODAY*, February 13, 2010, www.usatoday.com (accessed March 14, 2011); Jeffrey Spelman, Ashland University (personal communication, February 15, 2011) corrected the information reported in the *USA TODAY* article.
35. John Roman et al., *Impact and Cost-Benefit Analysis of the Maryland Reentry Partnership Initiative* (Washington, DC: Urban Institute, July 2007)
36. Stephanie Carmichael et al., "The Successful Completion of Probation and Parole Among Female Offenders," *Women & Criminal Justice*, vol. 17, no. 1 (September 2007), pp. 75–97.
37. Amy L. Solomon et al., *Putting Public Safety First: 13 Strategies for Successful Supervision and Reentry* (Washington, DC: Urban Institute, December 2008).

CHAPTER 9

Boot Camps and Jail-Based Community Supervision:

Unique Alternatives to Traditional Community-Based Corrections Practices

OBJECTIVES

1. Identify the major features of correctional boot camps.
2. Describe effective characteristics of boot camp programs.
3. Describe the research on correctional boot camps as a viable alternative to incarceration.
4. Explain the benefits of jail-based community service and work release programs.
5. Describe the basic elements of a jail reentry program.
6. Explain why jail-based substance abuse treatment and therapeutic communities are integral components of reentry.

OUTLINE

"While military boot camps train soldiers in unique military arts, the correctional boot camp's training focus should be educational, occupational, or tailored specifically to correct[ing] the behavior for which the offender is incarcerated. Like its military counterpart, the training environment should generate physical and mental stress to assist in preparing the prisoner for the pressures of constructive citizenship. Intensive supervision and success-oriented counseling and mentorship apply to both the military and corrections 'boot camp' environment."[1]

This was the comment of Lieutenant Colonel Bruce R. Conover, Chief of Corrections Branch Headquarters for the U.S. Department of the Army, when asked about the compatibility of military and correctional boot camp goals. While the comment underscores the differences between the two kinds of boot camps, Conover also notes the similarities: immersion in a stressful environment in order to prepare participants for the pressures of what lies ahead.

In this chapter, we take a close look at correctional boot camps and discuss the viability of this "shock incarceration" program and its impact on recidivism. Later in the chapter, we'll turn our attention to nonresidential programs for offenders under jail authority. While the operations of these two correctional programs differ considerably, both are popular alternatives to incarceration.

Overview and History of Boot Camps

Correctional boot camps are military-style programs wherein young offenders convicted of nonviolent crimes are confined for a short time, typically from 90 to 180 days. These are secure environments where an offender, often referred to as a "trainee," is exposed to regimented activities of physical training, close-order drill, inspections, and labor. Nearly all correctional boot camp programs incorporate discipline, such as requiring inmates to stand at attention and respond with "Sir, yes sir! Sir, no sir!" Additionally, correctional boot camps provide an array of activities such as life skills and academic education, vocational training, drug treatment, individual counseling, and work.

Although all boot camps share certain characteristics, they also show multiple variations in programming. They also vary significantly in cost, size, and effectiveness. Moreover, boot camps for adjudicated juveniles tend to differ from boot camps for adult offenders. In adult camps greater emphasis is placed on hard labor, while camps for juveniles are more apt to provide therapeutic components. Finally, new models are constantly evolving that differ from earlier prototypes. However, a common principle is that correctional boot camps serve as an intermediate sanction to reduce prison crowding by changing offenders' behavior and thereby deterring their further involvement in crime.

To provide a functional definition of boot camps, then, we list their major features:

- Serve as a cost-effective alternative to institutionalization
- Limit participants to young, nonviolent first offenders

- Have military drill and ceremony as a component of the program
- Promote discipline through physical conditioning and teamwork
- Instill moral values and a work ethic
- Promote literacy and increase academic achievement
- Reduce drug and alcohol abuse
- Ensure that offenders are held accountable for their actions
- Encourage participants to become productive, law-abiding citizens

Historical Roots of Correctional Boot Camps

The states of Georgia and Oklahoma are credited with being the first to introduce military practices into corrections. Georgia introduced the concept in 1983, when the state's Department of Corrections instituted Special Alternative Incarceration (SAI) to relieve the overcrowded conditions in prisons and jails. SAI required probationers to serve 90 days in prison with an additional period of postrelease supervision in the community. The initial phase of confinement was designed to provide a highly structured, regimented, military-style program in which offenders participated in strenuous physical conditioning and manual labor. When they completed this program, offenders were released to either general probation, intensive probation, or a residential program. The first SAI program was established at the Dodge Correctional Institution in Chester, Georgia, when 50 beds were committed to the program.[2]

In 1984, a military-style boot camp facility, called the Regimented Inmate Discipline (RID) program, was opened in Lexington, Oklahoma. It was established for first-time drug offenders and others who had been convicted of nonviolent offenses. In 1989, it was moved to the William S. Key Correctional Center, a 400-bed minimum-security facility in Fort Supply, Oklahoma, and provided bed space for 150 inmates. The program was designed for 18- to 25-year-old first-time, nonviolent offenders and involved a stay of about 120 days within a regimented, military-life atmosphere. The RID program was the first boot camp program accredited by the American Correctional Association.[3]

In 1985, Louisiana became the first state to establish a correctional boot camp for juvenile offenders. Developed in Orleans Parish, it modeled a basic military-style training format, and juveniles were required to wear uniforms and march to daily activities. This camp included a highly regimented schedule of discipline, physical training, and educational programming—this last feature generally distinguishing juvenile boot camps from adult boot camps. As juvenile crime escalated in the late 1980s and early 1990s, juvenile boot camps became popular with corrections officials, policymakers, and the general public. The idea was to introduce youthful offenders to self-discipline, adherence to authoritarian control and rules, and physical conditioning. Such environments were intended to maximize deterrence but in a less costly way than incarceration.

By the 1990s, military-style boot camps were being used across the United States. Policymakers and corrections officials of both the adult and juvenile correctional systems fully embraced the concept. Conservatives viewed boot camps as secure complexes that forced prisoners to conform to strict military-type rules, thereby teaching them self-discipline and the value of hard work. Others viewed boot camps as structured environments where offenders would benefit from education and vocational services as well as individual and group counseling.

Factors Influencing the Adoption of Boot Camps

In addition to the general popularity just described, three other forces greatly influenced the adoption of boot camps by local, state, and federal correctional agencies. These included "get-tough" revisions to sentencing practices, overcrowded conditions in confinement facilities, and the availability of federal and state funding. Among the get-tough laws, mandatory drug sentences, **three-strikes laws** for repeat offenders, and "truth-in-sentencing" laws that established presumptive sentencing stand out as powerful supports for boot camps. The reason is that as a consequence of restructuring the sentencing system in the United States, prisons, jails, and juvenile detention facilities became overcrowded and unmanageable. This opened the door for boot camps to be used to relieve such conditions. Last, through the 1990s, Congress authorized the U.S. Department of Justice to award multimillion-dollar grants to jurisdictions that endorsed planning, renovation, and construction of boot camps. In 1995, for example, 44 grants and $24.5 million were awarded to boot camp programs.[4]

Between 1990 and 1995, the number of prisoners participating in boot camps tripled. By mid-year 1995, there were 62 state-operated boot camps, two federally operated boot camps, and one privately owned boot camp. The majority were classified as minimum-security facilities and served a population of 8,968 persons. By region, 45 percent of all prison boot camp programs were in the South, 22 percent in the West, 16 percent in the Northeast, and 14 percent in the Midwest.[5] In addition to boot camps for adults, state and local agencies operated 30 juvenile boot camps, and larger counties operated 18 boot camps in local jails.[6]

Within a few years, 30 more boot camps were in operation across 31 U.S. states. The Bureau of Justice Statistics reported a total of 95 boot camps with 12,751 persons enrolled. The number of privately operated boot camps rose to 5, while states operated 87 facilities, and the Federal Bureau of Prisons operated three.[7] With the average offenders spending a little more than three months in a boot camp prison, more than 27,000 offenders could complete the program in a one-year period. [8]

Negative Evaluations and Offender Abuse

Advancing boot camps as a viable alternative to incarceration seemed unbridled in the United States. However, between 1996 and 2005, two forces bore down on the philosophy of **shock incarceration**, another label applied to this kind of short-term military-style confinement, and eventually caused a decline in the popularity of boot camps. These forces included the negative results of boot camp program evaluations and reports of offender abuse.

First, evaluations of adult and juvenile boot camp programs consistently showed that they did not produce the desired goals of reducing **recidivism**. Concurrently, several other evaluations indicated that offenders were being admitted to boot camps as a condition of probation, as opposed to being drawn from an otherwise prison-bound population. Still other research studies found that less than half the offenders who were admitted to boot camps actually completed the programs. Finally, with regard to cost savings, many studies confirmed that boot camp costs were comparable to prison costs.[9]

A 2003 National Institute of Justice study titled "Correctional Boot Camps: Lessons From a Decade of Research" presented 10 years of data analyzing whether boot camps were successful in reducing recidivism, prison populations, and operating costs. The report noted that although boot camps generally had positive effects on the attitudes and behaviors of inmates during confinement, these changes did not translate into reduced recidivism. Programs were often too brief to exert a lasting effect on inmates released to the community, and they lacked a strong treatment model or sufficient preparation for reentry into the community. Also, efforts by boot camps to achieve multiple goals contributed to conflicting results. For example, lengthening sessions so that more treatment programs could be included (which reduced recidivism) also undercut the discount in time served and prison bed costs.[10]

At the same time that evaluations were showing unfavorable results, stories of abuse began to surface. The area of greatest concern and controversy related to the harsh physical and verbal tactics of these military-style programs. Most media accounts of boot camps portrayed correctional staff as aggressive and threatening toward young offenders. Frightful stories of injury and death appeared from time to time in the media. Two of the most highly publicized stories of abuse involved the deaths of Gina Score and Martin Anderson.

Congresswomen Frederica Wilson speaks at a news conference in 2006 about the death of Martin Anderson, shown in the photo.

On July 16, 1999, 14-year-old Gina Score arrived at a military-style boot camp for teenage girls located at the State Training School in Plankinton, South Dakota. She had been admitted for a parole violation after being convicted of shoplifting. Five days after arriving at the boot camp, Score, who weighed 226 lbs at 5 feet 4 inches tall, collapsed from heat exhaustion near the end of 2.7-mile run/walk exercise. None of the three staff members supervising the morning physical training had more than elementary training in first aid, and none was ever trained or had dealt with heat exhaustion. Moreover, staff members left the girl on the ground for three hours because they thought she was pretending to be ill. When she arrived at a hospital later that day, Score's core body temperature was 108 degrees, which was the maximum measurement for the thermometer. The autopsy report concluded the cause of death as hyperthermia.[11] In February 2000, South Dakota agreed to pay Score's parents $1.25 million to settle a wrongful death lawsuit.[12]

On January 5, 2006, 14-year-old Martin Anderson was admitted to the Florida Bay County Sheriff's Boot Camp in Panama City, Florida. He had been trespassing at a school, which violated his probation imposed after he was adjudicated of helping his cousins steal their grandmother's car. Anderson died at the boot camp after guards forced him to inhale ammonia, which caused his vocal cords to spasm and shut off his air supply. A coroner initially determined Anderson fatally hemorrhaged because he had an undiagnosed sickle cell trait, a condition that can cause red cells to change shape and not carry oxygen when the body is under extreme stress. A second autopsy determined Anderson had died from oxygen deprivation caused when guards pushed ammonia tablets into his nose and covered his mouth.[13] In April 2007, the Florida Department of Juvenile Justice paid the Martin family $5 million, even though the guards and a nurse were acquitted of aggravated manslaughter charges.

The deaths of Martin Anderson and Gina Score were tragic events and represent a small rendering of the numerous reports of abuse that have occurred in both public and private military-style boot camps. A U.S. Government Accountability Office report released in October 2007 found thousands of allegations of child abuse at private residential treatment programs—often called "boot camps," "wilderness camps," or "behavior modification facilities"—around the country between 1990 and 2007. The report also examined in detail 10 cases of child abuse and neglect that resulted in death between 1990 and 2004.[14]

Boot Camps as a Policy Conundrum

Evidence-based corrections literature tells us the following about correctional boot camps:

1. We have an adequate body of scientifically rigorous research examining correctional boot camps.
2. The military atmosphere of correctional boot camps does not bring about individual-level changes in thinking, reasoning, or problem solving.
3. An aftercare component to correctional boot camp may reduce recidivism, but we have little information about the type of aftercare that existing programs provide. Thus, we do not know whether individual-level changes result from drug treatment, employment, or something else.
4. To date, we cannot say why the recidivism rates of some correctional boot camp participants are lower than others.
5. If the goal of correctional boot camps is to reduce recidivism, then we have little reason to continue their use.
6. If we have other goals for using boot camps, such as operating as back-end programs or to reduce prison crowding, then we need more research to see whether this is an effective strategy.
7. Research studies associated with cost benefit analysis have shown mixed results.

As you can see, the evidence does not strongly support the success of boot camps in promoting public safety. At the same time, one of the most pervasive problems challenging today's correctional system is its ever-increasing size. For example, by mid-year 2009, there were an estimated 504 sentenced prisoners per 100,000 U.S. residents. Meanwhile, jails report an increase of 2.6 percent new beds, bringing the total rated capacity to 849,544, which is equivalent to the average annual increase per year since 2000.[15] Regarding juveniles, the latest statistics show that more than 100,000 are confined in juvenile detention facilities. This growth in the juvenile and adult offender populations is paralleled by rising confinement costs. Consequently, boot camps and other intermediate sanctions have been viewed as necessary outlets to relieve an overburdened correctional system. Let's look at the conundrum these programs pose for policymakers and correctional officers.

Public Support and Practice

One driving force behind the abundance of boot camps has been their ability to show that military protocol can be infused into a correctional setting. The image of prisoners sitting around watching television, making phone calls, and eating free meals are replaced with images of discipline, esprit de corps, and hard labor. The appeal to the public is that boot camps possess "film-ability"; the typical media portrayal is of "programs that do not coddle prisoners."[16] On another level, boot camps are occasionally seen as an excellent vehicle for rehabilitation, given the restricted target groups and the emphasis on redirecting the individual through education, training, treatment, counseling, and enhancement of self-esteem. It's likely that as boot camps continue to be portrayed as secure environments where offenders are held accountable, public support will remain quite high.

In examining the nexus between public support and practice, we recognize three areas that are consistently cited as the principal goals of correctional boot camps: (1) to promote public safety while reducing prison crowding, (2) to create a less expensive alternative to prison, and (3) to reduce recidivism. State corrections officers value these goals. For example, when asked to rate the importance of boot camp program goals, corrections officials named deterring future crime and rehabilitating offenders as the two main goals (Exhibit 9.1).

As we have discussed, however, boot camp programs developed throughout the country with little regard to evidence-based practices. For example, one program, called CORE (Convicted Offenders Reentry Effort), a boot camp program in Travis County, Texas, claims to have developed the first county-level boot camp in the United States. Responding to the controversy over whether boot camps make a difference in preventing recidivism and getting inmates back on the right track, CORE claims that its "staff, probation officers, and the cadets themselves think the program does make a difference. Travis County's emphasis on the importance of providing a continuity of services for those in the boot camp program will, we hope, ensure that the CORE

EXHIBIT 9.1 Program Goals as Reported by State Corrections Officials[17]

	Not a Goal	Relatively Unimportant	Moderately Important	Important	Very Important	Average Rating*
Reducing crowding	3%	3%	38%	21%	35%	2.8
Reducing cost	0	3	24	31	41	3.1
Punishing offenders	21	14	45	21	0	1.7
Protecting the public	0	3	17	14	66	3.4
Deter future crime	0	0	0	21	79	3.8
Rehabilitating offenders	0	0	3	38	59	3.6
Reducing recidivism	0	0	7	52	41	3.3
Addressing public dissatisfaction	11	11	32	32	14	2.3

* Scale runs from 0 to 4, with 0 = Not a goal and 4 = Very important

program will be successful."[18] Nevertheless, a 1993 evaluation found no significant increases in moral development as a result of involvement in the boot camp program.[19]

When correctional agencies go beyond speculation and actually evaluate the merits of a boot camp program, they tend to conduct the evaluations themselves. The results are not widely circulated, and they tend to be self-serving. Of critical importance is the recognition that evidence-based research plays a key role in examining existing programs and guiding the implementation of future boot camp programs.

Public Safety and Reduced Prison Crowding

Boot camps were initially conceived as intermediate sanctions for offenders who otherwise would be incarcerated in jail or prison. Based on this assumption follows another assumption—that the resulting bed space will mean reduced crowding. In one of her many publications relating to boot camps in Louisiana, Dr. Doris MacKenzie and co-researchers found that offenders who went through the boot camp program, on average, served 11 months less than if they had gone to prison. This saved the prison about 154 beds per year, indicating that the program had potential for impacting the prison-overcrowding situation. As an added benefit, offenders who successfully completed the program reported that they learned valuable skills and that intensive parole was helpful in making the transition back to the community.[20]

However, in contrast to its original goal of reducing the number of prison-bound offenders, some offenders are sent to boot camps as a condition of probation, thereby causing a **net-widening** effect. The concept of net-widening has two dimensions: offender net-widening and systemic net-widening. Offender net-widening suggests that rather than being used as alternative sanctions, boot camps are being used to supplement an existing sanction. Adding the requirement that an offender successfully complete a 90-day boot camp as a condition of probation is contrary to the original intent of using boot camps for offenders who would otherwise have received more severe punishment. Systemic net-widening refers to the increased costs for correctional facilities as well as correctional staff that are required to operate the boot camp. So, while states search for innovative alternatives to address burgeoning prison populations, many offenders fail to successfully complete the boot camp program, only to have their probation revoked and be sent back to prison.

Creating a Less Expensive Alternative to Prison

In 1987, the Elayn Hunt Correctional Center in St. Gabriel, Louisiana, established the IMPACT (Intensive Motivational Program of Alternative Correctional Treatment), which is often referred to as a boot camp program. It consists of a minimum of 180 days in a highly regimented, tightly structured treatment program within a military model, followed by a period of intensive parole supervision. IMPACT was accredited by the American Correctional Association (ACA) in 1994 and was recognized in 1998 as an ACA Best Practice. Findings from a 1988, evaluation sponsored by the National Institute of Justice (NIJ) indicated that inmates who completed IMPACT believed they had learned valuable lessons and skills, and their positive attitudes grew during the time they were in the program. Moreover, cost savings per boot camp inmate were significant ($13,784) compared with the cost of longer-term incarceration, even though these savings were somewhat offset by higher costs for the community supervision phase ($5,956), thus netting a total of $7,828 saved for each offender who completed the program instead of going to regular prison.[21]

Several other studies, however, show that boot camps do not save money. For example, in 1996, the NIJ awarded a competitive grant to the National Council on Crime and Delinquency (NCCD) to conduct a national multisite impact evaluation of public and private boot camp programs. Regarding averted cost savings, researchers noted that because these programs were too small to capture a sufficient "market share" of the prison or jail population, they did not have an impact on population growth and the associated operating and construction costs. Furthermore, the study suggested that boot camps tend to be more staff and program service intensive than traditional correctional facilities. Consequently, unless a larger pool of incarcerated offenders is made eligible for these programs, they cannot function as a viable means for controlling prison crowding or reducing the costs of the correctional system.[22]

Reducing Recidivism

Of all the studies of boot camps, only one, in New York, found slightly lower recidivism rates for boot-camp graduates. In that study, researchers compared the return-to-prison rates of boot camp graduates with other inmates, finding that the graduates did as well as (or in some situations better than) parolees who did not participate or complete the program. However, the New York Shock Incarceration program included numerous components (e.g., aftercare and higher levels of staff training) that are not found in other boot camp prisons.[23]

It is not clear why empirical studies have overwhelmingly found no differences in recidivism between boot camp offenders and others, but some have speculated that short-term confinement in boot camps may not allow time for building participants back up after they have been broken down. Researchers have proposed that reducing recidivism requires "bridging services" for offenders when they return to the community.[24]

Should boot camps be abolished because they do not reduce recidivism? Although research has questioned the effectiveness of boot camps as a deterrent, evidence also suggests that as an alternative sanction, boot camps score at least as well as incarceration. Moreover, most offenders leave boot camps no worse off than when they were admitted. The addition of new programs may prove to be beneficial, especially in the juvenile justice system, where job training, education, and treatment protocols for younger, more impressionable offenders may have a better chance of influencing recidivism. Whether this occurs remains to be seen, but evidence thus far suggests that boot camps will not have much impact on recidivism. Given their popularity with the media, politicians, and correctional officials, however, the poor record of boot camp programs in reducing recidivism may not be so important. As noted by researcher Dr. Brent Benda, "boot camps might be labeled 'Teflon programs' because they seemingly are resistant to damaging evidence—empirical criticism simply does not stick."[25]

Overview and History of Supervising Jail Offenders in the Community

Jails are adult detention facilities that confine persons awaiting trial, sentencing, or transfer to state prison; they also confine those who are serving a sentence of one year or less. Jails also temporarily hold persons in a wide variety of other categories, including juveniles pending transfer to juvenile authorities, inmates housed contractually for federal or military authorities, and readmitted probation, parole, and bail-bond violators. With more than 12 million inmates released annually, jails have the most frequent contact with individuals being processed through the criminal justice system.[26]

In an additional role, jails are increasingly supervising offenders outside the jail facility. Exhibit 9.2 provides data collected by the Bureau of Justice Statistics regarding jail inmates from 2007, 2008, and at mid-year 2009.[27] Note that of the 837,833 total persons under jail authority in 2009, 8.38 percent (70,213) were supervised outside a jail facility. The largest number of persons in community-based programs under jail authority includes those involved with community service programs.

Typically, we think of community service as a program that uses offender labor to perform services throughout the community—for example, building playground equipment, cleaning up trash, or planting greenery at public parks. In such programs, low-risk, nonviolent offenders housed in minimum-security facilities (e.g., a jail annex) are selected to go out into the community and perform services under the supervision of jail staff. Local citizens generally support such cleanup-type programs, and they have been shown to reduce crime-related problems at the areas serviced. For example, since 1994, the Sheriff's Office in Bristol City, Virginia, has operated a jail-based clean-up program. The community has reacted very positively, and individuals often buy sodas and pizza for the clean-up crew. Moreover, fewer crime-related problems have been reported on the streets serviced by the jail residents. According to the sheriff, citizens have come to accept the jail residents and appreciate their work. Several neighboring Virginia counties have since adopted similar programs.

Other forms of community service allow offenders under jail authority to volunteer in the community in exchange for jail time. For example, in Dane County, Wisconsin, inmates perform community service while completing their sentences. As of February 1, 2009, Wisconsin's Huber law allows inmates who qualify to exchange 24 hours of community service for a day off their sentence.[28] Another program (the Work in Lieu of Jail Program) in Washington County, Oregon, allows offenders who are not lodged in

EXHIBIT 9.2
Persons Under Jail Supervision, by Confinement Status and Type of Program, Mid-year 2007–2009

Confinement status and type of program	Number of persons under jail supervision		
	2007	2008	2009
Total	848,419	858,407	837,833
Held in jail	780,174	785,556	767,620
Supervised outside a jail facility	68,245	72,852	70,213
Weekender programs	10,473	12,325	11,212
Electronic monitoring	13,121	13,539	11,834
Home detention	512	498	738
Day reporting	6,163	5,758	6,492
Community service	15,327	18,475	17,738
Other pretrial supervision	11,148	12,452	12,439
Other work programs	7,369	5,808	5,912
Treatment programs	2,276	2,259	2,082
Other	1,857	1,739	1,766

ALTERNATIVES TO INCARCERATION: AN EVIDENCE-BASED RESEARCH REVIEW

The purpose of this report is to concisely review the available scientific literature related to several correctional programs that are currently being used as alternatives to incarceration, with special attention to alternatives to jail incarceration. Read the report and then answer the following question.

What do you conclude about the way evidence is being used to determine the worth of correctional programs?

Visit CBC Online 9.1 at www.mhhe.com/bayens1e

the jail to work off their sentences eight hours each Saturday and Sunday at community projects. They clear undergrowth and brush; paint and make minor repairs to schools, park buildings and granges; and clear and repair damage to local cemeteries.[29] In CBC Online 9.1, we provide a link to a 2004 report by Justin W. Patchin, PhD, University of Wisconsin—Eau Claire, and Gary N. Keveles, PhD, University of Wisconsin—Superior, in which the authors discuss how policymakers have sought to identify appropriate alternatives that are better able to address the crime problem in a more cost-effective manner than jail incarceration.

Work Release

Many jails operate **work release** programs that afford offenders the opportunity to maintain employment even while they are confined. The jail resident is allowed to leave the facility for a specified number of hours to work and is required to return to jail at the end of the work day. Usually work release programs are limited to offenders who have been sentenced to a year or less in jail.

Work release not only has substantial potential as a reintegration program, but it also makes immediate and significant economic sense. Offenders who are working are taxpayers, meaning that they pay all applicable federal, state, and local taxes. They can also pay fines, court costs, and fees associated with their court case. Many jail work release programs require offenders to send a certain percentage of their pay to their dependents as support. Likewise, offenders on work release are required to reimburse the jail for room and board; thus, the jail is recouping part of the cost of incarceration. Depending on the size of the program, the amount collected via these reimbursement payments can be substantial. Also, work release inmates can be housed in minimum security quarters, which are far less expensive than the typical jail living unit.

Another potentially important benefit of work release is the financial safety net it provides for residents who have served a jail sentence. Typically, when offenders have been confined for a substantial length of time, they leave with very little money. The period immediately following release is a very uncertain one if the offender has no job, no savings, and no place to live. Jail work release programs provide offenders with a means of providing for themselves.

While many benefits can be derived from work release programs, these jail programs are not without their critics. Some say offender work programs take jobs from local workers. The argument is that companies needing workers will have no incentive to pay more than the minimum wage, especially in metropolitan communities where larger jails operate big work release programs and inmate workers are abundant. Others oppose work release because of the opportunity for jail residents to abscond. Still others argue that such programs do little to reduce the criminal behaviors of offenders. In the next section, we explore the effectiveness of work release as a means of reducing recidivism, followed then by a discussion of jail reentry programs.

Correctional work release centers and other evidence-based reentry initiatives can diminish corrections costs and improve public safety.

Effectiveness of Work Release

A 2004 report titled "Alternatives to Incarceration: An Evidence-Based Research Review" noted that "only one comprehensive study was identified that scientifically evaluated the effectiveness of work release."[30] That study, entitled "Work Release: Recidivism and Corrections Costs in Washington State," published by the National Institute of Justice in December 1996, found that a state work release program did achieve its most important goals: preparing inmates for final release and facilitating their adjustment to the community. The report further noted the following:[31]

- While in the program, most work release participants maintained employment, paid room and board, reconnected with their communities, and remained drug-free.
- The Washington work release program "has benefited enormously from a particularly close relationship with private industry."
- In terms of recidivism, only 22 percent of work release participants were rearrested within one year, compared to 30 percent of offenders who served their sentence as nonparticipants of the work release program.

An Eye Toward Reentry: Jail Supervision in the Community as a Rehabilitative Ideal

Although supervision is common for those leaving prison (i.e., parole), community supervision is often not considered for those leaving jail. This is because most jail detainees serve very short sentences for minor offenses. But increasingly, local communities and correctional officials are recognizing that nearly all offenders in jail are admitted with problems of substance abuse, mental health, or serious medical conditions including viral hepatitis, tuberculosis, and HIV. A survey conducted by the Bureau of Justice Statistics, for example, found that more than two-thirds of jail residents had substance-abuse problems.[32] What is more, 64 percent of jail residents reported having a recent history or symptoms of a mental health problem.[33] Finally, offenders with substance abuse, mental health, and other types of complex problems more often than not lack proper support systems (e.g., transportation, money). For these reasons, several local jurisdictions have created "reentry" programs.

According to the Community Oriented Correctional Health Services[34]—a nonprofit organization funded by the Robert Wood Johnson Foundation—the best reentry programs follow this pattern:

- Reentry planning starts on the inside and continues on release.
- The reentry plan is comprehensive yet realistic and feasible.
- The same reentry planner or case manager works with the detainee on the inside and on the outside and serves as an advocate for successful reentry.
- The program includes concrete linkages to comprehensive community resources that include health care, behavioral health care, and social services.
- The program includes connections to long-term health care and social support programs as needed.
- If a person is reincarcerated, reentry planning continues in an effort to better prepare the detainee for his or her next release.

Let's take a look at characteristics of effective reentry programs.

Reentry and Intake

Ideally, reentry services begin when an offender is booked into jail. Most jails conduct an evaluation of incoming jail inmates to determine if they pose a security risk and to assign living quarters. This **classification** process also includes an assessment of the offender's needs for substance abuse treatment, education, and other services. This assessment forms the foundation for programs offered to the offender while he or she is confined. It also shapes reentry planning and potential services to be provided in the community once the offender is released.

Reentry Programming and Strategies

The type of reentry planning prescribed for a jail resident depends on both risk and needs factors. Risk factors include such items as criminal history, severity of the crime committed, and behavior while confined. Needs relate to medical conditions and medication needs, psychological and emotional stability, educational background, and job history. A third factor, length of stay, is also considered in the reentry planning process. That is, reentry plans for jail residents who are detained for only a few days differ significantly for residents sentenced for several months or a year. Since the average length of stay is typically only a few weeks, reentry planning may be brief and consist of a simple review of risk and needs with recommendations for referrals to agencies in the community. For jail inmates who are expected to be confined for a longer period, comprehensive reentry plans can be developed as well as logistical plans.

Besides assessing offender characteristics, a reentry plan also considers appropriate intervention services. Typically, these include programs conducted by jail staff, community volunteers, or outside service providers that offer **in-reach programs** at the jail. Also considered are programs that provide continuity of care once the offender is released from jail. The availability of services in each of these areas is often determined by size of the jail. Small jails, for example, normally provide only limited programming, such as drug and alcohol awareness education and adult basic education.

Career Profile

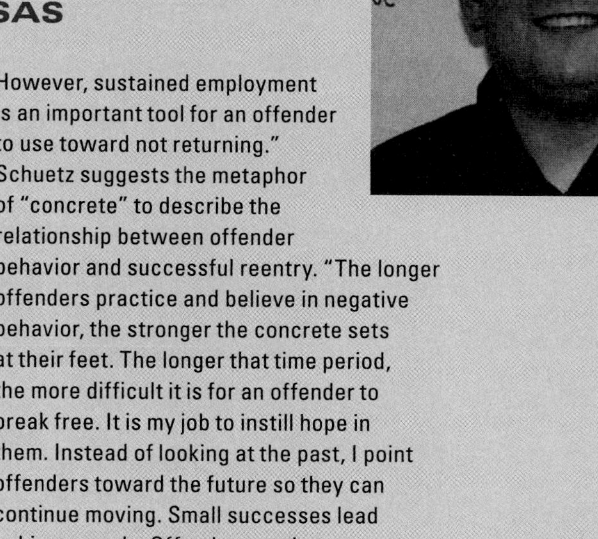

JOSEPH SCHUETZ: REENTRY OFFICER, SHAWNEE COUNTY, KANSAS

Joseph Schuetz holds the position of Work Program Coordinator and Reentry Officer at the Shawnee County Adult Detention Facility in Topeka, Kansas. He holds Baccalaureate degrees in Criminal Justice and Sociology from Washburn University. Officer Schuetz supervises jail inmates participating in the trustee program (those working inside the 500-bed jail facility), lawn maintenance program (those working with public works), and work release program (those working in the local community). He also supervises offenders participating in the reentry program.

Says Officer Schuetz, "Substance abuse, mental health issues, and family supports are all-important keys to helping the offender return from incarceration. However, sustained employment is an important tool for an offender to use toward not returning." Schuetz suggests the metaphor of "concrete" to describe the relationship between offender behavior and successful reentry. "The longer offenders practice and believe in negative behavior, the stronger the concrete sets at their feet. The longer that time period, the more difficult it is for an offender to break free. It is my job to instill hope in them. Instead of looking at the past, I point offenders toward the future so they can continue moving. Small successes lead to bigger goals. Offenders are keen on picking up small signals. If they believe in themselves, they can do almost anything."

Large jails, however, are more likely to provide in-depth programs and services. Exhibit 9.3 provides a list of programs offered at the 400-bed jail facility in Boulder County, Colorado. Note that this jail provides a multitude of programs including therapeutic counseling in anger management, communication skills, coping, assertiveness, domestic violence, and parenting skills. Health education is provided by the Boulder County Health Department on a weekly basis at no cost to the jail. Residents can also participate in adult basic education, GED preparation and testing, and college-level correspondence courses. An addiction recovery center offers evidence-based outpatient treatment services in the following areas:

- Inpatient Detoxification (Detox) Program: Provides safe detoxification from alcohol and/or drugs 24 hours a day, seven days a week. Provides referrals for HIV testing, family counseling, psychiatric assessment, and medical care.
- Intensive Teen Outpatient Program (ITOP): Provides drug and alcohol treatment to teenagers aged 14–17 years who are involved in the juvenile justice and social service systems and who are at risk for out-of-home placement.
- Impaired Driver Program: Provides drug and alcohol treatment services and promotes responsible behavior and better decision-making for individuals under court order for driving while impaired or intoxicated.
- Outpatient Services: Provides nonresidential drug and alcohol treatment and replaces substance abuse behavior with effective coping skills, life management skills, and alternatives to substance abuse.
- Specialized Women's Services (SWS) Program: Provides specialized drug and alcohol treatment services to pregnant and parenting women. Services include individual and group counseling and therapy, case management, testing and monitoring for drug and alcohol use, and psychiatric services.

The Boulder County, Colorado, jail partners with drug treatment centers in the community to improve inmates' health, increase opportunities for employment, and foster better family relationships. Do you think policymakers should support evidence-based jail-based interventions that are aimed at reducing recidivism, substance abuse, and homelessness?

Reentry Plans

When an offender's risks and needs are assessed and then gauged against available intervention resources, the process provides the basis for an individually tailored reentry plan. But like assessment instruments, reentry plans come in all shapes and sizes. Some plans are basic, only addressing the offender's need for housing, employment, and

EXHIBIT 9.3 Jail Programs Offered by the Boulder County Jail[35]

- Counseling Programs
  - Alcoholics Anonymous
  - Narcotics Anonymous
- Education Programs
  - Literacy
  - English as a Second Language (ESL)
  - GED Preparation & Testing
  - Life Skills Classes
  - Jail Education Training
  - Multiple Offender Program
  - BoulderReads!
  - Narcotics Anonymous
- Health Programs
  - AIDS Education
- Library
  - Library Services
  - Law Library
- Living Assistance
  - Focus: Transitional Program
- Jail to Community
- Recreation
  - Active Recreation
  - Passive Recreation
- Religious programs
  - Shekinah
  - Vine Life
  - Sunday Services
- Safehouse
- Substance Abuse Programs
  - Alcoholics Anonymous
  - Phoenix Project
- Yoga and Meditation
  - Prison Dharma

social service. The Rikers Island Discharge Enhancement (RIDE) assessment form, for example, is a one-page screening for individuals being transferred from court to the city jail at Rikers Island, New York. The document identifies housing, employment, education, health care, and other service needs. The housing section of the screening includes questions about what individuals' housing situations were immediately before arrest, whether they have ever been homeless, and whether they would like assistance with housing on release. Discharge planners use the screening, along with further assessments, to form a plan for an individual's transition from jail to the community.[36]

Other reentry plans are more elaborate and include information on medical treatment and diagnosis, with follow-up appointments, scheduled sessions with community counseling programs, and of course liaison information for required community corrections programs. The adult Transition Services Unit (TSU) of the Multnomah County, Oregon, Department of Community Justice uses a two-page transitional plan and referral form that contains sections for medical and mental health appointments and referrals. TSU also works with incarcerated offenders to provide reentry planning up to 120 days prior to their release. This process is facilitated by an in-custody interview, known as a "Reach In." Potential risks are identified during Reach In, allowing for the development of appropriate supervision plans and services, which are in place by the time the offender is released.

Exhibit 9.4 provides an abbreviated list of six intervention "tracks" that jails can use for various types of people in their custody. Track one jail residents receive a minimum level of reentry services, while those in track six receive the most comprehensive reentry planning. These tracks are described in detail in a publication titled "The Jail Administrator's Toolkit for Reentry,"[37] which also provides principles and guidelines to assist practitioners in preparing residents for transition from jail to the community.

EXHIBIT 9.4 Six Tracks for Reentry of Jail Residents

REENTRY TRACKS		SERVICES
Track One Low needs and/or very short stay	⇨	General resource information
Track Two Medium needs and/or longer stay	⇨	Reentry plan and general resource information
Track Three High needs and/or longer stay	⇨	Appointment for services, reentry plan, and general resource information
Track Four High risk and needs and/or longer stay	⇨	Coordination and collaboration of services back to the community, appointment for services, reentry plan, and general resource information
Track Five High needs	⇨	Extended care placement
Track Six	⇨	Reentry programs, coordination and collaboration of services back to the community, appointment for services, reentry plan, and general resource information

Programming and Treatment Models in Community-Based Jail Supervision

Treatment efforts that begin while offenders are confined will have little impact after release without follow-up in the community. Therefore, jails must broker services with community-based organizations to provide continuity of care. Examples of community-based interventions include support networks in areas such as job training, substance abuse treatment, and postrelease supervision, as applicable.

In addition to identifying aftercare services for jail offenders, staff must periodically evaluate progress, update treatment models and programming needs, and measure outcomes. Thus, jail staff must collaborate with community service providers to gather data and determine whether the programming being delivered is achieving its stated objectives. This also means that every program that is delivered to jail offenders (in jail and the community) must have clearly defined outcomes.

Job Training

Research has shown that ex-offenders have a high risk of unemployment and that an association exists between adult offender unemployment and recidivism.[38] Studies also show that low levels of personal, educational, vocational, and financial achievement—in particular, an unstable employment record—are among the major predictors of continued criminal conduct.[39] Compelling evidence thus supports the position that unemployment contributes to recidivism or the failure of offenders to successfully transition to the community.

Local and state public officials have responded to concerns regarding recidivism by passing legislation and policy reforms requiring employment training and job placement for offenders when they are released. Consequently, numerous local jails have allocated staff and support services to employment preparation and placement and to collaborating with community resource organizations.

Job Retention

According to a survey conducted by the Office of Correctional Job Training and Placement (OCJTP), job retention is most likely when jobs match offenders' skills and interests, when offenders have an enhanced level of social and problem-solving skills, and when offenders have realistic work expectations.[40] Of course, offenders face tremendous challenges finding and maintaining legitimate job opportunities because of low levels of education, limited work experience and vocational skills, poor attitudes, and a general reluctance of employers to hire people with convictions. These challenges are further compounded by arrest and incarceration periods, during which offenders disconnect from social contacts that could lead to legal employment on release.[41]

Case Management

The OCJTP developed a survey consisting of 23 closed-ended questions on several employment and retention-related topics. The survey was administered to 512 correctional practitioners and examined what they believed to be the most critical job-retention factors, retention obstacles, and job loss indicators. Seventy-seven percent of respondents indicated that case management is very important for offender job reten-

EXHIBIT 9.5
Ready4Work—Prisoner Reentry Initiative

Funded by the U.S. Departments of Labor and Justice and the Annie E. Casey and Ford Foundations, Ready4Work provides reentry services to almost 5,000 returning prisoners in 17 sites around the country. Services consist of employment-readiness training, job placement, and intensive case management, including referrals for housing, health care, drug treatment, and other programs. Ready4Work also incorporates a unique mentoring component, the theory being that mentors may help ease ex-prisoners' reentry by providing both emotional and practical support with navigating everyday barriers, such as finding a place to live, getting a driver's license, or figuring out how to commute to work. A summary report indicates that 60 percent of the participants obtained a job, and 60 percent of those who did were employed for three months. Outcomes from the initiative have been impressive, including recidivism rates 34 to 50 percent below national averages.[43]

tion; 13 percent termed it somewhat important. Moreover, case managers name the following as the most common job-retention obstacles for offenders:

- Substance abuse (cited by 68 percent of respondents in the OCJTP survey)
- Limited transportation (63 percent)
- Limited knowledge of workplace culture (34 percent)
- Limited support meaningful to the offender (29 percent)[42]

With these issues in mind, well-established offender employment organizations such as Ready4Work (Exhibit 9.5) include case management in their programs. Further, intensive case-management models include creating professional relationships with offenders and encouraging one-on-one personal attention by the case manager.

Substance Abuse Treatment

In our nation's jails, more than 66 percent of jail residents have substance abuse problems, and 50 percent of all convicted jail residents were under the influence of drugs or alcohol at the time of their offense. Drug abuse among residents does not vary significantly by race or gender, although it does vary by age, with nearly a third of offenders age 34 or younger having used drugs at the time of their offense. Only a small portion (6 percent) of inmates age 55 or older had used drugs when they committed their offense.[44]

Because a history of using alcohol and drugs is common to so many people in jails, it is important that addiction issues be addressed. Failing to capitalize on this opportunity minimizes the potential success of reintegration. In CBC Online 9.2 Dr. James A. Inciardi, PhD, Center for Drug and Alcohol Studies at the University of Delaware, notes that research suggests that for criminal offenders with long histories of substance abuse, the "therapeutic community" is likely the most viable treatment approach. Unfortunately, according to the U.S. Department of Justice, only 43 percent of jails provide any form of substance/alcohol abuse treatment (68 percent of those were referred only to self-help groups such as Alcoholics Anonymous (AA), Narcotics Anonymous (NA), or peer counseling).[45]

In Richmond, Virginia, a more comprehensive jail-based program, called BELIEF, helps residents with substance abuse problems and assists them in altering their negative social behavior, including addiction. A primary goal is to build a solid foundation for jail residents to successfully return to the community. The BELIEF program partners with several community-based agencies that focus on substance abuse and employment training, and these agencies provide services in jail and accept referrals upon release.

9.2

CBC Online

NIDA (NATIONAL INSTITUTE ON DRUG ABUSE)

Supported by a grant from the National Institute on Drug Abuse, this PowerPoint presentation titled, "Corrections-Based Treatment for Drug-Involved Offenders" by Dr. James A. Inciardi, Director of the Center for Drug and Alcohol Studies at the University of Delaware, provides information about therapeutic communities and suggests them as the most appropriate form of drug abuse treatment in correctional settings. Watch the PowerPoint presentation and then answer the following question.

Based on the information in the presentation, do you think offenders should be allowed to reside in a total treatment environment (i.e., a therapeutic community) isolated from the rest of the population?

Visit CBC Online 9.2 at www.mhhe.com/bayens1e

Using the 12-step recovery principles and a behavior modification model, a rehabilitation counselor and a substance abuse counselor work with each participant to address substance abuse issues and harmful behaviors. While confined, participants also take part in apprenticeship programs, vocational training, and on-the-job training provided by a local nonprofit organization that focuses on community economic development and job training.

BELIEF develops transition plans for all participants, with a focus on safe and sober housing, including recovery houses, substance abuse treatment, NA and AA meeting sites, and employment.[46]

Treatment Modalities

We have reported here on a number of treatment programs that address the needs of offenders transitioning from jail to the community. In particular, however, two evidence-based practices have shown promise. First, jail-based substance abuse treatment programs have been found to reduce jail costs and recidivism rates. An evaluation of the Hillsborough County Jail program in Tampa, Florida, for example, showed that in a one-year follow-up program, completers had fewer arrests and spent less time in jail than others who had not completed the treatment.[47] In another study in Polk, Woodbury, and Scott Counties in Iowa, clients were tracked by consortium staff for two follow-up interviews that occur approximately six and 12 months after admission to the jail-based substance abuse treatment program. The study found that the average daily cost for a client in the program was $30.19 compared to $64.02, which is the daily rate to house an inmate in a state prison facility in Iowa. Moreover, the majority of the jail-based treatment clients who were interviewed tended to maintain abstinence, did not get arrested, and obtained full-time employment.[48]

In general, jail-based substance abuse programs like the one in Tampa involve activities to develop cognitive, behavioral, social, vocational, and other skills that residents can use to overcome substance abuse and its related problems. Treatment involves helping residents consider thinking errors that lead to substance abuse and criminal behavior. In short, offenders are taught how to better understand the connections among thought processes, behavior, and consequences.

Another intervention that seems to work for substance abuse offenders are therapeutic communities (TCs), which are intensive, long-term, self-help, highly structured residential treatment modalities for chronic, hardcore drug users. The TC model has been shown to be effective in addressing the complex issues that determine chronic substance abuse. Offenders gradually learn to take responsibility for their actions and discard the negative patterns of thinking, feeling, and behaving that contributed to their drug use. This rehabilitative approach, therefore, requires multidimensional influences and training over an extended period of living in a 24-hour residential setting. In Washington County, Virginia, for example, a 1993 study conducted at the Adult Detention Center showed that jail residents who did not go through the Jail Substance Abuse Program (JSAP) were three times more likely to be reincarcerated within a 12-month period than inmates who completed the JSAP 30-day program and initiated aftercare, which saved the county thousands of dollars due solely to its impact on reduced jail terms.[49]

In another evidence-based evaluation, the Amity/Pima County Jail Program, a national demonstration program funded by the Bureau of Justice Assistance at the Pima County Adult Detention Facility in Tucson, Arizona, showed excellent results in lowering recidivism to drugs and crime. Offenders involved in drug treatment show marked improvements in knowledge of the treatment curriculum, in abilities to use drug-coping skills, and in psychological functioning. Particular improvement was noted in identifying personal high-risk situations, using coping skills for cravings, and identifying methods for disputing irrational beliefs related to drug use. Findings also indicated that even relatively short-term interventions (six to eight weeks) can provide inmates with important coping skills to manage high-risk situations and can increase their knowledge regarding the recovery process, health-related consequences of drug abuse, and relapse-prevention principles.[50]

Policy Implications

Over the past two decades, increases in jail populations across the country have mirrored that of state prisons. And as in prisons, much of the growth in jail population has been attributed to recidivism (i.e., both arrests for new crimes and revocations for technical violations of community-based sanctions). Local jails are better positioned than state prisons to provide a normative environment that facilitates the transition process. Shorter lengths of stay and the community location of most jail facilities translate into less time away from family, treatment providers, employers, and other social supports. The proximity of the jail to the home community also allows community-based providers to begin interventions with individuals prior to release, improving the chances that they will continue to receive care after release.

In recent years, evidence-based practices have increasingly revealed that interventions for offenders under jail authority can be successful when strategies address both the risks and needs of the offender. This is especially true of jail populations that receive treatment and support both before and after release. But should jails take on this additional role of treatment provider and broker of community services as part of its mission? After all, aren't jails simply short-term, temporary detention facilities where neither punishment nor treatment is a principal goal? Is it not the prevailing philosophy that the population leaves no worse off than when they entered? Perhaps, but advocating change in the functional role of local jails is based on a recognition that traditional methods of warehousing offenders have failed to accomplish any constructive purpose other than the perpetuation of some very expensive jail buildings. While policies that call for increased in-house rehabilitation programs, community services, and reentry do focus on the offender, the ultimate concern is for the next potential crime victim.

Across the country, policymakers are redefining the statutory provisions of jails to better reflect the multipurpose role of local detention. Consider the definitions of a jail in the states of Ohio and Nebraska, which are noted in Exhibit 9.6. While the statutory language does include the word "jail," the definitions also include workhouse, community residential facility, halfway house, and so on. States like Ohio and Nebraska that define jail more broadly are changing the traditional model of local detention.

Jails that emphasize treatment are likely to benefit from earmarked funds to develop diversion, treatment, and reentry programs. For example, the Second Chance Act of 2007: Community Safety through Recidivism Prevention[51] authorized $300 million in grant programs to facilitate successful reentry in the following ways:

- $110 million for adult and juvenile offender state and local reentry demonstration programs
- $40 million for grant projects to provide job training, mentoring, and transitional services
- $20 million for reentry courts
- $130 million in funding for substance abuse treatment, education and training, and mentoring

In the context of this initiative, reentry is envisioned as an evidence-based process that begins with incarceration and ends with successful community reintegration, defined by lack of recidivism. This process includes the delivery of a variety of evidence-based program services in both a pre- and post-release setting designed to ensure that the transition from prison or jail to the community is safe and successful.[52]

As a concluding thought about reentry, we note that if local jails are to successfully provide interventions for residents returning to the community, policymakers must understand the continuing burden that laws place on criminal offenders seeking a fresh start. Most states, for example, have enacted laws disenfranchising convicted felons and ex-felons. Additionally, other more basic barriers (e.g., loss of driver's license and restrictions that make offenders ineligible for certain types of jobs) hamper successful reentry. Consequently, community programs for offenders under jail authority may be as much about advocacy as about educating offenders. We leave this chapter by providing a synopsis of the Dutchess County, New York, Jail Transition Program, which has been recognized for significant recidivism reductions and contributing to the enhancement of public safety.

EXHIBIT 9.6
Statutory Definition of Jail

Ohio Revised Code: "Jail" means a jail, workhouse, minimum security jail, or other residential facility used for the confinement of alleged or convicted offenders that is operated by a political subdivision or a combination of political subdivisions of this state.[53]

Nebraska Revised Statute: Jail shall be defined to include a jail, house of correction, community residential center, work release center, halfway house, or other place of confinement of a person committed by any lawful authority to any suitable and appropriate residence, facility, center, or institution designated as a jail facility by the county.[54]

A SUCCESSFUL PROGRAM: THE DUTCHESS COUNTY, NEW YORK, JAIL TRANSITION PROGRAM

In Poughkeepsie, New York, the Dutchess County Jail (DCJ) is typically overcrowded, housing between 320 and 400 offenders in a facility with a rated capacity of 286. Annual admission rates are nearly 3,500, the average length of stay is over 30 days, and over 90 percent of those admitted transition directly from the jail to the local community. These realities, coupled with local recidivism rates ranging from 48 percent to 62 percent, led officials to initiate a jail transition program. This approach was based on "what works" practices that clarify offender needs, challenge old systems of belief, and link with external stakeholders to facilitate successful offender transition from the jail.

The DCJ Transition Program (DCJTP) is operated within a 50-bed, direct supervision residential facility. The DCJTP goals statement was developed to complement the departmental mission relative to long-term public safety with these goals:

1. Enhance public safety through the management of criminogenic risk factors, while considering the necessity for other types of interventions such as substance and/or alcohol treatment.
2. Facilitate the successful transition of offenders to our community.
3. Reduce recidivism.

The DCJTP Five-Week Plan

The DCJTP begins with the formulation of a plan for transition. During a five-week period, program officers and clinical staff build professional associations with each inmate to engage him or her in a process of self-disclosure and personal skill building. This dialogue is designed to examine and address known criminogenic risk factors. Correctional program officers manage all such efforts and form in-house case plans designed to assist in the development of a detailed plan for transition. Daily program outcomes are measured and reported formally at weekly, multidisciplinary case meetings.

The DCJTP Correctional Environment

The program takes place within a social learning context; therefore, pro-social correctional officers are trained in and practice the tenets of direct supervision. Correctional program officers and/or clinicians administer the Level of Service Inventory—Revised Edition/Adult Substance Use Survey (LSI-R/ASUS) protocols with each participant to determine criminogenic profiles, assist in classification decisions, and assign group placement. Professional clinicians and correctional officers also co-facilitate a variety of additional training and therapy that explores the application of life skills and associated difficulties.

Follow-up is a unique component of DCJTP. All participants agree to be tracked by correctional program officers for one year postincarceration. This component of the strategy was developed in response to the reality that 80 percent of all recidivism takes place within six months of release. Using the individual's transition plan as a basis for discussion, then, correctional program officers make contact with all program graduates and/or their families at least once per month for the year following release from jail. These contacts offer correctional staff the opportunity to check in and see if the plan for transition is being carried out or if further assistance is needed. The contacts are further intended to enhance pro-social family and personal networks that are likely to act as informal social controls. DCJTP staff believe that the combination of simple, direct supervision management coupled with the application of "what works" methodologies and community/family networking accounts for the successes of this strategy. However, without the effort and personal buy-in of the professionals who are associated with the DCJTP, these successes would be mitigated significantly. The professional relationships they develop with offenders are important to the program's success.

Outcomes of the Dutchess County Jail Transition Program Strategy

In 2008, researchers reported that for the three-year period beginning November of 1998 (initiation of DCJTP) through November of 2001, the DCJTP showed a 33 percent reduction in recidivism for participants. A follow-up study was conducted in 2006. Given the results of previous studies and the fact that DCJTP houses high-risk offenders, it was expected that these rates would be consistent with that of the general jail population. Indeed, the combined rate of recidivism for all inmates prior to their entry to the program was calculated at approximately 60 percent. However, after completing the DCJTP, this same group of offenders recidivated at a rate of only 25 percent. Fuller longitudinal analyses of these data are necessary to draw statistically significant conclusions; however, these analyses coupled with prior studies indicate that this approach shows great promise in its ability to affect offender behavior postincarceration.[55]

Summary

Correctional boot camps were intended to serve as a cost-effective alternative to incarceration and are typically limited to young, nonviolent, first time offenders. Boot camps vary in cost, size, and effectiveness. Boot camps for adjudicated juveniles tend to differ from boot camps for adult offenders. In adult camps greater emphasis is placed on hard labor, while camps for juveniles are more apt to provide therapeutic components.

Evidence-based research has shown that boot camps are for the most part ineffective in meeting program goals unless the program combines the military regimented practice of teaching self-discipline and teamwork with educational, rehabilitative, and aftercare programs. A few research studies have shown that boot camp participants learned better problem-solving and coping skills as a result of their boot camp experience. Only a few programs that offer aftercare supervision in the community have shown success in reducing recidivism.

Conceptually, boot camps are intermediate sanctions for offenders who otherwise would be incarcerated in jail or prison. Based on this notion, boot camps should reduce prison crowding, provide a less expensive alternative to prison, and lower recidivism. The policy implications of research are that correctional boot camps are a viable alternative to incarceration only in the sense that some individuals may benefit by not being submerged into prison culture. One concern from a policy standpoint is that boot camps may widen the net of correctional sanctions available for punishing offenders.

When jail-based residents clean up public places and perform community service, they make their communities more attractive, safer places to live, and the experience provides an opportunity for offenders to make amends to the community. Work-release programs allow offenders to work in the communities where they will return when released from jail. Besides the obvious benefits to the individual, wages earned from working can be applied to court costs, fines and fees associated with confinement.

The basic elements of a jail reentry program include assessing risk and need, determining availability of treatment services, and developing the reentry plan. Risk factors include such items as criminal history, severity of the crime committed, and behavior while confined. Offender needs relate to medical treatment and medication, psychological and emotional status, educational background, and job history. Treatment services include jail-based programs conducted by jail staff and community volunteers, service providers who offer in-reach programs at the jail, and community programs that provide a continuity of care once the offender is released from jail. Some reentry plans are basic, only addressing the offender's need for housing, employment, and social service. Others are more elaborate and include medical treatment and diagnosis with follow-up appointments, scheduled sessions with community programs for counseling, and of course liaison with required community corrections programs.

Two-thirds of jail residents have substance abuse problems, and half of all convicted jail resident inmates were under the influence of drugs or alcohol at the time of their offense. Jail-based substance abuse treatments initiate offenders to treatment that is considered crucial to the reentry process. Therapeutic communities (TCs), which are intensive and highly structured long-term residential treatment modalities for chronic, hardcore drug users, have been shown to be an effective method to address the complex issues that determine chronic substance abuse.

Key Terms

classification, p. 264
in-reach programs, p. 264
net-widening, p. 259
recidivism, p. 255
shock incarceration, p. 255
three-strikes laws, p. 255
work release, p. 262

Questions for Review

1. Trace the historical roots of correctional boot camps.
2. Describe the theoretical forces that greatly influenced first-, second-, and third-generation boot camps.
3. When program evaluations were conducted at correctional boot camps, what did they show?

4. Do evaluations and evidence-based studies show that correctional boot camps work as an alternative to confinement? Explain your answer.
5. What is work release? What concerns might the public have about jail residents being released to work in the community? What has evidence shown about such concerns?
6. What planning elements should be included in a jail reentry program?
7. Summarize the two evidence-based treatment modalities that have shown to reduce jail costs and recidivism rates.

Question of Policy

Setting Priorities for Reentry

The Center for Innovative Public Policies (CIPP) assembled two national work groups during May and June 2007 in western (Las Vegas, Nevada) and eastern (Orlando, Florida) locations to discuss current and future needs, challenges, and priorities for the nation's jails and to make funding recommendations to the Bureau of Justice Assistance. Composed of 45 sheriffs and jail administrators from jurisdictions throughout the country, the participants identified reentry initiatives as important, but only at a tertiary level compared to primary priorities (e.g., medical care and mental health services) and secondary priorities (e.g., workforce issues). They made the following recommendations regarding reentry:[56]

- Assure that federal funding is not targeted exclusively to state corrections, either by providing funding eligibility for local jails, or requiring state departments of corrections to work with jails and pass-through funding.
- Develop programs to make more productive use of "dead time" in jail to help prevent recidivism.
- Assist jails with developing transition plans (especially aftercare for persons with mental illness).
- Encourage jails to identify local resources and forge partnerships with other community services.

Given the low priority status of reentry by the sheriffs and jail administrators, how likely are reentry programs to be introduced on the local level without federal funding? Of the recommendations regarding reentry noted above, which stand out as most important?

What Would You Do?

Recently, the county built an annex on the existing jail site to accommodate a boot camp program for young offenders. The boot camp was created through an agreement between the county and the state to divert convicted offenders between the ages of 16 and 18 from being sent to an already overcrowded prison system. The jail receives $45 per diem from the state for each boot camp participant, and it monitors offenders for six months after release from the program. As the jail division manager responsible for population control, you discover from admission data that judges in your district have started to sentence first-time offenders to the county boot camp as a condition of probation. In fact, of the 38 new participants in the boot camp program in the past few months, one-third were committed to the boot camp by local judges after being convicted of minor property crimes. Consequently, in this period, the county lost $29,000 in revenue from state compensation that normally is used to offset operating costs for the boot camp program.

1 What problems could surface if this trend continues?

2 As the jail division manager, how would you handle the situation?

Endnotes

1. Doris L. MacKenzie and Eugene E. Hebert, *Correctional Boot Camps: A Tough Intermediate Sanction* (Washington, DC: National Institute of Justice, February 1996).
2. Gerald T. Flowers, Timothy S. Carr, and R. Barry Ruback, *Special Alternative Incarceration Evaluation* (Atlanta, GA: Georgia Department of Corrections, 1991).
3. Sue Frank, "Oklahoma Camp Stresses Structure and Discipline," *Corrections Today,* vol. 53, no. 6 (October 1991), pp. 102–105.

4. Michael Peters, David Thomas, and Christopher Zamberlan, *Office of Juvenile Justice and Delinquency Prevention Series: Boot Camps for Juvenile Offenders*, NCJ 164258 (September 1997).
5. James J. Stephan, *Bureau of Justice Statistics: Census of State and Federal Correctional Facilities, 1995 Executive Summary*, NCJ 166582 (August 1997).
6. Camille G. Camp and George M. Camp, *The 2000 Corrections Yearbook: Adult Corrections* (Middletown, CT: Criminal Justice Institute, 2001).
7. James J. Stephan, *Bureau of Justice Statistics: Census of State and Federal Correctional Facilities, 2000 Executive Summary*, NCJ 198272 (October 2003).
8. Marilyn D. McShane and Franklin P. Williams, *Encyclopedia of Juvenile Justice* (Thousand Oaks, CA: Sage Publications, 2002).
9. Jerald C. Burns and Gennaro F. Vito, "An Impact Analysis of the Alabama Boot Camp Program," *Federal Probation,* vol. 58, no. 1 (1995), pp. 63–67.
10. Dale Parent, *National Institute of Justice Research for Practice: Correctional Book Camps: Lessons from a Decade of Research*, NCJ 197018 (June 2003).
11. "Teenage Girl Run to Death in SD Boot Camp: Excerpt from Investigative Report Summary," *The Argus Leader,* in *Boot Camp for Kids: Torturing Teens for Fun and Profit* (Alamo, CA: Project NoSpank, August 1999). Retrieved from www.nospank.net.
12. Christian Parenti, "When 'Tough Love' Kills: Murder at Boot Camp for Teenager Offenders," *The Progressive Inc.* (October 2000).
13. Brent Kallestad, "Parents Want Charges in Boot Camp Death," *Associated Press* (February 9, 2006).
14. Gregory Kutz, *Residential Treatment Programs: Concern Regarding Abuse and Death in Certain Programs for Troubled Youth* (U.S. Government Accountability Office Report GAO-08-146T, October 2007).
15. Todd Minton, *Jail Inmates at Midyear 2009—Statistical Tables* (Washington, DC: Bureau of Justice Statistics, NCJ 230122, June 2010).
16. Adam Nossiter, "As Boot Camps for Criminals Multiply, Skepticism Grows," *The New York Times* (December 18, 1993), pp. 37–39.
17. Adapted from Voncile B. Gowdy, "Historical Perspective," in *Correctional Boot Camps: A Tough Intermediate Sanction National Justice Research Report* (February 1996).
18. Joyce Stevens, *The Travis County Boot Camp Program* (U.S. Department of Justice: National Institute of Corrections Library, 1989).
19. Loyal Freeman, "Boot Camps and Inmate Moral Development: No Significant Effect," *Journal of Offender Rehabilitation,* vol. 19, no. 3/4 (1993), pp. 123–127.
20. Doris MacKenzie et al., *An Evaluation of Shock Incarceration in Louisiana*, Final Report to The National Institute of Justice (August 1990).
21. MacKenzie and Hebert, *Correctional Boot Camps.*
22. James Austin et al., *Multi-Site Evaluation of Boot Camp Programs, Final Report*, NCJ 192011 (January 2002).
23. Cherie Clark, David Aziz, and Doris MacKenzie, *Shock Incarceration in New York: Focus on Treatment,* NCJ No. 148410 (Washington DC: National Institute of Justice, U.S. Department of Justice, Office of Justice Programs, 1994).
24. Mark Osler, "Shock Incarceration: An Overview of Existing Programs, *Federal Probation* (March 1991), pp. 34–42.
25. Brent Benda, "Introduction: Boot Camps Revisited: Issues, Problems, Prospects," in Brent Benda and Nathaniel Pallone (eds.), *Rehabilitation Issues, Problems, and Prospects in Boot Camp* (New York: Haworth Press, 2005).
26. Paige Harrison and Allen Beck, *Prison and Jail Inmates at Midyear 2005* (Washington, DC: U.S. Department of Justice, Office of Justice Programs, Bureau of Justice Statistics, 2006).
27. Adapted from Todd Minton and William Sabol, *Jail Inmates at Midyear 2008—Statistical Tables*, Bureau of Justice Statistics, NCJ 22570 (March 2009).

28. *2003 Wisconsin Act 141*, § 973.03(3)(am), Wisconsin Statutes.
29. *Washington County Sheriff's Office: Inmate Work Programs.* Retrieved from www.co.washington.or.us/sheriff/jail/wiloj.htm.
30. Justin Patchin and Gary Keveles, *Alternatives to Incarceration: Evidence-Based Research Review: A Summary of Findings*, Northwest Wisconsin Criminal Justice Management Conference (November 2004).
31. Susan Turner and Joan Petersilia, *Work Release: Recidivism and Corrections Costs in Washington State* (National Institute of Justice: Research in Brief, December 1996).
32. Jennifer C. Karberg and Doris J. James, *Substance Dependence, Abuse, and Treatment of Jail Inmates, 2002* (Bureau of Justice Statistics, NCJ 209588, July 2002).
33. Doris James and Lauren Glaze, *Mental Health Problems of Prison and Jail Inmates* (Bureau of Justice Statistics, NCJ 213600, September 2006).
34. Barry Zack and Katie Kramer, *Linking Reentry Planning to Community-Based Correctional Care* (Oakland, CA: Community Oriented Correctional Health Services, February 2009).
35. *Boulder County Sheriff's Office: Jail Programs*, Boulder, Colorado. Retrieved from www.bouldercounty.org/sheriff/jail/programs.htm.
36. "Reentry Policy Council: Rikers Island Discharge Enhancement," *New York City Department of Corrections* (New York, NY: The Council of State Governments Justice Center). Retrieved from http://tools.reentrypolicy.org/assessments/program/10.
37. Jeff Mellow et al., *The Jail Administrator's Toolkit for Reentry* (Washington, DC: Urban Institute, Justice Policy Center, 2008).
38. Peter Finn, "Job Placement for Offenders in Relation to Recidivism," *Journal of Offender Rehabilitation,* vol. 28, no. 1/2 (1998), pp. 89–106.
39. Don Andrews, "The Psychology of Criminal Conduct and Effective Treatment," in James McGuire (ed.), *What Works: Reducing Reoffending, Guidelines from Research and Practice* (West Sussex, England: John Wiley & Sons Ltd., 1998).
40. Melissa Houston, *Offender Job Retention: A Report from the Office of Correctional Job Training and Placement* (Washington, DC: National Institute of Corrections, July 2001).
41. Bruce Western, Jeffrey Kling, and David Weiman, "The Labor Market Consequences of Incarceration," *Crime and Delinquency,* vol. 47 (2001), pp. 410–427.
42. Melissa Houston, *Offender Job Retention.*
43. Chelsea Farley and Wendy McClanahan, *Ready4Work in Brief: Update on Outcomes; Reentry May Be Critical for States, Cities,* Brief, Issue 6 (Philadelphia, PA: Public/Private Ventures, May 2007).
44. Jennifer Karberg and Doris James, *Drug Use, Testing, and Treatment in Jails* (Washington, DC: Department of Justice, Bureau of Justice Statistics, NCJ 209588, 2005).
45. Doris Wilson, *Drug Use, Testing, and Treatment in Jails* (Washington, DC: Bureau of Justice Statistics, 2002).
46. Amy Solomon et al., *Life After Lockup: Improving Reentry from Jail to the Community* (Washington, DC: The Urban Institute, May 2008).
47. Ray Hughey, "Evaluation of a Jail-Based Substance Abuse Treatment Program," *Federal Probation,* vol. 60, no. 4 (1996), pp. 40[en]44.
48. Suzy Hedden, Kristina Barber, and Stephan Arndt, "Jail Based Substance Abuse Treatment Program: Cost Analysis Study," *Iowa Department of Public Health, Contract No. 5887JT04* (Iowa City, IA: Iowa Consortium for Substance Abuse Research and Evaluation, 2006). Retrieved from http://iconsortium.subst-abuse.uiowa.edu.
49. Center for Substance Abuse Research, "Washington County Explores a Structure for Success," *CESAR Reports* (University of Maryland at College Park, 2(2), 1992).
50. Ron Mullen et al., "Programs That Work: California Program Reduces Recidivism and Saves Tax Dollars," *Corrections Today Inc.* (August 1996). Retrieved from http://findarticles.com/p/articles/mi_hb6399/is_n5_v58/ai_n28673117/?tag=content;col1.
51. *Second Chance Act of 2007,* Pub. L. No. 110-199, 122 Stat. 657 (2008).

52. *Second Chance Act Prisoner Reentry Initiative FY 2009.* Competitive Grant Announcement BJA-2009-2095, U.S. Department of Justice, February 27, 2009.

53. Ohio Rev. Code Ann. § 2929.01(R).

54. Neb. Rev. Stat. 47[en]117.

55. Gary Christensen, *Our System of Corrections: Do Jails Play a Role in Improving Offender Outcomes?* (Washington, DC: National Institute of Corrections, January 2008).

56. Jeanne Stinchcomb and Susan McCampbell, *Jail Leaders Speak: Current and Future Challenges to Jail Operations and Administration: A Summary Report to the Bureau of Justice Assistance* (Naples, FL: Center for Innovative Public Policies, Inc., January 21, 2008).

CHAPTER 10

Residential, Day Reporting, and Drug Courts:

Offenders Living Among Us

OBJECTIVES

1 Trace the evolution of halfway houses in the United States.

2 Describe characteristics of various types of residential community-based programs.

3 Describe cognitive-behavioral therapies found in residential community-based corrections programs.

4 Name program characteristics common to day reporting centers.

5 Compare and contrast the effectiveness of residential community-based programs and day reporting centers giving emphasis to evaluation outcomes.

6 Explain the goals of drug courts and comment about the effectiveness of these alternative sanctions.

OUTLINE

On October 13, 2007, Grammy-winning rap artist Clifford J. Harris Jr. (also known as T.I.) was arrested by federal agents with the Bureau of Alcohol, Tobacco, Firearms, and Explosives. He was charged with felony possession of three unregistered machine guns and two silencers, and possession of firearms by a convicted felon. The arrest was made after Harris tried to purchase the guns from a bodyguard—turned cooperating federal witness—who at the time of the exchange was wearing a wire. Authorities then executed a search warrant of Harris's residence and found several rifles, pistols and boxes of ammunition. Harris, a repeat felony offender, entered into a plea-bargaining agreement with federal prosecutors and was sentenced to one year and one day in the Forrest City federal prison in Arkansas and ordered to pay $100,300 for federal weapons charges. After seven months of confinement in this minimum-custody facility, Harris was released and sent to a halfway house in Atlanta. His attorney described Harris's living conditions as "It's a restriction on your liberty, but it's a way for you to reenter into society and not be confined within a jail-type institution 24 hours a day."[1] Harris was released from the halfway house on March 26, 2010.

Previously, we discussed how work-release and reentry programs have been developed to provide structured correctional services for offenders transitioning from confinement to the community. In this chapter, we turn our attention to residential community centers and day reporting centers. We also consider drug court programs and explore their application to corrections. As you read this chapter consider whether you think these alternative sanctions to incarceration provide an adequate level of community safety as they attempt to rehabilitate offenders.

Residential Community-Based Corrections

Residential community-based corrections programs have become an integral part of the criminal justice system over the years. Many varieties of residential programs exist throughout the country and serve an equally diverse offender population. Sometimes referred to as reentry centers, community corrections centers, pre-release centers, or merely residential centers, the basic premise behind these correctional programs is to reintegrate clients into the community as successful, productive citizens.

Halfway Houses

One type of residential community correctional program is the **halfway house**. Halfway houses are designed to reintegrate persons released from prison or jail back into the community. Offenders are placed in a structured living environment that offers employment counseling, life skills training, substance abuse treatment, and other social services. The length of stay can vary because each person is evaluated on their readiness to return to the community, and their behavior while in the halfway house.

Halfway houses have an extensive history in America. It begins in the early 1800s when the Massachusetts legislature appointed a commission to study problems in the Pennsylvania prison system. The Commission recognized that ex-offenders were unsuccessful in transitioning from highly controlled prison environments back into their home communities because of the lack of available jobs and other resources. Because these offenders experienced problems with social readjustment and could not become legally self-sufficient, many returned to criminal activity. In 1820, the Massachusetts Commission recommended reforms to the prison system that included the establishment of the country's first halfway house facilities.[2]

Some evidence indicates that concurrent with the Commission's recommendation, religious and private volunteer groups began to help the poor with securing shelter and other basic needs, and that these efforts propelled the halfway-house concept. These groups provided ex-offenders with such services as temporary housing, food, clothing, and sometimes assistance in finding employment.[3] In 1845, the Quakers opened a halfway house in New York City, naming it after Isaac T. Hopper, an American abolitionist who is known as the father of the Underground Railroad. When this halfway house was opened, Hooper was active with the Prison Association of New York, working on behalf of men discharged from prison. The following year, a halfway house for women released from institutions opened in Boston.

While the movement toward establishing halfway houses continued into the early 1900s, state parole authorities opposed the concept. The basic objection was that these facilities provided an opportunity for prisoners to associate with each other, which was forbidden by parole regulations.[4] Moreover, there was a great deal of controversy about where halfway houses fit into the organizational structure of the correctional system. This was especially true of privately funded halfway houses, which were self-contained and isolated from correctional authorities. For these reasons, the development of halfway houses languished for much of the next half century.

It was not until 1965 that the halfway house movement was revived with the passage of the Federal Prisoner Rehabilitation Act (H.R. 6964), which established home furloughs, work-release programs, and community treatment centers. When he signed the bill into law, then President Lyndon Johnson commented:

> For the first time, the Attorney General of the United States has the authority to apply a full range of rehabilitative techniques to adult offenders. H.R. 6964, which I have today signed into law, allows him to (1) commit or transfer adult prisoners to residential community treatment centers (more popularly known as "halfway houses"), (2) grant prisoners leave for emergency purposes or to contact prospective employers, and (3) permit them to go into a neighboring community to work at paid employment or to obtain training. One or more of these techniques have been used successfully by the Federal Bureau of Prisons in dealing with youthful offenders, by several States and European nations, and by the military services. We expect similar success with adult Federal prisoners. This measure has been described as one of the most important pieces of legislation affecting the Federal prison system in the past 30 years. It is a beginning in the search for improving a correctional system that today sees one out of three parolees revert to crime. I have also signed today H.R. 2263, the Correctional Rehabilitation Study Act of 1965. If we are to find new and better ways to help parolees return to society and to a good and useful life for themselves and their families, we must have highly trained specialists at our disposal. The studies to be financed under this bill will tell us the kind of specialists we need, the number we must have, and what training we must provide for them.[5]

In 1964, the International Halfway House Association was created, which strongly influenced the growth of residential community corrections programs throughout the

THE INTERNATIONAL COMMUNITY CORRECTIONS ASSOCIATION

The International Community Corrections Association (ICCA) is a private, nonprofit, membership organization located in Washington, DC, that acts as the voice for residential and other community corrections programs.

After reviewing the various links found on ICCA's Web site, click on the "Public Policy" tab and under the heading of "Policy Position," read the document titled, "ICCA Policy Position on Community Responsibility and Engagement."

List five steps that ICCA proposes to facilitate community acceptance of responsibility and community engagement in the justice process.

Visit CBC Online 10.1 at www.mhhe.com/bayens1e

country. The association changed its name in 1989 to the International Association of Residential and Community Alternatives and later to its present name, the International Community Corrections Association (ICCA) (See CBC Online 10.1). The mission of ICCA is to promote legislation, establish regulatory policies, and support agencies that operate halfway houses and other community-based programs. In 2010, ICCA represented 1,500 adult and juvenile community-based programs and supported the following 2010 legislative agenda:

- Improve the capacity and utilization of community corrections through statutes and regulations that maximize the use of community corrections resources and minimize costly jail and prison use for nonviolent offenders. Pursue new legislation, specifically the *Community Corrections Improvement Act of 2010*, to increase community capacity.
- Secure adequate appropriations to support the programs of the Second Chance Act and the development of regulations supportive of its intent to reduce recidivism and increase public safety through jobs, housing, mental health and substance-abuse treatment, and strengthening of families for prisoners reentering society.
- Promote adoption of the President's Budget for 2011 calling for a $527.5 million increase that includes $100 million for Second Chance Act grants and increased funding to the Federal Bureau of Prisons for "confining offenders in . . . contract or community-based facilities."
- Support additional bills that strengthen pre-release transitional programming for inmates, service coordination upon release, and postrelease housing, employment, and education services.
- Improve the effectiveness of community corrections through statutes, regulations, accreditation, and standards that require delivery of appropriate services to achieve specific performance outcomes related to reduced recidivism.[6]

Much of the momentum for developing halfway houses comes from changes in correctional theory. For example, the work of Robert Martinson in the 1970s served as the opening for policymakers to abandon existing ideas of rehabilitation. Martinson's research was a review of 231 studies on correctional interventions in which he concluded with regard to then current policy, that "nothing works" to reduce recidivism.

SOMETIMES I'D RATHER BE IN JAIL

Neil Miller of Boston served 10 years for a rape he didn't commit. When Miller was released, his lawyer believed he would have an easier time with freedom because "he's so rational, so thoughtful." His lawyer was so wrong. As you watch this eight-minute video segment, consider the following questions.

What problems did Neil Miller experience when transitioning back into the community?

Should falsely convicted persons receive special compensation from the state?

Visit CBC Online 10.2 at www.mhhe.com/bayens1e

As a result, paradigm shifts occurred in correctional policy and practices. One such shift was to place less emphasis on rehabilitation and more emphasis on crime control. As a result, punitive sentencing practices that called for **reintegration** as a sentencing goal changed the focus from "fixing the offender" to a more complex recognition of shared responsibility between offender and community.[7]

Reintegration emphasizes the concepts of normality, community involvement, and resocialization for offenders transitioning from institutions to the community. A factor central to successful community reintegration is employment. An offender's ability to secure and maintain employment of course alleviates financial pressures, but it also provides various benefits to the community (e.g., allowing the offender to pay taxes, child support, and restitution). However, ex-offenders face a range of barriers to employment as discussed in chapter 8, and these in turn are barriers to successful reintegration. Specific employment-related barriers include lack of work experience, employer attitudes/restrictions, legal restrictions, reporting requirements, and drug and alcohol treatment and/or rehabilitation.[8] In a large-scale study involving 596 employers, 234 employment service providers, 176 corrective service workers, and 175 offenders, researchers found that apart from people with an intellectual or psychiatric disability, those with a criminal background were rated as being the least likely of disadvantaged groups to obtain and maintain employment. In addition to their criminal records, the study found, offenders were unable to gain employment because they were seen as less likely than the general workforce to exhibit the skills and characteristics relevant to employability.[9] In CBC Online 10.2, we provide a video presentation of the stigmas that offenders face when a criminal history significantly encumbers opportunities for attaining employment, traveling, voting, and entering and maintaining personal relationships.

While many of today's residential community-based programs maintain the original halfway-house philosophy of serving parolees who are transitioning back into the community, their role in the corrections system is now much broader. The scope of services extends to both offenders who are released from prison into residential community-based corrections facilities as a condition of parole or administrative release—often as a response to the crisis of prison overcrowding—and offenders from pretrial placements. This second group consists of offenders who are sentenced directly to residential community corrections facilities. In a third group are those offenders who are placed in a facility as a condition of probation or in response to a probation violation.

Additionally, these community-based programs now serve almost all categories of offenders with special needs:

- The developmentally disabled
- The mentally ill
- The elderly
- The physically handicapped
- Those with substance abuse problems
- Juveniles

Residential community-based corrections facilities are an attractive punitive option for the courts because they provide a restrictive setting with a high level of supervision, and they require offenders to comply with programming requirements. Staff provide around-the-clock monitoring of the movements, behavior, and actions of residents and they immediately report infractions. Residents are required to maintain employment, perform court-ordered community service, and submit to regular drug testing. Residential programs also typically employ some form of behavior modification that requires residents to earn privileges such as weekend passes or later curfew times.

The public is more receptive to residential corrections programs than to nonresidential programs because the sanction is closest to the total institutional setting. Moreover, existing evidence indicates that residential programs can operate at a cost below jail or prison. For example, a comparison study in Michigan showed the daily, per-person cost of prison to be $64.80 versus $35 for residential programs.[10] Other states report similar savings. In Exhibit 10.1, we provide a comparison of costs associated with prisons, halfway houses, and community-based correctional facilities in Ohio. Note that the cost of prison is nearly seven times that of halfway houses and nearly four times more expensive than other community-based correctional facilities. Although the per-day cost of prison is not that much higher than that of halfway houses, and lower than that of other community-based correctional facilities, the length of stay is what drives up the cost of prisons.

Residents working in the community can also pay restitution and complete community service work. The Ohio Department of Rehabilitation and Corrections notes that the 7,108 offenders in halfway houses in FY2009 earned $5,419,555; paid $12,676 in restitution; $59,688 in court costs; and $193,021 in child support. These offenders also completed 63,415 community service hours. These outcomes could not have been possible had the residents been incarcerated in prison.[11]

EXHIBIT 10.1 Cost Analysis: Residential Community Corrections and Prisons in Ohio

Type of Facility	Number	Total Offenders	State Funded Cost per Day	Average Length of Stay	State Funded Cost Per Offender
Prison	32	49,908	$68.60	704 days	$38,325
Halfway houses	23	7,108	$60.96	92 days	$5,608
Other CBC facilities	18	5,749	$80.10	124 days	$9,933

Source: 2009 Ohio Department of Rehabilitation and Correction Funded Community Corrections in Ohio Fact Sheet.

These cost savings, however, are not typical of all residential community-based correctional programs because there are so many types of programs. Obviously, programs with more intense supervision are more costly than programs with less intensive supervision. Programs with successful treatment programs are personnel intensive, highly structured, and very costly. Also, while some programs require offenders to pay program fees to help defray costs, others do not. Last, publicly run residential programs cost less per offender per day than private programs. In the next section we more closely examine several types of residential programs, giving particular attention to program characteristics. We end this section with an evaluation of program results.

Program Characteristics

Most residential correctional programs can be placed in two categories. The first category is referred to as the "transitional control" program, and its purpose is to closely monitor an offender's adjustment to community supervision. These facilities typically house small groups, and though they do not possess the characteristics of high-security correctional facilities—steel doors, uniformed officers, and barbed-wire fences—surveillance, risk management, and formal controls are top priorities. Program rules tend to be strict but are viewed as necessary to impart structure to the living situation and ensure order. Residents are placed in these facilities either as a result of a court order or the administrative action of a public agency such as a state department of corrections. Residents stay for varying lengths of time, but the basic aim for all is to provide support and ensure resident accountability.

This type of residential community-based corrections program does not serve special offender groups, such as sex offenders or offenders with mental health issues. The primary function of the staff is to provide a safe environment, intervene when they encounter problem behavior, and support residents in the reintegration process. Staff members typically include correctional case managers, counselors, food services workers, and clerical personnel. Many programs use volunteers from churches as mentors. Volunteers may provide life-skills classes and programs aimed at growth and at teaching the skills necessary to promote personal change. They may also help residents connect with businesses and nonprofit groups where they might find employment. Funding is provided through community- and faith-based organizations such as the Salvation Army and Volunteers of America, private and charitable donations, grants from foundations, and appropriations through local or state governments.

The Alternative Incarceration Centers (AIC) operated by Community Partners in Action, a nonprofit company in Hartford, Connecticut, exemplify this type of program. AIC provides service to pretrial defendants, offenders sentenced to them in lieu of incarceration, individuals assigned to them as a condition of early release from a correctional facility, and individuals requiring supervision as an alternative to reincarceration following failure on community supervision. The program offers the following benefits:

- Saves prison or jail beds for more serious offenders.
- Monitors individuals referred by the criminal justice system to community supervision.
- Restricts the offenders' freedom to protect public safety and, at the same time, establishes positive ties between the community and the offender.
- Offers residents self-help groups, informational workshops, community service options, and staff assistance in effecting positive change.[12]

Another good example is the Residential Reentry Center in Baltimore, Maryland. This reintegration program is managed by Volunteers of America Chesapeake, a faith-based, nonprofit corporation that provides services for offenders throughout Maryland, Virginia, and the District of Columbia, under contract with the Federal Bureau of Prisons. The program's goal is to assist male and female offenders in making a successful transition from prison to the community through pre-release and work-release programs. While in the program, each resident is required to be employed and must participate in the available support services, including educational programming, GED preparation, job search and placement services, substance abuse counseling, and referral to follow-up community services.[13]

The second category of residential community-based programs includes a strong treatment component to identify dysfunctional patterns of offender behavior. Such behavior-management therapies seek to help individuals understand the basis for their negative behavior and correct their faulty perceptions of themselves, their environment, or both. The goal is to reduce recidivism and assist offenders so they will desist from committing offenses. The concept of **desistance** is key to community reintegration and refers to the act of decreasing in the frequency, variety, or seriousness of offending.

The most widely recognized behavior-management approach for offenders is referred to as **cognitive-behavioral therapy (CBT)**, which is based on the idea that offenders think differently than nonoffenders, either because of a lack of moral reasoning or through dysfunctional information processing. The fundamental goal is to teach offenders cognitive skills and values that are essential for pro-social competence. Studies have shown that improved reasoning and pro-social thinking skills are related to reduced recidivism.[14]

Six cognitive-behavioral programs are widely used in the criminal justice system:

1. Aggression Replacement Training (ART) is a multimodal intervention originally designed to reduce anger and violence among adolescents involved with juvenile

Cognitive-behavioral programs are used in community-based corrections to treat offenders for substance abuse, anger, and their overall criminal attitudes. What weight would you give to an offender's risk level versus their treatment needs when developing a supervision plan?

justice systems. More recently, the model has been adapted for use in adult correctional settings. It has three components:

- Social-skills training (the behavioral component) teaches interpersonal skills to deal with anger-provoking events.
- Anger-control training (the affective component) seeks to teach at-risk youth skills to reduce their impulses to behave with anger by increasing their self-control.
- Moral reasoning (the cognitive component) is a set of procedures designed to raise the young person's sense of fairness, justice, and concern with the needs and rights of others.

2. Criminal Conduct and Substance Abuse Treatment: Strategies for Self-Improvement and Change (SSC) is a long-term, intensive, cognitive-behavioral-oriented treatment program for adult substance-abusing offenders. The treatment curriculum consists of 12 treatment modules that are structured around three phases of treatment:
   - Phase I: Challenge to Change. This phase involves the client in a reflective-contemplative process. A series of lessons is used to build a working relationship with the client and to help the client develop motivation to change.
   - Phase II: Commitment to Change. This phase involves strengthening basic skills for change and helping the client learn key methods for changing thought and behavior that contribute to substance abuse and criminal conduct.
   - Phase III: Ownership of Change. This phase, the stabilization and maintenance phase, is designed to reinforce and strengthen the client's commitment to established changes.
3. Moral Reconation Therapy (MRT) is a cognitive-behavioral treatment program for offenders, juveniles, substance abusers, and others with "resistant personalities." Although initially designed for criminal-justice-based drug treatment, MRT has since been expanded for use with offenders convicted of driving while intoxicated (DWI), domestic violence, and sex offenses. It includes parenting-skill and job-attitude improvement and addresses general antisocial thinking.

   Nine stages of anticipated growth and recovery are identified in the program:
   - Disloyalty: Typified by self-centered behavior and a willingness to be dishonest and blame and victimize others.
   - Opposition: Includes the same behaviors as "disloyalty," only occurring less often.
   - Uncertainty: Uncertainty about feelings for others; these individuals still make decisions based on their own pain or pleasure.
   - Injury: Destructive behavior still occurs, but recognition of the source of the problem also occurs; some responsibility for behavior is taken, and some decisions may be based on consequences for others.
   - Nonexistence: Feeling of alienation but with a few satisfying relationships; these individuals sway between making decisions based on formal rules and decisions based on pleasure and pain.
   - Danger: Commitment to goals and decisions based primarily on law and societal values; when regression occurs, these individuals experience anguish and loss of self-esteem.

- Emergency: Social considerations are made, but "idealized ethical principles" influence decision making.
- Normal: Relative contentment and the presence of positive goals that are in the process of being fulfilled; decision making based solely on pleasure and pain has been virtually eliminated.
- Grace: Decision making based primarily on ethical principles; only a small percentage of adults reach this stage.

4. Reasoning and Rehabilitation (R&R and R&R2) is based on the theory that offenders suffer from cognitive and social deficits. This program focuses on enhancing self-control, interpersonal problem solving, and pro-social attitudes. Participants are taught to think before acting, consider consequences of actions, and conceptualize alternate patterns of behavior. The program consists of 35 sessions, running from eight to 12 weeks, with six to eight participants. A shorter version of R&R, known as R&R2, is a specialized 15-session edition that targets those over age 18 whose antisocial behavior led them to social services or criminal justice agencies.
5. Relapse Prevention Therapy (RPT) was originally developed to prevent and manage relapse following addiction treatment. Designed to teach individuals how to anticipate and cope with relapse, RPT uses coping-skills training to teach clients self-management and self-control of their thoughts and behavior. This approach views addictive behaviors as acquired habits with biological, psychological, and social determinants and consequences. RPT is based on the principle that relapse is less likely to occur when an individual possesses effective mechanisms for coping with high-risk situations. With such skills, individuals experience increased self-efficacy and, as the length of abstinence from inappropriate behavior increases and effective coping with risk situations multiplies, the likelihood of relapse diminishes.
6. Thinking for a Change (T4C) uses a combination of approaches to increase offenders' awareness of self and others. The program begins by teaching offenders an introspective process for examining their ways of thinking and their feelings, beliefs, and attitudes. This process is reinforced throughout the program. Moreover, social-skills training is provided as an alternative to antisocial behaviors. The program culminates by integrating the skills offenders have learned into steps for problem solving, which becomes the central approach offenders learn for working through difficult situations without engaging in criminal behavior.

Cognitive-behavioral approaches have often been used in residential programs that target substance abuse and its associated problems. The Talbert House, a nonprofit community-based program serving the greater Cincinnati and Northern Kentucky area, is a good example. It was founded in 1965 with the opening of a halfway house, and today it provides multiple services to children, adolescents, and adults. A substance abuse treatment program called ADAPT (Alcohol and Drug Addiction Partnership Treatment) is a 15-month residential and outpatient program that provides assessment, treatment, and reintegration services for drug- and alcohol-addicted adults charged with drug-driven felony offenses. Services include chemical dependency education and treatment, criminality/behavior modification, frequent and random drug testing, vocational/educational services, family counseling, and a variety of supportive services. Another Talbert House program, the Turtle Creek Center, provides assessment, treatment, and transitional services for adult males in a residential halfway house setting. Programming includes community monitoring, cognitive-behavioral groups, substance abuse treatment, and employment services, as well as other specialized treatment services.[15]

A third example is the Probation Residential Center (PRC) operated by Community Programs, Inc (CPI), a private, nonprofit organization located in Waterford, Michigan. The target populations for PRC are nonviolent sentenced felons, nonviolent sentenced misdemeanants, parole violators, and probation violators. The program serves both male and female clients over the age of 17 who have substance abuse problems, and clients normally stay at the center for up to 90 days. The standard program at CPI includes the following:

- Cognitive treatment/behavioral intervention
- Substance abuse testing and treatment
- Adult education classes, plus high school diploma and GED instruction
- Living skills, including parenting and HIV/AIDS classes
- Psychological evaluations
- Rigorous physical training exercises for two hours, three times a week[16]

Program Results

Over the past several decades, residential corrections programs have expanded from the original idea of providing support to offenders transitioning from prison to the community into another type of intermediate punishment. With so many variations of residential corrections programs—for example, some housing only low-risk inmates, others admitting inmates of all risk levels; some offering a full complement of programs and services, others functioning strictly as work-release centers—evaluations can focus on a variety of issues depending on the purpose of the program. For example, in some communities, residential corrections programs exist to relieve overcrowded jails and prisons. In other jurisdictions, the primary intent is to provide a cheaper alternative to incarceration. Still other programs exist so that offenders can make reparations to victims and the community without the isolation of a prison-bound punishment. Notwithstanding these variations, program effectiveness is most commonly based on the extent to which it reduces recidivism. Let's look at the few evaluation studies we have that measure the effectiveness of community-based residential programs at reducing recidivism.

First, note that prior to the 1980s, evaluations of halfway houses provided only anecdotal evidence of the outcomes of these programs. Most studies used no comparison group but, instead, attempted to identify variables associated with successful completion of the program. For example, in 1978, Dr. Edward Latessa and Dr. Harry Allen conducted a national assessment of halfway houses and parole, concluding that halfway houses may be as effective as other parole programs and strategies, and perhaps more cost effective. But they went on to note that "Most, but fortunately not all, of the evaluation materials suffer from a range of methodological weaknesses and research failings, leading to the suggestion of caution in drawing conclusions about effectiveness."[17]

In one of the earliest large-scale studies of recidivism, the Federal Bureau of Prisons focused on federal prisoners released in 1987. The study found that offenders released through a halfway house had a recidivism rate of 31.1 percent, compared to a rate of 51.1 percent for those released directly from prison. The study also noted that offenders released from halfway houses were significantly more likely to find postrelease employment than persons released directly from an institution. Thus, while halfway-house release appears not to reduce recidivism directly, it does appear to reduce recidivism indirectly, by increasing postrelease employment.[18]

The most definitive evaluation of residential corrections programs occurred in 2002, when the Ohio Department of Rehabilitation and Correction (ODRC) sponsored a study of the treatment practices of 15 community-based correctional facilities (CBCF) and 37 halfway houses (HWH). Ohio's CBCFs are minimum-security locked facilities aimed at providing rehabilitative services to offenders. Ohio's HWHs are designed to serve adult offenders released from state prisons, probationers, and offenders sanctioned due to a violation of community supervision. The study also captured recidivism data, including rearrest and reincarceration for 13,221 offenders, 7,366 of whom were placed in either an HWH or CBCF facility. The remaining 5,855 offenders served as parolee comparison cases that were released from prison but not exposed to an HWH or CBCF program.[19] Key findings were that a program's ability to reduce recidivism among participants varied substantially depending on risk level of the offenders. Higher-risk offenders in all categories responded well to more supervision and programming, resulting in reduced recidivism. While programs showed a reduction in recidivism of 8 percent for high-risk offenders, low-risk offenders showed an average increase in recidivism of 4 percent.[20]

A follow-up evaluation was conducted in 2010. Like the 2002 study, data from HWH and CBCF program participants were compared to nonparticipants (parolees and ISP) using multiple measures of recidivism. The sample size was very large, consisting of more than 20,000 offenders. Moreover, researchers interviewed staff at 64 programs across the state of Ohio (20 CBCFs and 44 HWHs). The study found similar results to the previous study—that is, programs clearly produced more favorable results with high-risk offenders, and tended to increase recidivism for low-risk individuals. Recommendations from this study were that programs provide offenders with supervision and treatment levels that are commensurate with their risk levels (see chapter 4) and that those programs targeting low-risk offenders should change policy so as to discontinue this practice.[21]

So, which programs work in reducing the number of reoffenders? Research consistently shows that cognitive-behavioral therapy is associated with significant and clinically meaningful positive changes, particularly when therapy is provided by experienced practitioners. A number of studies have found that participants in cognitive-behavioral programs have recidivism rates that are 10 to 30 percent lower than rates for offenders who did not receive such services.[22] Research has also demonstrated that adult cognitive-behavioral treatment programs can be particularly cost-effective relative to other therapy models. Studies have estimated economic returns of $2.54 to $11.48 for every program dollar invested in cognitive-behavioral treatment, while punishment-oriented interventions have yielded returns of only 50 to 75 cents for every program dollar spent.[23] Perhaps the most-cited study of the effects of cognitive-behavioral therapy on the recidivism of adult and juvenile offenders is a meta-analysis of 58 experimental and quasi-experimental studies, which confirmed prior positive findings on the impact of cognitive-behavioral therapy, even among high-risk offenders. Moreover, inclusion of anger-control and interpersonal problem-solving components in the treatment program are associated with larger effects.[24]

Studies have also shown that programs containing a quality assurance component (i.e., better implementation and more fidelity to the treatment protocol) are most likely to see successful outcomes. For example, an evaluation of Washington State's research-based programs for juveniles found that courts judged to be competently delivering Aggression Replacement Training (ART) had 24 percent reductions in 18-month felony recidivism, which was considered significant, and a positive benefit-to-cost ratio of $11.66.[25] Given this information, further inquiry designed to identify the combination(s)

Career Profile

LORA HAWKINS COLE: DEPUTY COMMISSIONER OF COMMUNITY CORRECTIONS, STATE OF MISSISSIPPI

Lora Hawkins Cole is a graduate of Delta State University, Cleveland, Mississippi, with a bachelor of science degree in criminal justice and a master of education degree in guidance and counseling.

Cole currently holds the position of Deputy Commissioner of Community Corrections with the Mississippi Department of Corrections. She is a graduate of Leadership Mississippi; she was profiled in *Corrections Today*, the international magazine of the American Correctional Association (ACA), as one of six successful professional women in corrections; she was selected by the L.C.Q. Lamar Society as an emerging leader of the South; and she has been honored by the Mississippi Association of Professionals in Corrections (MAPC) with the President's Award and the Criminal Justice Professional of the Year Award.

Cole began her career in corrections at the Mississippi State Penitentiary in Parchman, Mississippi, in 1974 as a correctional officer/camp counselor. She was subsequently promoted through the ranks to the positions of case manager, case manager supervisor, programs coordinator, and superintendent of security. She was promoted to deputy warden in 1986 and relocated to Jackson, Mississippi, to serve at the Central Mississippi Correctional Facility (CMCF). While assigned to CMCF, she was named associate superintendent and later warden. She was appointed to her current executive position in the central office in October 2002. In this position, she is responsible for the administration of 17 community work centers; four restitution centers; Interstate Compact, which is the agreement between states to supervise offenders who are sentenced in one state but have requested to move to another state, usually for family or work reasons: the Intensive Supervision/Electronic Monitoring Program; Training; and the Division of Field Services, which includes probation and parole. Under Cole's leadership, each of the agency's 20 residential facilities as well as its Division of Field Services became and continue to be ACA accredited, all holding steady with scores of 100 percent.

Explaining the nature of the community-based residential facilities under her supervision, Cole says, "Within the corrections profession, community work centers (CWCs) are most commonly referred to as community residential facilities.

of elements in residential programs that most effectively reduces recidivism should include both the type of program(s) offered and the quality of program delivery.

In the next section we discuss day reporting centers. As you read, consider the similarities between day centers and residential programs. One might argue that the only difference between the two is that offenders participating in day reporting programs are allowed to live at home. If this is correct, why would jurisdictions prefer that some offenders be required to stay in a residential center?

Day Reporting

A **day reporting center (DRC)** is a nonresidential, community-based corrections program, typically for nonviolent offenders. The goals of a DRC include rehabilitating the offender through intensive programming, providing punishment in a cost-effective way, and ensuring community safety. These goals are met through a comprehensive

The purposes served by these centers are as diverse and unique as the missions designated by the various state and federal jurisdictions. Some commonalities of such centers include the following: residents live as a group in a housing facility that's located squarely within the local community, the residents are convicted felons who have been screened and classified as a minimum threat to the tranquility of the community, the residents work in community settings at regular paid employment or at unpaid job assignments for governmental or nonprofit agencies, residents are required to perform community service hours, employed residents may be required to pay a portion of the cost of their daily subsistence, residents may have regularly scheduled unsupervised furloughs, placement is generally a step between incarceration in a secure correctional institution and release to live as independent citizens.

"The Mississippi Department of Corrections (MDOC) has 17 CWCs, each of which has an average daily population of 100 inmates. The vast majority, 95 percent, were convicted of nonviolent crimes. They are assigned to work for state, county, and municipal governmental agencies at no salary. The most obvious benefit of the CWC is the annual savings of millions of labor dollars for the local taxpayers (approximately $21 million for FY2010). However, there are other benefits, such as the partnerships developed between the MDOC and other governmental agencies with the increased sharing of resources and improved communication. The program also creates opportunities for the public to observe inmates and develop more positive perceptions of them and their ability and propensity to work hard, contribute to society, and successfully reintegrate with civilian life. Moreover, as noted, the cost to the agency of placements at the CWCs is considerably less than that of incarceration in institutions.

"There are, of course, benefits to residents as well. Many benefit by developing or enhancing their individual work ethic. Some experience self-pride for a job well done for the first time ever. The gradual development of personal responsibility and the proper response to being allowed increased freedom is also of great benefit to the residents. And finally, CWCs provide an avenue for the residents to be housed in closer proximity to their families, making regular contact with their support system through visitation more likely to occur."

intake process, individualized treatment plan, and structured supervision. Programming involves in-house treatment and referral services, including education, vocational training, substance abuse treatment, and psychological services.

Day reporting centers originated in Great Britain in the early 1970s as a means of reducing prison overcrowding. In the United States, the first DRC was opened in 1986 by the Hampden County, Massachusetts, Sheriff Department. By 1995, 114 centers were established in 22 states,[26] and 1,283 persons were participating in day reporting while under jail supervision.[27] By 2008, 5,758 persons were participating in day reporting while under jail supervision.[28] These centers require offenders who are on pretrial release, probation, or parole to appear at a specific location on a regular, scheduled basis. Unlike residential community-based corrections centers, which require residency, DRCs serve offenders who return to their residences at the end of the day. DRC services may be provided by public or private treatment agencies or correctional agency staff.

Most DRCs have been established as a means of reducing rising jail and prison populations and the huge costs associated with those rising populations. However,

10.3

CBC Online

GEORGIA DEPARTMENT OF CORRECTIONS VIDEO LIBRARY: DAY REPORTING CENTERS

The Georgia Day Reporting Centers provide intensive supervision and behavioral interventions as an alternative to incarceration for probationers and parolees who are failing to adhere to standard supervision conditions. This eight-minute video is an overview of the day reporting program operated by the Georgia Department of Corrections. As you view the video, consider the following questions.

What is the completion rate of the day reporting center?

What is the purpose of an administrative hearing?

Does family participation play a role in the success of the residents?

Visit CBC Online 10.3 at www.mhhe.com/bayens1e

like halfway houses, DRCs can assist offenders' transition back into the community. For example, in September 2010, Santa Barbara County, California, opened a DRC to provide a community-based alternative to incarceration for ex-offenders who were arrested in the county and then released back into the region after spending time in custody.[29] In CBC Online 10.3, we provide an example of a DRC in Atlanta that sets as its goal the restitution, restoration, and rehabilitation of offenders.

Nationally, there has been a growing movement to expand DRCs as alternatives to incarceration, especially in tight economic times. Although research regarding the effectiveness of DRCs in reducing recidivism has found mixed results, a growing body of literature does support this claim.[30] One of the earliest studies to show positive results involved a program evaluation conducted by Edward Byrnes and Russ Van

Day reporting centers (DRCs) acclimate the nonviolent offender to the daily routine of reporting to a supervised environment within the community, where he or she is expected to adhere to a schedule and engage in productive activities. In addition to reducing jail crowding, what other benefits can DRCs provide to the criminal justice system?

Vleet of the Social Research Institute at the University of Utah.[31] Their study focused on the day reporting center in Salt Lake City, Utah, which has been operating since 1994. It serves high-risk/high-need offenders who abuse substances and have had technical violations or committed new offenses while on probation or parole. The goals of the day reporting center are to reduce offender recidivism and improve the ability of offenders to conform to community norms. Program activities are designed to improve coping skills, prevent relapse, improve job and employment skills, and promote a smooth reentry to the community. Specific program components include:

- Educational opportunities
- Development of employable skills
- Psycho-educational programming
- Substance abuse treatment
- Intensive mental health therapy
- Increased contact between the offender and staff

The DRC is open six days a week with flexible hours to accommodate both offender and programming needs. It is located near public transportation and other service agencies. Services are rendered on an individual basis to meet the needs of each offender, increase the potential for success, and reduce recidivism. Some offenders are regularly or randomly tested for drugs. All offenders receive more services than they would under normal probation or parole, and the referring agent is kept informed of the offender's progress or problems. Although operations have changed only slightly since the inception of the program, additional treatment groups dealing with domestic violence and sexual orientation have been added.

A program evaluation focused on 124 (41.7 percent) probationers and 173 (58.3 percent) parolees who attended the Salt Lake City DRC. Arrest records were examined to determine the number of criminal charges for a period of one year before and after the offenders received DRC services. These data were then used to calculate the recidivism rate within one year and to make pre- and post-DRC comparisons. The results showed a recidivism rate (new charge or technical violation) of 44.8 percent, with 55.2 percent of subjects remaining free of any charges for one year after receiving DRC services. When recidivism was examined in terms of technical versus criminal charges, a different picture developed. Of the subjects who had post-DRC charges, 34 (26.6 percent) had charges that were technical violations, leaving 99 with new criminal charges. Therefore, of the original 297 subjects, only 99 recidivated on criminal charges, resulting in a recidivism rate of 33.3 percent. Thus, two-thirds of all the subjects remained free of criminal charges for one year subsequent to receiving DRC services.

In addition to the possibility of reducing recidivism, a number of studies have found DRCs to be, at the very least, a less expensive alternative to incarceration and an effective method of relieving jail overcrowding.[32] Consider the Bucks County, Pennsylvania, DRC, which requires each offender who participates in the day reporting program while remaining at their home residence to be charged a $10/day fee. So, there is no cost associated with housing and the offender pays a fee for services. In comparison, the average cost to confine a person in the Bucks County Jail is $85 per day.[33] In 2000, the Sedgwick County Sheriff's Office in Wichita, Kansas, added almost 600 beds to its jail at a cost of $37.5 million. But by 2005, the county again needed to expand the jail. Rather than simply add more beds, the county opened a day reporting center and other alternatives for the judicial system, which were designed to divert people from the jail.[34]

EXHIBIT 10.2 Common Characteristics of Day Reporting Centers

1. Accepts primarily male offenders who (1) are on probation and have violated the conditions of probation, (2) abuse alcohol and other drugs, and (3) pose a low risk to the community.
2. Aims primarily to provide treatment and other needed services to offenders and to reduce jail or prison crowding in the community.

Respondents' Ratings of DRC Goals

	Not at all Important	Important	Somewhat Important	Very Important	Not Applicable	Average Rating
Access to treatment or services	0	0	6	48	0	3.9
Reduce jail/prison crowding	0	4	10	39	0	3.7
Build political support	3	5	16	27	2	3.2
Provide surveillance/ protect society	1	7	24	1	21	3.2
Punish offenders	12	23	10	2	7	1.8

3. Is open five days (about 54 hours) per week, and the program duration is about five months.
4. Serves fewer than 100 offenders at any one time.
5. Maintains a strict level of surveillance and requires frequent contact with offenders.
6. Directs successful offenders through distinct phases with increasingly less stringent requirements.
7. Tests offenders for drug use at least five times each month during the most intensive phase.
8. Provides numerous services on-site to address each client's employment, education and counseling needs.

Program Characteristics

Day reporting programs vary in terms of the type of offenders they serve and amount of time an offender spends in the programs. Some primarily function as staging areas from which offenders are sent out in work crews to perform manual labor in the community: grounds maintenance, building repair, and so on. Others chiefly offer educational opportunities. In many jurisdictions, their primary mission is to provide outpatient alcohol and drug abuse treatment of various intensities. Although their aims are diverse, however, all DRCs have two common elements:[35]

- A strong supervision orientation that requires DRC participants to regularly report to the center
- A complement of services (e.g., job placement, drug abuse education, individual counseling)

To collect more specific information on program characteristics, in the mid-1990s the National Institute of Justice conducted interviews and surveyed programs

Types and Locations of Services Offered by DRC

	Percentage of DRCs that Provide Service	Location of Service		
		At DRC	Elsewhere	Both
Job-seeking skills	98%	79%	13%	8%
Substance abuse education	96	69	17	14
Group counseling	96	80	12	8
Job placement services	93	62	34	4
Education	93	55	31	14
Drug treatment	92	31	54	15
Life skills training	91	92	6	2
Individual counseling	89	72	17	11
Transitional housing	63	13	81	6
Recreation and leisure	60	74	16	10

9. Requires offenders to perform community service.
10. Employs one line-staff member for about every seven offenders and has a relatively low staff turnover rate.
11. Costs approximately $20 per day per offender.

Average Daily Costs Per Offender

Average Daily Cost per Offender	Number of DRCs	Percentage of Reporting DRCs.
Less than $20	13	39%
$20–$39	11	33
$40 or more	9	27

Source: Robert Barnoski, *Outcome Evaluation of Washington State's Research-based Programs for Juvenile Offenders* (Olympia, WA: Washington State Institute for Public Policy, January 2004).

throughout the country. Exhibit 10.2 provides data of 11 items that characterize how respondents rated program goals, what services were offered, and what they cost per day. In Item 2, the goal that received the highest rating from respondents is to provide offenders with access to treatment or services, with reduction of jail and prison crowding rated second. With regard to services offered (Item 8), most are delivered in-house; the services least likely to be delivered in-house are drug treatment and transitional housing. Finally, Item 11 shows the average cost per day per offender was $35.04.

Day Reporting and Drug Treatment

Drug trafficking and drug abuse in the United States affect nearly all aspects of our lives. The economic cost alone is immense, estimated at nearly $215 billion.[36] The damage caused by drug abuse and addiction is reflected in an overburdened justice system. The most recent annual data from the Federal Bureau of Investigation (FBI) show that 12.2 percent of more than 14 million arrests in 2008 were for drug violations, the most common arrest crime category.[37] As a result of this widespread problem and the need for substance abuse intervention, many jurisdictions have established day reporting centers that offer substance abuse treatment as the core component of the program. Many of these DRCs have a unique relationship with drug courts and collaborate to specifically address the treatment needs of the growing number of substance abuse offenders. Let's take a look at the drug court movement in the United States and how several day reporting programs have partnered with the courts to provide drug treatment.

Drug Courts

The first **drug court** was established in Dade County (Miami), Florida, in 1989, with the goal of reducing substance abuse and criminal behavior while also freeing the court and corrections systems to handle other cases. Since then, the number of drug courts has grown each year, and such courts now exist in all 50 states (Exhibit 10.3). As of June 2009, there were 2,361 drug court programs operating in the United States.[38] While communities have shaped their drug court programs to fit local circumstances, the general purpose is to divert nonviolent, substance abusing offenders from prison and jail into treatment.

EXHIBIT 10.3 Drug Court Locations in the United States, July 2009

Source: National Institute of Justice, www.ojp.usdoj.gov/nij/topics/courts/drug-courts/map-of-drug-courts.htm, accessed 20 May 2011.

Drug courts rely on the collaboration of key players from multiple agencies: the judge and court personnel; prosecution and defense attorneys; probation and other community-based corrections agencies; and providers of treatment services. Moreover, drug courts are defined by their adherence to the 10 key components identified by the National Association of Drug Court Professionals:[39]

1. Drug courts integrate alcohol and other drug treatment services with justice system case processing.
2. Using a nonadversarial approach, prosecution and defense counsel promote public safety while protecting participants' due process rights.
3. Eligible participants are identified early and promptly placed in the drug court program.
4. Drug courts provide access to a continuum of alcohol, drug, and other related treatment and rehabilitation services.
5. Abstinence is monitored by frequent alcohol and other drug testing.
6. A coordinated strategy governs drug court responses to participants' compliance.
7. Ongoing interaction with each drug court participant is essential.
8. Monitoring and evaluation measure the achievement of program goals and gauge effectiveness.
9. Continuing interdisciplinary education promotes effective planning, implementation, and operations.
10. Forging partnerships among drug courts, public agencies, and community-based organizations generates local support and enhances effectiveness.

The drug court model assumes that most drug offenders are serious abusers and that drug usage intensifies other criminal activity. As a result, offenders are required to satisfy a multiphase treatment process, generally divided into a stabilization phase, an intensive treatment phase, and a transition phase. The stabilization phase may include a period of detoxification, treatment assessment, education, and screening for other needs. The intensive treatment phase typically involves individual and group counseling and other core and adjunctive therapies. The transition phase may emphasize social reintegration, employment and education, housing services, and other aftercare activities.[40]

Drug court programs typically run between six months and one year, though many participants remain in the program for longer. Unlike traditional treatment programs, becoming "clean and sober" is only the first step toward drug court graduation. Almost all drug courts require participants to obtain and maintain employment, meet all financial obligations, perform community service hours, and have an aftercare plan. In order for a defendant to enter the program, a plea agreement is usually required that suspends punishment pending completion of all drug court requirements. Most courts also require a fee to enter the program. In Clark County, Indiana, for example, defendants must pay $500 to enter to the drug court program. To graduate from this program, offenders must accomplish the following:

- Have 150 consecutive days of negative drug screens
- Attend all required sessions with treatment and ancillary service providers for 150 days
- Attend all self-help meetings and drug court review hearings
- Pay all fees or work them off through community service hours

- Have a residence approved by the drug court
- Complete a relapse-prevention program
- Fulfill all goals as stated in the individualized drug court treatment plan
- Have a plan for a personal support network after graduating from the program that includes volunteering to help others, participating in self-help groups, and following the plan to prevent a relapse[41]

In cases where individuals fail to meet the requirements of the drug court, they are returned to the criminal court to face sentencing on the guilty plea.

Research has shown that drug courts are associated with reduced recidivism by participants and result in cost savings. A study designed to look at the operations and outcomes of a single drug court in Multnomah County (Portland, Oregon) over a 10-year period (1991 to 2001) found that the program significantly reduced recidivism nearly 30 percent and saved the county more than $7.9 million per year.[42] A study of nine California drug courts showed that graduates had an average rearrest rate of only 17 percent. Eight of the nine drug courts in this study produced net cost benefits ranging from about $3,200 to over $20,000 per participant. For each year that a cohort of participants entered just these nine drug courts, the state realized a savings of more than $9 million.[43] A final illustration of the success of drug courts involves the treatment programs in Bakersfield, California; Creek County, Oklahoma; Jackson County, Missouri; and St. Mary Parish, Louisiana. Researchers analyzed the records of 2,357 offenders enrolled in those four drug courts between 1997 and 2000 and gathered additional information by means of interviews, surveys, and personal observations. Findings confirm what other studies have found: Successful completion of the drug court program is the variable most consistently associated with low postprogram recidivism. Overall, of those who were rearrested, 41 percent were among those who had been expelled from the program while only 9 percent were among those who had completed and graduated from it. In other words, the rate of post-program recidivism was considerably higher for terminated participants than for graduates across all four sites.[44] In CBC Online 10.4 we provide a video presentation of a district court in Virginia which has graduated more than 600 participants from the program, saving tax payers thousands of dollars.

With success stories abundant, drug courts have gained approval at the local, state, and federal levels. However, while drug courts are operating in most mid- and large-sized counties in the United States, most are very small and serve fewer than 100 clients annually. Also, many drug court programs reject offenders because of prior convictions. The Urban Institute estimates that of the millions of persons arrested each year on drug charges, only 30,000 are accepted into a drug court.[45] To counter this problem, some jurisdictions have developed drug court models that permit probation staff to craft individualized supervision plans. This way, the program can focus on higher-level offenders. Some of these hybrid programs have combined the philosophies of drug court programs with day reporting and other community-based programs. Let's look at a few examples.

The Randolph County District Court in Asheboro, North Carolina, administers a drug treatment court that is a voluntary program for drug dependent individuals facing substantial prison time. Eligible participants agree to enter an outpatient treatment program for a minimum of one year; most are provided free services by the Randolph County Day Reporting Center. The center provides substance abuse treatment and assessments, drug testing, education services, behavior modification courses,

10.4

CBC Online

HOW VIRGINIA DRUG COURTS SUCCEED

This 28-minute video produced by the 23rd Judicial District (Roanoke County) Court of Virginia features eight graduates of the drug court program who share their stories of struggling with addiction, their recoveries, and reconnecting with family, friends, and community. As you view the video, consider the following questions.

What harm did the drug offenders cause to their family and friends?

What are the advantages of completing a drug court program versus being sentenced to incarceration?

How did the intensity of the drug court program help these offenders?

Visit CBC Online 10.4 at www.mhhe.com/bayens1e

employment/job search courses, sex offender treatment, transportation, close supervision, and case management.[46]

The Clark County Community Corrections facility in Jeffersonville, Indiana, offers a 90-day treatment program designed to reduce recidivism rates among male offenders struggling with mental health and substance abuse disorders. Judges sentence criminal offenders directly to this "forensic diversion program," which is operated by Centerstone, a nonprofit agency that provides community-based behavioral health care. Programming runs from 8:00 A.M. to 9:00 P.M. daily; group and individual psychotherapy are the primary modes of service provision. Offenders receive individualized treatment, psychiatric consultations, and referrals for vocational training, housing, and social services. An aftercare component monitors released offenders for up to nine months in the community or placement setting, with periodic reporting to the referral source as appropriate.[47]

The drug court in Princeton, West Virginia, located in the Mercer County Day Report Center, was founded in January 2006. Drug court participants are referred to the center by officials in the legal system, but before the drug court judge will accept them into the program, nominees must voluntarily choose to participate. The Mercer County Day Report Center provides drug screening and counseling services for federal probationers. In 2008, the R.E.V. (Restart, Educate and Validate) program was initiated to help find temporary service-industry positions for drug court participants. Once offenders prove that they are capable and reliable workers, they are assisted in finding the means to attend college or vocational school to move into a lasting career.[48]

The Cowley County, Kansas, (Winfield) Community Corrections Day Reporting Program operates to provide a nonresidential drug and alcohol treatment program for offenders under the supervision of community corrections, court services, courts, and state parole. The drug court program in Winfield, which makes referrals to the community corrections day reporting center, was implemented in part in response to the passage of Senate Bill 14 Risk Reduction Initiative in 2007, which established three specific goals:

1. Increase public safety.
2. Reduce the risk level of probationers on Community Corrections supervision.
3. Increase the percentage of probationers successfully completing community corrections supervision.

Community-based corrections staff participate in the drug court team, which meets weekly before a drug court session to discuss participants' progress in their programs. The team consists of treatment providers; personnel from the county attorney's office, law enforcement, and probation; mental health staff; and any other social service organization that may be involved in the offender's life.

Policy Implications

As we have noted throughout this chapter, there is growing evidence that residential community-based and day reporting approaches can work for some offenders. In particular, reduced recidivism has been found, especially when programs include substance abuse treatment, employment services, and cognitive behavioral therapies. But has the broader application of residential community-based and day reporting programs widened the net of correctional control?

Although residential community-based and day reporting programs can be seen as more intrusive than regular probation or parole, it can be argued that overall these sanctions are targeting the correct offender population. The basic rationale for residential community-based and day reporting programs is that they should target a wide array of offenders because it's cheaper to provide services in the community than behind bars. This idea applies especially to parolees on conditional release because they are very likely to have their parole revoked and be sent back to prison. For example, on any given day, six out of 10 admissions to California prisons are returning parolees.[49] The same can be said with regard to those on probation, given that probation is no longer limited to first-time, nonviolent offenders who pose minimal risk to the community. Thus, residential community-based and day reporting programs are viewed as essential to the continuum of sanctions because they provide higher levels of offender accountability and greater public safety than do traditional probation and parole. Furthermore, residential community-based and day reporting programs incorporate treatment and services to assist offenders, which may not always lower recidivism, but do ensure a more agreeable and enlightened criminal justice system.

More and more, policymakers are questioning whether states are getting their money's worth out of prisons and whether imprisonment is the most effective means of achieving public safety, especially when it diverts increasingly scarce funds from other social services, some of which have been shown to prevent crime in the first place. From a policymaking perspective then, residential community-based and day reporting programs are appealing for several reasons. In addition to relieving jail and prison overcrowding, they are less expensive to operate than imprisonment. Moreover, there is the prospect that offenders in residential and day reporting programs will pay taxes, restitution, programs fees, and so on that otherwise would not be collected. Second, considering the level of risk a great many offenders represent—too much for probation but not enough for prison—residential community-based and day reporting programs are a viable sentencing option for medium-risk offenders. Lawmakers, judges, and the public generally support the value of a continuum of punishment options with graduated levels of supervision and punishment severity. Finally, if these alternative sanctions reduce the negative impacts of incarceration, offenders may have a better chance for rehabilitation.

Summary

The history of halfway houses in America is extensive. In the 1800s, a Massachusetts legislative commission recognized that ex-offenders were unsuccessful in transitioning from prison environments back into their home communities because of the lack of available jobs and other resources. At the same time, the efforts of religious and private volunteer groups to help the poor with securing shelter and other basic needs propelled the halfway house concept. In 1965, the Federal Prisoner Rehabilitation Act (H.R. 6964) established community treatment centers. Today's residential community-based programs extend to both offenders released from prison into residential facilities as a condition of parole or administrative release and offenders from pretrial placements.

Residential community-based correctional programs can be placed in two categories: those that provide transitional control and those with strong treatment components. Each has its own characteristics and objectives.

The fundamental goal of cognitive-behavioral therapies is to teach offenders cognitive skills and values that are essential for pro-social competence. Studies have shown that improved reasoning and pro-social thinking skills are related to reduced recidivism.

Day reporting centers (DRCs) have two common conditions for clients who participate in the program: a strong supervision orientation that requires participants to regularly report to the center and a complement of services (e.g., job placement, drug abuse education, and individual counseling).

Although research regarding the effectiveness of DRCs in reducing recidivism has found mixed results, a growing body of literature does support this claim. A number of studies have found DRCs to be, at the very least, a less-expensive alternative to incarceration and an effective method of relieving jail overcrowding.

Drug court is a multiphase treatment process lasting six months to one year, generally divided into a stabilization phase, an intensive treatment phase, and a transition phase. Research has shown that drug courts are associated with reduced recidivism and result in cost savings.

Key Terms

cognitive-behavioral therapy (CBT), p. 287
day reporting center (DRC), p. 292
desistance, p. 287
drug court, p. 298
halfway house, p. 281
reintegration, p. 284

Questions for Review

1. What role have halfway houses played in the establishment of residential community-based corrections programs?
2. What are the characteristics of residential community-based programs?
3. Which cognitive-behavioral therapies are most beneficial to offenders?
4. What are day reporting centers?
5. Have residential programs and day reporting centers been shown to be effective community-based sanctions? Explain your answer.
6. What are drug courts, and what has been their impact?

Question of Policy

Transition from Prison to Community (TPC)

Policymakers have sought to implement a variety of intermediate punishments to alleviate prison crowding and the financial burden of incarceration. So, from an economic point of view, residential community-based programs provide a cheaper correctional service than imprisonment. At the same time, we know that high-risk offenders who are required to participate in residential community-based programs have access to multiple services that better meet their treatment needs. That is, offenders placed in residential community-based programs receive intense treatment for substance abuse, education, employment assistance, and other services that help to reduce recidivism.

The National Institute of Corrections (NIC) launched its Transition from Prison to the Community (TPC) Initiative to apply the best practical thinking and research knowledge to the challenge of safely transitioning a growing number of offenders from prison to the community. NIC's goal was to incorporate the lessons of evidence-based practice, emphasize the importance of collaboration, and provide a practical tool for corrections agencies. The result was the development of the TPC Model, which has now been implemented in 14 states throughout the country.

Go to the Web site for TPC, which can be found at http://nicic.gov/TPCModel, and read the profiles and summaries of activities and progress. What are the TPC model components? What have the states accomplished in implementing the TPC model?

What Would You Do?

Budget reductions in the county's correctional system have led to a gap in your probation agency's ability to supervise offenders. One major issue your agency faces is the increased number of clients who require substance abuse treatment and the related need to maintain public safety. One way to address this problem is to use residential community-based programs to supplement services provided by the jail. The director of your probation agency has assigned you to participate in a committee that is planning a new residential community-based facility. As the agency representative, your task is to emphasize your agency's mission statement—namely, that probation is a business of not just punishment but corrections.

What does this mission statement mean?

What arguments would you use to convince other committee members to incorporate treatment services when planning a residential facility?

Endnotes

1. "Ain't No Such Thing as a Secret Snitch," *Vibe Magazine* (April 2009). Retrieved from www.swtlaw.com/PDFs/sadow/TIVIBEAPRIL2009.pdf. "NEWS XXcLusive: T.I. Released from Prison Today, Lawyer Confirms," *XXL Magazine* (December 2009). Retrieved from www.xxlmag.com/online/?p=66274.
2. John Conrad, *Crime and Its Correction* (Berkeley, CA: University of California Press, 1965).
3. John McCartt and Thomas Mangogna, *Guidelines and Standards for Halfway Houses and Community Treatment Centers* (Washington, DC: U.S Department of Justice, May 1973).
4. Oliver Keller and Benedict Alper, *Halfway Houses: Community-Centered Correction and Treatment* (Lexington, MA: Heath Lexington Books, 1970).
5. John Woolley and Gerhard Peters, *The American Presidency Project* [online]. Retrieved from www.presidency.ucsb.edu/ws/?pid=27251.
6. International Community Corrections Association. Retrieved from www.iccaweb.org/documents/Legislative_Agenda_2010.pdf.
7. Alan Rosenthal and Elaine Wolf, *Unlocking the Potential of Reentry and Reintegration* (Syracuse, NY: Center for Community Alternatives, 2005).
8. Joe Graffam et al., *Creating a Pathway to Reintegration: The Correctional Services Employment Pilot Program (CSEPP)* (Victoria, AU: Department of Justice, January 2005).
9. Joseph Graffam, Alison J. Shinkfield, and Lesley Hardcastle, "The Perceived Employability of Ex-Prisoners and Offenders," *International Journal of Offender Therapy and Comparative Criminology,* vol. 52, no. 6 (November 2007), pp. 673–685.
10. Marcus Nieto, *Community Correction Punishments: An Alternative to Incarceration for Nonviolent Offenders* (Sacramento, CA: California Research Bureau, May 1996).
11. Ohio Community Corrections FY2009 Annual Report. Retrieved from http://occaonline.org/pdf/OCCA%20FY09%20Annual%20Report.pdf.
12. Community Partners in Action [online]. Retrieved from www.cpa-ct.org/alternative.php.
13. Volunteers of America Chesapeake. Retrieved from www.voaches.org.
14. Paul Gendreau and Robert Ross, "Offender Rehabilitation: The Appeal of Success," *Federal Probation,* vol. 45 (1981), pp. 45–48.
15. Talbert House [online]. Retrieved from www.talberthouse.org/aboutus/whoweare.html.
16. Eliot Bates et al., "Probation Residential Center Assessment for Washtenaw County" (September 2010). Retrieved from www.ewashtenaw.org/

government/departments/cjcc/random_cjcc_documents/prc.html.

17. Edward Latessa and Harry Allen, "Halfway Houses and Parole: A National Assessment," *Journal of Criminal Justice,* vol. 10, no. 2 (1982), pp. 153–163.
18. Miles D. Harer, *Recidivism Among Federal Prisoners Released in 1987* (Washington, DC: Federal Bureau of Prisons Office of Research and Evaluation, 1994).
19. Christopher Lowenkamp and Edward Latessa, *Evaluation of Ohio's Community-Based Correctional Facilities and Halfway House Programs* (Cincinnati, OH: University of Cincinnati, Division of Criminal Justice Research, September 2002).
20. Ibid.
21. Edward Latessa, Lori Lovins, and Paula Smith, *FINAL REPORT: Follow-up Evaluation of Ohio's Community Based Correctional Facility and Halfway House Programs—Outcome Study* (Cincinnati, OH: University of Cincinnati, Division of Criminal Justice Research, February 2010).
22. Steve Aos et al., *The Comparative Costs and Benefits of Programs to Reduce Crime: A Review of National Research Findings with Implications for Washington State* (Olympia, WA: Washington State Institute for Public Policy, May 1999).
23. Ibid.
24. Nana Landenburger and Mark Lipsey, "The Positive Effects of Cognitive-Behavioral Programs for Offenders: A Meta-Analysis of Factors Associated with Effective Treatment," *Journal of Experimental Criminology*, vol. 1 no. 4 (2006), pp. 435–450.
25. Robert Barnoski, *Outcome Evaluation of Washington State's Research-Based Programs for Juvenile Offenders* (Olympia, WA: Washington State Institute for Public Policy, January 2004).
26. Dale Parent et al., *Day Reporting Centers,* vol. 1 (Washington, DC: U.S. Department of Justice, 1995).
27. Paige M. Harrison and Jennifer C. Karberg, *Prison and Jail Inmates at Midyear 2002* (Washington, DC: U.S. Department of Justice, April 2003).
28. Todd Minton and William Sabol, *Prison and Jail Inmates at Midyear 2008—Statistical Tables* (Washington, DC: U.S. Department of Justice, March 2009).
29. Sheriff's Department Day Reporting Center: Informational Meeting, Press Release 06141001, Santa Barbara County, CA (June, 2010). Retrieved online at www.sbsheriff.org/pr/06141001.html.
30. Christine Martin, Arthur Lurigio, and David Olson, "An Examination of Rearrests and Reincarcerations Among Discharged Day Reporting Center Clients," *Federal Probation,* vol. 67, no. 1 (2003), pp. 24–30. Also, Edward Byrnes and Russ Van Vleet, *The Utah Day Reporting Center: Success with Alternative Incarceration* (Salt Lake City, UT: University of Utah, Criminal and Juvenile Justice Consortium, 1998).
31. Jan Solomon, "Utah: The Utah Day Reporting Center—Success With Alternative Incarceration," in Monograph NCJ 178936: *Creating a New Criminal Justice System for the 21st Century* (Washington, DC: U.S. Department of Justice, Bureau of Justice Assistance, April 2000).
32. Amy Craddock, "Estimating Criminal Justice Costs and Cost Savings Benefits of Day Reporting Centers," *Journal of Offender Rehabilitation,* vol. 39, no. 4 (2004), pp. 69–98.
33. *County of Bucks Department of Corrections Annual Report 2009.* Retrieved from www.buckscounty.org/government/departments/Corrections/index.aspx.
34. Criminal Justice Comprehensive Master Plan for Sedgwick County [Kansas]. Retrieved from www.sedgwickcounty.org/SHERIFF/CJCC_Master_Plan.pdf.
35. Supra (See note 25).
36. U.S. Department of Justice National Drug Intelligence Center, *The National Drug Threat Assessment 2010* (Washington, DC: Office of Policy and Interagency Affairs, U.S. Department of Justice, February 2010).
37. *Crime in the United States, 2008* (Washington, DC: Federal Bureau of Investigation, September 2009).

38. National Institute of Justice: Drug Courts. Retrieved from www.ojp.usdoj.gov/nij/topics/courts/drug-courts/welcome.htm.
39. Drug Court Resources Series, *Defining Drug Courts: The Key Components* (Washington, DC: U.S. Department of Justice, Bureau of Justice Assistance, October 2004).
40. Ibid.
41. Clark County, Indiana Drug Treatment Court. Retrieved from http://clarkcountydrugcourt.com/handbook.pdf.
42. Michael Finigan, Shannon Carey, and Anton Cox, *Impact of a Mature Drug Court Over 10 Years of Operation: Recidivism and Costs (Final Report)* (Portland, OR: NPC Research, July 2007).
43. Shannon Carey et al., *California Drug Courts: A Methodology for Determining Costs and Benefits PHASE II: Testing the Methodology Final Report* (Portland, OR: NPC Research, April 2005).
44. *Drug Courts: The Second Decade* (Washington, DC: U.S. Department of Justice Office of Justice Programs, NCJ 211081, June 2006).
45. Avinash Singh Bhati, John Roman, and Aaron Chalfin, *To Treat or Not To Treat: Evidence on the Prospects of Expanding Treatment to Drug-Involved Offenders* (Washington, DC: The Urban Institute, April 2008).
46. Pamela Smith, personal communication (October 7, 2010).
47. Centerstone: Forensic Diversion Program. Retrieved from www.centerstone.org/services/Forensic%20Diversion%20-%20Specialized%20Services.
48. Charly Markwart, *Drug Court Reshaping Futures* (Bluefield, WV: The Princeton Times, January 2009).
49. Ryken Grattet, Joan Petersilia, and Jeffrey Lin, *Parole Violations and Revocations in California* (Washington, DC: National Institute of Justice, U.S. Department of Justice, October 2008).

CHAPTER 11

Special Populations:

Offenders with Mental Health Problems, Sex Offenders, and Women Offenders

OBJECTIVES

1. Trace the evolution of treatment for mentally ill persons.
2. Describe how communities can best reintegrate offenders with mental health problems into their communities.
3. Describe theories that explain why sex offenders offend.
4. List and explain services that community-based programs are providing to ensure public safety from sex offenders.
5. Describe theories that explain female criminality.
6. Describe gender-specific problems that women face in the criminal justice system.

OUTLINE

Phillip Alpert had just turned 18 when, after an argument with his 16-year-old girlfriend, he sent a naked photo of her—a photo she had taken and sent him—to dozens of her friends and family. The high school sweethearts had been dating for almost two and a half years. Alpert was arrested and charged with distributing child pornography, a felony to which he pleaded no contest; he was later convicted. His girlfriend was never in any legal trouble. He was sentenced to five years probation and required by Florida law to register as a sex offender.

According to an 800-person survey on ***sexting*** *from the Pew Internet and American Life Project, 15 percent of teens ages 12 to 17 who owned cell phones had received nude or nearly nude photos by phone. Four percent of the teens said they had sent out sexually explicit photos or videos of themselves.*[1]

Alpert's life is not easy as a registered sex offender, a label he will carry until the age of 43. He's been expelled from community college, he cannot travel out of the county without making prior arrangements with his probation officer, and he has trouble finding a job because of his status as a convicted felon. Each week he attends a class for sex offenders where he is joined by offenders who have raped and molested children. He has lost many friends and says he feels terrible about sending the photo of his ex-girlfriend, especially since they were once so close. Fox News conducted an interview with Philip Alpert, which is available at YouTube, titled "'Sexting' teenagers risk child-porn charges" (www.youtube.com/watch?v=0mEky0KdHPk).

In this chapter we discuss three special categories of offenders—offenders who have mental health problems, sex offenders, and women offenders. Each category includes a wide variety of offenders, ranging from the most violent to the least serious offenders, and at times they may cross over into more than one category. Consequently, these offenders have special treatment needs and public safety concerns that challenge the criminal justice system. Throughout the chapter we examine the history, theories, policies, and practices pertaining to these offenders. We also look at evidence-based practices that show promise for the supervision of these special offenders in the community.

Offenders with Mental Health Problems

Societies have been dealing with the problem of what to do about the care, treatment, and control of persons with mental health issues for centuries. Historically, they were viewed as being different from "normal" members of society, in much the same way as criminals are seen as being different from law-abiding members of society. Since maintaining social control and order is a major goal of the criminal justice system, if someone's behavior goes against the norms of society, then the act can sometimes cross over into the area of criminal behavior. It is at this point that persons with mental health problems become criminal offenders and become the responsibility of the criminal justice system. We begin this section with a history of mental health treatment and reform movements in the United States.

Historical Overview

In colonial America, the care, treatment, and control of persons with mental health illnesses were left almost exclusively to their families. Often, family members hid or sequestered the mentally ill person from the other members of the community, caging them or putting them in restraints to keep them from hurting themselves or others. If the mentally ill person was allowed access into the community and misbehaved, he or she might be treated as a criminal and subjected to corporal punishment, banishment, or even death.[2]

It wasn't until 1773 that the first institution, Eastern Lunatic Asylum, was constructed in Williamsburg, Virginia, to house persons with mental illnesses. This institution did not have a resident physician; it was simply a holding place for 20 mentally ill patients. Because facilities were so limited, many people with mental illnesses were left to fend for themselves on the streets. In 1816, a second psychiatric hospital was opened in Baltimore. Philadelphia, Boston, and New York soon followed suit with their own psychiatric hospitals. The institutional confinement of those with mental health issues had now begun and would last for the next 150 years.[3]

The 19th century became the high point for the building and development of asylums, both for persons with mental illnesses and for those who had committed crimes. Large institutions were built to confine both the insane and the criminal. The need for community security, along with the belief that those who were confined could be rehabilitated, were the compelling justifications for building these massive institutions. During this time, institutional confinement became the most common form of disposition for both convicted criminals and those with mental illnesses. But as social values began to change in this country, and as our understanding of mental illnesses increased, people slowly began to differentiate between criminal offenders with mental illness and those without.[4]

Laws in the United States began to reflect the societal assumption that if an offender was found to be mentally ill, that person should receive treatment rather than punishment. The problem became how to sort out individuals who had committed crimes and also suffered from mental health issues so they could receive treatment. If the mental illness was not detected, the offender would be included with offenders who did not have mental health issues and therefore would receive punishment instead of treatment. In 1818, New York passed a law that granted the transfer of insane offenders from prisons to the Lunatic Hospital at New York.[5] Then in 1833, the State Lunatic Asylum at Worcester, Massachusetts, was opened: more than half its 164 patients came from jails, almshouses, and prisons.[6] By the mid-19th century many states had passed similar laws mandating that persons acquitted by reason of insanity should be committed to mental hospitals and not be held in prisons; however, often these laws were simply ignored, and many mentally ill offenders were sent to prison.[7]

Dorothea Dix is noted as one of the most famous and successful psychiatric reformers in American history. She began a crusade in 1841 on behalf of mentally ill people after agreeing to teach a Sunday school class at the East Cambridge Jail near Boston. While there, she witnessed insane prisoners being held in the same facility as criminal prisoners. She also discovered that insane prisoners were housed in unheated cells. When she questioned correction officials about this, Dix was told that the insane didn't need heat. After that, she visited over 300 county jails, 18 prisons, and 500 almshouses, and reported to state legislators about the deplorable conditions she had observed at these institutions. Dix urged state legislatures to authorize the building of more psychiatric hospitals in which insane persons would be treated with compassion. Her crusade led to the opening of at least 30 state psychiatric hospitals. By 1880, 45 additional public psychiatric hospitals were opened in the United States.[8] In 1880, the first census of "insane persons" was conducted in the United States, and the survey identified 41,083 who lived at home, 40,942 who lived in hospitals and asylums for the insane, 9,302 who resided in almshouses, and 397 who were incarcerated in jails or prisons. At that time, severely mentally ill inmates constituted only 0.7 percent of the jail and prison population.[9]

Toward the end of the 19th century, studies began to show the link between behavior and various parts of the brain. During this time, the public also became more aware of how brain dysfunction was associated with aggression. The case of Phineas Gage received widespread attention when he was critically injured in a construction accident. An explosion drove a tamping iron through his head, and severed his frontal lobes from the rest of his brain. Although Gage survived the accident, he suffered a major personality change that was characterized by fits of violence and profanity. While Gage's accidental lobotomy resulted in disastrous results for him, physicians and scientists soon came to realize that for some people with mental illnesses, frontal lobotomies could actually be helpful.[10]

At the beginning of the 1900s, there were approximately 145,000 people housed in state mental hospitals. By 1955, that number reached an all-time high of nearly 559,000 patients. From 1960 to 1980 this number plummeted to less than 100,000 people.[11] This drop can largely be attributed to the **deinstitutionalization** movement. The deinstitutionalization movement embraced the idea that people with mental illnesses and mental retardation could best be treated in the least restrictive setting: in the community rather than in institutions. Deinstitutionalization became an even more realistic alternative in 1955 when the first antipsychotic medication, Thorazine, was introduced. Thorazine was considered the single biggest advancement in psychiatric treatment at that time, dramatically improving the prognoses of patients in psychiatric hospitals worldwide.[12]

In the initial stages of deinstitutionalization, states funded small community pilot programs for individuals who responded well to the new antipsychotic medications.[13] In 1963, the **Community Mental Health Centers Act (CMHCA)** was signed into law; this provided federal funding for community mental health centers.[14] The purpose of the CMHCA was to provide for community-based care as an alternative to institutionalization. Some states also saw this as an opportunity to close expensive state hospitals. Many patients, formerly warehoused in institutions, were moved to the community centers. By 1980 the federal government had supported the construction, initiation, and staffing of over 750 such community centers. As the number of community mental health centers increased, the number of patients in institutions dramatically declined—from approximately 450,000 in 1970 to 160,000 in 1980.[15] However, despite the good intentions of the CMHCA, it didn't work as planned. Congress noted that "thousands of people with mental illnesses were being discharged from state hospitals into communities that simply did not have the adequate services or expertise to support this population."[16] Most persons suffering from mental illness returned to their families, and thus, the family once again became the core of the nation's mental health system.

By the early 1980s, the policy of deinstitutionalization was being severely criticized by policymakers. A study by the Commission on Mental Health recognized that thousands of former patients were living in nursing homes, board-and-care homes, and other community institutions. These mostly private, for-profit facilities served the

EXHIBIT 11.1 Reform Movements in Mental Health Treatment in the United States[18]

Reform Movement	Era	Setting	Focus of Reform
Moral treatment	1800–1850	Asylum	Humane, restorative treatment
Mental hygiene	1890–1920	Mental hospital or clinic	Prevention, scientific orientation
Community mental health	1955–1970	Community mental health centers	Deinstitutionalization, social integration
Community support programs	1975–present	Community support	Mental illness as a social welfare problem (e.g., housing, employment)

functions that were once performed by state hospitals. Consequently, the commission recommended greater emphasis on the prevention of mental illness, better training and education of personnel to treat those who suffer from mental illness, better distribution of services around the country, and additional research to develop best practices.[17] Ultimately, Congress passed the Mental Health Systems Act, which was designed to develop community support programs, provide housing, and expand outpatient and community support services. As we note in Exhibit 11.1, this movement is viewed as the fourth cycle of institutional reform. Unlike the prior reform movements, however, community support programs are to offer direct care and rehabilitation for the chronically mentally ill by means of a system of existing social services agencies.

Today, an estimated 4.5 million Americans suffer from schizophrenia, bipolar disorder, and other mental illnesses. Of these persons, only about 40 percent actually receive treatment for their mental health problems on any given day.[19] This lack of treatment has resulted in homelessness, incarceration, and increased violence. A study conducted in 1993 found that 27 percent of patients released from a psychiatric hospital were involved in at least one violent act within four months of discharge.

Frank Sirotich, a professor of social work at the University of Toronto, studies crime and violence among persons with mental disorders. He argues that too much emphasis has been focused on discovering the correlation between persons with mental illnesses and those who are prone to violence. Instead, Sirotich advocates for theoretically based research focused on the processes that lead to violent and delinquent behaviors. Such research, he believes, will lead to the treatment, supervision, and support necessary to address and prevent violent and illegal behaviors by persons with mental illnesses and, ultimately, will minimize their contact with the criminal justice system.[20]

Contemporary Approaches to Treatment of Offenders with Mental Health Problems

Today, more persons with mental illnesses are confined to jails and prisons than state mental hospitals. The number of persons housed in state mental hospitals may be as low as 40,000, while an estimated 321,000 mentally ill inmates are being housed in

U.S. jails or prisons on any given day.[21] In a study of more than 20,000 adults entering five local jails, researchers documented **serious mental illnesses (SMIs)** in 14.5 percent of the men and 31 percent of the women, which taken together, comprises 16.9 percent of those studied—rates three to six times higher than those found in the general population.[22] These numbers seem to indicate that jails and prisons have become the alternative mental health hospitals.

Between 1980 and 1995, the U.S. population increased by only 16 percent, while the total number of incarcerated individuals in American jails and prisons increased by 216 percent. Although the vast majority of this increase can be explained by changing demographics, more stringent mandatory sentencing laws, and stricter drug laws, correlations between deinstitutionalization and increased jail and prison populations cannot be overlooked. In short, mentally ill persons are entering the criminal justice system in increasing numbers. Unfortunately, some of these people haven't committed crimes and are simply put in jail while they await appropriate placements. Of those charged, most are jailed due to misdemeanor charges. Often, police charge the mentally ill person with disorderly conduct when there is no other charge available. At times police officers initiate a "mercy booking" to admit a mentally ill person to jail so that the person will receive food, shelter, and protection from victimization. A recent study showed that homeless persons with mental disorders are apt to become victims in the streets; but physical barriers offer more protection than having a social guardian.[23] Sometimes family members of a mentally ill person ask to have this family member jailed because they believe it to be the most expedient way to obtain treatment. Today, over three-quarters of a million mentally ill people live in the community. Just 40 years ago these people would probably be living in public psychiatric hospitals.[24]

The pendulum continues to swing back and forth for those with mental health disorders, from living in the community, to becoming institutionalized, to deinstitutionalization, and now again back to institutionalization. However, now the institutions are

Legal counsel by an attorney with specific training to defend mentally ill persons is extremely important because evidence of a defendant's state of mind at the time of the criminal offense may lead to favorable treatment in sentencing. Should a person suffering from mental illness be afforded court-appointed counsel who is experienced in representation of persons with mental illnesses?

jails and prisons. The challenge is for our mental health care system to discover better solutions for treating mentally ill offenders.[25] Convicting a person who has a mental illness for committing a minor offense results in a criminal record for that individual. Thus, persons with mental illnesses may appear to have lengthy criminal histories when in reality they have not have received adequate treatment for their mental illnesses and thus acted inappropriately or aggressively, which in turn led to an arrest.[26] Such criminalization is doubly stigmatizing, as the individual now has both a mental illness and a criminal record.[27]

Stigmatizing persons who have major mental health disorders only increases the beliefs that all persons with mental illnesses are dangerous and that they belong either in hospitals or correctional facilities. As prevalent as this thought may be, many offenders are eventually returned to the community. Consider, for example, that a national probation survey estimated that 547,800 probationers suffered from mental illness. Most of these probationers were female, white, and between the ages of 45 and 54 years old.[28] Consequently, community-based corrections programs that offer mental health treatments, along with social and medical services, have been developed to enhance public safety while offenders are supervised in the community. These community-based programs offer more humane treatments and are less costly than incarceration. Moreover, they tend to have lower recidivism rates because these programs are highly structured, with multiple components, and each component targets a particular problem tailored to an individual's needs.[29] For example, a study of 337 mentally ill offenders released from Washington's state prisons in 1996 and 1997 showed that of those who received postrelease social or mental health services, only 10 percent committed new felonies against persons, and only 2 percent committed very serious crimes.[30]

Some communities are using **mental health courts** in an attempt to reduce recidivism rates among people with mental health disorders. Essentially, any special effort courts make to better address the needs of offenders with serious mental illness can qualify as a mental health court. Mental health courts are likely to involve criminal sanctions. However, more recently developed mental health courts focused on misdemeanants with mental illness. Some programs emphasize pre-adjudication mechanisms for disposition of charges, whereas other courts require guilty pleas for program entry.[31] So, there is really no typical mental health court model; what we can say is that all are comprised of a judge, court personnel, and treatment providers who come together to define the terms of participation, provide ongoing assessments, and determine resolution of cases when an offender successfully completes the court-ordered treatment plan. The goal of the mental health court is therapeutic; it attempts to increase the offender's participation in treatment, while decreasing involvement in the criminal justice system.

Mental health courts seem to be catching on. In 1997 only four such courts were operating in the United States: King County (Seattle), Washington; Broward County (Fort Lauderdale), Florida; San Bernardino, California; and Anchorage, Alaska. As of 2007, the United States had more than 175 in both large and small jurisdictions.[32] Communities start mental health courts with the hope that effective treatment will prevent participants' future involvement in the criminal justice system and serve both the individual and the community better than traditional criminal case processing. With these ideas in mind, mental health court planners and staff cite specific program goals, which usually fall into these categories:

- Increase public safety for communities by reducing criminal activity and lowering the high recidivism rates of people with mental illnesses who become involved in the criminal justice system.

11.1

CBC Online

CRIMINAL JUSTICE/MENTAL HEALTH CONSENSUS PROJECT

The Justice Center's Criminal Justice/Mental Health Consensus Project Report (Consensus Project Report) provides more than 100 recommendations, endorsed by law enforcement, judges, advocates, and corrections officials, for improving the response to people with mental illness who encounter (or are at high risk of encountering) the criminal justice system.

Once at the Web site, navigate the flowchart of select events experienced by a person with mental illness in the criminal justice system. Then identify several recommendations that are specific to community-based supervision.

Visit CBC Online 11.1 at www.mhhe.com/bayens1e

- Increase treatment engagement by participants by brokering comprehensive services and supports, rewarding adherence to treatment plans, and sanctioning nonadherence.
- Improve quality of life for participants by ensuring that program participants are connected to needed community-based treatments, housing, and other services that encourage recovery.
- Increase effectiveness of sponsoring jurisdictions' resources by reducing repeated contacts between people with mental illnesses and the criminal justice system and by providing treatment in the community when appropriate, where it is more effective and less costly than in correctional institutions.[33]

Evaluations of mental health courts have shown relative success. For example, in Broward County, Florida, defendants were twice as likely to receive services for their mental illness and were no more likely to commit new crimes, despite spending 75 percent fewer days in jail compared to comparable defendants.[34] Other studies have shown that persons who successfully complete their programs show reduced recidivism rates and violence even after they are no longer supervised by the mental health court. It seems that public safety is not compromised by using mental health courts, but that, perhaps, it is even enhanced. In North Carolina, contact with the mental health court was associated with fewer arrests regardless of whether the defendant completed the program. Overall, defendants had an average of 4.19 arrests in the two years before entering the program and 1.79 arrests in the two years after. Defendants who completed the program were arrested on average only once in the following two years, and 72 percent of them were not rearrested. The percentages were reversed for the noncompleters: Rearrests occurred for 81 percent of those who were expelled from the program and 63 percent of those who opted out.[35]

Expanding the use of the mental health court model shows promise as a way to more effectively manage offenders with mental health disorders in the community.[36] And researchers have also begun to explore the fiscal impact of mental health courts. A recent study of the Allegheny County Mental Health Court in Pennsylvania by the RAND Corporation found that the program did not result in substantial added costs—at least in the short term—over traditional court processing for individuals with serious mental illnesses. The findings also suggested that over the longer term, the mental health court may actually result in net savings for the government.[37] In CBC Online 11.1 we have provided a Web link to The Council of State Governments Justice Center, a national nonprofit organization that serves policymakers at the local, state, and federal levels from all branches of government. The center serves all states to promote effective data-driven practices—particularly in areas in which the criminal justice system intersects with other disciplines, such as public health—to provide practical solutions to public safety and cross-systems problems.

Another important consideration for offenders with mental health disorders who are incarcerated is to ensure that they make a smooth transition back into the community once they leave jail or prison. The ideal is to link community treatment providers with offenders while they are still confined. However, trying to navigate the bureaucratic maze to access benefits and services can prove overwhelming for anyone, but even more so for persons with mental health illnesses. Newly released offenders with mental illnesses often struggle to meet their basic survival needs, such as food, shelter, and job concerns. Consequently, discharge plans should include arrangements for aftercare services that continue their mental health treatment, provide for housing and a month's supply of their medications, and expedite reinstatement of social service benefits. They also benefit from being assigned to probation or parole officers who have had special training in supervising persons with mental health issues.[38]

An excellent example of an aftercare program for transitioning persons with mental illness from incarceration into community-based programs is the San Bernardino Partners Aftercare Network (SPAN). SPAN is housed on the grounds of San Bernardino County's West Valley Detention Center. The aftercare management team serves as a bridge for offenders as they are released from state custody and reintegrated into the community. SPAN provides a number of services such as early discharge planning so that the mental health needs of inmates can be assessed well before they are released. In addition, inmates receive a 14-day supply of medication when they are released to cover the period until they can meet with a mental health service worker. They also receive identification cards so law enforcement personnel and treatment providers will know that the person is part of the program.[39]

Another example of a best practice is a community-based corrections program that began in 2006, when the Colorado legislature approved a $1.3 million pilot program designed to provide medication and monitoring to inmates with mental illnesses. The program provides free medicine to two kinds of inmates: those who are being released from prison to community halfway houses, and parolees who break rules and are sent to community corrections facilities. The program has shown the potential to dramatically reduce recidivism among those who participate. In 2006, the year before the medication program began, 92 mentally ill inmates, or 56 percent of the offenders sent to community corrections facilities, violated rules or committed new crimes and were returned to prison. In the first two years of the medication program, only two mentally ill inmates, or 3 percent of the 61 prisoners getting psychotropic medications at community corrections facilities, were sent back to prison. The number of mentally ill offenders who were released from prison to community corrections halfway houses and then ended up back in prison also dropped, from 47 percent in 2006 to 37 percent in 2007 and 2008.[40]

Criminal Culpability for Those with Mental Disorders

It's tricky to determine the culpability of people who have committed crimes while also recognizing that they suffer from mental health disorders. For an act to be considered criminal, three general features must be considered. First, the *actus reus,* or the act itself, must be considered, with a determination that it violated a law. Then, the *mens rea,* or state of mind, of the offender at the time of the criminal offense must be taken into account. Finally, these two features must be concurrent. That is, for a crime to occur, the person must commit an act that violates the law while at the same time comprehending the consequences of his or her actions.[41]

In relation to offenders who suffer from mental illness, *mens rea* raises several points for the courts to consider. First, should the mentally ill be held responsible for criminal acts? If a mentally ill person is charged, how will the court determine if the defendant is sufficiently competent to stand trial? Defendants are declared competent to stand trial if they understand the nature of the charges they are facing and if they are able to participate in their own defense in a meaningful way. Typically, if a trial judge has reasonable doubt that a defendant is competent to stand trial, then the goal is for the defendant to receive mental health treatment until the defendant is declared competent enough to stand trial.[42]

There are distinctions between competency and the insanity defense. Persons with mental health disorders can be found competent to stand trial, but may still try to escape culpability by using some type of insanity defense. The insanity defense is a legal defense based on claims of mental illness or mental incapacity. States vary in their approach to the insanity defenses, and four states— Idaho, Kansas, Montana, and Utah—presently do not allow for any type of insanity defense.[43] In most states that do, the burden of proof is on the defense to prove beyond a reasonable doubt that the defendant meets that jurisdiction's standard test of insanity.

The standard test used by most states is the **M'Naghten Rule** or a modified version of the M'Naghten Rule. The guidelines for establishing insanity under the M'Naghten Rule were codified in the British courts in 1843. Daniel M'Naghten, the namesake of the rule, was a Scottish woodcutter who murdered the secretary to the Prime Minister (Sir Robert Peel) in a botched attempt to assassinate the Prime Minister himself. Apparently, M'Naghten believed that the Prime Minister was the main cause for his multiple personal and financial misfortunes. During his trial, nine witnesses testified that M'Naghten was insane. The jury acquitted M'Naghten, finding him "not guilty by reason of insanity." Under the M'Naghten Rule, a defendant is considered legally insane if at the time the crime is committed, the defendant did not know what he or she was doing or did not know that his or her actions were wrong.[44]

Several states now use the Model Penal Code (MPC) or a modified version of the MPC as their test of insanity. The MPC provides a standard for legal insanity that is a compromise between the strict M'Naghten Rule and the irresistible impulse test. Under the MPC standard, defendants are considered insane if at the time they committed the crime, they had a mental disease or defect that made them substantially incapable of either understanding the wrongfulness of the act or conforming their behavior to the requirements of the laws. The **irresistible impulse test** pardons defendants of culpability for a crime when they can distinguish right and wrong at the time of the crime, but due to their mental disease or defect they are incapable of controlling their actions. This defense is commonly used in crimes of revenge. While no state today relies solely upon the irresistible impulse test, Colorado does use it in conjunction with a modified version of the M'Naghten Rule, and Texas uses the irresistible impulse test in combination with the M'Naghten Rule.[45]

As noted earlier, Idaho, Montana, and Utah are among the states that do not allow for an insanity defense. Yet these states allow for a finding of "guilty but mentally ill" (GBMI). This verdict is equivalent to a finding of guilty, but it acknowledges that a defendant, although mentally ill, had sufficient possession of his or her faculties to be held morally blameworthy for the crime. Georgia, which provides for a modified version of the M'Naghten Rule, also accepts a verdict of GBMI. When a jury delivers a GBMI verdict, the judge may impose any sentence allowed under the law for that particular crime. Psychiatric treatment is usually part of the commitment order, and once the offender is cured, he or she is placed in jail or prison to serve any remaining portion of the sentence.[46] Kansas, the other state that does not allow insanity defenses, maintains an "incompetent to stand trial" statute that considers defendants' mental stability in determining whether they are able to defend themselves. In short, persons who are charged with a crime can be considered incompetent to stand trial if they are unable to understand the nature and purpose of the criminal proceedings or if they are unable to assist in their defense.[47]

Policy Challenges Regarding Offenders with Mental Health Issues

Trying to enact and implement policies that affect offenders with mental health issues means defining the targeted group. Within the criminal justice system, offenders can be defined as legally insane and legally sane, competent and incompetent. Complicating matters, mental health illnesses may stem from biological, psychological/psychiatric, or sociological factors, or from a combination of these factors. Moreover, the system must also respond to developmentally challenged offenders who are considered legally sane and competent to stand trial, even though they may possess an IQ score of only 69 or below. Somewhere between 4 and 9 percent of the prison population is comprised of developmentally challenged inmates.[48]

Another challenge for those making policies related to this diverse population relates to classification. Are offenders mentally ill persons who have a mental health problem or are they persons with a mental health problem who have committed a crime? **Labeling theory** highlights the importance of this question. This theory suggests that certain people are more likely than others to receive stigmatizing labels, such as deviant, criminal, or mentally ill, because they are considered to be outsiders due to behavior or other kind of difference. The dominant societal group can successfully attach the label to an individual because the group has more power than the individual. Once a person has become successfully labeled, however, his or her choices become restricted. Moreover, persons in this category come to accept the label until it becomes a self-fulfilling prophecy. The stigmatized person has now had his or her identity shaped through the process of social definition.[49]

While everyone has the potential to violate the law, the way lawbreakers are treated is determined by how society labels them. Most people agree that a criminal deserves punishment, while someone with a mental defect deserves treatment. Moreover, as you have seen, ideas about how those with mental defects should be treated has changed over time. Herein lies the problem: What do you do with persons who have mental defects and commit crimes? Which factor—the mental defect or the criminal conduct—takes precedence? Similarly, what are the best treatment alternatives for this and other types of special categories of offenders? In the next section, we turn our attention to society's response to those labeled as sex offenders.

Sex Offenders

According to the Bureau of Justice Statistics, at year-end 2005, more than 160,000 offenders in state prisons had been convicted of rape or sexual assault. The vast

ANGELA GOEHRING: SENIOR VICE PRESIDENT OF CLINICAL OPERATIONS, ARMOR CORRECTIONAL HEALTH SERVICES, INC., MIAMI, FLORIDA

Career Profile

Angela Goehring, RN, MSA, CCHP, is currently employed by Armor Health Services, Inc., Miami, Florida, as the Senior Vice President of Clinical Operations. Goehring has worked in the correctional health care system for nearly 25 years. According to Angela, "Health care professionals working in the correctional environment must first and foremost recognize the offender as their patient, with basic health care needs that parallel those patients found in the community. Detainees and offenders often present histories of being medically underserved, addictions to drugs and alcohol, and are generally noncompliant with prescribed plans of treatment and medication regimens. These 'special needs' patients require early intervention and resources that include, physician, nursing, dental, and mental health professional time. They also require diagnostics, treatment modalities, and medications in amounts disproportionate to the general population inmate. Correctional professionals could easily see this population as a drain on resources and a hindrance to the system; however, it is important to see the situation as an opportunity to participate in the mission of supporting the offender and providing him or her with every tool necessary for a successful reintegration. Identification of the special needs patient must begin during the initial booking phase in our nation's jails.

"Special needs patients require a discharge plan that facilitates bridging them, and their medical and mental health needs to the community. It is imperative this discharge plan be initiated in both the jail and prison setting and prior to the offenders' release into the community. Identifying community resources for the offender remains a challenge but with continued efforts and ongoing dialogue, bridges will come to fruition. A staff position dedicated to this process is necessary in each jail and prison setting. The discharge process should begin upon offender entry into the system, continue throughout his or her confinement, and produce a solid plan of care upon release that provides continuity and availability of services during and after the patient's transition into the community. The discharge plan must include correctional facility health care providers, community corrections professionals, and community health care professionals.

"All correctional professionals—institutional, health care, and community corrections—must accept advocating and identifying resources for special needs patients as their moral and ethical duty. Effective discharge planning provides the offender with access to needed health services and rewards the correctional professional with a feeling of a job well done. We must avoid leaving the task to the next professional and seize the opportunity when offenders sit before us to intervene, take action, and make a difference in the life of the special needs offender."

majority of these offenders will be released to communities. Additionally, more than 700,000 registered sex offenders are residing in communities across the United States. At year-end 2008, 12,629 adult sex offenders were tracked by the Global Positioning System (GPS) while on parole. More than half of those offenders (6,629) are in the state of California.[50] These numbers create a significant management challenge to criminal justice professionals. Let's look now at issues that community corrections agencies face when dealing with this special-category offender.

An Overview

Much like offenders with mental health issues, sex offenders are considered to be in a special category of offenders. A sex offender is someone who has been convicted of an offense that has a sexual element, such as unlawful sexual intercourse or unlawful sexual contact. Even though sex itself is a normal part of life, some sexual practices are viewed as deviant or even illegal. What distinguishes normal sexual behavior from deviant or illegal sexual behavior? Various standards based on statistical, cultural, religious, and subjective data, are used to make these distinctions.[51] Standards regarding sexual behaviors can also vary across time and place. That is, an act can be considered deviant or even illegal at one point in time and place but seen as perfectly normal at another time and place. Conversely, a behavior that in one time or place was legal can become criminalized. Moreover, behavior that is unacceptable in one jurisdiction may be acceptable in another. One example is prostitution, which is legal in licensed brothels in Nevada, but not in any other state.

Sex victims and sex offenders are as diverse as all other people. They include adults, children, males, females, old, young, white, minorities, lower class, middle class, upper class, strangers, family members, and every imaginable occupational status.[52] People often respond to sex offenders in explosive, emotional ways, especially if the media have published the identity and locality of an offender in the community, and if the offense was committed against a child or was particularly heinous. Communities are often paralyzed with fear when a sexual predator is known to be active in their area, especially because they fear for the safety of their children. Often, politicians and the press pick up on these fears to further their own agendas. Sex crimes give politicians a platform to run on, insisting that more legislation is needed to control such offenses and the media report on sex crimes because the public is so intrigued by such stories.[53]

When discussing what constitutes a sexual offense, the concept of consent is a central focus point. If one party to a sexual act has not consented (willingly given permission), then a sexual offense has likely occurred. Even if consent was given, it may be invalidated if it was given under force or duress, or if the person giving the consent did not know the full implications of what he or she was consenting to, or if the person was not of age to give consent. Consent may also be considered invalid if the parties involved are entering into a prohibited relationship as defined by law. Prohibited relationships may include relationships between family members (incest), those of the same sex (such as homosexuality), people who are unmarried (fornication), or people who are married to someone else (adultery). Even in marriage, a prohibited relationship may be claimed, such as spousal rape, when one spouse forces the other to have sex against his or her will.

Of all the statutes governing consensual sexual conduct, adultery and fornication are the least likely to be enforced. While the Model Penal Code recommends against criminalizing this conduct, state statutes that prohibit it still exist. The Minnesota statute on adultery reads as follows: "When a married woman has sexual intercourse with a man other than her husband, whether married or not, both are guilty of adultery and may be sentenced to imprisonment for not more than one year or to payment of a fine of not more than $3,000, or both."[54] While not prevalent, prosecution under such statutes can occur under the guise of protecting families and their stability. Our opening story is a good example of questionable prosecutor judgment. Philip Alpert was prosecuted but his girlfriend was not. Why?

Sex Offender Treatment and Supervision

One approach for dealing with low-risk sex offenders is consistent with the idea of restorative justice. As we have seen in previous chapters, restorative justice is a concept that focuses on the victim, the offender, and the community. All parties collectively agree to come together to resolve how best to handle the aftermaths of an offense. A big component of this approach is reintegrative shaming, which refers to friends and family confronting an offender with the consequences of his or her offense and allowing the offender to express remorse as part of reintegrating into society.[55]

Reintegrative shaming was first advanced in 1989 by criminologist John Braithwaite as an alternative to stigmatic shaming. Braithwaite asserted that stigmatic shaming, which is tied to labeling, tends to destroy the moral bond between the offender and the community, setting an offender apart as an outcast, therefore making it virtually impossible for that person to ever again become a trusted member of society. In contrast, reintegrative shaming is thought to strengthen the moral bond between the offender and the community, thus allowing the offender to be brought back into the community as a productive member after completing his or her court-ordered sanctions.[56]

While it's often stated that "once a sex offender, always a sex offender," a new prison-based treatment program for sex offenders in British Columbia, Canada, examines this assumption with what has been referred to as sex offender school. Sex offender school focuses on the principles of managing risks that lead to reoffending, developing a consciousness of one's crime cycle, and building self-discipline. Thus, one goal is to create the high-risk checklist—a list identifying an offender's 10 highest risk factors, be they thoughts, feelings or situations.[57] Using class exercises and techniques, participants develop crime cycle and relapse prevention plans aimed at recognizing their criminal identity as sex offenders. By the end of treatment, sex offenders, although not cured, accept that this identity will always be a central part of their makeup so it's up to them to accept this reality, exercise self-discipline, and keep themselves from participating in illegal sexual behaviors again. Before being allowed to participate in society once again, sex offenders must able to prove to the clinical experts, the professionals in the criminal justice system, and eventually the community that they can monitor their risks and control unwarranted behaviors.[58]

Similarly, the Texas Department of Criminal Justice operates a two-phase comprehensive education and treatment program for sex offenders. The first phase, the Sex Offender Education Program (SOEP), consists of a four-month curriculum for sex offenders who are determined to pose a lower reoffense risk or are being sentenced to a lengthy term of community supervision. The curriculum provides information on a variety of topics including healthy sexuality, anger and stress management, interpersonal relationships, and cognitive restructuring. The program assists offenders with building the necessary skills to begin phase two—the Sex Offender Treatment Program (SOTP), which consists of an 18-month intensive treatment program in a therapeutic community environment. The SOTP involves three treatment phases employing a cognitive-behavioral model. The primary goal of the program is to reduce the rate of reoffense and move participants toward a more pro-social lifestyle.[59]

In addition to these progressive approaches to treatment of sex offenders, two additional trends are garnering attention in the criminal justice community: risk containment as part of community supervision, and civil commitment. These are the programs we will discuss next.

Risk-Containment Programs. A risk-management approach that places great emphasis on sex offender accountability and public safety is the offender containment program. This type of program augments traditional community supervision strategies (i.e., home visits, job checks, surveillance) with polygraph examinations and targeted behavior-modification treatment. Because community supervision is considered a privilege, and one that involves some risk to the community, offenders must help contain that risk by waiving their right to confidentiality. The waiver allows for the sharing of important information regarding the offender's risk and treatment progress between the judge, probation and parole officer, offender, family members, significant others, and the victim's therapist, if deemed necessary. Professionals must be on the alert to respond to such information in order to minimize the offender's access to victims and high-risk situations. This model approach is conceptualized as having five parts:

1. A philosophy that values public safety, victim protection, and reparation for victims as the paramount objectives of sex offender management
2. Implementation strategies that rely on agency coordination, multidisciplinary partnerships, and job specialization
3. A containment approach that holds sex offenders accountable through the combined use of the offenders' internal controls and external criminal justice control measures, including the use of the polygraph to monitor internal controls and compliance with external controls
4. Development and implementation of informed public policies to create and support consistent practices
5. Quality control mechanisms, including program monitoring and evaluation, that ensure prescribed policies and practices are delivered as planned

This five-part model establishes a framework within which agencies and communities can develop practices that promote public safety and victim protection and assistance. Research suggests that many probation and parole agencies have adopted the containment model for supervision of sex offenders in the community. For example, a survey of 732 probation and parole supervisors nationwide found sex offender supervision practices that included a victim-centered, collaborative team approach with consistent policies and quality control mechanisms.[60] In 2001, the Center for Sex Offender Management provided case studies of promising practices to jurisdictions seeking to improve their sex offender management approaches. One example is Intensive Parole for Sex Offenders (IPSO) in Massachusetts, which uses a containment approach that combines treatment, intensive team supervision, electronic monitoring, and use of the polygraph. IPSO also uses active GPS to track offenders, allowing parole officers to monitor high-risk sex offenders in real time. As evidence of success, while 6 percent of offenders under IPSO supervision returned to prison for new charges and 35 percent returned for technical violations, none returned for new sex crimes.[61] IPSO costs nearly double what it costs to supervise non-IPSO parolees—or about $3,580 per year per parolee—because the program requires parole officers to have reduced caseloads and twice the number of contacts with each parolee. However, the intensive approach is still considerably less expensive than incarceration or inpatient treatment. For instance, in Massachusetts, incarceration cost nearly $43,000 per year per offender, and inpatient treatment beds cost almost $20,000 per year per offender.[62]

Civil Commitment. In 1990, the state of Washington passed the nation's first modern Sexually Violent Predators (SVP) civil commitment law. Since then many states have followed suit, passing similar laws and policies, also known as Sex Offender Civil Commitment (SOCC). SOCC allows the state to retain involuntary civil custody of a person who has been declared by a court to present future risks of engaging in harmful sexual conduct by virtue of having a mental abnormality or personality disorder. Following this commitment, sexual offenders are then remanded to the custody of mental health care authorities, who continue to provide treatment until they determine that the offender no longer poses a threat to society.[63]

Although SOCC has garnered support in the general population, it is controversial because of assumptions that sex offenders suffer from mental abnormalities that makes them more likely than non-sex offenders to recidivate. A few studies have explored this topic and identified factors that lead to recidivism. For example, one looked at 61 previous studies of sexual recidivism using a 4 to 5 year follow-up period. This research found that 13.4 percent of sex offenders recidivated with a sexual offense, and 12.2 percent recidivated with a non-sex offense.[64] The strongest predictors of sexual recidivism were related to deviant sexual interests and deviant victim choices. When comparing sex offenders and non-sex offenders, failure to complete treatment was a significant predictor of both sexual and nonsexual recidivism.[65]

Several courts have challenged the constitutionality of civil commitment laws, but to date, none has succeeded.[66] However, civilly committing sex offenders raises a number of issues, including the high cost of doing so. Virginia estimates civil commitments cost an average of $110,000 per person per year, while in New York that figure is over $200,000.[67] Other issues include the need for specialized training for staff and serious questions about the safety and well-being of other patients.

Sex Offender Registration

In 1996, after the brutal rape and murder of Megan Kanka by a neighbor who had previously been convicted of a sex crime, **Megan's law** was passed. This law encouraged states to expand their sex registries, making records available to the public and thereby incorporating an element of community notification.[68] By 1998, all states had adopted some type of community notification policy.[69] In March 1998, the Bureau of Justice Statistics (BJS) established the National Sex Offender Registry Assistance Program (NSOR-AP), which provided assistance to states so they could participate in the FBI's permanent National Sex Offender Registry (NSOR). The NSOR-AP also surveyed states regarding their sex offender registries (SORs) and found that California had the largest number of offenders in its registry, with over 88,000 registrants, while Texas came in second with almost 30,000 registrants. Moreover, the survey revealed that 22 states had collected DNA samples and maintained them as a part of their registry, and that as of February 2001, 29 states and the District of Columbia had created publicly accessible Web sites containing information on individual sex offenders in a searchable format.[70]

In 2006, Congress passed the Adam Walsh Child Protection and Safety Act, another piece of legislation to protect children and the public from violent sex offenders. Six-year-old Adam Walsh had been abducted from a Sears department store in Hollywood, Florida, in 1981 and was later found murdered. His death drew national attention, and his father, John Walsh, became an advocate for victims of violent crimes; he later became the host of the television program, *America's Most Wanted.*

Title I of the Adam Walsh Act became known as the **Sex Offender Registration and Notification Act (SORNA)**, which attempts to standardize registration and

BeenVerified is a public record database available through Web-based software that can be accessed for a fee.

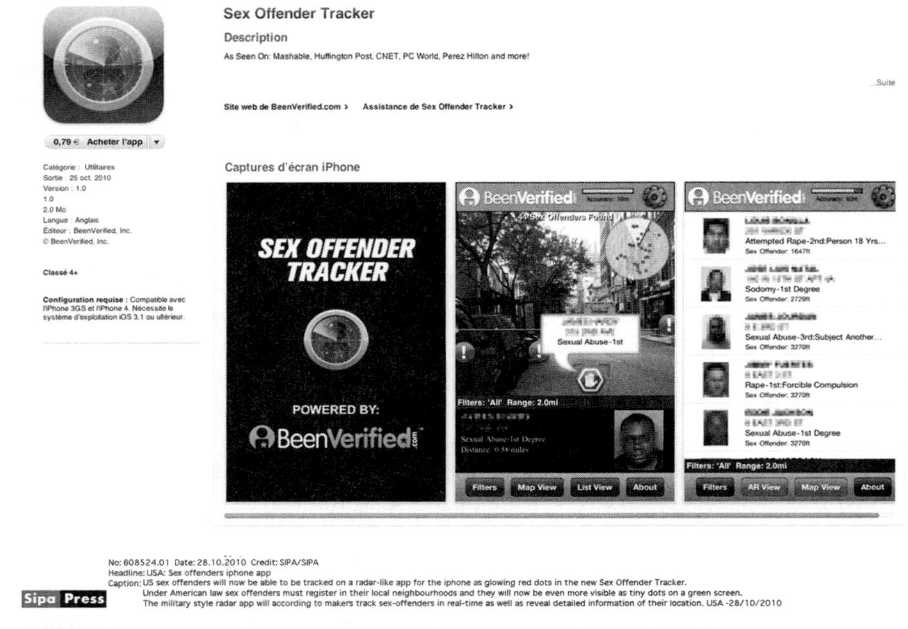

notification requirements across the country and provide for greater offender accountability and increased sanctions for noncompliance. Sexual offenses are categorized into three levels for registration purposes: Tier I Offenses require registration for 15 years and annual verification; Tier II Offenses require registration for 25 years and semiannual verification; and Tier III Offenses require lifetime registration and quarterly verification.[71] Today, all 50 states, the District of Columbia, and the principal territories including federally recognized Native American tribes have public sex offender registries that can be accessed via the Internet. Currently, the registry includes 704,777 sex offenders, most of whom live in the community while being supervised by either probation or parole offices. California has the most persons registered (118,692), for a per capita rate of 323 sex offenders per 100,000 people. Per capita, Oregon leads the country with 574 registered sex offenders per 100,000 people, and Delaware is next with 465 registered sex offenders per 100,000 people.[72]

While creating and providing public access to a sex offender registry may increase public safety, it can also lead to disastrous consequences for those whose names and addresses appear in the registry. In 2006, 20-year-old Canadian Stephen Marshall found the names and addresses of two sex offenders who lived in Maine by searching the online sex offender registry. After traveling to Maine to visit his father, Marshall borrowed his father's handgun and killed 24-year-old William Elliot and 57-year-old Joseph Gray. Gray had been convicted of sexually assaulting a child, and Elliot had been convicted of statutory rape (sexual intercourse with a person who is under the legal age of consent). What the sex offender registry did not explain was that Elliot, who was 19 years old at the time of his conviction, had committed statutory rape with his girlfriend, who had been just shy of her 16th birthday, the age of consent. After killing the two men, Marshall turned the gun on himself and committed suicide. This is an extreme case, but it reveals one face of the public reaction to sexual offenders: an atmosphere of moral panic that springs from the oft-mistaken belief that all sex offenders are either violent sexual predators, who are likely to engage in future predatory sexual behaviors, or pedophiles, who are sexually attracted to and then become molesters of children.[73]

Every year, 10,000 to 20,000 sex offenders are released back into the community. Sex offender management is an extremely complex issue that continues to pose vast challenges for state policymakers. To address these challenges, the Council of State Governments (CSG) has partnered with the Association of Paroling Authorities International, the American Probation and Parole Association, and the Center for Sex Offender Management to make up a Sex Offender Policy Board. This board and its work were made possible by a grant provided through the Bureau of Justice Assistance. In January 2007, after a yearlong study, the board presented its findings, concluding that a comprehensive approach to sex offender management includes assessment, appropriate treatment and supervision, and registration requirements. The board also found that while the public strongly supports having resident restrictions on where sex offenders can live, in reality there is no evidence to support that residence restriction is effective in preventing sex offenses. The board also emphasized the need to tailor treatment strategies to fit individual sex offenders; in other words, one-size-fits-all strategies were not found to be effective. Development of assessment tools that can successfully predict recidivism was also seen as a crucial component of sex offender management.[74]

Policies Related to Sex Offenders

Today, children have unlimited access to the Internet, and this has resulted in another type of crime: online sexual solicitation. In 2000, the findings from the first national study of online sexual solicitation of children were published. Researchers found that nearly 20 percent of children aged 10 to 17 had received at least one sexual solicitation in the previous year. This same study reported that 3 percent of children who regularly use the Internet had received aggressive sexual solicitations, including requests to meet in person. Another 3 percent reported that they had developed close relationships with adults online. Finally, the study found that in 75 percent of these cases, parents did not know their children were engaging in online relationships.[75]

By monitoring online solicitations, police have been able to initiate Internet sex stings and arrest sex offenders before they can meet potential victims. One former popular television program, *To Catch a Predator* (see CBC Online 11.2), revolved around the idea of using volunteer decoys to pretend they were underage minors and assist law enforcement in the capture of Internet child solicitors. The show ended shortly after one of the alleged predators, Louis Conradt, an assistant district attorney for Rockwall County, Texas, shot himself when a SWAT team appeared at his home to arrest him. This case illuminates some of the controversial questions regarding the use of Internet sex stings. Do they lead to crimes of enticement and entrapment? Should sexually explicit dialogue between an adult and a "pretend" minor be considered a crime?[76]

Another policy approach for dealing with sex offenders is the sentencing and/or legislative treatment option of using either chemical or surgical castration. The goal of this type of legislation is to decrease the risk of future sexual offenses by either chemically or surgically altering an offender's hormone and/or neurotransmitter levels so they will no longer desire to participate in their previous sexual offenses. Reoffending is a real

11.2

CBC Online

TO CATCH A PREDATOR

To Catch a Predator was a reality television show that featured a series of hidden-camera investigations by the television news magazine *Dateline NBC*. In 2006, the staff of this program collaborated with the Flagler Beach, Florida, Police Department to set up sting operations to expose men who used the Internet for sexual liaisons.

This two-part video shows the result. After viewing both videos, consider whether such televised sting operations serve the public good. Are there drawbacks to such television productions?

Visit CBC Online 11.2 at www.mhhe.com/bayens1e

possibility for some sex offenders. One study noted that after five years, the sexual recidivism rate for sex offenders ranged between 10 and 15 percent.[77] On September 17, 1996, California became the first state to sanction either chemical or physical castration for certain sex offenders who were being released from prison into the community. Since then, several states have followed suit; however, some allow for chemical castration only, and they also differ with regard to whether castration is seen as discretionary, mandatory, or voluntary.

Opponents of such legislation allege that it violates the First, Eighth, and Fourteenth Amendments to the U.S. Constitution. Other objections question (1) an offender's ability to give informed consent to castration, (2) the government's ability to diagnose which offenders can best benefit by castration, and (3) the financial costs to society. Perhaps the most troubling issue is whether castration really prevents sexual reoffending. Because castration legislation is relatively new, and only a limited number of castrated offenders have actually been released back into the community for any extended time, we have limited data on whether castration legislation has achieved its goal of decreasing sexual victimizations. However preliminary studies indicate that for certain sexual offenders, chemical or surgical castration does appear to decrease sexual reoffending.[78]

Sex offender policies are often influenced by rare, high-profile tragic cases. However, policymakers must enact laws that actually do promote public safety and don't merely give the public a false sense of security. Myths about sex offenders continue to flourish, such as the widespread belief that most victims are targeted by strangers, while in fact most victims are much more likely to know their perpetrators. These myths continue to influence policymakers and may have detrimental effects on public safety. Successful strategies take into account real data on sex offenders and the varying levels of risk they pose to the public.[79]

Women Offenders

An Overview

As a group, women typically commit fewer and less serious crimes than do men. In 2008, of the total number of people arrested, women constituted only 24.5 percent. For serious violent crimes, such as murder, forcible rape, robbery, and aggravated assault, only 18.3 percent were committed by women. Typically, adult women offenders are arrested for property offenses, such as larceny theft, and drug abuse violations. In

EXHIBIT 11.2 Arrest Trends by Sex, 1999–2008

	Male			Female		
	1999	2008	Percent change	1999	2008	Percent change
TOTAL	**6,279,139**	**6,083,494**	**-3.1**	**1,778,501**	**1,985,133**	**+11.6**
Murder and non-negligent manslaughter	6,636	6,292	-5.2	831	780	-6.1
Forcible rape	15,452	12,474	-19.3	179	148	-17.3
Robbery	54,658	64,844	+18.6	6,261	8,615	+37.6
Aggravated assault	228,525	202,645	-11.3	55,814	54,400	-2.5
Burglary	149,875	157,341	+5.0	23,106	29,055	+25.7
Larceny-theft	461,632	431,212	-6.6	254,629	308,011	+21.0
Motor vehicle theft	60,540	43,801	-27.6	11,331	9,344	-17.5
Arson	8,317	7,116	-14.4	1,373	1,291	-6.0
Forgery and counterfeiting	38,570	31,947	-17.2	24,253	19,631	-19.1
Fraud	114,020	80,973	-29.0	96,234	65,637	-31.8
Embezzlement	5,768	6,575	+14.0	5,634	7,039	+24.9
Stolen property; buying, receiving, possessing	56,110	53,172	-5.2	10,350	14,116	+36.4
Vandalism	135,146	137,165	+1.5	24,317	28,213	+16.0
Weapons; carrying, possessing, etc.	87,790	93,112	+6.1	7,492	7,480	-0.2
Prostitution and commercialized vice	19,762	12,133	-38.6	25,240	25,164	-0.3
Sex offenses (except forcible rape and prostitution)	48,800	40,876	-16.2	3,670	3,769	+2.7
Drug abuse violations	711,384	784,561	+10.3	155,256	185,201	+19.3
Gambling	4,481	2,227	-50.3	800	350	-56.3
Offenses against the family and children	65,172	51,268	-21.3	18,481	17,303	-6.4
Driving under the influence	714,457	667,017	-6.6	134,279	181,391	+35.1
Liquor laws	298,874	241,328	-19.3	84,444	89,999	+6.6
Drunkenness	370,924	347,399	-6.3	55,670	66,883	+20.1
Disorderly conduct	262,713	243,865	-7.2	82,332	89,530	+8.7
Vagrancy	13,302	12,037	-9.5	3,130	3,550	+13.4
All other offenses (except traffic)	1,687,374	1,724,690	+2.2	444,312	517,358	+16.4

Source: U.S. Department of Justice, Federal Bureau of Investigation.

2008, 34.8 percent of all those arrested for property crime were women. Other common arrests for women include driving under the influence, welfare fraud, check forgery, prostitution, and other varieties of petty offenses.[80] Exhibit 11.2 provides data on arrest trends by gender for selected crimes.[81]

As with men, women are most likely to be arrested while in their late twenties. In 2008, 357,045 women between the ages of 25 and 29 years old were arrested in the United States. This equates to 13.4 percent of all crime committed by women. With regard to age, the next largest groups of women arrested in 2008 included those between 30 and 34 years old (254,767), between 35 and 39 years old (240,832), and between 40 and 44 years old (219,643). Thereafter, arrests steadily decrease as age increases.[82]

Although gender is the most powerful variable to predict whether someone is likely to break the law, researchers did not begin including females in their samples until the late 1970s. Even when females were included, they were typically measured against male criminality standards. That is, theories were generated to explain male criminality, since males committed most of the crimes, and female criminality was judged to be less important and less interesting. This "invisibility" of female offenders, both historically and today, carries over into women's correctional facilities. The excuse given for the lack of vocational, educational, and counseling programs offered to incarcerated women is that women make up such a small percentage of offenders.[83] Nevertheless, women's incarceration rates have continued to rise since the 1980s. In 1980, only 12,331 women were under the jurisdiction of state and federal correctional authorities in the United States. By 2008, this number had increased to 114,852 women. During this same time period, men's incarceration rates increased from 303,643 to 1,434,800. So while women's incarceration rates increased over 9.3 times, men's incarceration rates increased only about 4.7 times. To put it another way, women's incarceration rates are increasing about twice as fast as those for men.[84] These dramatic increases do not necessarily mean that there have been dramatic increases in numbers of females offending, but rather that women are vulnerable to certain policies, such as mandatory sentences, due to their increasing involvement with drug-related or property crimes.[85]

To gain a better grasp on women's issues, one must understand the personal struggles they faced before they came into contact with the criminal justice system. When studies of incarcerated women are conducted, for example, researchers discover that women have themselves often been victims of crimes. Many women report being victimized as young girls living at home. Some suffer from mental illnesses brought on by enduring years of abuse. Some experienced violence and/or sexual abuse and felt they had to run away from home in order to protect themselves. However, once on the streets, they found they lacked the education and experience needed to obtain gainful employment. At this point, some turned to prostitution or other crimes to survive.[86] Often, these victims turn to alcohol and/or drugs to manage the pain they experience. In one study involving 456 adult female prisoners in Wisconsin, over 21 percent admitted that they drank alcohol on a daily basis. Over 27 percent of these incarcerated women reported that their current incarceration was due to an alcohol-related offense. About 80 percent of these inmates reported that they had used illegal drugs, and over 40 percent reported that their current incarceration was due to drug abuse.[87]

Special Issues Faced by Women Offenders

Of the millions of people admitted to U.S. jails and released back into the community each year, 12 percent are women.[88] Incarcerated women tend to be of color, poor, unemployed, and single mothers of young children. They often come from shattered families and have other family members who are also involved in criminal activities. Most have major drug abuse issues, along with multiple physical and mental health

Studies in correctional settings have found that women are typically underserved in all types of jail programming. What arguments would you make to advocate for gender-specific programming for women?

problems. As stated earlier, all too often, trauma is a contributing factor to their problems. Women in prison have typically experienced abuse, including sexual assault, domestic violence, and other forms of sexual, physical, and psychological abuse. Frequently, they serve relatively short prison sentences for committing nonserious, nonviolent crimes, and soon are released back into their communities. Most have not received much, if any, assistance to help them deal with their pathways to crime, nor are they given transitional services, thus almost guaranteeing that they will fail while on the outside and return to prison.[89]

A gender-specific problem that incarcerated women face is separation from their children. Nationally, 70 to 80 percent of female inmates have dependent children at the time of their incarceration, and most plan to be their children's primary caregiver when they leave prison. While both male and female inmates tend to be parents, women are much more likely than men to have custody of their children prior to incarceration.[90] And while the vast majority of children of incarcerated men live with their mothers, children of incarcerated women tend to live with their grandparents or other relatives, or they end up in foster care. The separation of a woman from her children has a significant bearing on her children's futures. Thus, children of inmates are five to six times more likely than their peers to become incarcerated themselves. Visitation policies and the long distances to prisons from their home neighborhoods often hinder visits between children and their incarcerated mothers.[91] Separation from their children also has a significant impact on incarcerated mothers. The longer the separation, the more role strain mothers experience from not being allowed to engage in mothering activities. The more mothers are allowed to participate in mothering activities while incarcerated, the better prepared they will be to resume the parenting role when they leave prison.[92]

Besides being victims of violence, many incarcerated women are riddled with health problems, such as infectious and chronic diseases, addictions, and mental health problems, all of which can profoundly affect their communities when they reenter. One study examined the life circumstances of adult females and adolescent males in the year following their release from New York City jails. The purpose of this study was to explore the pathways by which incarceration and reentry policies contribute to inequities in health and to identify policies that could improve community well-being by reducing recidivism rates. When the women jail inmates were asked at intake to reveal the primary problems they expected to face after release, 71 percent identified housing, 69 percent substance abuse, 65 percent inadequate income, 40 percent unemployment, 27 percent education, and 22 percent family problems related to their children. Unfortunately, policy does do not always take into consideration these concerns. For example, although having health insurance coverage was found to reduce recidivism and drug use (a concern among 69 percent of the women interviewed), New York State chose to terminate rather than suspend Medicaid coverage for jail inmates. A year following release from jail, only a little more than half (55 percent) of the women and about a quarter (23 percent) of the men had reinstated their Medicaid coverage. Considering the health problems surrounding this population, public policy may have led to adverse health and social consequences for these individuals, their families, and their communities. Postrelease employment—a concern for 40 percent of the women interviewed—also was found to significantly reduce rearrest rates. Thus, this study recommends that public health professionals develop employment, educational, substance abuse, health, and mental health programs and policies to assist jail inmates when they reenter the community.[93]

Women tend to be good candidates for community-based sentences because the crimes they commit are usually not as serious or violent as crimes committed by men; therefore, they pose less of a threat to the community. Even though 85 percent of convicted women are under some type of community supervision, community-based programs have historically been given little consideration. Criminal justice practitioners are faced with the pressure to reduce recidivism rates and keep communities safe, while at the same time staying within their budgets. Thus, they will need to rely more and more on evidence-based practices to determine what works best for the female offender population. One promising practice that uses cognitive skills to develop moral reasoning, is known as **moral reconation therapy (MRT),** which was an element in a study conducted at a community reentry center in the state of Illinois. In this study, researchers hypothesized that MRT would reduce recidivism for both male and female offenders, but that the reduction for males would be significantly greater than that for females because the therapeutic programs being used were built primarily on theories used to explain male criminality. However, data from the study showed a significant reduction in the risk of recidivism for all program participants. The risk to recidivate for males was lower in comparison to female offenders, but not significantly lower. One conclusion of this study was that to best produce behavioral changes and reduce recidivism in women, therapeutic programs must be based on developmental theories related to women. Moreover, for MRT to be most effective with women participants, a gender-specific component should be incorporated.[94]

Having a gender-specific program does not mean simply limiting programs designed for males to females only. A safe, trusting, and supportive environment is required to address the unique needs of women. And while correctional treatment programs have traditionally been evaluated by their ability to reduce recidivism, using only recidivism as a measurement of success is problematic. Variables such as the frequency of recidivism, the seriousness of the offense, the timing between first and subsequent offenses, and undetected offenses should also be included in the equation. Also, when evaluating women's success under community-based supervision, researchers often overlook the possibility that even though these women may not have committed any new, known offenses, they may be living in abusive relationships, having difficulties finding employment, or struggling to regain custody of their children—all factors that undermine a successful reentry.[95] The National Council on Crime and Delinquency supports the increased use of community correction programs but strongly recommends that a gender-responsive model be developed to provide intensive services related to needs for housing, job training and placement, parenting skills, education, substance abuse treatment, trauma-sensitive reentry, health care, and long-term follow-up. The council also recommends that community corrections become part of a larger reform effort that addresses sentencing policy, prevention and reentry programs, and intervention with children of incarcerated mothers, and that a public awareness campaign encourage community ownership of programming for female offenders.[96]

The Federal Bureau of Prisons recommends a strategy called the Inmate Skills Development (ISD) initiative to advance successful reintegration back to the community. This is a competency-based strategy designed to promote skill-building and inmate accountability, while addressing the multidimensional problems that challenge female offenders. This strategy consists of identifying core skills needed for successful reentry, assessing skills rather than relying solely on program completion, linking programs to specific reentry skills, allocating resources to inmates who possess the greatest skill deficiencies and face the greatest risk of recidivism, and sharing information to build community partnerships for a holistic approach in transitioning offenders. Women involved in such programs will be assessed with regard to daily living skills, mental health skills, wellness skills, interpersonal skills, academic skills, cognitive skills, vocational/career skills, leisure time skills, and character skills.[97]

Since a large portion of women offenders that leave incarceration or have been sentenced to community corrections are mothers, community-based programs for mothers—such as the one illustrated in CBC Online 11.3—are needed to assist them with parenting and emotional management skills. And these programs should be used in conjunction with other programs to address the multiple, overlapping needs of women. But for these programs to be effective, they need to go beyond teaching women offenders how to become better mothers; they need to teach them how to become self-sufficient, independent individuals. One program along these lines involves three phases. Phase one is an eight-week parenting class that explains the developmental stages of children and teaches appropriate types of discipline that fit each stage of development. Phase two offers a 16-week parent support group that focuses on the issues that impact female offenders. Finally, phase three is eight weeks long and addresses emotional deficits and how to manage stress. For such programs to work effectively, they should be conducted in the least restrictive environment possible and in close proximity to the participants' children. Even though these women may not have been ideal mothers, most will return to their children as their sole caretaker. To prevent the cycle of offending from being repeated with the next generation, it is important to support the mother-child relationship.[98]

As mentioned, substance abuse affects a large percentage of women offenders, and it is a complex issue stemming from a multiplicity of factors. Women entering community-based substance abuse treatment programs are less likely than men to be employed and are more likely to be dealing with past experiences involving emotional, physical, and sexual abuse. Women who are in substance abuse treatment programs

11.3

CBC Online

PURDY

PURDY is a 60-minute video of five offender mothers and their infants. The documentary explores the struggles of raising a child in an institution, the challenges the women face as they prepare to reenter the community, and the joy they experience as a bond develops between them and their infants.

After viewing the video, describe the residential parenting program at Washington State Corrections Center for Women.

Visit CBC Online 11.3 at www.mhhe.com/bayens1e

are more likely than men to be divorced, have child care responsibilities, and have low incomes. Compared with men, women participants are also more likely to abuse multiple substances, have a history of using crack and cocaine, and have co-occurring mental and physical health care issues. One study, involving 714 males and 169 females from a transitional case management study, revealed that females living in someone else's house were more likely to have had prior substance abuse treatment issues, suggesting that drug abuse and relapse are closely tied to their relationships with others. If a partner or other family member uses and abuses drugs, chances are that a woman living in that environment will also engage in these behaviors. Another result from this study showed that women with histories of hospitalization for health issues were 3.5 times more likely than men to have also had substance abuse treatment, suggesting that women offenders with substance abuse issues need access to health care to assist them in overcoming their multitude of problems.[99]

Policy Implications

Many offenders who fall into the category of special populations have a minimal, if any, prior criminal history and no history of violent behavior. These low-level offenders are consistently incarcerated but may be better served and less likely to recidivate if placed in community-based correctional programs that are better positioned to provide appropriate supervision and treatment strategies, recognizing that special types of offenders need specialized services. The challenge for policymakers is to recognize the multifaceted needs of special offenders and support the development of community-based correctional programs that will serve them.

One of the most difficult questions in the field of corrections is what to do with mentally ill offenders. Many offenders need professional mental health treatment, and compared with jails and prisons, mental health facilities are safer, less costly, and offer more humane options for nonviolent, mentally ill offenders. If mentally ill offenders are not diverted to mental health facilities, community-based corrections can provide specialized treatment through coordinated efforts with mental health providers. Team approaches involving corrections, law enforcement, and mental health professionals are often useful.[100]

A number of jurisdictions have established specialized court programs for low-level offenders who appear to suffer from mental illness. The goal of such programs is to assess defendants' needs for mental health treatment and divert them into proper treatment programs. Most can be supervised in the community, while others may require residential treatment. Still others will be convicted and sentenced to jail or prison, where they will receive medical attention. For these offenders, the key to long-term successful treatment is adequate reentry services. But many jurisdictions have failed to implement such services. Consequently, the most needed policy change perhaps relates to the supervision of mentally ill offenders after their release from jails and prisons. As an example of the lack of adequate supervision, a survey conducted by the National Commission on Correctional Health Care (NCCHC) found that nearly 71 percent of state correctional systems provided only a one-month supply of medications to offenders with chronic medical conditions (including mental illness) at the time of prison release. Thereafter, offenders are expected to obtain their own medication. Community-based corrections agencies, including parole agencies, do not fill in the gap either, as they are not required to provide medical care to offenders in the community.[101]

Another important challenge relates to the treatment of sex offenders. In recent years, sex-offender legislation focused on registration, community notification, civil commitment, and residence restrictions. The goals of such laws include increasing public safety, deterring offenders from committing future crimes, and providing law enforcement with additional investigative powers. When sex offenders are placed in community-based corrections, programs face the difficult dilemma of how best to accomplish punishment and rehabilitation while upholding public safety. Central to this challenge is holding sex offenders responsible for their actions while treating them to help them change their behavior. Given the serious nature of sex offenses, and their lifelong impact on victims, even a low reoffending rate may be too high. But estimates that community-based sex offender treatment costs about $5,000 per year—versus $20,000 per year per offender for incarceration—make community-based correctional programs an attractive alternative for low-level offenders. Policymakers should advocate for laws that are grounded in evidence-based practices and that will protect citizens as well as rehabilitate perpetrators in the most efficient and cost-effective manner.

With regard to female offenders, we have noted that they differ from their male counterparts in several key ways. In particular, most female felons were victims before they were offenders, most are single parents, and most were convicted of nonviolent drug or property crimes. Nationally, of those offenders living with their children prior to arrest, 46 percent of female offenders were living in a single-parent household, compared to 15 percent of male offenders. In many instances, the children in these households are minors. For example, more than half of the 10,000 women in California's prisons and 12,000 women on parole were living with their minor children prior to their arrest. Among those women, two-thirds were single parents. Research shows these children are at a higher risk of having behavioral problems and becoming involved in foster care and the criminal justice systems.[102]

With these concerns in mind, policymakers should be urged to develop gender-specific correctional strategies for women offenders that emphasize community-based corrections and that reconnect women to social services, employment, and their families. A few states have established alternative sentencing and residential placement for mothers who are to be incarcerated for relatively short periods. The purpose of such programs is to minimize harm to the family and to help stabilize the parent within the community setting. Such programs offer a new perspective on women's corrections with the goal of reducing the number of women who return to prison.

Summary

For years societies have been dealing with the problem of what to do about the care, treatment, and control of persons with mental health issues. During the colonial period, such problems were left up to the families. In 1773, however, the first institution was built in the United States to specially house persons with mental illnesses. This trend continued, and the 19th century became the heyday for the building of asylums, both for persons with mental illnesses and for those who had committed crimes. As the social climate changed in the United States, reformers considered that those who had committed crimes but also had mental illnesses should receive treatment rather than punishment. Science continued to make strides regarding how the brain affected behavior, and when the drug Thorazine was introduced in 1955, a push toward deinstitutionalization began. Although community mental health care centers were supposed to regulate the population that had been newly released from institutions, in reality they fell short of their goals, which resulted in lack of treatment for those with mental health problems. This lack of treatment led to increases in homelessness, incarceration, and violence for people with mental health issues.

Some communities strive to make better use of community treatment programs to lower recidivism by offering social and legal services, along with mental health treatments. Offenders who have mental health problems continue to challenge the criminal justice system. When being reintegrated to the community, it is helpful for these offenders with mental health problems to be assigned to probation or parole officers who have received special training.

Much like offenders with mental health issues, sex offenders have a unique set of characteristics and needs. Sex offenders are as diverse as the population itself. Their crimes cover a wide range of sexual offenses. Several theories try to explain why sex offenders offend, but because there are so many types of offenders and offenses, one theory cannot explain them all.

Sex offenders have the potential to hurt numerous victims, including children. For that reason, legislation has been enacted to establish and expand sex registries. However, having one's name on a sex registry labels that person and can lead to unintended consequences for the registered offender. Sex offending has now expanded by using the Internet to lure victims. Options for treating sex offenders range from castration to supervision and therapy. One-size-fits-all treatments do not work. In order for a treatment to be effective it must be tailored to fit the individual sex offender.

Even though women make up a small percentage of offenders, their numbers are increasing at a much faster rate than the rate for men. Women offenders bring with them their own special needs. In the past they were studied by using theories tested on male offenders only. Recently, however, theories have been developed that address female criminality. One such approach, the feminist or gendered pathways perspective, uses the voices of women to identify linkages between child and adult life events and traumas that may have led to criminality.

Most women have been victims themselves and have turned to substance abuse as a means of self-medication. Without the proper education and training, most cannot earn a good wage, even though most have children and plan to support their children when they are released from incarceration. Being a mother poses a set of unique challenges for women offenders. Most want to be good mothers, but they may need training in parenting skills. Most women are not serious, violent offenders and would be best served in community-based corrections where they can receive help for their problems and maintain bonds with their children.

Key Terms

Community Mental Health Centers Act (CMHCA), p. 312
deinstitutionalization, p. 311
irresistible impulse test, p. 317
labeling theory, p. 318
M'Naghten rule, p. 317
Megan's law, p. 323
mental health courts, p. 314
moral reconation therapy (MRT), p. 330
reintegrative shaming, p. 323
serious mental illness (SMI) , p. 313
Sex Offender Registration and Notification Act (SORNA), p. 324
sexting, p. 309

Questions for Review

1. How did the introduction of medicine and the deinstitutionalization movement influence the evolution of treatment of mentally ill persons in the United States?
2. How can communities best help offenders with mental health problems reintegrate back into their communities?
3. What theories are offered to explain why sex offenders commit sex crimes?
4. What services are community-based programs providing to ensure public safety from sex offenders?
5. What theories have been suggested to explain female criminality?
6. What gender-specific problems do women face in the criminal justice system?

Question of Policy

Why Care that People with Mental Illnesses Are Significantly Overrepresented in Jails?

Local jails have a constitutional mandate to accept all persons who are arrested by police and to provide adequate medical treatment for these defendants while in custody. However, these detention facilities are ill-equipped to meet the needs of those with serious mental illnesses. So why are so many mentally ill persons in jail?

1. Because state and local governments are facing significant budget shortfalls, spending for community-based mental health services continues to decrease. Consequently, persons with serious illnesses have nowhere else to be placed but jail.
2. Some people assume that persons with mental illness are more violent or dangerous. Consequently, they assume they need to be locked-up.
3. Why is it critical for policymakers to consider evidence-based practices that address what community leaders have long known: that people with mental illnesses are significantly overrepresented in jails?

What Would You Do?

In response to public concern about sex crimes, your state legislature has toughened penalties for sex offenders, increased funding for programs that treat sex offenders, and taken steps to ensure that more offenders receive treatment. However, basic descriptive information about the number of treatment programs in operation and the number of sex offenders who receive treatment is lacking. Also, legislators have asked whether sex offender treatment programs are effective in reducing the rate at which sex offenders commit additional crimes.

You have been given the task of addressing these concerns for your probation agency. You develop a preliminary list of questions that relate to the legislature's concerns: How has the number of sex offenders on probation changed in recent years? How much treatment do offenders typically receive and how much does it cost? What data does my agency keep to judge whether treatment works?

Can you identify two other questions relating to the legislature's concerns?

What methods would you use to collect the data necessary to answer these questions?

Endnotes

1. Amanda Lenhart, *Teens and Sexting* (Washington, DC: Pew Research Center's Internet & American Life Project, December 2009).
2. Nancy J. Beran and Beverly G. Toomey (eds.), *Mentally Ill Offenders and the Criminal Justice System* (New York, NY: Praeger Publishers, 1979).
3. E. Fuller Torrey, *Out of the Shadows: Confronting America's Mental Illness Crisis* (New York, NY: John Wiley & Sons, Inc, 1997).
4. Supra (See 1).
5. William Logie Russell, *The New York Hospital: A History of the Psychiatric Service 1771–1936 (Mental Illness and Social Policy; the American Experience)* (New York, NY: Columbia University Press, 1945).
6. Supra (See 2).
7. Albert Deutsch, *The Mentally Ill in America—History of Their Care and Treatment from*

Colonial Times (New York, NY: Columbia University Press, 1949).

8. Supra (See 2).
9. Frederick H. Wine, *Report on the Defective, Dependent and Delinquent Classes of the Population of the United States* (Washington, DC: U.S. Government Printing Office, 1888).
10. Risdon N. Slate and W. Wesley Johnson, *The Criminalization of Mental Illness* (Durham, NC: Carolina Academic Press, 2008).
11. Ibid.
12. Supra (See 2).
13. Chris Koyanagi, *Learning From History: Deinstitutionalization of People with Mental Illness as Precursor to Long-Term Care Reform* (The Henry J. Kaiser Family Foundation, 2007).
14. Hitesch C. Sheth, "Deinstitutionalization or Disowning Responsibility," *International Journal of Psychosocial Rehabilitation*, vol. 13, no. 2 (2009), pp. 11–20.
15. Steven Sharfstein, "Community Mental Health Centres," *Journal of the Royal Society of Medicine*, vol. 73 (March 1980), p. 219.
16. Ted Strickland, "Weapons of Mass Destruction," *Testimony of Congressman Ted Strickland Before the House Judiciary Subcommittee on Crime* (2000).
17. Joseph Morrissey and Howard Goldman, "Cycles of Reform in the Care of the Chronically Mentally Ill," *Hospital and Community Psychiatry,* vol. 35 (1984), pp. 785–793.
18. The American Presidency, "President's Commission on Mental Health Remarks on Receiving the Commission's Final Report" (April 27, 1978). Retrieved online at www.presidency.ucsb.edu/ws/index.php?pid=30714.
19. Hitesh Sheth, "Deinstitutionalization or Disowning Responsibility," *International Journal of Psychosocial Rehabilitation,* vol. 13, no. 2 (2009), pp. 11–20.
20. Frank Sirotich, "Correlates of Crime and Violence among Persons with Mental Disorder: An Evidence-Based Review," *Brief Treatment and Crisis Intervention,* vol. 2, no. 2 (2008), pp. 171–194.
21. H. Richard Lamb et al., "Treatment Prospects for Persons with Severe Mental Illness in an Urban County Jail," *Psychiatric Services,* vol. 58, no. 6 (2007), pp. 782–786.
22. *Justice Center Study Brief: Prevalence of Serious Mental Illness among Jail Inmates, Council of State Governments Justice Center* (2009). Retrieved from http://consensusproject.org/jcpublications/council-of-state-governments-justice-center-releases-estimates-on-the-prevalence-of-adults-with-serious-mental-illnesses-in-jails/MH_Prevalence_Study_brief_final.pdf.
23. Brent Teasdale, "Mental Disorder and Violent Victimization," *Criminal Justice and Behavior,* vol. 36, no. 5 (2009), pp. 513–535.
24. Supra (See 2).
25. Supra (See 14).
26. Supra (See 17).
27. Supra (See 9).
28. Paula Ditton, *Mental Health and Treatment of Inmates and Probationers* (Washington, DC: Bureau of Justice Statistics, July 1999).
29. Sheilagh Hodgins et al., "A Multisite Study of Community Treatment Programs for Mentally Ill Offenders with Major Mental Disorders: Design, Measures, and the Forensic Sample," *Criminal Justice and Behavior,* vol. 34, no. 2 (2007), pp. 211–228.
30. David Lovell, Gregg J. Gagliardi, and Paul Peterson, "Recidivism and Use of Services Among Persons With Mental Illness After Release From Prison," *Psychiatric Services,* vol. 53 (October 2002), pp. 1290–1296.
31. Patricia Griffin, Henry J. Steadman, and John Petrila, "The Use of Criminal Charges and Sanctions in Mental Health Courts," *Psychiatric Services,* vol. 53 (October 2002), pp. 1285–1289.
32. *Mental Health Courts: A Primer for Policymakers and Practitioners.* Retrieved from http://consensusproject.org/mhcp/mhc-primer.pdf.
33. Ibid.
34. Roger Boothroyd et al., "The Broward Mental Health Court: Process, Outcomes and Service Utilization," *International Journal of Law and Psychiatry,* vol. 26 (2003), pp. 55–71.

35. Virginia Hiday and Bradley Ray, "Arrests Two Years After Exiting a Well-Established Mental Health Court," *Psychiatric Services,* vol. 61 (May 2010), pp. 463–468.

36. Dale E. McNiel and Renee L. Binder, "Effectiveness of a Mental Health Court in Reducing Criminal Recidivism and Violence," *American Psychiatry,* vol. 164, no. 9 (2007), pp. 1395–1403.

37. Supra (See 30).

38. Supra (See 9).

39. *Emerging Judicial Strategies for the Mentally Ill in the Criminal Caseload: Mental Health Courts in Ft. Lauderdale, San Bernardino, and Anchorage* (Washington, DC: Bureau of Justice Assistance Document: NCJ 182504, April 2000).

40. Kirk Mitchell, "Drug Aid Benefits Prisoners Recidivism Cut for Mentally Ill Upon Return to Society," *The Denver Post* (September 2009).

41. Frank Schmalleger, *Criminal Justice Today: An Introductory Text for the 21st Century,* 10th ed. (Upper Saddle River, NJ: Pearson Prentice-Hall, 2009).

42. Supra (See 9).

43. *Insanity Defense.* Retrieved 3/29/2010 from www.enotes.com/everyday-law-encyclopedia/insanity-defense.

44. Supra (See 28).

45. *Insanity Defense.* Retrieved from http://legal-dictionary.thefreedictionary.com/Guilty+mentally+ill.

46. Supra (See 28).

47. Kan. Stat. Ann. §§ 22–3301 to 22–3302 (2010). Retrieved from http://kansasstatutes.lesterama.org/Chapter_22/Article_33/.

48. Harry Allen et al., *Corrections in America: An Introduction,* 11th ed. (Upper Saddle River, NJ: Pearson Prentice-Hall, 2007).

49. Howard Becker, *Outsiders: Studies in the Sociology of Deviance* (New York, NY: Free Press, 1963).

50. Lauren E. Glaze and Thomas P. Bonczar, *Probation and Parole in the United States, 2008,* (Washington, DC: U.S. Department of Justice, Office of Justice Programs, Bureau of Justice Statistics, December 2009).

51. Ronald M. Holmes and Stephen T. Holmes, *Current Perspectives on Sex Crimes* (Thousand Oaks, CA: Sage Publications, Inc., 2002).

52. R. Barri Flowers, *Sex Crimes: Perpetrators, Predators, Prostitutes, and Victims*, 2nd ed. (Springfield, IL: Charles C. Thomas Publisher, Ltd., 2006).

53. Supra (See 38).

54. See Minn. Stat. § 609.36 (2010).

55. Anne-Marie McAlinden, *The Shaming of Sexual Offenders: Risk, Retribution and Reintegration* (Portland, OR: Hart Publishing, 2007).

56. John Braithwaite, *Crime, Shame and Reintegration* (Sydney, Australia: Cambridge University Press, 1989).

57. Danny Lacombe, "Consumed with Sex: The Treatment of Sex Offenders in Risk Society," *British Journal of Criminology, vol. 48* (2008), pp. 55–74.

58. Ibid.

59. Texas Department of Criminal Justice: Rehabilitation Programs Division. Retrieved from www.tdcj.state.tx.us/pgm&svcs/pgms&svcs-sexofftrtpgm.htm.

60. Kim English, Suzanne Pullen, and Linda Jones, *Managing Adult Sex Offenders in the Community—A Containment Approach* (Washington, DC: National Institute of Justice: Research in Brief, January 1997).

61. National Governor's Association Center on Best Practices, *Issues Brief: Managing Convicted Sex Offenders in the Community* (April 7, 2008). Retrieved from www.nga.org/files/live/sites/NGA/files/pdf/0711SEXOFFENDERBRIEF.PDF.

62. Ibid.

63. Andrew J. Harris, *Civil Commitment of Sexual Predators: A Study in Policy Implementation* (New York, NY: LFB Scholarly Publishing LLC, 2005).

64. R. Karl Hanson and Monique Bussière, "Predicting Relapse: A Meta-Analysis of Sexual Offender Recidivism Studies," *Journal of Consulting and Clinical Psychology,* vol. 66, no. 2 (1998), pp. 348–362.

65. Ibid.

66. *Kansas* v. *Hendricks*, 521 U.S. 346 (1997).

67. Mental Health Association in New York State, Inc. (October 2006). Retrieved from www.mhanys.org.

68. *High Court to Test Sex Offender Law: Case Challenges Megan's Law Sex Offender Registries*. Retrieved from http://usgovinfo.about.com/library/weekly/aa052002b.htm.

69. Monica L.P. Robbers, "Lifers on the Outside: Sex Offenders and Disintegrative Shaming," *International Journal of Offender Therapy and Comparative Criminology*, vol. 53, no. 1 (2009), pp. 5–28.

70. Devon B. Adams, *Summary of State Sex Offender Registries, 2001* (Washington, DC: U.S. Department of Justice, Bureau of Justice Statistics, 2002). Retrieved from www.ojp.usdoj.gov/bjs/abstract/sssorao.htm.

71. National Sexual Violence Resource Center, *Sex Offender Management Policy in the States, Final Report: Strengthening Policy & Practice* (Winter 2010). Retrieved from www.nsvrc.org.

72. *Registered Sex Offenders in the United States Per 100,000 Population Map*. Retrieved from http://missingkids.com/en_US/documents/sexoffendermap.pdf.

73. Supra (See 48).

74. Supra (See 55).

75. David Finkelhor, Kimberly Mitchell, and Janis Wolak, *Online Victimization: A Report on the Nation's Youth* (Washington, D.C.: National Center for Missing & Exploited Children, June 2000). Retrieved from ww.unh.edu/ccrc/Child_Vic_Papers_pubs.html.

76. Supra (See 49).

77. R. Karl Hanson and Monique T. Bussière, "Predicting Relapse," pp. 348–362.

78. Supra (See 49).

79. Supra (See 55).

80. Meda Chesney-Lind and Lisa Pasko, *The Female Offender: Girls, Women, and Crime*, 2nd ed. (Thousand Oaks, CA: Sage Publications, Inc., 2004).

81. Table 33 of *Crime in the United States, 2008* (Washington, DC: U.S. Department of Justice, Federal Bureau of Investigation, September 2009). Retrieved from www.fbi.gov/ucr/cius2008/data /table_33.html.

82. Table 40 of *Crime in the United States, 2008* (Washington, DC: U.S. Department of Justice, Federal Bureau of Investigation, September 2009). Retrieved from www.fbi.gov/ucr/cius2008/data /table_40.html.

83. Joanne Belknap, *The Invisible Women: Gender, Crime, and Justice*, 3rd ed. (Belmont, CA: Thomson Wadsworth, 2007).

84. *Sourcebook of Criminal Justice Statistics* (2008). Retrieved from www.albany.edu/sourcebook.

85. Angela Wolf, "Reducing the Incarceration of Women: Community-Based Alternatives," *Special Report: National Council on Crime and Delinquency* (2006).

86. Meda Chesney-Lind and Nancy Rodriguez, "Women Under Lock and Key: A View from the Inside," *The Prison Journal*, vol. 63 (1983), pp. 47–63.

87. Martin Guevara Urbina, "A Comprehensive Study of Female Offenders: Life Before, During and After Incarceration," *Critical Criminology*, vol. 17, no. 3 (2009), pp. 217–219.

88. Ibid.

89. Supra (See 69).

90. Sandra Enos, *Mothering from the Inside: Parenting in a Women's Prison* (Albany, NY: SUNY, 2001).

91. Supra (See 69).

92. Phyllis E. Berry and Helen M. Eigenberg, "Role Strain and Incarcerated Mothers: Understanding the Process of Mothering," *Women & Criminal Justice*, vol. 15, no. 1 (2003), pp. 101–119.

93. Nicholas Freudenberg et al., "Coming Home from Jail: The Social and Health Consequences of Community Reentry for Women, Male Adolescents, and Their Families and Communities," *American Journal of Public Health*, vol. 95, no. 10 (2005), pp. 1725–1736.

94. Ann M. Schlarb, "A Comparison of the Effects of the MRT Cognitive Behavioral Program between Male and Female Parolees," *Cognitive-Behavioral Training Materials*, vol. 1 (2010), pp. 10–13.

95. Maeve McMahon, *Assessment to Assistance: Programs for Women in Community Corrections*

(Lanham, MD: American Correctional Association, 2000).

96. Supra (See 69).

97. Ruth T. Zaplin, *Female Offenders: Critical Perspectives and Effective Interventions,* 2nd ed. (Sudbury, MA: Jones and Bartlett Publishers, 2008).

98. Ibid.

99. Michele Staton-Tindall et al., "Gender-Specific Factors Associated with Community Substance Abuse Treatment Utilization Among Incarcerated Substance Users," *International Journal of Offender Therapy and Comparative Criminology*, vol. 53, no. 4 (2009), pp. 401–419.

100. Mary Shilton, *Targeting Special Populations: Tools for Building Effective Community Corrections* (Washington, DC: Center for Community Corrections, October 2000).

101. The National Commission on Correctional Health Care, *The Health Status of Soon-to-Be-Released Inmates: A Report to Congress* (2002). Retrieved from www.ncchc.org.

102. Little Hoover Commission Report, *Commission Urges Focus on Women Offenders* (December 2004). Retrieved from www.lhc.ca.gov.

CHAPTER 12

Community-Based Corrections for Juveniles: Giving Kids the Chance They Need

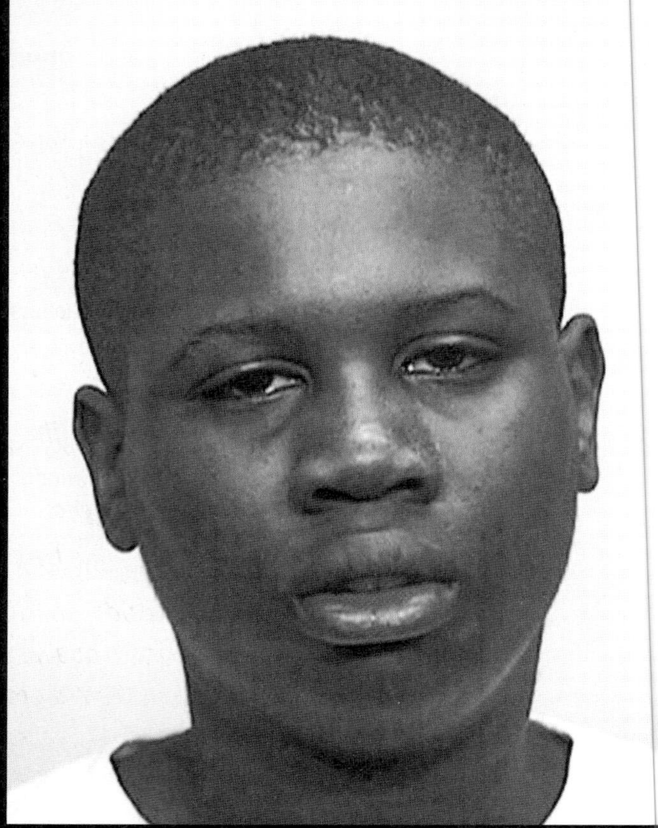

OBJECTIVES

1 Trace the historical roots of juvenile community-based corrections.

2 Describe the U.S. Supreme Court decisions that are significant in the history of juvenile rights.

3 Describe the methods for transferring youths to adult court.

4 List and explain the services provided by juvenile probation agencies.

5 Explain the importance of ISP and aftercare programs in juvenile community-based corrections.

6 Identify several innovative practices in today's juvenile community-based corrections agencies.

7 Describe gender-specific programming for female offenders.

OUTLINE

In 1999, 12-year-old Lionel Tate was arrested and charged with first-degree murder for the battering death of six-year-old Tiffany Eunick in Broward County, Florida. Tate claimed he was imitating professional wrestlers. Tate was a large boy for his age, nearly 6 feet tall and 166 pounds. Eunick weighed only 48 pounds. Medical experts testified that Tiffany had sustained a ruptured spleen, lacerations, damage to her rib cage, a fractured skull, brain contusions, a detached liver, and bruises all over her body. In 2001, Lionel Tate was convicted as an adult of aggravated child abuse and felony murder. At the age of 14, he became the youngest person in the United States to be sentenced to life in prison without parole. However, finding that Tate should have been mentally evaluated before trial, an appeals court overturned his murder conviction in 2004, and he was released from prison and placed on 10 years probation, including a year of house arrest and the requirement to wear an electronic monitoring device.

In September 2004, during his period of house arrest, Lionel Tate, then age 17, was taken into custody by police when they found him away from home at 2:00 A.M. carrying an eight-inch knife. For that, the court added five years to his probation and warned him that any future violations would not be tolerated. Less than two years later, Tate pled guilty to a gun violation after being arrested for robbing a pizza deliveryman. He was sentenced to 30 years in prison for violating his probation, and in October 2007, an appeals court upheld the sentence. On February 19, 2008, Tate pled no contest to the pizza robbery and was sentenced to 10 years. The sentence will run concurrently with his 30-year sentence for violating his probation.

As you read this final chapter, consider whether you think Lionel Tate should have been charged as a delinquent (instead of an adult) for felony murder. Might it have been better to place this 14-year-old in a boot camp, an intensive supervised probation program, or a treatment center for juveniles? Throughout the chapter, you will have an opportunity to consider this question as we explore the juvenile justice system, legal decisions, and policy changes that have occurred as a result of the rise and fall of juvenile crime in the past 25 years. We also discuss issues relating to community-based programs that have been developed for youths, some of which are gender-specific. In the final section of the chapter we explore the relationship between media coverage of juvenile crime and its potential impact on community-based corrections.

Evolution of Juvenile Community-Based Corrections

The Juvenile Justice and Delinquency Prevention Act (JJDPA) of 1974[1] provides the foundation for a discussion of community-based corrections for youthful offenders. The JJDPA is the primary vehicle through which the federal government sets standards for state and local juvenile justice systems. It also provides direct funding for states, research, training, technical assistance, and evaluation. The basic tenets of the JJDPA involve the

12.1

CBC Online

A PIVOTAL MOMENT: SUSTAINING THE SUCCESS AND ENHANCING THE FUTURE OF THE JUVENILE JUSTICE AND DELIQUENCY PREVENTION ACT

This September 2009 report from the Coalition for Juvenile Justice provides the results of a national survey on the federal-state partnership that underlies the impact of the JJDPA.

After reading the report, can you identify the major findings relating to the history of funding JJDPA programs? Which of the recommendations made to the President and Congress do you think will best build on the successes of JJDPA programs and confront emerging challenges for juvenile justice?

Visit CBC Online 12.1 at www.mhhe.com/bayens1e

separation of adults from juvenile offenders in correctional settings and the provision of community-based services for **status offenders** (e.g., those charged as truants or runaways). The statute contains four core requirements: (1) **deinstitutionalization** of status offenders; (2) separation of juveniles from adult offenders; (3) removal of juveniles from adult jails and lockups; and (4) attention to reducing minority confinement.

Due in large part to the JJDPA, juvenile justice reform gained momentum in the 1970s toward achieving the requirements just listed. Children charged with noncriminal **status offenses** and nonoffenders, such as dependent, neglected, and abused youths, started to be diverted from secure detention facilities, which were reserved only for youths who posed a direct safety risk to themselves and the community. A report from the General Accounting Office indicates that as a result of the 1974 law, the number of status offenders detained for longer than 24 hours has been reduced by almost 95 percent in all states that participated in the program.[2] If a child was charged with a criminal offense, detention in an adult jail facility was merely a temporary arrangement until he or she could be transported to a **juvenile detention facility**. If held in a jail awaiting transportation, the young offender was housed separate from the adult offenders. For the first time juvenile offenders were better protected from the psychological and physical abuse sometimes associated within a jail environment where they were more likely to be assaulted by adults than by other children in juvenile facilities.[3] CBC Online 12.1 provides additional information about the federal-state partnership on Juvenile Justice and Delinquency Prevention.

The drive toward reducing the negative effects of secure detention for status offenders and the push toward separating juveniles from adult offenders were further supported when deterrent-based programs failed to accomplish their intended goals. The Juvenile Awareness Project provides an example of a deterrent-based program. Started in the 1970s, it embodied a simple concept: Employ fear to deter youths from committing crime. To do so, it brought youngsters to New Jersey's Rahway State Prison to hear about life there from convicts who were sentenced to 25 years to life. However, several studies of this program found that scaring youngsters with the brutalities of prison life did little to enlighten them about the effects of involvement in crime.[4]

Concurrent with the enactment of the federal JJDPA, some juvenile court judges began to address deficiencies within the juvenile court systems in their own local jurisdictions. In 1977, for example, David Soukup, a juvenile court judge in Seattle, Washington, asked community volunteers to become trained advocates for abused and neglected children in court. His initiative started the Court Appointed Special Advocate Program (CASA). In 2008, more than 68,000 CASA volunteers served more than 240,000 abused and neglected children through 1,018 program offices throughout the country.[5] In 2004, a study of CASA representation was conducted to examine the shorter- and longer-term impacts of CASA volunteers on children and families in contact with the child welfare system. The findings indicate that children with CASA volunteers received significantly more services than children without volunteers. On average, parents of children with a CASA volunteer also received a significantly greater number of services than parents of children without a CASA volunteer. The findings also suggest that children who were assigned a CASA volunteer had far more risk factors and were in more dangerous situations than children who were not assigned a CASA volunteer. This is an essential point to consider when comparing children with and without a CASA volunteer on case outcomes and measures of well-being.[6]

The importance of the JJDPA and CASA and other such programs becomes apparent when we consider that abused and neglected children are more likely to be arrested for criminal behavior as juveniles, more likely to be arrested as adults, and more likely to be arrested for a violent crime.[7] With these thoughts in mind, we turn our attention to how research, crime rates, and private sector involvement have influenced the evolution of juvenile justice.

NCCD Research on State Systems

Perhaps the greatest legacy of the JJDPA is that funding to state and local juvenile justice programs has made the treatment of young offenders more humane through diversion from confinement and supervision in the community. Community-based programs have proven to be cost-effective solutions for a large number of delinquent youths. Alternatives to secure detention include intensive supervised probation, day reporting programs, and adolescent treatment centers. All have reduced crowding in institutions, cut the costs of operating juvenile detention centers, shielded young offenders from the stigma of institutionalization, and helped to maintain positive ties between juveniles and their families and community.[8] Moreover, research has consistently shown that well-structured community-based programs for juveniles can reduce recidivism more effectively than traditional correctional programs and at less cost.

The classic example of this effect involves the Massachusetts Department of Youth Services (DYS),* which in 1972 closed its training schools for juveniles and developed a wide range of structured community-based programs for the majority of the state's committed youths.

In studies of this change, researchers compared the outcomes of youths released from the newly established community-based programs with a group released from training schools before the 1972 reforms were enacted. They concluded that "regions that most adequately implemented the reform measures with a diversity of programs did produce decreases in recidivism over time."[9] In 1989, a second study of the Massachusetts community-based system was conducted by the National Council on Crime and Delinquency (NCCD). The results of this study revealed that recidivism rates were equal to or lower than most jurisdictions throughout the country. Compared to the pre-DYS period, youths in the post-DYS period showed a significant decline in the incidence and severity of offending in the 12 months after entry into DYS community programs. NCCD also found that the Massachusetts approach was cost effective, saving an estimated $11 million annually by relying on community-based care.[10]

---

* The closing of the Massachusetts training schools and other reforms by Dr. Jerome Miller are generally regarded as the most revolutionary and meaningful in American juvenile justice history.

Another relevant NCCD research project focused on the Utah juvenile justice system, which implemented community-based programs after a lawsuit against the state's 450-bed Industrial School. Using a pre- and post-test design, researchers found that youths who were placed in community-based programs had dramatic declines in their rates of reoffending. Addressing a common public fear, the researchers concluded that "Utah's policy of community-based corrections did not worsen public safety."[11] The study also indicated that Utah's policies toward community-based corrections saved the state money. It was estimated that a one-time expenditure of nearly $33 million in construction funds and another $10 million in operating costs would have been needed to accommodate juvenile offenders if confinement policies had taken precedence over community-based corrections.[12]

Research studies using meta-analysis techniques have come to similar conclusions regarding the effectiveness of community-based programs. To begin, Dr. Mark Lipsey's meta-analysis of 443 studies of juvenile programs (373 of which were published between 1970 and 1987 and included data from both correctional institutions and community-based environments) is perhaps the most comprehensive meta-analysis of delinquency studies to date. Lipsey found that rehabilitative treatments in community settings reduced recidivism more effectively than treatments in custodial institutions.[13] Overall, he found that the more effective programs:

- Provided larger amounts of meaningful contact (greater treatment integrity) and were longer in duration (higher dosage).
- Were designed by a researcher or had research as an influential component of the treatment setting.
- Offered behavioral, skill-oriented, and multimodal treatment.[14]

In another study, Dr. Lipsey and his colleagues from the Peabody Research Institute at Vanderbilt University selected a subset of 200 studies on serious offenders from previous meta-analysis studies of interventions for both noninstitutionalized and institutionalized serious offenders. They found that certain types of treatment were more effective than others in decreasing recidivism (e.g., individual counseling, training in interpersonal skills, and behavioral programs), and that the effective ones decreased recidivism by 40 percent for noninstitutionalized offenders.[15] Exhibit 12.1 lists some of the types of treatments for noninstitutionalized and institutionalized offenders, with the most effective shown first.

The Fluctuation of Juvenile Crime Rates

In the 1970s and 1980s, alternative programs for juveniles targeted primarily status offenders and less serious delinquents. Juveniles who were alleged to be delinquent were normally routed through the family court system, and every effort was made to divert them from secured detention. Title 18 U.S.C. 5039 provides the authority for this approach:

> No juvenile committed, whether pursuant to an **adjudication** of delinquency or conviction for an offense, to the custody of the Attorney General, may be placed or retained in an adult jail or correctional institution in which he has regular contact with adults incarcerated because they have been convicted of a crime or are awaiting trial on criminal charges. . .. whenever possible, detention shall be in a foster home or community based facility located in or near his home community.[17]

But from mid-1980 through the mid-1990s, a disturbing upward trend in juvenile crime coupled with news accounts of school shootings and other serious crimes by

EXHIBIT 12.1 Treatments for Juvenile Offenders in Order of Effectiveness[16]

Treatment Used with Noninstitutionalized Offenders		Treatment Used with Institutionalized Offenders
Individual counseling; Interpersonal skills	← **Positive** effects—consistent evidence →	Interpersonal skills; Family-style, behavior modification group homes
Multiple services; Restitution, probation/parole	← **Positive** effects—less consistent evidence →	Behavioral programs; Community residential; Multiple services
Employment related; Academic programs; Advocacy/casework; Family counseling; Group counseling	← **Mixed**—but generally positive effects with inconsistent evidence →	Individual counseling; Guided group counseling; Group counseling
Reduced caseloads, probation/parole	← **Weak**—or no effects with inconsistent evidence →	Employment related; Drug abstinence; Wilderness/challenge
Wilderness/challenge; Early release, probation/parole; Deterrence programs; Vocational programs	← **Weak**—or no effects with consistent evidence →	Milieu therapy

children began to heighten public fears. Pressured by public opinion and politics to get tough on juvenile crime, police across the country arrested an increasing number of juveniles. In 1965, there were 58 arrests for violent crimes for every 100,000 minors under age 18, according to U.S. Justice Department statistics. In 1985, the rate was 139 per 100,000, and by 1994, it had risen another 66 percent to 231.[18] Perhaps the most notable of these juvenile crime increases centered on the arrest rate for murder, which increased by 110 percent between 1987 and 1993.[19] Reacting to such evidence, state and federal legislators passed laws that made the juvenile system more punitive and that allowed younger children and adolescents to be transferred to the adult system for a greater variety of offenses and in a greater variety of ways. Lionel Tate, from our opening story, is an example of someone to whom this more punitive approach was applied. In fact, his home state of Florida is near the top of the national chart when it comes to the number of youths transferred to adult court each year. From 2001 to 2006, Florida tried between 2,500 and 3,000 youths as adults.[20]

Meanwhile, across the country, the rate of detaining youths increased even faster than arrests. From 1985 to 1995, the number of juveniles confined in detention centers rose by 74 percent. A snapshot of juvenile offenders detained on one day in 1995 showed that only 29 percent of the youths had allegedly committed a violent crime. Another 30 percent were detained for property, public order, and "other" offenses. A mere 7 percent were locked up for drug offenses, and only one-sixth of those were detained for selling or distributing drugs. The majority (34 percent) were detained for status offenses and/or technical violations of conditions of probation.[21]

Although the get-tough philosophy certainly fueled the increased use of detention, most local juvenile justice systems simply had no alternatives to confinement. The limited number of possible placements at emergency shelters, **foster care** homes, and other noncustodial care programs caused many juveniles who were arrested for minor infractions to be placed in detention facilities. Moreover, children in need of care (those who had been neglected or abused) were often placed in local detention centers. Consequently, the overcrowding in detention centers increased steadily from 1985 to 1995, so that by 1995, 62 percent of juveniles behind bars were housed in an overcrowded facility.[22] In the meantime, the costs associated with operating these facilities began to skyrocket, as it was not unusual for rates to exceed $100 per diem.

The growth in the number of juvenile violent crime arrests that began in the late 1980s peaked in 1994. Between 1994 and 2004, the juvenile arrest rate for Violent Crime Index offenses (i.e., murder, forcible rape, robbery, and aggravated assault) fell 49 percent. As a result, by 2004, the juvenile Violent Crime Index arrest rate was at its lowest level since at least 1980. From its peak in 1993 to 2004, the juvenile arrest rate for murder fell 77 percent.[23] However, in 2005 and 2006, juvenile arrest rates, particularly Violent Crime Index rates, increased, as did fears that the country was on the brink of another juvenile crime wave. However, the latest data—from 2007—show increases in some offense categories but declines in most, with most changes being less than 10 percent in either direction.[24]

Despite declining juvenile crime rates, concerns about serious, violent, and chronic juvenile offenders, sometimes referred to as "**superpredators**," have led states to pass legislation aimed at ensuring that these youths receive maximum terms of confinement. Waiver of youths to the jurisdiction of criminal court, sometimes referred to as the process of juvenile **certification**, has emerged as a powerful symbol of the transformation of juvenile justice.

Private Sector Involvement

For the past 20 years, private agencies have played a role in nearly every area of the juvenile justice system, from secure detention services to community-based services. Both private for-profit corporations and private nonprofit agencies have evolved from being partners that provided collateral services for local and state government agencies and have now become mainstream, primary-service providers of justice programs. In many cases, the principal reason for the conversion from public to private juvenile services has been money. The House Fiscal Agency, a nonpartisan legislative service that provides research, statistics, and assessments to lawmakers, estimated that by privatizing juvenile services, the state of Michigan could save $3.5 million in the first year and $7 million long term.[25] And in response, in 2009, a Michigan legislator proposed to privatize the state's juvenile justice system. Cost reductions have not been the only impetus toward privatization, however. Greater emphasis on private services has occurred because of research that indicates that such programs are perhaps better equipped to succeed in the juvenile justice system.

In 1999, the Office of Juvenile Justice and Delinquency Prevention (OJJDP) sponsored a study of private sector involvement in juvenile justice systems. Survey participants represented 41 jurisdictions, including Puerto Rico and the Federal Bureau of Prisons. Of the total number of jurisdictions, 81 percent indicated they had at least one currently active private sector contract. The highest percentage of respondents (85 percent) had contracts with private nonprofit agencies; 76 percent had contracted with for-profit agencies; 49 percent had contracted with public nonprofit agencies; and 20 percent with public for-profit agencies. Nine jurisdictions indicated they had private sector contracts with other types of agencies/entities, the largest proportion of these being with professional individuals.[26] In the area of juvenile probation, 10 states have turned to private agencies to supervise youths adjudicated of misdemeanant offenses.[27] In Philadelphia, for example, recent data suggest the average sentence with private probation providers was two months for juveniles.[28]

Research of private sector involvement typically shows that juvenile programs are at least as effective as publically operated programs. For example, in a cost-benefit analysis of the Family Resource Unit, a private sector agency program in Springfield, Missouri, that provides treatment for adjudicated juvenile delinquents and status offenders and their families, the Missouri Division of Youth Services completed a study that measured recidivism and any further delinquent behavior among 203 families completing one of the short-term family therapy programs. Follow-up data were collected at 30 days and again six months after completing one of the family treatment programs. Only 33 (16 percent) of the juveniles had committed new law violations at the six-month evaluation. Twenty (almost two-thirds) of the 33 failures had committed new offenses by the 30-day follow-up. Researchers noted that in view of the traditionally high reports of recidivism among troubled, ineffective, and often dysfunctional family groups (60–80 percent recidivism six months after leaving most training schools), the Missouri Program seemed to be successful in rehabilitating juvenile offenders and their families.[29]

In another study of 8,400 juvenile offenders released from correctional facilities in Florida between July 1, 1997, and June 30, 1999, researchers explored the effects of facility management type (private for-profit, private nonprofit, public state-operated, and public county-operated) on recidivism outcomes and costs. A cost-benefit analysis showed that the short-run savings offered by for-profit over nonprofit management are negated in the long run due to increased recidivism rates. However, the study also found that while for-profit correctional facilities performed worse than state, nonprofit, and county facilities with respect to recidivism, they may still be desirable as a public policy tool since they come at a lower cost to the state. That is, the study found that $6,000 and $11,500 less per release than the average cost for a comparable release from a nonprofit and a state-operated facility, respectively.[30]

The Juvenile Justice Process versus the Adult System

The first juvenile court in the United States was established in Chicago in 1899, in response to concerns that juvenile law violators were being treated no differently than adult criminals, subjected to harsh punishment, and confined in jails and prisons with adult offenders. The business of the new court though was guided by the doctrine of ***parens patriae***, ensuring the state acted in the best interest of the child. In this family court system, judges were not interested in due process or establishing guilt and innocence. Rather, they were given great latitude to individualize care for child miscreants.

Establishing a juvenile court meant that corrective measures would emphasize treatment and rehabilitation, in contrast to the adult system, which concentrated on punishment. Social services agencies, schools, and community-based organizations would provide services to both juveniles who were at-risk of committing crimes and juveniles who had committed crimes. As we have noted, though, the juvenile justice system has experienced significant modifications during the past 30 years. Perceptions of a juvenile crime epidemic in the 1980s and 1990s fueled public scrutiny of the system's ability to effectively control juvenile offenders. Thus, the principles of separate courts, detention facilities, judicial procedures, and laws created with the intent of protecting and rehabilitating juveniles have bent to the point that differences between the adult and juvenile justice systems are often blurred.

Despite the commonalities, a few distinctions can be made between the processes used in juvenile versus adult court systems. First, the juvenile system maintains a variety of pretrial mechanisms to provide services for youths based on their individual needs while accounting for concerns of public safety. The goal is to divert youths from the court's jurisdiction at the earliest possible stage. One method of rerouting a delinquency case involves juvenile intake and assessment, a system for determining which services in the community (formal or informal) are most appropriate for youths who are in police custody. During an intake screening, a specialist collects information about the seriousness of the offense, prior record of delinquency, family and community ties, and legal mandates in order to determine whether the youth should be released to his or her family, referred to a community service, or placed in custodial care at a detention facility. Such procedures are done in Lakewood, Colorado, at the Jefferson County Juvenile Assessment Center for youths who are brought there by law enforcement officers. Key areas assessed include mental health, substance abuse, family violence, school functioning, and peer relationships.[31] In 2005, 301,200 cases (18 percent of all delinquency cases) across the country were dismissed at intake, generally for lack of a legal base. An additional 26 percent (447,400) of the cases were handled informally, with the juvenile agreeing to some sort of voluntary sanction (e.g., restitution).[32]

Another area in which the criminal and juvenile justice systems differ is bail. When an adult is arrested, he or she is typically (1) remanded to jail; (2) released with a set bail amount; or (3) released on his or her own recognizance. Juvenile offenders, however, are normally not eligible for bail,* so the judge must decide either to release the youth to the custody of a responsible adult (usually parents), or to remand to a juvenile detention facility. While constitutional limitations on preventive pretrial detention exist for adults, preventive detention of juveniles could be described as limitless. In *Schall* v. *Martin*, the U.S. Supreme Court ruled that pretrial preventive detention of juveniles under New York's Family Court Act did not violate the "fundamental fairness" requirement of the Fourteenth Amendment's Due Process Clause.[33]

The juvenile justice system also differs from the criminal justice system in the area of confidentiality, which has two aspects: confidentiality of records and confidentiality of proceedings. Confidentiality was practiced by most early juvenile courts, where it was deemed unfair to label a juvenile as a criminal because such a characterization would inhibit a youth's rehabilitation.[34] However, as juvenile crime became more violent, community protection and the public's right to know have displaced confidentiality and privacy issues as underpinnings in the juvenile court system.[35]

Consider the following scenario that has been developed to illustrate the public availability of juvenile records. As you read the scenario about confidentiality and juvenile records, be aware that access to juvenile records is not peculiar to Florida. In fact, three very popular online sources of national criminal records include the Instant Background Check (www.instantbackgroundreport.com/?hop=jkwent3); Criminal Check (http://criminal-check.com/?sp=0); and The Criminal Registry (www.criminalregistry.org/index.php?hop=jkwent3&xsite=CriminalRegistry&xtarget=&xpath=index&gc_source=g).

---

* Presently some states such as Georgia, Colorado, and Oklahoma allow juveniles to have the same rights to bail as adults.

Confidentiality and Juvenile Records

Josh Taylor of North Bay, Florida, was informed that his niece had been turned down for a part-time job after an employer ran a background check and came across information about the girl's arrest for a misdemeanor as a juvenile. Mr. Taylor searched through the Florida Department of Law Enforcement's online public records database (at www.fdle.state.fl.us/CriminalHistory) and quickly found misdemeanor records of other juveniles. Florida's law requires a $24 fee for public access to criminal history records. In other words, as long as they pay the fee, anyone can peruse the criminal history database maintained by the Florida Department of Law Enforcement and buy a copy of an individual's state criminal record. Searching by name, racial group, age, or gender, a person can collect information about people charged as juveniles with minor offenses. Critics say the public disclosure of juvenile misdemeanor records is wrong and should be stopped. They argue that online posting of criminal records, civil filings, and traffic and other minor offenses stigmatizes youths.

The last distinction between the adult and juvenile systems relates to the legal processes involved in judicial decision-making. In the juvenile system, adjudication hearings are used to establish the facts in a delinquency case and to decide whether to place the juvenile under the supervision of the court. In a criminal proceeding, the goal of the court is to determine guilt or innocence of the alleged offender. Also, criminal courts are normally open to the public, whereas juvenile courts operate primarily in private. Last, during the dispositional phase of the juvenile system, the court determines an appropriate settlement to the case based not only on the severity of the offense but also on many other factors including the social, psychological, and individual needs of the youth. In the criminal justice system, severity of crime and criminal history are the key factors to be considered at sentencing.

Legal Decisions Affecting Juvenile Justice

As you've just learned, the juvenile courts have characteristics unique to the administration of justice for youths. However, several U.S. Supreme Court rulings, such as *Kent* v. *U.S.*, *In re Gault*, *In re Winship*, *McKeiver* v. *Pennsylvania*, and *Breed* v. *Jones* (see Exhibit 12.2), have formalized procedures in juvenile court and furthered the movement to guarantee due process rights for juveniles accused of crime at the same level provided for adult defendants. The same is true of a number of state court rulings. One example arose in 2008 when the Kansas supreme court ruled that juveniles have a constitutional right to a jury trial under the Sixth and Fourteenth Amendments, and also under the Kansas constitution.[36] Kansas also became the 11th state to rule that when juveniles face serious punishment, they—like

Since the 1960s, the U.S. Supreme Court has continued to introduce constitutional due process into the juvenile justice system. The effect has been that juvenile court closely resembles adult court, and the trend continues today as Kansas and New Hampshire have recently passed laws allowing juveniles the right to a jury trial in juvenile court. Should the juvenile justice system be abolished altogether?

12.2

CBC Online

NATIONAL CENTER FOR JUVENILE JUSTICE (NCCJ)

The NCCJ provides descriptive information and analysis regarding each state's juvenile justice system, illustrating the differences between the 51 separate juvenile justice systems in the United States.

Go to the Web site and review the highlights of your state's juvenile justice system. Which policy or legal decisions are unique to your state?

Visit CBC Online 12.2 at www.mhhe.com/bayens1e

adults—are entitled to jury trials. The other 10 states that provide jury trials for juvenile offenders include Alaska, Massachusetts, Michigan, Montana, New Mexico, Oklahoma, South Dakota, Texas, West Virginia, and Wyoming. CBC Online 12.2 provides descriptive information and analysis regarding each state's juvenile justice system, illustrating the uniqueness of the 51 separate juvenile justice systems in this country. Two of the most important legal issues are trying juveniles as adults and issues related to the Eighth Amendment—cruel and usual punishment. Thus, we will next look at court decisions that impact these issues.

Trying Juveniles as Adults

Transferring juveniles to criminal court is not a new phenomenon. Since the inception of the juvenile court in 1899, judges have always identified certain youths, particularly those accused of violent and serious crimes, to be transferred to adult courts.[46] From a historical perspective, even though the primary goal of sentencing in the early juvenile courts was to rehabilitate rather than to punish, some jurisdictions are thought to have now rejected widely held principles about adolescent behavior and culpability. They instead favor laws that contain provisions for treating children as adults. However, obtaining an accurate picture of the orientation of our nation's juvenile courts is difficult because of the lack of research on the contemporary juvenile court, including the philosophies and practices of intake officials, judges, prosecutors, defense attorneys, and those who administer and work in the juvenile correctional system.[47] What we do know is that in more recent history, proponents of transferring youths to adult court claim that such laws are necessary to reform an outdated juvenile justice system initially created to deal with truants, not violent predators. Critics often counter that waiver laws unjustifiably consign too many youths to the adult system, and that there is great potential for overuse.[48] Thus, the question of which youths should be transferred to the adult, criminal court and which should be adjudicated within the juvenile justice system has always existed.[49] In CBC Online 12.3, two experts debate whether juveniles should be tried and sentenced as adults.

States have established various laws that allow juveniles to be tried as adults, and these laws can be sorted into three basic types: judicial waiver, statutory exclusion, and concurrent jurisdiction (see Exhibit 12.3). Judicial waiver laws permit juvenile court judges to remove certain youths from juvenile court jurisdiction to be tried as adults in criminal court. There are three broad categories for judicial waiver: discretionary, presumptive, and mandatory. Most states (45) have discretionary judicial waiver

EXHIBIT 12.2 Significant U.S. Supreme Court Decisions Affecting Juvenile Justice

1. *Kent* v. *U.S.*, 383 U.S. 541 (1966)

   "The *parens patriae* philosophy of the Juvenile Court is not an invitation to procedural arbitrariness."[37]

   "The [waiver] hearing must measure up to the essentials of due process and fair treatment."[38]

   RULE: Before a minor is transferred to adult court, the child is entitled to an informal hearing where the trial court must articulate the reasons for the transfer so that the child can have an adequate record for appellate review.

2. *In re Gault*, 387 U.S. 1 (1967)

   "The child and his parents must be advised of their right to be represented by counsel and, if they are unable to afford counsel, that counsel will be appointed to represent the child."[39]

   "[A]dmissions and confessions by juveniles require special caution" as to their reliability and voluntariness, and "[I]t would indeed be surprising if the privilege against self-incrimination were available to hardened criminals, but not to children."[40]

   RULE: In a **juvenile delinquency** trial, children are entitled to (1) notice of the charges, (2) a right to counsel, (3) a right to confrontation and cross-examination, and (4) a privilege against self-incrimination.

3. *In re Winship*, 397 U.S. 358 (1970)

   "A person accused of a crime . . . would be at a severe disadvantage, a disadvantage amounting to a lack of fundamental fairness, if he could be adjudged guilty and imprisoned for years on the strength of the same evidence as would suffice in a civil case."[41]

   "Where a 12-year-old child is charged with an act of stealing which renders him liable to confinement for as long as six years, then, as a matter of due process . . . the case against him must be proved beyond a reasonable doubt."[42]

   RULE: Proof beyond a reasonable doubt, which is required by the Due Process Clause in criminal trials, is among the essentials of due process and fair treatment required during the adjudicatory stage when a juvenile is charged with an act that would constitute a crime if committed by an adult.

4. *McKeiver* v. *Pennsylvania*, 403 U.S. 528 (1971)

   "[A] jury trial would entail delay, formality, and clamor of the adversary system, and possibly a public trial."[43]

   "Equating the adjudicative phase of the juvenile proceeding with a criminal trial ignores the aspects of fairness, concern, sympathy, and paternal attention inherent in the juvenile court system."[44]

   RULE: A trial by jury is not constitutionally required in the adjudicative phase of a state juvenile court delinquency proceeding.

5. *Breed* v. *Jones*, 421 U.S. 519 (1975)

   "Although the juvenile court system had its genesis in the desire to provide a distinctive procedure and setting to deal with the problems of youth, including those manifested by antisocial conduct, our decisions in recent years have recognized that there is a gap between the originally benign conception of the system and its realities."[45]

   RULE: Hearing a case in both juvenile and criminal court constitutes double jeopardy.

provisions, in which the juvenile court judge is authorized, but not required, to waive jurisdiction over a juvenile to clear the way for criminal court prosecutions.[50] The second type, presumptive waiver, is currently available in 15 states. The juvenile bears the burden of proof in a presumptive waiver hearing. That is, if a juvenile meeting age, offense, or other statutory criteria triggering the presumption fails to make an adequate showing against transfer, the juvenile court must send the case to criminal court. The mandatory waiver applies to cases that meet certain age, offense, or prior record criteria. In mandatory waiver cases, proceedings against a juvenile are initiated in juvenile court. However, the juvenile court has no other role than to confirm that the statutory

SHOULD TEENS WHO COMMIT SERIOUS CRIMES BE TRIED AND SENTENCED AS CHILDREN OR ADULTS?

This PBS video presentation features Marsha Levick, legal director of the Juvenile Law Center in Philadelphia, Pennsylvania, and Paul Pfingst, district attorney of San Diego, California. These two experts debate whether juveniles should be tried and sentenced as adults. At the center of the discussion is the Florida court case of Nathaniel Brazill, who shot his middle-school teacher in May, 2000, when he was 13 years old. Brazill was tried as an adult, convicted of second-degree murder, and sentenced to 28 years in prison.

After viewing this video, debate the issue. What rationale is presented for and against trying juveniles as adult offenders? Which side do you support?

Visit CBC Online 12.3 at www.mhhe.com/bayens1e

requirements for mandatory waiver are met. Once it has done so, it must send the case to criminal court.[51]

The second type of transfer involves statutory exclusion laws (also known as direct file), which automatically grant criminal courts original jurisdiction over certain classes of cases involving juveniles. At present, 29 states have statutory exclusion provisions in which state legislatures have in effect predetermined the question of the appropriate forum for prosecution and essentially have taken the decision out of both prosecutors' and judges' hands.[52]

The final type of transfer is referred to as concurrent jurisdiction or blended sentencing. Fifteen states currently empower juvenile courts to impose adult criminal punishment on certain categories of serious juvenile offenders. Most of these laws authorize the court to combine a juvenile disposition with a suspended criminal sentence, which functions as a guarantee of good behavior. If the juvenile cooperates, he or she will remain in the juvenile sanctioning system; if not, he or she may be sent to the adult one. Another 17 states have criminal blended sentencing laws under which criminal courts, in sentencing transferred juveniles, may impose sanctions that would ordinarily

EXHIBIT 12.3 Methods for Transferring Youths to Adult Court

Judicial Waiver	The most common provision for transfer; the juvenile court judge has the authority to waive his court's jurisdiction over the case and have it sent to adult court. Some states refer to this procedure as "certification" or "remand."
Statutory Exclusion	Statutory provisions that mandate that certain cases are automatically tried in adult court. In these cases, no other transfer mechanisms or extenuating circumstances are considered.
Concurrent Jurisdiction	Prosecutors have the discretion to file juvenile cases in adult court. Such authority is also referred to as "prosecutorial discretion" or "direct file."
Doctrine "Once an Adult, Always an Adult" (OAAA)	Under such laws, youths who have been previously tried as adults are automatically prosecuted in adult court for any subsequent offense (minor misdemeanors are typically excluded). Thirty-four states have OAAA provisions in place.

be available only to juvenile courts. Criminal blended sentencing provides a mechanism whereby juveniles who have left the juvenile system for criminal prosecution may be returned to it for sanctioning purposes. Again, sometimes the return to the juvenile system is only conditional, with a suspended adult sentence serving as a guarantee of good behavior.[53]

Collectively, the transfer mechanisms have had their impact on juvenile justice. In 1996, juvenile court judges waived 10,000 delinquency cases, 47 percent more than in 1987 but 18 percent (3,000 cases) less than in 1994, the peak year.[54] Since 1994, the number of cases judicially waived declined 47 percent (6,900 cases in 2005). One caveat to note here is that the decrease in judicial waivers by judges is in large part due to direct files and other nonjudicial transfer laws. That is, criminal cases that might have been subject to waiver proceedings in previous years were undoubtedly filed directly in criminal court, bypassing the juvenile court altogether.[55]

In 2009, the Lyndon B. Johnson School of Public Affairs at the University of Texas-Austin released a study titled "From Time Out to Hard Time: Young Children in the Adult Criminal Justice System." It contains the most up-to-date literature and facts about treating children under the age of 12 as adults. Below, we have listed some of the key findings.

- In more than half the states, it is legal for children under age 12 to be treated as adults. In 22 states plus the District of Columbia, children as young as seven can be prosecuted and tried in adult court.
- In many states a child charged with a crime in adult court may be held in an adult jail while awaiting trial and may be sent to an adult prison upon conviction. On a single day in 2008, 7,703 children under age 18 were held in adult local jails and 3,650 in adult state prisons.
- The United States stands almost alone in the world in the punitiveness toward children. The researchers found no instances where countries other than the United States handed down 20- and 30-year sentences for children under 13.
- Research clearly shows that treating children who are this young in the adult system creates nothing positive—neither for children nor for public safety.
- While judges in the adult system often have little discretion in sentencing children, those in the juvenile court system have many options. Juvenile courts are fully capable of handling even the most serious young offenders.
- Taxpayers save money by treating children within the juvenile justice system. One researcher found that $3 was saved for every $1 spent on the juvenile system.[56]

Cruel and Unusual Punishment for Juveniles

When interpreting the Eighth Amendment's cruel and unusual punishment clause, the U.S. Supreme Court has acknowledged that it will rely, at least in part, on prevailing public opinion when making its determination of whether a particular punishment is cruel and unusual. This relationship between public opinion and the Eighth Amendment's cruel and unusual punishment clause has also been relevant to the Court's disposition on the subject of capital punishment and juveniles.

In 1988, the constitutionality of the juvenile death penalty was initially decided in *Thompson* v. *Oklahoma*.[57] William W. Thompson, when he was 15 years old, actively participated in a brutal murder. Because he was a child as a matter of Oklahoma law, the district attorney filed a statutory petition seeking to have him tried as an adult, which the trial court granted. Thompson was then convicted and sentenced to death, and the Court of Criminal Appeals of Oklahoma affirmed. However, the U.S. Supreme Court held that there is an "evolving standard of decency" dictating that the execution of offenders 15 years old and younger was unconstitutional under the Eighth Amendment.

The following year, in *Stanford* v. *Kentucky*,[58] the Court ruled that the Eighth Amendment does not prohibit the execution of 16- or 17-year-old offenders tried in criminal court. Kevin Stanford was 17 years old at the time that he committed murder, first-degree sodomy, first-degree robbery, and receiving of stolen property. He was certified as an adult and ultimately convicted and sentenced to death.

In March 2005, in *Roper* v. *Simmons*,[59] the Court determined that executing juveniles who were under the age of 18 at the time of their crime constituted cruel and unusual punishment in violation of the Eighth and Fourteenth Amendments. The Court also reaffirmed the necessity of referring to "the evolving standards of decency that mark the progress of a maturing society" to determine which punishments are so disproportionate as to be cruel and unusual. The Court further reasoned that the rejection of the juvenile death penalty in the majority of states, the infrequent use of the punishment in states where it remained on the books, and the consistent trend toward abolition of the juvenile death penalty demonstrated a national consensus against the practice. That ruling affected 72 juvenile offenders in 12 states.[60]

The final cases that have had a tremendous impact on the juvenile justice system are *Graham* v. *Florida* and *Sullivan* v. *Florida*.[61] These Court cases raise the issue of whether the U.S. Constitution's prohibition on cruel and unusual punishment bars a sentence of life without parole (LWOP) for crimes committed by juveniles. Taking the cases in the order in which the Court heard them, let's begin with the case of Terrance Graham of Jacksonville, Florida.

In July 2003, Graham and two accomplices went to a restaurant in Jacksonville with the aim of robbing it. When the manager would not give them money, one of the juveniles hit him with a steel bar; Graham then fled the scene. Graham had previously been involved in several burglaries in the Jacksonville area. Two months later, Graham was arrested and charged (as an adult) with one count of burglary with an assault or battery—a serious felony that could have led to a maximum sentence of life. He was also charged with attempted armed robbery. He pleaded guilty to both, and was given three years on probation added to nine months in county jail. Six months after getting out of jail, Graham was again arrested, this time on charges of felony home-invasion robbery and eluding police. Prosecutors also charged him with violating his probation for the first crime. Graham, who at the time was 17 years old, admitted to the eluding charge and, when asked by police, admitted other robberies. By the time his sentencing occurred, he was 19. The judge imposed the sentence of life without possibility of parole. Relying on the Court's decision in *Roper*, Graham's attorneys argued that it would be cruel and unusual punishment under the Eighth Amendment to sentence him—or any juvenile—to life without parole. The First District Court of Appeal rejected the argument, stating that a term of years in prison was not "grossly disproportionate." Graham then petitioned the Court for a writ of certiorari, which the Court granted on May 4, 2009.

In 1989, 13-year-old Joe Sullivan was tried as an adult and convicted of raping and robbing a 72-year-old woman in Florida; he was sentenced to life without parole. At sentencing, the prosecutors listed 17 crimes in the prior two years, and noted that the youth had spent time in juvenile detention facilities. The judge concluded that, given the record and the sexual battery conviction, Sullivan should be treated legally as an

12.4

CBC Online

WHEN KIDS GET LIFE

Human Rights Watch and Amnesty International report that more than 2,000 inmates are serving life without parole in the United States for crimes committed when they were juveniles; in the rest of the world, only 12 juveniles are serving such sentences, according to figures reported to the United Nations' Convention on the Rights of the Child. This *Frontline* video presentation profiles five individuals who have been sentenced to life without parole as juveniles.

After viewing the presentation, discuss the implication of a 2006 Colorado law that did not include the retroactive application of ending the practice of sentencing juveniles to life without parole.

Visit CBC Online 12.4 at www.mhhe.com/bayens1e

adult under Florida law. Consequently, he was sentenced to life in prison for that crime. In the current appeal of his sentence, his attorneys argue that the practice of sentencing juvenile offenders to life imprisonment without the possibility of parole has been rejected by every nation in the world except the United States. The state of Florida argues that the U.S. Constitution allows a life sentence in such a brutal case and that the Court has never before factored age into considerations about when such a sentence is permissible. Under Florida law, the state supreme court could not review the appeal, and Sullivan petitioned the U.S. Supreme Court, which granted a writ of certiorari on May 4, 2009.

In May, 2010, the Court handed down its biggest Eighth Amendment ruling in noncapital cases in a long time, by ruling that it is unconstitutional to sentence a juvenile offender to life in prison without parole when the crime does not involve murder. The opinion is based on the Eighth Amendment's ban on "cruel and unusual" punishment. The vote was 6–3, reversing and remanding *Graham*. In the *Sullivan* case, the Court ruled that the Eight Amendment does not permit a juvenile offender to be sentenced to life in prison without parole for a nonhomicide crime. The immediate impact of the decision will be felt in the 11 states that are incarcerating at least one of the 129 inmates sentenced to LWOP for a nonhomicide committed as a juvenile. Those states are: California, Delaware, Florida, Iowa, Louisiana, Mississippi, Nebraska, Nevada, Oklahoma, South Carolina, and Virginia. The federal government also has six inmates serving juvenile LWOP sentences.[62]

Thus, these rulings reflect a trend in the Court of being increasingly lenient towards the punishment of juvenile criminals. It also leads to the next logical question: What about juveniles who commit murder? Should a sentence of life without parole for these juveniles be unconstitutional as well? To address this question, we provide in CBC Online 12.4 the video profiles of five juveniles serving life without possibility of parole.

Juvenile Probation and Aftercare

Probation remains the cornerstone of the juvenile justice system, with 67 percent of all delinquency cases placed on probation.[63] Probation is the conditional release of an adjudicated youth into the community, under supervision of a probation officer. It is conditional because it can be revoked if certain conditions are not met. Though probation is most often thought of as a disposition for juvenile offenders, most states allow probation as a disposition for status offenders as well. For status offenders referred to court, however, strict limitations are typically imposed on the length of the probation period. In California, for example, a status offender can be placed on probation for a period not to exceed six months. Idaho places a three-year limit on the amount of time a status offender can be placed on probation.[64]

Ideally, probation combines both the corrective and restorative aspects of the juvenile justice system. The goal of juvenile probation is to improve the ability of youths to live productively in the community while holding them accountable for their actions. This approach promotes public safety while focusing on the individual needs of the youth. To meet this goal, local and state agencies that administer juvenile probation provide a continuum of services ranging from intake assessment to aftercare. In Exhibit 12.4, we provide examples of distinctive services provided by juvenile probation agencies across the country. Note that some of these services are more closely aligned with public safety concerns while others are more rehabilitative.

At the heart of all probation is assessment and supervision. That is, probation programs conduct predisposition investigation, recommend appropriate court dispositions for juvenile delinquents, and supervise those youths placed on probation. In the next section we turn our attention to assessment reporting and the probation agreement. Then we discuss how case management, intensive supervised probation, and aftercare services function to provide a foundation for successful probation.

Assessment Reporting and Probation Agreement

Like the risk and needs assessment conducted prior to sentencing in the adult court system, a predisposition report is completed for the juvenile court system after a youth is convicted of an offense. Typically, a probation officer prepares the report after making inquiry into the background, criminal history, and family circumstances of the defendant. The goal is to accurately reflect information regarding the social, medical, psychological, and educational history of the juvenile being assessed. The predisposition report also includes information on the probability that the juvenile will commit further delinquent acts and recommends a disposition.

In Exhibit 12.5, we provide an example of a predisposition report. Typically, the first page of the report serves as a fact sheet with information necessary for the court to determine a disposition. In addition to the primary function of reporting to the juvenile court, the predisposition assessment can also be used to develop initial supervision strategies and case management plans for youth placements. Note that each section of the report contains criteria that are useful for this dual purpose:

- Information on family and other social supports
- Offense, prior criminal record, history of delinquency, or referrals to child protection agencies
- Mitigating or aggravating circumstances that should be taken into account
- Medical and mental health needs
- Substance use/abuse
- Employment history
- School performance and conduct
- Estimated recidivism risk

EXHIBIT 12.4 Juvenile Probation Services in Selected Jurisdictions

Jurisdiction	Service	Brief Description
Jefferson County, New York	Intake assessment	A preliminary procedure related to Family Court regarding Juvenile Delinquency and Persons in Need of Supervision. Intake is a screening process to determine which cases can be properly adjusted or referred to Family Court.
Harris County, Texas	Therapeutic counseling	Professional, licensed therapists provide counseling to juvenile probationers and their families.
San Diego, California	Community response officer program	Probation officers are stationed at various law enforcement agencies throughout the county. These officers participate in truancy and warrant sweeps and work with law enforcement agencies to divert at-risk youths from the juvenile justice system.
Allegheny County, Pennsylvania	Electronic monitoring/ home detention	An alternative to keeping juveniles in secure detention is release utilizing electronic monitoring or home detention. This service is also used for increased supervision of youths placed in community intensive supervision. This program is operated by the probation department.
Hennepin County, Minnesota	Sole sanction-community service	An early intervention program for youngsters with less serious offenses whose only sanction from the court is to perform a specified number of unpaid community work service hours. The child's individual plan is verified, and compliance is monitored by staff with assistance from volunteers and interns.
Jackson County, Missouri	Victim empathy program	An educational program designed to teach juvenile offenders about the human consequences of crime. Juveniles learn how crime affects the victim in order to increase the juvenile's awareness of the negative impact of their crime on their victims and others; encourage juveniles to accept responsibility for their delinquent actions; and provide victims and victim service providers with a forum to educate juvenile offenders about the consequences of delinquent behaviors.
Polk County, Iowa	Early services program	A wrap-around program for youths who have been referred to Juvenile Court Services. The diversion program is designed to deliver mental health evaluation and treatment services to the children and their families prior to formal involvement with the court.
Douglas County, Nevada	Aftercare	Weekly group and individual counseling by a staff psychologist is offered to youths who have completed their probation requirements, China Springs or Aurora Pines programs, Western Nevada Regional Youth Center, or any state facility. The intention is to preserve the effort they have put into their programs, build resiliency skills, and lower risk factors directly related to their relapse or rearrest.

When a youth is recommended for probation, a second page of the predisposition report is completed that provides a number of conditions for the court's consideration. Exhibit 12.6 displays a sample juvenile court supervision agreement. In addition to general conditions of probation (e.g., abide by a curfew; attend probation meetings; abstain from drug/alcohol use), the court specifies other special conditions. For example, the youth may be ordered to work community service hours and/or pay money to

EXHIBIT 12.5 Example of a Predisposition Report (Fact Sheet)

Predisposition Report		Juvenile Identification Number: JV2010-		
Juvenile Name—Last:		First:	Middle:	
Alias (AKA):		Date of Birth:		Age:
Most Current Address: ____ Street ____ City State Zip				Sex:
		Telephone Number:		
		Cell Phone Number:		

Current Caretaker and Relationship:

Street ____ Telephone Number ____

City State Zip ____ Cell Phone Number ____

Mother's Name (Last, First, Middle Initial):

Street ____ Telephone Number ____

City State Zip ____ Cell Phone Number ____

Father's Name (Last, First, Middle Initial):

Street ____ Telephone Number ____

City State Zip ____ Cell Phone Number ____

Current Offense/Prior Adjudication(s)/Disposition Information

Docket Number	Initial Charge(s)	Final Charge(s)	Disposition
____	____	____	____
Docket Number	Initial Charge(s)	Final Charge(s)	Disposition
____	____	____	____

Reports Attached Current Complaint ☐ Previous PDR ☐

Functional Equivalent Reports Attached

Educational Assessment ☐ Substance Use/Abuse Evaluation ☐

Mental Health Evaluation ☐ Psychological Evaluation ☐

Other(s) ____

Recommendations: Confinement ☐ Alternative Placement ☐ Probation ☐

EXHIBIT 12.6 Predisposition Report (Supervision Agreement)

IN THE MATTER OF: ____________________

Juvenile Identification Number:
JV2010- ____________________

CONDITIONS OF PROBATION

In accordance with the provisions of Title II-Section I of the Juvenile Code, the court has placed you on probation. You are hereby advised that under law, the court determines the terms and conditions of your probation. In fact, if you do not follow the rules set forth by the Juvenile Probation Officer, the court can modify and/or revoke your probation.

IT IS THE ORDER OF THE COURT that beginning ____ **day of** ____________**, 2010,** and for a period of __________ months or until the juvenile's eighteenth birthday, you shall strictly comply with and obey the following conditions of Probation:

1. You will not violate any laws of the United States or any City, County or State.
2. You will report to the Juvenile Probation Department in person **once** per month during the normal working hours, or as instructed by the Probation Officer for the entire term of your probation, and obey all rules and regulations of the probation department.
3. You will attend school and obey school rules and regulations; or you will attend an accredited G.E.D. course until successful completion if approved by the Probation Department and the Juvenile Court.
4. You will be in your home at all times except when attending school and can only leave when accompanied by a parent or guardian, except for church functions or school activities such as an athletic contest and then only with the consent of parent or guardian.
5. You will not associate in any way with persons who have violated the law. Also, you will not have any contact with the victim, or his family in this case, either in person, in writing, by phone or any other method.
6. You will avoid use or possession of narcotics or habit forming drugs, paraphernalia, inhalants, alcoholic beverages, and cigarettes.
7. You will participate in group and individual counseling with a contract service deemed appropriate by the Probation Officer and remain in the program until properly discharged by the authorities.
8. You will submit to random urine surveillance a minimum of ***1*** time per month.
9. You will permit the Probation Officer to visit you at home or elsewhere at any time.
10. You will complete a minimum of **45** hours of community service restitution.

COURT COSTS, PROBATION FEES, RESTITUTION

The FOLLOWING fees have been assessed and require payment, unless otherwise waived by the court.

- The court finds you able to pay the court fees of **$25.00**.
- The court finds you are able to pay a monthly probation supervision fee of **$15.00**.
- The court finds you are able to pay restitution or reparation in the amount of **$**__________.

It is therefore ordered that you must pay a total fee of **$**__________ prior to being released from probation.

the victim, if the victim suffered losses as a result of the crime. The youth may also be ordered to submit to an evaluation and/or attend counseling, or if the offense warrants, submit a biological specimen for DNA testing.

Case Planning and Management

To effectively supervise juvenile offenders in the community, a probation officer must be able to develop case plans that are commensurate with the risk levels, diverse needs, and circumstances of the youths placed on their caseload. Specifically, prioritizing higher-risk juvenile offenders for higher-intensity supervision will be more likely to reduce recidivism than providing that same level of supervision to their lower-risk counterparts.[65] Moreover, programs that provide intensive supervision coupled with treatment-oriented programs have proven to reduce the rates of recidivism far better than those programs that did not offer both in combination.[66]

A number of promising research-supported assessment tools allow probation officers to establish a **case plan** for juvenile offenders. For example, the Youth Level of Service/Case Management Inventory (YLS/CMI) is widely used for assessing general risk and developing individualized supervision plans among justice-involved youths. The YLS/CMI was developed in consultation with experienced probation officers and other juvenile justice professionals to ensure its practicality. The completed YLS/CMI produces a detailed survey of risk and need factors and links these factors to the development of a case management plan.

In Idaho, for example, the Department of Juvenile Corrections uses the YLS/CMI to determine the criminogenic and mental health needs of juvenile offenders.[67] In Alaska, the Department of Health and Social Services' Division of Juvenile Justice implemented the use of YLS/CMI in probation services statewide to assist in making intake decisions. Probation officers in that state perform the assessment for youths referred to the formal court process, those who have been placed on informal probation, and those who have been referred to the Division repeatedly within a two-year time frame. The instrument helps determine supervision levels and craft appropriate case plans. Reassessments are conducted at regular intervals to ensure that services are effectively addressing the youth's risks and needs.[68]

Other types of assessment instruments can be found across juvenile justice systems throughout the country. These case planning tools provide a written document or road map for supervision and constitute the first step toward a comprehensive strategy for juvenile probation.

Once a case plan is established, the next step involves case management, a process by which probation officers:

- Continuously reassess an offender's risks, needs, and strengths
- Plan activities
- Facilitate offender participation and completion of planned activities
- Monitor offender performance and enforce compliance to the court order
- Broker /link to community resources and services[69]

The basic principles of case management point to a multifaceted role for the probation officer. They are in essence the eyes and ears of the court, serving as both compliance officers and brokers of services. Probation officers monitor, counsel, and coordinate service delivery so that youths successfully complete probation. According to Chris Kingsley, senior trainer and senior program associate at the Center for Youth and Communities at Brandeis University:

> Case managers serve as surrogate parents, role models, counselors, social entrepreneurs, and political advocates. They nag, cajole, prod, and encourage clients. They pressure institutions to act responsibly or lubricate the gears between institutions. They make referrals, and monitor client fit. They deal with the client's family life; work and school; and social services and public institutions. They alter client behaviors strengthening client capacity to exercise self-determination and autonomy.[70]

RANDY MCWILLIAMS, JUVENILE PROBATION OFFICER, 46TH JUDICIAL JUVENILE DISTRICT, VERNON, TEXAS

Randy McWilliams is a juvenile probation officer for the 46th Judicial Juvenile District, which is a three-county district in north central Texas. Vernon is the county seat of the district and is a relatively small farming community. McWilliams has been in the probation field for 13 years since graduating with a bachelor of science degree in criminal justice from Midwestern State University in 1996.

Mr. McWilliams explains that "the Texas juvenile probation system is based on the rehabilitation of juvenile offenders to keep them out of the adult system. I find [this job] personally fulfilling because this system is about helping children better themselves, keeping them in the community, and not strictly about punishment or locking them up." Further, he says, "if anyone is interested in a fulfilling career in the criminal justice system, has a desire to help children, and enjoys the legal system, then juvenile probation might be the perfect career."

Career Profile

Intensive Supervised Probation

While most juveniles are placed on standard probation, some offenders require closer supervision and may be placed on intensive supervised probation (ISP). Generally, the purpose of ISP is to provide an intermediate sanction between standard probation and secure detention. In the juvenile justice system, ISP serves as an alternative sentence for youths whose crimes are not severe enough to warrant confinement and yet are too serious for them to be placed on regular probation. When placed on ISP, youthful offenders are strictly monitored and held accountable for their compliance with terms of probation and law-abiding behavior. In Arizona, for example, juvenile intensive probation differs from regular probation in the increased frequency of contact, the requirement to actively participate in 32 hours of structured programs per week, the restrictions concerning unsupervised time away from home, and the lower officer-to-probationer caseload ratio.[71]

Successful juvenile ISP integrates effective interventions with risk-control strategies. Effective interventions are those that have been found to reduce recidivism. Merging control (e.g., contingency management and graduated responses) with rehabilitation (e.g., cognitive behavioral interventions) has provided a basis for a new generation of community corrections programs, known as intensive rehabilitation supervision (IRS).[72] Such programs, which tie intensive supervision with treatment, have been used in homes, schools, and other community-based organizations, and they have been shown to be viable options for certain adjudicated delinquents who otherwise would be confined.[73] The Anti-Gang and Drug Abuse Unit (AGDAU) in Peoria, Illinois, provides an example.

The AGDAU is a four-phase intensive supervision program that targets juvenile offenders placed on probation for gang-related behavior or substance abuse offenses. All participants have extensive criminal histories or are at risk of incarceration or residential placement. Essential to the program are its small caseloads, articulation of distinct graduated phases to structure youths' movement through the program, substance abuse assessments, and behavioral controls, such as electronic monitoring, curfews, home confinement, and random drug testing. The goal of this program is to prevent recidivism.

An evaluation of this ISP program by the Center for Legal Studies at the University of Illinois found that during the first year following program completion, 63 percent of the participants who successfully completed the program were not arrested for a new offense, compared with only 44 percent of those who were unsuccessful in the program. The factors that appeared to have the strongest correlation to successful program completion were regular school attendance, gender (if female), lack of mental health problems, initial assessment of low risk, and the extent of prior involvement in the juvenile justice system (i.e., age at program entry, number of prior offenses, and length of prior probation terms). The older a participant was at the time of first involvement in the criminal justice system and the fewer prior offenses he or she had, the more likely the participant was to successfully complete the program.[74]

Another intensive supervision approach is referred to as Multi-Systemic Therapy (MST)—a home- and family-oriented treatment program that targets juvenile offenders and their families who need help reducing a youth's antisocial behavior, such as poor school performance, poor choice in friends, family conflict and other home issues, substance abuse, and mental health issues. Typical MST participants are 11- to 16-year-old juvenile offenders who are at risk of out-of-home placement. Normally, the duration of home-based MST services is approximately four months, with multiple therapist–family contacts occurring weekly.

MST has been found to be effective in meeting its primary goals of decreasing antisocial behavior, improving family relations and school performance, and saving money by reducing the use of out-of-home placements such as residential treatment and incarceration. The first controlled study of MST with juvenile offenders was published in 1986, and since then, numerous randomized clinical trials with violent and chronic juvenile offenders have been conducted. In these trials, MST has demonstrated several benefits:

- Reduced long-term rates of criminal offending in serious juvenile offenders
- Decreased recidivism and rearrests
- Reduced rates of out-of-home placements for serious juvenile offenders
- Extensive improvements in family functioning
- Decreased behavior and mental health problems for serious juvenile offenders
- Favorable outcomes at cost savings in comparison with usual mental health and juvenile justice services[75]

In addition, the National Registry of Evidence-Based Programs and Practices (NREPP), a service of the Substance Abuse and Mental Health Services Administration (SAMHSA), recently published a review of five studies that measured the effectiveness of MST. In Exhibit 12.7, we highlight results of these studies relating to post-treatment arrest rates, long-term arrest rates, and long-term incarceration rates.[76] Moreover, several government agencies (e.g., U.S. Public Health Service, National Institute on Drug Abuse, and the National Institutes of Health) have identified MST as an approach that shows considerable promise in the treatment of youth criminal behavior, substance abuse, and emotional disturbance. These conclusions are based on findings from 18 published outcome studies.

EXHIBIT 12.7 The National Registry of Evidence-Based Programs and Practices Review of Multi-Systemic Therapy (MST) for Juvenile Offenders

Post-Treatment Arrest Rates

Description of Measures

Archival arrest records were collected from the South Carolina Department of Youth Services approximately 60 weeks after referral to treatment, which was on average about 46 weeks following completion of MST treatment. In another study, postprobation arrests for the four years following MST treatment were obtained from state police records.

Key Findings

Compared with youths receiving treatment as usual, youths receiving MST were arrested about half as often in the post-treatment period. Recidivism rates were 42 percent for the MST-treated youths compared with 62 percent for youths receiving usual services. In a second study, MST was more effective than individual therapy in preventing rearrests for violent offenses during the follow-up period.

Long-Term Arrest Rates

Description of Measures

Juvenile and adult criminal arrest records were collected at 4.0 and 13.7 years following MST treatment versus individual therapy (IT) or usual services.

Key Findings

At the end of four years of follow-up, the rate of criminal recidivism (rearrest) for the MST completers (22 percent) was less than one-third the overall rates for IT completers (71 percent). At 13.7 years after treatment, MST participants (then aged 29 years) showed significantly lower rates of criminal recidivism (50 percent) than comparable youths (81 percent).

Long-Term Incarceration Rates

Description of Measures

Incarceration histories were collected following treatment from archival databases (e.g., juvenile justice records) and from sentencing information (e.g., days sentenced to confinement).

Key Findings

MST participants had on average 73 fewer days of incarceration than youths receiving usual services. More than two-thirds (68 percent) of youths in the usual-services group were incarcerated after treatment, compared with only 20 percent of the MST group. Almost 14 years after treatment, MST youths were sentenced to fewer than half as many days of incarceration as the comparison youths.

Aftercare

Within the realm of juvenile probation lies a segment of community-based corrections typically referred to as **aftercare**. In the simplest of terms, aftercare involves the reintegration of confined youths back into the community with the goal of averting recidivism. Aftercare begins with planning before the offender is discharged into the community and culminates with the completion of the probation period. Some of the more successful aftercare programs found in juvenile probation services follow a theoretical model of corrections known as Balanced and Restorative Justice (BARJ). BARJ-based programs focus specifically on crime and recognize three parties with equally important roles and stakes in the justice process: offenders, victims, and communities. The balanced approach mission addresses the public need for (1) accountability measures that attempt to restore victims and provide meaningful consequences for offensive behavior; (2) offender rehabilitation and reintegration; and (3) enhanced public safety protection.[77] Restorative justice requires an active partnership with the community.

EXHIBIT 12.8 The Balanced Approach

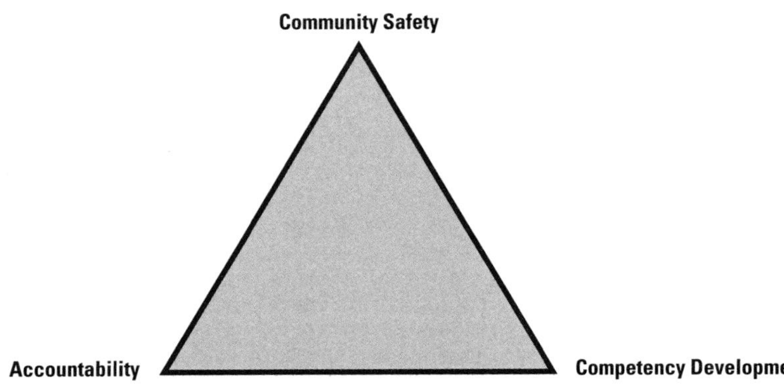

Client/ Customer	Goals	Values
Victims	Accountability	When the offense is committed, the juvenile offender is obligated to the victim and the community.
Youth Development	Competency	The juvenile offender should be more capable when leaving the juvenile justice system than before entering.
Community	Community Safety	Juvenile justice has a responsibility to protect the public from offenders in the system.

Source: Adapted from Dennis Maloney, Dennis Romig, and Troy Armstrong (1988). Juvenile Probation: The Balanced Approach. Reno, NV: National Council of Juvenile and Family Court Judges. Reprinted in Gordon Bazemore and Mark Umbreit (1997). *Balanced and Restorative Justice for Juveniles: A Framework for Juvenile Justice in the 21st Century.* Washington, DC: Office of Juvenile Justice and Delinquency Prevention.

Under this framework, the plan takes into account the injury to the victim and the community and works to repair that injury to the highest degree possible (see Exhibit 12.8).

In the framework of aftercare, several research-based models have been developed for transitioning youths from confinement back into the community. Most notable is the Intensive Aftercare Programs (IAP) model, which combines the most innovative policies and practices identified nationally.[78] Both surveillance and treatment services are central to this approach.

Moreover, five principles underlie the successful reintegration of youths into the community:

1. Preparing youths for increased responsibility and freedom in the community
2. Facilitating youth-community interaction and involvement
3. Working with both the offender and targeted community support systems (e.g., families, peers, schools, employers) on qualities needed for constructive interaction and the youths' successful community adjustment

EXHIBIT 12.9 Intensive Aftercare Program (IAP) Model

The Colorado IAP, which is operated by the Colorado Department of Human Services, Division of Youth Corrections (DYC), serves delinquent youths from the greater metropolitan Denver area including the counties of Arapahoe, Denver, Douglas, and Jefferson. The program serves youths from the Lookout Mountain Youth Service Center (LMYSC), a secure facility located in Golden. All IAP participants are housed in a single cottage and receive individualized care based on specialized assessment techniques. Project staff includes three IAP client managers who provide intensive case management from institutional referral through community reentry and beyond. Program components include a range of services provided at each stage of the reintegration process (i.e., institution phase, institution transition, community transition, and aftercare), including educational, special educational, and vocational services; counseling/mental health counseling; drug/alcohol prevention services; life skills; community service work; and transportation. A system of graduated sanctions and incentives is an integral component of this program.

Nevada's IAP, also known as Fresh Start, is operated by the Nevada Youth Corrections Services Youth Parole Bureau in Clark County (Las Vegas). High-risk youths participating in Fresh Start are housed at the Caliente Youth Center, one of Nevada's two secure facilities for juvenile offenders, located about 150 miles northeast of Las Vegas. All IAP participants are placed in Beowawe Cottage ("B" Cottage) and receive services from the case managers. However, the program's case management system has been adapted to address a situational factor: the long distance between the secure facility and the community. Youths take courses in a prerelease curriculum devoted to social skills training. The program has implemented a system of positive incentives and graduated sanctions to emphasize accountability. Sanctions range from community service for minor misconduct to curfews, house arrest, and brief confinement for more serious offenses. Community outreach trackers support the youth center staff by providing additional monitoring.

Virginia's IAP project is referred to as the Intensive Parole Program (IPP). It is operated by the Virginia Department of Juvenile Justice (DJJ) and serves high-risk youths from the City of Norfolk who have been committed to the department and placed at one of two central Virginia facilities (i.e., the Beaumont and Hanover Juvenile Correctional Centers). The initial phase of treatment begins at the Reception and Diagnostic Center, where juveniles are assessed to determine if they are high-risk offenders, based on a locally developed and validated risk assessment instrument. The IPP Management Team, composed of nine DJJ staff, is responsible for the development and implementation of each youth's treatment plan. Virginia has developed a coordinated transition to aftercare process that involves (1) the use of local group homes as "halfway back" residential facilities and a continuum of graduated parole supervision levels; (2) provision of services immediately upon the youth's return to the community; (3) an aftercare planning process that begins shortly after commitment and involves institutional, aftercare, and community agency staff; and (4) communication mechanisms that facilitate an integrated case management process across both the institutional and the aftercare transition stages.

Source: David Altschuler, Troy Armstrong, and Doris MacKenzie (1999). *Reintegration, Supervised Release, and Intensive Aftercare.* Washington, DC: U.S. Department of Justice, Office of Justice Programs, Office of Juvenile Justice and Delinquency Prevention.

4. Developing new resources and supports where needed
5. Monitoring and testing the youth and community on their ability to deal with each other productively[79]

The IAP model was tested in three jurisdictions: the Denver metropolitan area in Colorado; Clark County (Las Vegas), Nevada; and the City of Norfolk, Virginia (see Exhibit 12.9 for descriptions of each of these programs). A total of 435 juveniles were involved in the evaluation that took place from fall 1995 through summer 2000. None of the three sites found statistically significant differences between the IAP and control groups in the prevalence of reoffending. However, positive outcomes were found when examining various intermediate outcomes, including aftercare adjustment. In Colorado and Nevada, IAP youths were significantly less likely than control group youths to test positive for substance abuse while on supervision. And in each site, IAP youths were significantly more likely than controls to be involved in vocational training for at least two months during aftercare. Finally, in Colorado and Virginia, a substantially larger percentage of

IAP youths remained in school for at least two months. The Virginia IAP also had a larger percentage of youths employed for two or more months while on aftercare.[80]

Innovative Community-Based Supervision of Juveniles

To be effective over time, community-based supervision must include interventions that enhance those positive aspects, however limited, of the social environment in which youths live. Or, as stated in the ODJJP annual report, "[S]eriously delinquent youth can be maintained in their communities only as long as their social environment is carefully designed to provide them with structured support and supervision."[81] Based on this notion, several innovative community-based programs for juveniles show promise. While this list is far from exhaustive, it does represent some of the best contemporary practices in the supervision of youthful offenders in the community.

Alternatives to Detention (ATD) Programs. In New York City, it costs nearly $171,000 to confine one youth in a detention center for one year, while it costs only $9,000 to $12,000 annually to send a child to a community-based alternative program.[82] To help counter the costs of detention, the New York City Department of Probation, in partnership with the Department of Education, developed the Alternatives to Detention (ATD) program. ATD provides community-based supervision and educational services for youths awaiting trial in family courts. An evaluation of the operation revealed that over 90 percent of youths in the ATD program successfully complete the program, with successful completion defined as remaining arrest-free and attending their court hearings.[83]

Similarly, the ATD program in Portland, Maine, was created to help address overcrowding in the detention unit at the Long Creek Youth Development Center. Funded by an OJJDP Juvenile Accountability Block Grant,* this program provides supervision for youths in the community so that they can be released from detention while awaiting their appearance in court. Services include a reporting center and intensive case management. The program's effectiveness is illustrated by the following statistics:

- 90 percent of youths leaving the program successfully completed program requirements.
- Only 12.5 percent of youths reoffended while in the program.
- 90 percent of youths with a goal of finding employment were placed in jobs.
- All youths appeared in court as scheduled and none interfered with the court process.[84]

Home Detention and Electronic Monitoring. Home detention requires youths to remain at home during specific time periods. It is often used in conjunction with electronic monitoring (EM) to enforce curfew and other conditions of home detention. The positive aspects of home detention and EM include allowing delinquents to maintain community ties and enabling families to stay together. The theory is that youthful

---

* Juvenile Accountability Block Grants (JABGs) are administered by the OJJDP, and their goal is to reduce juvenile offending through both offender-focused and system-focused activities that promote accountability. OJJDP distributed approximately $42 million in FY2008 under the JABG program. OJJDP and the JABG program are helping local and state jurisdictions provide enhanced options such as restitution, community service, victim-offender mediation, and restorative justice sanctions.

offenders in such programs have greater opportunity for reintegration into the community, less risk of reoffending, and less overall cost to the community.

Assessments of home detention and electronic monitoring programs have shown favorable results when evaluated as an alternative to incarceration. In a study of a detention program in Tuscaloosa, Alabama, researchers compared the behaviors of 29 juveniles assigned to home detention with those of 57 juveniles held in secure institutional detention while awaiting court hearings. Findings showed that youths placed on home detention were no more likely to recidivate than youths placed in secure detention.[85] In another study of 560 youths from Lake County, Indiana, who were court-ordered to home detention, researchers found only 7 percent of first-time offenders had failed to meet program requirements. Also, those assigned to electronic monitoring had a higher program completion rate and a lower recidivism rate than youths who were not electronically monitored.[86]

Day Reporting Centers. These highly structured, community-based, nonresidential programs for juvenile offenders allow youths to return home at night. Since residential care is not offered, costs are lower for day reporting centers than for halfway houses and other facility-treatment programs that offer housing. Treatment services include individual and group counseling, educational and vocational training, employment counseling, substance abuse treatment, and community resource referrals.

Studies suggest that day treatment may be a promising option for delinquent youths. For instance, the Bethesda Day Treatment Center in West Milton, Pennsylvania, provides up to 55 hours of services per week from 8:30 A.M. to 7:45 P.M. to delinquents and status offenders. Treatment services focus on life skills, career opportunities, and individual, family, and group counseling. A study revealed that program participants had a recidivism rate of only 5 percent in the first year after discharge, far lower than state and national norms.[87]

Another benefit of day reporting is the reduction of costs compared with incarceration. Consider for example, that as of March, 2009, the Department of Corrections and Rehabilitation's Division of Juvenile Facilities (DJF) housed 1,637 offenders in six institutions at an estimated cost of approximately $234,029 annually per juvenile inmate.[88] To counter the exorbitant cost of confinement, the Merced County, California, probation department, which supervised 4,500 adult and juvenile offenders on felony probation, opened a day reporting center (DRC) for offenders aged 13 through 18. In 2008, the center managed up to 25 individuals daily.[89] An evaluation of the DRC after one year showed that 84 percent of clients who went through the program were employed or involved in school. In addition, of the offenders who had exited the program, there has been a 36 percent drop in assessed risk. Also, attendance rates to classes and counseling sessions have been very high.[90]

Juvenile Drug Courts. Juvenile drug courts (JDC) are intensive treatment programs established within and supervised by juvenile courts to provide specialized services for eligible drug-involved youths. JDCs represent the coordinated efforts of justice and treatment professionals to actively intervene and break the cycle of substance abuse, addiction, and crime. As such, the JDC judge maintains oversight of each case and works as a member of a team that comprises representatives from treatment, juvenile justice, social services, school and vocational training programs, law enforcement, probation, the prosecution, and the defense. Together, the team determines how best to address the substance abuse and related problems of the youth and his or her family.[91] As of 2009, 459 juvenile drug courts existed across the country.[92]

In a 2004 study in Maricopa County, Arizona, researchers used data from three years (October 1997 to November 2000) to examine how legal and social variables affect delinquency and drug use patterns once juveniles enter drug court treatment. A comparison group comprised of youths on standard probation was used to measure potential differences. Findings reveal that youths in drug court were less likely than those in the comparison group to commit a subsequent delinquent act.[93]

School-Based Probation. In school-based probation, the juvenile probation officer is located directly in a school rather than in the traditional courthouse environment. This model allows the probation officer to check attendance, discipline records, and other information about probationers on a daily basis, as well as to check with teachers about academic progress. School-based programs are underway in a number of locations and preliminary evaluations show promising results.

Pennsylvania's school-based probation program began in 1990 at Allentown through the support of the Pennsylvania Juvenile Court Judges' Commission and the Pennsylvania Commission on Crime and Delinquency. Roughly 150 school-based probation officers work in the program and have served more than 16,000 juveniles.[94] An initial evaluation found that the average school-based probation client was similar in demographic and offense characteristics to regular probation clients; however, youths placed on school-based probation spent significantly more time in the community without charges and/or placements. Placement cost savings per school-based probation client were projected at $6,665 per year.[95] Due to these encouraging findings and an infusion of state funding for specialized probation programs beginning in 1998, school-based probation has expanded to more than two-thirds of Pennsylvania counties.

In 2001, the National Center for Juvenile Justice conducted a follow-up evaluation of school-based probation in five Pennsylvania counties and found that participants viewed the program as effective in meeting its objectives, particularly in decreasing absenteeism, suspensions, and school disciplinary referrals. Over 90 percent of the probation respondents and 79 percent of the school administrators believed the program is effective in reducing recidivism among probationers.[96]

Gender- and Culture-Sensitive Programs for Juveniles

In the past two decades, the number of girls entering the juvenile justice system has risen at a rate much higher than that for boys. The proportion of delinquency cases that involved females was 19 percent in 1985; and 27 percent in 2005; by 2007, it had increased to 29 percent.[97] Also, during this period, female caseloads increased more than male caseloads for each of the four general offense categories (i.e., person, property, drug, and public order offenses), and the number of court dispositions for probation increased from 14 percent in 1985 to 24 percent in 2005.[98]

Reacting to increases in arrests of girls, OJJDP began to fund programs that were gender-tailored to female juvenile offenders. The 1992 reauthorization of the OJJDP Act of 1974 required states to examine their juvenile justice systems and identify gaps in their ability to provide services to juvenile female offenders.[99] Let's examine some of the gender-related issues involved.

Gender-Specific Services

Girls and boys experience many of the same risk factors, but they differ in sensitivity to and rate of exposure to these risks. For example, for girls, the key risk factors for delinquency and incarceration are family dysfunction, trauma and sexual abuse, mental

Courts are increasingly requiring gender-responsive community-based strategies to reduce girls' involvement in violence and delinquency. Do you think such strategies will reduce the number of girls involved in the juvenile justice system?

health problems, high-risk sexual behaviors, school problems, and affiliation with deviant peers.[100] Boys are more vulnerable than girls to develop attention-deficit and hyperactivity disorder (ADHD), learning disabilities, delayed communication skills development, or even higher levels of callous-unemotional traits, which are all factors associated with a heightened risk for developing delinquent and disruptive behaviors.[101] Girls and young teenagers who are victims of physical and sexual abuse often turn to drugs and alcohol to mask their pain.[102] As a result, girls may have different programming needs when considering conditions of probation.

At the national, state, and local levels, there is a movement to use gender-specific programming designed to get and keep adolescent girls on a positive developmental track. Six guiding principles underlie gender-specific services in all phases of the corrections system:

- Principle 1: Gender. Acknowledge that gender makes a difference.
- Principle 2: Environment. Create an environment based on safety, respect, and dignity.
- Principle 3: Relationships. Develop policies, practices, and programs that are relational and promote healthy connections to children, family, significant others, and the community.
- Principle 4: Services and supervision. Address substance abuse, trauma, and mental health issues through comprehensive, integrated, and culturally relevant services and appropriate supervision.
- Principle 5: Socioeconomic status. Provide women with opportunities to improve their socioeconomic conditions.
- Principle 6: Community. Establish a system of community supervision and reentry with comprehensive, collaborative services.[103]

The Connecticut Judicial Branch, Court Support Services Division (CSSD), has developed and evaluated statewide initiatives that are providing **gender-responsive** services to girls. The Girls Probation program is CSSD's most recent effort to strengthen and enhance probation services for girls. This innovative, specialized probation model is research-based and relies on the following principles:

- Female responsive: The model accounts for the realities of girls' lives, including their emotional, intellectual, and physical development, socialization, and individuality.
- Strengths-based: It requires staff to see what is good about girls in order to help them help themselves.
- Trauma-informed: It trains staff to understand the prevalence and impact of trauma on girls' lives and to work actively to prevent system-level trauma.
- Culturally competent: It is sensitive to cultural differences.
- Family-centered: It addresses girls' needs within the context of their families and communities.
- Relational: It works to help girls achieve success within, not outside, a relational context.

CSSD has dedicated 13 full-time gender-specific probation officers to the program and established a policy that caseloads will not exceed 25 girls. Dedicated caseloads allow officers the time necessary to address the specific needs of the girls. A project coordinator oversees day-to-day operations and coordinates project goals, objectives, and outcomes including training, resources, technical assistance, and quality assurance.[104]

Some communities are working with at-risk youth and their families to determine both gender and culturally sensitive issues that should be considered for treatment purposes. For example, in 2003, a needs assessment was conducted to determine the attitudes and beliefs of Cambodian American youth in Seattle, Washington, toward alcohol, drugs, sexuality, and promiscuity, and how those issues relate to family and social context. The state of Washington has the third-largest Cambodian refugee population in the United States, with most Cambodian Americans living in Seattle/King County. Findings revealed that many Cambodian American youths do not fit the stereotypes of other Asian youths, such as lower incidents of criminal activity and almost no juvenile delinquency.[105] For example, the average Cambodian American youth interviewed knew of 12 other youths and 13 adults who used and abused alcohol and drugs. Also, 83 percent became sexually active at the age of 16 or younger, compared to 33 percent of American youth in general. Using this data, the Help Each Other Reach the Sky (HERS) youth program of Seattle developed a comprehensive gender-specific program with the goal of reducing risk factors that cause Cambodian American girls to become perpetrators and victims of antisocial behavior and violent acts. Youth selection into HERS is based on family and individual risk factors, such as a history of drug abuse or gang activity among relatives. Programming includes intensive case management, mental health services, job skills training, employment and career exploration opportunities, tutoring, and counseling to teenage Cambodian American girls.[106]

Assessment of Girls' Programming

While program providers and juvenile justice administrators have increased their equitable and unique programming for girls, little research and evaluation is available on whether and how much gender-specific programming helps or hinders girls on probation. Below, we highlight two gender-specific intervention programs that have been evaluated and show promise in reducing delinquency.

The Reaffirming Young Sisters Excellence (RYSE) program of the Alameda County, California, probation department operated between 1997 and 2001 as an intervention program designed to address both gender and cultural factors in girls' programming. The RYSE program consisted of intensive treatment interventions and supervision of girls, ages 12 through 17, who had been adjudicated within the Alameda County juvenile court as they completed their restitution and community-service requirements. RYSE served more than 450 girls and was based on the premise that programming and interventions directed toward gender-specific needs would be more effective than traditional (probation) services. RYSE had two primary objectives: (1) preventing girls whose cases have been adjudicated in the Alameda County juvenile court from returning to the justice system; and (2) promoting the development of girls' social competencies so they can sustain crime-free and economically secure lifestyles.[107]

The immediate outcome results of a study of the RYSE program were encouraging. While the girls were receiving intensive services, they had a lower recidivism rate than the control group. Longer-term outcomes were less positive, however, as RYSE girls transitioning back to traditional probation showed similar failure rates to those of the control group.[108] In short, there was no evidence to suggest the RYSE program was more effective than traditional probation in reducing recidivism for all girls. However, the program did significantly reduce recidivism for African American and Hispanic girls in the treatment group. Also, girls in the RYSE program were more than 50 percent likely to complete probation and make restitution during the intervention period than girls in the control group. Many probation officers noted that the program improved the girls' attitudes toward substance use and education. Finally, the girls in the study claimed that they developed greater interpersonal skills, particularly with other girls.[109]

The San Diego County Probation Department served as the lead agency for the Working to Insure and Nurture Girls' Success (WINGS) program, which is a program that provides gender-responsive services to girls between the ages of 12 and 17½ who are minimally involved in the juvenile justice system. WINGS clients (798 girls) were provided with a comprehensive array of services that combined home visiting and center-based services. Some core program components included mother-daughter mediation, transportation, and a variety of gender-specific programs that addressed such issues as academics, alcohol and other drug use, anger management, and vocational/career support. Successful program completion was defined as participation for a minimum of six months that included the client completing her case plan and not receiving a new charge resulting in custody of 90 days or more. An evaluation of the program revealed that a significantly smaller percentage of WINGS clients (1 percent) received institutional commitments for a new offense compared to the control group (4 percent). WINGS clients were also more likely to attend school on a regular basis (70 percent) compared to those in the control group (45 percent). Finally, fewer WINGS clients were recorded as failing (18 percent) during their participation in the program compared to those in the control group (30 percent). Unfortunately, because of funding cuts in 2002, the WINGS program ceased to exist.[110]

Policy Implications

Since the 1990s, a trend in legislation and policy has continued to blur the line that distinguishes the juvenile justice system from the criminal justice system. Once considered as family courts that gave greater emphasis to rehabilitating youths, today's juvenile courts more closely resemble the adult criminal justice system. While many factors have contributed to this transition, a critically important dynamic relates to the impact of the media on the public's assumptions about youth violence. That is, sensationalized media accounts of juvenile crime create panics that lead to public misperceptions about youths. As a result, a fearful public is more apt to support more punitive responses to youth crime.

There is a substantial disconnect between the public's perceptions of juvenile crime and the reality of juvenile crime statistics. Although juvenile crime is still a major social problem, juvenile crime rates began decreasing in the late 1990s. Between 1999 and 2008, for example, juvenile arrests fell 16 percent.[111] Moreover, in 2008 juveniles accounted for only 16 percent of all violent crime arrests.[112] However, the fondness of the media for reporting violent crime prominently and often, despite several years of decreases in crime, creates a **media myth** about juvenile crime.

This is especially true of high-profile cases like the one featured in our opening story, which extend the emphasis on negative stories about kids (i.e., "if it bleeds, it leads").[113] Consider for example, a study that found that nearly one-third (31 percent) of the crime stories focus on juvenile crime. Most of these stories spotlighted violent crime (particularly murder), and nearly 80 percent were covered in the first block of the newscast.[114]

A consequence of the media myth is that exaggerated perceptions regarding the violence of juvenile crime may influence juvenile justice policy. That is, the more television news exposes the public to juvenile crime, the more the public may question less punitive treatments. In a recent study of perceptions about community-based rehabilitation versus imprisonment, researchers conducted a statewide telephone survey of nearly 500 voting-age Louisiana residents selected via random digit dialing. The results showed that television viewing was associated with the perception that juvenile (and adult) crime is increasing when, in fact, it has been decreasing. Television viewing was also associated with inflated perceptions regarding the percentage of juveniles imprisoned for violent crimes. Finally, heavier exposure to television news was associated with greater support for more punitive solutions (i.e., imprisonment rather than rehabilitation).[115]

Public perceptions regarding young people have been affected by media portrayals of youth violence and youth crime. Why does the media misrepresent the vast majority of kids this way?

Since media portrayal of juvenile crime can distort public perception, agencies that operate community-based programs must initiate a campaign for accurate public information. One way to bridge the gap between perception and reality is to make the public better aware of successful research-supported interventions. Community-based programs that rely on evidence-based practices to promote community safety should be advanced to counterbalance news coverage that evokes images of incorrigible offenders for whom rehabilitation programs are fruitless. Information that needs to become available to the public includes the nature of effective best practices found in community-based programs, the adverse effects of incarceration, and the impact of incorporating gender, race, and class sensitivity in interventions for young people.

Summary

Two major influences in the evolution of community-based corrections for juveniles and the doctrine of *parens patriae* are the Juvenile Justice and Delinquency Prevention Act (JJDPA) of 1974 and evaluation research studies.

Several U.S. Supreme Court rulings, such as *Kent* v. *U.S., In re Gault, In re Winship, McKeiver* v. *Pennsylvania,* and *Breed* v. *Jones* have formalized procedures in juvenile court and furthered the movement to guarantee due process rights for juveniles accused of crime at the same level provided for adult defendants.

States have established various laws that allow juveniles to be tried as adults, and these laws can be sorted into three basic types: judicial waiver, statutory exclusion, and concurrent jurisdiction.

Probation programs conduct predisposition investigation, recommend appropriate court dispositions for juvenile delinquents, and supervise those youths placed on probation.

Intensive supervised probation (ISP) serves as an alternative sentence for youths whose crimes are not severe enough to warrant confinement and yet are too serious to be placed on regular probation. Successful aftercare programs are couched within core principles of a theoretical model of corrections known as Balanced and Restorative Justice (BARJ). BARJ-based programs focus specifically on crime and recognize three parties with equally important roles and stakes in the justice process: offenders, victims, and communities.

Innovative community-based programs for juveniles include alternatives to detention programs, home detention and electronic monitoring, day reporting centers, drug courts, and school-based probation.

At the national, state, and local levels, there is a movement to use gender-specific programming designed to get and keep adolescent girls on a positive developmental track.

Key Terms

adjudication, p. 344
aftercare, p. 363
case plan, p. 360
certification, p. 346
deinstitutionalization, p. 342
foster care, p. 346
gender-responsive, p. 369
juvenile delinquency, p. 351
juvenile detention facility, p. 342
media myth, p. 372
***parens patriae*, p. 347**
status offenders, p. 342
status offenses, p. 342
superpredator, p. 346

Questions for Review

1. What are the important events that led to the development of juvenile community-based corrections in the United States?
2. Describe the key legal decisions affecting juvenile justice and the implications of these cases on *parens patriae.*
3. Is the death penalty for juveniles considered cruel and unusual punishment? What about life without parole?
4. Describe the risk/needs assessment process and provide examples of services provided by juvenile probation agencies.
5. Explain intensive supervised probation and aftercare programs for juveniles.
6. Describe three community-based programs within the juvenile justice system that show promise in terms of achieving their stated mission and goals.
7. What are gender-specific programs and why are they needed for juveniles?

Question of Policy

Waiver Laws for Juveniles

Instead of being placed in a juvenile detention facility without chance for bail, a juvenile offender waived to adult court could be eligible for ROR or other types of pretrial release. But when we consider the extralegal criteria typically used by a judge to determine pretrial release (e.g., employment, property ownership), bail that would be manageable for an adult may be unattainable for a youth. Consequently, although juvenile offenders may be certified to stand trial as an adult, it's questionable that youths, especially from low-income families, really enjoy the right to bail. Moreover, from what we know about the adverse relationship between pretrial detention status (i.e., release on bail versus jail confinement) and sentencing, it would appear that bail reform for juveniles should be an essential part of the policy debate about waiver laws.

Should ancillary social effects, such as the unlikely possibility of bail, be considered by policy makers before enacting waiver laws for juveniles? If you were asked to weigh in on a discussion of this issue, what concerns would you express?

What Would You Do?

You are the newly appointed program director for juvenile services at a large county probation department that provides court services for both adult and juvenile probationers. You are directly responsible for the supervision of 14 juvenile probation officers, six surveillance officers, one social worker, and two clerical staff. The juvenile probation program provides intake assessment, predisposition reporting, and supervision services. Ancillary services for case management include drug treatment, anger management counseling, and life-skills training. The court administrator informs you that the county will receive a substantial monetary grant from the state to fund a new aftercare program at your agency for juveniles being released from the state Juvenile Correctional Facility. These are 16- and 17-year-old boys who are considered medium-risk offenders, having been adjudicated delinquent and confined primarily for drug-related crimes.

What concerns do you have about extending juvenile services to include aftercare for juvenile offenders under state jurisdiction?

Would you attempt to develop an aftercare component that balances social control and treatment features? Why or why not?

Endnotes

1. Juvenile Justice and Delinquency Prevention (JJDP) Act (1974 et seq.). 42 U.S.C. § 5601.
2. Leonard P. Edwards, "The Juvenile Court and the Role of the Juvenile Court Judge," *Juvenile & Family Court Journal,* vol. 43, no. 2 (1992), p. 11.
3. Martin Forst, Jeffrey Fagan, and T. Scott Vivona, "Youth in Prisons and Training Schools: Perceptions and Consequences of the Treatment-Custody Dichotomy," *Juvenile and Family Court Journal,* vol. 40, no. 1 (1989), p. 9.
4. James Finckenauer and Patricia Gavin, *Scared Straight: The Panacea Phenomenon Revisited* (Prospect Heights, IL: Waveland Press, Inc., 1999).
5. History of the CASA Movement. Retrieved from www.nationalcasa.org/index.asp.
6. *Evaluation of CASA Representation: Research Summary* (Fairfax, VA: Caliber Associates, January 2004).
7. Cathy S. Widom and Michael G. Maxfield, *An Update on the Cycle of Violence* (Washington, DC: National Institute of Justice Research in Brief, February 2001).
8. James Austin, Kelly Dedel Johnson, and Ronald Weitzer, *Alternatives to the Secure Detention and Confinement of Juvenile Offenders* (Washington, DC: U.S. Department of Justice: Juvenile Justice Practices Series, September 2005).
9. Robert Coates, Alden Miller, and Lloyd Ohlin, *Diversity in a Youth Correctional System* (Cambridge, MA: Ballinger Publishing, 1978).
10. Barry Krisberg, James Austin, and Patricia Steele, *Unlocking Juvenile Corrections* (San Francisco, CA: National Council on Crime and Delinquency, 1989).
11. Barry Krisberg et al., *A Court that Works: The Impact of Juvenile Court Sanctions* (San Francisco, CA: National Council on Crime and Delinquency, 1988).
12. Ibid.
13. Mark Lipsey in D. Rosenbaum (ed.), *Juvenile Delinquency Treatment: A Meta-Analytic Inquiry into the Variability of Effects in Community Crime Prevention: Does it Work?* (New York, NY: Russell Sage Foundation, 1992).
14. David Altschuler et al., "Reintegration, Supervised Release, and Intensive Aftercare," *Juvenile Justice Bulletin* (Washington, DC: Office of Juvenile Justice and Delinquency Prevention, July 1999).
15. Mark W. Lipsey, David B. Wilson, and Lynn Cothern, "Effective Intervention for Serious

Juvenile Offenders," *Juvenile Justice Bulletin* (Washington, DC: Office of Juvenile Justice and Delinquency Prevention, April 2000).

16. Supra (See 16).
17. 18 U.S.C. § 5035.
18. Rochelle Stanfield, *Pathways to Juvenile Detention Reform: The JDAI Story* (Baltimore, MD: The Annie E. Casey Foundation, 1999).
19. Howard Snyder and Melissa Sickmund, *Juvenile Offenders and Victims: 2006 National Report* (Washington, DC: Office of Juvenile Justice and Delinquency Prevention, 2006).
20. Florida Department of Juvenile Justice, *2005–2006 Department of Juvenile Justice State Profile Database.* Retrieved from www.djj.state.fl.us/Research/Delinquency_ Profile/0506_Profile.html.
21. Ibid.
22. Ibid.
23. Howard Snyder, *Juvenile Justice Bulletin: Juvenile Arrests 2004* (Washington, DC: Office of Juvenile Justice and Delinquency Prevention, December 2006).
24. Charles Puzzanchera, *Juvenile Justice Bulletin: Juvenile Arrests 2007* (Washington, DC: Office of Juvenile Justice and Delinquency Prevention, April 2009).
25. Minehaha Forman, *The Michigan Messenger: Mich. House GOP Plan to Privatize Juvenile Justice Services Leaves Out High-Security Delinquents* (Washington, DC: The Center for Independent Media, September 2009).
26. Robert Levinson and Raymond Chase, "Private Sector Involvement in Juvenile Justice," *Corrections Today* (April 2000), pp. 156–159.
27. Christine Schloss and Leanne Alarid, "Standards in the Privatization of Probation Services: A Statutory Analysis," *Criminal Justice Review,* vol. 32 (2007), pp. 233–245.
28. E. P. Mulvey, C. A. Schubert, and H. L. Chung, "Service Use After Court Involvement in a Sample of Serious Adolescent Offenders," *Children and Youth Services Review,* vol. 29 (2007), pp. 518–544.
29. Albert Roberts and Michael Camasso, "Juvenile Offender Treatment Programs and Cost-Benefit Analysis," *Juvenile & Family Court Journal,* vol. 42 (1991), pp. 37–48.
30. Patrick Bayer and David Pozen, "The Effectiveness of Juvenile Correctional Facilities: Public versus Private Management," *Journal of Law & Economics,* vol. 48 (October 2005), pp. 549.
31. Jefferson County Juvenile Assessment Center in Lakewood, Colorado. Retrieved from www.jeffcojac.org/jeffcojac_whatwedo.htm.
32. Melissa Sickmund, *Delinquency Cases in Juvenile Court, 2005* (Washington, DC: Office of Juvenile Justice and Delinquency Prevention, June 2009).
33. *Schall* v. *Martin*, 467 U.S. 253 (1984).
34. Tamryn Etten and Robert Petrone, "Sharing Data and Information in Juvenile Justice: Legal, Ethical, and Practical Considerations," *Juvenile & Family Court* (1994), pp. 65–89.
35. Patricia Torbet et al., *National Center for Juvenile Justice, State Responses to Violent Juvenile Crime* (Washington, DC: Office of Juvenile Justice and Delinquency Prevention, July 1996).
36. *In re* L.M. 186 P.3d 184 (Kan. 2008) Kansas Supreme Court No. 06-96197-A.
37. *Kent* v. *U.S.*, 383 U.S. 541 (1966).
38. Ibid.
39. *In re* Gault, 387 U.S. 1 (1967).
40. Ibid.
41. *In re* Winship, 397 U.S. 358 (1970).
42. Ibid.
43. *McKeiver* v. *Pennsylvania*, 403 U.S. 528 (1971).
44. Ibid.
45. *Breed* v. *Jones*, 421 U.S. 519 (1975).
46. David Tanenhaus, *Juvenile Justice in the Making* (New York, NY: Oxford University Press, 2004).
47. Donna Bishop, "Public Opinion and Juvenile Justice Policy: Myths and Misconceptions," *Criminology & Public Policy,* vol. 5, no. 4 (October 2006), pp. 653–664.
48. Donna Bishop, "Juvenile Offenders in the Adult Criminal Justice System," in M. Tonry (ed.), *Crime and Justice: A Review of Research* (Chicago, IL: University of Chicago Press, 2000), pp. 81–167.

49. Brandon Applegate, Robin King Davis, and Francis Cullen, "Reconsidering Child Saving: The Extent and Correlates of Public Support for Excluding Youths from the Juvenile Court," *Crime & Delinquency,* vol. 55, no. 1 (January 2009), pp. 51–77.

50. Benjamin Adams and Sean Addie, *OJJPD Fact Sheet: Delinquency Cases Waived to Criminal Court, 2005* (Washington, DC: Office of Juvenile Justice and Delinquency Prevention, June 2009).

51. Patrick Griffin, *National Overviews: State Juvenile Justice Profiles* (Pittsburgh, PA: National Center for Juvenile Justice 2008).

52. Ibid.

53. Ibid.

54. Anne L. Stahl, *OJJPD Fact Sheet: Delinquency Cases in Juvenile Courts, 1996* (Washington, DC: Office of Juvenile Justice and Delinquency Prevention, May 1999).

55. Supra (See 43).

56. Michele Deitch et al., *From Time Out to Hard Time: Young Children in the Adult Criminal Justice System* (Austin, TX: The University of Texas at Austin, LBJ School of Public Affairs, August 2009).

57. *Thompson* v. *Oklahoma*, 487 U.S. 815 (1988).

58. *Stanford* v. *Kentucky*, 492 U.S. 361 (1989).

59. *Roper* v. *Simmons*, 543 U.S. 551 (2005).

60. U. S. Supreme Court: *Roper* v. *Simmons*, No. 03–633 (Washington, DC: Death Penalty Information Center, 2009). Retrieved from www.deathpenaltyinfo.org/u-s-supreme-court-roper-v-simmons-no-03-633.

61. *Graham* v. *Florida* (Apr. 10, 2008) U.S. Supreme Court Docket: 08-7621. *Sullivan* v. *Florida* (June 17, 2008) U.S. Supreme Court Docket: 08-7621.

62. John Kelly, "Will Ruling Save All Lifers?" *Youth Today* (June 2010). Retrieved from www.youthtoday.org/view_article.cfm?article_id=4031.

63. Sarah Livsey, *OJJPD Fact Sheet: Juvenile Delinquency Probation Caseload, 2005* (Washington, DC: Office of Juvenile Justice and Delinquency Prevention, June 2009).

64. Linda A. Szymanski, *Probation as a Disposition for Status Offenders* (Pittsburgh, PA: National Center for Juvenile Justice, April 2006).

65. Donald Andrews and James Bonta, *The Psychology of Criminal Conduct,* 4th ed. (Cincinnati, OH: Anderson, 2007).

66. Steve Aos, Marna Miller, and Elizabeth Drake, "Evidence-Based Adult Corrections Programs: What Works and What Does Not," *Washington State Institute for Public Policy* (January 2006), pp. 1–19.

67. Ibid.

68. National Center for Juvenile Justice, *Alaska State Juvenile Justice Profiles* (2006). Retrieved from www.ncjj.org/stateprofiles/.

69. Patricia Torbet, *Building Pennsylvania's Comprehensive Aftercare Model: Probation Case Management Essentials for Youth in Placement* (Pittsburgh, PA: National Center for Juvenile Justice, March 2008).

70. Chris Kingsley, *A Guide for Case Management of At-Risk Youth* (Waltham, MA: Brandeis University, Heller Graduate School, Center for Human Resources, 1989).

71. Rob Lubitz, Fred Santesteban, and Brett Watson, *Juvenile Intensive Probation Supervision (JIPS): Fiscal Year 2008 Annual Report* (Phoenix, AZ: Arizona Supreme Court: Juvenile Justice Services Division, January 2009).

72. Paul Gendreau, Francis Cullen, and James Bonta, "Intensive Rehabilitation Supervision: The Next Generation in Community Corrections?" *Federal Probation,* vol. 58 (March 1994), pp. 72–78.

73. William Barton and Jeffrey Butts, "Viable Options: Intensive Supervision Programs for Juvenile Delinquents," *Crime & Delinquency,* vol. 36, no. 2 (1990), pp. 238–256.

74. Sharyn Adams, "The Impact of Intensive Juvenile Probation Programs," *Illinois Criminal Justice Information Authority,* vol. 6, no. 1 (August 2002), pp. 1–2.

75. Scott Henggeler, *Treating Serious Anti-Social Behavior in Youth: The MST Approach* (Washington, DC: U.S. Department of Justice, Office of Justice Programs, Office of Juvenile Justice and Delinquency Prevention, May 1997). Cindy Schaeffer and Charles Borduin, "Long-Term Follow-Up to a Randomized Clinical Trial of Multisystemic Therapy With Serious and Violent Offenders," *Journal of Consulting*

and Clinical Psychology, vol. 73, no. 3 (2005), pp. 445–453; Scott Henggeler et al., "Four-Year Follow-up of Multisystemic Therapy With Substance Abusing and Substance-Dependent Juvenile Offenders," *Journal of the American Academy of Child and Adolescent Psychiatry,* vol. 41, no. 7 (July 2002), pp. 868–874.

76. Substance Abuse and Mental Health Services Administration, *National Registry of Evidence-based Programs and Practices.* See Intervention Summary at http://nrepp.samhsa.gov/programfulldetails.asp?PROGRAM_ID=102#description.

77. Gordon Bazemore, Kay Pranis, and Mark Umbreit, *Balanced and Restorative Justice for Juveniles: A Framework for Juvenile Justice in the 21st Century* (Washington, DC: U.S. Department of Justice, Office of Justice Programs, Office of Juvenile Justice and Delinquency Prevention, August 1997).

78. David Altschuler and Troy Armstrong, "Aftercare, Not Afterthought: Testing the IAP Model," *Juvenile Justice,* vol. 3, no. 1 (1996).

79. Troy Armstrong, *Achieving Positive Results with Serious Juvenile Offenders in a Reintegrative Framework: Strategies Essential for Rehabilitative Effectiveness with the Intensive Aftercare Program (IAP) Model* (Sacramento, CA: Center for Delinquency and Crime Policy Studies, June 2003).

80. Richard Wiebush et al., *Implementation and Outcome Evaluation of the Intensive Aftercare Program* (Washington, DC: Office of Juvenile Justice and Delinquency Prevention, March 2005).

81. Patricia Chamberlain, "Comparative Evaluation of Specialized Foster Care for Seriously Delinquent Youths: A First Step," *International Journal of Family Care,* vol. 2 (1990), pp. 21–36.

82. Mishi Faruqee, *New York Juvenile Justice Coalition: Proposals for Reform 2007* (New York, NY: Correctional Association of New York, 2006).

83. Mishi Faruqee, *How Can New York City Save Money and Improve Its Juvenile Justice System?* (New York, NY: Correctional Association of New York, 2008).

84. OJJDP Annual Report 2008, *How OJJDP Is Serving Children, Families, and Communities* (Washington, DC: Office of Juvenile Justice and Delinquency Prevention, 2009).

85. John Smykla and William Selke, "Impact of Home Detention—A Less Restrictive Alternative to the Detention of Juveniles," *Juvenile and Family Court Journal,* vol. 33, no. 2 (May 1982), pp. 3–9.

86. Sudipto Roy, "Five Years of Electronic Monitoring of Adults and Juveniles in Lake County, Indiana: A Comparative Study on Factors Related to Failure," *Journal of Crime and Justice,* vol. 20, no. 1 (1997), pp. 141–160.

87. James C. Howell, *Guide for Implementing the Comprehensive Strategies for Serious, Violent, and Chronic Juvenile Offenders* (Washington, DC: Office of Juvenile Justice and Delinquency Prevention, May 1995).

88. Daniel Macallair, Mike Males, and Catherine McCracken, *Closing California's Division of Juvenile Facilities: An Analysis of County Institutional Capacity* (San Francisco, CA: Center on Juvenile and Criminal Justice, May 2009).

89. Patrick Hyde, "Merced County, CA Turns to Day Reporting for Relief," *Journal of the California State of Counties* (January/February 2009), pp. 26–28.

90. Behavioral Interventions Incorporated, *Unique Merced County Day Reporting Center Marks First Anniversary—Center Proving Effective at Reducing Criminal Risk* (April 2009). Retrieved from www.bi.com/node/71.

91. Bureau of Justice Assistance Monograph, *Juvenile Drug Court: Strategies in Practice* (Washington, DC: U.S. Department of Justice, Office of Justice Programs, BJA, 2003).

92. National Drug Court Initiative (2009). Retrieved from www.ndci.org/research.

93. Nancy Rodriguez and Vincent Webb, "Multiple Measures of Juvenile Drug Court Effectiveness: Results of a Quasi-Experimental Design," *Crime Delinquency,* vol. 50, no. 2 (May 2004), pp. 292–313.

94. Patrick Griffin, "Juvenile Probation in the Schools," *In Focus,* vol. 1, no. 1 (1999), pp. 1–12.

95. David Metzger, *School-Based Probation in Pennsylvania* (Philadelphia, PA: University of Pennsylvania, Center for Studies of Addiction, 1997).
96. Patricia Torbet et al., *Evaluation of Pennsylvania's School-Based Probation Program* (Pittsburgh, PA: National Center for Juvenile Justice, 2001).
97. Supra (see 26 and 28).
98. Ibid.
99. Juvenile Justice and Delinquency Prevention Act of 1974. 42 U.S.C. § 5601 et seq. (Section 223(8)(B)(i-ii) and Section 223(8)(B).
100. Dana Hubbard and Travis Pratt, "A Meta-Analysis of the Predictors of Delinquency among Girls," *Journal of Offender Rehabilitation,* vol. 34 (2002), pp. 1–13.
101. Celeste Simoes, Margarida Matos, and Joan Batista-Foguet, "Juvenile Delinquency: Analysis of Risk and Protective Factors Using Quantitative and Qualitative Methods," *Cognition, Brain, Behavior: An Interdisciplinary Journal,* vol. 12, no. 4 (December 2008), pp. 389–408.
102. Susan McCampbell, *The Gender-Responsive Strategies Project: Jail Applications* (Washington, DC: National Institute of Corrections, April 2006).
103. Ibid.
104. Wethersfield, CT: Court Support Services Division, *Sanctions Update: 2008*. Retrieved from www.jud.ct.gov/cssd/pub/SU_winter08.pdf.
105. Warya Pothan, *Informal Assessment: At-Risk Cambodian Youth in Seattle* (Seattle, WA: The University of Seattle Medical Center, July 2003). Also see Futoshi Kobayashi, *Model Minority Stereotype Revisited* (1999). Retrieved from www.eric.ed.gov/ERICDocs/data/ericdocs2sql/content_storage_01/0000019b/80/15/e0/75.pdf.
106. Elaine Morley et al., *Comprehensive Responses to Youth At Risk: Interim Findings From the Safe Futures Initiative* (Washington, DC: Office of Juvenile Justice and Delinquency Prevention, November 2000).
107. Thao Le, Isami Arifuku, and Michell Nunez, "Girls and Culture in Delinquency Intervention: A Case Study of RYSE," *Juvenile and Family Court Journal,* vol. 54, no. 3 (2003), pp. 25–34.
108. Barry Krisberg, *Juvenile Justice: Redeeming Our Children* (Thousand Oaks, CA: Sage Publications, 2005).
109. Ibid.
110. Cynthia Burke, Sandy Keaton, and Susan Pennell, *Addressing the Gender-Specific Needs of Girls: An Evaluation of San Diego's WINGS Program* (September 2003). Retrieved from www.sandag.org/uploads/publicationid/publicationid_899_3916.pdf.
111. Charles Puzzanchera, *Juvenile Arrests 2008* (Washington, DC: Office of Juvenile Justice and Delinquency Prevention, December 2009).
112. Ibid.
113. Mark Soler, *Public Opinion on Youth, Crime, and Race: A Guide for Advocates* (Washington, DC: Youth Law Center, October 2001).
114. Danilo Yanich, "Kids, Crime & Local TV News: A National Study," *Crime & Delinquency,* vol. 51, no. 1 (January 2005), pp. 11–12.
115. Robert Goidel, Craig Freeman, and Steven T. Procopio, "The Impact of Television Viewing on Perceptions of Juvenile Crime," *Journal of Broadcasting and Electronic Media,* vol. 50, no. 1 (March 2006), pp. 119–139.

glossary

acculturation a process in which members of one cultural group adopt the beliefs and behaviors of another group.

actuarial assessment the second era in the assessment of risk/needs that focuses on the science of applying mathematical and statistical methods to assess risk.

adjudication a judicial hearing wherein guilt or innocence is determined either by the child's admission or by trial by a court or jury.

aftercare the delivery of community-based services to offenders who have been released from confinement in a correctional facility.

anomie a theory of the sociological school of criminology that asserts individuals become criminal when there is a breakdown of social norms.

arraignment involves the reading of a charge and the entering of a plea of guilty or not guilty by the defendant, usually at the defendant's first court appearance.

Arrestee Drug Abuse Monitoring (ADAM) a survey conducted by the U.S. Department of Justice to gauge the prevalence of alcohol and illegal drug use among prior arrestees.

atavism a term used to suggest that criminals are physiological throwbacks to earlier stages of human evolution.

atavistic a term used by Cesare Lombroso, founder of the positivist school of criminology, to describe criminals as biological throwbacks to an earlier evolutionary stage, and people more primitive or less highly evolved than their noncriminal counterparts.

back-end offenders a term commonly used to refer to convicted persons who are being released from a correctional sanction within the criminal justice system (e.g., parolee).

biological school of criminology an explanation of criminal behavior that deals with evolutionary and genetic influences on criminal behavior.

boot camps an intermediate sanction typically used for young offenders that provides structured and military-like activities focusing on discipline, physical labor, and education.

breathalyzers devices for estimating blood alcohol content from a defendant's breath.

case investigation the first major role of probation officers consisting of preparing the presentence report (PSR) that provides detailed information on the offense and the defendant's criminal history and characteristics.

case plan a written document that describes the social and child welfare services and corrective activities to be provided by state and local agencies.

case planning a process of identifying dynamic risk factors requiring intervention, prioritizing placement in programs and treatment, and assembling the supervision team.

casework/medical model a philosophy of offender treatment that regards criminal behavior as a disease to be treated and that views probation officers as social workers engaged in counseling with their "clients," the probationers.

certification the process by which delinquents are transferred to adult court for criminal prosecution. If certified to the adult court for prosecution, the child may be treated like an adult defendant.

classical school of criminology an explanation of criminal behavior that asserts that crime is a matter of individual choice and individuals rationally calculate the benefits of committing crime against its potential costs.

classification a process of separating offenders into discrete groups in such a way that the offenders in the same group are similar or close to each other on certain common characteristics in order to effectively supervises and manages them.

cognitive restructuring a problem-focused intervention that emphasizes changing the way one perceives, reflects, and thinks through modeling, graduated practice, role-playing, reinforcement, and concrete verbal suggestions.

cognitive-behavioral therapy (CBT) a type of psychotherapy based on the idea that individuals' distorted thoughts lead to dysfunctional emotions and problem behaviors. CBT is used in community-based corrections programs to reduce recidivism and increase pro-social behavior by changing the offenders' thoughts, attitudes and beliefs through research-based cognitive programming.

cognitive-behavioral treatment (CBT) a problem-focused intervention that emphasizes skill training to change the way an individual perceives, reflects, and thinks.

cognitive transformation the process of changing the way a person perceives, reflects, thinks about life, reasons, and solves problems—before moving toward a different way of life.

collateral contact the contact with anyone other than the offender who can provide information relevant to the supervision of the case.

community brokerage model a philosophy of offender treatment that calls attention to the influence of the social environment on offending behavior and in which probation officers turn to community resources for therapeutic, employment, social, educational, and vocational interventions.

community corrections a philosophy of correctional treatment that embraces decentralization of authority from state to local levels, citizen participation in program planning, design, implementation, and evaluation, redefinition of the population of offenders for whom incarceration is most appropriate, and emphasis on rehabilitation through community programs.

community corrections acts (CCAs) state laws that give economic grants to local communities to establish community corrections goals and policies and to develop and operate community corrections programs.

Community Mental Health Centers Act (CMHCA) a law passed by Congress to provide federal funding for community mental health centers for the purpose of establishing community-based care, as an alternative to institutionalization.

community service a court-ordered intermediate sanction, often imposed by the judge as a condition of probation, to work a certain number of hours for a civic or nonprofit organization, without being compensated, as reparation to the community.

conditional-un/supervised release a court-ordered, conditional release of a defendant from confinement but not under community supervision by a pretrial services officer.

conflict theory a critical theory that argues that law is a social-control mechanism that reflects the values and interests of the dominant group and crime is inevitable in capitalist societies because certain groups become marginalized and unequal.

criminogenic refers to risk factors associated with the prediction of recidivism.

critical theory an umbrella term in the sociological school of criminology that believes knowledge is influenced by human interests and reflects the power and social relationships within society; that science is influenced by values of the scientist and the scientific community; that the goal of research should be a more just and democratic society; and that crime is a result of the way society is organized.

day fine a dollar amount that is based on both the severity of the crime and an offender's daily earnings.

day reporting center (DRC) an intermediate punishment that requires mandatory attendance at a non-residential facility on a daily or otherwise regular basis at specified times depending on the level of supervisions and treatment required in order to participate in activities such as substance abuse counseling, social skills training, or employment training.

deinstitutionalization the process of replacing long-stay psychiatric hospitals with community mental health services for those diagnosed with mental disorders. The term was also used in the Juvenile Justice and Delinquency Prevention Act of 1974 to describe the mandate to remove juvenile status offenders from secure detention facilities.

demonstration programs grant programs designed to support criminal justice reform and synthesize knowledge that emerges from these funded activities.

desistance a process in which the frequency of crimes decelerates and exhibits less variety.

detainer a request from one criminal justice agency to another asking the agency to hold the offender for the requesting agency or notify the agency when the offender's release is close at hand.

determinate sentencing a prison sentence with a fixed term of imprisonment that can be reduced by good-time or earned-time credits. Also called presumptive sentencing.

deterrence a theory of justice that states that if the consequences of committing a crime outweigh the benefit of the crime itself, the individual and/or the general population will refrain from committing the crime.

differential association theory a theory of the sociological school of criminology that argues that criminals learn to commit crimes just as they learn any other behavior and that a person becomes delinquent when there is an excess of definitions favorable to violation of the law over definitions unfavorable to violation of law.

differential reinforcement theory a theory of the sociological school of criminology that asserts that learning criminal behavior depends on the feedback people receive from their environment and how they evaluate their own behavior through interaction with significant other people and groups.

discretionary parole early release based on the paroling authority's assessment of eligibility.

diversion an alternative to prosecution which seeks to divert certain offenders from traditional criminal justice processing into a program of supervision and services.

drug court an intermediate sanction and specialized court that handles cases involving drug-addicted offenders. The program includes random drug testing, judicial supervision, counseling, educational and vocational opportunities and the use of sanctions and rewards.

due process of law can be operationally defined as law in the regular course of judicial proceedings that is in accordance with natural, inherent, and fundamental principles of justice. A defendant is afforded all substantive and procedural protections that the law presently provides.

dynamic risk assessment the third era in the assessment of risk/needs that addresses both the treatment linkages and case-specific strategies for offender supervision by introducing dynamic criminogenic need items that are linked to general personality theory and the learning of criminal behavior.

evidence-based corrections (also **evidence-based practices**) the application of social scientific techniques to the study of everyday corrections procedures for the purpose of increasing effectiveness and enhancing the efficient use of available resources.

failure to appear a court issued bench warrant for a defendant's arrest because he or she has missed a scheduled court appearance.

feminist theory a critical theory that argues that traditional criminological theories, which are created primarily by men and used men as their subjects, cannot be generalized to explain women's criminality.

fine a financial penalty requiring an offender to make payments to the court. A fine is usually based on the seriousness of the crime committed but can also be based on the offender's income.

foster care a form of substitute care, usually in a home licensed by a public agency, for children whose welfare requires that they be removed from their own homes.

front-end offenders a term commonly used to refer to persons entering a correctional sanction within the criminal justice system (e.g., probationer).

gender-responsive refers to correctional policies and programs geared to differences between men and women. The policy acknowledges that problems are likely to arise if these differing needs are not adequately met.

general conditions (of probation) restrictions that all probationers are subject to (e.g., refrain from criminal activity).

general deterrence a theory of justice that states that punishment serves a useful purpose because it restrains the population as a whole.

get-tough era a reference to legislation and policies developed in the 1980s and 1990s to deal with crime in the United States.

halfway house a residential center where offenders work in the community and pay rent while undergoing counseling and job training.

home confinement/house arrest an intermediate sanction that restricts offenders to their residence in one of three ways: under curfew, home detention, or home incarceration.

in re a Latin phrase meaning "in the matter of." When "*in re*" appears in the title of a court case, it means that the case does not have formal opposing parties. The use of *in re* refers to the object or person that is the primary subject of the case. The phrase is often used in cases involving juveniles.

incapacitation a theory of justice that focuses on restraining offenders from committing additional crimes by isolating them, generally in jail or prison.

indeterminate sentencing a term of incarceration that does not state a specific period of time or release date, but rather a range of time, such as "five-to-ten years."

in-reach programs community-based providers that deliver services in the jail setting.

intensive supervision probation (ISP) an intermediate sanction with frequent contact between offenders and their supervision officers.

intermediate sanctions criminal sentences that fall between standard probation and incarceration.

irresistible impulse test an insanity defense in which defendants claim they should not be held criminally liable for their actions and that they broke the law because of their inability to control those actions.

jail weekender programs allow offenders to serve their sentences of confinement only on weekends (i.e., Friday–Sunday).

just deserts a theory of justice that states that criminal acts are deserving of punishment and that offenders are morally blameworthy and deserving of punishment.

juvenile delinquency any act that would be considered criminal, if not for the fact that it was committed by a juvenile. A juvenile is defined in the U.S. Code as a person under the age of 18.

juvenile detention facility a place of temporary care for juveniles in judicial custody pending court disposition.

labeling theory holds that deviance is not an inherent characteristic of humans but that that the majority population tends to negatively label minorities as deviant when they diverge from norms.

law violation one of two reasons that probation or parole is revoked is offenders commit a new crime.

level of service inventory-revised (LSI-R) an objective, quantifiable instrument that provides a consistent and valid method of predicting risk to re-offend, and a reliable means of measuring an inmate's change over time through readministration. The LSI-R provides insight into which inmates should receive the highest priority for treatment regardless of their specific problem areas.

liberation hypothesis a feminist theory that argues that the women's movement brought about greater involvement of women in criminal activity.

M'Naghten Rule a test for criminal insanity that assumes a defendant is not guilty by reason of insanity if, at the time of the alleged criminal act, he or she did not know that what she or he was doing was wrong.

mandatory parole early release after a time period specified by law, good-time provision, or emergency releases.

Marxist theory a critical theory that argues that crime occurs as a result of the conflict between those who own the material forces of production and the wage laborers who produce the goods.

media myth a term used to describe the media's continued portrayals of images and information that are not based on fact. A "media myth" is created when whole groups of people are misrepresented because the extreme actions of a few dominate the media.

Megan's law an informal name for laws in the United States requiring law enforcement authorities to make information available to the public regarding registered sex offenders.

mental health courts long-term community-based treatment programs that rely on mental health assessments, individualized treatment plans, and ongoing judicial monitoring to address both the mental health needs of offenders and public safety concerns of communities.

Model Penal Code (MPC) a statutory text developed by the American Law Institute to assist legislatures in updating and standardizing states' penal law.

moral reconation therapy (MRT) a cognitive skills program to develop moral reasoning.

motivational interviewing a style of offender-centered counseling that facilitates changes in behavior based on negotiation rather than conflict in which the offender, not the probation officer, articulates the benefits and costs involved, and a collaborative relationship between the probation officer and the probationer, in which they tackle the problem together.

National Crime Victimization Survey (NCVS) used to collect information from victims on nonfatal violent and property crimes, reported and not reported to the police, against persons ages 12 and older from a nationally representative sample of U.S. households. It produces national rates and levels of personal and property victimization.

need principle one of three risk-need-responsivity principles that highlights the importance of criminogenic needs (attributes of offenders that are strongly correlated with risk of recidivism, such as who an offender associates with and whether an offender uses substances) in the design and delivery of treatment.

neoclassical school of criminology a revision of the classical school of criminology that championed the need for judicial discretion in considering age, criminal history, mental condition, and external forces.

net-widening refers to a situation in criminal justice in which individuals who previously would have received an informal disposition are now dealt with by the justice system simply because, with the existence and expansion of sanctions, there is a "suitable" correctional program now available to handle them.

neutralization theory a theory of the sociological school of criminology that focuses on the words and phrases offenders use to justify or excuse lawbreaking behavior, such as claiming an action was in self-defense.

offender notification forum a reentry program that brings together parolees with federal, state, and local law enforcement officials, community representatives, and various service providers to discuss the consequences and available service options relevant to crime desistance, and to alter the parolee's perceptions of law enforcement.

offender supervision the second major role of probation officers consisting of monitoring the probationer's activities through office meetings, alcohol and drug testing, and home and work visits and holding offenders accountable by making sure they understand the consequences of violating the criminal law.

parens patriae a Latin phrase used to describe the power of the state to act in place of the parents for the purpose of protecting the property and person of a child.

parole a period of conditional supervised release in the community following a prison term and may be either discretionary or mandatory.

parolee a criminal offender who has been conditionally released from prison to serve the remaining portion of his/her sentence in the community.

paroling authority a person or correctional agency (often called a *parole board* or *parole commission*) that has the authority to grant, revoke, and discharge from parole.

pathways to crime theory a feminist theory that identifies women's abuse, early family life, children, street life, and marginality as the most common avenues for producing and sustaining female criminality.

positivist school of criminology an explanation of criminal behavior that asserts that criminal behavior is explained by factors beyond the individual's control.

power-control theory a feminist theory that predicts that patriarchal families are characterized by more gender differences in delinquent behavior than egalitarian families.

pre-arraignment all of the steps conducted prior to the arraignment.

predatory crime a violent crime with a human victim, such as murder or rape; contrasted with victimless crime, such as drug use, gambling, or prostitution.

pretrial assessment a system of screening services and investigation that may lead to community supervision for selected defendants who otherwise would be in jail while awaiting trial.

pretrial failure defined as failing to appear for scheduled court dates, having new charges filed while under pretrial supervision, and/or failing to abide by conditions of pretrial supervision.

pretrial release defined as a non-monetary alternative to detention for defendants who are unable to post bail.

pretrial services a function of the courts that takes place after a person has been arrested and charged with a crime and before he or she goes to trial. Pretrial services officers focus on investigating the backgrounds of these persons to help the court determine whether to release or detain the defendant while they await trial.

prisonization a process whereby the inmate takes on the norms and values of the prison environment and loses the ability to successfully reintegrate into society after prison.

probation the conditional release of an adjudicated offender into the community, under supervision of a probation officer. It is conditional because it can be revoked if certain conditions are not met.

professional/clinical assessment the first era in assessment of risk/needs that believed that as community corrections officers gained knowledge and experience, they developed an intuitive sense, or a "gut" feeling, of what an offender's risks and needs were and what the probability was that he or she might reoffend.

psychological school of criminology an explanation of criminal behavior that posits that criminal behavior is the result of mental disturbance, intelligence, personality, or impulsivity.

rational choice theory a theory of the classical school of criminology that asserts that an individual makes a rational choice to commit a crime by weighing the risks and benefits.

recidivism a measure of return to criminal activity. It is often used interchangeably to refer to re-arrest, re-conviction, and re-incarceration. Some recidivism studies count all re-arrests as recidivism, others count only re-conviction or only a return to incarceration, and some studies track all three events.

reentry the transition offenders make from prison or jail to the community. It is a collaborative partnership between the prison or jail and the community in transitioning an inmate from custody back into the community.

reentry court a specialized court that manages the return to the community of individuals released from prison, using the authority of the court to apply graduated sanctions and positive reinforcement, and to marshal resources to support the prisoner's reintegration.

rehabilitation a theory of justice that attempts to alter the attitudes and behaviors of offenders and change criminal lifestyles into law-abiding ones by using medical and psychological treatments and social-skills training.

reintegration the most recently used term to define the transition from incarceration to life outside an institution, in a community.

reintegrative shaming a refinement of social learning theory that argues that offenders can be reintegrated back into society as law-abiding citizens through words or gestures of forgiveness or ceremonies that decertify the offender as deviant.

release on recognizance (ROR) a nonmonetary method by which a person charged with a crime is released upon his or her promise to appear in court (sometimes involving special conditions such as remaining in the custody of another person or abiding by travel restrictions) and answer a criminal charge.

remote location monitoring (also referred to as *electronic monitoring*) an intermediate sanction with periodic or continuous surveillance of an offender through electronic means such as an ankle bracelet, voice verification, or GPS.

residential community centers (RCC) an intermediate sanction where offenders live in minimum-security residential facilities that provides them with housing, treatment services, and access to community resources for employment and education.

responsivity principle one of three risk-need-responsivity principles that states that styles and modes of treatment must be matched to the preferred learning style, motivation and abilities of the offender.

restitution a process by which offenders are held accountable for the financial losses they have caused to the victims of their crimes.

restorative justice a theory of justice that emphasizes repairing the harm caused by criminal behavior.

retribution the infliction of punishment on those who deserve to be punished.

retributive justice a theory of justice that states that everyone should get what they deserve.

revenge (also known as *vengeance*) a harmful act taken in response to criminal victimization.

revocation the formal termination of an offender's conditional freedom.

revocation hearing a due process hearing conducted by the court or probation authority to determine whether the conditions of probation or parole have been violated.

risk assessment the process whereby offenders are assessed on several key variables empirically known to increase the likelihood of committing an offense.

risk principle one of three risk-need-responsivity principles that asserts that criminal behavior can be reliably predicted and that treatment should focus on the higher-risk offenders.

risk-need-responsivity model (RNR) an approach for identifying high-risk offenders from low-risk ones and intervening effectively; the model is based on the theory of general personality and cognitive learning.

routine activities theory a theory of the classical school of criminology that argues that crime occurs when there are motivated offenders, suitable targets, and an absence of capable guardians.

salient factor score (SFS) a risk assessment instrument to estimate an offender's prison sentence and likelihood of success or failure on parole following his or her release from prison.

self-control theory a theory of the sociological school of criminology that argues that criminal behavior is a result of impulsive behavior, a tendency in all humans to break rules and make rational choices about whether to do so.

sentencing guidelines standards for determining the punishment that a convicted criminal should receive based on the nature of the crime and the offender's criminal history.

serious mental illness (SMI) defined as a diagnosable mental disorder found in persons aged 18 years and older that is so long lasting and severe that it seriously interferes with a person's ability to take part in major life activities.

Sex Offender Registration and Notification Act (SORNA) a federal mandate codified under 42 U.S.C.16911 that requires U.S. jurisdictions to update their sex offender registration laws to conform to federal guidelines.

sexting the act of sending sexually explicit messages or photographs, primarily between mobile phones.

shock incarceration involves a short period of confinement during which young offenders convicted of less serious, nonviolent crimes are exposed to a demanding regimen of strict discipline, military-style drill and ceremony, physical exercise, and physical labor.

social contract philosophy the belief that people give up pursuing their own interests in favor of forming a social contract with the government that provides them with order, structure, and the right to use force to maintain the contract.

social control theory a theory of the sociological school of criminology that stresses the idea that people commit delinquent or criminal acts because the forces restraining them from doing so are weak, not because the forces driving them to do so are strong.

social disorganization theory a theory of the sociological school of criminology that asserts that persons become criminals when they are isolated from mainstream culture and instead immersed in impoverished and dilapidated neighborhoods that have their own sets of norms and values.

social learning theory a theory of the sociological school of criminology that argues that behavior may be reinforced not only with rewards and punishments, but also with expectations that are learned by watching what happens to other people.

social reaction theory (labeling theory) a theory of the sociological school of criminology that argues that official efforts to control crime often increase crime.

sociological school of criminology an explanation of criminal behavior that shifts the discussion to external forces affecting individual behavior.

special conditions (of probation) restrictions that certain types of offenders are subject to (e.g., mandatory treatment for substance abuse offenders).

special-needs offenders offenders who exhibit unique physical, mental, social, and programmatic characteristics that distinguish them from other offenders, such as sex offenders, substance abusers, domestic violence abusers, and offenders who present particular treatment needs and management issues.

specific deterrence a theory of justice that states that punishment serves a useful purpose because it restrains the individual offender.

Speedy Trial Act a statute that imposes a series of time limits upon a court and prosecutors for carrying out the major events in a criminal case to ensure that the defendant receives a speedy trial.

split sentence criminal punishments that sentence probationers to a combined short-term incarceration sentence immediately followed by probation.

status offender a child charged with an offense not classified as criminal, or with an offense applicable only to children.

status offense refers to non-criminal misbehavior, which would not be criminal if committed by an adult (e.g., truancy, runaway). The behavior is an offense only because of the minor's status as a minor.

substance abuse treatment a special condition the court imposes that requires an individual to undergo testing and treatment for abuse of illegal drugs, prescription drugs, or alcohol. Treatment may include inpatient or outpatient counseling and detoxification.

superpredator a term to label a new breed of antisocial, radically impulsive, and brutally cold-blooded youths who commit violent crimes and generally wreak havoc on communities.

supervised release implies frequent and intensive contact between the supervising agency and the defendant. For example, these conditions may include the defendants participating in a drug treatment or counseling program or working with a vocational counselor to secure employment.

surety bond an agreement made between one or more persons and a bond agent where the bond agent agrees to post the necessary bail so that a defendant can be released from jail.

tariff fine a fixed dollar amount applied to every offender for a particular crime regardless of the offender's income level or ability to pay.

technical violation one of two reasons that probation or parole is revoked if offenders do not comply with noncriminal rules such as paying restitution, meeting with the probation officer, or continuing prescribed treatment.

three-strikes laws state statutes that require a mandatory and extended period of incarceration to offenders who have been convicted of a serious criminal offense on three or more separate occasions.

truth in sentencing (TIS) a term to describe laws targeted primarily at increasing the severity of sentencing for violent offenders by either increasing the proportion of violent offenders sentenced to prison, increasing the length of their punishment, or both. These laws were designed to reduce the apparent disparity between the sentence imposed and time served.

Uniform Crime Report (UCR) a nationwide, cooperative statistical effort of more than 17,000 city, university and college, county, state, tribal, and federal law enforcement agencies voluntarily reporting data on crimes brought to their attention. Since 1930, the FBI has administered the UCR Program and continues to assess and monitor the nature and type of crime in the United States.

victim impact statement refers to a written or oral report commonly used at sentencing that describes the impact of the crime on the victim and the victim's family.

work release a community-based correctional program that enables offenders to hold jobs in the community during the day, returning to their institutions at night.

working alliance an effective relationship between a change agent and a client, with negotiated goals and a mutual willingness to compromise to meet the goals or maintain a viable relationship.

credits

Chapter 1 Opener: Photos courtesy of *The Fulton County Daily Report*. Copyright © 2010. ALM Media Properties, LLC. Further distribution without permission is prohibited. All rights reserved; p. 6: Courtesy of Ryan Egg and Michael Torres; p. 9: Courtesy of Jesse Montgomery; p. 17: Courtesy of Howard Zehr; p. 18: © John Smykla

Chapter 2 Opener: © Photo by California Department of Corrections/Getty; p. 34: © Aaron Roeth Photograph; p. 40: Courtesy of Beverly Morgan; p. 46: © Mikael Karlsson/Arresting Images RF

Chapter 3 Opener: © George Pimentel/FilmMagic/Getty; p. 60: © Brand X Pictures RF; p. 63: © Brand X/Getty RF; p. 66: © The McGraw-Hill Companies, Inc., Christopher Kerrigan, photographer; p. 70: Courtesy of Matthew Crow; p. 79: © Brand X Pictures RF

Chapter 4 Opener: © Randy Pench/Sacramento Bee/MCT via Getty; p. 94: Courtesy of Latia Thomas and Laurie Dihota; p. 102: © Manchan/Getty RF; p. 104: Courtesy of Beth Robinson; p. 110: © Ryan McVay/Photodisc/Getty RF

Chapter 5 Opener: © Mark Wilson/Getty; p. 119: Courtesy of Kimberly Rieger; p. 125: U.S. Census Bureau, Public Information Office (PIO); p. 138 (top): © AP Photo/Jason DeCrow; p. 138 (bottom): © Dallas Morning News

Chapter 6 Opener: © Jon Kopaloff/Getty; p. 154: © Ryan McVay/Getty RF; p. 166: © Corbis RF; p. 168: Courtesy of Dan Petersen; p. 174: © Visions America/Joe Sohm/Getty RF

Chapter 7 Opener a: © AFP/Getty; Opener b: © AFP/Getty; p. 191: © Mikael Karlsson/Arresting Images RF; p. 199: Courtesy of Kelli Matthews; p. 202: Courtesy of Chastity Manning and Michael Davidson; p. 208: Courtesy of Joseph Herczog and Linda Jordan

Chapter 8 Opener: © Darren Carroll/Sports Illustrated/Getty; p. 229: © James Hardy Photo Alto/Punchstock RF; p. 238: © Jacobs Stock Photography/Getty RF; p. 240: Courtesy of Rick Robinson; p. 245: © Larry Mainer

Chapter 9 Opener: © John Eastcott & Yva Momatiuk/Photo Researchers; p. 256: © AP Photo/Phil Coale; p. 263: © McGraw-Hill Companies, Inc., Mark Dierker, photographer; p. 265: Courtesy of Joseph Schuetz; p. 266: © Gerald Bayens

Chapter 10 Opener: © Ben Rose/WireImage/Getty; p. 287: © Ingram Publishing/SuperStock RF; p. 292: Courtesy of Lora Cole; p. 294: © Joel Gordon

Chapter 11 Opener: © Ricardo Ramierez Buseda/Orlando Sentinel/MCT/Getty; p. 313: © George Frey/Getty; p. 319: Courtesy of Angela Goehring; p. 324: © SIPA/SIPA/Newscom; p. 329: © Thinkstock/Comstock Images/Getty RF

Chapter 12 Opener: © Broward County Sheriff's Office/Getty; p. 349: © Brand X Pictures RF; p. 361: Courtesy of Randy McWilliams; p. 369: © Spencer Grant/Photo Edit; p. 372: © Ryan McVay/Getty RF

case index

subject index

S